Frederick Wiseman by The Philadelphia Inquirer/Amy Huntoon.

─────────────Reality Fictions
The Films of Frederick Wiseman

THOMAS W. BENSON
AND
CAROLYN ANDERSON

SOUTHERN ILLINOIS UNIVERSITY PRESS
CARBONDALE AND EDWARDSVILLE

Edited by Yvonne D. Mattson
Designed by Laura D. Niemann
Production supervised by Natalia Nadraga

Library of Congress Cataloging-in-Publication Data

Benson, Thomas W.
  Reality fictions : the films of Frederick Wiseman / by Thomas W.
Benson and Carolyn Anderson
      p.   cm.
  Bibliography: p.
  Includes index.
  ISBN 0-8093-1364-2
  1. Wiseman, Frederick—Criticism and interpretation.
2. Documentary films—United States—Criticism and interpretation.
I. Anderson, Carolyn, 1939–   II. Title.
PN1998.3.W57B46 1989
791.43′0233′0924—dc19   88-17613
                                                             CIP

The paper used in this publication meets the minimum requirements of
American National Standard for Information Sciences—Permanence
of Paper for Printed Library Materials, ANSI Z39.48-1984. ♾

—For our daughters
Daisy and Sarah Benson
Kisa and Kimi Takesue

Contents

Figures

Preface

Frederick Wiseman has been making documentary films for twenty years; for most of those twenty years we have been watching the films, teaching them in our classes, and occasionally writing about them. Finally, we saw that our work was leading us to attempt a full-length study of the films. There are too many films to give each a detailed analysis; rather than trying to squeeze in brief treatments of each film, we have chosen several of the films as representative of the aesthetic and rhetorical problems Wiseman has raised. We have attempted to give words to the interpretations that the films seem to invite, and the rhetorical structures by which those interpretations are induced; and we have gone behind the rhetorical structures of the films to offer a glimpse of the people and processes behind the films. Since Wiseman's films speak to his audiences so deeply of their own experiences of American institutional life, it seemed important to examine in context the issues of ethics and epistemology, and the elements of convention, craft, collaboration, finance, distribution, and legal restraint that constrain the production and reception of the films.

In the years during which we have developed the various parts of this book, many colleagues and students have offered encouragement and advice. Professors Richard Gregg, Gerard Hauser, and William Rawlins of the Pennsylvania State University and Fern Johnson, Jack Shadoian, Hermann Stelzner, and Richard Stromgren of the University of Massachusetts, Amherst, commented on early drafts of various chapters. Other colleagues and students, a group too large to identify individually, have encouraged us with questions and suggestions, and we deeply appreciate their support. This project was partially funded by grants from the Institute for the Arts and Humanistic Studies, the College of Liberal Arts, and the Department of Speech Communication at The Pennsylvania State University and by a faculty research grant from the University of Massachusetts. Our department chairs and deans—first Robert Brubaker and Stanley Paulson and then Dennis Gouran and Hart Nelsen from Penn State, and Barnett Pearce and Glen Gordon from U-Mass—provided additional support. The manuscript for this book was edited on the mainframe computer system at Penn State and relied during its preparation on Bitnet, an interuniversity electronic mail system. For computer assistance at our universities, we thank Donald Laird, Gerald Santoro, William McCane, Glen Kreider, William Verity, Tom Minsker, Kevin Jordan, Judy Smith, and Pat Driscoll. Wayne McMullen and Joe Gow each spent a summer as our research assistants at Penn State. We are grateful to typist Sylvia Snape, Ellen Levine from WNET/13, Jane Willoughby of Allan King Associates, and to Florence Boisse-Kilgo, Larry Fay, Judy Trochi, David Robinson, Barbara Sweeney, Catherine Egan, Catherine McGee, Len Siebert, and Tasha Cooper.

Dozens of people kindly shared information, opinions, and memories regarding Wiseman's films. They include Cathy Anderson, Kent Carroll, Ken Colpan, Kevin Crain, Anne Fischel, Ellen Feingold, Oliver Fowlkes, Charles Gaughan, Phil Glassanos, Phil Green, Dean Hargrove, Hal Himmelstein, Katherine Kane, Frederick A. King, Robert Kotlowitz, Michael Leja, Jemethy MacKaye, Lorna Marshall, John Morrison, Barry Nigrosh, P. J. O'Connell, Francis X. Orfanello, Anne O'Toole, Michael Perlman, Jerry Rappaport, John Roberts, Deac Rossell, Jay Ruby, Richard Rush, Sylvia Schenfeld, and Judge Kenneth A. Turner. We are grateful to the staff of the Southern Illinois University Press for their help and support on this large and complicated project, and especially to Kenney Withers, James Simmons, Susan Wilson, and Yvonne Mattson. Special thanks go to cinematographers John Marshall, Richard Leiterman, William Brayne, and John Davey for their candid interviews and to Karen Konicek of Zipporah Films for her helpfulness. We thank James Hallowell, who is credited in the films as Oliver Kool, Ollie Hallowell, Ali Kul, or James Hallowell, and who has volunteered for many years as Frederick Wiseman's assistant and still cameraman, for trying to arrange an interview with us—in the end, Hallowell declined our request for an interview when Wiseman urged him not to talk with us.

We must say a word about our relationship to Fred Wiseman. This book is not an authorized study of Wiseman's films. Wiseman cooperated with our universities and granting agencies in leasing copies of some of his films, and over the course of several years, in person, by telephone, and in writing, he has answered many of our questions. But Wiseman is in no way responsible for any of our interpretations, either in the analysis of the films, or in the account we give of their production and distribution. In the *Titicut Follies* case, he was in a particularly difficult position, because the history of those events involved so many disputed recollections, so many charges and counter-charges of bad faith, and of course an ongoing legal restriction of the film. For the most part, Wiseman preferred not to discuss the *Titicut Follies* case with us. To do so, he told us, might have seemed to place him in the position of collaborating with our version of the story, or in the equally difficult position of being quoted as disputing our version. In the summer of 1987, Wiseman read a nearly final version of the first two chapters of this book and offered some corrections dealing with factual matters in a memorandum to the authors, with the understanding that this did not commit him to a view as to our interpretation of the case. He declined our requests for an extensive interview on his work and declined to provide photographic reproductions from the films. We have tried hard to respect Wiseman's privacy, and we think it is clear how much we respect his work. On the other hand, he has often said that his works are about public issues and exist in the public sphere and that where the public's right to know conflicts with other interests, the public's right to know must usually prevail. Wiseman's actions and assertions have made his films and his working methods into public issues, the legitimate subjects of critical analysis and searching inquiry.

Wiseman, and others, as participants in the *Titicut Follies* case, will no doubt disagree not only with some of our interpretations, but with some of our allegations as to the facts. We have relied, in our account, on the published record, on trial transcripts, and on interviews and correspondence with participants. Even a trial transcript, although it is taken under oath, is not a transparent record of the events it describes, since it occurs in an adversarial setting—it is making history, not just reporting history. Whatever the limits of various documents and the unreliability of human memory, the story is important and needs to be told. Our version is offered in good faith as one supported by the record. We make it public here in the spirit of scholarly inquiry, in the hope that where it is wrong it will be refuted.

We are grateful to the institutions, associations, and journals that have allowed us to present early versions of our work to audiences who contributed to shaping what is presented here. For invitations to lecture, we thank our colleagues at the University of Texas at Austin, Auburn University, the University of Maryland, Rhodes College, and Hampshire College. Chapters in various stages of preparation have been presented at meetings of the Speech Communication Association, the Eastern Communication Association, the Society for Cinema Studies, the Popular Culture Association, the Speech Communication Association of Pennsylvania, the Conference on Discourse Analysis (Temple University), the Conference on Culture and Communication (Temple University), the Society for the Study of Social Problems, the Image Ethics Conference and the International Conference on Visual Communication at the Annenberg School of Communications, University of Pennsylvania. For permission to reprint our work, we thank *Communication Monographs, The Quarterly Journal of Speech, The Journal of the University Film Association,* and *Current Research in Film.*

We are grateful to our families—Margaret, Daisy, and Sarah Benson, and Andy Anderson, Kisa and Kimi Takesue—for their encouragement and support.

It takes a special kind of trust, courage, and generosity to say yes to a documentary filmmaker. And so, finally, we wish to thank all the people who have allowed Wiseman, his crews, and the rest of us into their lives that we might all better understand American institutions and ourselves.

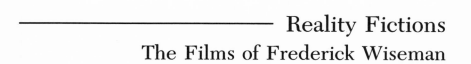

Reality Fictions
The Films of Frederick Wiseman

Chapter 1

Reality Fictions and the Rhetoric of Documentary

Frederick Wiseman is the most successful independent documentary filmmaker currently working in the United States. His work rivals that of the most distinguished originators and practitioners of the genre. And yet Wiseman stands apart from the documentary film movement as such; he has not started a movement or even a group of filmmakers, has no followers, and may be impossible to imitate. He has stretched the limits of what counts as documentary film to the point where it has challenged what at one time appeared to be fairly settled matters of style, practice, and politics, of the relations of documentary to its subjects, its audiences, its means of knowing, and its claims as art.

This book is our attempt to write a preliminary history and criticism of the body of work that Frederick Wiseman has often referred to as *reality fictions*. The term was used by Wiseman as early as 1974 and at one level is a fairly obvious way of referring to the same problem John Grierson pointed to when he said that documentary film was about "the creative treatment of actuality."[1] One works from social actuality but necessarily imposes form upon that actuality, turning it into what may be implied by the terms *art* or *fiction*.

Wiseman has sometimes used the term *reality fiction* to disclaim a responsibility to represent social actuality "objectively." At other times, he seems to use the term to advance his claim to be making "art," with all that term implies about artistic freedom, complexity, and worth in a romantic and modernist frame. At still other times, Wiseman has turned the phrase against its apparent roots in other attempts to name a hybrid form that emerged in the 1960s in film, journalism, and fiction: an inventory of such terms would include the cinema verite of French documentarians Jean Rouch and Edgar Morin; the direct cinema associated with Americans Robert Drew, Richard Leacock, Albert and David Maysles, and Donn Pennebaker, and with the Canadians grouped around Allan King (who once referred to his work as "actuality drama"); the nonfiction novel of Truman Capote; and the novel-as-history, history-as-novel of Norman Mailer. Wiseman at one time referred

1

to his work as "reality dream," and only later as "reality fictions"; later, he commented that he had used the term *reality fictions* as a parody of attempts to label what he and other documentary filmmakers were doing.[2]

Wiseman's use of the term *reality fictions* is characteristic of his relations to the press and public. At times, he has used the term as an apparently serious attempt to point to the inevitably constructive nature of documentary film. At other times, he has used the term in a more combative way, either to disclaim any responsibility to maintain a literal accuracy to the "reality" he records on camera and tape or to assert the claims of his films to be regarded as art and to be read with the same level of interpretive complexity as serious fiction. He has also used the term as an apparent thrust at the implied claims to truth of cinema verite and direct cinema. Coming full circle to pull the rug out from under those of his own admirers who were willing to take up the banner of "reality fiction" on his behalf, Wiseman has also said that "partially in reaction to the concept of cinema verite, I came up with my own parody-pomposity term called reality fiction."[3] Wiseman's use of the term *reality fiction* seems less like a claim upon film theory than a way of pointing at the inevitable tension between social actuality and film form. Wiseman is not a film theorist. Similarly, this is not a book primarily about film theory, nor is it an attempt to locate the theory of a form called "reality fiction," as a theoretical entity, a genre, or a comprehensive explanation for the whole body of Frederick Wiseman's documentary work. Our approach will draw from and perhaps contribute to theoretical, genre, and auteurist approaches to film, but we do not see it as being located primarily in any one of those well-known domains.

Our approach to Wiseman's work is drawn, broadly speaking, from a rhetorical perspective. A rhetorical approach is nowadays widely understood as being interested in the way meanings are constructed and communicated through a variety of symbolic actions and processes. In ancient Athens and Rome, rhetoric had to do with the theory and practice of public, spoken argument. As the rhetorical tradition has evolved through the nearly two thousand years since the theories of Plato, Aristotle, and Cicero, it has come to be used as a way of referring to what Kenneth Burke has called "symbolic inducement," that is, to the ways in which humans make meanings out of the forms they construct and perceive in the world.[4]

A rhetorical perspective points the critic-historian at the whole enterprise of communication. Essential to a rhetorical inquiry is the notion that it is justified by an interest in actual human practices. At one end of the process, people sit before their television screens, or in auditoriums, watching Wiseman's documentaries, making sense out of them, experiencing the thoughts and feelings that the films somehow arouse. Critics try to find words to describe what that audience experience may be like, understanding, of course, that words are only an approximation and that every person experiences the films to some degree idiosyncratically. And yet the films are social constructions and as such invite shared experiences. The rhetorical critic inquires into that shared experience, not by surveying audience response, and not simply by reporting the critic's subjective, impressionistic responses, but by interrogating the film itself, regarding the film as a constructed invitation to a complex experience of thoughts and feelings. At best, the film is an "invitation" rather than a "cause" of its viewer's response—a critic can describe the film badly or describe insensitively the response that the film seems to invite in its audience. And of course the viewer may decline the invitation. Properly executed, however, a rhetorical criticism, in identifying both the experience of the film and the way in which the film brings about that experience, may open the film to discussion in a way audiences and filmmakers might find useful. It is beyond the scope of the rhetorical method to determine with finality how viewers would see a particular film, and it is against its spirit to reduce the alleged "meaning" of a film to a stale didacticism; it is against the very ethics of rhetoric as a view of the world to attempt to dictate to viewers how they must see a film, but part of the ethical obligation of the rhetorical critic is to attempt to persuade viewers, on occasion, how they should view a film; the rhetorical perspective is meant to prompt inquiry as part of the process of enabling choice. We shall, in this inquiry into Wiseman's films, attempt to retain an attitude that is interrogative rather than declarative or imperative.

Frederick Wiseman's documentaries are both artistic experiences and social documents. The films speak to us about the politics of American institutions, and about difficult legal, social, educational, scientific, and other public matters. After their first showings on public television, they are widely seen in secondary distribution in classrooms. Because they speak so profoundly and with such a liberating freshness of the experience of institutional politics and the petty oppressions of everyday life, it seems especially important to understand not only what they say and by what cinematic/rhetorical means they construct their meanings, but also how they come to be made, through the whole process of identifying subjects, locating willing institutions, securing consent to film, collaboratively recording the sound and images that will make up the film, gaining access to funding and air time on public television, maintaining an independent distribution company, and coping with the legal and other challenges that sometimes arise in dealing with controversial material. These matters are of considerable historical interest to those who make or study documentary films, but they must also be a concern to anyone who would make use of documentary as a way of knowing something about the issues and institutions it depicts.

At every step in the process of production and distribution, the filmmaker, no matter how independent, is making choices that constrain the form of the work and its reception and interpretation by the public. Frederick Wiseman has been notably successful as an independent producer of documentaries. As is clear from his films, and from his many interviews, he regards independence as a central issue in human experience. When we mentioned to him, for example, that we were interested in his films, in how he maintains the freedom and independence to make them, and in the constraints within or against which he finds himself working, he replied, "What constraints? There are no constraints. I get the money and I make the films. There are no constraints." Such a reply is valuable as evidence of Frederick Wiseman's view of the world and of his work, but it cannot brush aside the question of how his films come to be as they are. Clearly at the center of the whole enterprise are Wiseman's intelligence, sensibility, and willpower. But readers who are interested in Wiseman's films not only as expressions of his character, chapters in his autobiography, but also as social documents, may wish to consider the whole series of shaping forces that intervene in various ways between the institutions Wiseman observes and the films we see on the screen.

Take, for example, the question of Wiseman's cameramen.[5] Four brilliant cinematographers, each with independent credentials, have worked on Wiseman's films. John Marshall, Richard Leiterman, William Brayne, and John Davey are not merely transparent windows for Wiseman's vision; in the work of each—and this persists into the finished films—are embedded each man's way of working with subjects, working with Wiseman, seeing the world through a lens. And so, for the understanding of any one of the films, it is perhaps useful to have some idea of the working methods of each of these cameramen. Their accounts of the process of filming differ from Wiseman's, as it is perhaps natural that they should. They clearly respect Wiseman as a filmmaker and enjoyed working with him, partly because they felt they were given considerable freedom and support. They felt able and encouraged to make their own special contributions to the films. And yet in Wiseman's interviews, the cameramen are not mentioned by name; Wiseman typically gives the sense that the cameramen are at virtually every moment simply carrying out his very specific directions about what to shoot and how to shoot it. Surely it cannot be both ways. Surely Wiseman's account tells us something about his image of his own independence. Consider further the matter of the cameramen at the level, not of the individual films, but across the films. It seems clear that because of Wiseman's methods of work, there is nowhere for a cameraman to go in his collaboration with Wiseman except to repeat the process or get out. For all the pleasure and professional satisfaction they clearly took in working with Wiseman, three cinematographers were eventually replaced: John Marshall, because of a dispute about *Titicut Follies;* Richard Leiterman, because he had other work to do when Wiseman wanted to film *Law and Order;* William Brayne, apparently, because the documentary work was becoming a dead end, and he could pursue other interests only by breaking with Wiseman.[6] Each of these cameramen had his own reasons for moving on, and we do not wish to suggest, except for the special case of John Marshall, that there was any particular dissatisfaction on either side of the arrangement. But the working pattern, the pattern of independence, that makes Wiseman's films possible also seems to make it inevitable that after a time either Wiseman or his cinematographers will see that it is time to break up the partnership. We do not presume to judge this pattern, but it does seem to be a responsibility, not only to the historical record but also to an adequate critical understanding of the films, to see that a working arrangement, created by Frederick Wiseman out of some combination of personal preference, economic necessity, and industry practice, from time to time results in his hiring a new cinematographer—and that this considerably alters the way the films look, and therefore what they *mean* for the viewer as an experience. This example of the cinematographer as a constraint both upon the look of a particular film and upon the viewer's interpretation can be repeated for every phase of the production process; we have tried to give an account of those that seemed most important and that were reasonably accessible to us, and we have tried to do so without suggesting that any of these constraints *determined* the films or their interpretation.

To arrive at a view of the films as inviting a viewer's experience, and then to push backwards to inquire into how that experience was brought about, it seemed necessary to us to deal with various layers separately. A viewer's experience of the film takes place as a result of, but usually without any particular knowledge of the real world of the subject, the actual intentions of the filmmaker, or any of the various technical and administrative processes of production and distribution. Hence, it seemed that some of the films needed to be treated, for the most part, from the viewer's perspective. Chapters 3 through 9 take this essentially audience-oriented perspective on eight of Wiseman's films and consider various ways of reading each film. Rather than repeating the same intepretive strategy for each film, we have tried to shift our approach in such a way as to set forth, for each film, a reading that was true to the particular film and yet also contributed to reading the other films in Wiseman's work. Each, we think, can stand on its own as a partial reading of the film being examined; together, the chapters are intended as an account of the various reading strategies that Wiseman seems to invite for each of the films. This approach clearly has the danger of lacking symmetry, so that the reading of any given film is not strictly parallel to the reading of any other, but the alternatives seemed to us unacceptable: either we could write a long book about just one film, which would considerably restrict the usefulness of a book intended to inquire into the work of a filmmaker; or we could impose an artificial symmetry that would force us to leave out of consideration matters that seem to press themselves upon the viewer.[7]

Chapter 2 considers in some detail the circumstances under which Wiseman's films have been made, distributed, and, in the case of *Titicut Follies*, subjected to a variety of legal proceedings. The chapter offers a historical account of Wiseman's first documentary and of the largely successful attempts of the Commonwealth of Massachusetts to restrict its exhibition. The trials of *Titicut Follies* raise crucial and ongoing issues about the relation of social documentary to its subjects and audiences and provide a rare opportunity to see the issues of documentary ethics, consent, filmmakers' intentions and methods, and exhibition argued in an adversarial setting, and under oath. Our account of the *Titicut Follies* case, relying on interviews, journalistic accounts, and especially on the legal record, including the *Commonwealth v. Wiseman* transcript, provides a special opportunity to consider the issues and forces that independent documentarians must contend with in shaping their work.

In the course of our research for this book, we conducted extensive interviews with each of Wiseman's four cinematographers, as well as with Robert Kotlowitz, vice-president at WNET and an important institutional advocate for Wiseman; an early draft of the book contained a long chapter including those interviews. Considerations of space have forced us to drop that chapter. We have tried to seek a balance between the realities of production and distribution, on the one hand, and the freewheeling speculativeness of the films themselves, on the other hand, without homogenizing them. The technical apparatus of film and the politics of public broadcasting have much to do with the form and the very existence of the films, which of course constrains viewer perceptions, but viewers typically cannot read a film's history directly in the film itself. Cinematographer Richard Leiterman recalled that both he and Wiseman were self-consciously pursuing the issue of gender and sexuality in filming *High School,* which seems in part to confirm our reading of the film. But is a reading of a text confirmed just because a filmmaker agrees with a critic? Or disagrees? In our interview with William Brayne, he discussed a shot in *Basic Training,* interpreting it in such a way as to make our own reading of the shot, in its context, seem like a typical academic "overreading." Does a cameraman's description of the literally descriptive or merely narrative intention of a shot mean that the shot bears no other meanings? Our own view, which seems consistent both with traditional accounts of film history and theory and with Wiseman's work, is that the shot—and all others—must inevitably be read in the context of the unfolding experience of the film and that, especially in a Wiseman documentary, the audience is put in the peculiar position of having to "overread" all the shots or not being able to make sense of them at all. But once overreading begins, where does it end? If we can make sense of the films only by going beyond the narrative and descriptive levels, does that mean we are forced, or invited, to read there anything at all? Are the films merely inkblots? We think not.

One of the major contributions of Wiseman's films is their ongoing speculation about American institutional life, a speculation that is rigorously organized and managed by the filmmaker. The films are a form of social discourse, it seems to us, but never rigidly didactic, inviting the spectator not so much to accept an argument as to participate in a vision, to share an attitude, to experience a recognition.

Our own work is presented as a partial history and a partial interpretation of Frederick Wiseman's work, as a conversation with that work and with our readers. In saying that this book is an interpretation, we do not mean to claim that what we are saying is what Fred Wiseman would say if he chose, explicitly, to interpret his own work—as he has usually refused to do. Our work necessarily differs from Wiseman's partly in that it takes upon itself an obligation that his stance and circumstance deny him: namely, the obligation to state potential interpretations of the films and their construction explicitly, so that they may be subjected to further argument. Similarly, we recognize that our own method and tone differ from Wiseman's. We have no wish to substitute our own meanings for his, but it also seemed wrong to us to try to imitate him or compete with him. It is worth noting as a feature of Wiseman's art that he tempts his viewers and critics to congratulate themselves on how smart they are; it is no less a feature of his art to make the claims of viewers and critics to wisdom, insight, or interpretive authority feel foolish and hollow. For just as he positions us as voyeurs of human folly, he entices us to be connoisseurs of our own foolishness. Wiseman's films are often joyously, even arrogantly, assertive of their own brilliance; but they are as often comically, even sardonically, reflexive about their own limits, sometimes pushing the comedy of those limits near the edge of despair. Let us begin the story where he did, with *Titicut Follies*.

Chapter 2

Documentary Dilemmas
The Trials of *Titicut Follies*

Frederick Wiseman's first documentary, *Titicut Follies* (1967), is the only American film whose use has court-imposed restrictions for reasons other than obscenity or national security.[1] *Titicut Follies* is a bitterly critical documentary account of the prison hospital for the mentally ill at the Massachusetts Correctional Institution at Bridgewater.[2] After allowing Wiseman access to the institution to shoot the film, the Commonwealth of Massachusetts took him to court to prevent the film from being exhibited. Because the struggle for control of *Titicut Follies* entered the courts, a debate regarding the intentions, procedures, and effects of this film was made public. By examining that debate and constructing from it a history of *Titicut Follies*, told primarily from the public record, we hope to offer a sense of the complex interaction that takes place among filmmakers, subjects, and audiences in the negotiation for the meaning and use of documentary films. Familiarity with this volatile context is essential in understanding the influence and worth of Wiseman's remarkable documentary series.

No later Wiseman film has met with the organized resistance leveled at *Titicut Follies*, but many of the questions raised about the Bridgewater documentary continue to be asked about subsequent films. The legal battle regarding *Titicut Follies* provided Wiseman and his numerous supporters an occasion to explain and to defend the film in a manner that has not been repeated. Still, the style Wiseman developed while working on *Titicut Follies*, in the sense both of working procedures and of filmic construction, has remained essentially consistent across his documentary productions.

We present the history of *Titicut Follies* as a narrative in generally chronological order, with each section of the chapter organized around a central dilemma. These dilemmas are not unique to the case of *Titicut Follies*, but endemic to the documentary enterprise, and especially to the form known as direct cinema, which Wiseman has so greatly influenced.

The Politics of Asking and the Myth of Informed Consent

Speaking before a university audience a decade after the 1967 release of *Titicut Follies*, Fred Wiseman was questioned about the controversial documentary. He quipped, "Bridgewater, like any maximum security prison, is not the kind of place you parachute into and hide in the hills and make forays into the cell blocks when nobody's looking. [Hesitation] It took a year for me to get permission to make *The Follies*."[3] The filmmaker's sarcasm anticipates and mocks any suggestion of clandestine filmmaking in the *Titicut Follies* project. The film's history begins not with claims of journalistic rights, although such rights later became the filmmaker's primary legal defense, but with what Wiseman has called the "politics of asking."[4] Whether one sees the litigious and often acrimonious history of *Titicut Follies* as a demonstration of an unfortunate, avoidable breakdown in communication, an exercise in cross purposes and sensibilities, or an example of personal betrayal, consent—as bureaucratic procedure, ethical imperative, and oral contract—is the key concept of the first stage in the film's history.

There is wide consensus that consent is not valid unless it was given under conditions free of coercion and deception, with full knowledge of the procedures and anticipated effects, and by someone competent to consent. A documentary filmed at a state institution with characteristics of both a maximum security prison and a mental hospital strained each condition of validity. Still, the incarcerated subjects stood a chance of gaining if the film led to improved conditions at Bridgewater. In documentaries dedicated to social reform, consent negotiations with persons in power are particularly problematic, since full disclosure of intent could easily result in withdrawal of support. The balance of risk and benefit thus presented a dilemma of procedural ethics for the Bridgewater documentarians.

Wiseman began his pursuit for permission to film a documentary at Massachusetts Correctional Institution-Bridgewater, a permission required by state law,[5] by the most direct and standard of procedures: he personally contacted the superintendent of the facility. Identifying himself as a member of the instructional staff in sociology at Brandeis University, Wiseman telephoned Superintendent Charles Gaughan in the spring of 1965. Their conversation concerned Wiseman's instructional work in the area of legal medicine. That May, Wiseman met with Gaughan to discuss a potential documentary film. In his capacity as a Boston University law instructor, Wiseman had first visited Bridgewater in the spring of 1959, shortly after Gaughan's appointment. Later Wiseman recalled, "Ever since I began to take law classes to Bridgewater, I'd wanted to do a film there."[6]

Although Wiseman was a novice filmmaker in 1965, he held impressive personal and professional credentials upon which to draw in presenting himself to state officials. He was the only child of Jacob Leo Wiseman, a distinguished attorney who practiced law in Boston for sixty years, and

Gertrude Kotzen Wiseman, administrator of the psychiatry department at Children's Hospital in Boston. Jacob Wiseman had immigrated from Russia as a child; he later became a leader in Boston's Jewish community and a staunch Republican.[7] Jacob's son Frederick received a classic New England education: Boston Latin, Rivers Country Day School, Williams College, Yale Law School. After Fred Wiseman graduated from Yale, he worked briefly in the Massachusetts attorney general's office and then was drafted. While in the army, he served as a court reporter for the judge advocate general's office in Fort Benning, Georgia, and Philadelphia. After his military discharge in 1956, Wiseman spent two years in Paris, where he first studied at the Sorbonne on the G.I. Bill and then worked for an American attorney. While in France, Wiseman bought a movie camera and shot eight-millimeter film of life in the Parisian streets.[8] Returning to Boston in 1958, Wiseman was a research associate at Boston University's Law-Medicine Institute and, later, a lecturer at Boston University's Law School; he received a Russell Sage grant in 1961 to study in the department of Social Relations at Harvard; in 1963, Wiseman was awarded a National Institute of Mental Health grant, which coincided with his appointment as a research associate in the Sociology Department at Brandeis University.

Wiseman's experience as a film producer began in 1960 when he purchased the film rights to Warren Miller's novel *The Cool World* for five hundred dollars. An adaptation of Miller's grim story of Harlem street youth was produced by Wiseman, directed by Shirley Clarke, and released in 1964. Wiseman's experience with *The Cool World* convinced him that he wanted to direct and that "there was no mystery in the process."[9]

Holding an undergraduate degree from Harvard and two graduate degrees, Charles Gaughan had worked as a social worker, a community organizer, and an administrator for the State Commission on Alcoholism and the State Department of Public Health before going to Bridgewater in 1959. During his superintendency, he had been conducting an active and largely unsupported campaign to improve the antiquated, understaffed facilities at Bridgewater.

A large, complex facility with 139 buildings spread over 1,500 acres, MCI-Bridgewater was divided into four divisions with four distinct populations: a state hospital for the criminally insane (with approximately 600 men), a prison department for alcoholics sentenced by the courts and voluntarily committed for drug addiction and inebriety (with 600 to 1,000 men), a facility for defective delinquents suffering from gross retardation (with around 150 men), and a treatment center for the sexually dangerous (with around 150 men).[10] Although only approximately 15 percent of the total population had ever been convicted of a crime—many were sent there for a twenty- to thirty-day observation period—the institution was administered by the Department of Correction, rather than the Department of Mental Health. These two state units, often representing quite different and even contradictory goals, participated in a precarious alliance at Bridgewater. Correction officers were accustomed to taking medical instructions from doctors and security commands from supervisors. In 1965 the oldest of Massachusetts' twelve mental hospitals and the most confining, Bridgewater served as a threatened destination to patients or inmates in order "to allay difficulties in other mental health or correctional facilities."[11] Institutions like Bridgewater became "Siberias"[12] for correctional and medical staffs, who were frequently undertrained, underpaid, and overworked. Doctors who were marginal within their own profession often provided the treatment in such institutions.[13] In the mid-sixties, Bridgewater used the services of foreign physicians practicing on partial licenses. At the time *Titicut Follies* was filmed, two psychiatrists and one "junior physician" cared for six hundred men in the hospital section of MCI-Bridgewater.[14] Gross shortages existed in all personnel areas: security, medical, nursing, and social work. It was not uncommon during the early 1960s for a state official to visit MCI-Bridgewater, publicly express outrage at the miserable conditions, demand reform, promise support, and then go on to other projects.

Encouraged by Gaughan's expressed interest in a Bridgewater film project, Wiseman, accompanied by *Boston Herald Traveler* journalist George Forsythe, returned to the institution in early June. Forsythe had previously visited Bridgewater with a district court judge and at the time had indicated a special interest in the prison department and its treatment of alcoholics. Wiseman and Forsythe spoke to Gaughan of grant funding, broadcast on National Educational Television (NET), use of the film by institutions and organizations, and the possibility of tracing an alcoholic inmate from the initial court disposition to confinement at Bridgewater. Other subthemes were discussed. Superintendent Gaughan was particularly eager to educate the citizenry about the variety of services at Bridgewater and the difficulties the staff encountered in providing those services adequately. At that time, both Wiseman and Gaughan assumed that heightened public awareness would improve conditions; both subscribed to the Griersonian notion that a documentary film could be a direct agent of change. Both saw opportunities in the documentary tradition of social indignation.

Seeing Wiseman's documentary proposal as an extension of his courageous informational campaign, Gaughan became Wiseman's "internal advocate."[15] Gaughan introduced Wiseman to James Canavan, the public relations director for the Department of Correction, at a meeting in mid-June, at which Canavan screened a documentary made at MCI-Walpole and Wiseman showed *The Cool World*. Gaughan later recalled describing the Walpole film as "didactic" and expressing the hope that a Bridgewater film would "not follow that general outline" (*Commonwealth of Massachusetts v. Wiseman*, tr. 4:19). Wiseman's recollection of Gaughan's reaction to the screening session suggests a sensibility and an optimism rare, if not misplaced, in a prison administrator.

After viewing both films, Mr. Gaughan . . . said . . . he did not want a film made like the one that had been made at Walpole because . . . it was a phony film, that it only expressed one point of view, that it had no depth and that it didn't accurately portray, as far as he knew, the conditions at Walpole and . . . it was more a public relations job. He said the kind of film he wanted made at Bridgewater was a film that would be beautiful and poetic and true, and . . . that *The Cool World* was such a film. . . . He also said . . . that there was no film that I could make at Bridgewater that could hurt Bridgewater. (Tr. 13:20)

Wiseman had Gaughan's firm support by midsummer, but that was not enough; the project required the approval of the department head. Therefore, Gaughan talked to his immediate supervisor, John A. Gavin, on Wiseman's behalf. Gavin's recent appointment as Commissioner of Correction by Governor John Volpe had followed the controversial dismissal of a well-respected, reform-minded penologist. After meeting with Gavin and two of his deputies in August, Wiseman sent a letter of request to film, accompanied by a five-page proposal to Gavin.

Dated August 19, 1965, and written under the letterhead "Wiseman Film Productions" (with Wiseman's home address in Cambridge), the letter announced that the proposed film on Bridgewater "would be made for showing on NET," would also be available "for teaching and training purposes," and was under negotiation for NET or foundation funding.[16] Although the letter implied that releases would be obtained, it did not mention who would collect the releases or who would be released from liability. Judgments as to competency were delegated, however. Wiseman wrote, "No people will be photographed who do not have the competency to give a release. The question of competency would in all cases be determined by the Superintendent and his staff and we would completely defer to their judgment."[17]

The letter included an offer of additional information beyond the enclosed proposal and closed with self-references of respect, gratitude, and hope: "appreciative of a chance to talk with you . . . very grateful for the courtesies extended . . . by you, Superintendent Gaughan, and Mr. Canavan . . . I look forward to hearing from you."

The attached proposal, although certainly not belligerent, displayed the confidence that flows from elaboration and enthusiasm. It fluctuated between specificity and vagueness, between predictions of a rather routinely scripted documentary and plans for an ambitious and determinedly innovative work. Counsel for the state would later seize upon details of the proposal as promises unkept.[18] Superior Court Judge Harry Kalus, in his summary of facts found by the court, included three of the ten paragraphs of the proposal as "pertinent excerpts."

This will be a film about the Massachusetts Correctional Institution at Bridgewater. Bridgewater is a prison for (1) the criminally insane, (2) defective delinquents, (3) alcoholics, (4) narcotics addicts, (5) sexual deviates, (6) juvenile offenders. The prison therefore has a cross-section of the problems confronting the state in dealing with a wide range of behavior of individuals whom the state must (1) Punish, (2) Rehabilitate, (3) Treat, (4) Segregate. The purpose of this film is to give people an understanding of these problems and the alternatives available to the state and its citizens.

The story of the film would be that of *three people*—an inmate most of whose adult life had been spent at Bridgewater; a youthful offender committed from the Roxbury District Court for a 35 day observation period (Judge McKenney, Chief Judge of the Roxbury, Massachusetts, District Court, has granted us permission to photograph the sentencing); and a Correctional Officer intimately concerned with the day to day functioning of the institution. In showing the day to day activities of these *three people* it will be possible to illustrate the various services performed—custodial, punitive, rehabilitative and medical as well as the conflicting and complementary points of view of prisoner, patient, guard, family, legislature, etc.

This will be a film about a prison and the people who are in it and those that administer it, as well as their families, friends, and the institutions, groups, agencies and forces within the community that either aid or hinder the custody, rehabilitation, punishment and return to community life of those who have been sentenced by the courts to prison. [emphasis added by Kalus][19]

Kalus did not mention Wiseman's unrealized prediction that the documentary would be "written by George Forsythe," but he did note Wiseman's listing of consultants: Superintendent Charles Gaughan and Brandeis sociology professors Morris Schwartz, John Seely, and Maurice Stein. The proposal also mentioned employing two more staples of the traditional educational film, neither of which was used: interviews and professional actors—"if it becomes apparent that a significant segment of the reality of prison life is impossible to obtain from a participant." Yet running throughout the outline was the promise (or threat) of a self-consciously poetic work that would tap the metaphoric potential of Bridgewater and attempt innovation in both content and form. Thus, two voices emerged: one a cautious traditionalist, the other a restless experimenter. Wiseman straightforwardly stated:

Bridgewater will be shown as an institution where conflicting and complementary forces within the larger community . . . meet.

Implicit in all our experience is an awareness of how similar problems have been dealt with in other countries, therefore . . . the prison itself becomes a metaphor for some important aspects of American life.

The technique of the film . . . will give an audience factual material about a state prison but will also give an imaginative and poetic quality that will set it apart from the cliche documentary about crime and mental illness.

The bringing together of seemingly disparate material [audio and film footage from two different sources] will be used to provide a kind of condensation and counterpoint necessary to make the film dramatic.

Wiseman's summary of his intentions—in their radical willingness to challenge conventional notions of confinement and in a simultaneous effort to praise the status quo—exhibited the complex, even contradictory, impulses that characterize the entire proposal. "Therefore, the content and structure of the film will [among other goals] dramatize the sometimes great, and often slight, differences that exist between those inside and outside of prisons and mental hospitals and to portray that we are all more simply human than otherwise . . . [and will] develop an awareness of . . . the dedicated and skillful work involved in the attempt to provide rehabilitation and dure *[sic]*."

It was the proposal of an intelligent, imaginative, eager producer-director; it was a declaration of possibilities too numerous to find their way into a single film. Therefore, it is easy to imagine how a dedicated, optimistic administrator, weary of the didacticism of state-sponsored projects, might read his own dreams into this proposal *and* how anyone committed to the smooth running of a frequently criticized and routinely underfunded state department might see the documentary as one more risk easily avoided. Whatever their reasons, Gaughan continued to support the project and Gavin, after first notifying Wiseman that he would "explore aspects of doing the film with his staff," wrote a letter of denial to film (Ex. 3).

Gavin's letter to Wiseman stated that he had made a careful judgment, after "considerable discussion with [his] staff and others regarding the total implications of such a film . . . and with full awareness of several complications which may arise." Although Gavin's reasons were vague, his answer was clearly no. "I am sorry to inform you that I cannot permit the filming of this story."

Gavin's letter emphasized his "careful review of [the Wiseman] proposal," but at the subsequent legislative hearing regarding the film he testified that there was no enclosure with the Wiseman letter of request (which began, "I am enclosing a statement of the proposed film on Bridgewater"). At the trial, Gavin said that his earlier testimony had been in error. He had received the proposal, but only "scanned" the memo of request and referred the Wiseman correspondence to Deputy Commissioner Falls, supposedly accompanied by an interoffice memo written by Gavin which stated that "it is also understood that nothing will be filmed or included that is not approved by the Department of Correction" (Tr. 3:82).

Certainly many requests pass through the office of a state department head. It is possible that the initial decision to deny was made not by Gavin, but by a staff member. Saying no is a routine duty for many assistants, and no documentary film had ever been made at Bridgewater, so it was a request with no precedent of approval; however, the letter does bear Gavin's signature. Gaughan did not receive a copy of the denial and later testified that he did not realize that Gavin had reached a decision that summer (Tr. 4:147).

For a less determined filmmaker, a denial from the Commissioner of Correction's office would have meant the end to the project, but Wiseman did not accept no as his answer. At Gaughan's suggestion, Wiseman made arrangements to contact Lieutenant Governor Elliot Richardson. Widely regarded as a shrewd politician and a gentleman, Richardson was an important bridge figure in Massachusetts politics in the 1960s. A Brahmin by education, social background, and personal style, Richardson nevertheless sided with the liberal Democrats on many civil rights issues that were dividing the nation and the Commonwealth. In the 1964 campaign, John Volpe had promised Massachusetts voters that if the Republican "team" were elected, Elliot Richardson, as lieutenant governor, would have heavy responsiblities in the areas of health, education, and welfare.[20] Volpe did narrowly achieve the reelection he had been denied in 1962, and Richardson also was elected by a slight margin in what was "increasingly a one-party Democratic state."[21] As lieutenant governor, Richardson had visited Bridgewater twice in 1965. Appalled by conditions at the prison hospital and the lack of public interest in improving them, he pledged his support for their reform.

In the fall of 1965, Katherine Kane, a young liberal Democrat who held a seat in the Massachusetts General Court (the state legislature) from the influential Beacon Hill district of Boston, arranged for Richardson and Wiseman to meet. Kane and her husband had invested in *The Cool World* and strongly supported Wiseman's creative aspirations and his expressed goals of institutional reform. Describing Wiseman as an accomplished documentary filmmaker, Representative Kane asked Richardson to see Wiseman, which he did, in early October. On meeting Wiseman and reading his written proposal, Richardson telephoned Gavin, said he knew Wiseman personally, and asked the commissioner to reconsider his earlier decision about the Bridgewater documentary. Several months later, in January of 1966, Kane, a member of the Committee on Public Welfare and of the Special Commission on Sentencing and Release, telephoned Gavin to indicate her support of the Wiseman project. Later, under oath, both Gavin and Richardson strongly denied that any political pressure had been exerted on Gavin.

Gavin did reconsider his decision. In late January, the commissioner met with Wiseman and Gaughan and gave his verbal go-ahead for the film, pending advice from the state attorney general regarding whether he had the *right* to approve such a project. There is no written record of this meeting; the reconstructions of the three participants are in disagreement regarding crucial facts. According to Gavin, Wiseman agreed that any release of the film would be contingent on the final approval of the Correction Department (Tr. 3:89–90, 119). Wiseman has consistently denied such contingencies, claiming that the only conditions agreed upon were that the film crew would be accompanied by a Bridgewater staff member at all times during filming; that only competent inmates and patients would be photographed, with competency determined by the prison staff; and that several individuals (notably Albert De Salvo, the self-claimed "Boston Strangler") would not be photographed (Tr. 14:63). There was no written contract. Within the week,

Gavin wrote Attorney General Edward Brooke for a legal opinion. Although the letter was written under the MCI-Bridgewater/Gaughan letterhead and cosigned by Superintendent Gaughan, Gavin never referred to the Bridgewater official in the text of the letter; all five first-person references were singular (Ex. 4). Once again, Gavin exhibited an unusual style of indicating, while somehow simultaneously rejecting, joint decision making with Gaughan. A combination of assertiveness and caution is a bureaucratic phenomenon; certainly the tendency to court and abdicate responsibility was pronounced in Gavin's consent style. Subsequent trial testimony revealed that Gaughan had written "almost all" of the text (Gaughan, tr. 4:159). Gavin had made a few changes, which Gaughan adopted, then the superintendent drafted the letter, signed it, and served it to Gavin for his signature.

Earlier Gavin had asserted his power to say no to Wiseman, but he later doubted his right to say yes. Gavin signaled his awareness of potential legal complexities when he wrote Brooke: "I have told [Wiseman] that I would give him permission to make the film. Provided, however, that the rights of the inmates and patients at Bridgewater are fully protected. . . . I would very much appreciate your views on the question of whether or not I can give permission to do this" (Ex. 4). In describing the precautions Wiseman would take, Gavin mentioned the photographing of only those who were competent to sign releases, which Wiseman had promised in his letter of request. The commissioner did not mention Wiseman's stated expectations that the Bridgewater staff would determine competence. Gavin also claimed that Wiseman had assured him that he would "obtain a written release from each inmate and patient whose photograph is used in the film," an assurance that Wiseman never made in writing and consistently denied (Tr. 4:103–4).

There is no indication by joint address or carbon copy notation that Wiseman was sent a copy of Gavin's letter to Brooke, but Wiseman was aware of the request. The lawyer-filmmaker actively sought a favorable legal opinion when he visited Brooke personally at the attorney general's office in late February or early March. There he was informed that an opinion was being prepared.

Brooke's advisory opinion, dated March 21, 1966, quoted a Massachusetts General Law that designated the superintendent as the party responsible for prisoners.[22] Brooke then stated: "Unless your rules or regulations provide otherwise, the granting of the requested permission would be within the discretion of the Superintendent of the Institution at Bridgewater, who is cosigner of your request. There does not appear to be any provision, whether statutory, constitutional or common law, to the effect that a *consenting* inmate at the Institution may not be photographed (assuming that such an inmate is mentally competent to give his consent)" (Ex. 5).

Brooke cited legal decisions that supported both the jailer's duty to exclude intruders and his large discretionary powers "in determining at what time, under what circumstances, and what persons not having legal authority may be permitted to enter the jail or to have access to prisoners." Brooke thus informed Gavin that it was not the commissioner's decision, but Gaughan's. Again, oddly, copies were not noted.

The same day—March 21—Gavin sent a copy of the Brooke letter and a cover letter to Gaughan. The commissioner's letter of transmittal indicated that he still perceived himself as a vital link in the Commonwealth's decision chain. "On the basis of the attached, you have my permission to proceed to make appropriate arrangements with Mr. Wiseman and get started with the usual precautions" (Ex. 5a).

Here Gavin doubly qualified his responsibility by noting that his approval was based on Brooke's opinion and contingent on Gaughan's following "the usual precautions." These precautions, left unspecific then, became rigorous indeed in Gavin's later testimony before the legislature: "The usual precautions are that no faces are shown in any of our institutions in filming, that no man's picture is shown under any conditions unless he signs a legal release, that he has to be competent to sign such a legal release and that the filming of such inside an institution would be supervised."[23]

A week after the release of Brooke's opinion, Wiseman went to Gaughan's office, where he obtained the (oral) consent that was now Gaughan's to give. It had taken a year to get, but Fred Wiseman finally had his permission to make a documentary film at MCI-Bridgewater. Although not an attorney, Gaughan later claimed he explained the conditions of Brooke's advisory opinion when he gave a copy of it to Wiseman and that the lawyer-filmmaker said, in substance, "I can live with that." Gaughan later insisted that these conditions included a final right of approval by the state; Wiseman has been equally insistent in denying any censorship agreement. Such conditions are not stipulated in the advisory opinion. The opinion does quote Gavin's assumption that Wiseman would be responsible for obtaining releases from all photographed persons. Wiseman never made objection to that expectation in the meeting with Gaughan or in writing later. Charlie and Fred, as they addressed each other by then, seem to have assumed an equal familiarity with and acceptance of each other's intentions regarding the Bridgewater film. It was an assumption that would prove unfounded for both of them.

The same day that Brooke and Gavin issued their approval of the film project, NET wrote Wiseman to offer advice and the possibility of broadcasting a completed film, but denied funding. Wiseman's request for foundation support was also rejected, so he turned to the most common financing method known to the independent filmmaker: a combination of personal investment by crew and friends and lab credit. By this time, George Forsythe had been more or less replaced by David Eames, another journalist and a Cambridge neighbor of Wiseman's. The two men had met earlier in the year and Wiseman had interested Eames, then a free-lance journalist with some peripheral movie experience, in the Bridgewater project, yet Eames never saw the formal proposal Wiseman had sent Gavin until litigation against the film began; neither did John Marshall, the film's cinematographer and codirector, see it.[24] Since there was neither scripted dialogue nor narration in the film, Eames's contribution as a writer per se was limited to composing letters to potential investors in the spring of 1966. As associate producer, Eames joined Wiseman in the difficult task of being frank, yet encouraging, with potential investors. Eames claimed, "We told the investors that there was little likelihood of it being a commercial success" (Tr. 7:34), yet they also indicated that they hoped to return initial investments.

Although not officially incorporated until the following November, the Bridgewater Film Company (BFC) was formed to handle all business transactions connected with the film project. A letter to a potential—and subsequent—investor assured him that "all the proceeds from the sale of the stock are to be used for the sole purpose of producing, distributing, and otherwise turning to account the documentary film tentatively entitled Bridgewater" (Tr. 7:36). Five personal friends of the director—Carl Binger, Henry Kloss, Stephen Paine, Douglas Schwalbe, and Warren Bennis—invested a total of ten thousand dollars. Wiseman, Eames, and John Marshall, who joined the crew that spring, each contributed to the financing of the film and received no compensation for labor. Following an independent tradition, the production budget was sparse. Cinematographer John Marshall had two sixteen-millimeter cameras; Wiseman, doing sound for the first time, used Marshall's Nagra recorder; Eames assisted by changing magazines and tapes, keeping records, and providing a VW van for transportation between Bridgewater and Cambridge.

Of the three-person crew, cinematographer and codirector Marshall was certainly the most technically experienced filmmaker and even his experience was limited. He had worked briefly as a cameraman for NBC in Cyprus and made ethnographic films in Africa. Marshall was best known and respected for *The Hunters* (1958), part of a family research project among the San (Bushmen) begun in 1951 when Marshall was still a high school student.[25] In 1966, Marshall—then in his midthirties, as were Wiseman and Eames—was a Harvard graduate student in anthropology.

When questioned about his motives in making *Titicut Follies*, David Eames testified that he wanted "to gain a great deal of experience in filmmaking, particularly in the documentary field. . . . Another motive was, by making the film, to try to let the public at large understand some of the conditions and problems and situations at Bridgewater which we had observed while filming there" (Tr. 7:146). Certainly when Wiseman and Eames were formally presented to the Bridgewater staff at a special meeting called April 6, 1966, for the expressed purpose of introducing the film project, it was not as men looking for some documentary film training. Their stated goal was to "educate" the public about the institution. The superintendent asked the staff members present to cooperate fully with the film crew and, according to the testimony of Gaughan and correction officers, assured them that the state had been guaranteed final approval rights (Tr. 4:40). Wiseman has contested both the guarantee and its announcement at the meeting of prison personnel. After an introduction by Gaughan, Wiseman screened *The Cool World* for the staff, answered several questions from the audience, described the noninterventionist methods of film making that would be employed and the technical innovations that made them possible, thanked the staff in advance for their cooperation, and told them that he hoped the group assembled in the prison auditorium would be among the first to see the completed Bridgewater film. Neither the filmmakers nor the superintendent gave any instructions for determining competency or for release procedures. It was made clear that anyone who objected would not be filmed, yet it was also made clear that the superintendent wanted all personnel to support the film project.

In late April, the crew began shooting footage at a rehearsal of "The Titicut Follies." An annual inmate-patient-staff variety show, "The Titicut Follies was a kind of religious event at Bridgewater in the sense that it was something that the inmates and the staff looked forward to six months before it happened and talked about afterwards."[26] ("Titicut" is the Indian name for the area in which the institution is located.) According to his own testimony, the superintendent had been eager to have scenes from "The Follies" included in the film; he was especially pleased that approval had come in time for the spring event to be filmed, since he felt it would provide some lightness (Tr. 4:168–69). Before any footage was shot, David Eames told the performers in the review about the documentary project in general, indicating that the film crew would try not to interfere with any activity while they filmed at Bridgewater. He explained the technical procedures of the filming and said that anyone who did not want to be photographed should indicate so (Tr. 13:64–65). It was an introduction that the filmmakers repeated again and again over the next few months.

Portions of each of the four performances of "The Titicut Follies" were filmed. During some performances, a friend of John Marshall's and a fellow anthropologist, Timothy Asch, operated a second camera. Edward Pacheco, a senior corrections guard who was the producer, director, and a featured performer in "The Follies," expressed an interest in escorting the filmmakers. Wiseman spoke to the superintendent on Pacheco's behalf. The director later recalled telling Gaughan, "I thought it possible that Mr. Pacheco would be an important person in the film because I felt that he had a great deal of charm and personality and was photogenic and I very much admired his manner with the inmates because he seemed to treat them so cordially, so affably, and so individually" (Tr. 13:67). Pacheco received the guide assignment and became so devoted to it that he sometimes accompanied the film crew on his days off.[27] Soon on a first-name basis with the filmmakers, Pacheco often jokingly addressed Wiseman as "landsman."[28] Eddie Pacheco became another internal advocate for Wiseman.

The three filmmakers were issued passes to the institution signed by the superintendent; their presence became routine, expected. With the exception of several minor restrictions (for example, no filming of Albert De Salvo), Gaughan permitted the crew to film anyone, anywhere in the institution. This freedom was curtailed when Dr. Harry Kozol, the director of the treatment center for the sexually dangerous, made strong objections in writing to any filming there without compliance with explicit written conditions.[29] Neither Gaughan nor Wiseman challenged Kozol's right to make these restrictions; no footage was shot at the center. (In the completed film, several patients from the center appeared in a chorus number in "The Follies," which was noticed and criticized by Kozol.) Kozol's demands that filming privileges—and he definitely saw them as just that—be subject to explicit, written conditions contrasted sharply with the implicit, oral nature of many other supposed agreements between the Bridgewater administration and the film crew.

Known as "the movie men," "the boys from Channel 2" (the Boston NET channel), "the candid camera crew," "the TV guys,"[30] Wiseman, Marshall, and Eames found the correction officers, inmates, and patients generally cooperative and extremely curious about the film-making equipment and the process of movie making. No hidden cameras or microphones were ever used, but the use of relatively new high-speed film (which enabled shooting in entirely natural light) and telephoto lenses made it possible for the filmmakers, at times, to go unnoticed without being surreptitious. The directional microphone that Wiseman operated could, on occasion, pick up sounds the ear could not.[31] Yet most of the time it was perfectly clear what Marshall was filming and Wiseman was recording. Rarely did anyone object. The people of Bridgewater permitted the filmmakers to record their lives. They filmed Commissioner Gavin delivering a lecture at the training school for corrections officers at Bridgewater; they filmed Superintendent Gaughan conducting an interview with an inmate and being interviewed by Wiseman (off-camera). Soon after their arrival, the crew began to receive suggestions from guards of situations or persons that would be "interesting" to include in the Bridgewater movie. Following such leads, the crew photographed a skin search on Ward H, a high school tour of the institution, a physician interviewing a recent arrival, the same physician force feeding an inmate, a man who sang standing on his head, a burial.

There were rare objections to filming particular activities; most of these were raised by staff members on behalf of inmates or patients. Father Mulligan's request that an inmate's confession not be recorded was followed; Officer Moran's objection to the photographing of his interview of a boy under age was honored.[32] Officer Lepine later claimed he objected to the filming of nude men and was supposedly told that they would be shown only from the waist up—Wiseman denied the promise and Marshall said the agreement was misunderstood.[33] In each of these cases, prison personnel acted in their role of *parens patriae*, making consent decisions for the confined men.

In all of the consent negotiations, staff consent was assumed. Correction officers had been told by their superiors to cooperate with the photographers. One staff member, preparing a corpse for burial, objected to being filmed. Wiseman later claimed the man was reluctant because he was an unlicensed mortician, who feared the disapproval of local undertakers (Tr. 13:104–5). Wiseman testified that no inmate ever *said* he did not want to be photographed, and any inmate who expressed an unwillingness to be photographed by a gesture such as "waving away the camera, putting a hand over the face, turning around, turning a coat collar up" was not photographed (Tr. 13:132).

Marshall has described his camera work at Bridgewater, not as an activity "directed" by Wiseman, but as an emotional, personal contact he had with the people photographed.[34] He has claimed he was always sensitive to the desires of his potential subjects, yet also remembers that once he began shooting, it would have taken "a hand in front of the lens" to stop him.[35] Yet the competency of these men to consent remained highly problematic. No objections to filming were made based on determinations of incompetence to consent by the professional staff or by the correction officers who accompanied the filmmakers, which leads one to speculate that the guards had never been given the charge of determining competency, which Wiseman said he assumed. It was, not incidentally, a charge for which prison guards were unqualified.

It is not difficult to believe Gaughan's claim that he assumed the guards were with the filmmakers for security purposes only, although Gaughan was never able to clarify exactly when or by whom competency was to have been determined in his scheme of things. Nor is it difficult to believe Wiseman's claim that he was willing to invest considerable amounts of his time, money, and energy only because he assumed that anything the crew was allowed to shoot and record he would be allowed to use in the Bridgewater film. In at least one instance—a filmed incident in which guards taunted a distraught man in a sequence which became central to the case against the filmmaker—Wiseman claimed he asked the accompanying correction officers if it would be all right to film and he was told that it was.

Added to the vagueness of the consent procedures during filming were the related, and equally vague, conditions involving releases. There was never any written agreement specifically determining who would be expected to sign a release, to whom the releases would run, what form they would take, or who would expedite this process. In Wiseman's letter of August 19, 1965, he intimated that releases would be taken, but did not promise responsibility for collecting them when he wrote, "No people will be photographed who do not have the competency to give a release." Gavin's letter to Brooke, included as an interior quote in the Brooke decision, stated that

"Mr. Wiseman has assured me that . . . he will obtain a written release from each inmate and patient whose photograph is used in the film." Yet the attorney general did not explicitly state that his opinion rested on the necessity of obtaining releases.

A release is a precautionary measure; it is a protection from liability and, therefore, assumes a position potentially antagonistic to that of the releasor. Although the state's later position would be that its officers assumed that releases running to the Commonwealth had been obtained, at no time during their period at Bridgewater did the film crew receive a release form, directions for formulating one, or inquiries about such collection. When filmed, neither Commissioner Gavin nor Superintendent Gaughan asked to sign a release or questioned why releases were not being presented for signatures. Gaughan later testified that he did not know what a release was when the matter was first discussed in January, 1966.

In the spring of 1966, Wiseman, a member of the Massachusetts bar, drafted the following:

> That in consideration of the sum of $1, lawful money of these United States, to me in hand paid by the Bridgewater Film Company, with offices at 1694 Massachusetts Avenue, Cambridge, Massachusetts, and for other good and valuable considerations [sic], receipt of which is hereby acknowledged, I hereby grant to the aforesaid, the Bridgewater Film Company, its successors and assigns, the right to use my name and likeness and to portray, impersonate or simulate me and to make use of any episode of my life, factually or fictionally, in a motion picture tentatively entitled Bridgewater. This grant shall extend to remakes and reissues of the aforesaid picture, to television rights and to all phases of the exploitation of the aforesaid picture, including publicity, advertising, promotion and the like. (Ex. 19)

A form similar to the one Wiseman used during the filming of *The Cool World*, this release provided wide artistic latitude for the filmmaker and legal protection for BFC investors. Eames and Wiseman obtained signed releases from some 106 individuals, most of them staff members (Tr. 7:127). No one was ever paid the one-dollar release consideration (Tr. 7:39).

Despite a filmmaker's intentions, the procedures of direct cinema filming, whereby a small crew becomes as inconspicuous as possible, often mitigate against efficient release operations. This efficiency is further curtailed when an incident of heightened emotional import has been filmed. Of course, just such incidents are most in need of the protection to subject and filmmaker afforded by a signed release. At the trial David Eames answered a question about "missing" releases. "At the time of filming these individuals there was either too much commotion or confusion or too much activity involved in the filming to make it appropriate or, indeed, possible at that time to approach them" (Tr. 6:144). And, when asked about another instance, he stated that "the obtaining of a release from this inmate was at the time, in my mind, secondary to other duties that I had to perform at the time, such as mechanical or technical duties" (Tr. 6:148).

The direct cinema adage of "shoot and record now—decide later" worked against a systematic cataloging of persons photographed and releases obtained; however, there were "scenes" that Wiseman felt fairly sure would be in the final edit, even as filming ended in late June. Eames volunteered to return to Bridgewater to obtain a release from an individual who had previously refused to sign one, but had been the focus of several provocative filmed incidents. Eames and Wiseman agreed that Eames would get a release from anyone else that he happened to see that he "recalled not having gotten a release from during the filming" (Tr. 6:173). During that haphazardly organized trip, Eames obtained three or four releases from patients at the treatment center for the sexually dangerous who had been filmed during a performance of "The Follies."

Eames did not get a signed release from the inmate identified as No. 54 in the trial proceedings, but referred to in the film by name—Vladimir. This young inmate took advantage of the filming to state his case, frequently saying, "I want to say this to the camera" (Tr. 13:116). In at least three situations, two of which were included in *Titicut Follies*, Vladimir was filmed complaining to the staff about his treatment. Yet, when first asked to sign a release, he told Eames "he would sign it on the condition that [the filmmakers] arrange to get him out of Bridgewater and not until then" (Tr. 6:170). Eames recalled that in August Vladimir "said he would not sign a release until I showed portions of the film to members of the federal government and until I arranged to have him deported out of America and back to another country" (Tr. 6:174). Vladimir's demands, despite, and even because of, their outrageousness, showed a rare lucidity. This subject realized his reproduction on celluloid was something valuable to a filmmaker; it was a commodity to be negotiated. He did not sign a release; yet his frustrated attempts for a transfer from Bridgewater did become a central part of *Titicut Follies*.[36] Vladimir's story is a capsule version of the complexity of the consent dilemma.

Throughout the spring and summer of 1966, Wiseman and Marshall received dailies from their New York developer, DuArt Film Labs. Neither Gaughan nor Gavin ever asked to see any of the rushes, and the filmmakers did not volunteer to show any footage to them. So unfamiliar was Gaughan with the process of filmmaking that he later claimed he assumed no film was developed until the filming was entirely completed. Whether because he trusted the filmmakers' judgment and good will or believed in the state's right of final censorship, the superintendent did not interfere in any way with the filming itself. Although Gaughan testified that he reminded Wiseman of his agreements with the state on a number of occasions during the filming period, the filmmakers' freedom while shooting is apparent from the footage they took with them when they left MCI-Bridgewater.

Artistic Dilemmas: The Paradox of Reality Fiction and the Aesthetics of Uncertainty

Eleven months elapsed between the time the film crew finished shooting and recording sound at MCI-Bridgewater (June 29, 1966) and the completed editing of the film, which Wiseman would call *Titicut Follies*. While the images and voices that John Marshall and Fred Wiseman had captured on celluloid and tape remained frozen in time—raw material from which Wiseman was constructing a film—the country, the state of Massachusetts, the Boston-Cambridge area, and MCI-Bridgewater reeled in a period of flux and conflict.

The political tensions of 1966–67 created a context of discord that the Bridgewater documentary entered and extended. A national trend to reject the programs and supporters of the Great Society in the elections of 1966 spread into Massachusetts. Republicans won four top state offices: John Volpe was reelected governor by a huge plurality; Elliot Richardson narrowly won the attorney general position vacated by Edward Brooke, who was elected to the U.S. Senate; Francis Sargent replaced Richardson as lieutenant governor. Democrats retained their control of the state legislature; Representative Katherine Kane was reelected to the Massachusetts General Court. State political feuds took on an edge of particular seriousness, even bitterness, as politicians and their constituencies became polarized over national issues such as civil rights and military involvement in Vietnam. The busing of school children to integrate Boston schools continued to divide the city.[37]

Not surprisingly, given its large student population, Cambridge became a center of antiwar activity, the Berkeley of the East Coast. In April of 1967, Martin Luther King, Jr., and Benjamin Spock, accompanied by reporters, visited sympathetic Cambridge residents in a search for volunteers in the antiwar campaign. Among homes visited were those of the Wiseman and Eames families. Attorney Zipporah Wiseman, wife of the producer-director of the Bridgewater film, pledged her support to these two national leaders emblematic of civil disobedience. Here is an account of that visit, as published in a Boston paper:

> The Marty and Benny show begins at the Wiseman's place, the first act in a season-long extravaganza that is to be known as the Vietnam Summer Happening. It is an anti-war production which could put the stars on a Presidential ticket in 1968. . . .

> Of course when Mrs. Wiseman opens the door she doesn't get just Marty and Benny. She also gets about 40 newspaper and television reporters in her living room. Plus several hecklers in the front yard who call themselves the Sons of Liberty and sing an old hit, "The Star Spangled Banner," to try to upstage Marty

and Benny. . . . The first doorbell ringers [out of thousands of volunteers] are Marty and Benny on Martin Street in Cambridge, and it is disappointing because it is a setup. The Wisemans have been informed that they are to be visited, and they are known sympathizers. . . . Mrs. Wiseman says, "We're honored by your visit. . . ." And the Marty and Benny Show moves on, driven by honest concern and despair through a bewildered country that respects their accomplishments but doesn't know what to think of them now.[38]

Against this general background of political volatility in 1966–67 came the sudden explosiveness of several incidents at Bridgewater. After the film crew left the institution, Superintendent Gaughan continued his personal campaign for attention and increased funding for the forgotten men at Bridgewater. The legislature was appropriating ninety million dollars for state-wide mental care already; Volpe had promised to introduce measures to establish one hundred mental health centers in the state, which would divert funds from Bridgewater. Then Dominic Rosati, a suspected murderer, was found naked and dead in his cell at Bridgewater. An examination revealed that he had died of rat poison. The reaction to his cause of death and the revelation that some men at Bridgewater were kept naked because they were possibly suicidal provoked a cycle of wide media coverage, a public outcry about the conditions and the need for reform, and a legislative investigation that resulted in minor changes in some procedures at the prison hospital. During the January 1967 investigation prompted by the scandal, a legislative committee heard Superintendent Gaughan, medical and legal experts, and social workers describe Bridgewater as "a 'dungeon' throwback to the Dark Ages."[39] Attorney F. Lee Bailey, whose client Albert De Salvo, the self-proclaimed Boston Strangler, was sent to Bridgewater, declared, "The entire institution should be leveled and I'd be happy to do it with my own plane."[40] Once again, criticism of conditions at Bridgewater filled the Boston newspapers. By the end of January, the legislature had responded by appropriating $3.5 million for a new building at Bridgewater.

Still another weakness in the antiquated institution became obvious when De Salvo and two other inmates escaped from Bridgewater in February 1967. Superintendent Gaughan appraised the security situation. "We're holding murderers in what amounts to a hen coop."[41] A Boston journalist described public reaction to the escape: "Bay State citizens were laughing the laugh of sarcasm, of dismay, of complete digust with responsible officialdom."[42] Still another special legislative commission was formed to investigate the conditions at Bridgewater, and once again, the pattern of reaction to particular events, rather than a general concern for treatment, prevailed.

During the many months that Wiseman was editing the film—a period of intense criticism of the conditions at Bridgewater and a time of personal vulnerability for the superintendent—Gaughan called the filmmaker at least half a dozen times to check on the documentary. Each time Wiseman told the concerned administrator that the work was going very slowly (which it was) or that he had just returned from or was going out of town (which was common for him during that period). Wiseman made no offer to show Gaughan any of the footage, nor did the superintendent demand to see it.[43] Commissioner Gavin had no contact whatsoever with Wiseman during the editing period. In the spring of 1967, at Gaughan's suggestion, senior correction officers Edward Pacheco and Joseph Moran visited Wiseman at his office in Cambridge. There Wiseman introduced them to his associate editor, Alyne Model, showed them a sequence of the film in which Pacheco appeared, and took them to lunch at a Cambridge restaurant. Their meeting was cordial, but Pacheco and Moran returned to Bridgewater with little new information regarding the final film, other than an assurance that there was indeed some developed film that had been synchronized with a sound track and that the mysterious business of movie making was in progress.[44] Since the prison guards had presented themselves as friends stopping by Wiseman's work place for a casual visit, they could do no more than ask general questions, to which they received friendly but vague answers from the filmmaker.

Wiseman's evasiveness—which was later characterized by the state as irresponsible—may also be explained, at least partially, on circumstantial grounds. Like so many other uncertainties in this case, there had never been an agreement between Wiseman and Gaughan as to *when* the project would be completed. One of the advantages for Wiseman of not receiving funding was that he did not have an editing deadline, yet the price of this independence was that he, like most free-lancers, had to support himself and the film while the work was in progress. Wiseman continued to hold his position as associate in sociology at Brandeis. The same spring (1966) that he began shooting the Bridgewater film, he and an associate, Donald Schon, formed a private consulting company, The Organization for Social and Technical Innovation, Inc. (OSTI), which conducted a variety of research jobs (an evaluation of the report of the National Crime Commission before it was published; the Model Cities proposal for Greenville, Mississippi; a study of urban transportation problems for San Diego) during the period that Wiseman was also working on the Bridgewater film project.[45] Wiseman would later refer to OSTI's efforts over a five year period, and to the work of most middle-level professionals who did policy research during the Johnson era, as a "grand boondoggle."[46] The OSTI projects paid some of the Bridgewater film bills but made it impossible for Wiseman to devote full time to the overwhelming process of editing forty hours of footage into an hour-and-a-half film.

In terms of sheer bulk, the physical material Wiseman had to manage was considerable: approximately two hundred boxes of four-hundred-foot reels of film, approximately two hundred boxes of the original one-quarter-inch audio tapes and then, after the transfer for editing purposes, approximately two hundred boxes of four-hundred-foot reels of magnetic tape. It "filled six or seven quite large bookcases."[47] Alyne Model, the only salaried staff member, was hired as an associate editor but she was essentially a cutter, making splices at Wiseman's direction. Marshall claims he played an active part early in the editing process, but Wiseman later "threw [him] out of the editing room."[48] Marshall has codirector's credit on the film itself.

Directed and Produced
by FREDERICK WISEMAN

Co-directed and Photographed
by JOHN MARSHALL

Editor
FREDERICK WISEMAN

Associate Editor
ALYNE MODEL

Associate Producer
DAVID EAMES

Recently published credits of Wiseman's films do not mention Marshall as codirector.

Producer: Frederick Wiseman
Director: Frederick Wiseman
Photography: John Marshall
Editor: Frederick Wiseman
Associate Editor: Alyne Model
Associate Producer: David Eames.[49]

To Wiseman, the process of editing soon became an entirely individual enterprise.

> I don't believe in this whole business of testing out a film with an audience, or asking somebody else what they think, or even showing it to a small group and asking for their reactions. It's not that I'm not interested in their reactions, but after you've worked on a film for a year and have made the selections you have made, you are the one who knows what works and what doesn't work better than anybody else. Which is not to say that you are absolutely right about it; but if you've been at all hard with yourself about the material you really have a sense of what works and what doesn't and why.[50]

Yet at this beginning point in Wiseman's career as an editor, he was not quite so sure of "what worked" or "why." Although he had toyed with editing eight-millimeter films, and was somewhat involved in the editing of *The Cool World*, he had no training in the craft. His personal inexperience as a professional editor slowed down the process of editing; yet in many ways his missing apprenticeship also proved to be an advantage because it forced— and freed—him to experiment with the material unbound by traditional rules. The interest he developed in his 8mm experiments "in trying to accumulate little reality episodes and trying to cut them together in a way that dealt with some of the complexities of the issues of a place"[51] remained a central concern in *Titicut Follies* and in his subsequent series of documentaries on American institutions.

The editing was a time of personal autonomy for Wiseman. Long before he finished editing the film, Wiseman began to act like a filmmaker who had the right to make both artistic and business decisions. Although releases signed in the spring and summer of 1966 had run to the Bridgewater Film Company, the papers of incorporation were not drafted by Wiseman and signed by David Eames (president), John Marshall (treasurer), and Heather Marshall (secretary) until November 14 of that year. The company was run informally. It had no bylaws, no formal meetings, no minutes, no stock certificates, no balance sheet, yet it was organized to handle all commercial aspects of the film.[52] Wiseman assumed that the film and sound track taken at Bridgewater were the property of the corporation, although no formal documents were executed (Tr. 14:51). The company served as a medium of investment and also a means to protect the interests of the investors, a group that included the film crew. The papers of incorporation included provisions for the issuance of 1,200 shares of common stock, but no stock was ever issued.[53] Wiseman was not a stockholder himself and held no official position in the company.

Wiseman's experience as producer of *The Cool World* had taught him some important business lessons about introducing an independent feature.[54] Film festivals provide access to potential distributors and various opinion leaders in the film world. Beginning in April of 1967, Wiseman submitted the film in twelve international film festivals. Later, *Titicut Follies* was accepted at festivals in four cities: Florence, Mannheim, New York (all 1967), and Edinburgh (1968). It won awards at two: first place for the best documentary feature at Mannheim; the critics' prize and film best illustrating the human condition at the Festivale dei Popoli in Florence. Wiseman acted as a free agent, negotiating for the yet uncompleted film's exhibition. In a series of letters, Wiseman wrote that he "had complete independence" and "no interference" while making the film at Bridgewater, which he described as "about various forms of madness."[55] Writing to a festival committee on May 26, about the time he completed the final edit, Wiseman anticipated criticisms of *Titicut Follies* when he offered a series of disclaimers. "The *Titicut Follies* does not seek to judge or condemn; it is not meant as an expose of backward mental health or prison practices nor is it a circus freak show."[56] Even though Wiseman already sensed that motives he denied would be imputed, he was eager to have his film seen. No one was more eager to see it than Superintendent Charles Gaughan.

How Gaughan initially reacted to the finished film has been disputed. On June 1, 1967, the superintendent and approximately ten of Wiseman's friends met at a studio in Boston and saw the long-awaited documentary. Gaughan recalled that "when the film was completed there was almost complete silence for a period of minutes" (Tr. 4:51). When the silence was finally broken, it was by praise from Wiseman's friends, some of whom later testified in support of the documentary. Whether carried along by a general climate of praise or in response to a direct statement by the superintendent, Wiseman's impression was that Gaughan liked the film (Tr. 14:15). Gaughan testified that on June 1, he "was very surprised at the trend or the new theme that the film had developed . . . was amazed at that degree of nudity . . . questioned whether the degree of nudity was legal under state or federal laws . . . questioned the representativeness of a number of scenes that were used" and challenged whether the man being tube fed could be justified as representative (Tr. 4:52).

After considerable discussion with Eames, Wiseman decided in late May to call the documentary *Titicut Follies*. But the title and credits had not yet been added to the print screened on June 1, nor had the sound been mixed.[57] Otherwise, the film was complete. Gaughan later claimed that he did not raise more objections on June 1 because he did not realize that he had seen a completed film. The superintendent also testified that he had not asked Gavin to accompany him to the screening because he thought that he was going to see an unfinished film (Tr. 4:203). Given Gaughan's confusion about the "rushes," his total unfamiliarity with the editing process, and the highly innovative form of the completed film, this explanation is plausible. In addition, the tension between the superintendent and the commissioner regarding the documentary project from the outset would make Gaughan less than eager to involve Gavin at preliminary stages of decision making. The superintendent asked that the film be shown to Richardson, and Wiseman said he would take care of that as soon as possible.[58]

The screening Wiseman arranged on June 27 was attended by Gaughan, Elliot Richardson (then attorney general), Richardson's driver, and Assistant Attorney General Frederick Greenman. Again, reconstructions of reactions to the screening differ. Wiseman testified that "Mr. Gaughan said to me that, having seen the film a second time, he wanted to tell me again how much he liked the film and how powerful he thought it was" (Tr. 14:15). The filmmaker also recalled that Gaughan was pleased that Richardson also liked the film because the superintendent anticipated that he would need the attorney general's support. Wiseman's account of his conversation with Gaughan after the film screening is a poignant description of political vulnerability. "Mr. Gaughan also said that he didn't want to get into any difficulty over his job with Commissioner Gavin, that he had two sons, one of whom was in medical school or about to enter medical school, and a daughter in college; that he hoped that if Mr. Gavin was concerned and angry with him about the film that the Attorney General's appreciation of the film would neutralize opposition that Mr. Gavin might have toward Mr. Gaughan for having allowed the film to be made" (Tr. 14:15–16). Wiseman recalled that Greenman "asked whether sub-titles or a narration would be of any value in explaining the film to people who were unfamiliar with Bridgewater and the Attorney General said he thought that the film would lose its impact if there were any sub-titles or narration" (Tr. 14–11).

Richardson later testified that either he or Greenman had suggested subti-tles or narration (Tr. 12:139) and that the film he saw in June "did not appear to be a finished film" (Tr. 12:151). Almost a decade after the June 27, 1966, screening, goaded by the ugliness of a sensational trial, the two articulate, strongwilled attorneys were even more staunch in their disagreement over what was said and what it meant. Here is Wiseman in *Civil Liberties Review*: "Richardson thought the film was great. He understood it, understood what I was trying to do with it, and congratulated me warmly. The superintendent asked him whether I should show it to anybody else in the state government, and Richardson said no, not even the Governor, who was then John Volpe. The conversation took place in a sound studio. Unfortunately, it wasn't recorded."[59] Richardson replied, "When I first saw the film, I raised at once the problem of the rights of the individuals shown. I asked Wiseman whether he had obtained releases from all of these people, and he replied that he had. I reminded him the film would have to be shown to the commissioner of correction, and Wiseman promised me not to release it pending this re-view."[60] In this particular exchange, Wiseman had the last word. "Mr. Rich-ardson is a man of intelligence and sensitivity caught in the conflict between his political career and his private reactions. Both he and I know what his reaction to the film was. It is too bad he doesn't have the courage to say in public what he said in private."[61]

In the summer of 1967, relations between these two men had not yet festered into bitterness. State officials seemed unaware that they were dealing with a filmmaker who would never succumb to compromise; Wiseman seemed unaware that he would not continue to have support in high places. Yet questions of liability surfaced when Richardson mentioned having Al Sacks of the Harvard Law School see the film. Gaughan later testified that the suggestion was made in Wiseman's presence at the June 27 meeting (Tr. 4:57), but in a July 5 letter to Wiseman, the superintendent wrote, "A day or two after the showing of the film to the attorney general, Fred Greenman called me . . . to tell me that . . . the attorney general had suggested that Professor Al Sacks should be invited to the next showing of the film" (Tr. 5:25). Greenman called Gaughan about the film several times during the summer; he also met with Wiseman in July and they discussed a memoran-dum the attorney general's office was preparing about the superintendent's liability regarding the film. The attorney general's office was obviously aware of the completed Bridgewater documentary and alert to the potential legal problems its exhibition might engender.

The commissioner's office did not share this awareness. If we consider Gavin's early opposition to the project, the out-of-sight, out-of-mind posture of his office was somewhat surprising; but there were no inquiries regarding the progress of the Bridgewater film project from the department office and no information was offered. At the June 27 screening, Gaughan told Wiseman to try to show Commissioner Gavin the film (Tr. 4:58). The superintendent's July 5 letter cautioned, "Let us keep in mind that at some point the Commissioner will have to be drawn in" (Tr. 5:21). The language of this letter indicates that Gaughan's identification with Wiseman remained strong; yet the commissioner was not "drawn in" by Wiseman or Gaughan or Richardson that summer.

Wiseman proceeded as a filmmaker who had the right to make autonomous distribution and exhibition plans. Cinematographer Haskell Wexler was able to help at this point. He later recalled, "A friend of mine, Fred Wiseman, made a film called *Titicut Follies*, for which I arranged to get distribution with Barney Rossett, who now owns the Grove Press."[62] Wexler and Wiseman had both worked—Wexler as director of photography, Wiseman as co-writer—on a Hollywood feature, *The Thomas Crown Affair* (1968).[63] In 1967, Wexler was a well-respected cinematographer who had recently won an Academy Award for his camerawork on *Who's Afraid of Virginia Woolf?* (1966). A member of a noted and wealthy Chicago family, Wexler has long been associated with radical politics. He is best known for *Medium Cool* (1969), a fictional film about a news photographer's growing sense of political responsibility set in the real action of the Chicago Democratic National Convention of 1968, which he coproduced, directed, wrote, and photographed.[64]

Wexler was impressed with *Titicut Follies*, especially the camera work of John Marshall.

> It's a fantastic film, it makes you see what cinema-verite can do. John Marshall was the cameraman—I hadn't heard of him before. You see, the problems of shooting cinema-verite are so different. Not just the shooting but the cutting too. Ordinarily when you are shooting, when things stop happening you cut the camera . . . what really good cinema-verite guys do—or learn to sense—what John Marshall does—is when things seem to have stopped, you keep rolling, and move in a little on a face, and about four or five times in the film everything would stop, he would move in on a face and then you *see* the change happening, and then something would start again. When you get that moment, I don't think there is anything in films that I have ever seen, that can match it.[65]

Wexler called his long-time friend Barney Rossett, described the Bridgewater documentary as "extraordinary," and urged that the publisher see the film with a view to distributing it.[66] In 1967, Grove Press was distributing between 200 and 250 motion pictures and was expanding its 16mm line. As owner of the aggressively nontraditional Grove Press, Rossett had experienced the political harassment and litigation that could result from publishing and distributing controversial products. Grove had published Henry Miller's *Tropic of Cancer* when the book was banned in Massachusetts and elsewhere and had fought, successfully, all the way to the Supreme Court for its First Amendment rights.[67] In 1965, the cover of Grove's political magazine, the *Evergreen Review*, featured Che Guevara as a sort of "Man of the Year." Soon after, Grove's offices in Greenwich Village were bombed, supposedly by anti-Castro Cuban exiles. During the 1960s the FBI, the CIA, and the army kept Rossett and Grove Press under surveillance and maintained files on them.[68]

Rossett, a man accustomed to risk and a staunch supporter of the right of artists and journalists to take risks, met Wiseman at Grove's New York offices on August 16. Along with Edith Zornow, of Grove's film division, Rossett saw *Titicut Follies*. He told Wiseman that he liked the documentary very much and that he would get back in touch with the filmmaker. Rossett then consulted Wexler and still another influential mutual friend, attorney Ephraim London, about distributing *Titicut Follies*. Wexler and London both encouraged Rossett to proceed. It was Rossett's understanding that Wiseman "had permission to make the film and have it distributed."[69] Rossett later recalled under oath that "right from the very first time I saw it in August . . . [I assumed Grove was] dealing with something which the producer-director-owner had the right to sell."[70]

During this same period, Wiseman was also making other distribution plans. He hoped to introduce *Titicut Follies* at the Venice Film Festival in late August or early September. By midsummer, he still had not heard from the selection committee. (The film was not accepted.) During the third week of July, Wiseman submitted a print of *Titicut Follies* to the New York Film Festival, scheduled for late September. Wiseman informed the festival director by letter that he had secured releases from all the people in the film or from their authorized representatives. Within a month of that submission, festival codirector Amos Vogel notified Wiseman that his documentary was accepted in the "Social Cinema in America" division. Edith Zornow was a member of the festival selection committee; Rossett and Vogel were friends and colleagues. As founder of Cinema 16, a longstanding showcase for independent films, Vogel was one of New York's most influential champions of avant-garde film. Parts of Vogel's manuscript that would later appear in book form as *Film as a Subversive Art* were first published in the *Evergreen Review*.[71]

Richardson later claimed that he had never been told about the festival entries and characterized Wiseman's negotiations with Grove Press as deceptive.[72] He asserted that during the summer of 1967, "we were exploring possible compromises, such as the obscuring of identities and the adding of subtitles to explain various scenes."[73] It is not entirely clear what parties are included in Richardson's remembered "we," but filmmaker Frederick Wiseman was making no compromises that summer. Or later. One can interpret the director's intransigence and its consequences in a variety of ways, but the *Titicut Follies* Wiseman screened for Gaughan and Richardson,

Rossett and Zornow, in the summer of 1967 was identical to the film that as of this writing rests impounded in the Suffolk County Court House, while its duplicates are shown, under unique restrictions, to Massachusetts audiences.[74]

Confronting the Paradox of "Reality Fiction"

In his proposal for a "Bridgewater film," Fred Wiseman predicted that the documentary technique he envisioned would "give an audience factual material about a state prison but [would] also give the film an imaginative and poetic quality that [would] set it apart from the cliche documentary about crime and mental illness."[75] There would be considerable debate regarding the "quality" of the imaginative and poetic dimensions of *Titicut Follies*, but the documentary that Wiseman first screened on June 1, 1967, provided an audience with factual material *shaped* by an individual who had created a product unlike others that had preceded it. On a variety of levels, *Titicut Follies* was and, less so, still is subversive and will always be paradoxical.

From the time Wiseman first approached Gaughan through all the litigation surrounding the subsequent film, attention has been directed toward the potential—then actual—content of the Bridgewater film. Henry Breitrose has observed that "it is an aesthetic of content that drives the documentarian, and the rule that for the audience a documentary is as good as its content is interesting is difficult to falsify."[76] In *Titicut Follies* Wiseman subverts conventional educational documentary expectations of content; he educates his audience by revealing what has previously gone unseen and unheard. No Wiseman film better fits the following Bill Nichols description than *Titicut Follies:* "Wiseman disavows conventional notions of tact, breaking through what would otherwise be ideological constraints of politeness, respect for privacy, queasiness in the face of the grotesque or taboo, the impulse to accentuate the positive. . . . Wiseman's 'tactlessness' allows him not to be taken in by institutional rhetoric; it helps him disclose the gap between rhetoric and practice. But this lack of tact also pulls Wiseman's cinema toward the realm of voyeurism."[77]

In *Titicut Follies* Wiseman shows a Bridgewater inmate in shots of full frontal nudity as he is tormented by guards into a rage of personal revelation; he includes footage of another nude inmate being carelessly force-fed; he presents an interview of a child molester, which reveals actionable information about the inmate's crimes. These are but three of the scenes in the film that have made the filmmaker vulnerable to charges of voyeurism. Wiseman foregoes the soothing, sensible, concerned voice of the authoritative narrator, common to most educational documentaries of the period, for the dark comedy of such passages as this soliloquy by an inmate:

> Charles Goodman, biddlegah, Volpe, Lt. Governor Richardson, biddlegah, McCormick, biddlegah and all members on parole. Biddlegah. I want all those men arrested biddlegah. Immediately. 168 pounds now down to 96 pounds, and all

those known biddlegah. Deputy Brewer and all those known, John F. Powers, Volpe, Charles McCormick, Deputy Brewer all go back to von Braun. Palestine, give money sheckle. Biddlegah, biddlegah, President Johnson, biddlegah, all interest, Japanese, Japanese. We know the truth, biddlegah, twenty billion dollars, Charles Gaughan, biddlegah and now death. I point out to you I am Christ Jesus and I am called Borgia. Kennedy who is now biddlegah in truth Christ Jesus. I say in Mississippi niggers over to this fuckin part of the country. You no good John F. Kennedy. I say you stink. No good we send them back to England. We don't send them back to Mississippi back to prison. We put a sign up niggers we don't want to see your fuckin heads here. Finished.

Because Wiseman abandons the convention of a narrator's actual voice on the sound track, some have assumed that he consequently abdicates his own directorial "voice." In a second-order memory of the filming of *Titicut Follies*, French documentary pioneer Jean Rouch complained, "I would like [Wiseman] to say something, say what his thesis is. . . . In *Titicut Follies* there isn't any [commentary or 'guiding hand'], it's a certified report, which could perhaps be interpreted as a cynical and sadomasochistic report. I asked John Marshall . . . what was Wiseman's reaction in the face of all that, did he take pleasure in it, was he happy? And John Marshall said that there was a fascination with horror, which is a strange fascination and which should have been expressed."[78]

Beginning with *Titicut Follies*, Wiseman's work "represents a radical restructuring of the viewing experience."[79] He simultaneously challenges us not to look away, to experience life at Bridgewater, to see and hear what it "is," and also to figure out what it means, to us as individual viewers and to the filmmaker, by discovering the structure he has developed. This duality comes through even in rejections of the film. Judge Harry Kalus called the film "a nightmare of ghoulish obscenities" and "a hodge-podge of sequences," thus responding to *Titicut Follies* emotionally as a shocking dream and formally as an (unsatisfying) collage.[80]

In interviews, Wiseman has shown little patience with questions of influence, claiming he does not read social science literature because he is not good at foreign languages and that he reads the "usual writers"—naming George Eliot and Nathanael West.[81] He is especially fond of the density of characterization and situation in Eliot's work and recalls spending most of his time in law school reading novels in the Yale library. While in Paris for three years in the late 1950s, Fred and Zipporah (Chippie) Wiseman attended plays or movies five or six nights a week, so he was familiar with a wide variety of American and western European theatrical and cinematic material.[82] He has always been personally—and deliberately—isolated from the "film scene," but when he made *Titicut Follies* he had seen and admired many of the early direct cinema films of Robert Drew and Richard Leacock.[83]

Titicut Follies colleague and friend David Eames recalls, "I don't think Fred had any notion that this project, so vaguely conceived, so loosely defined, so fuzzy and wacky and chancy, would turn out to be, a long year later, a film called 'Titicut Follies.' Which is not to suggest he didn't know what he was doing. He did, after a fashion. 'There's a film there, there's a film there,' he would tell me. Part of his genius lies in his unilateral trust in his own instincts and his unswerving dedication to them."[84]

From the outset, Wiseman was inevitably confronted with a central dilemma of realist art: "The secret of art lies in betrayal."[85] Like every other contemporary filmmaker, Wiseman had access to technology that made him come to his own terms with a metaphysical paradox: he could produce something of his own making out of the physical material that had recorded the words and actions of other people. During the year Wiseman spent editing the Bridgewater footage and sound, he might have been ethically bound by a sense of fairness, or artistically bound by his own ability and imagination, or technically bound by footage shot with a single camera of unstaged action, but he was free to treat the material creatively. Keenly aware of this shaping function, Wiseman has always dismissed claims of cinema verite or film truth by documentarians as presumptuous at best and described his films as "reality fictions" or "reality dreams," thus calling attention to their paradoxical nature. "Your imagination is working in the way you see the thematic relationships between various disparate events being photographed, and cutting a documentary is like putting together a 'reality dream,' because the events in it are all true, except really they have no meaning except insofar as you impose a form on them and that form is imposed in large measure, of course, in the editing. . . . In that framework, you can make a variety of movies, and it's the way you think through your relationship to the material that produces the final form of the film."[86]

Wiseman realizes that the abstractions that emerge in the structure of the film are constructed. Wiseman gives himself two related, but quite different challenges: first, to structure understandable sequences and, second, to structure an understandable total film out of those parts. He allows himself great liberties in restructuring the time and space of the original material. Here is still another description by Wiseman of the freedom of the editorial process:

> So you are fiddling around with both the relationship between real time and film time or edited time, and you are fiddling around with the positioning and you are saying that these sequences happened in relation to each other when in fact they had no relation to each other either physically or temporally. You are creating a fiction based on non-fiction material that these things are related to each other, but they may be related to each other only in your mind. And the success of the film depends on the extent to which the whole film creates the illusion that these events have in fact some connection with each other. But it can create that illusion if in fact the process that led you to the conclusion that there is a relationship seems to have some validity in terms of the final form of the film.[87]

Although Wiseman has often said that the relationship between the pieces in his films "should be something other than a linear one,"[88] the tyranny of the projector dictates that his films move through real time, and so the most obvious connections are in images and sounds that directly follow one another. Wiseman has chosen not to work with split screen, multiple projection, superimposition, or various other flamboyantly obvious strategies to suggest simultaneity or relatedness. With some exceptions, which usually occur in the early films, he limits himself to the most austere and subtle ways of suggesting association. By various types of fragmentation—some ingenious and others quite routine—he manages to comment on the limitations of linear time progression and to suggest patterns of circularity and repetition.

John Marshall remembers that, during the early stages of editing, he, Wiseman, and Eames had long talks about how to structure the Bridgewater film and that together they worked out an editing outline of sorts. Wiseman disputes that recollection. "I never worked on an editing outline with Marshall."[89] Marshall, who now prefers sequence films "without bones," has recalled some of the "bones" or structuring principles in *Titicut Follies:* the idea of the follies, the movement from the front to the back wards (with progressively more helpless occupants), the return to various individuals.[90]

Assuming that Marshall was the primary decision maker, but seeing another anatomy, Nancy Ellen Dowd has written:

> I am aware of the argument which insists that Marshall has given a conventional structure to the film, selecting three or four major characters upon whom to focus (the foreign shrink, the head warden, the chinless psychologist, and Vladimir) and has even created a primitive plot (Vladimir's efforts to be released), in order to orient the audience, or to create a framework upon which to suspend the small isolated scenes. I do not believe this to be the case. . . . [Instead] Time encloses itself in a transparent and unsuspected framework as it proceeds in an overlapping stitch V-pattern from itself to itself. . . . The suicide itself [mentioned early in the film, the body seen on a television monitor] will never be spoken of again, and the victim will not appear until the middle of the film (the apex of the V) when the overlap stitch will be very tight and repetitive, cutting from the man being fed to the same man being embalmed. The structure loosens again; much later we see the burial of this same inmate and the movie ends with a scene from the Follies.[91]

Dowd's singular reading of the film as structured around one suicide indicates how seductive the "popular conventions" of character and plot remain for viewers, even when used "unpopularly."

Two scholars—Liz Ellsworth (Elizabeth Jennings) and Susan Heyer—have written detailed synopses of the entire film, and, in doing so, have commented on what they consider the organizational structure of *Titicut Follies.*[92]

Neither Ellsworth nor Heyer treated the Follies scenes as separate, structural divisions. (The musical variety show or a "rehearsal" for it is featured in shots 2–3, 59, 117, 163–64.) An account of these pieces would result in a

Figure 2-1

Structure of *Titicut Follies*, as interpreted by Jennings-Ellsworth and Heyer.

JENNINGS-ELLSWORTH	HEYER		
Part 1: Admission Shots 2–35 (17:00)	Act I A world of folly	Scene 1 Scene 2 Scene 3	Music show Strip search Interview
Part 2: Free time Shots 36–43 (3:11)	Act II Guard-inmate relationships	Scene 1 Scene 2	Yard montage "Chinatown" duet
Part 3: Routine day Shots 44–59 (15:50)		Scene 3 Scene 4 Scene 5	Daily confrontations Guards' conversation Musical show insert
Part 4: Who's crazy Shots 60–73 (10:21)	Questions of authority, sanity Personal madness and national mores	Scene 5 Scene 7 Scene 8	Role reversal Vietnam argument "The Ballad of the Green Berets"
[end of reel one]			
Part 5: Force-feeding Shots 74–97 (7:52)	Act III	Scene 1	Force-feeding Burial
Part 6: Birthday party Shots 98–117 (6:46)		Scene 2	Birthday party
Part 7: Trying to get out Shots 118–34 (3:40)	Contrasts in competence, care, and concern	Scene 3	Psychiatrist's appointments Vladimir's review
Part 8: Hopeless cases Shots 135–46 (3:40)		Scene 4 Scene 5	Al's bath Serious problems
Part 9: Getting out Shots 147–64 (10:13)	 Blaming the victims	Scene 6 Scene 7 Scene 8 Scene 9	The Last Rites Borges' monologue Upside-down incantation Funeral The final bow

spiral pattern, which seems to us the general shape of the film and one of the sources of its intrinsic despair. Many of their comments reveal that both of these thoughtful writers were well aware of the systemic nature of the film; yet it is difficult to describe the continuous loops in *Titicut Follies* using sequential prose.

Usually Wiseman has been reluctant to comment on why he included anything in his films, preferring that the documentaries speak for themselves and that his audiences do likewise. He is even more reluctant to discuss what he shot and recorded, but kept out of his films, and why. *Commonwealth v. Wiseman* provided the rare occasion when Wiseman discussed his artistic motives as evidenced in his editing decisions.

Wiseman testified that he "wanted to put the audience for the film in the state hospital"; he "wanted to put the audience in the midst of Bridgewater immediately" (Tr. 13:142,148). The filmmaker emphasized that he intended to tap the experiential potential of direct cinema recording techniques. In other testimony, various individuals described footage that was shot and not used, footage that could have provided Wiseman with the material for a completely different style of documentary. Some of these outtakes are worth describing in detail, because they indicate that while at Bridgewater, Wiseman was still not yet sure of what would become the "Wiseman style," let alone sure of what particular pieces would be used in what final pattern. Wiseman and Marshall were keeping their artistic options open. Marshall recalled that he and Wiseman filmed many interviews. "We did that kind of like a safety net. If you couldn't hook things together with the pictures and the events and the Follies as a recurrent theme, if that didn't work, you could always use an interview, but we didn't want to. We didn't want to make a talking heads movie."[93] Consequently, they had the material to construct another type of documentary about Bridgewater when editing began.

Much, although not all, of the unused footage could be grouped into three kinds of documentary material. The use of the first would have led Wiseman toward constructing a more traditional documentary; the second provided material for a more modernist or reflexive documentary; and the third could have been used in either style, but did not fit the rigorous direct cinema style Wiseman chose while editing the Bridgewater footage.

In contrast to fulfilling Wiseman's desire to put the audience in the midst of Bridgewater, each of these three kinds of unused material might have distanced a potential viewer. The first category—which would have filled the expectations of many typical documentary formats—consisted of several types of essentially expository footage: an interview of Gaughan by Wiseman (off camera) about the institution and its programs and goals; a speech by Gavin at the officers' training school across the street from the prison; a guided tour conducted by Eddie Pacheco for students from Whitman-Hanson High School in which the corrections officer explained the funding problems of the institution and the subsequent picnic on the Bridgewater grounds; various scenes that established a general sense of perspective and context. Thus, Wiseman had the material to make his film "educational" in a more standard form or more bitterly ironic and personally damaging to Gavin and Gaughan by juxtaposing theory and practice in the most heavy-handed style of the expose film, had he so chosen.

The director-editor also had the footage to create a reflexive documentary, a type of film that by 1967 was common among avant-garde filmmakers. With footage of Vladimir turning to the camera in several different situations and saying that he wanted to use the film to get out of Bridgewater and of a guard repeatedly looking into the camera and saying, "We have failed, but it's not us in here who have failed, it is you out there," Wiseman could have made a camera-as-catalyst movie. There are several instances in the film of some acknowledgment of the camera's presence: the guard who is holding the inmate as he is force-fed looks directly at the camera, as if to indicate, "What can I do?"; the elderly man who sings "Chinatown" seems to be performing for the film crew. But the general style of *Titicut Follies* is observational and noninterventionist.

A third type of unused material could fit either of the two documentary styles mentioned. When Dr. Ross made his rounds, accompanied by the film crew, he would state for the camera the history of each individual and give a very brief statement concerning his condition. Because this footage conveys information in the authoritative manner of the expert or the typical television news reporter, it could have been used in the traditional educational format. The material would also have fit—but less easily so—in a documentary self-consciously examining documentary conventions and how people do imitations of media roles when they are filmed themselves.

Rejecting the possibilities of either a straightforward, "direct address" documentary in a traditional mode, or the aggressive introspection of the reflexive documentary, Wiseman depended upon various types of comparison for his organizational matrix. The director testified that a central motive in making the documentary was to discover for himself "what echoes of the larger world did one find at Bridgewater" (Tr. 13:141) and then to represent those echoes in his work. He "wanted to show something about the people that are confined [at Bridgewater] and their similarity or dissimilarity to people on the outside" (Tr. 13:141). Marshall has recalled that Wiseman was "very much into analogy" and frequently spoke of Bridgewater as a microcosm of the imposition of the state on individuals' lives.[94]

A last example of outtakes illustrates Wiseman's central organizing and thematic principle of comparison and his reluctance, for whatever reason, to move beyond the suggestive to blatant examples of role reversals in noting similarities between the keepers and the kept at Bridgewater. In a letter dated April 26, 1967, he described the Bridgewater film as organized around a skit from "The Titicut Follies" in which a psychologist and an inmate sentenced for murder reversed their roles (Tr. 15:80). Wiseman eliminated the skit from his final cut, but he retained the suggestion of similarities between the staff and the inmates and patients.

As finally edited, the documentary makes an issue of uncertainty. That theme is introduced immediately. The first sound we hear is a group of male voices singing "Strike Up the Band" and then, slightly later, we see, by a panning movement of the camera, a row of men singing in what seems to be a theatrical performance. They stand in front of the glittering letters "Titicut Follies" attached to a stage curtain. The audience is given no background information.

Throughout the film, we must figure out what is happening by clues within the text that are more similar to those planted in fiction films than in documentaries, but without any help from stars and stereotypical actions and consequences. Both the content and the form of the text suggest meaning, but the interpretive possibilities are vast. We gradually discover that we are watching the activities at a prison, then at a prison hospital for the mentally ill, but this information is never stated directly. Reading backward and forward, we note that some of the men in the opening chorus number are guards, some inmates; others we are never sure about.[95]

After the musical prologue, Wiseman compares two prison activities, using the obvious technique of crosscutting back and forth between two events, which are identifiable as separate and assumed to be simultaneous. A young man is interviewed by a prison staff member, presumably a psychiatrist (actually a "junior physician," a foreign doctor with a limited license); a group of men, mostly elderly, are stripped of their clothing and searched. Wiseman testified that here he was intercutting the material to compare "an emotional search with a physical search," both of which he considered violence against a person (Tr. 13:146). It is a juxtaposition many have noted, some in complaint for its lack of subtlety. Yet in the dialectical spirit that informs the entire work, Wiseman, according to his testimony, was also constructing a contrast here between youth and age, between a "young man being born into Bridgewater" (Tr. 13:147) and the old-timers, a contrast that has gone unmentioned by critics. Again, following conventions of fiction, Wiseman cuts on dialogue for emphasis:

INMATE: I want to get some help.   *Close-up of patient/inmate.*

DR. ROSS: I guess you will get it here.   *Close-up of Ross.*

                                          Direct cut to the faces of old men
                                          presumably neglected for years.

In an example of the editorial irony that runs throughout the film, Wiseman suggests "the kind of help or the lack of it that this man might expect to get at Bridgewater" (Tr. 13:148).

In describing the interview scene, Wiseman pointed out one of the most frustrating limitations of this documentary style for the editor: the incomplete or technically unusable footage or sound track. After the interview, the inmate was confined to his cell, nude, because he was mistakenly described as suicidal. Yet the footage acknowledging that confinement error was too "jiggly" to use,[96] a consequence of shooting unstaged action on the run. Also dialectical is Wiseman's inclusion of the guard tousling the young man's hair in a gesture of friendliness, just before he locks him into his cell. In this crucial scene, the editor introduces the theme of isolation as the camera remains while the inmate stares forelornly out of his cell window. The next cut is dictated by narrative conventions: we see what the featured person supposedly sees as he looks out his cell window—activities in the prison yard. Again, conventionally, a sound bridge connects the two scenes. The innovation that Wiseman attempts and accomplishes in *Titicut Follies* is achieved through the unconventional use of the formal conventions of the illusionary narrative cinema.

Many of Wiseman's organizational principles are standard: the movement from birth to death, entry to exit. Wiseman recalled, "One of the things that provides a structure for the film is, in a sense, the range of activities from birth to death within the context of the institution" (Tr. 13:147). Since Wiseman's perception was that most men get out of Bridgewater in a pine box, he ended the film with a funeral sequence (Tr. 13:149). The actual last shots of the film are of "The Titicut Follies," but the variety show footage can be seen as a prologue and epilogue, framing the other events and commenting on them. The very last image is of a young inmate-patient performer in stage makeup and costume, smiling and clapping; we are left with the suggestion that he will waste his life in Bridgewater.

Some of Wiseman's metaphors are obvious. Later he would see them as weaknesses of the film.[97] Despite the obviousness that the "Follies" performances function metaphorically, they still have relatively open metaphoric meaning to various audiences. Some of Wiseman's intended associations are far less obvious. For example, he explained connecting a discussion between Pacheco and another guard about the past use of tear gas to quiet a violent inmate and an excerpt of Pacheco singing "Chicago" on the double associational level of reminiscence and violence. Wiseman explained, "Chicago, of course, has not only been a scene of considerable violence at one time, but it was also by way of a reminiscence of a life other than Bridgewater" (Tr. 13:162).

For Wiseman, as editor, the connections existed first emotionally and intellectually, then physically in the sense of joining the physical material. For the audience member, the process is reversed. The connections are physically there, as the projected film moves through actual time and space. Whether the viewer then approximates, matches, or negates the emotional-intellectual process that led Wiseman to join the pieces in the first place depends on a variety of factors, some of which Wiseman cannot control. Wiseman is well aware of the subjective nature of "rational" connections.

"What's involved in the editing process is thinking your way through the material, and thinking not simply in a deductive way but in an associational way. And trusting those little thoughts that pop up at the edge of your head about the possible connections between sequences. And then finally seeing whether it works. It's an interesting combination of the highly rational—or what you think is rational—and the highly non-rational in the sense of the associative."[98]

Provoked by Wiseman's connection of the filmic material, each viewer is challenged to construct associations, bringing to the film a personal and social history as perceptual context. All films operate this way to some extent, but, because of the density of the images and sound track, their resemblance to the actual lives of the audience members at the level of social actions, and Wiseman's comparative nonintervention, the experience seems intensified in viewing Wiseman documentaries. *Titicut Follies* is particularly sensitive to "social" readings.

There are some sequences in *Titicut Follies* when Wiseman is obviously guiding the viewer through didactic editing. The most flagrant example of editorial point making occurs when an inmate being force-fed by a physician so unconcerned with the patient's well-being that he lets a cigarette ash dangle over the funnel is intercut with images of the same inmate, now dead, being carefully prepared for burial. The extreme contrast between the two kinds of treatment is made obvious by the crosscutting. It is an example of 1960s editing at its most obtrusive, a style Wiseman soon abandoned.

Although Wiseman did not mention this particular juxtaposition in his trial testimony about his thematic goals, he did describe at length the contrast he noticed between guards and the professional staff at Bridgewater in terms of their genuine concern for the inmates, and how he tried to convey that impression cinematically.

> One of the reasons that Mr. Pacheco appears so frequently in the film is because, in my view, he was one of the people at Bridgewater, more frequently found among the staff of correction officers than among the professionals, so-called, the professional staff of psychiatrists and social workers, who expressed genuine warmth toward inmates and treated them on an individual basis. And I was trying to use Mr. Pacheco in this film as an "everyman," as a touchstone, as someone who the audience would identify with, as someone who had reasonable standards of decency and who was generally concerned. (Tr. 13:156–57)

Contrast that proclaimed goal of identification with Pacheco to Elizabeth Jennings's comments, which are more extensive than most, but typical.

> The "Star Guard," with a little help from Wiseman, comes off as the least sane of the "sane" characters. Wiseman allows him to return throughout the film with his compulsive lip movements and dramatic, egotistical gestures. In the middle *Titicut Follies* performance he sings "I Want to Go to Chicago" with a partner who is never identified as an inmate or employee. In isolation, the guard's expressions

and gestures would make it hard to decide whether or not he's an inmate himself. In the birthday sequence he gives an encore of "I Want to Go to Chicago," then prances out of the room singing a line from "So Long for Now." In the last *Titicut Follies* shots, he gestures dramatically, looking diabolical in bottom lit extreme closeup. Wiseman allows the guard to build suspicion of his own sanity until we suspect that he really does belong on the same stage with the inmates. The final, diabolical shot convinces us.[99]

Jennings's comments suggest the viewer's dilemma that Wiseman provokes by using several types of quite different conventions in editing his films. Because he employs many Hollywood editing conventions, he invites the critics to look for clues like lighting and angle, which the fiction filmmaker usually controls, but which are often beyond the control of the documentary filmmaker.

There is also the reverse problem of underreading. Does Wiseman present a viewer with too much visual information to expect him or her to read the images "successfully" at the editing tempo he imposes? *Titicut Follies'* overall editing rhythm is much slower than the average fiction feature (32 seconds compared to 7.5 seconds average shot length for American features in the 1964–1969 period),[100] yet this average is skewed by five shots (out of 164) that are longer than two minutes. Exactly half of the shots are less than 20 seconds and 82 percent are less than 50 seconds, which is rapid for a film that provides no typical exposition. Even a sensitive critic who has gone through the extraordinary effort of creating a shot by shot analysis of *Titicut Follies* can "underread" its text. If Elizabeth Jennings considered Pacheco's partner "unidentified" as inmate or employee in the Chicago number, what possibility would the first-time viewer have of possessing the knowledge Wiseman presumes in the following testimony: "And the way the scene is shot, the camera is on the chest and face of Mr. Pacheco and the inmate and then the camera draws back and you see Mr. Pacheco's keys on his belt and you know that despite the friendliness that these two men displayed toward each other, it is not Mr. Pacheco singing with another correction officer but he is singing with an inmate. . . . And that scene, to my mind, represented . . . a care and concern and an intimacy and a respect for the inmates" (Tr. 13:163).

Among the sequences in *Titicut Follies* that demanded particular "justification" from Wiseman is one that illustrates how a director's extrafilmic information about an event recorded might possibly blind the director-editor to meanings that seem obvious to some viewers who have no information on the situation filmed beyond the text. It also demonstrates how a film builds its own internal expectations. Very quickly *Titicut Follies* establishes an expectation of shock.

Under oath, Wiseman offered a benign description of the yard scene that occurs early in the film: Men are lined up around the walls of the courtyard. There is little activity in the middle of the yard, "no relatedness, no conversation." An elderly man plays "My Blue Heaven" on the trombone, "not to any audience, but to a hydrant." The song title strikes Wiseman as ironic, as does the fact that another inmate, some distance away, is "shaking his head" and "listening very attentively to the music" (Tr. 14:117–19).

Many viewers of *Titicut Follies*, including Judge Kalus, did not interpret this scene as a complex presentation of both isolation and attempts at connection among lonely men, but as prurient voyeurism. They assumed the "listener" was photographed while masturbating. Wiseman, and several guards, testified that this was not the case. Marshall said that this interpretation of the man's actions never occurred to him while shooting the film; Wiseman has claimed he did not edit with this characteristic in mind, since he was familiar with the "real" nervous habits of this particular inmate.[101] However, masturbation had been made an issue earlier in the film.

DOCTOR: You know what masturbation is. How often do you masturbate?
INMATE: Sometimes three times a day.
DOCTOR: That's too much. Why do you do this when you have a good wife and she's an attractive lady. She must not have given you too much sex satisfaction.

Left out of Wiseman's testimony about intentions were any references to material that dealt with political figures or religion, although both are part of the audio track and there is footage of the last rites being administered by the chaplain and also a funeral service. Eddie Pacheco tells a joke about Father Mulligan as part of "The Follies" prologue. Wiseman also omitted mentioning any interest in formal experimentation either as a goal in making the movie or as an art-for-art's-sake argument in defense of the completed work. And he certainly did not ever say—as he would several years later in an interview—that he himself considered *Titicut Follies* "often funny."[102]

The state also avoided mentioning the possible subversiveness of Wiseman's use of politics, religion, formal experimentation, and humor in *Titicut Follies*. It is not clear from the public record when Richardson and his staff decided to move against the film legally or exactly why they made that decision. If the film itself motivated this action, then the decision could have been made at any time after the screening on June 27. The *Titicut Follies* shown in late June was materially identical to the documentary that the Commonwealth would try to ban in late September.

In early September 1967, two bills attending to the plight of the forgotten men at Bridgewater, both of which had been submitted by Elliot Richardson, were near final passage in the Massachusetts General Court. This legislation would require: (1) legal civic commitment at Bridgewater; (2) periodic psychiatric and legal reexamination of inmates; and (3) authorization for the Massachusetts Defenders Committee to represent indigent inmates in these hearings. Although state legislators and journalists were still oblivious to the Bridgewater documentary, they once again expressed their shock and surprise and called out for reform, when, in August, a Superior Court hearing resulted in the transfer of fifteen men illegally confined at Bridgewater, some of whom had been held for decades.

Meanwhile, Fred Wiseman was negotiating with Grove Press on terms for distribution of *Titicut Follies*. Wiseman testified that during the first week of September, he informed both Gaughan and Greenman that the documentary had been accepted at the New York Film Festival and that arrangements were being made to screen the film publicly there. Both Gaughan and Greenman denied receiving any such information.[103] Since Wiseman did not notify either office by letter, this detail was, like so many other details in the film's history, one man's memory against the memories of others. State officials claimed that the letter to them that announced the New York screening came from an unlikely source: a former state resident unconnected to production of the documentary.

By early September, film critics had previewed the films scheduled for screening at the New York Film Festival later that month. The first published review of *Titicut Follies* appeared in the September 9 issue of the *Saturday Review*. Critic Arthur Knight generally praised the film, but ended his piece by questioning its uncompromising frankness. "*The Titicut Follies* is, to be sure, a film of our times, a startling example of film truth. But, inevitably, it must raise the ethical question: Where does truth stop and common decency begin?"[104]

Knight was the first person to define the Bridgewater documentary publicly as a potential or actual "problem." Thus began a repetitious pattern, in which the press acted as mediator between *Titicut Follies* and a public drawn into vociferous support or opposition, without having seen the film. Soon after the publication of the *Saturday Review* article, Mildred L. Methven, a former Massachusetts social worker then living in Minnesota, wrote a letter of complaint, based on Knight's description of the film (which included the erroneous claim that hidden cameras had been used in the filming) to Commissioner Gavin, with copies sent to Governor Volpe, Senator Edward Kennedy, and the Civil Liberties Union-Massachusetts (CLUM). This letter was Gavin's first indication that the film had been completed; it was Volpe's first indication that a documentary had been contemplated or filmed at MCI-Bridgewater. Both Gavin and Volpe were angered by the situation and doubly insulted that their offices had been left uninformed. Volpe contacted Richardson, who said he had been unaware of plans for a public showing of *Titicut Follies*. Gavin called Gaughan to inquire about why he had been excluded from the screenings. Gavin later testified, "I felt that protocol would demand that they invite me to view the film in view of the fact that I was the one that [Wiseman] had all the dealings with to get permission to do this film" (Tr. 3:38). Gavin would later see advantages to his exclusion, but at this point he was irritated that his approval had not been sought.

Within days, Wiseman, too, had shocking news from an unexpected source. In a convoluted example of the press feeding on itself, a reporter from the Quincy *Patriot Ledger* called Wiseman regarding a front-page article that had appeared in the September 16 *Ledger*. The author of the article, having been alerted by Knight's review to the existence of *Titicut Follies* and its scheduled showing, had interviewed several members of the Bridgewater staff about the documentary. The article quoted Gaughan as saying that the state's three censors would have to pass on the Bridgewater film before it could be shown at Lincoln Center.[105] Dr. Ames Robey, the former medical director at Bridgewater, was quoted as having said that he had a written agreement with Wiseman that gave Robey a right to review the portions of the film in which he appeared before the film was shown. Now it was Wiseman's turn to be upset. He claimed that he not only had never agreed to the state's right to censor the film, but that the topic had never even been mentioned before. When contacted by Wiseman, Gaughan denied making the censorship claim to the *Ledger* reporter.[106] Wiseman then contacted the attorney general's office and pressed Greenman to schedule a meeting of the attorney general, the superintendent, the commissioner, and the filmmaker "so that if there were any issues, they could be discussed openly and frankly."[107]

Obviously, there were some issues. The film still had not been shown publicly, but it soon would be. The *New York Times* had already carried an announcement for the Lincoln Center screening of *Titicut Follies* and a subsequent discussion of the film as part of the "Social Cinema in America" program on September 28. If there was going to be a frank and open discussion among these men it would have to be when they met at the attorney general's office on September 21.

When Fred Wiseman arrived at Richardson's office, he was accompanied by attorneys Alan Dershowitz and Gerald Berlin. Wiseman had originally hired Dershowitz, a member of the Harvard Law School faculty, to represent him. Since Dershowitz was then not a member of the Massachusetts Bar, he suggested they "bring in Gerald Berlin."[108] At that time, Berlin was serving as chairman of the Civil Liberties Union of Massachusetts. He had previously served as an assistant attorney general under Democratic Attorney General Gerald McCormack. Wiseman and his counsel met with Attorney General Richardson; Assistant Attorney Generals Greenman, Ward, and Campbell; Commissioner Gavin; and Superintendent Gaughan. Gavin later recalled that Richardson did most of the talking, which seemed reasonable to the commissioner, since he assumed that Richardson had called the meeting (Tr. 3:153).

Beginning on fairly congenial terms, the meeting soon became a forum for all parties to express the feeling that each had been uninformed, if not deceived, about crucial matters. Attorney General Richardson and his staff claimed surprise—and dismay—regarding the New York Film Festival screening; Wiseman was concerned about censorship claims that had been reported in the state press; Gavin was extremely upset that he had not yet seen *Titicut Follies*. As Gavin later recalled, he "didn't want, from what [he had] heard of the nudity in the picture and so forth, the Commonwealth to be made a laughing stock nor the Commissioner of Correction" (Tr. 3:164). Gavin said that he did not want to "compromise the governor."[109] Berlin noted that under Brooke's advisory opinion, there had been no necessity for showing the film to Gavin. The argument of protocol was then advanced as a counter. Assistant Attorney General Greenman later testified that at this meeting Gavin "said words to the effect that . . . simple dictates of common courtesy and protocol would have been to show him this film" and that "it had been the understanding" that Gavin had a right of approval and "the last word."[110] Wiseman later testified that at this meeting, state officials made no claims of any censorship agreement, but argued from protocol and what seemed to them common understanding of the way the state operated.

To the lawyers present—seven of the nine men—it was not courtesy nor protocol, but rather the legal aspects of the arrangements that demanded close attention. Richardson spoke at length about responsibilities: the responsibility of the Commonwealth to protect the rights of the inmates and patients at Bridgewater and the responsibility of his office to advise Gavin and Gaughan as to the legal implications of their responsibilities. Often making reference to a legal memorandum that Greenman had prepared, Richardson voiced concern for the inmates' right of privacy. Dershowitz suggested that perhaps there might be some conflict of interest in the state representing both the Department of Correction and the individuals at Bridgewater. Consequently, he advised that individual guardians be appointed for each inmate shown in the picture before any determination was to be made as to what, if anything, should be done to protect them. Richardson said that he thought the law professor's analysis "ingenious," but felt the state should not evade its responsibility to the inmates.[111] While discussing the matter of liability, Richardson asked Wiseman for information regarding the releases that he and David Eames had obtained. On advice from counsel, Wiseman refused to give the attorney general the signed releases, to show him a blank release form, or to give him information about the contents of the form.[112]

If any one of these men had been optimistic about the chances of reaching some accord about the public screening of the Bridgewater documentary when the meeting began, they had much less reason for optimism one-half hour later when the meeting ended with Richardson telling Wiseman that he was "turning him down."[113]

Hours after the crucial meeting at the state house, Wiseman met with his colleagues Eames and Marshall. That same evening Commissioner Gavin, his three deputies, James Canavan (the public relations director for the Department of Correction), and the filmmakers saw *Titicut Follies* at a screening room in Newton. The next day, Gavin received a hand-carried opinion from the attorney general; he immediately wrote Wiseman to notify him that "in accordance with the agreement that you have with Superintendent Gaughan and me that it will not be shown without our approval . . . [you do] not have approval to show this film to anyone."[114] For the first time, censorship privileges were mentioned in writing; they were claimed as an a priori agreement. This letter to Wiseman, along with an enclosed copy of Richardson's letter to Gavin, was sent by registered mail to a Cambridge address that was no longer Wiseman's residence. It was returned, marked "unclaimed," approximately ten days later. Since a copy of the letter was sent to Berlin, Wiseman's attorney, there is little doubt that Wiseman eventually saw the commissioner's letter, but he did not receive the registered letter on September 22. That day the filmmaker was in New York negotiating with Grove Press for distribution rights to *Titicut Follies*. While Gavin was assuming that state administrators held veto rights regarding the exhibition of the Bridgewater documentary, Wiseman was assuming rights of his own. The Commonwealth of Massachusetts would need more than letters of disapproval to keep Fred Wiseman from showing the documentary that he had made. That would demand the support of the courts.

The Conundrum of Competing Rights

On Friday, September 22, 1967, the attorney general's office moved with dispatch and force against *Titicut Follies*. In a single day, Attorney General Elliot Richardson sent an opinion to John Gavin; the Commissioner of Correction then wrote Wiseman that he did not have approval to show the film to anyone; Assistant Attorney General Frederick Greenman filed a bill of complaint in the Superior Court of Suffolk County (Boston) on behalf of the Commonwealth, Gavin, and Superintendent Gaughan to temporarily restrain Wiseman, his agents, and attorneys from entering into any contracts or agreements that would permit the showing of *Titicut Follies*. The bill also petitioned that Wiseman and his associates be permanently enjoined from "exhibiting, showing, or causing to be shown, or authorizing the showing of said film entitled 'The Titicut Follies' to any audience, group, person or persons without prior approval in writing by the plaintiffs."[115] The bill, filed and entered in the equity docket on September 22, included the signatures of plaintiffs Gaughan and Gavin. The commissioner later testified that he had not signed the complaint until around seven o'clock that night (Tr. 3:58). The following Monday, Greenman filed a motion to amend the bill in equity, adding the Bridgewater Film Company, Inc., as a party respondent.[116] The next day, September 26, counsel for the attorney general filed papers in the New York Supreme Court to halt the showing of *Titicut Follies* in that state. The Commonwealth sought both a temporary and a permanent injunction against the showing of the film in New York.

In retrospect it seems that the time for compromise between the Commonwealth and Wiseman—if indeed there ever had been such a time—had come and gone at the crucial meeting on September 21. Once legal action commenced on September 22, the Commonwealth of Massachusetts and Frederick Wiseman became locked into adversarial positions that have never relaxed.

In a special night session of the Suffolk Superior Court on September 22, Justice Joseph Ford, without having seen the Bridgewater documentary, put a temporary restraining order on the exhibition of *Titicut Follies* in Massachusetts. The temporary restraining order was granted without notice to or presence of Wiseman's counsel.[117]

A motion also progressed swiftly through the New York Supreme Court. The Commonwealth filed the motion on September 26; New York Supreme Court Justice Francis T. Murphy, Jr., viewed the film the next day; Murphy heard arguments and reached a decision on September 28. During the hearing, with Murphy's knowledge and during a recess called for that purpose, counsel for the defendants (Richard Gallen representing Grove Press; Ephraim London on Wiseman's behalf) offered—as they had done two days before—a six week delay in further exhibition of the film if the Commonwealth would permit the New York Film Festival screening that evening.[118] According to Wiseman's later testimony, Justice Murphy advised counsel for the Commonwealth, Roger Hunting, to agree to the compromise so that parties might have time to resolve their differences outside of court.[119] Hunting called Richardson; the attorney general refused the offer, stating that he was responsible for the full protection of the privacy of the Bridgewater inmates.[120] The hearing continued. Its conclusion: Murphy denied the request to enjoin the showing of *Titicut Follies* in New York. In announcing his ruling, Murphy pointed out that both sides had agreed that the film "has social significance."[121] The Commonwealth responded with continued determination by filing a second motion for injunctive relief in New York, now naming two inmates—Albert Dagnault and James Bulcock (both of whom are shown nude in the film)—as coplaintiffs. The second motion claimed that the defendants (The Lincoln Center for the Performing Arts, Inc.; The Bridgewater Film Company, Inc.; Frederick Wiseman; Grove Press, Inc.; and Barney Rossett) had taken advantage of the order denying the first motion for an injunction by then arranging for the commercial showing of the film. In the second New York hearing, the defense argued primarily on First Amendment grounds, claiming the widely recognized principle that freedom of expression was not diminished when a communication was sold for profit. On October 2, a second New York justice, Saul S. Street, denied the motion for injunction, arguing that insufficient evidence had been entered by the Commonwealth to exercise the drastic power of the restraining order. According to Justice Street, "The question as to whether there was an oral agreement is not for the court to decide at this juncture on this motion, the question as to whether or not the patients have any claims or rights remains. They are wards of the Commonwealth of Massachusetts. The Commonwealth could not surrender their vested rights, whatever they may be; they survive the showing of this film."[122] The Commonwealth of Massachusetts had failed in its legal efforts to block exhibition of *Titicut Follies* in New York state and thereafter abandoned the campaign to suppress the film through this route.

While the Commonwealth was petitioning Massachusetts and New York courts to enjoin the exhibition of *Titicut Follies,* Wiseman was equally aggressive in making immediate arrangements to protect the film. Directly following the critical meeting in the attorney general's office on September 21, Wiseman, Eames, and Marshall met at the Eames home in Cambridge. According to Eames and Marshall, Wiseman did not mention that earlier in the day Gavin had claimed a right to approve the film.[123] Wiseman did say that the commissioner was eager to see the film and, indeed, Gavin saw the documentary that very night in the presence of the filmmakers. At the screening in Newton (which was also the first viewing of the final cut for Marshall), neither Gavin nor his deputies said anything about censorship rights.[124] The night of September 21, Wiseman's colleagues must have been aware that state officials were not pleased with the Bridgewater film, but the trial testimony indicates that they had less than a full account of the meeting at the attorney general's office earlier that day. In preparation for negotiation with Grove Press executives the next day in New York City, Marshall brought Wiseman a copy of the contract that Marshall's parents had negotiated on his film *The Hunters,* to be used as a guide.[125] Eames and Wiseman seemed to have left for New York with the support, if not the active participation, of their cinematographer; however, according to Wiseman's testimony, on September 20, Marshall expressed concern about the absence of corporate bylaws and told Wiseman that he planned to consult counsel about his role as an officer in the Bridgewater corporation (Tr. 15:27).

Although Wiseman was not an officer of Bridgewater Film Company (BFC), which held all rights to the film *Titicut Follies,* he spoke on behalf of the film in the negotiations with Grove and signed contracts. The question of ownership was complicated for these three colleagues. Exhibit 20, a letter to an investor, stated, "The ownership of the film is divided 50-50 between the investors who provide the total $30,000 capital requirement and the above-listed incorporators [Eames, John and Heather Marshall] of the Bridgewater Film Company." Eames was president, John Marshall treasurer, and his wife, Heather, clerk. The state would later try to prove Wiseman an untrustworthy associate and suggest that he held no corporate office or owned any corporate stock to avoid anticipated liability. When questioned about his lack of corporate involvement with the BFC, Wiseman offered an altruistic account:

> There were several reasons, the principal reason being that Mr. Eames and Mr. Marshall had put up a considerable amount of cash themselves and spent a lot of time working on the film without any compensation. And I was going to receive

the principal credit for the film as the producer and director and editor. And this was the way that their interest in the film would be protected and the monies that they had advanced and the labor that they performed would be protected. In addition, the corporation was formed because we needed more money to complete the film and it was thought that we might be able to get some investors, which we subsequently did. (Tr. 15:21)

Despite his lack of corporate status, Wiseman continued to take charge of all negotiations when he and BFC president David Eames went to New York. Wiseman asked Grove Press for fifty thousand dollars for the exclusive rights to distribute *Titicut Follies* "in all sizes and gauges of film for all purposes in the United States and Canada."[126] Grove offered fifteen thousand; they agreed upon twenty-five thousand dollars. The film company was to receive 50 percent of theatrical gross receipts and 75 percent of any television sale, after expenses were "taken off the top," which, according to Grove Film Division head Edith Zornow, was "a standard industry deal."[127] On agreement to spend at least ten thousand dollars in advertising, Grove was to have "complete control of the matter and means of distribution."[128] There was no written contract signed that day with Grove, but, according to all those present at the negotiations (Wiseman, Eames, Zornow, Grove president Barney Rossett, and Grove's general counsel Richard Gallen), there was an oral agreement made on Friday, September 22, to transfer distribution rights for *Titicut Follies* from BFC to Grove and all details of the Friday meeting which were "commemorated" in the memo of September 25 were agreed to on September 22.[129]

That Friday in the Grove offices there was no mention of the Thursday meeting at the attorney general's office or of any present or potential legal problem regarding exhibition.[130] Rossett later recalled, "I don't remember anything specifically, but the gist of the whole thing right from the very— right from the very first time I saw it *[Titicut Follies]* in August until then [22 September] was that we were dealing with something which the producer-director-owner had the right to sell that which he was speaking to us about."[131]

The meeting with Grove had been scheduled earlier in the week. It is impossible to know whether Grove's offer would have been altered or even withdrawn had the company known that the Commonwealth would petition for injunctions against exhibition in Massachusetts and New York. Grove Press was certainly no stranger to censorship problems; indeed, the company prided itself on its firm support of controversial publications, but litigation is always expensive and Grove was also a business. In the subsequent trial, the state would try to establish that Wiseman had deceived, among many others, the president of Grove Press. When questioned about whether Wiseman had indicated on or before September 22 that there might be a dispute about film rights, Rossett's reply suggests business-as-usual. "My answer is, unfortunately, a very vague one. It's entirely possible that he did, but if he did I do not recall it. However, in any endeavor that we are involved in, where we are dealing with creative people, I always take it for granted that there is the possibility of problems arising."[132]

The meeting concluded, Eames and Wiseman left a print of *Titicut Follies* with Grove. Wiseman immediately called Marshall to tell him about the agreement. According to Eames's testimony, the BFC treasurer was "extremely pleased" with the contract terms (Tr. 7:92). Wiseman, now alone, went to the offices of attorney Ephraim London for an appointment made earlier in the week. There, Wiseman made arrangements to retain London as his counsel. The distinguished New York attorney had earned an important place in film history with his successful defense in 1952 of the Italian import *The Miracle (Burstyn v. Wilson)*.[133] The United States Supreme Court decision in *Burstyn v. Wilson* is commonly regarded as the beginning of First Amendment protection of film. In 1963 Arthur Mayer wrote, "Today we all turn to Ephraim London for advice on censorship matters."[134] Perhaps Wiseman would have been equally successful in the New York courts without the celebrated attorney as his counsel, but Wiseman doubtlessly had expert legal advice. In London's office, a letter to DuArt Film Labs (the processor of all the Bridgewater footage) authorizing prints for Grove Press was prepared and signed by Wiseman. He returned to the Grove offices with this letter, met Eames there for his signature, then hand-delivered the order to the lab.[135] Still more arrangements were made over dinner with a representative of Springer Associates, the firm handling the public relations work for the Lincoln Center Festival. It had been a long, productive day for the producers of *Titicut Follies*, just as it had been for officials of the Commonwealth.

While Wiseman remained in New York, Eames returned to New England and discovered that all was not well. Over the weekend of September 23–24, the BFC president received a call from John Marshall, whose attorney had advised him to resign from the BFC. According to Eames, Marshall "said he didn't want to hurt the film in any way and he wanted what was best for the film and he hoped that his action or his contemplated action wouldn't affect the film adversely" (Tr. 7:85).

On Monday, September 25, the day that Wiseman and Eames signed what they would later term the "memo of agreement" with Grove Press, Marshall heard (on a local newscast) about the injunction against *Titicut Follies*. That day, John and Heather Marshall each wrote a letter of resignation to David Eames, president of Bridgewater Film Company, Inc. Notarized in New Hampshire, the letters protested the contract with Grove Press and the planned showing at Lincoln Center.[136] In telephone conversations with both Eames and Wiseman that day, Marshall allegedly claimed that he and his wife sent the letters on the advice of counsel, but he was "still with the film 100%" and hoped that they understood "he really didn't mean it [the protest] literally."[137] Not surprisingly, the state would seize upon the Marshalls' resignations to suggest that Wiseman at best had been a careless businessman, at worst that he had betrayed a friend and a colleague. In testimony, Eames and Wiseman presented the resignations as something akin to a legal technicality, which had no serious consequences and fostered no ill will. In private, according to Marshall, Wiseman was furious.[138] It is uncertain whether the resignations damaged Wiseman's ethos in the eyes of the trial judge, but they could not have helped it. Whatever the director felt personally about the resignations of John and Heather Marshall, he did not let their real or feigned protest deter his plans for the first public showing of *Titicut Follies* at the 1967 New York Film Festival.

Although Frederick Wiseman's work was not yet well known to the New York film milieu, there was probably considerable anticipation regarding the first public screening of *Titicut Follies* among this influential group. The Lincoln Center promotional material described the Bridgewater documentary as "explosive" and, as early as September 17, noted that Wiseman *and* Ephraim London would discuss the film after its festival screening, a sure clue of potential litigation.

Even before its first public showing, and before the Commonwealth began moving against its showing on September 22, *Titicut Follies* had been presented to audiences and viewed as a litigious film. Eight prints had been made of the film (Wiseman, Tr. 14:47), and by mid-September *Titicut Follies* was familiar to some members of the film community. The film had been shown at the Flaherty Film Seminar in Harriman, New York, in early September,[139] at three press screenings in conjunction with the festival, and had been reviewed in the national press. On September 22, 1967, it became known to a larger public when excerpts were broadcast on Channel 13 in New York. By September 27, *The New York Times* had reported the injunctive pleas by the Commonwealth. Justice Murphy reached his decision only hours before the scheduled 6:30 P.M. screening on September 28. A crowd stood in line for tickets to *Titicut Follies*; several hundred people "waited in the rain even after all tickets had been distributed."[140]

The advertisement that appeared in New York papers in early October announced *Titicut Follies* as a film "cleared by the Supreme Court of New York for showing at the Lincoln Center Film Festival."[141] Not only did the advertisement proclaim victory in a past legal struggle, but promises of public exhibition became part of the Grove Press defense in the second New York hearing, held on October 2. In his affidavit in opposition to the injunction, Grove counsel Richard Gallen, wrote, "It is impossible to calculate the damage to the film and to the reputation of the distributor that would follow if people who read the advertisements for the picture and come to the theater are unable to see the film."[142] Gallen presented a variety of arguments, mostly from the point of financial harm—the wheels of commerce were in motion and it was unjust to stop them. Gallen also denied the Commonwealth's claim that Wiseman had personally and contemptuously handled the commercial exhibition plans. "The negotiations for the theater and the arrangements for the exhibition of the film were made by the Distributor of the film, and Mr. Wiseman had nothing whatever to do with it."[143]

Injunctive relief was again denied to the Commonwealth, and *Titicut Follies* began a six-day commercial play on October 3 at the Cinema Rendezvous, a small first-run Manhattan theater, where it was shown six times a day to a total daily audience of approximately 300 people and grossed a total of eight thousand dollars.[144] The advertisements showed how a company protects itself financially and legally while marketing a potentially litigious product: The film was released by a newly formed corporation—the Titicut Follies Distributing Co., Inc. All references in the ads to the content of the film were quotations: "Relentless expose of a present-day snake pit, it deserves to stand with works like Upton Sinclair's *The Jungle* as an accusation and a plea for reform" (*Time*). "Makes *Marat/Sade* look like *Holiday on Ice*" (Vincent Canby, *New York Times*). A recorded message at the theater urged the caller "not to miss seeing the film which the state of Massachusetts attempted to keep from the public."[145]

Edith Zornow of Grove next placed the film at the Carnegie Hall Cinema, another small Manhattan movie house. It was advertised as an "engagement extended by popular demand."[146] Booked as a four-wall arrangement (whereby the distributor pays a sum for what amounts to theater rental and advertising control for a specific time and then keeps all profits, in contrast to a usual distributor-exhibitor split of admission receipts), *Titicut Follies* played seven times daily from October 14 to November 4. Attendance was comparable to that of the first run. From the commercial screenings in New York, Grove and Titicut realized gross revenues of $31,798.50 and, after payment of expenses, a net profit of $14,451.61.[147] The Carnegie Hall Cinema advertised the documentary by quoting Richardson, among others. The attorney general denied he had described the film as "superb" and requested that the theater remove his name from the marquee, which it did.[148] Grove had hoped to show *Titicut Follies* commercially in key cities throughout the country and to reopen it at the Carnegie Hall Cinema later in November, but those plans were canceled because of the continuing legal action against the film in the Massachusetts courts.[149]

Titicut Follies was among approximately one hundred films from the United States submitted to the Mannheim Film Festival and one of the five American entries selected to compete with sixty or seventy international films. On October 15, a friend of Ephraim London's attending the West German documentary festival notified London, who in turn notified Wiseman, that *Titicut Follies* had been awarded first prize for the best feature-length documentary. Immediately incorporated into the ad campaign, the international recognition was used as a credential of serious worth from then on. Other pretrial screenings during the fall of 1967 included a much publicized Boston showing to the Massachusetts General Court (a screening that required the passage of a special resolution), a private screening to some

Massachusetts newsmen in Providence, Rhode Island,[150] a public showing at the Museum of Modern Art in New York City,[151] and an exhibition to three jointly assembled classes at Yale Law School, which was followed by a discussion with the filmmaker.[152] From its completion at the end of May through its public exhibition in the fall of 1967, probably fewer than ten thousand people worldwide had seen *Titicut Follies*.

The film's total audience as of the end of 1967 could have been easily multiplied tenfold by a single broadcast on National Educational Television (NET). Such a broadcast would have given Wiseman the opportunity to fulfill his proposal of educational broadcast to state officials and investors and to gather important supporters to the cause of exhibition. Of course, such a broadcast would also have added some opposition. Some time before November 10, Zornow had an offer to broadcast *Titicut Follies* on NET, but, unsatisfied with the financial bid, she refused.[153] In the closing days of the trial, Wiseman announced a pending NET offer to broadcast *Titicut Follies* (Tr. 15:141). Had a law suit against the film not been in progress, he has since claimed, the Public Broadcasting Laboratory would have run *Titicut Follies* as its first show.[154]

The Rush to Judgment outside the Courts

On the day that the attorney general's office filed the first request for an injunction against *Titicut Follies* in New York, the qualifying election for mayor claimed the attention of most Bostonians. School Committee Chair Louise Day Hicks and Secretary of State Kevin White were the victors; Beacon Hill Representative John Sears, the first Republican candidate for mayor in over twenty years, was a surprising third. All of the ten candidates had tried to appeal to the frustrations of the Boston electorate, but Hicks had tapped a particular discontent. "With a record turnout . . . she picked up the 'anti' vote. It was against a strong mayor, John Collins. It was against the Boston concept of urban renewal. And it was against Negroes."[155] That last week of September, Boston's two favorite sports—baseball and politics—competed as excitements. A comment by a local journalist indicates the Boston habit of thinking of the two activities as comparable professional games, the attitude among the professional class that a Hicks victory would be regressive, and the common notion that Boston was in a period of transition and, therefore, under national scrutiny. "During the last two months the country has watched Boston, trying to determine whether the Red Sox had progressed enough to win, and whether the town had progressed enough for Louise to lose."[156]

That theme of "the whole country's watching" showed up frequently in remarks regarding *Titicut Follies*. Early on, various people defined the situation as one of national concern. At the critical meeting on September 21, Commissioner Gavin said he feared that the release of the Bridgewater documentary would result in the Commonwealth's becoming a national "laughing stock" (Tr. 3:164). In an October 3 letter to the editor of the *Boston Herald Traveler*, responding to a strongly negative editorial about the documentary, Representative Katherine Kane accepted Gavin's assumption of national interest, but turned his argument inside out, claiming that the documentary would offer Massachusetts an opportunity to show its public courage and sincere interest in reform. The only political figure to remain consistently supportive of Wiseman, Kane argued that suppression of the film would make Massachusetts a "laughing stock" and thus also appealed to the provincial desire to gain the respect of the larger world.[157]

Formed in February of 1967 and chaired by Democratic Senator John J. Conte, the Governor's Study Commission on Mental Health distributed a pamphlet to fellow lawmakers and the press on September 27. Its report described the grossly inadequate facilities at Bridgewater, outlined recommendations for the construction of a new 450-bed hospital there, and suggested changes in some mental-penal laws. The group generally supported the growing feeling among reform minded legislators and citizens that the Bridgewater hospital for the criminally insane should be transferred from the Department of Correction to the Department of Mental Health. The special commission saw itself as a qualified, authorized fact-finding and advisory group and thus saw Wiseman as a usurper of their authority even if he were granted the role of reformer. Vice-chairman Robert Cawley claimed that the showing of *Titicut Follies* undermined the commission's three-year effort to recodify the state's mental health and commitment laws.[158] In early October, Representative Cawley, a Democrat from West Roxbury (a working-class section of Boston), announced his eagerness to conduct a legislative hearing regarding the conditions at Bridgewater and the circumstances under which the documentary was made. That interest was not shared by his co-chair and thus the decision to have a hearing became the first of a new round of political struggles. Like all the other disputes in this controversy, it had personal, partisan, procedural, and ideological dimensions.

Cawley's co-chair, Republican Senator Leslie Cutler, opposed the hearings, as did Attorney General Elliot Richardson. They both claimed that the hearings would quickly turn from an investigation of conditions at Bridgewater into a trial of persons involved in the film project and, since litigation against the film had begun, that action should proceed through the courts without the interference of testimony gathered elsewhere. While they had a valid point about due process, their reasons for making it were challenged by some Democrats as partisan and self-protective. They did not persist in their objections.

Four levels of conflict were obvious by the time the hearings began: (1) the struggle for control of *Titicut Follies;* (2) the struggle for control of MCI-Bridgewater; (3) the struggle for control of the legislative and executive branches of the Commonwealth; (4) the struggle for ideological control. The

Bridgewater documentary, ostensibly connected only to the first, narrow struggle, became evidence and excuse for continuing and accelerating broader conflicts. The history of *Titicut Follies* is inexorably bound to the uses made of it.

Long before the trial verdict was issued in *Commonwealth v. Wiseman,* even before the legislative hearings began, the public judged *Titicut Follies.* By the first week of October, the editorial staff of the *Boston Herald Traveler* began assigning blame. A tone of vituperation was established quickly and never abandoned.

> Responsibility for this debacle rests with the prison officials. . . . It is now up to the Attorney General to exhaust all legal remedies to right the wrong. And it is up to the Governor and the Legislature to consider whether the corrections officials responsible should be allowed to go on making blunders without sharing in the consequences.[159]

> It is not possible for Gavin and Gaughan to escape responsibility for the astonishing incident, which is certainly without precedent in the commonwealth, and it will be surprising if there is not a clamor for their scalps by the families of the mental incompetents involved.[160]

> While some believe both Gavin and Gaughan should be fired for their parts in the incredible filming incident, it is the consensus that, at the very least, some kind of disciplinary action is in order.[161]

> One public official who has seen the film [The *Herald Traveler* writers had not] predicts that if members of the Legislature ever get a look at it "they will be out looking for a hanging rope."[162]

No legislator was looking for that rope more zealously than Representative Cawley. Using the Boston media, especially the *Herald,* as a willing tool, he made a series of accusations regarding the filmmakers' procedures and motives. He claimed that someone had invested $250,000 in the film, that it had been made entirely for commercial gain, that Wiseman had used hidden cameras, that *Titicut Follies* was anti-Catholic. All these claims were made before the co-chair saw the documentary. He then made a highly publicized trip to New York to see the film, after which he accelerated his resistance to its exhibition.

Before the hearings, a pattern of charge and countercharge was established. Once started, the accusations spread and infected everyone involved in the project. In response to Cawley's accusation of "deep personal involvement," Richardson charged that Wiseman had "doublecrossed the Commonwealth."[163] The attorney general further suggested that there may have been "a deliberate scheme" to exploit the banned-in-Boston theme for financial gain.[164] Wiseman, "shocked and dismayed at the intemperate, abusive and untrue personal attack made against [him] by the attorney general" said that

Richardson acted "contrary to high professional standards established by the American Bar Association in that an attorney does not take his case to the media and personally attack the other party when the matter is pending before the courts."[165] Gavin wrote Volpe and blamed Richardson and Kane for influencing his decision regarding permission for filming.[166]

By the time the hearings began on October 17, "the prospect of massive damage suits against the commonwealth, possibly running into the millions of dollars,"[167] was widely discussed. Although there was blame enough to go around, the state and its officers would have been protected if they could pin the blame on Wiseman.

The *Titicut Follies* controversy was characterized as the "biggest political flap to hit the state since the wrangle a year [before] for the state medical school."[168] John Volpe chose to ignore the uproar, commenting only that he was "concerned with the looseness" in the handling of the documentary project.[169] At the request of the general court, which had passed a special resolution for this purpose, the attorney general's office obtained a modification of the restraining order so that the legislature and the governor would be able to view *Titicut Follies*, but Volpe left for a national governors' conference in mid-October without having seen the film.

The majority of the 280 members of the general court, however, eagerly watched at least some of *Titicut Follies* the morning the special legislative hearings by the State Commission on Mental Health commenced. Richard Gallen, counsel for Grove Press, hand-delivered a print of the documentary. Broadcast and print journalists, barred from the screening by armed guards, clustered outside Gardner Auditorium to question exiting legislators on their reactions to the film. Those who left early were interviewed first. All those who made an early exit, and many others, expressed outrage; a few praised the emotional power of *Titicut Follies* and felt the film, if edited, should be seen by the public. "Although they would talk only behind their hands, Republicans in the audience said that the Democratic majority would 'look for somebody to hang.' And the obvious target, they said, was State Attorney General Elliot L. Richardson."[170] Democrats found the *Titicut Follies* controversy a perfect excuse to level the general charge of "moral insensitivity" against the current Republican administration. It was a charge that had been successfully used against the former Democratic administration by the Republicans in the previous election campaign. This intensely partisan and extremely hostile environment was the context of the *Titicut Follies* hearings.

Testimony was taken under oath. Although never used—"invitations" sent to individuals were sufficiently persuasive—subpoena powers, at Representative Cawley's request, had been voted by the legislature. From the outset, Cawley seized the role of head prosecutor. Co-chair Cutler, who had, at Richardson's request, first opposed the hearings, now pushed to have state police assigned to an investigative detail connected with the hearings. A state trooper, sent to New York, conferred with foundation officials regarding

Wiseman's alleged grant proposals. State troopers questioned financial backers of the documentary at their homes, which Wiseman described as harassment. When asked at the hearing whether a trooper's visit to the Marshall home had frightened her, Heather Marshall replied that the officer's questions had not been more upsetting than those posed at the hearing in progress, and they were not bothering her.[171]

The hearings began on October 17 and ended on November 9, but were in session for only eight days. During the recesses, there was much speculation in the press regarding potential witnesses (for instance, Representative Katherine Kane and U.S. Senator Edward Brooke) and probable agendas. Disorganized at best, an abuse of power at worst, the hearings occupied the attention of the general court for three weeks, then evaporated when the Senate failed to approve the House recommendation for a second probe of *Titicut Follies* to be conducted by a special committee on correctional problems.

First to testify was Commissioner John Gavin. He presented himself as someone only remotely connected to the documentary project and, therefore, not culpable of anything more serious than taking the suggestion of superiors (Richardson and Kane), assuming his subordinate (Gaughan) was responsible, and trusting that the filmmaker (Wiseman) would keep his word, which he claimed included a commitment to editorial control by the state. The second day of the hearings, October 18, Gaughan defended himself against Gavin's implication of mismanagement by attacking Wiseman for misrepresentation and duplicity. Here is an example of the style of questioning that was standard procedure throughout the hearings: "Asked pointblank by Sen. Francis McCann (D-Cambridge) if he felt that 'Wiseman and his production company tricked you and did not keep their agreement,' Gaughan answered, 'I very definitely do.' "[172]

After Gaughan's testimony, the commission called for a one-week recess, which led the filmmaker to complain that the press would have a week to feed off the correction officials' allegations, while he would have no opportunity for a rebuttal. The hearings were continued five days later, but behind closed doors, which brought another complaint from Wiseman's newly retained counsel. In one of many indications of the haphazard procedures of the hearings and their responsiveness to pressure, the testimony of three correction guards was then repeated in an open session that same afternoon. Officers Gadry, Pacheco, and Banville claimed that they had also been misled by Wiseman. The following day, three members of the Bridgewater professional staff—Harry L. Kozol; his administrative assistant, Richard Boucher; and the chief clinical psychologist, Ralph S. Grafolo—appeared. Dr. Kozol, the director of the treatment center for the sexually dangerous and a faculty member at Harvard Medical School, had anticipated legal problems regarding invasion of privacy connected with the film making and, when the filmmakers would not agree to written safeguards and acceptance of liability, he denied them access to his unit. Hungry for a hero, many lauded Kozol's foresight and used this incident as proof that the hospital would be in better hands if administered by the Department of Mental Health. That some of Kozol's patients were included in the final film (in group scenes of the variety show actually shot before the directive was issued) was used as further proof of Wiseman's bad faith. Kozol himself claimed, "If the Department of Correction had adopted my attitude, there would have been no Frederick Wiseman and no film."[173] For some, blame was not enough.

On October 25, Fred Wiseman read a formal statement before the commission, a standing-room-only crowd of onlookers, and television cameras. He denied the charges against him that had accumulated over several weeks in and outside of the hearings. Under advice from his attorney that to do so would violate the injunction, he refused to turn over the unused footage demanded by Cawley. The following day, the commission asked that Wiseman, Kozol, Gavin, and Gaughan all return, so that they could be questioned together about their conflicting testimony. When asked if he objected to the multiple questioning, Wiseman's attorney, James St. Clair, replied, "This is an august body and should not be engaged in games. We have courts of law where conflicts can be tried before judge and jury."[174]

Tension between Cawley and Wiseman had begun weeks before. In reference to Cawley's prehearing accusations, Wiseman claimed that Cawley was exploiting the controversy for political gain and using the hearings as a platform from which to campaign for the secretary of state position, which would be vacated if Kevin White were elected mayor of Boston in November.[175] During Wiseman's testimony, Cawley's comments became so abusive that St. Clair objected to the legislator's exhibiting "personal animosity" toward the witness and to the "truth or consequences" tone of the questioning.[176]

But the low point in the hearings had not yet been reached. Testimony from David Eames, president of Bridgewater Film Company, Inc., predictably supported what Wiseman had said, yet the accusations of commercial exploitation continued. Representative Amelio Della Chiesa charged that *Titicut Follies* was produced "to make millions of dollars at the expense of the poor souls at Bridgewater State Hospital."[177] The BFC president's reluctance to accept Della Chiesa's offer to "give all of the film to the Commonwealth for the $30,000 it cost and forget the whole thing"[178] was interpreted as "substance" to the view that financial gain was the filmmakers' primary motive.

Richardson agreed with prison officials in claiming misrepresentation on Wiseman's part and denied Wiseman's contention that Richardson had told the producer that he need not show the film to anyone, including the governor. That denial was expected; what was unexpected was the discovery on November 2, during the testimony of cinematographer John Marshall, that Timothy Asch, a teacher in the Newton public schools, a lecturer in anthropology at Brandeis University, and a friend of Marshall's, had been audio taping and filming parts of the hearings. Asch was directed to take the witness stand. When questioning revealed that he had briefly assisted John Marshall in filming part of the Bridgewater documentary,[179] commission members impounded the audio tapes and still and moving picture film that Asch and nine of his students from the Ethnographic Research Center at Brandeis had taken of the hearings. Asch requested legal counsel, and the hearings recessed in a state of confusion and suspicion.

The response to Asch revealed the depth of the fear and animosity some felt toward the members of the Bridgewater Film Company. Asch was immediately charged with deception by Representative Cawley. Asch claimed he had represented himself as being both from the *Brandeis Justice*, the university newspaper, and as doing free-lance work.[180] Cawley's response was that the commission had been misled into thinking that Asch was a "member of the working press."[181] Early in the hearings, Wiseman had joked with reporters that some would try to make him into a Rasputin.[182] To those who claimed "Beatniks Aided, Insane Aren't"[183] and described *Titicut Follies* as a "montage of sex,"[184] Wiseman *was* a Rasputin. Rumors circulated that the footage taken at the hearing might be intercut into the documentary "to embarrass the legislature [sic] process or to exploit [the] committee."[185] To prevent this from happening, confiscation and destruction were suggested.

Based on a photograph of Asch printed in the Boston dailies, Cawley claimed that several legislators had identified Asch as a man who had "posed as a representative of Massachusetts House Speaker John F. X. Davoren's office,"[186] had accompanied a legislative tour of the Fernald School the previous spring, and had taken hundreds of photographs of retarded children. It was assumed that these photographs would now be used by Asch in an exploitative manner. Another flurry of accusations began. Attorney General Richardson said that he would "launch a full investigation and take action aimed at protecting the privacy of retarded children and other patients at the Waltham facility."[187]

A week later—November 9—Asch took the stand again to repeat a statement he had made several days before to the press. Asch claimed, "Prior to the story which appeared in Friday's newspapers, based on Rep. Cawley's statement, I had never had occasion to hear of the Fernald School. . . . Since the allegation that I took pictures there is false, the more serious allegation that I posed as a member of Speaker Davoren's staff is doubly false."[188]

People who considered themselves entitled to privileged information about *Titicut Follies* were disappointed and insulted when they learned what they considered important information directly affecting them at the same time as, or even after, the general public. Gavin (via a letter) learned of the documentary's release through a review written by an "out-of-stater."[189] Wiseman said he first found out that the state was claiming censorship rights through reading a news story in the Quincy *Patriot Ledger*.[190] Marshall discovered when watching a television news program that an injunction had been filed against the film.[191] Asch read in the Boston dailies about the allegation that he had posed as a legislative staff member on an inspection of a state facility.

From the outset, surprise and suspicion ran throughout the press accounts of the details that became the *Titicut Follies* "story." Quickly, media gatekeepers determined the importance of a cluster of details and seized the opportunity to define the situation: it was labeled a controversy. Two common metaphors—combat and theater—shaped the earliest discussions of the film and became self-fulfilling prophecies.

The Boston press played the *Titicut Follies* drama as tragedy, melodrama, slapstick, comedy of the absurd. The easy ironies suggested by the film title swiftly found their way into print. Circumstances surrounding the making of the documentary and then the investigation into those circumstances both became known as the Beacon Hill follies. A cartoon presented a hesitant hearing witness peeping through a curtain as "Titicut Follies, Act II."[192] A headline claimed, "Cawley Blooms as 'Follies' Star."[193]

During Wiseman's legislative testimony, Cawley challenged him to defend the "educational" worth of various sequences, which the legislator implied were sensationalized. Wiseman replied, "I am not going to review each scene with you on this occasion. The film speaks for itself."[194] But, because of the temporary restraining order, *Titicut Follies* could *not* speak for itself in Massachusetts. Instead, many spoke at great length about it. Since privacy invasion was one of several charges against the filmmakers and since their central defense was the public's right to know, descriptions of the film in the press created a journalistic dilemma. It was difficult—if not impossible— for a writer to discuss the film without becoming hypocritical or evasive. Wiseman's counsel attempted unsuccessfully to include issues of *The Beacon* (the MCI-Bridgewater newspaper) as a trial exhibit to establish that public identification of inmates and patients was routinely practiced by the state.[195]

The Boston media also fed—or even created—an appetite for information about Frederick Wiseman himself. Previously unknown to the general public, in contrast to the appointed and elected public officials involved in the controversy, Wiseman was especially vulnerable to stereotyping. The Boston *Record American* discovered and printed the lawyer-filmmaker's answer to the Massachusetts bar exam question about why he wanted to become a lawyer.[196] Eager to position Wiseman in an ideological camp, Boston dailies deemed as newsworthy that the Wiseman and Eames families had welcomed Benjamin Spock and Martin Luther King, Jr., into their homes,[197] that Wiseman's wife had signed a petition urging people to vote "yes" on the referendum to end the war in Vietnam,[198] that Wiseman wore his hair "cut long in back like an artist's."[199] It is difficult to see the following description of the Wiseman-produced *The Cool World* as anything but an attempt to tap pools of discontent: "The picture depicts all white people as evil, and all Negroes as good."[200] There was considerable comment about Wiseman's coolness and his wit.[201] A portrait emerged of a liberal intellectual, a Cambridge radical; the same evidence was thus used for and against Wiseman as an individual. Some who formed judgments of the man bypassed the press and made direct contact with Wiseman. The director said he personally received many letters and calls of support. He also received a large amount of hate mail, much of which he classified as "anti-kike letters," and calls threatening him and his family.[202] Gavin also received death threats, which were headlined by the *Record*, unreported by the *Globe*.[203]

The Boston press served as the locus and the prime participant in the debate regarding the film. Often functioning as press agent for unreliable informants, the Boston dailies printed accusations and later retractions as central components of news stories. The *Titicut Follies* controversy thus fed on itself. Exploiting the media's insatiable need to know, Richardson and Wiseman both called prehearing press conferences. On October 13, Wiseman distributed a folder to members of the press with his press release, copies of the New York court decision, reviews of the film, and letters of praise from various citizens and mental health organizations. Both Wiseman (October 22) and Richardson (October 29) were interviewed about *Titicut Follies* on Boston radio station WEEI's "Bay State Forum." Gaughan, previously known for his candor with the press, did not follow the suggestion that he, too, have a press conference. Attacked on all sides, Gaughan withdrew from the challenge to manage press impressions and to control some of the information flow.

Undaunted by not having seen *Titicut Follies*, citizens of Massachusetts used letter-to-the-editor sections in Boston papers as an arena for debate regarding the documentary and what they perceived to be related issues. Often the controversy surrounding *Titicut Follies* functioned as a springboard from which to launch a discussion of a related topic. The letters expressed a considerable range of attitudes, often presented with cynicism or anger. Definitions of the problem varied significantly. The contradictions in consensual values evident in the letters illustrate how problematic the legal notion of "community standards" was in connection with obscenity in the late 1960s. The privacy issue confounded the presence of nudity in *Titicut Follies*. Considerable opposition to the film seemed to come from a constituency that would have been offended by any public exhibition of nudity, or any use of what was considered offensive language, and thus saw nudity and profanity themselves as issues. Amid the diversity, two clearly defined positions emerged and rigidified as the controversy continued. The arguments and judgments in the letters often echoed the editorial voices of the Boston papers, which, in turn, had followed the legal pattern of advocacy and judgment.

Both sides argued that the villainous opposition was hiding behind a legitimate civil right to cloak the real situation and personal deviousness. Advocates of general exhibition claimed the state had raised the privacy issue and moved aggressively against the film, not to protect the inmates as it claimed, but to protect itself from the political embarrassment of being shown defective both in its management of Bridgewater and in the handling of the film. Advocates of the ban claimed that the filmmaker had raised a false free speech issue to conceal a serious violation of the state's trust in which he had misrepresented himself and exploited the helpless inmates of Bridgewater for financial and professional gain.

The three Boston dailies—the *Globe*, the *Herald Traveler*, and the *Record American*—all devoted substantial attention to the *Titicut Follies* story, but there were appreciable differences among the three in the character of that attention.[204] Each set a tone immediately, a tone in keeping with the general position of the paper, and remained fairly consistent throughout the coverage.

Of the three newspapers, the *Globe* was the calmest, most disciplined voice. Still in September, a *Globe* editorial acknowledged a civil rights dilemma in the *Titicut Follies* case and called for a compromise "to clear up these cross-purposes between the right to privacy and the public's right to see the film."[205] In subsequent editorials, the *Globe* staff supported the film (October 18), spoke of the unfairness of the legislative hearings (October 19) and, during the trial (November 20), speculated that the zeal exhibited in the investigation of *Titicut Follies* flowed "less from civil libertarian sentiment than from a collective guilty conscience concerning conditions at Bridgewater."[206] Ray Richard's "The 'Titicut Follies' Film: Anatomy of a Controversy"[207] is an example of the analytic journalism that the *Globe* prided itself on. The *Globe* was the only Boston paper to follow the litigation concerning the film through the 1970s.[208]

The *Boston Record American* formed an early judgment regarding exhibition of *Titicut Follies* and consistently maintained its position. An editorial on October 19 argued that the film was an exploitative invasion of privacy and advocated corrective and punitive action. A tabloid with a predominantly working-class readership, the Hearst-owned *Record* practiced what is sometimes euphemistically known as New York-style journalism. Emotional, politically conservative, the *Record American* aggressively played the role of assistant prosecutor against Wiseman and the Bridgewater Film Company.

Also extremely accusatory of Wiseman and strongly dependent on emotional appeals, the *Boston Herald Traveler* did commission a lengthy guest commentary written by an academic who would later appear as a witness for the defense and a long, analytic piece that included a positive review of the film.[209] The characteristic *Titicut Follies* piece in the *Record American* was a liberal-baiting commentary by Thomas C. Gallager. No single journalist set himself up as a judge more than Gallager. Wiseman was not the only person involved in the documentary project whom Gallager found guilty, although he condemned the director-producer of *Titicut Follies* with particular fury.

Gallager and others were strongly critical that *Titicut Follies* was being shown commercially in New York. Several assumptions seemed to underlie the protest of commercial exhibition: that all films exhibited commercially made vast sums of money; that no one would pay to see a film for "educational" reasons; that broadcast on ETV would somehow not have been public exhibition. The fact that a single ETV broadcast would probably reach a much larger and more juvenile audience than a year of exhibition on the art theater-film society-university classroom circuit was lost on the *Herald Traveler* writers. Both the *Herald Traveler* and the *Record American* picked up the double-bind logic that Representative Cawley used against the films of Wiseman and Marshall. If they made no money, they were "flops"; if they made money, they were exploitations.

Although *Titicut Follies,* in this early period, had no commercial public screenings in the United States outside of New York—and exhibition ended there on November 4, 1967—the film was much discussed in the national press through the fall and into 1969.[210] Some critics found the film a violation of norms of privacy, responsibility, fairness, or technical skill, but the majority of reviewers considered it powerful social criticism. *Titicut Follies* became a national cause célèbre, attracting interest and support rare for any documentary, especially one made by a heretofore unknown filmmaker. A witness for the defense in *Commonwealth v. Wiseman,* critic Richard Schickel, stated in cross examination, "I do not think that this film would have been reviewed in *Life* had not it become a subject of controversy in the courts" (Tr. 16:97).

Counsel for the plaintiffs tried to hold Wiseman responsible for whatever critics had said about the film. It was a responsibility that Wiseman firmly and consistently disclaimed, yet he was willing to use reviews as evidence in support of the film. In the "Answers of the Respondent Frederick Wiseman to the Petitioner's Original Bill in Equity," Wiseman attached reviews from *The New York Times, Newsweek, Cue,* and *The Christian Science Monitor.* He or his counsel wrote, "The Respondent says that . . . the film has been consistently recognized as a powerful document of vast social sweep and artistic integrity. A sampling of critical reviews and commentary by social scientists dealing with the power, quality, and truth of the film are annexed hereto and marked Exhibit B."[211] During the fall of 1967 and the winter and spring of 1968, *Titicut Follies* became a rallying point for various publics. Wiseman has claimed that he received letters and calls from many inmates and their families expressing their support of the film and its exhibition.[212] There were no organized prisoners' rights groups that defended or opposed *Titicut Follies* in 1967–68, nor were any such groups active inside Bridgewater. The *Titicut Follies* Defense Fund, headed by Reverend Harvey Cox of Harvard Divinity School, reflected support for the film at its most organized. Predominantly, but not exclusively, composed of individuals involved in professional, academic, and artistic work in the New England-New York area, this group provided a number of trial witnesses for the defense and also discussed the film in a national forum, which, in turn, broadened the support. Various organized groups, such as the Playboy Foundation, joined the defense cause. But there were constraints on the effectiveness of such support. It was of minimal value legally since the trial judge would not hear arguments in defense of the film as a social document or as art. It was probably counterproductive, emotionally, among some publics. People like Cox, an active and outspoken leader in draft-resistance counseling, were perceived as part of a general conspiracy by a substantial Massachusetts constituency. For this group, the fact that much of the national press responded positively to the Cox pro-exhibition position became not proof of its validity, but proof of an attitude that a handful of liberals controlled the national media.

A decade after the trials, Superintendent Gaughan recalled the film's supporters with bitterness:

> The "Hippy group" who were so supportive of Wiseman at the time were widely in vogue. I felt that my position, based on the truth and capable of substantiation by various documents, did not require great vocalization. Our testimony was given to the courts, as required by law, and we came out very successfully.
>
> I felt that Wiseman's Titicut Follies and other items of that sort are now part of modern history. They were part of the breakdown of the morality and convictions of the great mass of Americans. Today, one wonders what moral obligations and duties the average American has. We are bombarded by a highly prolific variety of media, anxious to make a dollar, which caters to our most jaded sensibilities. To rationalize these events with constitutional interpretations belies the farcical. Regrettably, this type of interpretation appears most prevalent in the academic group who are the group most divorced from normal American reality.[213]

It would be a mistake to characterize all judgments regarding exhibition of *Titicut Follies* as clearly and cleanly halved, with each unit possessing established markers of social/economic class and political/ideological attitudes. No group better belies such facile division than the American Civil Liberties Union (ACLU) and its state affiliate, the Civil Liberties Union of Massachusetts (CLUM). With a membership mostly drawn from the political left-of-center, the organization is dedicated to the preservation and full implementation of the Bill of Rights.

Frederick Wiseman was a member of ACLU-CLUM in September 1967 when Mildred Methven sent the CLUM office a copy of her letter of complaint regarding *Titicut Follies*. That same week, Wiseman engaged Gerald Berlin, the CLUM chairman, as his personal counsel, an arrangement obviously unknown to the Boston journalist who wrote in early October that "despite this invasion of privacy of the patients involved, *[Titicut Follies]* has produced only silence in the ranks of the liberals, and the civil libertarians. In fact, one of their number, Rep. Katherine D. Kane (D-Beacon Hill), has staunchly defended the film. There have been no cries of outrage from the Civil Liberties Union of Massachusetts, or its articulate chairman, Atty. Gerald A. Berlin. . . . The only individual who has come to the defense of these sick people is Republican Atty. Gen. Elliot L. Richardson."[214]

The beginning of the legislative hearing coincided with the appearance of these claims and observations in the *Herald*:

> . . . the controversy has damaged the image of the Civil Liberties Union . . . [which] appears to harbor less concern for the demented patients at Bridgewater than for the beatniks in Cambridge. It has chosen to stand mute in the "Titicut Follies" controversy.
>
> Moreover, its chairman, Berlin, has turned up as the lawyer for the producer of the film. . . . [Rep. Cawley] sought to contact Luther Macnair, the executive director of [CLUM], to suggest he view the film.
>
> Where was Macnair?
>
> Over at the Boston Common, watching for any violations of the civil liberties of the draft card burners.[215]

Even without Gallager's public baiting, even without the introduction of a partisan struggle regarding responsibility for the film, the position of the CLUM on the *Titicut Follies* case would have been complicated. On October 20, a cartoon appeared on the *Herald* editorial page entitled "Titicut Follies-Another Act." It featured "Attorney-Chairman Berlin" astride two white horses (labeled "Attorney for Titicut Follies Producer" and "Chairman of Civil Liberties Union") racing in opposite directions. That same day, Berlin resigned as Wiseman's counsel. Berlin has said he withdrew because of "personal disagreement over management of the case."[216] Wiseman recalled that Berlin "told me that he could no longer represent me because the CLUM would lose contributions if he did so, and besides he now thought that I didn't have a good case and suggested that I give it up. I left the office furious because his primary obligation was to me, his client, and not to CLUM. I then retained other lawyers who were not professional civil libertarians."[217]

Berlin has declined to respond to Wiseman's accusations, but others have attested to Berlin's scrupulousness in handling the case and in avoiding any possible conflict of interest.[218] Plaintiffs' counsel took Berlin's deposition in preparing *Commonwealth v. Wiseman* for trial, but did not call him as a witness.[219]

By late October, CLUM had not taken a position regarding exhibition of *Titicut Follies*. The CLUM Executive Committee explained its silence in a press release on October 28 that included the following statements:

> The versions as to what actually happened, and under what agreements, are contradictory and confused, and until these facts have been clarified in a dispassionate forum, resolution as to the relative weight to be accorded to competing civil liberties are premature and indeed harmful. This in short is the reason, and the only reason, for the failure of the [CLUM] to add its voice to the hue and cry concerning the film. . . .
>
> The termination of [Berlin's] relationship with Mr. Wiseman is in no respect the result of criticism of his conduct within the Union. On the contrary, we endorse his participation as a lawyer, and we are in total disagreement with suggestions in the press that it has been inconsistent with the purposes of our organization.

The CLUM board had not seen the documentary, and therefore stated, "Under these circumstances expression of a judgment on our part at this time would be highly presumptuous. . . . The decisional process can be entrusted only to the judiciary." CLUM suggested that it might take a position in an *amicus curiae* brief, if the case were later filed with an appellate court. It presented its carefulness as superior to the haste of other judgments: "We do not believe that we, or the public generally, are in a position to render judgment at this time."[220]

CLUM did file a friend-of-the-court brief in the appeal of *Commonwealth v. Wiseman* before the Supreme Judicial Court of Massachusetts in the spring of 1969.[221] Signed by CLUM counsel Henry Paul Monaghan and prepared by the five-member board, the brief continued in the cautionary tone of the 1967 press release: there were competing civil liberties claims; the union board had still not seen the film; the court, after having seen *Titicut Follies*, would have to be the judge. The brief objected to the extremity of the injunctive relief entered in the superior court and suggested that—if the supreme judicial court found that there were specific privacy invasions—the film itself should be altered or audiences be limited to specialized groups in order that competing civil liberties might be balanced. The truth or falsity of the oral contract question was not considered critical.

In 1974, Wiseman characterized CLUM's "Solomon-like solution" as a position "against the film" and recollected with considerable bitterness, "The moral insensitivity and cowardice of CLUM and its chairman were for me the worst part of the *Follies* case. . . . The national ACLU stayed out of the case. All I could get at the New York office were a few stale ironies from the staff general counsel."[222]

A chain of letters appeared in the *Civil Liberties Review* following the publication of Wiseman's remarks: Richardson claimed that concern for the privacy of the inmates had led CLUM "to file its *amicus* brief supporting the state".[223] Wiseman answered that CLUM never supported the state's position that *Titicut Follies* should be banned and that, since the board of CLUM had just voted unanimously (on May 8, 1974) to support an action to be brought in the state and federal courts to have the film shown without restriction, he hoped that Richardson would "support this CLUM postion so that they can continue to have a comity of interests."[224] Ellen Feingold (then president of CLUM) criticized Wiseman's discussion of the role of CLUM in the legal struggle over *Titicut Follies*. "[His] statements oversimplify just where his films excel—in showing an issue objectively in its complexity." She outlined the CLUM position: "It is clear in retrospect that the court's attempt at balance resulted in prior restraint. . . . The Union is still trying to find a balance among competing issues, but we have shifted emphasis and are working actively to lift the ban on public showing. The problem posed by violation of the patients' privacy still troubles us."[225]

Executive Director John Roberts said that the major reason for the shift in CLUM's position regarding *Titicut Follies* was that the privacy concern had waned with age.[226] By 1984 even Elliot Richardson saw no reason why exhibition should continue to be restricted.[227] Yet the privacy concern has also intensified with age, since some of the inmates and patients pictured in the film have since been released from Bridgewater. Alan Reitman has called the right of privacy "the new zone of civil liberty" and has wondered how the ACLU might help "to rein in technology's power to surveil, record, and disseminate the details of a person's life . . . yet [use] that power for positive purposes."[228] In 1976, the CLUM board established a policy regarding direct representation. "Staff lawyers may accept any case in which there is a clear civil issue and no competing civil liberties interest."[229]

On November 1, 1967, while the legislative hearing involving *Titicut Follies* continued, four Bridgewater guards (Charles J. Cullen, Carlton G. Shaw, Edwin F. Spencer, and George L. Parent) filed a defamation suit in federal court in New York against Titicut Follies Distributing Co. Inc.; Grove Press, Inc.; and F and A Theaters. They sought an injunction to prohibit current and future distribution and exhibition of the documentary, then playing at a commercial movie house owned by F and A Theaters, and claimed damages of eight hundred thousand dollars (one hundred thousand dollars for each officer on each of two counts). *Cullen* invoked a New York privacy statute that provided grounds for such action if "a person, firm or corporation . . . uses for advertising purposes, or for the purposes of trade, the name, portrait or picture of any living person without having first obtained the written consent of such person."[230] The guards claimed they had not signed releases and had been deceived by the filmmakers about the type of film being made and the plans for its future use. *Cullen v. Grove Press*,[231] although certainly having much in common with previous and subsequent litigation involving *Titicut Follies*, nevertheless presented some legal questions not posed in other cases. Here was (1) a defamation suit (2) filed in Federal Court (3) against three New York firms engaged in the distribution and exhibition of *Titicut Follies* (Wiseman and BFC were *not named* as defendants), (4) seeking damages for state employees pictured in the documentary because (5) their privacy had allegedly been invaded by their presentation with nude inmates. Obscenity was not stated as grounds for action, but implied by a description of the film as a "montage of sex" by counsel for the plaintiffs, Robert F. Muse, and by the filed claim that Grove Press "is engaged principally in the sale and distribution of salacious printed materials that have an overbearing emphasis on the carnal aspects of sex."[232]

Federal District Judge Walter R. Mansfield heard the case only two weeks after the November 1 filing and announced his decision by the end of the month. Prepared in some haste, the case for the plaintiffs set for itself the formidable task of proving libel and/or invasion of privacy not only sufficient to realize damages for the guards, but also injunctive relief. That the case failed should come as no surprise, especially after previous petitions for injunctive relief had been denied by two New York supreme court justices.

Cullen's suit responded to predicted and actual comments such as those of NBC-TV *Today* reviewer Judith Crist, who, questioning the possible bias of *Titicut Follies*, asked "Are all the attendants sadistic morons?"[233] The guards claimed that the documentary holds them "up to ridicule, contempt and scorn in all respectable segments of our society and community," because (among other reasons) inmates are presented as "indistinguishable from the guards" and the film "has been edited . . . to emphasize certain erotic aspects of nudity and overtones and suggestions of indifference and brutality on the part of the Correction Officers as a class of which your plaintiffs are members."[234]

Neither the complaint nor the other pleadings offered any proof that the filmed events were false or distorted, let alone proof of the defendants' knowledge of the documentary's alleged falsity or reckless disregard of the truth, thus failing to comply with the holding of the U.S. Supreme Court decision reached earlier that year in *Time, Inc., v. Hill.*[235] Faced with *Time*, the plaintiffs made the general claim in oral argument that "the film does not give a true and balanced impression of conditions at Bridgewater but distorts conditions thereby emphasizing the bizarre and failing to show other aspects that would explain the scenes that are portrayed and thus put them in proper context."[236]

Based on the trial judge's own viewing of the film, the testimony of the producer-director (whose academic and professional experiences the judge found relevant), Wiseman's offer (declined) to show the court the balance of the eighty thousand feet of film shot at Bridgewater, the "imposing array of affidavits" from experts in various fields and film critics, Mansfield found *Titicut Follies* not a false report. Mansfield, the son of a former mayor of Boston, wrote, "By its very nature the subject matter is such that a chronicle of it must to some extent be gruesome and depressing in character, and in this case the picture fulfills such anticipation." He found the allegation of invasion of privacy, based on the guards' appearances in scenes (for example, and most particularly, the "skin search") in which inmates or patients are pictured nude, not worthy of consideration. No proof to support the allegation of inflammatory advertising was offered. Because of the nature of the filming (at such a close physical distance), the judge assumed consent at all times on the part of the guards.

Responding to the questions of obscenity, "at best hinted at in the plaintiffs' reply," Mansfield found that "the nudity appears in each instance to form an integral part of an episode that is of legitimate public interest. . . . There are no commentaries or actions that could be construed as an appeal to any prurient interest in sex, and this Court does not believe that the material is so patently offensive as to affront community standards."

The judge further found the contentions (sharply disputed by the film-makers) that the film crew suggested actions or scenes for the film, that the guards participated in scenes with naked inmates subject to an understanding that only the "upper extremities" of inmates would be photographed, and that the film would be exhibited only for "educational purposes," even if true, not grounds for injunctive relief or damages. Mansfield held that "the conditions in public institutions such as Bridgewater for the care of the criminally insane, including the physical facilities, conduct of employees, and type of treatment administered to inmates, are matters which are of great interest to the public generally. Such public interest is both legitimate and healthy." Mansfield found the distribution and exhibition of *Titicut Follies* protected by the First Amendment.

Although the federal judge emphatically denied the guards' motion, Mansfield kept the judicial door open to further considerations. "This conclusion does not, of course, constitute an adjudication of rights of non-parties, such as individual inmates claiming violation of their own personal rights or state officials suing for breach of contract, if any, with respect to conditions for exhibition of the film."

Several weeks before the Bridgewater guards filed their damage suit against the distributors and exhibitors of *Titicut Follies*, there had been speculation in the Boston press that the Commonwealth would be sued for damages. Journalist Thomas C. Gallager reported that Representative Caw-ley had been "advised by legal experts" that there was a "prospect of massive damage suits against the Commonwealth, possibly running into the millions of dollars, by patients whose rights of privacy have been violated, and mem-bers of their families."[237] Legal scholars later claimed that releases were only for the filmmakers' protection, since the state was immune from tort liability (invason of privacy itself),[238] but that the state, as guardian, also has a duty to protect the rights and interests of its wards—failure to do so is grounds for suits for money damages. A sensitivity to the legal vulnerability of the state was one of several reasons that Dr. Harry Kozol objected in the spring of 1966 to filming at the division under his direction. During the summer of 1967 and into September, the question of the state's liability, through Gaughan, had been raised at meetings between Wiseman and the attorney general's office.

Announcing the preparation of *Cullen v. Grove Press*, the *Herald Traveler* further stated that "it was understood from one reliable source that 'perhaps 100, perhaps even more' libel and other suits would be brought in Massachu-setts on behalf of the inmates."[239] As of this writing, only one such case has gone to trial. The suit, entered on behalf of thirty-five inmates pictured in *Titicut Follies* against Wiseman and Bridgewater Film Company, Inc., sought five million dollars in damages for alleged invasion of privacy and breach of contract. The action was taken technically through guardians appointed to represent the inmates, thirty of whom were no longer at Bridgewater. Assistant Attorney General Donald Wood was counsel for Charles W. Gaughan, guardian of one of the patients. Attorneys Paul Tamburello and Neil Chayet represented the others. The 210-page statement of the case, filed November 3, 1969, was the lengthiest entered to that date in Suffolk Superior Court.[240]

In a seventy-two page decision, Judge Robert Sullivan rejected all 560 claims made on behalf of the inmates. He ruled in Wiseman's favor on First Amendment grounds, finding that conditions at Bridgewater were "all matters of news and of great public concern."[241] Sullivan refused to grant the inmates a share in the profits of the film (then twenty-seven thousand dollars) since there was no evidence of any contract or any agreement that subjects in the film were to be paid. To the claim made on behalf of the inmates that the film's public showing had added "psychological harm" to the subjects, the judge responded, "This court has been asked to place a dollar value on an almost imperceptible change in degree of insanity. Such a task is impossible."

Legal scholars point out that definitions of privacy are "necessarily subjective, abstract, elusive," but "whatever its form, an invasion of privacy is presumed to have an adverse effect on an identifiable person's psychological well-being."[242] Sullivan's decision provokes the basic question: Could a person judged legally insane be found (legally) to have had his or her privacy invaded under *any* circumstances? In *Commonwealth v. Wiseman*, the defense argued against the state positions that inmates (a) were incompetent to give consent and (b) had suffered an invasion of privacy, claiming that if competent to give consent, then the subjects' privacy had been waived; if incompetent, then the subjects could not suffer the mental anguish claimed by privacy invasion.

The next legal question regarding damages would seem to be whether a person, presumed sane and released from Bridgewater, would suffer current mental anguish when his past condition is made public. So far no damage suit filed by a former inmate or patient himself has gone to trial. In the spring of 1977, approximately ten days after *Titicut Follies* was shown at the University of Massachusetts-Boston, through the sponsorship of a civil liberties class, a member of the student body came to the class to protest the then new practice of showing the film on Massachusetts campuses. The student had been an inmate at Bridgewater in 1966 and, although he claims he tried to avoid the camera and did not give his consent to be filmed, he is clearly identifiable in the documentary.[243] As of this writing, he has not filed suit for damages.

A month after the Commonwealth filed its first papers petitioning for an injunction against the exhibition of *Titicut Follies*, Suffolk Superior Court Justice Joseph Ford ordered the suit "first case out" on the list for hearings the following month and thus moved *Commonwealth v. Wiseman* to trial in slightly less than two months.[244] Normally, the Commonwealth would have been represented by its attorney general, but, since Attorney General Elliot Richardson was a potential witness in the case, all early motions and other legal papers were signed by Assistant Attorney General Frederick Greenman, chief of the Division of Health, Education, and Welfare. Two attorneys from Ropes and Gray, Richardson's former law firm—Edward B. Hanify (the son of a former superior court judge) and George C. Caner, Jr.—were appointed as special assistant attorneys general, and they acted as counsel for the Commonwealth in the trial.

James D. St. Clair and Blair L. Perry of Hale and Dorr represented Wiseman and BFC. In 1967, St. Clair was remembered as Joseph Welch's assistant in the Army-McCarthy hearings; he would later be known as Richard Nixon's Watergate lawyer. He is highly regarded within the legal community; a lawyer's lawyer, St. Clair has been described as "all case and no cause."[245]

Grove Press was represented by John Larkin Thompson, whose first major task was to disengage his clients (Grove and Titicut Follies Distributing Co., Inc.) from the state court proceedings. In a pretrial conference, Thompson argued that the case against them should be tried in a federal court. St. Clair argued against the removal, saying that it would be a burden for the Commonwealth to conduct two trials.[246] The plaintiffs, eager to move to trial against Wiseman, did not oppose the separation petition. The trial judge allowed the severance; however, U.S. District Court Judge Francis J. Ford later remanded the case against Grove back to the Suffolk Superior Court, where it was heard in the spring of 1968.

Oliver Wendell Holmes's century-old reminder remains worth considering when one tries to understand *Commonwealth v. Wiseman:* "The life of the law has not been logic: it has been experience. The felt necessities of the time, the prevalent moral and political theories, intuitions of public policy, avowed or unconscious, even the prejudices which judges share with their fellow-men, have had a good deal more to do than the syllogism in determining the rules by which men should be governed."[247] The controversy that swirled around *Titicut Follies* outside the courtroom reflected serious divisions regarding what might be called necessities and substantial differences in moral and political theories. Those tensions found their way into the court presided over by Judge Harry Kalus. Born in Russia, raised in three different working-class neighborhoods of Boston, Kalus worked as an upholsterer while he attended Suffolk University Law School. He was later elected to the general court (Democrat, Ward 12), served as an assistant corporation counsel for the city of Boston and then as legislative counsel to Governor Maurice J. Tobin before Tobin appointed him a district court judge.[248] In 1962, he was elevated to the superior court by Governor John Volpe. Hardworking and conservative, Kalus was "a real Commonwealther," a man dedicated to serving his state.[249] Throughout the *Titicut Follies* trial, Kalus played an active role, not just in making determinations regarding evidence and procedure, but also in questioning witnesses (for example, posing forty-one sequential questions to witness for the defense Richard Schickel; tr. 16:82–91). At one point, counsel for the defendants would raise an objection to one of the judge's questions; at another, Kalus would apologize for his intrusions.[250]

During the pretrial conference on November 17, 1967, which was mostly dialogue between St. Clair and Kalus, St. Clair defined the situation as a case "without any substantial precedent . . . [in which] substantial issues are going to get resolved . . . [and thus] the case has significance beyond the parties themselves" (Tr. 1:36). St. Clair's interest in the case came through in his description that "there are many, many issues. It is a very unusual case and I find it very fascinating. . . . I have a feeling that this case is going to grow more complicated rather than less" (Tr. 1:33). Later in the conference, Kalus remarked to the defense counsel, "Well, you said this was going to be a thorny trial, it certainly is" (Tr. 1:59). These men of the court seemed to agree that legal dilemmas would confront them; at that point in the trial, they seemed eager to meet the challenge.

The first confrontation was a decision regarding the screening of the documentary itself. All agreed that the trial judge should see *Titicut Follies*, but Kalus wondered if the injunction against the film did not also apply to him. St. Clair assured him that the court did not enjoin itself. He also claimed that it would not be an open and public trial if the screening were private and that the issuance of the temporary injunction by another judge who had not seen the film had been not just inappropriate, but unconstitutional. Throughout the lengthy trial—eighteen trial days, sixty-four exhibits, 2,556 pages of proceedings (plus another two days of nontranscribed oral arguments)—counsel for Wiseman and BFC would maintain the position contained in their pretrial request for an open screening of *Titicut Follies*.

THE COURT: Then for the benefit of the public only?

MR. ST. CLAIR: For the benefit of the integrity of the judicial system, as I view it. (Tr. 1:65)

The judge denied the request.

Because of the litigation in New York and federal courts, the legislative hearings, and the extensive press coverage of the controversy, the entire trial of *Commonwealth v. Wiseman* was, in a nonlegal sense, a series of rejoinders or second pleadings. For example, the first witness, Commissioner John A. Gavin, was questioned about his answer to a question asked in the legislative hearing based on an attribution in a newspaper based on an interview. For the plaintiffs and the defendants *Commonwealth v. Wiseman* covered a great deal of old ground, but it was not the same legal ground.

Commonwealth v. Wiseman was not a defamation case, and it was not filed as an obscenity case. The plaintiffs (the Commonwealth of Massachusetts, with Superintendent Gaughan and Commissioner Gavin in their official capacities, and James C. Bulcock, through Gaughan as his guardian) alleged that the defendants (Frederick Wiseman and Bridgewater Film Company, Inc.) had breached an oral contract and invaded the privacy of the named inmates. The petitioners claimed that all receipts from the film should be held in trust for the inmates, but there was no plea for damages per se. Rather, they sought to enjoin exhibition of *Titicut Follies*.

A description of the *Titicut Follies* project by Edward Hanify in his opening remarks serves as an outline of what the state claimed were promises unkept. "The project then . . . [promised to be] an educational film about the Massachusetts Correctional Institution at Bridgewater, probably financed by the support of a national foundation, the ultimate film to use only the photographs of inmates and patients who were legally competent to give releases, with the film maker bound to obtain written releases from each inmate and patient whose photographs were used in the film, and the final film, prior to public release, to be subject to the approval of Superintendent Gaughan and Commissioner Gavin" (Tr. 2:10).

The general defense position regarding the allegation of breach of contract was that there were no conditions actually agreed upon that had been breached, that there had been no agreement regarding censorship by the state, and that, even if there had been a censorship agreement, it would be unconstitutional and, therefore, legally unenforceable.

Let us consider each subpart of the charge. Since Wiseman did not obtain foundation funding and since *Titicut Follies* had been exhibited theatrically in New York, the state's position was that Wiseman and BFC "attempted to engage in commercial traffic with tragedy in violation of Wiseman's basic agreement with the Commonwealth and petitioners Gavin and Gaughan."[251] The state argued not only that *Titicut Follies* was a sensational, exploitative product of dubious educational value, but also that Wiseman and his associates had intended, from the outset, to create such a product. Because of the nature of the allegation, questions regarding motives were allowed and became central to the arguments of both sides. David Eames, the associate producer and president of BFC, was called as a witness for the state and was presented as someone lacking the academic and technical credentials necessary for educational film making who had been misled by Wiseman— a characterization Eames strongly denied. John Marshall, whose deposition had been taken by the state, was not called to the witness stand by the state or the defendants.[252] Still, the resignations of Marshall and his wife were much discussed during direct examination of Eames and cross-examination of Wiseman. Counsel for the state implied that these resignations cast serious doubt on the integrity of the enterprise. Marshall, an articulate, well-educated member of a wealthy Cambridge family devoted to anthropological research, was not present to claim or disclaim allegiance to the educational worth of the project.

Wiseman, the central witness for the defense, naturally asserted the legitimacy of his motives, the BFC procedures, and the final film. The producer-director was on the witness stand for almost three full days. Unshaken by the aggressive cross- and recross-examination, Wiseman maintained that he had met all contractual agreements. He claimed that, along with the "loneliness and isolation and despair at Bridgewater," he also wanted the film to disclose "the tenderness and the concern and the genuine interest that was expressed on the part of people like Superintendent Gaughan and the correction officers" (Tr. 13:141–42). His answers were usually direct, often extremely detailed. A response to his counsel's question regarding his editing strategies lasted for twenty-five minutes.[253]

The defense argued that, although foundation support had been denied, the investors and crew continued to see the project as an educational endeavor. Arrangements with Grove Press were necessary to recover the expenses of making the film and to guarantee its exhibition. The defense was in the delicate position of presenting *Titicut Follies* as essentially a noncommercial project, according to the terms of the agreement, and also arguing its First Amendment protection for any commercial use or intent. The defense presented a group of witnesses with established academic credentials, all of whom contended that *Titicut Follies* had considerable educational value—a university dean (Gerhart D. Weibe), a professor of psychiatry (Leon Shapiro), and a professor of social psychology (Morris Schwartz).

The agreement to film only competent persons was a matter of written contract and went undisputed as a condition by the defense. The state, therefore, tried to prove that some individuals in the film were incompetent at the time filmed and thus conditions were violated. Lengthy expert testimony by Samuel Allen, the director of clinical psychiatry and acting medical director at Bridgewater State Hospital, and Samuel Tartakoff, a retired physician who had been director of the Division of Legal Medicine for the Massachusetts Mental Health Department, was entered by the state to support its contention that the BFC had filmed incompetents, including the named plaintiff.

The defense offered the evidence, also in writing, of Wiseman's proposal that competency would be determined by state personnel, who would accompany the filmmakers at all times. Wiseman's defense sidestepped the burden of proving that the subjects were, in fact, competent by referring to the consent procedures in which competence was assumed by the BFC crew unless the superintendent or his staff said otherwise, which was never the case. Eames and Wiseman both testified that they were not sure of the definitions of competency or sanity before they went to Bridgewater and became increasingly unsure of them after their time at the institution (Tr. 6:160–66; 15:136). Cross-examination of the doctors in reference to the subjects' mental reports revealed how rarely the men at Bridgewater had received psychiatric examinations. One of the men filmed had not been given a psychiatric examination for more than eight years, and it had been more than six years since his last physical exam.[254] St. Clair stated that "Bridgewater is a prison; whether or not it is a hospital is a question of fact for the Court" (Tr. 8:14). The defense questioned the particular credentials of the expert witnesses and the general capacity to determine sanity. St. Clair quoted the venerable Justice Frankfurter: "Only one proposition seems certain, that is, that sanity and insanity are concepts of incertitude" (Tr. 8:12).

The discussion of sanity also pertained to releases and indicated how intertwined the legal, medical, and ethical questions are in the *Titicut Follies* case. In cross-examination, Dr. Tartakoff acknowledged that insanity is essentially a legal, not a medical description (Tr. 8:5). Yet he was willing, at the request of state counsel Caner, to apply that term to individuals pictured in *Titicut Follies*. Since, by law, a contract made by an insane person is voidable, releases signed by incompetent inmates and patients could be set aside. Caner also challenged the legality of releases made out in the spring and summer of 1966 to a corporation (BFC) not legally organized until the following fall. Even if no releases were voided for such reasons, the state introduced the evidence that only eleven or twelve of the sixty-two identifiable inmates had signed releases.[255] Staff members had signed the balance of the 106 releases, but their releases were not questioned or discussed.

The defense claimed that since Attorney General Brooke had not explicitly mentioned releases in his opinion (releases were mentioned in the Gavin request that was part of the correspondence from Brooke) and since no release form had been offered by the state, there had been no agreement regarding releases. St. Clair argued that the state "cannot have it both ways" (that is, to argue as *parens patriae* on behalf of the inmates and to have a right protectable by a release, which assumes a position antagonistic to that of the releasor; tr. 8:33). The defense maintained that all who were pictured gave their consent, albeit unwritten in many cases. The BFC attorneys introduced canteen receipts and cash account records as evidence that MCI-Bridgewater officials assumed that the inmates were sufficiently competent to allow them to make these kinds of contractual agreements. The records were not accepted as exhibits, but were marked for identification.

The most heavily argued section of the breach-of-contract allegation was the contention by the state that Wiseman had agreed to state approval prior to the release of the Bridgewater documentary. Much of the testimony of Charles Gaughan and James Gavin spoke to the point that Wiseman had agreed to this condition. Elliot Richardson and Frederick Greenman firmly and forcefully testified that they, too, had assumed that *Titicut Follies* would not be shown publicly without state approval and that Wiseman was well aware of that condition. Thirteen correction officers, including two who had been named plaintiffs in *Cullen v. Grove*, testified that they had, at some time in the presence of the BFC crew, heard state approval as a condition of film making mentioned by Superintendent Gaughan, the crew, or both. The defense argued "the complete lack of any objective conformation [sic] of any right of censorship" (Tr. 2:35) and that this condition, although consistently claimed untrue by Wiseman and Eames, would be unlawful, if true.

The allegation of invasion of privacy was filed in the name of one inmate, James Bulcock, who is shown nude with his genitals exposed and is provoked by guards into revealing personal information about himself. The scene involving this man and his interaction with the guards, who shave him and return him to his cell, lasts for six minutes and forty-five seconds and is one of the lengthiest in the film.[256] Bulcock, who was known in the trial as No. 3, had been confined to Bridgewater for twenty-five years and had no known living relatives. Around October 1, 1967, Superintendent Gaughan signed a petition to be made the man's legal guardian; they never met. Inmate No. 3 did not sign a release form. Based on his records, an examination by Bridgewater staff members prior to the trial, and his observed behavior in the film, he was classified by Allen and Tartakoff as incompetent at the time of filming. In arguing invasion of privacy, counsel for the plaintiffs implicitly emphasized two areas of the privacy tort—intrusion and public disclosure of private facts—but did not explicitly refer to a privacy tort. Although only one individual inmate was a named plaintiff, Hanify's opening remarks indicated that the privacy invasion would be argued in plural terms. "It is the view of the Commonwealth that essentially [Titicut Follies] displays nude and incompetent inmates at Bridgewater in the process of manifesting their hallucinations, their abberations, their mad ravings and their basic mental diseases in circumstances depriving them of spiritual and physical privacy" (Tr. 2:21). Both Gaughan and Richardson testified that they had registered complaints about privacy invasion with Wiseman as early as the previous summer.

The defense pointed to case law that found that confinement itself limited privacy. St. Clair and Perry argued that filming introduced no invasions of privacy substantially greater than those routinely experienced by the men at Bridgewater. Although not allowed in evidence by the trial judge, footage taken by the BFC crew showed a high school tour of the facility in which students observed nude inmates. The footage included students looking into No. 3's cell, which had a name plate over the door. Here is the defense cocounsel attempting to present the defense argument:

THE COURT: Would you state that again?

MR. PERRY: That the right of privacy, your Honor, is often stated in terms of a right to be let alone. It is our position that those people so unfortunate as to be at Bridgewater have a right not to be let alone, in other words, that they have been abandoned by society, in effect, and . . .

THE COURT: That would be the most monstrous proposition I have ever heard. (Tr. 15:157)

Continuing that argument, the defense claimed that inmate No. 3's medical treatment had actually improved considerably after the release of the film and that the acceleration in attention was not coincidental. Thus, they argued, disclosures of such deplorable conditions would be in the inmates' and patients' best interests. Bulcock did not appear as a witness. He had been sent a notice of deposition by the defense, but there is no Bulcock deposition filed with the case records.[257] No family member served as a witness for the plaintiffs or the defense.

Counsel for the defense accused the Commonwealth of hypocrisy in the case in general and in particular details like the use of numbers rather than names in the trial testimony. St. Clair argued that "it is the privacy of the Commonwealth that is being sought to be protected here, not the privacy of these poor, unfortunate individuals" (Tr. 2:23).

The main defense, of course, was on constitutional grounds. St. Clair and Perry invoked the First Amendment. "It is our position that under the law of this Commonwealth, there is no recognized right of privacy; that to the extent that one ever would be or could be recognized, it is subordinate, as the Court has indicated in the Themo case, if recognized, to a right of people to know or a right of disclosure in a matter of public interest" (Tr. 15:156). Defense counsel argued that the public has a right—and a duty—to know what transpires in a public-supported institution. They contended that public scandal cannot be revealed without scandalous revelation.[258]

Although the case was not filed on an obscenity charge, St. Clair anticipated obscenity claims when he said in his opening statements that "this is not a case . . . that involves any pornography. There is not even any suggestion that this would attract any prurient interest on the part of anybody. This is a factual film" (Tr. 2:34). There was a shadow charge of obscenity throughout the trial. Obscenity originally meant beyond the bounds, offensive. In the *Titicut Follies* case, two vague terms—privacy invasion and obscenity—often blurred into a general complaint of offensiveness. Witnesses for the plaintiffs made frequent reference to the general amount of nudity in the film (correction officer Lepine testified that there are at least seven inmates shown nude who are clearly identifiable and about eleven others shown nude, but not easily identifiable); to an interview in which an inmate discusses his sexual behavior (some of which is actionable); and to a scene in which an inmate is allegedly shown in an actual or implied act of masturbation. Wiseman was asked to write out a description of an outtake considered too offensive to be discussed aloud in the courtroom. The description, from a Wiseman affidavit in previous action in a New York court, states, "For example, there is the line-up for showers. Approximately fifteen or twenty men at a time are taken naked from their cells, many of them with their genitals in various states of erection."[259]

Defense witnesses attesting to the value of *Titicut Follies* as news (Louis Lyons, print journalist, director of the Neiman Fellowships at Harvard, and WGBH-TV [Boston NET] news commentator), social document (experts from the fields of sociology, psychology, law, and medicine), and art (Richard

Schickel, author and film critic for *Life* magazine, and Willard Van Dyke, documentary filmmaker and director of the film division of the Museum of Modern Art) followed the pattern of First Amendment defense in many obscenity cases. Between 1967 and 1971, the U.S. Supreme Court reversed obscenity convictions in thirty-nine cases in which a majority of the Court, applying separate tests, decided that the material in question was not obscene. What became known as the LAPS test was the "test" whether a work, taken as a whole, lacked literary, artistic, political, or scientific value and could, therefore, be denied First Amendment protection; however, Kalus stated that *Commonwealth v. Wiseman* was not an obscenity trial and refused to let a social psychologist continue testimony, ruling that "the question of whether the film has any value as a social document is irrelevant to the issues in the case."[260]

When questioned about the necessity of having subjects identifiable in the film, Wiseman did not call upon poetic license as his defense; he defended his choices on informational/educational grounds. Schickel's testimony in cross-examination sounded a great deal like that in an obscenity case, yet the *Life* critic avoided an explicit art-for-art's sake position (Tr. 16:44–98). Willard Van Dyke, the last witness in the trial, made a distinction, which he claimed to be a commonly held one, between instructional and educational documentaries. The filmmaker said instructional films were didactic and did not challenge a viewer to think. Van Dyke described *Titicut Follies* as an educational documentary, because, rather than telling, it helps "someone to understand" (Tr. 17:26).

Before the attorneys presented their final arguments, the trial judge mentioned "certain issues of law and fact and mixed law and fact issues" that they might wish to address: (1) the question as to the status of the plaintiff parties; (2) "almost a threshold question and a fact question"—whether there were any conditions imposed on Wiseman concerning the privilege or permission to make the film; (3) the question of representation by Wiseman as to the purpose for which the film was to be used; (4) whether commercial use of the film allowed the defendant to claim free speech; and (5) whether anyone could sign a release for the persons filmed who were mentally ill.[261]

Final arguments were presented before the court on December 14 and 15, 1967; briefs and memoranda of law were filed December 22. It now became Judge Harry Kalus's responsibility to render a judgment. Don Pember describes the considerable power given to judges in cases under equity: "The rules and procedures under equity are far more flexible than those under the common law. Equity really begins where the common law leaves off. Equity suits are never tried before a jury. Rulings come in the form of judicial decrees, not in judgments of yes or no. Decisions in equity are (and were) discretionary on the part of judges. And despite the fact that precedents are also relied upon in the law of equity, judges are free to do what they think is right and fair in a specific case."[262] It did not take the court long to consider its judgment. On January 4, 1968, Judge Harry Kalus issued his "Findings, Rulings and Order for Decree."

Kalus found that Frederick Wiseman and Bridgewater Film Company, Inc., had breached an oral contract with the Commonwealth of Massachusetts and invaded the privacy of James C. Bulcock. Kalus wrote:

> The film product which Wiseman made . . . constitutes a most flagrant abuse of the privilege he was given to make a film. . . . There is a new theme—crudities, nudities and obscenities. . . . It is a crass piece of commercialism—a contrived scenario—designed by its new title and by its contents to titillate the general public and lure them to the box office. The film is 80 minutes of brutal sordidness and human degradation. It is a hodge-podge of sequences, with the camera jumping, helter-skelter, from the showing of an inmate in an act of masturbation to scenes depicting mentally ill patients engaged in repetitive, incoherent and obscene rantings and ravings. The film is excessively preoccupied with nudity, with full exposure of the privates of these persons. There is no narrative accompanying the film, nor are there any subtitles, without which the film is a distortion of the daily routine and conditions at the Institution. Each viewer is left to his own devices as to just what is being portrayed and in what context.[263]

Regarding the issues that he had mentioned before final arguments, Judge Kalus found that (1) the Commonwealth and Gaughan as guardian had status; (2) there were conditions imposed on Wiseman by the state; (3) Wiseman had misrepresented his purposes; (4) no free speech claim was legitimate here; and (5) the men at Bridgewater had a right to be left alone. Writing the first decision in Massachusetts legal history based on the right to privacy, Kalus said that "this right of privacy rests upon the most elementary principles of natural law. . . . The true rule is that equity will protect the personal and intangible rights of an individual just as it will enjoin the violation of a person's property rights."[264] He dismissed the First Amendment claim. "No amount of rhetoric, no shibboleths of 'free speech' and the 'right of the public to know' can obscure or masquerade this pictorial performance for what it really is—a piece of abject commercialism, trafficking on the loneliness, on the human misery, degradation and sordidness in the lives of these unfortunate humans."[265]

Kalus not only found for the Commonwealth, but the outraged judge exceeded its demands for injunctive relief. He modified the bill of complaint by deleting the words "without prior approval in writing by the plaintiffs" and ordered the respondents to deliver to the Commonwealth "the balance of the film footage (the original negative and any and all prints thereof), together with sound tapes, taken by them at Bridgewater."[266]

On December 28, 1967, the Commonwealth had filed a motion for enlargement of the injunction, to force Grove/Titicut to discontinue distribution of the documentary. Judge Kalus reserved judgment on the Commonwealth's petition concerning the disposition of the income and profits from the commercial exhibition of *Titicut Follies* until the conclusion of the suit against the respondents Grove Press, Inc., and Titicut Follies Distributing Co., Inc.

A hearing regarding the disposition of income was held on May 23, 1968. Daniel Mahoney, attorney for Grove and Titicut, was the only witness. Kalus ruled against the trust requirement, stating that it would be "inappropriate, if at all legally permissible, for the Court to order that any and all of the inmates at Bridgewater share in any profits made by the several respondents in the showing of a film" (Tr. 18:39). Kalus went on to state that there could be no pooling of a fund, since each person "is entitled to recover for himself, and alone, for such damages he has proved he has sustained and suffered" (Tr. 18:40).

Kalus ordered a permanent injunction against the showing of *Titicut Follies* in Massachusetts, directed the Commonwealth to destroy the unused Bridgewater footage, and dismissed the bill without prejudice to the petitioner (the guardian of Bulcock) to bring an action at law for damages. The final decree of the Suffolk Superior Court, entered on August 6, 1968, by Justice Harry Kalus, was a clear and almost complete victory for the Commonwealth.[267]

The same day that the final decree of the superior court was entered, denying the petition that the receipts and profits from *Titicut Follies* be held in trust for the men at Bridgewater, the Commonwealth appealed the decree to the supreme judicial court (SJC). Yet certainly the respondents, Frederick Wiseman and Bridgewater Film Company, Inc., had been more—to use the language of the Commonwealth appeal—*aggrieved* by the Kalus decree. Within the week, Blair L. Perry had claimed an appeal for his clients. *Commonwealth v. Wiseman* was scheduled for the May sitting of the supreme judicial court.

As cross-appellants, the petitioners (the Commonwealth) argued: (1) The showings of *Titicut Follies* by Grove and Titicut were illegal; (2) Grove and Titicut should account for the profits made by the film to the inmates whose rights of privacy were violated by its showings (the brief listed gross revenues of not less than $31,798.50 and net profits of not less than $14,451.61); and (3) the petitioners had standing on behalf of their wards to reach the profits from the film. The Commonwealth claimed that "the constructive trust remedy is peculiarly appropriate in the case at bar because of the difficulty incompetents are likely to encounter proving compensatory damages in a tort action."[268] The petitioners suggested that the court should determine how the profits would be distributed to the inmates or their representatives.

The brief for the respondents (Wiseman, et al.) raised questions of both fact and law. Counsel for Wiseman and BFC argued: (1) The findings upon which the decree was based were not supported by the evidence and were misleading (twenty-one detailed challenges to the court's findings were listed); (2) there was no material breach of contract by Wiseman; (3) the petitioners had no interests which were entitled to equitable protection; (4)

no right to privacy is infringed by the film; (5) the film is protected by the First and Fourteenth Amendments to the U. S. Constitution; (6) any restrictions imposed upon Wiseman as a condition of his being permitted to make the film are void and unenforceable because of the First Amendment; (7) Article 16 of the constitution of the Commonwealth of Massachusetts [which protects freedom of speech] prohibits any injunction against showing of the film; (8) the basic principles of equity and public policy compel that *Titicut Follies* be permitted to be shown to the public, regardless of the conditions under which filming was permitted; (9) the Commonwealth should be barred from relief in this case by reason of its unclean hands and inequitable conduct; and (10) the evidence did not warrant the relief granted by the trial court in the final decree.[269]

As appellees, the petitioners (the Commonwealth) argued: (1) *Titicut Follies* violated the conditions on which permission was granted; (2) the conditions of the contract (as found by the trial court) were constitutional; (3) showings of the film were properly enjoined as a continuing invasion of the rights of privacy of the inmates shown; (4) the injunction against the continued showing of the film is not an invalid prior restraint on First Amendment rights; (5) the Commonwealth had standing to obtain an injunction enforcing the contract and protecting the inmates' rights of privacy; and (6) the Commonwealth should not be barred from relief by "unclean hands."[270] In other words, they supported the trial judge's finding of fact and law.

In addition, three organizations—the American Sociological Association (ASA), the American Orthopsychiatric Association (AOA), and the Civil Liberties Union of Massachusetts (CLUM)—filed *amicus curiae* briefs with the supreme judicial court. The ASA argued that the film is an important document which can be effectively used by professional groups for research, instruction, and discussion; and that any asserted right of privacy on behalf of the inmates does not preclude, as a matter of law, professional viewing and use of the film.[271] A broader argument in support of exhibition was entered by counsel for the AOA, who claimed: (1) The interests of the patients at Bridgewater, and of the mentally ill elsewhere, require that *Titicut Follies* be widely shown; (2) the interests of society in free discussion prohibit the enjoining of the film; (3) the Commonwealth and its officials have a clear conflict of interest in claiming to act for the patients in initiating censorship of a film critical of a state mental institution; and (4) the supposed contract cannot constitutionally authorize prohibition of the film.[272] The third brief filed by a friend of the court presented an abstract discussion of the issues, but gave limited support to the Wiseman appeal. CLUM made the following points: (1) The rights to personal dignity and privacy of the inmates of Bridgewater may be violated by unlimited distribution of this film; (2) some injunctive relief may be appropriate on the facts of the case; but (3) even if some injunctive relief were appropriate in this case, the decree entered in the superior court was too broad.[273] The Massachusetts Supreme Judicial Court had indicated its willingness—if the proper case presented itself—to consider whether and, if so, to what extent any nonstatutory right of privacy existed within the Commonwealth. Court watchers assumed that *Commonwealth v. Wiseman* was such a case.

Appeals were heard on May 6, 1969. On June 24, the Massachusetts Supreme Judicial Court issued its decision. All five justices agreed to modify the final decree, so that the injunction prohibited the showing of *Titicut Follies* to the general public, but allowed specialized audiences (legislators, judges, lawyers, sociologists, social workers, doctors, psychiatrists, students in these or related fields, and organizations dealing with the social problems of custodial care and mental infirmity) to see the documentary. The court regarded the film as a "collective, indecent intrusion into the most private aspects of the lives of these unfortunate persons in the Commonwealth's custody."[274] Still, it acknowledged the value of the film as a social document and allowed that "the film may indirectly have been of benefit to some inmates by leading to improvement of Bridgewater."[275] Preservation of the unused footage by BFC was allowed.

For the first time in its 277-year history, the SJC recognized a legally enforceable right of privacy in Massachusetts; however, the court explicitly stated that the right was recognized only to the extent of the factual situation presented in the particular case. Therefore, the court itself refused to define the situation as one of legal precedent. Justice Cutter, who wrote the decision, explained the modification as an attempt to balance conflicting public and private interests, probable good and possible harm. The court required that Wiseman add a brief explanation to the film that "changes and improvements have taken place in the institution since 1966."[276] The court held that a constructive trust based upon receipts for past showings of the film was unwarranted, since it was not an appropriate basis of recovery for any individual inmate who may have suffered ascertainable damage.

A number of legal scholars writing about *Commonwealth v. Wiseman* have seen the SJC modification as a legal improvement over the lower court decision, but they question the arguments the higher court used to explain its solution to a legal dilemma. David L. Bennett and Phillip Small wrote in the *Suffolk Law Review* that "It is difficult to comprehend how the court could have decided the *Wiseman* case without resolving the underlying problems raised by the First Amendment. . . . It appears illogical to dismiss First Amendment considerations in one part of the case by merely relying on the breach of contract, and then balance the private interests of the inmates against the public interest in another part of the case. . . . The court appears to have achieved the best of both worlds in its ultimate result, but neglects the need for rational consistency in reaching this result."[277] The *Harvard Law Review* noted:

Although the Supreme Judicial Court specifically disclaimed giving any weight to the interests of the Commonwealth . . . it seems likely that the state had an undue influence upon the final decision. A preliminary question never reached by the court, for example, was whether the government should have been permitted to act as legal guardian for the prisoners. . . .

[The required announcement regarding improvements] is a pernicious and, understandably, unique requirement. Such an announcement would in no way benefit the inmates, for whose sake the suit was supposedly brought, and would serve only to improve the image of the Commonwealth and the Department of Correction. Indeed, insofar as the audience takes the announcement to mean that conditions at Bridgewater are now acceptable, the inmates would be harmed.[278]

And, finally, a comment in the *Columbia Law Review* states that "ironically, [the] first judicial recognition of a right to privacy in Massachusetts is designed to protect the sensibilities of the criminally insane from the effects of a disclosure which can only improve the squalid circumstances of their lives. The only interests clearly protected are the dignity of the Commonwealth and the public image of her agents. . . . 'Titicut Follies' is an unfortunate case."[279]

Certainly Grove Press and Titicut Follies Film Distributing Co., Inc., considered *Commonwealth v. Wiseman* an unfortunate case. In the summer of 1971, the same day that the U.S. Supreme Court announced its decision to allow the publication of the Pentagon papers, a Boston paper also announced that Titicut and Grove had filed a civil suit in federal court against the Attorney General of Massachusetts (then Robert H. Quinn), Justice Harry Kalus, the SJC judges, Gavin, and Gaughan for "an impermissible prior restraint on free expression."[280] The defendants filed a motion to dismiss the case, a dismissal which Judge Frank J. Murray allowed the following spring.[281] As of this writing, no individual who does not fit into one of the specialized groups allowed to see *Titicut Follies* has filed a suit against the Commonwealth, protesting the elitist position of the current regulations.

Hardly any dispute ever goes to trial unless there is real fervor pushing at least one side forward. In the litigation involving *Titicut Follies*, strong feelings motivated all parties to the original argument. That passion continues. For two decades, the Commonwealth of Massachusetts and Frederick Wiseman have remained consistent in their claims, tenacious in their willingness to initiate or resist litigation.

In the spring of 1980, the office of still another Massachusetts Attorney General (Francis X. Bellotti) moved for a supplemental order to enjoin Wiseman from exhibiting *Titicut Follies* at the Saxon Theater as part of the "Boston Jubilee 350" (an event organized by a deputy mayor of Boston, Katherine Kane). U.S. District Judge Rya W. Zobel denied the motion for supplemental relief.[282]

Wiseman has been denied two petitions for *certiorari* to the United States Supreme Court. In 1983, his attorney, Blair Perry, was preparing a third appeal.[283] The first request, based on several First Amendment issues, was filed in the fall of 1969. Wiseman claimed that the Massachusetts decision limiting showings of the film to professional audiences is "a unique pernicious form of censorship"; he asked whether a state can "ban the showing to the public of a documentary film revealing conditions in a state institution on the theory of enforcing restriction imposed upon the filmmaker by the state as a condition of permitting the filming." Finally, the appeal claimed the *Wiseman* decision conflicted with the principles established in *Time, Inc., v. Hill*.[284]

Twice Wiseman has been just one vote short of the needed four for review of *Commonwealth v. Wiseman* by the U.S. Supreme Court.[285] Justices Harlan, Douglas, and Brennan voted to hear the first Wiseman appeal. Justice Harlan explained the reasons why he voted to grant *certiorari* and set the *Wiseman* case for plenary consideration:

> The balance between these two interests, that of the individual's privacy and the public's right to know about conditions in public institutions, is not one that is easily struck, particularly in a case like that before us where the importance of the issue is matched by the extent of the invasion of privacy. . . .
>
> A further consideration is the fact that these inmates are not only the wards of the Commonwealth of Massachusetts but are also the charges of society as a whole. It is important that conditions in public institutions should not be cloaked in secrecy, lest citizens may disclaim responsibility for the treatment that their representative government affords those in its care. At the same time, it must be recognized that the individual's concern with privacy is the key to the dignity which is the promise of civilized society. . . .
>
> [The conclusions of the Massachusetts Supreme Judicial Court] represent a measured and thoughtful attempt to grapple with a difficult and important problem. Yet they demonstrate the importance of review by this Court for they sharply focus the dimension of the question presented by this case. The question at this juncture is not whether the Supreme Judicial Court was correct or incorrect in striking the constitutional balance, but merely whether this Court should grant certiorari. I fail to see how, on a complex and important issue like this, it can be concluded that this Court should withhold plenary review. The case for review is strengthened by the fact that a distinguished federal judge refused to enjoin in New York the showing of this very same film. This is not of course the traditional conflict that requires this Court to step in, but it underscores the difficulty and importance of the issues that are apparent both from reading the decision of the Massachusetts court and a viewing of the film.
>
> I am at a loss to understand how questions of such importance can be deemed not "certworthy." To the extent that the Commonwealth suggests that certiorari be denied because petitioners failed to comply with reasonable contract conditions imposed by the Commonwealth, that question itself is one of significant constitutional dimension, for it is an open question as to how far a government may go in cutting off access of the media to its institutions when such access will not hinder them in performing their functions.[286]

The second petition for *certiorari* was filed for October term 1970 and denied December 7, 1970. National Educational Television was allowed to file an *amicus curiae* brief in support of the petition for rehearing. Again, Wiseman had three favorable votes (Justices Harlan, Brennan, and Blackmun). Justice William O. Douglas, who had previously voted in favor of review, withdrew from consideration because excerpts from his book *Points of Rebellion* had appeared in the *Evergreen Review*, a Grove Press publication, and he wished to avoid any possible conflict of interest.[287] Wiseman argued for a rehearing on the grounds that the important free speech issues should be considered in the initial stage by a full nine-man bench, but to no avail.[288] *Wiseman v. Massachusetts* was never heard by either the Warren or the Burger Court.

In July 1987, Wiseman returned to the Suffolk Superior Court, filing a motion to permit showing of *Titicut Follies* to general audiences. Wiseman's attorney, Blair Perry, argued that the motion should be allowed because (1) the applicable law had changed (regarding prior restraint) and (2) the facts had changed (few of the inmates shown in the film and identifiable are still living; attitudes of society toward public disclosure of conditions in an institution such as Bridgewater have changed; officials of the Commonwealth who sought to suppress the film are no longer in office; the original release of the film was credited with resulting in significant improvements at Bridgewater).[289]

The Commonwealth responded that it supported the showing of *Titicut Follies* to the general public "as long as a procedure is first imposed and followed to its conclusion to locate the inmates and patients depicted in the film, notify them of the pending motion and provide representation, as needed and separate from the Commonwealth to protect their privacy rights."[290] According to the state, consent by subjects or their guardians should be a prerequisite of public release. After twenty years, the Commonwealth moved to the position that Alan Dershowitz held during the crucial meeting at the attorney general's office on September 21, 1967, before any litigation had begun against *Titicut Follies*. During the fall of 1987, the attorney general's office attempted to locate the inmates and patients who appear in *Titicut Follies*. By mid-December, representatives of the Commonwealth determined that "of the 62 inmates so identified as appearing in the film, 28 are deceased; two are in custody at M.C.I., Bridgewater; one is in custody at M.C.I., Concord; four are in other institutions operated by or licensed under the Department of Mental Health; four are in nursing homes and six are believed to reside in private residences. The remaining seventeen have not been found despite diligent efforts, and all or some of them may be deceased."[291] The Commonwealth requested that a guardian *ad litem*—a guardian appointed for the purpose of a suit—be appointed to represent the interests of persons whose photographs are included in the film and who may be under some present disability. Wiseman's attorney and the attorney general's office agreed to nominate Mitchell J. Sikora, Jr., a member of the Massachusetts bar who had served in a similar capacity in a number of other cases. Judge Andrew G. Meyer appointed Sikora as guardian *ad litem* on December 17, 1987.

Early in January 1988 newspapers throughout the Commonwealth ran the following announcement:

Titicut Follies

Legal proceedings have started again on "Titicut Follies," a film made at M.C.I. Bridgewater in 1966. Exhibition of the film is enjoined to anyone other than certain specialists or professionals. The film's producer has asked the Suffolk County Superior Court to permit the film's showing to the general public.

The Court has appointed a guardian ad litem to represent the interests of certain persons whose photographs are shown in "Titicut Follies." If you believe you or someone you know is shown in the film, please immediately call or write Stephen A. Jonas, Deputy Chief, Public Protection Bureau, Department of the Attorney General, One Ashburton Place, 19th Floor, Boston MA 02108, (617) 727–4878.[292]

The Commonwealth's announcement led to the discovery of two or three men who had not been found by the earlier search of state records.[293] In April 1988, Sikora began to prepare his report, to be based on a review of parts of the trial transcript, a viewing of the film, interviews with the men pictured, and a search of state departmental and agency records. Men found competent by the guardian *ad litem* would make their own decisions, with the aid of counsel if they desired, regarding general exhibition of the documentary. Sikora was directed to report to the court on behalf of anyone he considered incompetent and to determine whether public exhibition of *Titicut Follies* would harm or benefit each person. Meyer's order made it clear that the report, recommendations, and opinions of the guardian *ad litem* would be advisory only. Meyer also ordered that the guardian "shall not disclose the names and addresses of the named persons to any members of the public (including, without limitation, the press or media) without further order of the Court. In his report to the Court, the GAL [guardian *ad litem*] shall refer to named persons by initials or other means appropriate to avoid public disclosure of their names and addresses."[294]

The Contradiction of Restricted Exhibition

Despite Wiseman's efforts, as of this writing, the exhibition status of *Titicut Follies* has remained fixed since 1969. Hence, Wiseman, as a filmmaker and a businessman, is confronted with the problematic situation of simultaneously marketing his film, of following the restrictions of the modified decree, and of preparing himself for a possible Supreme Court review or action on his motion before the superior court. The Commonwealth, on the other hand, is caught in the awkward position of enforcing a ban that can function as a promotional device.

Before its exhibition was legally restricted, *Titicut Follies* was shown at several film festivals and had a brief run in commercial theatres, which is unusual for a documentary film. After the Kalus decision of January 1968, Grove did not book *Titicut Follies* in any commercial theaters. In the May 1968 trial of the respondents, Grove Press, Inc., and Titicut Follies Distributing Company., Inc., the Commonwealth objected to screenings of *Titicut Follies* at the Florence Festivale dei Popoli and at St. Elizabeth's Hospital in Washington, D.C. and charged the New York companies with contempt. Grove was, therefore, aware that the Commonwealth was carefully monitoring distribution of *Titicut Follies*. Judge Kalus found no evidence to support the contempt charge. He refused to accept newspaper articles describing the exhibition of the film as evidence of contempt, since one could not infer admission had been charged based on the articles. The judge also refused to reevaluate the film's merits after it won two prizes at the Italian film festival. Kalus said the prizes "may be very interesting as a commentary on our times and on those who make literary judgments as to artistic value, but I doubt whether it has any relevancy" (Tr. 18:37).

In June 1969, after the Massachusetts Supreme Judicial Court modified the Kalus decree to permit exhibition of the film to selected professional audiences, Grove marketed *Titicut Follies* on the nontheatrical university film society-museum-classroom circuit as a winner of several international awards. Speaking several months after Grove's distribution contract with Wiseman and BFC expired on December 31, 1976, the director of the film division for Grove Press said that Grove had initiated a voluntary policy of limited distribution nationally "to insulate Wiseman, a Massachusetts resident, in the on-going case against the film's exhibition in Massachusetts."[295] During the nearly ten years when Grove held exclusive distribution rights to *Titicut Follies,* the company sold approximately 110–120 prints of the documentary. University libraries, medical schools, law schools, and teaching hospitals were the typical buyers, frequently following a pattern of renting the film several times, then deciding to purchase it, since the rental fee was $100 and the purchase price went from $500 in 1968 to $600–700 in 1976.[296] Although Grove did not file records with the clerk of the Suffolk County Court regarding all screenings—as Wiseman did and does—the film seems to have been generally, if not exclusively, exhibited to the professional groups named in the modified decree during the period when Grove held the distribution rights.

After Films, Inc., bought the distribution rights to most of the titles in the Grove film collection in the midseventies, Grove expended little effort in marketing its remaining film holdings, which included *Titicut Follies.* Wiseman has been blunt about his dissatisfaction with Grove in numerous interviews. "You never get accurate reporting, you never get any money and all that sort of stuff." His solution: "Because I've been screwed so badly in distribution, I set up my own distribution company, Zipporah Films."[297]

In a 1974 interview, Wiseman said that "the conditions under which I can show the *Follies* [in Massachusetts] are so restrictive that I have not shown the film rather than comply with the terms of the restraining order."[298] The terms of the SJC restraining order have changed only once since the modified decree of 1969; that change was the result of an appeal filed by Wiseman's attorney the year he founded his own distribution company. On November 5, 1971, Blair Perry argued before the SJC that provisions regarding restricted exhibition were unnecessarily burdensome for the defendants. Within a week, the SJC bench decided that, at the option of the defendants, the provisions could be modified, but only in the following respects:

(a) notices of future showings of the film (to categories of persons permitted to see it) may be combined in a single advance notice covering the next succeeding thirty days; (b) notices of such showings in Massachusetts need be filed only three days in advance of such showings, respectively, in instances where longer notice is impracticable; and (c) reports of showings, after the event, may be made by filing a written report . . . during the first seven days of each calendar month, covering showings during the next preceding calendar month.[299]

The terms of the restraining order did not change between 1971 and 1977. But first distribution control, then exhibition patterns, did change. Wiseman began to show *Titicut Follies* in Massachusetts.

When Zipporah Films began distributing *Titicut Follies* as of January 1, 1977, the company instituted a comprehensive reporting system for all screenings of the documentary nationwide. Since 1977, prospective exhibitors of *Titicut Follies* have received some close variation of the following instructions:

By order of the Supreme Judicial Court of Massachusetts, TITICUT FOLLIES may be shown only to legislators, judges, lawyers, sociologists, social workers, doctors, psychiatrists, students in these or related fields, and organizations dealing wih the social problems of custodial care and mental infirmity.

TWO statements regarding the screening of TITICUT FOLLIES must be completed in full, signed and returned as specified.

The first statement must be completed and received in Boston along with the rental agreement form at least *12 business days* prior to your scheduled screening date. No prints will be shipped before the statement has been received. Please check the appropriate categories; no additional categories may be added.

The second statement, which confirms your intended screening of the film, will be enclosed in the film case and must be completed and returned *immediately* following your screening. It must arrive in Boston no later than *five days* following the screening.

Prints of TITICUT FOLLIES are available on both a rental and long term lease to anyone who wishes to show the film in compliance with the Final Decree of the Supreme Judicial Court.

Should you have any questions concerning the procedure please do not hesitate to contact us.[300]

The first statement is a declaration of intent to screen *Titicut Follies* to an audience composed only of people who meet the qualifications as defined in the final decree; the second statement is an acknowledgment that the documentary was seen only by persons meeting the court specifications. For Massachusetts screenings only, Wiseman's company requires that the exhibitor demand that each audience member sign an individual statement claiming membership in at least one of the designated categories. The exhibitor is admonished to collect these affidavits before the film begins, deny admittance to anyone who does not sign such a form, and return all signed statements with the print of *Titicut Follies* to the Zipporah office immediately following the screening. In this way, Wiseman and his company meet the personal knowledge stipulation of the decree, since Wiseman is legally responsible for verifying that each person who sees the film is a member of one of the allowed groups.

Zipporah files a statement of intent for each scheduled screening and then either a statement of cancellation or, far more often, a statement that *Titicut Follies* was shown as described. All statements are filed with the clerk of the Suffolk Superior Court in Boston; copies are sent to the attorney general's office. Audience member affidavits are not required by the decree and remain in Wiseman's possession. Although Wiseman himself has signed some of the statements, especially for the foreign screenings in the 1974–77 period and for showings at his studio, most statements bear the signature of "an authorized person claiming through him," that is, a Zipporah staff member. Since 1977, the authorized person has changed—Jennifer Ettling, Iris Berry, Gayle Taylor, (then Gayle Taylor-Sutton), Ann Kahn, Karen Konicek—but the tedious clerical routine has not. Each statement also contains a notice to the clerk of the court that requests that the form be returned to the Zipporah office if it is not accepted for filing.

Those filed statements leave a paper trail marking where, when, and to whom *Titicut Follies* has been exhibited since January of 1977. The trail indicates that a 1968 prediction that "soon *Titicut Follies* will be of interest only to movie buffs, organizers of film festivals, and . . . social historians and anthropologists" underestimated the long-term interest in the film.[301] According to the filed statements, students and working professionals in sociology, law, medicine, and social work most frequently compose the audience for the film, but the actual breadth of the audience is not ascertainable, especially when the film is screened, as it is infrequently, for general audiences.

The first year that Zipporah distributed the film was the most active in rental exhibition in the 1977–87 period, with approximately 160 rental screenings nationwide in 1977; 1978 followed in rental volume, with only a slightly lower number of bookings. Reductions in rental totals may disguise actual increases in screenings, since regular exhibitors will often lease a print after several rentals. Rental activity in Massachusetts has been far greater than in other states.

Before 1977, *Titicut Follies* had been screened in the Commonwealth only to select groups and individuals. After 1977, the groups broadened, but continue to comprise a viewing elite, following the lines drawn by the Supreme Judicial Court of Massachusetts. The SJC stipulation on audience composition institutionalized the exhibition of the film; members of groups, rather than individuals, see *Titicut Follies* in Massachusetts, since the film is booked almost exclusively in institutional viewing situations. An individual involved in arranging one of the first Boston screenings, at the University of Massachusetts-Boston in the spring of 1977, described a "sense of paranoia around the showing," with Zipporah Films anxious to have the *Titicut Follies* print returned to the distributor's office by taxi immediately after the screening.[302] Such nervousness has diminished as Boston screenings in academic environments have become increasingly common, but careful monitoring continues.

The first screening of *Titicut Follies* in Amherst, Massachusetts, was sponsored by the law program at Hampshire College on April 5, 1977. When delivered, a print of *Titicut Follies* includes, among other exhibition directions, the notification that the scheduled screening cannot be advertised in any way. If an exhibitor planned to advertise, the message is somewhat late in arriving. The Hampshire showing was perhaps not advertised, but certainly it was announced publicly, among other places, in the *Five-College Calendar*, a monthly publication available to the Amherst, Hampshire, Mt. Holyoke, Smith, and University of Massachusetts-Amherst communities. The announcement indicated that the screening was free and would be followed by a panel discussion of mental-health and law experts.[303] There was no indication of any audience restrictions. At the screening, audience members were asked to sign individual affidavits before the film began in a manner that resembled a request for signatures on a petition. An individual could easily have neglected to sign an affidavit without being recognized or refused admission.

A flier posted in various locations on the University of Massachusetts-Amherst campus announced a free showing of *Titicut Follies* on May 6, 1982, at the Hampden Student Center, Southwest Residential College. The flier included a long excerpt from Robert Coles's laudatory description of the documentary, labeled the film as "banned in Massachusetts," and cautioned audience members that each would have to sign a statement acknowledging membership in one of the allowed categories in order to see the film. The dormitory showing was cosponsored by the Hampden Board of Governors and the Human Services Program as part of the prison film series and was attended largely by students enrolled in a one-credit colloquium in criminal justice. Two student moderators, both exconvicts, distributed and collected affidavits from all audience members, but no attempt was made to verify the status of those who sought admission and no one was turned away. One of the student moderators, Jerry Sousa, who had been confined at Bridgewater on two occasions, led a discussion following the film. He was not at Bridgewater when *Titicut Follies* was made, but claimed he spoke for the men pictured in the documentary when he advocated exhibition in the cause of reform. He knew some of the men in the film and discussed their lives with no hesitation. A graduate student in anthropology in 1982, Sousa had recently won a settlement against Walpole, Massachusetts, prison guards who had brutalized him; he planned to participate in a maltreatment case to be filed against Bridgewater guards.[304]

Others in the prison studies program at the University of Massachusetts-Amherst have also been regular users of *Titicut Follies*. In any other state, such regular use would encourage an institution to have its own copy of *Titicut Follies*. For copyright protection, Wiseman retains property rights for the documentary; therefore, an organization or individual actually leases a print, rather than purchases it, although for practical purposes the lease is equivalent to purchase. The Zipporah lease contract, however, stipulates that the film must be exhibited "in its entirety without the addition or deletion of any matter" and that it may be exhibited "only upon premises owned or controlled by the exhibitor." Grove had offered a life-of-print sale and did not attempt to control use of prints. In the late 1970s at Zipporah, a lease was for five years or the life of the print, whichever came first. At the end of five years, the print was recalled or the long-term lease was renegotiated. The change in terminology between the Grove and Zipporah offices is more than a semantic technicality; it is indicative of a general difference in attitude toward control of *Titicut Follies* and other Wiseman films. Since 1983, life-of-the-print contracts are available only to institutions unable to lease for the five-year period. Prices are somewhat higher than lease contracts for such arrangements. Renewals of leases for additional five-year periods are available at 50 percent of current lease prices. Replacement prints are available at a 10 percent discount of current lease prices. Zipporah has obviously discovered that Wiseman's documentaries have regular users over decades.

In 1967, Grove sold copies of *Titicut Follies* for $500. In 1977, the price of a leased print from Zipporah was $900; in 1987, $1,200. The rental cost for high schools or charity/civic/church organizations has remained at $100, while the college/corporation/government agency rental fee has increased from $125 to $150. Videotape lease copies of *Titicut Follies* ($900) became available (outside of Massachusetts) for the first time in 1983 but as of April, 1984, only one tape of *Titicut Follies* had been leased.[305] Pirated videotapes have been a problem for Wiseman, as well as for others, for years; this is one of several reasons he demands an immediate return of a print after its rental screening(s).[306] However, what is unique to *Titicut Follies* is that a pirated tape presents problems beyond lost revenue: Wiseman loses control over the exhibition situation and audience composition, for which he is responsible. Screenings of pirated tapes are thus illegal in several senses of the word. Since access to video recorders is increasing, it is not suprising that Zipporah does not offer rentals in video format.

Of course, the most common source for unauthorized videotaping is not from a rental tape, but off-broadcast. *Titicut Follies* and *High School* are the only Wiseman documentaries that have not been aired nationally on NET-PBS, although the Public Broadcasting Laboratory "almost ran [*Titicut Follies*] as its first show."[307]

Wiseman is faced with the dilemma of expediting the procedures for reaching the allowed audience for *Titicut Follies* in direct and efficient ways so that his business will operate smoothly and profitably, yet also arguing that the terms of the edict are unduly complicated at best and unconstitutional at worst. Wiseman is thus trying to reach an audience as large as possible and as often as possible in Massachusetts, while simultaneously claiming that the Massachusetts public is being denied its constitutional right to see the Bridgewater documentary. The air has never completely cleared of the early charge of commercialism; Wiseman must continually protect himself from that charge, even though he is operating a business.

For Zipporah Films to remain solvent and retain exclusive distribution control of the Wiseman films, it is necessary to market the documentaries aggressively. Independence has its price. The annual Zipporah brochure is an example of stylish promotion—the graphic design is handsome; the excerpts from critical reviews are impressive; the directions for ordering the films are clear. Additional materials such as reprints and film reviews, brochures, and still photographs are available to exhibitors from the Zipporah office on request. For *Titicut Follies* exhibitors, these materials are considered informational rather than promotional. Among the reprints of *Titicut Follies* reviews that are issued by Zipporah are Robert Coles's lengthy piece from *The New Republic*, Richard Schickel's *Life* review, the *Newsweek* article about the controversy surrounding the film, and a description of the ban written by Harvey Cox and published in *Playboy*. The Zipporah brochure contains no editorial description of the content of *Titicut Follies*, as it does with all other Wiseman films. It suggests *Titicut Follies* as a possible selection for courses in health, medicine, psychology, social work, legal studies, philosophy and, with all other Wiseman titles, in cinema studies and sociology-anthropology. The filmmaker himself is marketed as well: "Mr. Wiseman is available for lectures and workshops. Requests for guest appearances should be made well in advance."[308]

After its New York screenings in the fall of 1967, Grove Press did not book *Titicut Follies* in commercial theaters. There were some public showings with admission charges in states outside of Massachusetts while Grove held the distribution rights to the documentary, but these were usually film society showcases on university campuses. Zipporah brochures announce that all Wiseman films are for nontheatrical use only, yet rates for screenings where there is an admission charge are listed: $150 or 50 percent of the gross box office receipts, whichever is greater. What seems to be a contradiction is actually an accommodation for film society and art house exhibition.

Very soon after Wiseman took distributive control of *Titicut Follies*, he made arrangements for a public showing in a commercial Massachusetts theater. After contacting several theater owners, Wiseman scheduled the first public Massachusetts showing of the restricted film at the Pleasant Street Theater in Northampton.[309] The small (135 seat) theater had just opened under new ownership in the college town the previous November, but it already was establishing a reputation for innovative programming of American revival films, contemporary European features, and various types of alternative cinema. Owned by two former professors with extensive film society experience, the Pleasant Street Theater had a sophisticated ambiance, a liberal clientele, and a 16mm projector. Like the rest of western Massachusetts, the provincial art theater and its operations were of no interest to the Boston press and public.

In what co-owner John Morrison described as "leisurely four-walling," Zipporah and Pleasant Street agreed on a rental price of $75 for each of four showings on February 14 and 15, 1977, as long as there were more than forty people in the audience. There were far more than forty people in each audience; several screenings could not accommodate all those who wished to purchase tickets at the special events price of $3, an amount dictated by the Zipporah office. Three Zipporah staff members were present at all showings; they taped the introductory message about the required affidavit signatures each time it was delivered. Affidavits were collected from all audience members at each screening. The exhibition of *Titicut Follies* had been advertised by fliers and in newspapers, which mentioned the special premiere status of the engagement and also the audience restrictions.

The following week, another set of fliers and advertisements announced that *Titicut Follies* was "back by popular demand," a typical promotional phrase, but either a mistaken or a subversive description for a *Titicut Follies* audience.[310] For the February 21–22 engagement, Zipporah charged the Pleasant Street Theater $100 a show; however, the crowds at the theater were not nearly as large as they had been the previous week. No showing had an audience demand that could not be met in the tiny theater; only four of the five showings had more than forty patrons. There were no complaints about the showings registered with the management, nor did any complaints about the screenings or the audience restrictions appear in the local press. The affidavits seemed a silly technicality not worth protesting in a community known for its civil rights protests.

Even after these benign public showings, Zipporah Films did not book *Titicut Follies* as part of Wiseman retrospectives in the Boston-Cambridge

area during 1977. Institute of Contemporary Art curator Michael Leja wished
to include *Titicut Follies* in the museum retrospective in the fall of 1977, but
was told by Wiseman that the filmmaker-distributor was not yet ready to
test the court order with a public showing.[311] Similarly, the Bridgewater
documentary was excluded from a Wiseman retrospective at the Orson
Welles Cinema in Cambridge that same fall.

The Boston public showing test came in May of 1980 when *Titicut Follies*
played at a large public theater during "Boston 350," a city-wide birthday
celebration organized by a deputy mayor of Boston, Katherine Kane. As part
of the Boston 350 festivities, the Sack theater chain, the Boston Museum of
Fine Arts (MFA), and the city of Boston jointly sponsored screenings of films
written, produced, directed, or starring current or former Boston residents.
For a thirty-five-cent admission charge, Boston moviegoers could see films
of Boston's own and be treated to guest appearances of the local celebrities.
The suggestion to include *Titicut Follies*, if Wiseman agreed, came out of a
group discussion of the festival organizers from the mayor's office, the Sack
theaters, and the MFA.[312] May 12 was designated as "Fred Wiseman Day"
and as early as May 7, Boston newspapers announced that *Hospital, High
School,* and *Titicut Follies* would be screened as part of the month-long
Jubilee 350 Film Festival at the Saxon Theater.[313] Located in the heart of the
theater district in downtown Boston, the Saxon originally was a site for stage
plays; it operated as a cinema for only several years. On May 8, a Boston film
critic, after garbling the documentary's legal history, wrote that the inclusion
of *Titicut Follies* in the Jubilee 350 was possible because "it falls under one
of the many exceptions that allow the film to be shown for 'educational
purposes.' It's the film in the festival that any serious film-goer shouldn't
miss."[314] That same day, another Boston paper reported that a spokesman for
the attorney general's office said he was unaware of the planned showing of
Titicut Follies and had no comment. In the same article, Wiseman was quoted
as saying, "People will have to decide for themselves whether they're in the
categories allowed to see the film. But they will be told if they are not, they
are not allowed to see the film."[315] By May 9, the two planned Boston
screenings of *Titicut Follies* were described in an Associated Press story as
"under terms supposedly allowed by the Court."[316] Advertisements for the
screenings in the Boston papers carried the disclaimer, "Shown under terms
of restraining order."[317]

Two weeks before the May 12 play dates, Sack submitted the required
statement announcing plans for two screenings of *Titicut Follies* to the clerk
of the court and the attorney general's office, but the statement of intent
apparently had gone unnoticed until members of the Boston press brought
the screenings to the attention of the attorney general's office. On Friday
afternoon, May 9, Assistant Attorney General Anthony P. Sager of the Civil
Rights Division filed an affidavit in which, among other statements, he
recounted a telephone conversation with Alan Friedberg, president of Sack

Theaters, earlier that same day that confirmed the scheduled showings of *Titicut Follies* at the Sack's Saxon Theater. Friedberg had told Sager that a notice regarding the viewing restrictions would be placed in the box office and that before each showing the theater manager would announce that anyone in the theater who was not a member of one of the listed categories would be asked to "leave the theater so as to satisfy the requirement of the Court."[318] Sager also stated that, based upon information received from Superintendent Gaughan, he believed the inmates who appeared in *Titicut Follies* had been released to the community or transferred to civil facilities.

Assistant Attorney General Robert H. Bolin, Jr., moved for an injuction against the showing of *Titicut Follies* at the Saxon Theater. The Commonwealth's motion for supplemental relief implicitly questioned the general audience's motives for seeing the film and its ability to effect change. "The scheduled showings of 'Titicut Follies' in the Boston Film Festival do not primarily serve the purpose of informing an audience of professional persons with a serious interest in the rehabilitation of mentally ill persons and with the potential capacity to ameliorate the conditions and treatment of mentally ill persons in institutions."[319] That same day, May 9, U.S. District Judge Rya W. Zobel denied the motion for injunctive relief.

Three hours before the afternoon showing of *Titicut Follies* on May 12, the Civil Rights Division of the attorney general's office hand delivered copies of a sternly worded letter to Zipporah Films and the Sack Theaters executive office, suggesting that the Saxon management get full identification from each person attending the showings of *Titicut Follies* at 3:00 and 8:00 P.M. that day. Although the Saxon ignored the suggestion, anyone who did not sign an affidavit was denied entrance. A private police guard was stationed outside the theater for this purpose. A representative from the attorney general's office, attempting to enter the theater without signing an affidavit, was not admitted. A *Boston Globe* reporter interviewed six patrons before the matinee screening, all of whom had signed the document, but none of whom belonged to the professions listed on the form.[320] Six people admittedly comprise a very small sample, but one gets a scent of audience autonomy. According to a spokesperson for Wiseman, "technically, [anyone who signed the affidavit under false pretenses] could also be hauled into court for violating the edict."[321] But no action was taken by the attorney general's office against theater patrons. The court order regarding specialized audiences seemed a paper tiger to the Boston audience. Here, as in other showings of *Titicut Follies*, the force of the court order has been diluted.

In sharp contrast to the press furor regarding the exhibition of the film in the fall of 1967, the Boston press commented little about the public showings of *Titicut Follies* in May of 1980. Two days after the screenings, the film seemed to have been forgotten. There were no printed letters to the editors of Boston newspapers criticizing or praising the screenings.

On May 22, 1977, Assistant Attorney General Sager filed a request for the production of documents concerning the composition of the audience to which *Titicut Follies* was shown: "(a) on May 12, 1980 at 219 Tremont St., Boston, Mass.; (b) on April 10, 1980, at Twentieth Century Fox, Beverly Hills, California; (c) on April 6, 1980, at Facets Multimedia, Chicago, Illinois; (d) on April 14, 1980, at Columbus Branch Library, Tucson, Arizona, (e) on February 4, 1980, at 3657 Springfield Road, Indianapolis, Indiana; (f) on December 16, 1979, at Panorama Studios, Vancouver, B.C."[322] Wiseman was also requested to produce "all documents pertaining (a) to the showing(s) of 'Titicut Follies' from December 27, 1971, to the present at any commercial establishment, public accommodation, or other place to which the public usually may gain admission (such as a movie theater, public library, or public auditorium) or (b) to the nature of the audience at any showing(s) at such places."[323] The attorney general's office had, surprisingly, missed the Pleasant Street Theater screenings in its review of the exhibition statements, but its request for production of documents would have revealed these showings, if followed. It was not. The Commonwealth's motion for a hearing as to this request before the superior court department of the trial court was denied; but the request itself served as a reminder of the continuingly rigid position of the attorney general's office toward the exhibition of *Titicut Follies*.

There were no additional public screenings of *Titicut Follies* in Massachusetts between May 1980 and April 1987. A Wiseman retrospective sponsored by the Institute of Contemporary Art and held at the Coolidge Corner Theater in Cambridge in the fall of 1982 omitted *Titicut Follies* from the series. The guest curator of the retrospective, Ned Rifkin, made a special note of this omission and the court-ordered reasons for it in the series program notes.[324] On May 4, 1987, the John W. McCormack Institute of Public Affairs and the College of Public and Community Services at the University of Massachusetts-Boston cosponsored "*Titicut Follies* Twenty Years Later" at the JFK Library. The free program consisted of the screening of *Titicut Follies* (simultaneously in two auditoria, with the audiences divided into one auditorium for those with invitations and another for the general public, all of whom were required to sign the usual affidavit), light refreshments, and a public forum moderated by Charles Nesson of Harvard Law School. Panelists (all of whom received a framed poster announcing the event) included June S. Binney (supervising attorney at Bridgewater State Hospital), John W. Briggs, Jr. (associate commissioner and general counsel, Department of Correction), George C. Caner, Jr., Judi Chamberlin (chairwoman, National Committee on Patients' Rights), Alan Dershowitz, Blair Perry, Wesley Profit (forensic director, Bridgewater State Hospital), Harvey Silvergate, Howard Simons (former managing editor of the *Washington Post* and curator of the Nieman Foundation, Harvard University), and Frederick Wiseman. During the panel discussion, Wiseman estimated that between 150,000 and 200,000 people had seen *Titicut Follies*.

In a state bulging with law schools, medical schools, colleges, and universities, it seems that in the 1980s most individuals looking for an opportunity to see *Titicut Follies* in Massachusetts could probably find one more easily than an opportunity to see other documentaries made in 1967, or 1977, for that matter. There have been no published complaints in recent years from Massachusetts residents "unqualified" to see the documentary and unwilling to lie about their professional status on affidavits, yet demanding a right to see the Bridgewater documentary. The continuing struggle over exhibition freedom on Wiseman's part seems to be far more an issue of constitutional principle than a matter of actual audience denial.

As long as the conditions of the restraining order remain in effect, there will be a paper stream between the secretaries at Zipporah Films and those at the office of the clerk of the Suffolk Superior Court. At the court house, the roles of the Commonwealth as plaintiff, judge, and keeper of the records all merge. In that temple of red tape, the file for *Commonwealth v. Wiseman* is just one more pile of papers, left on the floor and stuck into a corner because it is too cumbersome to be shelved with the other files. In true civil-servant style, the woman assigned to the record keeping does not file equity docket No. 87538 with the equity cases that have been disposed. Those dockets are filed one floor up from her desk and she must enter statements into the No. 87538 docket on a routine basis. Yet, since it is stamped "disposed," the *Titicut Follies* docket is not allowed in the pending files in the area where she works. Dilemma seems too grand a term for what a file clerk is to do with a case that was legally closed in 1971, but remains obviously open to the routine additions that are her responsibility. Entries in the *Titicut Follies* docket exceed 2,700.[325] The statements will keep rolling in as long as the court order remains and Wiseman exhibits the film. There is no place for such an anomaly as the closed, yet open, *Titicut Follies* docket in the institutional maze, but the government worker assigned to administering the case clerically has found a way to ignore the rules and make her job more reasonable. In a gesture right out of a Wiseman film, this woman has found a place for the *Commonwealth v. Wiseman* docket: in the middle drawer of her own desk, next to a change of shoes and an umbrella.

Dilemmas of Construction and Use

Titicut Follies has much to teach about the dilemmas of documentary construction and use. Dilemmas of negotiation immediately confront a filmmaker who proposes a potentially controversial documentary project: how does one convince people to consent to participate in a film, to sponsor its production, to work on its crew, to support it financially without using guile, misrepresentation, or coercion when risk is not only possible, but probable? The dilemma of consent is partly practical (how to get it), but essentially ethical (how to get it fairly and then not abuse it). Without the participation of social actors, the documentary form known as direct or observational cinema could not exist. Without the informed consent of the subjects, the form lacks ethical integrity; without freedom for the filmmaker, it lacks artistic integrity. The dilemmas of documentary construction are both procedural and artistic. The mix of the two creates its own dilemma: Wiseman could not have made any documentary film about Bridgewater without the active participation of others; he could not have made *Titicut Follies* without independence. Thus, Wiseman relied upon cooperation while filming; he demanded independence while editing. He expected the impossible. In turn, subjects and audiences often expect the impossible from his work. Reviewing the steps of the constructive process and the eventual use of *Titicut Follies* reveals not just its dilemmas, but the dilemmas that shape the documentary enterprise.

To film a Bridgewater documentary, Wiseman had to get permission from others before he could approach the individuals who would be social actors on screen to obtain their consent. Even in this most bureaucratic of settings, the supposed state rule for institutional consent procedures (head of institution—department head—governor's office) was not followed. Governor John Volpe's office was unaware of the project's existence. This violation of protocol made the film susceptible to criticism.

Another chain of consent particular to this case, but quite possibly common in its variance from the orthodoxy of official procedures, was substituted. Lieutenant Governor Elliot Richardson's and Representative Katherine Kane's intercessions changed the permission structure, yet the chain in use retained hierarchical features. Bridgewater was not a closed system, an important consideration when identifying the subject of the film and reactions to it. Wiseman later disclaimed any political motivations in making the documentary, yet he was willing to use the influence of friends who held elective office in order to gain permission to film. It is arguable whether a film about a publicly supported institution can ever be apolitical, whatever its maker's stated or unstated intentions. Thus, both in the narrow sense of partisan politics and in the larger sense of political philosophy, those who had assisted Wiseman were identified with and held accountable for the final product.

The exact, final terms that were being consented *to* by both the state and the filmmaker are vague. It is difficult to imagine a filmmaker with the fierce independence Wiseman later displayed ever consenting to state censorship as an initial and continuing condition of filming. It is also difficult to imagine a state official like Commissioner John Gavin not expecting final state control. It is equally surprising that a sophisticated politician and experienced lawyer like Attorney General Edward Brooke would not anticipate Superintendent Charles Gaughan's position as a man caught in the middle and, therefore, suggest the legal protection of a written contract. Certainly Wiseman, himself an attorney, understood the legal importance of a written contract, but its absence also had advantages for him. Nowhere in writing was there any claim by Wiseman of the rights of the press or the public's right to know; nowhere in writing was there any claim by the state to a right of censorship. In their delay in clearly asserting what were later claimed as rights, both Wiseman and the Commonwealth of Massachusetts positioned themselves for an inevitable confrontation.

The consent pattern had both vertical and horizontal dimensions. Every link in the consent chain was a potential breaking point, but also a point of obligation. Individuals could say no—as the filmmakers claimed—but they were expected to say yes. Often the individuals filmed said nothing. Silence was considered consent. Staff members had been directed by their superiors to cooperate with the filming. Although privacy and consent are usually discussed as individual matters, they have social as well as personal dimensions.

Many social activists advocate protection in inverse relationship to power; many documentary film projects work the other way around.[326] John Galliher thinks that some of the controls on research to protect human subjects "limit both research and consequent criticism of officials."[327] He argues against the protection of superordinate subjects when "studying up" and cites Wiseman's "muck-raking" films as successful attempts at learning about the powerful.[328] Wiseman does not see protection, selective or otherwise, as his obligation or his privilege. Just the reverse, he puts the responsibility and—in Wiseman's view of the world, an equally important word—the *choice* of protection or disclosure on his subjects and their guardians.

Since some of the subjects to be photographed were wards of the state in a prison mental hospital, both freedom to consent and mental competence, on which legal competence rests, became highly problematic. In court, the Commonwealth cast doubt on the competency of some of the subjects in the film. Wiseman's defense took the position that the filmmakers assumed *all* subjects were competent unless specifically informed otherwise by the superintendent and his staff at the time of shooting.

In all his subsequent documentary films, Wiseman's consent procedures have remained stable, with two crucial modifications, both of which provide Wiseman legal protection and were prompted by the litigation surrounding *Titicut Follies*. After initial conversations with administrators, Wiseman summarizes his plans in a letter in which he mentions why he wants to make the film, the filming procedures, the types of events that might be filmed (indicating that these examples are merely suggestive), and the duration of filming and editing. He explicitly states his claim of complete editorial control over the completed film. The persons (or person) in charge of this initial permission decision sign(s) Wiseman's letter, thus indicating consent to the filming agreements in this contract of sorts.

On the advice of his lawyers, Wiseman has not obtained written releases since *Titicut Follies*. Before or, more frequently, just after shooting a sequence, Wiseman audiotapes his explanation that he is making a film for public television that will be widely seen by the general public and may be shown theatrically. He explains that he will not use all the film he shoots and offers to answer any questions. If an individual consents, Wiseman asks for a full name, address, and phone number. Thus, he has a contemporaneous record of subject assent.[329] The procedure of consent before, during, or immediately after the act of filming creates a situation of trust in the filmmaker's judgment, rather than a situation of truly informed consent. Subjects who say yes to the film in a camera sometimes say no to the film screened. Ideally, consent is processural, not contractual.[330] But the process of making meaning of filmic images continues into the viewing situation and beyond. It is a never-ending process; neither subjects nor filmmaker can ever fully anticipate audience response.[331] Subjects cannot anticipate their own reactions to the responses of others.[332] Even Calvin Pryluck, an outspoken critic of many direct cinema procedures, admits that "obviously a filmmaker's commitment to a subject cannot be open-ended."[333] As Pryluck himself is aware, his suggestion of collaborative editing diffuses, rather than solves, the ethical dilemma of informed consent.

There are ways of constructing documentaries that incorporate the consent of crew members, subjects, sponsors, and financial backers into the editing process for reasons that range from democratic idealism to artistic indecision. Fred Wiseman did not work that way with *Titicut Follies*, or with any of his later films. He thoroughly rejects collaborationist cinema when he constructs his personal "reality fictions." If we consider Wiseman's entire career, editorial autonomy may be seen as a central feature of a pattern of independence that has remained consistent.

Titicut Follies set Fred Wiseman on the path to distinction as a documentary filmmaker. Did it help or hurt the inmates at Bridgewater? Charles Gaughan thinks *Titicut Follies* had negative effects on plans for the new hospital at Bridgewater (which did open in December 1974). He remembers the film project with bitterness:

> I can only reiterate that, instead of being of help, he [Wiseman] was responsible for our almost complete loss of the whole venture. Many months preceding the bringing out of his film, we had had a media campaign initiated by the Mass. Medical and the Mass. Bar Associations. We also had had the escape of Albert De Salvo and a series of other front page events. These basically enabled us to tell our story and secure the cooperation of the Legislature and the Governor's office. Wiseman's lame and highly peculiar method of breaching the problem was initially considered as a violation of faith in the professional organizations involved. However, as a result of the series of court hearings and their legal criticism of Mr. Wiseman, the work initiated by others, went forward.[334]

Speaking at the time of the legislative hearing, Dr. William Chasen of the Massachusetts Medical Society also thought "if anything [*Titicut Follies* has] hurt our cause."[335] When the governor's special commission filed a comprehensive Bridgewater reform report on the eve of the New York commercial showing of *Titicut Follies,* Volpe claimed that he did not know about the film until after he had appointed a commission to develop a construction program for Bridgewater.

Looking back on events years later, many people who are familiar with MCI-Bridgewater, the Departments of Correction and Mental Health, and Commonwealth operations think *Titicut Follies* played a small, but positive, role in improvements at Bridgewater. A correction department official has said it is hard to conclude that the film itself is an agent of change, but it did publicize the issue of forgotten people.[336] The legal counsel to the psychiatric staff at McLean Hospital sees *Titicut Follies* as part of a chain of events that led to improved conditions.[337] A psychiatrist with the Mental Health Department speculates that the legal action in right-to-treatment cases had more effect on changes than the documentary.[338] In addition to the new hospital facility, changes since the documentary include a reduction in population from approximately eight hundred to around three hundred men and the negotiation of medical personnel contracts with various teaching hospitals. Shortly after the documentary was released, approximately three hundred men were transferred from Bridgewater when the superior court sat on the grounds for months and conducted hearings.[339] Although some consider the recent changes at Bridgewater more apparent than real, all agree that vast improvements have been made since Charles Gaughan first became superintendent. Fred Wiseman, who is often asked in interviews and public question-and-answer sessions about the improvements effected by the film, gives some variation on this answer: "I no longer have the view that I had in the beginning that there might be some direct relationship between what I was able to show in these films and the achievement of social change. . . . I guess I've gone very far away from the liberal cliches and bromides that I started with, especially the simpleminded social work view of help and intervention."[340] He speaks of change working in oblique, subterranean ways and labels as presumptuous the claims of others that the new hospital at Bridgewater was a direct result of *Titicut Follies.*[341] Nevertheless, in the affidavit accompanying Wiseman's 1987 motion to release the film to general exhibition, a motion filed amidst news reports of recent violent deaths of inmates at Bridgewater, he claimed:

> One of my primary reasons for making the film "Titicut Follies" was to try to bring about improvements in the way in which inmates of M.C.I., Bridgewater, were treated, by showing conditions at M.C.I., Bridgewater, to members of the public. I have been told that as a result of the making of the film, and the public interest which was engendered by the initial public exhibition of the film, conditions at M.C.I., Bridgewater, were improved significantly for a period of time (in that additional staff members were hired, new buildings were built, and some inmates who had been held at the M.C.I. for many years were released from the institution). I have no personal firsthand knowledge that this is true, but of course I am pleased

that the film has been credited with bringing about various improvements in conditions at the institution. . . .

. . . I believe that showing of the film "Titicut Follies" to members of the general public at this time would help to arouse public concern about the conditions at M.C.I., Bridgewater, and thus would help to bring about changes in conditions there and lessen the probability of additional deaths of the types described above or other injuries to inmates there.[342]

James F. Gilligan, a psychiatrist who later became treatment director at Bridgewater and then consultant to the new treatment program there thinks *Titicut Follies* changed the moral climate, so that a group of lawyers started a class action suit and the courts then ordered the state to build a new facility and provide better treatment. Gilligan argues that the controversy surrounding *Titicut Follies*, despite the pain it brought the central participants, also was of good use to them. "Ironically, for all the *sturm und drang*, I think the controversy helped Wiseman. I think Wiseman's film helped Bridgewater, and yet neither party could see this [so great were their feelings of betrayal]."[343]

Those feelings of betrayal surface again and again in Wiseman interviews. "The lesson of *Titicut Follies* for me was cowardice, and the biggest coward of all was Elliot Richardson."[344] In Wiseman's office, an old newspaper photo of Richardson being sworn in as ambassador to England by Gerald Ford hangs above the toilet.[345] Richardson does not mention *Titicut Follies* in a book-length political memoir which examines the difficult political choices of his life.[346] Katherine Kane "really [does] not remember much about it, since it was so long ago."[347] It was a long time ago, yet Wiseman and Marshall still do not speak to each other. Marshall is proud of his work on *Titicut Follies* and recalls the experience of working with Wiseman with fondness.[348] Yet he is also critical of Wiseman's work, claiming that, especially in the early films, the sequences are not rich enough, people and situations not followed closely enough, to permit audiences to draw inferences.[349] Eames remembers the filming of *Titicut Follies:* "Working alongside Fred when he is shooting is a singular experience, perhaps like being invited to ride with Santa in his sleigh on Christmas Eve. A lot of hard work is required; the hours kept are odd and long; the trip is likely to take you places you never expected to be, involve encounters you never imagined with people you otherwise wouldn't believe; you may count on plenty of mishaps and screwups and moments of high farce. I never had so much fun."[350]

The uses of *Titicut Follies* will continue to grow—a coffee house in Berkeley and a hotel on Martha's Vineyard have been named after the film—but mostly it will be used for the educational purposes originally intended by Wiseman and Gaughan. The reasons for constructing and using documentaries are various; they are tied to complex motives both personal and social and are ultimately unknowable. Projects begin in a mood of cooperation that sometimes diminishes as choices are made and disappointments accumulate. The Bridgewater film project began without easy cooperation, without full disclosure of goals and consequences, among individuals and institutions that held different, even contradictory, values and sensibilities.

Some of the problems *Titicut Follies* faced, and faces, were particular to the film itself, but many were related to the general social and political climate of the times and to tensions at the heart of all realist art. The litigation concerning the documentary has allowed us to overhear a debate among participants about expectations, intentions, procedures, and disappointments that goes on privately in many documentary projects. The litigation has forced the courts to consider a cluster of relationships among filmmakers, subjects, and audiences, and to strike a balance among competing constitutional rights. Those who care about documentary film need to attend to and participate in the debate on these issues.

The history of *Titicut Follies* reveals a substantial gap between the ideal of informed consent and the practice of direct cinema. Would the general good have been better served had *Titicut Follies* not been made? We think not. We believe the general good would be better served if *Titicut Follies* could be shown without restriction. Alone, Wiseman's first film is a work of considerable social and artistic value; as part of his ongoing documentary series, *Titicut Follies* is of even greater worth. The struggle for control of this film tells us much about documentary film and its social context. We are fortunate that Wiseman's experience with *Titicut Follies* did not extinguish his desire or his ability to explore other American institutions. Sometimes comically, but more often sadly, the history of *Titicut Follies* fulfills a central promise of Frederick Wiseman's original Bridgewater film proposal: "To portray that we are all more simply human than otherwise."[351]

Chapter 3

The Politics of the Double Bind
High School

The room darkens, the title flashes briefly on the screen, and then we are traveling along a suburban street listening to Otis Redding sing "Dock of the Bay" ("sitting on the dock of the bay, wasting time . . ."). Then there is a chain-link fence, a parking lot, and a factory-like building. A brief glimpse of a crowded hallway; we are in the school. Then a teacher's face, and the first speech of the film. "First thing we want to do is to give you the daily bulletin. You might be surprised. A little notice that you think doesn't concern you might change your whole life. It might decide what college you'll go to, or it might decide what activity. And then Joyce has a few things to say, right, Joyce? All right. The thought for the day: 'Life is cause and effect. One creates his tomorrows at every moment by his motives, thoughts, and deeds of today.' And this question of cause and effect, you know what they say, you might read something that might change, uh, your life."

Cut to a woman's face. She pronounces a sentence with exaggerated clarity, in Spanish, emphasizing the word *Existentialista*.

"Wasting time." "Cause and effect." *Existentialista*. We are less than two minutes into Frederick Wiseman's *High School* (1968). There has been no explanatory narration, nor will there be any, but already we have heard a series of statements that may serve not so much as the theme of the film than as its epigraph. In this chapter, we shall attempt a close reading of *High School*, arguing that the film offers a powerful rhetorical appeal that is realized through the structure of the film.

In a 1974 interview with Ira Halberstadt, Wiseman commented that his films, though based on real events, are constructed fictions presenting a theory about the material being considered.

WISEMAN: So you are creating, hopefully, a form which has a life of its own, and that form is a fiction because it does not exist apart from the film.
HALBERSTADT: How would you describe the way in which you work?
WISEMAN: Well, it's the structural aspect that interests me most, and the issue there is developing a theory that will relate these isolated, nonrelated sequences to each

other. That is partially, I think, related to figuring out what each sequence means and then trying to figure out how it either contradicts or adds to or explains in some way some other sequence in the film. Then you try to determine the effect of a particular sequence on that point of view of the film.

Presumably, if a film works, it does so because the structure works. . . .

That overall statement is what the point of view of the film is. And what the point of view of the film is, is also an expression of a theory or an attitude toward the experience that constitutes the film. In relating the sequences in a particular way, you are developing a theory which in turn provides a form for this kind of experience. The abstractions you are dealing with are abstractions that are related to the structure of the film and that emerge from the structure of the film.[1]

High School calls upon viewers to exercise a variety of skills to derive meaning from the experience. They must draw upon their skills as viewers of film, acquainted with the elements of film language, and they must be able to look through the film language to the social behavior recorded there—the use by human beings of speech and gesture in a context familiar to most viewers. Our question then becomes: How does Wiseman draw upon the skills and contexts of his viewers to invite them to experience a particular complex of meanings as they view *High School?*

If we are to make any sense of what *High School* means for its audience, we must take two risks. One is the risk of assumed linearity, the other of overinterpretation. *High School* is a film, not verbal discourse. The film argues, but does so in the context of a concrete audiovisual experience. As a film, and especially as a film often placed with others in the tradition called cinema verite, *High School* is coherent, but as a film it borrows from actuality an awkward concreteness that resists the forms of linear, propositional argument. We shall argue that *High School* is about power, but shall try to do so in a way that does not reduce the film to an oversimplified pseudolinearity, or broaden the concept of power until it is without any sort of coherence whatsoever. In film, the formal is always at war with the material, and it is in the filmmaker's resolution of the relation of form and matter that particular meanings emerge.

The risk of overinterpretation arises from critics' temptation to impose meanings for their own convenience. Selecting a detail here or there and calling it a symbol is a particularly antiaesthetic form of criticism, a kind of shell game in which critics substitute their own obsessions or ambitions for the common language of art or literature, for the common evidence of the senses, and for the common sense of the audience. As a general rule, an element should be admitted to critical interpretation as a symbol only if the context requires it, either through repetition of the same or parallel or contrasting symbols, or when failure to account for the symbol makes the element in question incoherent, implausible, or distracting.

In order to answer the question of how *High School* achieves meaning, we will offer a detailed analysis of two levels of symbolic activity: the film as a structure and the social behavior recorded in the film as another structure. The film is a rhetorical structure about a rhetorical structure. In order to avoid confusion, however, it is important to be clear about the perspective of this analysis. The only evidence we have about the actors in the film comes from the film itself. Hence, although we will comment in detail upon the behavior of the actors in the context of the film, we can make no claims for the referential accuracy of the actions depicted. We know, of course, that the actors behaved as we see them. The film is evidence of that. But the behaviors we see are contextualized by Wiseman and are out of the context in which they occurred for the participants. The film was shot at Northeast High School, Philadelphia, in 1968. But in the comments that follow about the meanings of the social behaviors recorded in *High School*, we make no claims about Northeast High School, about the intentions of its teachers and students, or about their relations to each other.

High School may be more or less accurate about Northeast High School. It may also be more or less accurate about "high school" as a generalized institutional experience shared by virtually every American who sees the film. The film is a powerful experience for most viewers, and its power probably derives at least in part from the viewers' experience of high school, and from the conviction that the film is a more or less accurate depiction of Northeast High School. Still, this chapter is about *High School*, and not about Northeast High School or "high school."

Because this chapter is about the way meanings are constructed in *High School*, it is important to be clear about *whose* meaning we are talking about and *what* meaning we are attributing to the film. Whose meaning? Even at the formal level, rhetorical criticism inquires not simply about the "meaning in the text," but about the meanings that audiences are invited to experience as they engage the text. We are not, here, particularly interested in the psychological predispositions of the filmmaker, although the film provides considerable inferential evidence about the filmmaker's rhetorical intentions. The meaning of the film is not in "what the filmmaker meant," although, as we shall try to show, the meanings experienced by the audience are constructed by the filmmaker, who is also constructing what Wayne Booth calls the "implied author."[2] Partly, audiences make sense of films by asking what the filmmaker meant, and that part of the audience's understanding, drawn from what it sees and hears in the film, must also be taken into account in a rhetorical reading. The matter is complicated still further, since a film is not actually authored by one person. Frederick Wiseman produced, directed, edited, and recorded sound for *High School*; Richard Leiterman ran the camera. In most of the discussion that follows, with obvious exceptions, we will write of Wiseman as the implied author, the consciousness understood by an audience as behind the film; thus, we will speak of "Wiseman's camera," rather than trying to sort out, in tracking the audience's ongoing experience of the film, who was actually contributing how much to the construction of that experience. We will return to the issue of Wiseman's collaboration with his cameramen in chapter 10, at which point Leiterman's contribution to the construction of *High School* will again become an issue.

We cannot speak with authority about the way the behaviors of the characters in the film may reveal the psychologies of those characters as real people. *High School* is a created reality. But for the audience of *High School*, the characters may seem real, and their behaviors significant, both socially and psychologically, just as the audience may, perhaps must, attend to the social and psychological evidence it finds in the film about that other character, the unseen but implied author. It is into the seeming reality of *High School* that we are inquiring. Our perspective is an audience perspective. But the evidence for the audience's responses, as well as the evidence for the filmmaker's designs upon that audience, will be sought in the film itself. One of the special merits of Wiseman's films is that, properly understood, they are models of the responses that audiences are invited to make to them— and that those responses stretch the generic boundaries of documentary film and public rhetorics. We cannot claim, of course, that our analysis represents what all audiences will make of the film—Wiseman makes his audiences work hard, and not all of his viewers will be willing to play the part of his ideal reader. Still, even those who resist that part, or who are not up to playing it, are responding in terms of what the film offers them, and not simply randomly. To concede that each of us responds individually is not to say that we do not also respond socially, sharing meanings together.

Most of the themes we will discuss as forming the fabric of *High School* have been mentioned by other writers: power, authority, identity, alienation, sexuality, boredom. What we hope to do is to develop the presence and the function of these thematic elements in more detail than previous writers, to show how the details of the film relate to each other to form a structure, and to offer an account of how the structure may invite a rhetorical response.[3]

High School is a film about power as it is exercised in an institution whose ostensible mission is to educate.[4] An audience is invited to perceive the institution's exercise of power as absurd and hurtful. Wiseman reveals his theme and invites us to share in a bitter laughter about the packaging of American adolescence through a remarkable filmic structure built upon accumulation, comparison, and contradiction. This seemingly simple, open, episodic film can be seen, upon close examination, to exhibit a startling coherence, based upon a series of dialectical relations that gain force with each additional sequence. As Wiseman has said, *High School* "is both a theory of and a report on what I have learned."[5]

The beginning and ending of the film show the school as a factory turning out a product. In the first sequence, a series of traveling shots, Wiseman opens the second shot with a close-up of the back of a milk truck advertising "Penn Maid Products," a pun for the Pennsylvania made products turned out by the school. And when the school first appears (figure 3–2, frames 2, 3), it looks like a factory.[6] The end of the film shows us the product: students adapted to military service, which seems to stand as a symbol for alienated conformity. The middle of the film explores how the factory processes its students into willing members of the social order. Wiseman revealed in his interview with Rosenthal that this pattern was consciously imposed on the film: "You begin the film showing a factory process, and you end with a view of the perfect product."[7]

The theme of power is introduced unmistakably in scene 6 (see figure 3–1 for a list of the scenes in the film). Scene 6 is the first in which we see an extended face-to-face interaction. A student attempting to get excused from compulsory gym class is confronted with the power of the school in the person of an administrator.[8] The administrator sits behind a desk, the stereotype of a retired drill sergeant. His heavy face is topped by a crew cut and he speaks in commands. He is framed in the shot so that we see his face and next to it, on the wall, a picture of the American flag (figure 3-2, frames 21–25). The student protests, and the administrator rises from his chair, pointing finger and fist at the student's face as he approaches. "Don't you talk and you just listen." Again he orders the student to report for gym. Then he repeats his order. Barely audible, the student says, "I said I would." This continued bit of protest, which the administrator rightly translates as "I said I would; stop scolding me," draws an immediate response. "You're suspended." The oppressiveness of the school is symbolized in unmistakable terms in this sequence—the school has the right to order these students around, and they must not only obey, but do so without argument or insolence. There are other scenes in which oppressive power is revealed, or in which school officials are engaged not in instruction but in admonition. In scenes 10 and 24, the administrator of scene 6 is again acting the role of school disciplinarian. In scene 11, we follow a teacher on hall patrol duty as he examines passes and regulates hall traffic. In scene 25, a mother and daughter attend a disciplinary conference with a school official. But while these scenes—6, 10, 11, 24, 25—are about power, discipline, and control of students, they are only five scenes out of a total of forty-three in the film. What of the other thirty-eight?

The power exercised so absurdly and hurtfully by the institution is not simply the power to discipline as it is represented plainly in scenes 6, 10, 11, 24, and 25, although these scenes serve the function of placing power unmistakably before the viewer. Power in the high school extends beyond discipline and punishment to the power of the school and its representatives to control the setting and define the situation. Their power is the power they try to achieve over the lives, the minds, and spirits of their charges. Such power is exerted in virtually every scene of *High School*, through all the means of face-to-face communication: language, gesture, costume, setting. And it is a power that is exercised in ways much more pervasive than simply requiring students to accept a single and simple code of thought and behavior.

Figure 3-1

Scenes in *High School*

1. Exterior traveling shots along streets to exterior of Northeast High School. Sound: Otis Redding singing "Dock of the Bay."
2. Interior: hallway with students.
3. Male teacher reading daily bulletin.
4. Female Spanish teacher discussing existentialism.
5. Orchestra.
6. A school administrator directing a student to report for gym class, then suspending the student.
7. Hallway with students.
8. Male French teacher discussing French and American domestic life.
9. Father and mother in administrator's office, protesting their daughter's failing grade.
10. School administrator (same man as in scene 6) convincing student who talked back to a teacher to accept punishment.
11. Male teacher patrolling hallway.
12. Girls exercising in gym to "Simple Simon Says."
13. Female teacher reading "Casey at the Bat."
14. Girls in gym taking batting practice.
15. Boys in cooking class.
16. Rehearsal for school fashion show.
17. Test in typing class.
18. Male teacher telling a classroom of boys about family life.
19. Woman lecturer discussing promiscuity to auditorium of female students.
20. Two teachers scolding a girl about the length of a dress she chose for a formal dance.
21. Girls hanging from rings in gymnasium.
22. Female teacher lecturing on poetic devices in Simon and Garfunkel.
23. Hallway: girl walks by, then woman pulls trash bin down the hall.
24. The administrator of scenes 6 and 10 reprimands a student who hit another student.
25. A mother, her daughter, and a female teacher discussing the girl's "messing around."
26. A female counselor with parents and their daughter, discussing plans for college.
27. The parents of scene 9, with their daughter, meeting with the administrator who also appeared in scene 9.
28. Hallway, with janitor.
29. Teachers in lunchroom discussing foreign aid.
30. Administrator of scenes 6, 10, and 24 teaching a class on labor-management relations.
31. Teacher of scene 3 discussing social issues and attitudes with a class.
32. Girl singers being led through scales by male teacher.
33. Students and teacher in discussion about Northeast High School.
34. The teacher of scene 13 reading the thought for the day.
35. Hallway: a policeman looks at his watch.
36. School auditorium: boys in costumes of girl cheerleaders.
37. A gynecologist lecturing to auditorium of male students.
38. Animated scenes from instructional film about venereal disease.
39. Exterior: Vietnam veteran and coach discussing the wounding of a former student.
40. Boys in gym playing ball game.
41. Boy astronauts at the end of simulated flight.
42. Drum major with band and color guard.
43. Woman reading letter from school alumnus about to be dropped into Vietnam.

Figure 3-2

Frames from *High School*

(Frames 1–20)

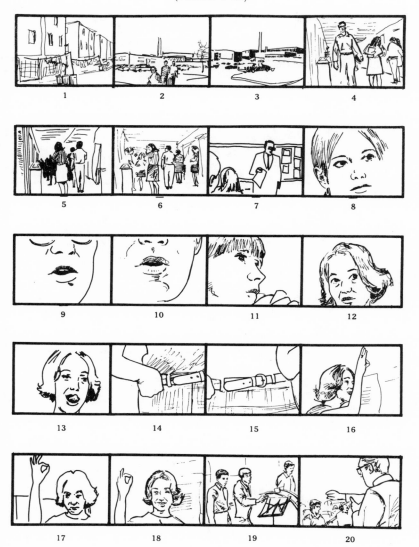

Figure 3-2

(Frames 21–40)

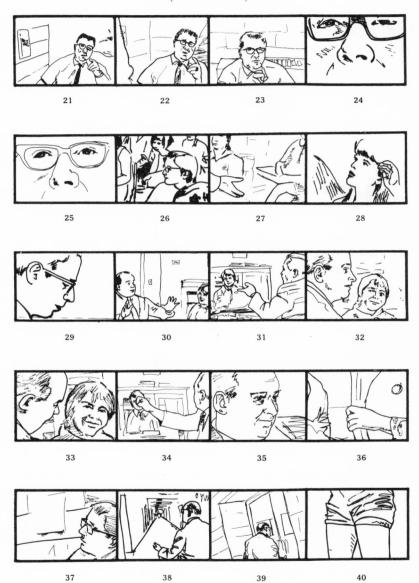

Figure 3-2

(Frames 41–60)

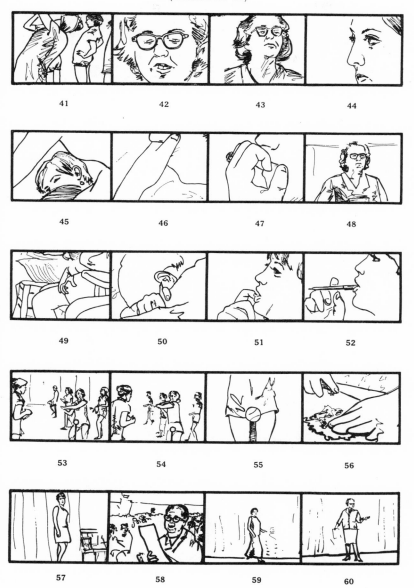

Figure 3-2

(Frames 61–80)

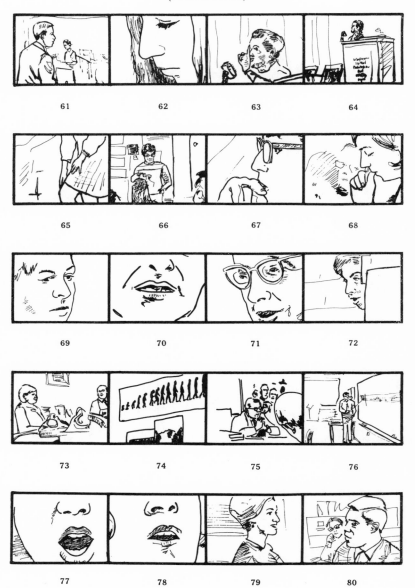

Figure 3-2

(Frames 81–99)

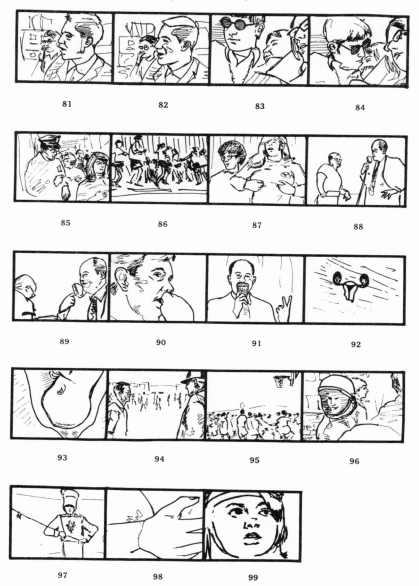

The school presented by Fred Wiseman is one in which students are required to obey a code that is by its very nature contradictory, from their point of view. Whatever they do is likely to be a mistake. The students are thus not merely required to obey a rule: they are required to be mixed up, stupid, confused, in the wrong—and subject at any time to the authority of the school. The school does not simply tell the students what to do; it tells them who they are. The school, of course, does not achieve total control. It does not have the students full-time, nor is it entirely competent to extend its confusion; moreover, its agents do not, truly, seem to understand the situation they seem to control. And the students have their own resources of subversion and alienation. Hence, the school does not produce robots, but rather very confused, oddly loyal, and self-sacrificial human victims, ready to take their places as the next generation of housewives, beauticians, astronauts, soldiers, secretaries, and high school teachers.

At its most damaging, the school exercises its power through a method that is similar to what Gregory Bateson and others have called the double bind.[9] The double bind was first posited as part of an interpersonal dynamic that contributed to the development of schizophrenia. In the double bind, the victim is repeatedly sent inconsistent messages by those in authority in a situation where the victim must make some response to the messages, but is prohibited from noticing or drawing attention to the contradictory nature of the messages, or withdrawing from the situation. The result is that the victim becomes schizophrenic. Wiseman does not, of course, claim that Northeast High School is breeding schizophrenics. Many authorities on the double-bind hypothesis have argued that the double bind is a characteristic pattern of human interaction that appears in families and institutions, where it operates as a pattern of control and a source of distress, but not necessarily as a cause of schizophrenia. In this milder, endemic, institutional sense, the structures of power that Wiseman discovers in the school fit the double-bind hypothesis remarkably well. We use the term *victim* in this chapter with some misgivings. A major contribution of the double-bind literature is to indicate that the psychological distress of one person is not to be *blamed* on another person, but rather that those who exhibit extreme distress and those who contribute to it are acting together in a communicative situation in which both share responsibility, and it follows that altered patterns of understanding and interaction may at least partly redeem the situation. The double-bind hypothesis was emphatically not an attempt to shift the blame for schizophrenia from a medical problem to a double-binding villain. Does *High School* cast the students as victims and the teachers as villains? It seems to us that the teachers are certainly criticized and held responsible for their double-binding communication in a rigidly hierarchical situation; on the other hand, they, too, are simply carrying out the routines of an institution. And the students, though they sometimes offer tiny gestures of resistance, on the whole seem willing to play the role offered them by the system, by sinking into apathy and passivity. For both double-bind theorists and Wiseman, the roles of double-binder and double-bound victim are social roles that can be addressed at an ethical level because they can partially be altered, even though their systemic character makes it difficult.

One of the ways the school exercises double-binding control is through the use of language, making nonsense of ordinary discourse. Teachers and administrators invoke contradictory commonplaces to gain momentary advantage, remove words from their proper signification, reduce poetry to technique, and just plain miss the point of their own sanctimonious homilies.

In scene 10, an administrator (whom we saw in scene 6) is talking with a boy, Michael, who has been sentenced to a detention for talking back to a teacher.

MICHAEL: I don't feel I have to take anybody screaming at me for nothing.

ADMINISTRATOR: No, well, there's a point to that, but in the meantime it's time you showed a little character of your own. Right?

MICHAEL: Yes.

ADMINISTRATOR: I would take the detention and then you can come back and say, "Now, I took the detention, may I speak with you?"

MICHAEL: I can't just, I can't speak to—

ADMINISTRATOR: Well, you can try.

Michael returns to a description of the situation that got him into trouble, and tries to show that he was not in the wrong. The administrator returns to his own agenda:

ADMINISTRATOR: See, we're out to establish something, aren't we?

MICHAEL: Yes.

ADMINISTRATOR: We're out to establish that you can be a man and you can take orders. We want to prove to them that you can take the orders.

MICHAEL: But, Mr. Allen, it's all against my principles; you have to stand for something.

ADMINISTRATOR: Yes. But I think the principles that are involved here, I think it's a question now of, of proving yourself to be a man. It's a question here of how do we follow the rules and regulations. If there's a mistake made, there's an approach to it. I think you don't fight with a teacher, I think you ask permission to talk, and you ask him to listen to you. Now this is what you didn't do. Now if you had taken your detention, and, after all, they didn't require much from you. The teacher felt you were out of order, and in her judgment you deserved a detention. I don't see anything wrong with assigning you a detention. And I think you should prove yourself. You should show you can take the detention when given it.

MICHAEL: I should prove that I'm a man and that's what I intend to do by doing what I feel, in my opinion, is what I—is right.

ADMINISTRATOR: Well, are you going to take the detention or aren't you? I feel that you should.

MICHAEL: I'll take it, but only under protest.

ADMINISTRATOR: All right then, you'll take it under protest. That's good.

Michael does not seem to realize what has happened to him. The administrator has twisted an act of protest by reversing Michael's meanings, suggesting that Michael "establish that you can be a man and you can take orders," when Michael obviously wants to prove to himself that he can pursue his rights and, equally important, pursue what is right. The administrator's tactic of seeming to agree with the student, seeming to take his side, is particularly insidious. It is in bad faith and makes nonsense of the language by which the student is attempting to understand his reality. The administrator appears to be motivated by the urge to clear his agenda of this administrative problem. Institutional order takes precedence over education, but that order is maintained in the name of education.

Linguistic nonsense also occurs in scene 9, where a father and mother are discussing their daughter's grade with another administrator. The father shows that the daughter earned high marks on her papers, even being told that one was "fabulous," only to find that she had failed the course. He seeks an explanation and is met, not with a clear inquiry into all the elements that went to make up the grade, but with obfuscation.

ADMINISTRATOR: I can only say this. That the teacher, in reading these papers, thought they were fabulous, but that the total mark involves more than just these papers. That's all I can tell you.
FATHER: Well, I think this is a rather unique situation, wouldn't you say so? Rather unique?
ADMINISTRATOR: Will you be happy if I say it's unique?
FATHER: I'd be happy.
ADMINISTRATOR: I would say somewhat unique.

The administrator speaks good sense when telling the father that grades are based on many types of student performance. As with the administrator in scene 10, he seems to announce a principle, a commonplace, that in itself is unobjectionable. But in this case he uses it as a cloak to prevent further inquiry. The commonplace is "all I can tell you," rather than the introduction to an examination of the other work done by the daughter. And then the dialogue loses focus and turns into complete nonsense, as father and administrator spar over whether the sequence is "rather unique" or "somewhat unique"—both, of course, meaningless qualifications of a word whose usefulness depends upon its absoluteness. But the discussion of *unique* is not mere silliness, nor simply Wiseman's disdainful recording of the linguistic inadequacies of father and administrator. The passage we have quoted appears to be a negotiation in which the father is trying to open up an inquiry and the administrator keeps finding ways to shut it down. The administrator first tells the father, in response to an inquiry, "I can only say this. . . . That's all I can tell you." This stonewalling is responded to by the father with another attempt to open the inquiry: "Well, I think this is a rather unique situation, wouldn't you say so?" The administrator's response to this question is a masterful bit of flak catching. In response to what appears to be an attempt to open the dialogue, the administrator says, "Will you be happy if I say it's unique?" Now, the administrator's reply seems to say two things: it indicates that his main aim is to stop the discussion ("will you be happy if . . ."), but he also makes an implicit offer: he seems to offer to say that the situation is unique if the father will accept that. When the father accepts the offer, the administrator welches; instead of agreeing, as he implied he would, that the situation is "unique" or even the father's weaker "rather unique," he takes the ground gained by having gotten the father to agree to the bargain and then takes a little more: "I would say somewhat unique." This is cheating. But it is extremely effective, because it is so subtle and so apparently trivial that the father cannot notice what has been done to him. To quibble over a "somewhat" would be ridiculous; to concede the "somewhat" is to agree not to notice that he has been cheated of a bargain he and the administrator had implicitly agreed to. So the father keeps his half of the bargain, accepts the "somewhat unique," and accepts what goes with it. He does not pursue this tactic any further. To accuse the administrator of bad faith because he does not keep his bargains would be excessive in the conversation itself, but the father obviously feels the force of what has happened to him, even if he cannot explain it. And perhaps something similar happens for the audience thanks to Wiseman's willingness to show us the dynamics of everyday argument.

Scenes 20 and 25 present an unresolved contradiction of commonplaces that we are invited to see as confusing and inconsistent. In scene 20, a girl is told not to be individualistic, and then in scene 25 another girl is told not to go along with the crowd. Another bit of linguistic confusion is introduced in scene 34, when a teacher reading the thought for the day seems to miss the point of it completely. The function of these linguistic absurdities in the film is not simply to show the teachers and administrators as inept. In each sequence, the misuse of language occurs in a setting where it confuses the issue. Students subjected to such language are at a disadvantage in the power game that the whole school is playing with them. In the world of the film, as in the world Alice finds in Wonderland, words and their meanings are under the arbitrary control of those at the top of the hierarchy, with the result that the person in charge stays in charge. And in this world where they cannot do anything right, it is no wonder that the responses of the students are pinched and apathetic—small acts of misbehavior or cautious conformity.

We have argued that *High School* is a film about power, a power exercised through direct control of behavior, as well as more subtly through the definition of setting and situation, and the confusion of issues by obfuscating language. These elements alone may be enough to account for the apathy of the students and the rage on their behalf that we are likely to feel as viewers. But there is more to the film than this.

In *High School,* the theme of power is related to a pervasive secondary theme of sexuality and gender. Thematically, the film might be taken as a set of binary structures relating power and sex in a guiding proposition: in *High School*, those who have social power maintain it by engaging those with an emerging sexual potency in a double bind. Students are ostensibly told to grow up and accept the responsibilities of adulthood, but they are subjected to constant warnings about the dangers of adult sexuality—they are told to grow up, but not to grow up, to take responsibility for themselves, but to take orders. The contradiction that seems so silly when heard at the level of power alone ("be a man and take orders") becomes devastating when the power of the school invades the confused sexual identities of its students. The confusion created by the double binding of the school's contradictory directions results in the apathy, alienation, juvenility, and inversion that are evident in the behavior of the students. Almost every scene in the film deals with some element of the curious relation between sex and power in the school, and the few remaining scenes deal with related issues.

We are claiming that most of the audience is moved by a rhetorical structure that has not previously been adequately described. *High School* is about institutional power—that much has been evident to every viewer and critic. But the vehicle by which that meaning is made into a powerful experience is the relation of power to sexuality through a series of mostly invisible but powerfully affecting rhetorical structures.

High School invites viewers to experience the structural relations of the themes of power and sexuality, and the subordinate manifestations of these themes in distorted interpersonal communication, twisted language, confused identities, militarism, regimentation, anti-intellectualism, and boredom. But the film is more than its themes. Critics can abstract themes from the film, but to present each theme separately, together with examples that support its presence in the text, would seriously distort Wiseman's structure and misrepresent the audience's probable experience. Instead of a theme-by-theme approach, we will proceed scene by scene through the film, presenting a detailed explication that will suggest the ways in which Wiseman invites his viewers to structure the meanings of *High School* as experiences, ideas, and attitudes. The structure of the film, we shall argue, reveals the interpretive actions, both intellectual and emotional, that the audience is invited to perform in response to it. The film is not simply the repository of meanings; it is an instrument for the evocation of those meanings, as rhetorical experiences, in the audience. Wiseman not only demonstrates, but also induces us to experience, the relation of the personal, private, and unconscious elements of our identities and desires to the public, institutional, and political level at which communities are enacted and social control is maintained.

The presence of sexuality in *High School* is exceedingly complex, ranging from possibly accidental dirty jokes to a general awareness of the human body, the formation of gender identities, and an undercurrent of courtship rituals. Though some of the sexually relevant scenes are unmistakable, as when a gynecologist lectures on the dangers of sex, most of the instances we will cite are marginal in their intimations. It is impossible to divine Wiseman's intentions or predispositions with any certainty, and equally impossible to be certain that an ordinary viewer would ascribe a sexual relevance to much of the material. Since Freud, it has been all too easy for a critic to find sexual symbolism in every random tree, telephone pole, and railway tunnel. It is well to remember Freud's reminder that sometimes a cigar is just a cigar. We will argue that the repetition of sexual elements, and the way they are placed in the context, is likely to predispose the viewer to decode them in something like the way we are describing. But we must strain the reader's credulity further by arguing that the sexual material works on the viewer of the film much as it works on the student in the school: for the student, it exists as part of the double bind that reinforces the school's power while remaining just at the edge of consciousness. For the film viewer, the sexual material is also usually just out of conscious awareness, inviting us to feel angry about the power of the school without quite realizing quite why we feel so angry.

Our description of the rhetorical structure of *High School* is intended primarily to seek the meaning of this film. In arguing that the viewer can "have" the experience of the film without "getting it" in a self-conscious way, we are also attempting to show how Wiseman provides a model for his own peculiar rhetoric of documentary, relating conscious to unconscious, discursive to filmic, public to private, factual to fictional. Can we prove that audiences would get the film this way, that they would agree with our interpretation of his work, and, if they did, that they would agree with Wiseman's "theory" of high school as we interpret it? No. Although presumably it would be possible to survey audience response, such a survey is beyond our purpose. Insofar as we are describing probable audience response, we are attempting to propose both a probable experience of the film and the way it is brought about. Readers of this chapter, it seems to us, can best decide for themselves whether our account matches their experiences. Our job, we think, is to try to get it right, but not to insist that we have it right. In the spirit of criticism and, it seems to us, in the humanistic spirit of Wiseman's documentaries, one does one's work—itself an appeal for understanding— and rests final judgment not with the critic or the poll taker or even the filmmaker, but with the viewer.

High School speaks in a rhetorical vernacular in which concepts of alienation and repression become the commonplaces of audiences who have never read Marx or Freud. Alienation and repression are part of the conceptual apparatus of *High School*, but Wiseman does not require of the audience a first- or even second-hand knowledge of philosophy or psychology; the concepts have seeped into ordinary discourse as part of the apparatus of contemporary conventional knowledge.

As soon as Wiseman enters the school, he presents the issue of bodily awareness. In scene 2, a hallway, we see students walking. A girl stops and looks into her handbag (frame 4). Then she turns to look into a glass, perhaps a glass doorway, and combs her hair (frames 5 and 6). She is performing a grooming activity that is not particularly significant in itself, but that will accumulate with other images in the film into a repeated pattern of gender-specific self-stroking and grooming. A *meaning*, once established, begins to absorb neutral or ambiguous signs. So with the theme of sexuality in *High School*, many gestures that are, in themselves, neutral seem to take on relevance to the general awareness of sex, gender, and bodily regard that pervades the film.

In scene 3, a teacher reads the daily bulletin. The speech in this sequence is accompanied by a visual undercurrent of bodily attention. The first shot of the sequence presents the teacher in a midshot (frame 7). Wiseman cuts to a close-up of a female student, looking at something off camera (frame 8). By the logic of film, the next shot should reveal what she is looking at. Cut to frames 9 and 10, a close-up of the teacher's mouth, then cut to frame 11, another student gazing with concentration at the teacher's mouth. It would be forcing the issue to argue that these images unambiguously—or exclusively—represent sexuality. But they do guide our awareness. Attention is focused, by the intercutting of a gaze and its object, the teacher's mouth, on the existence of some sort of relation between eyes and lips. At one level of significance, one might translate this as a kind of irony—looking at the presumable source of education and hearing from it instead these bored homilies. Or one might at the same time see the relation established here as part of Wiseman's metafilmic strategy of playing one sense against the other. Instead of ear to mouth, or eye to print, we are given a mixed sensory link, which habituates us to Wiseman's actively ironic attention. When the authority of institutional decorum asks us to listen, Wiseman also invites us to look; when the same decorum invites us to look away, Wiseman keeps looking, keeps listening.

In a fictional film, the gaze of these girls might also be understood as a foreshadowing of sexual desire. But we are not in a fictional film, are we? No, Wiseman never abandons the generic credibility of documentary altogether, but he constantly employs the conventions of fiction to liberate our imagination and guide our speculation. Even in frames 7–11, the film, if it is to be read even at the diegetic or story level, must be read as continuous in time according to the conventions of film narrative. Yet the film was shot with a single camera, and so the continuity we must assume in order to read the scene requires us to use our fictional imagination while retaining our documentary orientation. Something similar happens when the editing of the scene contextualizes some shots as subjective, point-of-view shots within the larger context of the implied author's perspective, which is objective (in the sense of outside the subject), but subjective (in the sense of bearing an attitude), real-time (in the sense of bound to the chronology of ongoing events by a single camera), but omniscient (in the sense of having been reassembled into a new coherence after the events have taken place). This mixture of generic conventions enables us to exercise the power of fictional identification and imagination within the larger realization that what we are seeing is rooted in and bears upon actual experience.

The hints of scenes 2 and 3 are made more explicit in scene 4. We cut to a woman talking in Spanish. She tilts her head, her eyes widen (frame 12), and then her tongue, pointed, caresses her upper lip (frame 13). Then, without a cut, the camera tilts down to reveal, in frame 14, the teacher's hand on her belt, thumb hooked into the belt and hip thrust to the side. The camera pans right, across the belt line, to discover the teacher's elbow (frame 15). Later in the same scene, the teacher leads the class in choral repetition of Spanish words, keeping time with her hand making the "ring gesture" —thumb and index finger forming a circle, tips touching, with the other fingers erect (frames 16–18). The ring gesture is repeated four times in one shot.

The widened eyes and protruding tongue are unmistakable courtship routines, and it is significant that the cameraman, Richard Leiterman, instantly recognizes this and tilts the camera down to discover the rest of the pose—the teacher's hand hooked in her belt. At the very least, such courtship routines seem to call attention to the gender of the actor and imply that gender is somehow relevant to the interaction that is taking place. Do they imply more than gender identification in this scene?

Albert Scheflen has pointed out that gestures whose origin and frame of reference have to do with courtship are not always used as the instruments of seduction or courtship. Instead, they are converted into "quasi-courtship behavior," in which courtship behaviors are qualified to make clear that they are not seductive, but rather meant to encourage a positive interaction. According to Scheflen, social occasions often require the maintenance of a sense of mutual attractiveness and attentiveness. "This state is necessary to group cohesion and the completion of tasks that are not immediately gratifying. Some of the different terms used to describe this state are attractiveness, attentiveness, sociability, readiness to relate, and quasi-courtship."[10] According to Scheflen, quasi-courting behavior is always available as a way of increasing the sense of attentiveness in groups, and a corresponding complex of decourting behaviors is available to lessen the degree of involvement.

It is not clear, by the time one has reached the fourth scene in *High School,* how a viewer is likely to understand the courtship behaviors of the Spanish teacher. Would they be seen as simple quasi-courtship intended to maintain a high level of attention among the students to the group task? Or would they be seen, consciously or not, as having a seductive quality? It must be remembered that we are not searching for what the behaviors meant in the actual classroom situation, but for how they are likely to appear to a viewer of the film. Surely the film viewer would not be likely to think that the teacher was actually trying to seduce her students. But possibly the teacher's behavior does at least cross over into an ambiguous area of sexual awareness. On film, it looks like a parody of a rock star's routine, sketched in a simple gesture. As film viewers, we have been trained by all our film watching to look for signs of sexual involvement on the screen. Bing Crosby, priest though he seemed, allowed us romantic fantasies in his partnership with Ingrid Bergman in *The Bells of St. Mary's* (1945). The involvement was not sexual, but there was about it an element of romantic longing that was rendered perfectly safe by the use of priest's collar, nun's habit, and Hollywood convention. But Dustin Hoffman and Anne Bancroft demonstrated another, more consequential pattern of courtship in an early scene from *The Graduate* (1967). Bancroft, as Mrs. Robinson, engages in a highly ambiguous display of sexually aggressive noninvolvement that contrasts with Hoffman's desperately juvenile decourting behaviors. Finally, when the audience has been given a chance to explore the special pleasures, the dangerous excitement, of wondering whether Bancroft is really courting, can be trusted, or is worth desiring, Hoffman, as Ben, asks, "Mrs. Robinson, you're trying to seduce me. Aren't you?" She maintains control of the situation, prolonging the terror of the young man, by replying, "Well, no, I hadn't thought of it." As it turns out, she has thought of it, of course, but her reply reminds us that courtship behavior is useful partly because it is deniable and that the risks of responding to quasi-courtship behavior as if it were courtship can be considerable. Both Ben and the audience, and presumably these high-school students, too, are likely to have trained themselves to avoid noticing courtship behavior in situations where it is unexpected or inappropriate—but not noticing can itself be a confusing process to the person who is trying not to notice.

The ambiguity and deniability of courtship behavior can work both ways. On the one hand, they allow couples negotiating courtship to test the situation without explicitly acknowledging what is happening. This permits a face-saving withdrawal if it is needed. But because we learn that courtship behavior is ambiguous, noncourting behavior may be mistaken for courtship and attract unwanted attention. In *High School*, Wiseman encourages us to experience the feeling of censoring our awareness of courtship, and the tensions that follow upon such self-censorship. As film viewers we have been trained to be aware of the signs of courtship. Whether the behaviors of a particular actor are likely to be seen as courting, quasi-courting, or ambiguous depends upon one's experience in watching films, one's social experience, and the context the filmmaker provides for the images. The Spanish teacher's behaviors are at least quasi-courting. And as Wiseman develops his context, they seem to go beyond quasi-courting to contribute to an atmosphere in which social power is expressed through the exchange of signals having to do with sexuality and its confusion, repression, or inversion.

The Spanish teacher's ring gesture also has a variety of possible meanings. In *Gestures: Their Origin and Distribution*, Desmond Morris and his associates trace the meaning of the gesture in several European cities. They found that the gesture meant "OK—good" to 700 informants; "orifice," anal or vaginal, to 128 informants; "zero—worthless" to 115 informants; and "threat" to 16 informants. Morris and his associates also found that the gesture was used as a "baton signal," where speakers were making a fine point or requesting greater precision in some way.[11]

In the context of the Spanish class, the baton signal appears to be the most appropriate interpretation of the ring gesture: the teacher is keeping time with the raising and lowering of her hand and signaling the need for precision with the ring. But in the context of the courtship gestures that have just preceded it, the ring gesture may be seen by Wiseman and the viewer as ambiguously referring also, in some measure, to the "ok," "orifice," and "threat" aspects of the gesture. And even if the ring gesture is understood only as the baton signal, the earlier presence of the courtship behaviors— widened eyes, tongue thrust, hand in belt, hip swing—creates a complex of meanings that goes beyond simple group attentiveness. The behaviors that we have observed in this scene are not performed mutually by teachers and students, but rather are the behaviors of a person in authority signaling a relation to a classroom of students. One way to test what may seem our overreading of the teacher's behavior is to imagine how it would look if one of the students performed exactly these behaviors in this context—the inappropriateness would be startling. Aggressive quasi-courtship behaviors, together with the baton signal, assert the relation of power and sexuality. Further, Wiseman has chosen a situation in which the response of the students is mechanical: they are a chorus, repeating by rote the words that the teacher is pronouncing.

Wiseman uses the baton signal as a bridge to scene 5. He cuts from the hand of the Spanish teacher beating time with the ring gesture to an orchestra (frame 19) being led by another teacher (frame 20). This cut not only reinforces, through parallelism, the interpretation of the Spanish teacher's ring gesture as a baton signal, but also indicates to the audience that the filmmaker is likely to seek meaningful associations when he cuts from one scene to another.

In scene 8, a French teacher is discussing, in French, the domestic life of France and America. As he talks, Wiseman's camera and editing build another courtship relationship. In frame 26, the girl in the foreground raises her left hand to stroke the back of her head, a preening gesture. The camera pans left to frame 27, in which the teacher is presenting his palm, another courtship gesture. Wiseman cuts from frame 27 to frame 28, an even more definite courtship gesture by a girl who preens her hair while presenting her palm. In American culture, this palm-forward hair preening is a strong courtship gesture and is reserved exclusively for females.[12] Wiseman cuts from frame

28 to frame 29, a close-up of the teacher's face. The framing and cutting relate these two shots not only to indicate that the two faces are regarding one another, but that one dominates the other. The girl in frame 28 is looking slightly upward and occupies a diagonal lower-right segment of the screen. The teacher in frame 29 occupies an upper-left diagonal section and looks down.

In scene 9, the sexual comedy is complicated by an element of pathos. A mother and father are trying to understand why their daughter failed a course. This is the same scene we examined earlier, in which the administrator conceded to a "somewhat unique" situation. In our earlier examination of the scene, we concentrated on the way language was manipulated to maintain control of the situation. An examination of the speech in relation to the images of the scene reveals the presence of an even more humiliating struggle. In frame 30, the father is pleading his case, palms held forward in a defensive gesture. The administrator replies (frame 31), with his elbow on the desk, arm blocking his body, fingers pointed toward the father, palms up—he is shrugging off an inquiry and using his desk as a prop to his authority. The father (frames 32 and 33) leans forward slightly to press his point. Mother is looking on with an encouraging grin. This time, the administrator responds with greater gestural emphasis (frame 34), extending his right arm and forming a fist. Then the administrator attacks:

ADMINISTRATOR: Because she failed on all these tests. We can only judge on the basis of performance. You may have hidden talent in you, sir, but if you don't perform, then we don't know.
FATHER: That's true.
ADMINISTRATOR: And the world will recognize you only by your performance.
FATHER: That's true, that's true.

As the administrator presses his argument directly, turning from the daughter to the question of the father's hypothetical performance, the father begins to concede, "That's true," and Wiseman moves in for a close-up. The father's eyes widen, and he appears to be on the verge of tears (frame 35). The father then bows his head in apparent submission. Leiterman tilts down and pans right to a close-up of the mother's hand, which is grasping the vertical wooden member back of her chair. Her hand gently strokes the post up and down (frame 36). The scene then cuts to a close-up of the mother's face, then cuts to the father's face, still almost in tears, and then the camera pans right across the desk to a tight close-up of the administrator's fist. End of scene.

Wiseman captures here the personal defeat of the father when the administrator turns from his "What can I do?" approach to a direct challenge of the father's performance. But the ambiguity in American talk about the word *performance*, when applied to an adult male, allows Wiseman another chance to stress the relationship between power and sexuality. The administrator has challenged the father's manhood, with startling results: the father is reduced almost to tears, and Wiseman shows the mother stroking her chair in a gesture that, in the filmic context, invites an interpretation of it as a sexual caress.

The next scene, scene 10, has already been discussed in the context of the way the teachers twist the language. It is in this scene that Michael is encouraged to be a man and take orders. Earlier, we discussed how the scene represented linguistic distortion, but we can see now that in the developing context of the film, the appeal to Michael's manhood is consistent with the sexual sub-theme of the film, in which students are encouraged to be confused about their developing gender identities and their desires, in order that they can be more easily controlled by the teachers and administrators.

The next six scenes are linked to amplify Wiseman's meditation on sex and power. In scene 11, a male teacher is patrolling the corridors, asking to see passes, and stopping to tell one student to finish a telephone conversation (frame 38). Wiseman cuts to a girl walking down the corridor, then back to the teacher. The cut makes it appear that the teacher is girl watching. The teacher continues down the corridor, and music is heard on the sound track. The teacher stops at a double door and looks through the windows in the door (frame 39). By the logic of film, the next shot should reveal what he is looking at. Wiseman cuts to scene 12, where the camera is recording close-ups of girls exercising in a gymnasium to a recording of "Simple Simon Says," the song that faded into the sound track at the end of scene 11. Wiseman's cutting makes it appear that the teacher of scene 11 is looking through the window at girls' bottoms (frames 40 and 41).

From the regimented but sexually charged athleticism of scene 12, Wiseman cuts to scene 13, in which an English teacher is reading "Casey at the Bat" in a mechanical, singsong voice (frames 42 and 43). As the teacher continues to read, Wiseman explores the attitudes of the students in the classroom. He discovers the girl in frame 44, her heavy eye makeup imitating a maturity at odds with the innocence implied by the poem. From frame 44, Wiseman cuts to the sleepy inattention of the girl in frame 45, then pans to the face of a boy with his hand over his mouth (frame 46). The boy moves his hand, stroking his lips with his knuckles (frame 47). Wiseman cuts back to the teacher (frame 48), then cuts to two girls and pans down to focus on one whose hand rests on her half-exposed thigh (frame 49). A moment later Wiseman presents a close-up of a boy asleep, his head resting on his arms (frame 50). The logic of film might tell us that the next image will show us what he is dreaming about. Wiseman cuts to the face of a girl who is caressing her opened lips with her finger (frame 51). As the shot continues, the girl takes her finger out of her mouth and begins to suck on the end of her pen (frame 52). All of these images in scene 13, when seen in the context of the sexual imagery preceding this scene, seem to add up to a description of a world in which the teachers drone on and on against a background filled with the unacknowledged sexual daydreams of the students. The daydreams are turned inward, finding their expression in a visible but tacitly ignored pattern of self-stroking. The inverted sexuality implied by the self-stroking of scene 13 creates the link to scene 14.

In scene 14, Wiseman returns to the gymnasium. In the foreground, a girl is taking batting practice with a softball perched on a flexible post. In the opening shot of the scene (frame 53), she whacks at the ball. Then the girl at the left of the frame puts another ball on the post (frame 54). Whack again. Wiseman then cuts to a close-up of the ball on the post (frame 55). Whack.

Scene 14 is linked to the preceding scene by the theme of baseball. But there is another link. By placing the camera so that the ball is framed at the batter's crotch, Wiseman escalates the sexual joke. The implication is that the sexual confusion engendered by the school's use of power (oppression) and sex (repression) turns these women into what street talk calls "ball-breakers," mutilating for themselves whatever chance they might have for a fully mature sexual intimacy. In our view, an audience would be unlikely to get this implication, since it depends for its force not upon the social sensitivity that makes us aware of courtship behaviors but upon a visual pun. Still, it is hard to doubt that Wiseman understood the implications of the batting practice scene.

The ball-breaking joke of scene 14 is taken one step further when Wiseman cuts from frame 55 to frame 56, the first shot of scene 15. In extreme close-up, we see a pair of hands, a knife, and chopped nuts. We realize that this is a cooking class and think that we have gone from girls batting balls to girls chopping nuts. The joke gets yet another twist as Wiseman cuts back to reveal that it is indeed a cooking class, but that the chopper is a boy. The sexual destruction of scene 14 carries forward to an implied self-mutilation in scene 15. Once again, it seems unlikely that an audience would catch this joke, but it is also clear that Wiseman has allowed very few accidents into this film: the framing and cutting are highly structured, and the interpretations we have offered for scenes 14 and 15 are supported by everything that comes before and after them in the film.

The home economics teacher of scene 15 appears as the central character of scene 16 and provides a link between the two scenes. But there is also a thematic bridge. In scene 16, the teacher instructs a group of girls who have designed and constructed dresses and who are rehearsing for a fashion show. Everything the teacher says encourages the girls to see their own bodies as imperfect objects which must be costumed and manipulated so as to project an illusion of grace and beauty. The teacher advises girls not to wear culottes if they have heavy legs, asks another girl to find someone with slimmer legs to wear her outfit, and suggests that another girl wear pink stockings to make her legs seem slimmer (frames 57 and 58). Another girl crosses the stage (frame 59) and we hear that she has "a weight problem," and then she is congratulated on designing her costume to disguise the problem. Then the teacher takes to the stage and gives a short lesson in how to walk, stand, and turn gracefully (frame 60). The teacher is obviously a woman of good humor, affection, and modesty, but the message she is sending to the girls is consistent with the rest of what Wiseman shows us: success is the result of treating one's self as an object.

Scene 16 ends as the teacher asks, "Any questions?" Wiseman cuts to scene 17 as another teacher asks, "Any questions?" (frame 61). We are in a typing class, looking over the shoulder of an adenoidal and pasty young teacher who presides over several rows of machines. Wiseman indulges himself in a standard rack-focus shot down a long row of typewriters that draws our attention once again to the regimented quality of the high school. But he also discovers, in the midst of these machines, a Veronica Lake close-up (frame 62) that reminds us of the presence of adolescent sexuality.

In scene 18, a male teacher is describing to a group of boys the sociology of American families, emphasizing the division of responsibility between mothers and fathers. The scene is a straightforward lesson in gender roles.

In scene 19, Wiseman reveals, in close-up, a woman speaking about sex to an auditorium of girls (frame 63). Her speech is slightly disorganized, but constitutes a clear warning about the dangers of sexuality and promiscuity. She tells the girls to practice self denial. As the speaker rambles on through her warnings, Wiseman slowly zooms out on the speaker, to reveal her in a long shot behind the lectern (frame 64). A motto engraved on the lectern serves as Wiseman's ironic caption for the scene: "Whatsoever thy hand findeth to do, do it with thy might."

Scene 20 has already been mentioned in the discussion of distorted language. But it must also be mentioned here in the context of sex and gender, since the girl who is being reprimanded is accused of wearing too short a skirt to a formal dance. In frame 65, she demonstrates where she thought the hem should be. Two teachers tell her, and then tell her again and again, how wrong she was. One of the teachers, a woman, describes the sacrifices she makes to convention in wearing a formal dress. "I can't walk in it, I can't get in a car comfortably." It is not clear whether she is bragging or complaining, but it is clear that her sacrifice gives her the right to criticize the student, and that the student has been presented with a rule that confuses her not only about "style" and "individuality" but also about what it means to be a woman.

The critical woman teacher of scene 20 provides the bridge to scene 21, in which she is the gym teacher encouraging a group of girls to see how long they can hang with bent arms from sets of rings. To the girls who let go first she says, "Oh boy, you're feminine. Let's go." As she counts off the seconds, she shouts encouragement to those who hang on longer. "Tarzan!" "Super Tarzan!" Whatever these girls do is wrong. If they opt for femininity, they fail at the classroom task by falling off the rings too early. If they opt for success, they forfeit their femininity and become "Tarzans."

Critics have disagreed about what Wiseman intends with scene 22, in which a teacher describes the poetry of Simon and Garfunkel (frame 66).[13] Is she to be contrasted with the teacher who read "Casey at the Bat" in scene 13? Critics who believe so point out that she has chosen material that is relevant to her students. But perhaps here "relevancy" is only an unsuccessful attempt to co-opt her students. As we hear her describe the song, the camera records a poster on the wall: "Rock with Shakespeare." And on the blackboard the song is reduced to mechanics: theme, metaphor, images, figurative language. The teacher's sincerity is evident, but she is not the only well-meaning teacher in the film who may be contributing to the boredom and alienation of her students. The attitudes of the students who listen to the song are also unclear. Taken out of context, they might seem to be merely attentive (frames 67 and 68). But in the context of the other images in the film, the self-stroking of the students seems to hint at an infantile tactility in contrast to the teacher's attempt to rationalize song into technique.

In scenes 24 through 27, Wiseman develops the theme of communication between generations as it occurs in the context of confusion about sex and power. This group of scenes is set apart from the rest of the film by two transitional scenes: scene 23 shows a woman dragging a trash bin down a school corridor as the music from scene 22 fades out. Scene 28 shows a janitor working in a corridor. The corridor scenes provide a structural reinforcement for setting apart scenes 24 through 27, and their thematic similarities help to reinforce the coherence of this group of scenes.

In scene 24, the administrator from scene 6 is reprimanding a student who started a fight (frame 69). The student replies with formality, speaking in what sounds like military courtesy, as he begins and ends most of his replies with "sir."

ADMINISTRATOR: Hey, you, turn around, pal.
STUDENT: Sir.
ADMINISTRATOR: Don't sir me. Don't feed me that sir business.

* * *

ADMINISTRATOR: That's why you're going to be suspended, for throwing the first punch.
STUDENT: Yes, sir.
ADMINISTRATOR: Don't give me that yes sir business. I don't like the sir business, you know why? Because there's no sincereness behind it.

The administrator's demand to be treated with respect is perhaps reasonable, and he is perhaps even justified in asking the student to refrain from using "sir." But in the context of the film, his demand that the student be sincere is absurd. A communicative practice frequently associated with double binds is the paradoxical injunction "Be spontaneous." Such a command cannot be obeyed. Similarly, if the student were sincere in this situation, he might tell the administrator just what he thought of him, which would get him in even worse trouble. The command "Be sincere," though perhaps not structurally impossible to obey, as the "Be spontaneous" command is, would nevertheless be dangerous to obey and is clearly not what the administrator wants. Whatever the student does in response to the demand to be sincere is going to be disobedient.

In scene 25, a mother and daughter are in a disciplinary conference with a female administrator. When the girl says she was just "messing around," the mother wants to know what that means. The term, of course, is impossible for the girl to define. Then the girl is told by what standards she should govern her conduct. The mother says that respect for adults is most important. The administrator tells the girl to be an individual, to lead the crowd away from trouble. Either advice is perfectly sensible, but in a film where we have been alerted by Wiseman to look for contradictions, it appears that this girl is getting contradictory advice: be an individual but respect and obey adults. And when placed in the context of the film as a whole, it is clear how difficult it is for the students to discover a general standard of conduct. The girl in scene 20, whose skirt was too short, was told that she ought to conform. "Around here we are going to do what the majority decides." But here another girl is told that she should not go along with the crowd. What rule applies? Wiseman seems to invite us to take the point of view of the students, from which the demands of the adults are double binding. The adults speak a different language, and they make impossible demands. It is not surprising that the students respond with apathy. As if to emphasize the adults' garbled speech and distorted vision, Wiseman focuses on the tense, thin-lipped mouth of the mother (frame 70) and the coke-bottle glasses of the administrator (frame 71).

In scene 26, a girl and her parents are discussing college plans with a counselor. As if to emphasize the barriers to communication, Wiseman frames the counselor peeping out from behind a row of books (frame 72).

In scene 27, the mother and father of scene 9 are shown with their daughter and the administrator. Wiseman jokes about the difficulties of communication by framing father and daughter so that two telephones loom up between them in the foreground of the shot (frame 73). But the joke is given an extra twist when the administrator tries to construe a remark of the father's about his daughter's strength as insulting to the girl, and she contradicts the administrator by saying that it pleases her.

Scenes 29 through 34 are grouped between the corridor transitions of scenes 28 and 35. In this group of scenes, the dominant element appears to be the discussion of social issues and attitudes, though the contexts of power, sexuality, and communication are also interwoven into the form and substance of the scenes. Once again, the teachers are made to look absurd. In scene 29, a group of teachers in the lunchroom discuss foreign aid. They agree that foreigners ought to be more grateful for American help. Wiseman makes one teacher look foolish by recording him as he drips food on the heel of his hand and licks it off.

In scene 30, the administrator we saw handing out discipline in scenes 6, 10, and 24 is teaching a class about labor-management relations. Why, he asks, were unions necessary? The correct answer, it turns out, is "lack of communication" and "lack of security," which of course is precisely the condition of the high school. After the scenes in which we have already seen this teacher, his comments on communication and insecurity have an ironic edge. And Wiseman plays another visual joke in scene 30. The scene opens with a shot of a chart on the wall at the back of the classroom. The chart represents the rise of man from ape to *Homo sapiens* (frame 74). *Homo sapiens* is on the right side of the frame. The camera then begins to pan to the left, from *Homo sapiens* to ape, and comes to rest (frame 75) on the teacher dispensing homilies about social studies. The effect has been to descend from homo sapiens to ape to teacher. From a bulletin board behind him, Leonid Brezhnev, Jackie Onassis, and Ho Chi Minh look over his shoulder.

In scene 31, the teacher who read the daily bulletin in scene 3 and who dribbled his food in scene 29, discusses poverty and race relations with his class. How many, he asks, would join a club in which a minority of members were black? The students glance around at each other and most raise their hands. How many would join if an equal number of blacks and whites were in the club? The students glance at each other again. Fewer hands go up. If blacks were in the majority? More glances. Fewer hands still. Then the teacher tells the students not to worry, that there is no right or wrong answer, and that he is just trying to determine attitudes. His statement seems disingenuous in the atmosphere of conformity revealed by the visual messages. As if to reinforce our sense that the teacher's questions about attitudes are not an open search for values but rather are transformed by the situation into an exercise in peer pressure, Wiseman cuts to scene 32, in which a music teacher (frame 76) leads a class through the scales. As the teacher stands at the blackboard pointing to one note after another, Wiseman cuts to extreme close-ups of disembodied mouths singing out in chorus the names of the notes (frames 77 and 78). The dominant tone of scene 32 has to do with regimentation, although in the context of the film as a whole, in which Wiseman has established mouths as having sexual relevance, it appears that the close-ups shown in frames 77 and 78 help to maintain the film's undertone of misdirected eroticism.

In scene 33, a teacher (frame 79) is discussing Northeast High School with a group of students. The students speak out against the moral and intellectual atmosphere of the school, and it appears that here at last is a sign of rebellion that runs counter to the rest of the film in which students have been badgered into passivity. But Wiseman dashes our hopes. Although the students make brave speeches, they are unable to get through to the teacher or each other. A black student is recognized by the teacher and begins to talk about the school, saying that "morally, socially, this school is a garbage can." But before he has a chance to finish, the teacher interrupts him and makes a speech of her own. Wiseman keeps the camera on the black student's face as the teacher's interruption continues (frames 80–82). He stops speaking, then looks on with surprise, and finally displays a cowed grin. A young woman looking on over his shoulder contemplates his reactions, and as she does so her hand moves from her chin to her mouth.

At another point in the scene, Wiseman shows what seems at first to be an exception to the atmosphere of stifled sexuality that he has constructed throughout the rest of the film. A student in dark glasses makes some disparaging remarks about the school. He has been sitting with his arm around a girl. The girl cuddles towards him (frame 83), and he kisses her on the forehead (frame 84). Is this to be taken as a healthy display of affection? In context, we think not. The student's wisecracking attitude about the school, his beads and dark glasses, are, it is true, signs of rebellion from the confines of the school, but the dark glasses, beads, and kiss appear in the context of the classroom discussion as a demonstration rather than as an authentic act of politics or human intimacy. The girl is part of his audience, and part of the costume that he displays to the rest of his audience. He is not, in this context, capable of authentic affection, but instead comes off as a smug pseudo-rebel playing it cool. If Wiseman's rhetoric has been successful up to this point, the audience will not simply condemn the student for his inauthenticity, however. If viewers have been persuaded that the school has abused its power, then the school must seem to blame for the poverty of his response. If the school is to blame, he is simply another one of its products, groping unsuccessfully for a way to become fully human in a political situation that robs him of that opportunity.

Scene 35 returns once more to the corridor as students crowd through it between classes. In the foreground, a policeman looks at his watch in apparent boredom (frame 85).

The film's undercurrent of concern about sexual repressiveness continues with scene 36, which opens with a shot from the rear of an auditorium, looking toward the stage. Amid cheers and music, a group of cheerleaders runs down the aisles and begins to dance on the stage (frame 86). When Wiseman moves in for a closer look (frame 87), we see that this is a group of boys dressed in girls' cheerleading outfits.

In scene 37, a man who seems perfectly cast as a stereotype of the male chauvinist gynecologist is warning an auditorium filled with boys about the dangers of sexual intercourse (frames 88 and 89). He stands in the classic posture of male dominance: arm akimbo, hand on hip, fingers pointing to his genitals. Wiseman cuts to a boy in his audience, who is apparently worried by the warnings of the doctor (frame 90). But the tone taken by the gynecologist is at odds with his message. At the same time that he warns the boys about the dangers of pregnancy, he brags about his access to female genitals. He talks about inserting his fingers into vaginas, and says, with a smirk on his face, "I happen to be a gynecologist and I get paid to do it." He holds up the fingers that have explored so many women (frame 91) and tells the boys to use birth control or to abstain.

The danger of sex continues as a theme in scene 38, where Wiseman shows excerpts from an animated film that explains the consequences of venereal disease (frames 92 and 93). An adult male narrator, the prototypical documentary voice of authority, warns the students that "a girl with gonorrhea can become a mother; but this creates another problem: when the baby is ready to be born there is danger that she may transmit the disease to the child when it passes out of her body." This brief scene is typical of Wiseman's working technique, because it is capable of signifying at so many levels. At the purely descriptive level, it is another case of instruction and is grouped in terms of manifest content with another scene of hygienic and perhaps slightly menacing description of sexuality. At the larger thematic level, it makes explicit the links among sexuality, authority, and autonomy. A viewer's sense of the significance of the scene may well end at either of these levels, and the film is a coherent whole even if one does not go beyond them—in this sense, further speculation is not forced upon the viewer. But it seems characteristic of Wiseman's method, and of the frame of mind into which he casts his viewers, that further speculative and metaphorical interpretations are encouraged at every turn. Each scene is a restatement and variation on the major themes of the film as a whole; the film and each of its parts show the institution as a microcosm of its society. The society gives birth to these students and transmits its diseases to them, so the gonorrhea scene becomes another way of saying what is said in different ways in all the other scenes of the film. What works in terms of the scene's discursive contribution to the film as a whole also makes sense at the sequential level: immediately following the warning about the transmission of gonorrhea, Wiseman cuts to frame 94, where he introduces a young man speaking with an older man. We have been prepared by the voice-over accompanying the animated film to consider how social diseases are transmitted from one generation to the next, so the situation in scene 39, in which a former student in military uniform visits with a high school physical education teacher, seems another example of the transmission process, but here raised to a higher metaphorical level: the subject of discussion in scene 38 is the transmission of gonorrhea to an infant; the subject of scene 39 is the mutilation of a former high school student in Vietnam. Hence the two scenes seem in many ways tightly connected to one another, despite the retrospective sense that scene 39 is the beginning of a new sequence of scenes grouped together by militarism. Wiseman encourages his audiences to probe his films for multiple patterns of coherence, at the same time that they are rejecting the static coherence of institutional rhetoric. In scene 38, he adds yet another layer of speculation by contrasting the animated sex-hygiene film to his own documentary, hence inviting the audience to compare the invigorating, anti-institutional rhetoric of his documentary to that of the stodgy, authoritative, instructional film being shown to the students.

The last five scenes of the film are tied together by their common emphasis on the theme of militarism, though even here there are hints about the way sexuality and body imagery mingle with the theme of violence. These five scenes seem to build towards Wiseman's vision of the product of the school: good soldiers. This is not to say that Wiseman reduces *High School* to an antimilitaristic tract. Rather, the scenes of militarism help to symbolize and summarize the alienation that grows out of the experience of the school as he depicts it.

The concluding section of the film begins with a pair of scenes that are related to each other by a typical Wiseman irony. In scene 39, a Vietnam veteran is standing at the edge of a playing field talking with a coach (frame 94). They are discussing the wounding of a former student, and for a moment it appears that the coach, who obviously feels sympathy for the wounded man, is hinting at a tone of regret about the war. Then Wiseman cuts to scene 40, where the same coach is refereeing a violent game between two massive teams who fight to move a huge ball back and forth in a gymnasium (frame 95), and it is evident that the coach is encouraging the students to learn the skills of battle.

In scene 41, three boy astronauts emerge from a simulated flight in a space capsule (frame 96). The military ambience of the scene is clear, but the military theme is synthesized with the issue of gender identity when the boys remove their space helmets. One of the boys who has been assisting from outside the capsule cries, "The beard! Look at the beard!" The astronauts have raised a stubble in their days of simulated flight. They are men.

There is another bit of byplay in the astronaut scene that demonstrates how to be a man. As the boys emerge from the capsule, one of the students on the sidelines, apparently asking for a pose so that he can take a picture, asks the teacher in charge of the group to put his arm around one of the astronauts. The teacher obviously hears the request, but chooses to ignore it, saying instead that he will help the astronaut remove his helmet. The request for a physical display of affection between the teacher and his student is emphasized by the way it is brushed off. Later in the scene, a woman gives one of the boys a motherly kiss.

In scene 42, a drum major (frame 97) prances onto a stage, then stands before the camera and pumps his baton, held vertically before his body, up and down in rhythm to the music. The militarism of the scene is parodied by the jerking motions of the boy's symbol of authority. Wiseman then cuts to an ambiguous close-up (frame 98), as a hand grasping a rifle butt moves back and forth in the frame, revealing on each swing a patch of uniform on the torso of the person with the rifle. Then Wiseman completes his joke by panning up to reveal that the rifle is in the hand of a pretty girl (frame 99), and our expectations about gender are once more reversed, as they have been in some earlier scenes.

In the final scene, Wiseman reveals what all the preceding scenes add up to. The school principal is standing behind a lectern reading a letter to a group of teachers in the school auditorium. The author of the letter is a young man about to be dropped behind enemy lines in Vietnam. In his letter, he tells how much the school has meant to him and says that he has bequeathed his military life insurance to a scholarship fund for the school. Of his attitude toward himself as a man and a soldier, he says, "I am only a body doing a job." The principal comments, "Now, when you get a letter like this, to me it means that we are very successful at Northeast High School. I think you will agree with me."

The final scene of *High School* completes Wiseman's design. It is important to observe that Wiseman chose to reserve the principal's reading of Bob Walters's letter until the final scene. Had the letter scene come at the beginning of the film, as the first scene, say, or the second, it would have served as a heavy-handed announcement that this film was going to show how the school made "good soldiers," that is, tractable adults. Had Wiseman tipped his hand in this way, the audience experience would have been very different. It would have been clear that Wiseman disapproved of the school and that the audience was expected to do the same. The body of the film would have served as proof for a more or less clearly stated proposition. By structuring the film as he has, Wiseman allows the audience to work its own way through the ambiguous discomforts of the school's oppressiveness and repressiveness. In this way, the film becomes an experience before it becomes evidence. When the letter scene is finally presented, the audience can gasp at the revelation that the school meant, all along, to produce "good soldiers." And the audience can clinch the job of persuasion it has been allowed to perform upon itself by congratulating itself that its theory about the school is confirmed by the principal's reading of the letter. The placement of the letter scene is the climactic stroke in Wiseman's rhetorical design.

The design is more complicated than it appears, because it has to achieve a delicate balance between obscurity and overstatement to convey its impressions. Wiseman's rhetorical structure can best be appreciated if we review his "theory" about Northeast High School and then describe how an audience can be expected to experience the presentation of that theory in *High School*.

Wiseman's "theory," of course, resists simple verbal expression. That is why it is expressed in a film rather than an essay. But at the risk of reductionism, the theory seems to run as follows: In Northeast High School, the teachers and administrators work to control the students. They control the students in the school, and they try to build a system of control that will last the students for a lifetime. Control is exercised by constantly placing students in a double bind, where the students receive inconsistent directions in a situation in which they must try to obey the directions, but in which they cannot call attention to or even conspicuously notice what is happening. Power is exercised in the high school through direct orders, the imposition of a routine, humiliating reprimands, absurdly manipulated language, mechanical teaching that reduces learning to a stultifying process of repetition, and, most hurtfully, through a constant confusion of thought and feeling about sex and gender. The students are unable to bring any of the school's tyrannies into a clear enough focus to combat them directly. The student response, for the most part, is to disconnect, to resort to daydreams, narcissism, and apathy.

That this statement of Wiseman's theory is approximately correct has been borne out, we hope, by the detailed examination of the film. But the viewer of the film does not have the same experience as a student in the high school, nor does he or she have the same experience of the film as a critic who takes it apart bit by bit on an editing table. A rhetorical examination of Wiseman's film would be seriously incomplete if it were to stop with a statement of what a critic is able to discover in the text. To stop here, to allege that a detailed examination, having revealed Wiseman's "theory," has thereby revealed the structure of his rhetoric, is to ignore the audience and to be guilty of overreading. Even if a critic can find a significant detail and can relate it to other details to argue that it is part of a pattern, one's understanding of a work of rhetoric is inadequate without some attention to what an audience would be likely to make of the detail and the pattern.

The success of *High School* as a rhetorical structure seems to depend upon the audience's apprehending the film at different levels of consciousness. At the conscious level, the audience understands that *High School* is about power, and it sees the students being oppressed, reprimanded, manipulated, humiliated, miseducated, and bored. But audiences typically are not consciously aware of the prevalence of sex and gender as elements of the film. Rather, the recurring images of courtship and the repressive warnings about the dangers of sexuality are mostly just beyond conscious awareness. Although they are out of conscious awareness, the sexual themes of the film magnify the audience's felt discomfort with the film they are experiencing, because for the audience, as for the students, the presence of sexuality in interpersonal and intrapersonal conduct is at the core of the sense of self but carefully blocked from conscious attention.

The presence of sexuality as an issue in *High School* seems to function as a way of deepening the audience's feelings about those parts of *High School* that they do allow themselves to notice: the parts that have to do with the exercise of power. It is the genius of the film that it enables viewers to reexperience the tensions of adolescence and to adopt sufficient distance from that experience to condemn the high school for its role in enforcing an institutional tyranny. But *High School* does not create so much distance from the experience that it makes the whole "theory" of repression immediately clear to viewers. It is the great strength and the great weakness of filmic persuasion that it can create an experience, and an attitude toward that experience, but that it would be likely to diminish the felt response to the experience and the attitude if it were to provide a clearly stated, linear explanation of its point of view. Wiseman helps us to feel the institutional claustrophobia and the sexual panic of these teenagers, giving us just enough distance from them to feel outraged on their behalf, and perhaps somewhat liberated from the remembered defeats of our own adolescent years. The power of the double bind is diminished when the victim can call attention to what is happening.

If Wiseman had been explicit about the suggested meanings of his treatment of sexuality, the power of his film as an appeal to shared experience would be dissipated. Suppose that in scene 4 (frames 12–18), a voice-over commentator told us that this teacher was employing courtship behaviors that were likely to be confusing to her students. Our immediate response would be, quite properly, suspicion of the claim, arguing that this particular teacher is shown out of context, that it is reasonable to explain her behavior simply as a way of making faces and gestures to retain the amused attention of her students, and that, in any case, she may have been mugging for the camera. However, Wiseman never tells us that these are courtship behaviors, and we are unlikely to notice them at a conscious level. Rather, they exist for us just out of conscious awareness, as they tend to do in face-to-face interaction, making us vaguely attentive to our sexuality and hers but never conscious of what is happening.

Similarly, if Wiseman had pointed out the courtship gestures of scene 8 between the French teacher and the two girls in his class (frames 26–29), we would object that there was a cut between these images and that we have no way to be sure that teacher and students were actually directing these gestures at each other, or that they were particularly significant. And so on with the other scenes in which attention to sexuality and gender identity hovers just at the edge of conscious awareness.

Some of the scenes having to do with sex, as we have argued, are likely to be almost totally disregarded by the audience, as in scene 15, when boys in cooking class are chopping nuts, or when, in the first shot of the film, Wiseman shows a street scene with garbage cans and a line of laundry on which there hangs a football jersey with the numeral 69 (frame 1). But if all the scenes about sexuality were as obscure, marginal, or symbolic as this, constituting a sort of private joke, our argument would be reduced to critical overreading and, even if convincing, would not be very interesting from a rhetorical point of view, since it would treat the text and the images simply as a challenge to the ingenuity of the critic, a sort of secret code planted in the work by an artist. Although Wiseman does crack some private jokes in *High School*, most of his sexual imagery has a rhetorical function, inviting the viewer to experience a tension that can occur only when the images are apprehended, but when part of the experience is kept out of conscious awareness.

The most explicit statements of sexual warning in the film are, of course, available to viewers at a conscious level. The lecturer of scene 19 and the gynecologist of scene 37 are stating directly what so many other scenes in the film display implicitly: sex is dangerous and is better left to adults, who seem to hold the secret of its powers or who, having attained sexual maturity, are seemingly beyond desiring it.

If our description of *High School*, of Wiseman's "theory," and of the audience's experience is convincing, then we can claim to have discovered something of the rhetorical structure of *High School*. What tentative, final assessment can be made of the film? An evaluation of Wiseman's *High School* must acknowledge the immense power of the film to evoke the experience of adolescence and to call into question the power exercised by high school. But Wiseman's rhetorical success is achieved at the expense of certain contradictions.

Wiseman takes advantage of the conventions of cinema verite to create a sense that we are observing social reality. The photographic surfaces of the film bespeak an atmosphere of naturally occurring behavior. There are no actors, no special lights, no enormous film crews. The feel of actuality is present as a condition of the recording of the images. The whole film feels open and observational. And yet the documentary texture of the film is contradicted by its dialectical structure. It is not simply that the filmmaker has selected these images from among the many hours he recorded. The film is not simply selected; it is carefully constructed within and between scenes to take advantage of the conventions of narrative and documentary film making to imply sequence, causation, and point of view. Wiseman employs the conventions of cinema verite to establish the evidentiary value of his images, to assure us that what we see is true to the material reality of Northeast High School. Then Wiseman draws upon the structural conventions of narrative and documentary film to relate the images so that they take on meanings they would not have if seen in isolation or at random, or perhaps even if studied ethnographically in the ongoing context in which they occurred for the participants. Are such combinations of generic conventions for the filmmaker's purposes objectionable?

Insofar as Wiseman leaves his viewers believing that they know the truth about a particular group of human beings who taught and studied at Northeast High School in 1968 he may be misleading. But insofar as he uses Northeast High School as a source of images out of which to fashion a film that evokes for his viewers the conflicts of their own adolescent years and thereby helps them to understand and transcend those conflicts, perhaps Wiseman is speaking a larger truth. This is not the place to debate with Wiseman the merits of American secondary education or the accuracy of his depiction of the school. But some brief comments on the matter are relevant to understanding *High School*. Wiseman's condemnation of the oppressiveness and repressiveness in Northeast High School is not simply a call for permissiveness or sexual freedom. All societies educate their offspring to cope with systems of contradictions, and Northeast High School is not to be blamed insofar as it presents to adolescents the necessity to face the tensions of social and sexual maturity. Insofar as Wiseman indicts high school, he seems to charge that the school perniciously invades the territory of the family, simultaneously abandoning its own calling to uphold intellectual standards and due process and that, rather than simply exercising the discipline necessary to get on with the job of educating, the school places the students into a double bind from which there is no escape except into the claustrophobic, dizzying haven of their own narcissistic passivity.

But *High School* speaks out for the importance of the individual through a filmic method that ridicules some individuals and fragments others. The teacher who reads "Casey at the Bat," the one who licks a bit of food from the heel of his hand, and the one who gives a lesson in how to walk gracefully down a hallway—all of these people are caught at moments when they look foolish. And at other times, Wiseman uses extreme close-ups of eyes or mouths to make a point in his description of a scene, at the expense of fragmenting the subject. Wiseman has fabricated a humanistic vision out of fragmentary bits and pieces of behavior and physiognomy. His humanism is compromised by his occasional willingness to sacrifice the full humanity of his subjects to make a point.

Wiseman does not, it seems to us, particularly encourage his viewers to experience the film as an indictment of a particular group of people, or of this particular school. Rather, he moves the action of interpretation, though based in microscopic observation of social behavior, to a higher level of abstraction. We usually do not learn the names of the students and teachers, and the structure of the film inclines the spectator to be more interested in what they are doing than who they are. Part of Wiseman's special gift is that he is able to evoke attention to the institution. The film is not simply an aggregation of micro-biographical vignettes; it is an inquiry into the repeated patterns of interaction that the members of this institution, both teachers and students, employ to constitute and maintain a human invention we call "high school." Still, the inquiry into the high school is not all abstraction: it is vividly embodied in the real people who are the subjects of this film, with incalculable effects for both subjects and viewers. As viewers, we must somehow deal with the tensions among our attitudes towards these people: we judge them, laugh at them, admire them, and feel a lingering embarrassment at peeping into their lives.

What of the subjects? Although Wiseman's fictional techniques invite us vicariously into a hypothetical consciousness that is attributed to these teachers and students—as if we were seeing into the minds of fictional characters—

our response to the film, if it is to have anything other than voyeuristic or aesthetic dimensions, must always include the knowledge that this is a real institution and that these are real people. Do they really act this way? Do they really feel this way? Does it matter?

In Wiseman's account, Philadelphia school officials were satisfied with the film until they began to learn that other viewers saw the film as critical of the school. Then they objected to it and threatened him with legal action. With rare exceptions, the film is not shown publicly in Philadelphia. In an interview with the editorial staff of *Film Library Quarterly*, Wiseman said that "generally students like the film, but teachers are mixed about it, and parents are often bewildered, if not furious."[14] In an interview with Alan Rosenthal, Wiseman concedes that the film is highly critical of the school and reveals that although he had no particular thesis in mind when he entered the school, his method was to seek out the conflict between ideology and practice in the places where power was exercised—a method that seems likely to discover such conflicts. In an interview with Alan Westin, Wiseman talks at some length about his criticism of the school, even at one point referring to "some of the formal ideologies that are being mocked in *High School*."[15] Answering a question about whether his films are ambiguous and generate differing responses, Wiseman says:

> I think all the films have a well-defined point of view. My point of view toward the material is reflected in the structure of the film—the relationship of the sequences to each other and the themes that are developed by this particular order. However, a person's reaction to the film in part depends on his values and experience. Since the reality is complex, contradictory, and ambiguous, people with different values or experience respond differently. I think that there should be enough room in the film for other people to find support for their views while understanding what mine are. Otherwise I'd be in the propaganda business.[16]

In the Rosenthal interview, Wiseman gives his account of the conflict with school officials that led to restrictions upon showings of the film in Philadelphia.[17] As Wiseman tells the story, the school principal, after the film had been finished and had begun to earn favorable reviews that were critical of the school, claimed a right to censor the film. Still fresh from the legal difficulties of *Titicut Follies*, Wiseman says, he accepted the advice of his lawyers to avoid showing the film in Philadelphia. The film has otherwise been shown without restrictions and was broadcast on WNET, New York's public television station.

In 1985, a student wrote to Northeast High School for their views on the film after an interval of almost twenty years. A teacher sent the following letter in reply. We offer it here, even though it may be mistaken in some of its historical details, as an indication of the way an institution recalls the experience of being represented by a Wiseman film, and of the way the institution loses both its own memories of the event and its access to the historical record, even as the film survives to be taken as a shared memory of a time and place.

Your letter regarding the film "High School U.S.A." did reach my principal, Francis Hoban, but as the administration of the school has undergone many changes in almost twenty years, there are only a few department heads who remember that era and who saw the film. As one of the few, I shall try to answer your questions.

1. Frederick Wiseman appeared at our school one day and asked to film our activities as that of a "typical high school." Dr. Mabel Haller, our principal at that time, referred him to the office of the Superintendent of Schools, Dr. Mark Shedd. Dr. Haller was subsequently told by the Superintendent's office to give full cooperation to Mr. Wiseman.
2. To my knowledge, no written statement of any kind was ever signed. People knew of Mr. Wiseman by reputation, but few had seen his previous work. Dr. Haller said that she had requested that she see the film before it was shown publicly, and I believe that she did when it was completely finished. I do not know of any document ever being signed by Mr. Wiseman and the School District.
3. I believe that the school officials felt that the publicity would be good for our educational system, so that they put few blocks in the way of Mr. Wiseman. Moreover, Dr. Shedd was an administrator who believed in free and open communication.
4. The student body was simply told that films would be made of the activities in the school. Our students always have been cooperative to visitors.
5. Mr. Wiseman and his aides filmed for six weeks, took tons of film. There was a slight delay in public showing because of the injunction, but the film began to be shown about four months after it was finished.
6. The film was never shown legally in Pennsylvania anywhere. However, a group of 5–6 of us went to Harvard University to see a showing of it. Our reactions were horror and resentment at the lies shown. I will explain this in more detail after I answer your questions.
7. See #3 above for places in the area where the film was shown. One of our former teachers, in the film, saw it in the San Francisco area.
8. Since I was in the school at the time of the filming, and later saw the film in the Boston area, I will share with you some memories:

Mr. Wiseman and his cameramen were everywhere in the school during the six-week period. They spent a half hour filming one of our teachers at the rexograph machine, but it never got into the film. They were friendly, perservering, and businesslike.

When I saw the film that they had edited, however, I had to say that it was *not* our school that they had filmed. Instead, they had written a scenario of a high school where conformity and dictatorship reign, then proceeded to weed out of thousands of feet of film only those things which would match *their* concept of a high school. In other words, they never looked at our school objectively at all.

Example #1: The film begins with a garbage truck and the back trash of the school.

The scene is meant to convey *their* idea of the worth of present education.

Example #2: A Spanish teacher is shown having the students repeat the word "existentialismo" a couple of times. The camera close-up is of her hand fiddling with a belt while she does so. *None* of the rest of a very interesting lesson of Spanish literature and philosophy is shown at all, and the impression given is that the teacher *just* has them repeat.

Example #3: An English teacher recites "Casey at the Bat," apparently interminably in the film, because the camera keeps returning to her. In reality, the recitation took a few moments, and then the class discussed the poem.

Example #4: A counselor who wears thick glasses is shown leaning toward a student. The glasses are so magnified by the camera lens that the counselor looks grotesque. This was a woman who gave sincere and constant help to the students.

I could go on and on with examples — a doctor who was shown with his finger pointed in an erotic position (I believe he sued them) when he had spent his own time helping to orient students in a lecture on sex education, for example.

At the end of the film showing at Harvard University, there was a discussion period. We from Northeast H.S. did not reveal ourselves until almost the end. Surprisingly, the reaction of many members of the audience was that they were glad to see that there was a school which set rules for its students. This reaction came not only from adults in the audience, but from students on a panel.

I do not, personally, disagree with the general philosophy of Mr. Wiseman's films. We *do* have too much conformity, setting of rules, and dictatorship in schools. However, . . .[18]

Northeast High School is a big-city, comprehensive high school of about 3,000 students. Our students come from many economic and social classes. A large percentage come from one-parent households, usually a mother who is working. Presently 40% of our students are of minority races. There is little background of family stability or training. The one unifying factor in the school is the feeling that education can bring success and happiness, if only by providing material things. In many cases, the school has been the only place where the student has learned that he must have self-discipline to succeed, that he must learn to *bend* in a group situation. Self-discipline and the art of compromise were not in fashion twenty years ago, but as I look back on 24 years at Northeast High and 36 years in a big-city school system, I feel that these qualities are just as important as individualism and self-interest.

I hope this letter has not come too late for your use.

The letter is signed by "(Miss) Sylvia Schenfeld, Department Head, Foreign Languages."

The paradoxes and anomalies of Wiseman's rhetorical method are flaws in *High School,* but they are flaws that share their existence with a comic vision that goes beyond the lampooning of Northeast High School to make an important statement about American social experience. Perhaps the best response to *High School* is to be charitable to Northeast High School and at the same time bitterly alert to the uses of power and repression revealed by the film. If we can do this, perhaps we can at the same time be alert to the potential deceptiveness of Wiseman's rhetoric and still celebrate his brilliant achievement. It is too much to ask that Wiseman resolve all the social and aesthetic paradoxes he has uncovered. We can, without forfeiting the right to continue the debate about Northeast High School, *High School*, and "high school," acknowledge Wiseman for creating a rhetorical masterpiece.

Chapter 4

Narrative without Story
Basic Training

Liz Ellsworth describes the next development in Wiseman's evolution as an independent producer: "*Law and Order* (1969), *Hospital* (1970), and *Basic Training* (1971) were funded in varying proportions by PBS, WNET Channel 13 in New York, and income from rentals. Wiseman says he began distributing his own films after deciding there was little risk involved, because distributors made money from his films and paid none to him. After *Basic Training*, Wiseman contracted with WNET to do one documentary each year for five years. The contract has been renewed once."[1]

Law and Order, filmed in the Kansas City Police Department, extends Wiseman's interest in forms of institutional control, but introduces a strong element of doubt, frustration, and impotence. Wiseman has said that he went to Kansas City looking for "the pigs," but that police brutality in the film turned out to be "part of a more generally shared violence and not something isolated and unique."[2] Clearly Wiseman's description of his own method of work was beginning to articulate more explicitly what was latent and mixed in the earlier films, and now he was self-consciously shifting from a stance that emphasized social reform of abusive institutions to one that emphasized empirical complexity, increasing neutrality, ambiguity, and a deliberate view of himself as learning from the experience of filming rather than using film to illustrate preconceived theoretical or political positions. Wiseman's view of his relations with his material was accompanied by a vision of his relations with his audience. In interviews and speeches, Wiseman began to talk more and more of the ways in which he tried to induce his audiences to work out the meanings of the films for themselves and said that for him to suggest solutions for the problems described in his films would be condescending. He told Alan Westin, "It's not my wish to impose solutions: that would be presumptuous."[3]

Hospital (1970), filmed at New York City's Metropolitan Hospital, is one of Wiseman's most widely admired films, gloomy and comic. It was also the occasion of one of the finest pieces of critical writing on Wiseman's films.

First published in 1978, Bill Nichols's "Frederick Wiseman's Documentaries: Theory and Structure" revolves around a close reading of a "segment" from *Hospital* which Nichols describes as dealing with "hospital/social-deviant interactions."[4] Nichols's scrupulously detailed reading explores how Wiseman constructs an apparent spatial and temporal continuity from shots and sound-tracks that abridge extrafilmic reality. "The textual system," he writes, "is metaphoric (poetic) more than metonymic (narrative or expository), and sup-plemental or associative more than strictly additive." As for the politics of Wiseman's films, Nichols comments:

> Wiseman does not seem to have developed [his filmic techniques] for overtly formal or political ends. Politically, Wiseman's choice of an "ensemble of social relations" is extremely narrow and fails to examine the larger ensemble circum-scribing the boundary between institutions and the public or the characteristics of class struggle found at that boundary itself. Nonetheless, the structure of his films carries a set of theoretical and ideological implications with it. Among them, it seems to me, is the political challenge to gauge the significance of his focusing on constraints more than on linear causality and to understand how this focus is related to historical materialism, especially to the constraints of ideology on social role-playing.[5]

Of his own method of semiotic analysis of Wiseman's films, Nichols comments that the method is better at identifying the formal patterns in the films than it is at understanding how viewers might decode such structures. In a semiotic study, Nichols says, "stress falls on the pattern of organization distinctive to the text as a whole and its effect, but lacks explanatory power to account for the effect of transparency, those short-circuits that mis-take sign for referent and mis-recognize the nature of the whole. To account for this level as well and, even more, the interaction of different levels, will require forms of analysis capable of founding themselves upon the untenable terrain of contra-diction and paradox, terrain for which we have little more than small-scale aerial survey maps at present."[6]

Nichols's comment here is perhaps too modest, for his essay is full of close analysis and of intriguing hints about how viewers make sense of Wiseman's films. Nevertheless, we agree that purely formal, semiotic analysis, for all that it is capable of showing, falls short of providing a full view of the films and the way they invite spectators to respond. That task, we think, requires the rhetorical eclecticism we are attempting to work out in these pages, drawing upon the rich heritage that stems from the rhetorical tradition, with its interests in art and politics, form and effect, invention and reception, text and context, imagination and concrete reality, in the tension between public discourse and private desires, and the inescapably juxtaposed appeals to belief and action on the one hand and to the pleasures of aesthetic engagement on the other. We have tried to suggest in the chapter on *Titicut Follies* how the realities of the institution observed and the forces that constrain the production and reception of documentary contribute to the way the film looks and the way it is seen. These we have grouped under the logic of the term *dilemmas*, suggesting both the conflicting groups and competing values that impinge on the film and the oxymoronic terms that govern the debate: informed consent, reality fiction, restricted exhibition. In our analysis of *High School*, we have tried to show how paradox functions through the double bind to structure observations of the world of the school and to constrain the interpretive actions of the film's viewers. In this chapter, we offer a close reading of *Basic Training*, with a special view towards exploring how aesthetic and rhetorical structures work, in Nichols's words, to undertake the burdens of "realist narratives and documentaries" that "risk . . . a purely imaginary relationship" of spectator to text.[7]

Basic Training is an apparently simple film that resists critical simplifications. Wiseman draws upon our skills and habits as film viewers to make us think we are watching something familiar, then stretches our perceptions and broadens our curiosities. And somehow Wiseman develops a structure and style that imply his own point of view but still allow us to believe that our puzzlements, surprises, and revelations are our own.

This sense of ourselves as active participants in social observation provides a large part of our pleasure in Wiseman's films. Critics who enjoy Wiseman often write about him as if they were claiming a friend: we love to discover an artistic sensibility that tells us something we know but have not heard this way before. We enjoy the Wiseman we discover in these films—the "implied author," in Wayne Booth's phrase.[8] But we also enjoy ourselves in Wiseman's films—the character whom Wolfgang Iser, following Booth, calls the "implied reader" and for whom Edwin Black uses the term *second persona*.[9] Indeed, in the body of journalistic and academic criticism of Wiseman's films, the dominant impression is that once Wiseman has been honored as a hero of documentary intelligence, the critic gets on with ignoring Wiseman, preferring instead to treat the characters and actions represented in the films as if they were unmediated reality, and as if the critic's attitudes were based on that reality, rather than upon Wiseman's discourse. In short, Wiseman makes us feel clever, even as he makes us feel guilty—both of which may be taken as pleasures, if the guilt we feel is experienced aesthetically, as a catharsis rather than as a spur to reflection and responsibility.

In an interview, Wiseman once described the way in which his films were, for him and his audiences, a direct form of social inquiry. "You start off with a little bromide or stereotype about how prison guards are supposed to behave or what cops are really like. You find that they don't match up to that image, that they're a lot more complicated. And the point of each film is to make that discovery. Before the film the tendency is to simplify. The discovery is that the actuality is much more complicated and interesting. The effort in editing is to have the completed film reflect that discovery."[10] Audiences with whom we have watched Wiseman's films seem to take genuine pleasure in the bromides that form the films' starting points: the idealistic promises of the institutions and Wiseman's conflicting revelation that the institutions do not live up to their promises, that they engage in a variety of practices to manipulate and coerce their clients in ways convenient to themselves. The antibureaucratic stance that audiences so quickly respond to is, as Wiseman says, a bromide. Audience pleasure in Wiseman's antibureaucratic stance may be a variation of what Aristotle says about the orator's use of maxims: "People are delighted when [the orator] succeeds in expressing as a general truth the opinions they entertain about special cases. . . . Another advantage, and a greater, is that [the maxim] invests a speech with moral character. . . . Now maxims always produce the moral effect, because the speaker in uttering them makes a general declaration of ethical principles; . . . so that, if the maxims are sound, they give us the impression of a sound moral character in him who speaks."[11]

But Wiseman's films do not develop as simple amplifications of antibureaucratism: rather than using the bromide as a proposition for which his films then become merely the evidence, Wiseman treats antibureaucratism as a truth needing qualification, as a starting point from which to introduce increasingly complex speculations about everyday institutional life and our attitudes and strategies for dealing with it. The matter is complicated still further by the obvious fact that Wiseman's films have achieved considerable success in the institutional bureaucracy of public television. We advance this reminder not simply in an attempt to maintain the historical record, and certainly not to accuse Wiseman of hypocrisy or inconsistency, but rather as a way of pointing to the complicated position in which audiences are placed as they interpret these films: what does it mean to see and appreciate Wiseman's antibureaucratism as a television viewer who has no hope whatever of addressing the public television audience and for whom Wiseman's antibureaucratism must therefore be read, contextually, as part of the "reality fiction?" Wiseman's viewers are invited to identify with his antibureaucratic attitudes, and clearly do so with great pleasure; and yet in doing so, they must, even as they identify with Wiseman, actively not notice that he relates to the bureaucracy very differently than they do, or they would not be watching the film. The problem seems to be part of what Burke has called "the bureaucratization of the imaginative," which imposes form upon inspiration in order to communicate it, but at the risk of mystifying its own operations.[12]

In what follows, we shall try to reconstruct the interpretive actions that spectators are invited to create in response to *Basic Training*. We cannot, admittedly, offer such a reconstruction with any certainty that our own interpretation is authoritative. Indeed, although we will offer an interpretation, part of our claim is that audiences respond in various and often unpredictable ways and that they are responsible for their own interpretations. But the role of the critic, in part, is to make interpretation arguable, engaging in the sort of postfilmic discourse that accepts the film's invitation to become a community of interpreters, not necessarily with a single interpretation but certainly with an impulse to debate the meaning and the merit of the vision offered by the filmmaker. In seeking to make sense of Fred Wiseman's documentaries, we admittedly can never establish beyond doubt—nor should we perhaps attempt to discover—what the films mean for or about the filmmaker, or what they do or should mean for his audiences. And yet, in the spirit of the American anarchist Paul Goodman, we will offer an argued interpretation in the conviction that "the need to make sense *is* the craving for freedom."[13]

Basic Training shares with Wiseman's earlier documentaries a formal, perhaps even generic, similarity. Like the earlier films, *Basic Training* is about an institution and deals with fundamental issues of social control and human autonomy. All the films are episodic, and though some characters recur, there is no single line of narrative development featuring a single character or group of characters. There is no "narration" as that term is used in film criticism to designate voice-over explanations of what we are seeing on the screen. But Wiseman's films, although they display generic similarities, show, when looked at individually, considerable variations on familiar techniques. And although the films usually seem at least dubious about the institutions they observe, the features of the institutions and the films' attitudes towards them vary widely. *Basic Training* is more nearly narrative than the earlier four films and is much less confident in its analysis of the ills of the institution it observes. *Titicut Follies* displays a reformist zeal in its depictions of conditions at Bridgewater. *High School*, though not reformist, seems to offer a strongly critical analysis of the institutional double binds used to achieve social control. *Law and Order* and *Hospital* begin to provide much more reflection about their own processes and to introduce more doubts about the predispositions of filmmaker and viewer who are looking for easy ways to condemn institutions. In *Basic Training*, the viewer seems to be deliberately presented with a foiled narrative and an argument that constantly doubles back upon itself.

Wiseman both uses and subverts our ordinary expectations of film form to influence our perception of his films. He both teaches us how to watch his films and confounds our willingness to reduce them to conventional formulas. Critics often adopt the convenience of reducing Wiseman's films to the form they subvert, or reach for analogies that distort Wiseman's actual structures. For example, Liz Ellsworth's useful reference work on Wiseman is at its best when she provides a complete shot list of a film. In cases where she does not, she often condenses the form to a simplicity that, while logical enough, belies the probable experience of the film for a viewer. And Nichols, perhaps Wiseman's most perceptive critic, sweeps aside too many complexities with his characterizations of the films as "mosaics," "inkblots," and as narrative within episodes and experimental as overall structures.[14]

Nichols's "mosaics" and "inkblots" are mutually contradictory, and neither accounts for the form or the experience of the films, it seems to us. *Mosaic* suggests a form that is both spatial and determined: that is, it exists in space, whereas a film exists in time. Moreover, a mosaic is an integrated image in which no single stone bears any meaning whatsoever but which, taken as a whole, any two competent viewers will regard as virtually identical from a semantic, iconic perspective. On the other hand, an *inkblot* is undetermined, a mere stimulus to the projection of the underlying concerns of the interpreter. Nevertheless, Nichols's argument is too useful and suggestive to be dismissed as jargon, and we will therefore return to it again in the chapters that follow. And Nichols is right to invoke metaphors for Wiseman's films that draw attention to strategies of perception enacted by viewers who invent what they see by assembling bits and pieces into a coherent interpretation and by processing what they see through their own predispositions.

The difficulties of structure are not resolved by attempting to reduce *Basic Training* to a narrative or descriptive sentence or two. Ellsworth says that Wiseman "follows recruits through training from their arrival as civilians to their graduation as soldiers."[15] But this suggests a clearer narrative than the film provides. The film does begin with arrival and end with a graduation ceremony, but we do not follow a clearly identified few recruits through their basic training—although several faces show up here and there in the film. It seems essential to our experience of the film that we are not able to follow clearly the progress of particular recruits at all points in the film. If we take the film to be a narrative, we must (as spectators often do) restructure what is before us on the screen, or we must dismiss it as incompetent and incoherent. But in our drive to apprehend the film as a complete form, as coherent and meaningful, we can also, instead of seeing it as a failed narrative, see it as composed of episodes, encounters, and moments that repeat, vary, and extend themselves on thematic as well as narrative planes.

Ellsworth implicitly recognizes the difficulty of reducing the film to narrative form. Her chapter on *Basic Training*, instead of providing the shot-by-shot transcript of some of her other chapters, and presumably in the interest of economy, proposes a ten-part synopsis (fig. 4-1).[16] The logic of Ellsworth's ten parts appears to have at least as much to do with thematic categories as with narrative sequence. Wiseman's own transcript, as prepared from the finished film, divides the film into eighty-one "scenes" (fig. 4-2).[17]

Basic Training seems to require of us, as spectators, an interpretive action that is both narrative and discursive, both fictional and factual. The film would not make sense without our being able to tie together its narrative connections, but narrative alone does not make sense of the film.[18] *Basic Training* begins with a group of recruits disembarking from buses at what is obviously an army base. We do not learn until later, in context, that this is the U. S. Army Training Center at Fort Knox, Kentucky. We are introduced to themes before persons, repetitive processes before narrative continuities.

The opening scenes at first appear to be the standard set of "you're in the army now" jokes of countless documentary and fiction films. Recruits troop

Figure 4-1

Basic Training:

Ellsworth Synopsis

Part 1: Processing
  Shots 1–46 (6:38) [corresponds to scenes 1–15 in the Zipporah transcript].
Part 2: Physical and Mental Fitness.
  Shots 47–84 (7:19) [scenes 16–24].
Part 3: Skills for War
  Shots 85–131 (9:53) [scenes 25–37].
Part 4: Misfits
  Shots 132–148 (8:16) [scenes 38–43]
Part 5: Men behind the Uniforms
  Shots 149–171 (8:44) [scenes 44–55]
Part 6: Conformity
  Shots 172–191 (13:37) [scenes 56–61]
Part 7: Baptism
  Shots 192–201 (3:51) [scenes 62–65]
Part 8: Indoctrination
  Shots 202–221 (6:26) [scenes 66–69]
Part 9: Practice for Vietnam
  Shots 222–283 (11:50) [scenes 70–79]
Part 10: Confirmation
  Shots 284–313 (5:48) [scenes 80–81]

off a bus in their motley civilian clothes and are immediately processed into a categorical anonymity. In the first words on the sound track, a lieutenant leads the recruits through a barracks, assigning bunks: "Number 33, the top bunk. Number 34, the bottom bunk." In the next scene, a tailor measures a recruit and calls out: "Fourteen . . . thirty . . . thirty-five . . . twenty-nine."

Then long hair falls before electric clippers. These are obligatory scenes: we know how to smile to ourselves about the standardization of humanity implied by the reduction of these young men to hairless aggregations of numbered parts. And these scenes begin to set up the terms of our relation to the material: we are not following particular men from one scene to the next and so we pay attention not to the continuity of characters but to the immediacy of what is before us and to its place in a more abstract process.

The invitation to consider process is implied by the camera work and cutting: we have to work to find its rules and are, throughout the film, never quite sure when a scene will end, nor what sort of scene might follow. And yet this film has a considerable narrative energy. We are carried forward from one scene to another in a pattern that seems to follow a temporal progression. But the temporal progression, insofar as we are likely to read it into the pattern of the film, is not that of conventional fiction, in which what happens in one scene motivates what comes in the next. Rather, we seem to follow the pattern of training, a cycle presumably imposed from outside the

---

Figure 4–2

Basic Training
Scenes as listed in Frederick Wiseman's Transcript,
Zipporah Films (1971)

Scene 1: Reception Center; trainees get off bus.
Scene 2: Reception Center; barracks.
Scene 3: Reception Center; clothes fitting.
Scene 4: Haircuts.
Scene 5: ID photos.
Scene 6: ID card machine.
Scene 7: Personnel interview.
Scene 8: Smallpox vaccination.
Scene 9: Trainees running with uniforms.
Scene 10: Reception Center; sewing tags on uniforms.
Scene 11: Class picture.
Scene 12: Sergeant at Reception Center.
Scene 13: Auditorium; orientation by commanding general.
Scene 14: Running to company.
Scene 15: Orientation.
Scene 16: Wake-up.
Scene 17: Latrine; shaving.
Scene 18: Dental colonel; outside.
Scene 19: Dental television demonstration.
Scene 20: Exercise.
Scene 21: Crawling.
Scene 22: Bar hanging.
Scene 23: Rifle rack.
Scene 24: Marching.
Scene 25: Range demonstration.
Scene 26: Picking up ammo.
Scene 27: Rifle firing.
Scene 28: Receiving brass and ammunition.
Scene 29: Marching.
Scene 30: Trainee receiving marching instructions.
Scene 31: Trainee marching with platoon.
Scene 32: Photographer.
Scene 33: Marching.
Scene 34: Bayonet demonstration.
Scene 35: Trainees in field with bayonets.
Scene 36: Trainees respond to bayonet instructor's commands.
Scene 37: Pugil demonstration.
[Scene 38: Marching. This scene is not listed in the Zipporah transcript, but a
    numeral is skipped to account for it.]
Scene 39: Private and Lieutenant.

Figure 4–2 *(Continued)*

Scene 40: Private and First Sergeant.
Scene 41: First Sergeant and another trainee.
Scene 42: First Sergeant on telephone.
Scene 43: Private and chaplain.
Scene 44: Pt run.
Scene 45: Groin-hitting practice.
Scene 46: Boxing.
Scene 47: Crawling.
Scene 48: Eating, washing, and resting.
Scene 49: Drill Sergeant and trainee.
Scene 50: Trainee on hill.
Scene 51: Trainee under tree.
Scene 52: Men sleeping.
Scene 53: Trainee describing Louisville recreational trip.
Scene 54: Karma.

[End of Reel One]

Scene 55: Marching.
Scene 56: Trainee and family.
Scene 57: Lieutenant and Private.
Scene 58: Private and Sergeant.
Scene 59: Lieutenant's promotion.
Scene 60: Sergeant addressing trainees.
Scene 61: Marching.
Scene 62: Outside gas chamber.
Scene 63: Inside gas chamber.
Scene 64: Outside gas chamber.
Scene 65: Marching.
Scene 66: Auditorium.
Scene 67: Marching.
Scene 68: Chapel.
Scene 69: Marching.
Scene 70: Sergeant addressing trainees about Claymore mines.
Scene 71: Hand-to-hand combat practice.
Scene 72: Man-to-man demonstration.
Scene 73: Marching.
Scene 74: Make-up.
Scene 75: Day crawl.
Scene 76: Night crawl.
Scene 77: Infiltration course.
Scene 78: Marching through jungle.
Scene 79: V. C. village.
Scene 80: Graduation.
Scene 81: Marching, band music.

events we are witnessing, its major acts part of a logic beyond the control of the participants.

The slightly comic tone of the first scenes is supported by the forward rush of observations. After the haircut comes a moment before a camera for an identification picture, a head-on mug shot, followed by a close-up of a hand being fingerprinted, and then we see a machine producing an endless strip of plastic-laminated ID cards. Another photo session occurs a few moments later. This second photo session contrasts with the first, and, we may notice, with Wiseman's photography.[19] The second photo session (scene 11) is an official portrait, in uniform, the sort that will lead to a picture of Private Somebody in the hometown paper. The recruit is encouraged to smile: "Say pooh, pooh." Then, to a black soldier, "John, we need a big smile now. Say something nice about George Wallace, huh?" The army's needs in these two photographs are obviously different: one is a functional identification device, the other a part of ongoing public relations. The contrast between them so early in the film serves to alert us both to the potential for inconsistency in the army's discourse and to that other visual discourse—Wiseman's—which is neither merely descriptive (like the ID photograph), nor an artificially stimulated, smiling, public-relations treatment of the institution. The two photographic sessions, then, both distance Wiseman's film from the sorts of photographic practices they embody, and they also distance Wiseman's film from the institution itself.

The record of the camera's and the editor's visual attention is going to be an important part of our experience of *Basic Training*, but as in other Wiseman films the language of the film's subjects is equally important, as the next three scenes remind us. In scenes 12–15, the recruits are addressed by a sergeant, a general, and a first lieutenant. The language—and its staging by both Wiseman and the army—conveys a powerful, if ambiguous, sense of hierarchy and multiple realities. The sergeant leads the men through a question-and-answer series in which the text seems less important than its form.

SERGEANT: The way you will address me is either yes, [here we cut from a shot of the assembled men to a close-up of the sergeant] or no, sergeant. Is that clear? [The sergeant, filmed from almost straight on in a close-up, sings his instructions and questions in a high-pitched, bored monotone, the vowels extended—a voice to carry to a large group outdoors].
SOLDIERS: Yes, sergeant [raggedly].
SERGEANT: Let's try that again, all together.
SOLDIERS: Yes, sergeant. [The chorus is now more nearly in unison.]
SERGEANT: Does everyone here have all of his clothing in his duffle bag?
SOLDIERS: Yes, sergeant.
SERGEANT: Does everyone here have an ID card and dog tags in his possession?
SOLDIERS: Yes, sergeant.

SERGEANT: Do you now have everything in your possession you had while in the
    reception station?
SOLDIERS: Yes, sergeant.
SERGEANT: Are you sure?
SOLDIERS: Yes, sergeant.

Although the questions appear directly functional, making sure that the
procedures have not slipped up, one feels the strong sense of how difficult it
would be to answer this series of questions with anything but "Yes, sergeant."
The lesson of this interaction, at least for us as spectators, seems to have
more to do with the mass, mechanical responses of the men than with the
double-checking that seems evident at the surface of the text. It is simply not
possible to imagine a trainee replying to the sergeant's "Are you sure?" with
a "Well, let me take another look in my duffle bag just to make sure." It is
almost equally impossible to imagine a recruit daring to say, "No, sergeant,"
when the answer to the question is so obviously "Yes, sergeant." We have
been prepared for this reading of the scene by the previous scenes of mechanical processing. This scene in turn prepares us to attend to the relational
dimensions of the talk that is to follow, for the way it feels to fit into the
pattern of interactions which the army is instructing these men to follow.
Wiseman's technique seems to enable us to adopt a multidimensional perspective that, in this scene, encourages us to imagine the experience of these
trainees, who are hustled without much explanation from one procedure to
another; to imagine (probably more if we are male than female viewers) what
it might be like for us to experience this process; and also to stand apart
from the process, and to view it with detachment and irony, as something
happening to other people, to people who are both real and characters in a
story. And for some viewers, especially at the time of the film's release, an
immediate political context emerged: these men were in training as American
soldiers during a controversial war. We think it is fundamental to Wiseman's
method of building meanings, and of shaping our experience as viewers, that
he creates ambiguities and tensions among the opinions and desires and
points of view that we bring to and experience in *Basic Training*.[20]

In the very next scene, we witness an orientation session addressed by
the commanding general.

	Midshot of a uniformed, bald man, in a large interior space. His arms are raised, and he looks away from the camera to his right. He gestures with his arms, and we hear the first notes of a fanfare.
A four-note fanfare, played on a trumpet.	
	At the fanfare, a large number of men who have been seated in the

background rise to their feet and stand at attention.

The fanfare immediately becomes a march, the army song, "When the Caissons Go Rolling Along."

The main body of men are standing on the flat floor of the large gymnasiumlike space; other men stand on risers on camera left; there is an aisle at center screen, and the camera takes a step to its right to look down the aisle to gain a better view of what the conductor saw when he looked in that direction.

The march continues.

A small group of men marches quickly up the aisle towards the camera, which follows them by panning to the right as they pass it on camera right. The men rapidly walk up a short flight of steps to a stage, which is next to the camera position at stage left.

The march continues.

Once the men have mounted the stage, the camera pans back, very rapidly, to its left, to a close shot of the conductor, who is watching the stage. He gestures again, and the tune changes.

Another march.

We remain on the conductor for several seconds, then the camera pans to its left and slightly downwards to reveal the first rows of the military band. Two saxophonists in army fatigues are seated in the front row; the black saxophonist on camera left, draped over his instrument, peers up at the conductor.

The camera pans back to the right, and, when it finds the conductor, pans up slightly to frame his upper body as he continues to conduct the march, which he now brings to a conclusion.

Cut

GENERAL: Good morning, gentlemen. [He speaks in a conversational tone, his voice amplified by the microphone.]

A midshot of a middle-aged man in fatigues, standing at a lectern, the legend on which identifies him as the commanding general. A microphone is mounted on the lectern. The camera is now located slightly stage right, and slightly below the general's eye level.

There is a pause, during which the general looks patiently down at the lectern.

TRAINEES: Good morning, sir [from the off-camera voices of the trainees].

GENERAL: There you go. I want to welcome you this morning to Fort Knox; and the U. S. Army Training Center Armor. I do that in an official sense, on behalf of the Commanding General of the Armor Center, and, in an official sense also, because your country needs your services. I also extend

Cut to a shot from the front of the auditorium that takes in the symmetrical rows of hundreds of faces.

to you a welcome on a person to person basis, so to speak.

The general continues his brief orientation speech, as we see close-ups of trainees listening. Then the march music begins again, and Wiseman's camera follows the general and his staff as they stride quickly down the aisle toward the back of the hall.

This is a complicated scene, both as read and as simply experienced, below the level of conscious "translation." The general's tone of voice and his bearing are dignified and graceful. But the scene is framed in such a way that we place almost equal emphasis on the staging of the orientation as on its "content": the scene begins and ends with music that is more than background; it is part of the foreground of the scene and calls our attention to the general's speech as a performance buoyed up by background music. The long first shot of the scene, opening with the conductor, turning to watch the ascent of the stage, then turning back to the players and the conductor again, further emphasizes this theme of performance. And it does something more. The turning back of the camera, to look directly at the band members we had seen before, as it were, only out of the corner of our eye, introduces a tone of wandering attention, a refusal to attend only to the official aspect of the orientation. Wiseman's camera looks behind the curtain to find the source of the wizard's thunder and finds, in this case, the curious figure of a black saxophonist, who seems oddly out of place here, as if he belonged, instead, in a jazz band. This momentary gaze, which amounts almost to a double take, glancing back as it does to take in what was only tangentially visible earlier in the shot, makes unmistakable a stylistic, tonal quality that is slightly odd. This oddness is comic, but it is also perceptually disturbing, since it seems to present us with a world in which things do not fit neatly together. The oddness of this double-take shot, which evolves into a pervasive element of the film as a whole, does much to account for the film's lingering, just-out-of-consciousness fascination. Wiseman has at times commented that he is interested in discovering the surreality of everyday life. It may be that the film's oddness is also partly explained by what the Russian formalists have called "defamiliarization," and what Burke calls "perspective by incongruity." Both of these notions describe the way artists may, largely by formal and stylistic means, alter our habitual way of apprehending "reality" and thereby make it newly visible.[21] Wiseman's stylistic oddness here assumes not only an aesthetic dimension, in which we may inhabit the world of the film as an artistic experience in its own right, but a political one, since the film's viewpoint contrasts with that officially presented by the army. It is not that Wiseman is arguing against the army, but that he does not adopt its style of perception, does not cooperate with its theatricality.

Wiseman's style in the general's orientation scene also makes unmistakable another, more familiar, stylistic dimension of the film—irony. The cut to the mass of listening soldiers just as the general is about to offer them his "personal" welcome is clearly ironic, an obvious joke and an assertion of style, and hence establishes our relation to whatever follows in this film as potentially ironic. The timing of the cut is an implicit claim about the film-maker's relation to his material, over which he asserts an omniscience of point of view more characteristic of Hollywood narrative than of single-camera documentary: note that the cut to the general's audience occurs *before* the general says "on a person to person basis." This cut ahead of the joke is in a class, as narrative technique, with opening a scene with a shot of a telephone, which then rings: the narrator knows that the phone is going to ring, and the technique tells us we are in the hands of an omniscient narrator. Consider the difference in implied point of view if the scene were presented instead as a real-time, single-camera documentary might film it: here, the camera would remain on the general until he said "person to person" and then would pan right to reveal the anything-but-personal mass of men. Even such an alternate example as this, of course, would be an assertion of the cameraman's rhetorical intentions, a reminder to us that the camera is being operated with an active and ironic intention. In both cases, the maneuver would be ironic, but one asserts a narrative consciousness that is aware of what is going to happen next, and the other asserts the authenticity gained by seeming to claim that it is merely following the action.

The rhetorical inducements offered by the general's orientation scene are exceedingly complex. Because the scene occurs early in the film, it is still part of our orientation on how to watch the film. What are we to make of it? In some ways, the effects of the double-take pan and the ironic cutting are parallel in that they undermine the official rhetoric of the army. But in other ways, they place us as spectators in a curious position. The film seems to assert both Wiseman's control over our perceptions and the unreliability of those perceptions—to insinuate, even more disturbingly, Wiseman's control over the camera and the cutting, and his refusal to make clear to us just how we are to read the film. He causes us, here, to doubt both the army's version and our own perceptions, but he has not yet made it clear whether he is going to present us with a coherent alternative perspective, particularly a perspective that addresses the politics of basic training or the larger politics of Vietnam. It is too early in the film for us to know whether the author is asserting control over our perceptions with a promise of some resolution or whether he will ask us to settle for our doubts. All of these adjustments that we must make as the audience, trying to discover what is happening in basic training and trying to negotiate the terms of our relation to Wiseman's rhetoric, occur much more rapidly than they can be stated here. Does that mean we are engaged in a laborious overreading? Perhaps. But many of the adjustments we make in daily human interaction occur as rapidly and as ambiguously. A face-to-face conversation proceeds at several simultaneous planes of meaning in multiple sign systems, both verbal and nonverbal, both intentional and out-of-awareness. In such conversations, we continually respond to signs that we could not testify to having been aware of. There is no reason to suppose that the structures of film, and of our interaction with it, are less complex, nor that audience members can or should be able to make a simultaneous "translation" of all filmic meaning into explicit, verbal terms.

After the general's orientation, we cut to the trainees running, and then to another interior. What was implicit in the "yes, sergeant/no, sergeant" of scene 12 and the irony of the general's orientation now seems to be translated for the trainees directly. A young officer standing at a lectern, speaking with the patient and slightly scolding realism of one who has been through all of this before, says:

> I'm Lieutenant Hoffman, your company commander. The best way to go through basic training is to do what you're told, as you're told, and there'll be no problems. When you start trying to fight the system, that's when you get into trouble. So if you go along with the system, it's fine. When you buck it, you come into the problems. I know some people come in and they're rebellious. They didn't want to come in the army. They don't think it's worth it, and they're against the war and all this. It's a little too late for that now. You're here. If you want to come out of here in two or three years, whichever your enlistment is, no problems, go along. That's all we ask. Go along. You'll learn, learn how to become a soldier.

Hoffman's directness about going along seems to offer a rereading of the general's orientation speech and to provide a way of taking note of the sorts of discourse that we are likely to hear in this institution. The three scenes of sergeant to general to lieutenant make sense as a sequential narrative, but they also are so markedly different as modes of talk that they alert us to talk itself as a subject of the film. Wiseman's treatment of the general's orientation asserts its theatricality, and this raises the issue of what is to count as reality and who is going to define it; in the lieutenant's orientation, the men are asked to accept the army as real and to adapt to that as an irresistible fact. But even though the men, and we, may *regard* the army as a fact, Wiseman has prepared us with his treatment of the general to see the lieutenant's speech as an appeal to belief. If they believe that the army is their inescapable reality, they will be easier to control. Hoffman's speech also seems to function as a narrative foreshadowing in the film: his mention of rebelliousness sets us up to see this both as a continuing concern of the officers and an indication that later scenes will dramatize the issue of rebelliousness and its consequences and alternatives.

In the sergeant/general/lieutenant orientation scenes, Wiseman has established another narrative convention for the film as it will develop. Each of these scenes employs a pattern of cutaways and reaction shots characteristic of narrative cinema. As the technique is employed here, the sound track appears to be continuous, while the camera cuts between the source of the sound, in these cases the speaker, and his listeners, who are either responding ("yes, sergeant") or, more often, simply listening, in close-ups or tight shots of two or three faces.

The next group of scenes also appears to be linked narratively and thematically. A sergeant walks through the barracks, awakening the sleeping trainees. In the next sequence, we see mirrored, fragmented close-ups of men shaving as we hear a voice giving instructions. The voice runs throughout the scene and gives it its temporal unity. We soon cut to its source: a sergeant matter-of-factly instructing a trainee in how to clean urinals, toilets, and sinks. "See, you get a lot of soap powder and stuff that builds up down in here, and it turns yellow. And then underneath, you gotta sometimes pass your hand underneath here, you see. It's all slime. That's where people try to shoot from way back over there, and it drips over the sides. I'm not afraid to put my hand in it." As the sergeant's voice continues, Wiseman cuts away for a close-up of the mirrored face of a young man brushing his teeth, followed by another close-up of a man shaving, then cuts back to the sergeant. The early-morning shaving and tooth brushing have a quality of domestic familiarity that is made odd both by their depiction in the mirrored close-ups and by the way they are contextualized as part of the sergeant's instructions. The tooth brushing and shaving are part of the routines these men brought with them to the army; the need for a disciplined routine of sanitation is the result of their strange new setting.

The next scene is part of the characteristic structure of *Basic Training*, in which Wiseman first makes an ironic joke at the army's expense and then turns the irony upon the spectator. The men are standing outside a small building, being addressed by an officer. "Very shortly you're going to move into the building, and you're gonna see about a fifty-minute television program. The first half of this television program will be a lecture in which they will tell you about how you can receive dental treatment while you are in the army. . . . The second half of the program will be a practical exercise in which you will participate yourself." Wiseman cuts to the inside of the building, where the seated men are watching a television program that, incredibly and hilariously, instructs them in how to brush their teeth—which the preceding scene has shown us they already know how to do. The sequence of scenes makes the army appear ridiculous, a classic example of the routinization of a task the men are perfectly capable of doing on their own. Our laughter at this point also invites us to identify with the soldiers, who must, themselves, see the joke, since they have just come from brushing their teeth at the barracks, but who cannot, as we can, laugh at the incongruity. The television sound track tells them, "We'll be brushing back and forth on the front teeth. Put the tooth brush in your mouth. Good, short, fast strokes, back and forth." To a musical accompaniment from the instructional video, on which young men in close-up are brushing their teeth, we cut to group shots of the recruits, seated in the classroom, gazing at the screen and brushing their teeth. Then we cut to a close-up of a recruit brushing, brushing, then another—and we see unmistakably that the recruit in this second close-up has evidently broken and diseased front teeth. The confidence with which we have been enjoying Wiseman's joke on the army is undermined by the evident need of this recruit for dental care. Then we cut to a black recruit, vigorously and apparently contentedly brushing his strong teeth, and the camera pans down to discover his booted foot tapping to the music. Wiseman has set us up to see the dental instruction as both unnecessary and resented, then shows us that it is neither.

A cut pitches us into a rapid sequence of scenes that extend into combat training itself. The sequence, which might be dismissed as a mere transition from the dental instruction (which in retrospect seems the last scene of the film's introduction) to combat training itself, is of considerable formal interest and an example of Wiseman's method of employing the mechanisms of film aesthetics to achieve complicated understandings. The merry music of the tooth-brushing sequence gives way to a metrical and strenuous beat, as a sergeant leads the men in push-ups. Then the trainees crawl through a field of soft earth, flat on their bellies, heads slightly raised, trying to master the awkward movement as an unseen sergeant (whose voice we may recognize as that of the sergeant who instructed the trainee in the sanitation detail in scene 17) gives rapid-fire instructions. "Ready, go. Get your butts up. Get off your elbows, young man. Get off your elbows. Get those shoulders off the ground. Move that ass. Kick them feet. Let's go, let's go. Get off them knees over there. I don't want you on your knees. Get on there. Reach out. Turn around. Don't go over there. Reach out. Kick in. Dig it in. Dig 'em in. Pull with your hands." The sergeant's short, loud sentences, the cutting from high-angle shots to close-ups from ground level of the men crawling, gives this short scene a sense of strain and rush and for the first time seems to imitate the motions required under fire. A cut from the crawling scene places us at a low angle, looking up at a row of men who are hanging from a series of horizontal bars. They advance obliquely, hand over hand, as the only sound we hear is the slight squeek of the dowels in their wooden frames. And then from this strain and noise, we cut to silence and a close shot of a row of rifle butts in a rack, visually echoing the row of advancing men. Still in silence, we cut to a wider shot and observe one of the rifles being pulled from a rack and handed to a trainee who then turns and walks out of the frame. Then we cut to a low-angle midshot of a sergeant holding a rifle in his hand and raising it above his head. The rapid alternation of complex rhythms that have preceded this first view of the weapons lends the silence of the rifle rack a mysterious quality, which might without exaggeration be called sacramental, as the sergeant lifts the rifle silently over his head and prepares to speak. Clearly, these men are about to be introduced to a mystery, and Wiseman has achieved this understanding at the level of feeling rather than of argument. But the sacramental, mysterious moment, for all its effectiveness, quickly passes. It is not underlined or overstated, but gives way to the complex core of the film, which extends and amplifies the materials of the introductory sequences.

In scene 23, the trainees are introduced to their weapons. We cannot tell as the scene begins that it will develop into an extended and complicated drama. Perhaps our attention is first drawn to the information the sergeant is conveying about the weapon he holds in his hand, and the curious rhetoric with which he addresses the men. "An M-16 A-1 weapon. Not to be confused with the M-16. Now, study it very carefully. Nut for nut, screw for screw, rivet for rivet, and you will find that it is exactly, exactly, my friends, the same as the one I have in my hand. Millimeter for millimeter, square inch for square inch, the weapon you have in your hand is exactly the same as the weapon I have in my hand." That the sergeant takes pride in the sameness of the weapons is not surprising to us, since it has already been clearly established as a value, and a method, of the army to develop these trainees into interchangeable parts. The sergeant's use of the rhetorical figure repetition, which gives his speech a curiously formal quality, seems fitting to the theme he is developing, as its echoes and restatements mimic the idea that one weapon is equivalent to another. A dark-skinned recruit asks the sergeant, "Have these guns been used bef—[his words are cut off by a small flurry of voices]. "Guns! . . . rifle . . . weapon . . . you're in the army." The sergeant responds:

SERGEANT: All right. This [pause] is an M-16 A-1 weapon. Rifle. Piece. Or what have you. At no time, for any circumstances, will you refer to this piece of metal I have in my hand as a gun. A gun is a high trajectory weapon.

TRAINEE: I'm sorry.
SERGEANT: It's all right.

The sergeant's answer to the trainee appears both technical and rhetorical, in the sense that there is a technical distinction maintained between guns and rifles, but the context makes it clear that knowing this difference is part of being in the mystery, among the users of a special vocabulary. The sergeant's employment of synonymy—weapon, rifle, piece—is as formal a use of language as the series of paired repetitions in his opening speech.

The trainee pushes ahead—he, too, is trying to be understood.

TRAINEE: Has this weapon, have these weapons ever been used before?
SERGEANT: Last cycle.
TRAINEE: To kill people, I mean.
SERGEANT: Not yet.

When he finally manages to finish the sentence that was interrupted by the short lecture on nomenclature, the trainee is misunderstood and so sharpens his question: "to kill people, I mean."

The trainee's question is now clear, but we do not know why he is asking it. Is this merely idle curiosity? Another sergeant, who clearly does not think so, who seems to interpret the trainee's question as a reluctance to consider shooting another person, exercises what he seems to see as his duty to set the trainees right. We have no reason to think the sergeant is wrong in his interpretation of the trainee's question, although his response raises questions that are central to our understanding of the film. This second sergeant makes an extended reply to the trainees, a reply marked by the same rhetorical figures used by the first sergeant who spoke in the scene—repetition and synonymy. This similarity in rhetorical style once again seems to emphasize the unity of the army as a place where people speak a special language.

[We hear the second sergeant's voice before we see him.] I don't know. I, we're getting pretty heavy on this discussion right here, and

Cut to the trainee who asked whether the weapons had been used to kill.

it's like discussing religion.

Cut to the second sergeant, whose voice continues throughout the scene. His back is to the camera. He wears a helmet and carries one of the weapons. He is walking away from the camera, then, on the word "religion," turns to face the trainees, whom we see standing before him.

I don't discuss it with anybody because I don't believe I have any right to discuss whether or not you should kill a man or you should not kill a man. But I do know one thing, gentlemen. If a man attempts to shoot me, kill me, slay me, or murder me, I definitely will attempt to stop him in the closest and fastest way possible. Now there's a lot going on about this nowadays, and I do believe you've got a right to sound off about it. What I'm saying is, when you get out in the jungle of Vietnam, I don't

believe the thought of killing a man will enter your mind, if you get hit

On these words, the camera steps slightly to the front of the sergeant and pans to frame his face in close-up; another noncommissioned officer stands in the background.

from three sides. Automatically the only thing that's gonna go into your mind is self-preservation. This is a touchy subject here also, gentlemen, but I know one thing. You probably won't have anything in your mind except survive, survive, survive. The man is out to kill you, gentlemen.

Ninety-nine per cent of the time

Cut to the rifle-rack trainee, head down; he looks up sharply.

the man is as scared as you are. Ninety-nine per cent of the time,

Cut back to a close-up of the sergeant.

if you say he's not gonna kill you, you're gonna go to Camranh Bay in a body bag.

Cut to a close-up of a trainee.

You understand? I'm telling you this

Cut to a close-up of the rifle-rack trainee.

so I can see you again in two years.

Cut to a close-up of another trainee.

This stuff will not get it, gentlemen. I'm not going to go into it any more,

Cut to a shot of several trainees.

it's getting pretty heavy right now. But I'm going to tell you something right now. If you want to come back from Vietnam, you might as well grow up and take a good look at the

Cut to the sergeant.

man that's gonna kill you, because
he'll do it in a second, gentlemen.
The man comes up, no, not all the
time he doesn't want to kill you.
I haven't run into one of them yet,
gentlemen, but I do believe I've
given some serious thought about
the other enemy. The man on the
other side. What are his feelings
towards killing me? Gentlemen, it's
a pretty hairy subject, but I'm
gonna tell you again. If you want to
get back from Vietnam, you better
learn how to use this black lickin'
stick and use it properly. Learn how
to keep it clean. How to fire it.
When to fire it. When not to fire it.
When not to fire it. And you better
listen up.

[Soldiers singing]: Ain't no use in
marching back . . .

*Cut to exterior long shot of soldiers,
marching, carrying rifles.*

The orientation lecture by Lieutenant Hoffman has prepared us for any evidence of rebelliousness on the part of the trainees, and so it does not, perhaps, seem unreasonable to assume, from a narrative point of view, that the sergeant is correct in understanding the trainee's question as expressing reluctance to fight in Vietnam. Wiseman's cutting during the second sergeant's speech makes the men appear subdued and reflective, as if soberly acknowledging the truth of the sergeant's remarks. Except for the curious trainee. The trainee does not answer, but Wiseman cuts to him twice during the sergeant's admonition. The cutting during the scene reinforces the trainee's narrative connection to the sergeant's speech and sustains the dramatic tension of his position as a subordinate being addressed by a superior. We are invited to imagine his position in the situation, in which he is not able to answer back.

But the scene is more complicated than this. From a narrative point of view, there is a certain pleasure, both formal and political, in seeing an apparent rebel contend with the system. The trainee seems to have asked not just "have these weapons killed?" but "*should* they kill?" Although the sergeant's interpretation of the trainee's question guides our own to this conclusion, our point of view is different from that of the sergeant, who jumps into the discussion early, before there has been any explicit questioning of the system or the war. We share the sergeant's expectation of trouble, but we welcome what he is clearly worried about. The sergeant's speech displays both the system's anxiety about the merest hint of protest and its constant, institutional mission of maintaining and justifying its control over the trainees.

And yet the sergeant, although his tone and attitude do not invite further discussion and clearly seem to silence the men, does not simply order them into silence. Rather, he explicitly acknowledges the "right to sound off about it," though he places that right in the category of things better not talked about ("it's like discussing religion"). The sergeant is clearly speaking a sort of truth, and he restates, in terms of survival in Vietnam, the need for "going along" introduced in the orientation scenes. But the grounds of belief and the justification for obedience have shifted here. In the lieutenant's orientation, the men were asked to go along because the army had become their reality: "You're here." For the sergeant at the rifle rack, the reality has shifted from the army to Vietnam, a distant and future place, a place where the reality is the threat of death. The sergeant places viewers in a narratively difficult position. In one sense, we desire to see at least some of the trainees rebel against the institution. But the sergeant convincingly reminds us that in realistic terms, these trainees are more likely to survive in Vietnam if they learn the lessons of basic training. In this sense, our desires are in conflict with each other: we wish for drama (which means that somebody will get in trouble or fail), and yet we may feel forced to acknowledge that, once in the army, it is better for these young men to succeed. This reading of the film is certainly not going to be that of every viewer, but it seems to us to explain, in large part, the formal structure of the film, which then becomes a series of challenges to what we may think we know or desire on narrative and political levels. A presumably liberal and antiwar public television audience will be alert for Wiseman's exposure of the methods by which the army coerces and persuades young men to obey; but that same audience is placed by Wiseman's filmic structures in the difficult and contradictory position of wishing for the young men to succeed in becoming good soldiers. The rest of the film plays variations on these formal and thematic patterns: the comic oddness of the institution; the special language of the group; the contradictory impulses to narrative conflict and pragmatic adaptation.

The scene at the rifle rack is followed by a series of scenes in which narrative and thematic elements overlap and interconnect in a complicated way. Let us first note some of the separate strands of this series and consider how they overlap. The rifles and their use tie together a cluster of scenes at a rifle range and, after some intervening scenes, at bayonet and pugil training. The rifle is fired by a demonstrator with a comic commentary describing his actions, as he shows the mildness of the weapon's kick by firing with the butt against his groin and chin. During this demonstration, we hear the trainees laugh at the jokes, but we also see close-ups of their serious faces. One of the faces, sober and attentive, is the trainee from the rifle rack. The men then fire the weapons themselves, each move controlled by an amplified voice. At bayonet practice, they again learn a series of mechanical moves, and then practice thrusting the bayonets at targets as they yell loudly. The trainee who seemed doubtful about killing at the rifle rack is shown thrusting and yelling with apparent fierceness. Then the men, dressed in padded helmets and gloves, engage in mock combat with clubs that are padded at both ends. We learn from the sergeant who is addressing the men that this is called pugil. The men are told to start and stop at the sergeant's whistle, and they pummel each other as other trainees call out to encourage them. "Hit him hard. Hit him. Hit him. Hit him in the head. In the head. In the head." The sergeant's whistle blows, but one of the trainees keeps on fighting. When he stops, the sergeant tells him, "You just done exactly what I told you not to do." "What's that?" asks the trainee. "You stop when I blow the whistle." The camera is focused on the sergeant as he reprimands the trainee, who has stepped off-screen right. He says, "But I didn't hear the whistle, drill sergeant." The drill sergeant replies, "Don't tell me that. Get out of here." The camera pans right to the trainee, who turns away from the sergeant, helmet in one hand, pugil stick in the other. It is the curious trainee from the rifle rack. Cut.

What are we to make of these scenes? We had presumably supposed, along with the sergeant at the rifle rack, that the trainee was reluctant to fight, but, seeing him at the bayonet field and pugil demonstration, he seems to be eager, perhaps overeager, to fight. Has the training converted him? There does not seem to have been enough intervening training to entirely change a real objector. Is he merely a rebel bucking the system? Perhaps, but we do not have much evidence for that, either. Is he just another young man who asked a naive question at the rifle rack and was misinterpreted, and who really did not hear the sergeant's whistle in the confusion of pugil training? We do not know, and it is perhaps now clear to us that we do not have enough evidence to decide one way or the other. What we—and the army—thought we knew was obviously an overreading or a misreading of the trainee's first question, but what his attitudes really are we have no way of knowing. In a film in which few characters reappear, and then always unpredictably, a character's reappearance becomes an element of narrative coherence at which we, the audience, may grasp. But having offered us the coherence that may be represented by the curious trainee, Wiseman takes away that coherence by forcing us to discover that we do not know what his actions mean. Here, the power of narrative, as form, is turned against itself, not simply as an aesthetic complication, although it surely has pleasures to offer on that level, but also as a rhetorical speculation, serving to undermine our confidence that we know how to understand basic training and all that it represents. We do not want to give the impression that this is some sort of subtle, artistic stunt that Wiseman has embedded in the film for a critic to uncover. The treatment of this trainee, structurally subtle, aesthetically sophisticated, and rhetorically powerful as it is, works first at the level of pure narrative experience, rather than of retrospective paraphrase. Wiseman puts us in the position, as first-time viewers, of trying to make sense of the world of basic training, of getting the feel of a powerful institution and the ambiguity of everyday experience. The resources of fiction, including especially the way in which narrative forms shape our desires, our sense of time, and our understandings of human motive, are brought to bear not as pure fiction but as modes of knowing everyday social reality. In *Basic Training,* Wiseman uses narrative and fictional techniques, including the free manipulation of the actualities of time and space, to create the feeling that reality resists the attempts of a film audience to reduce it to simple narrative coherence.

Let us step backward in the film's time to pick up another narrative thread. We followed the trainee from the rifle rack in scene 23 to the pugil demonstration in scene 37. In scene 30, we are introduced to a character who seems at first to exist primarily for our amusement: the sad sack soldier who cannot march in step. A sergeant is drilling a lone recruit in marching and pivoting. The sergeant calls out the cadence and the drill, a loud and towering figure barely maintaining his patience with the small, awkward, and bespectacled trainee who marches back and forth before him. "Left, right, left. Don't pause when you pivot. Left, right, left, rear—Har! You rushed it again. Left, right, left, rear—Har! Hands down at your side. Left, right, left. Rear—Har! You can do better than that. You had it down. Now you're slipping up again. Left, right, left, rear—Har! Left, right, left, rear—Har! Demonstrator halt. You're gonna have to think about what you're doing, Hickman, or you'll never make it. Okay, now join your platoon." Hickman, during these orders and admonitions, paces back and forth, not quite catching the rhythm. When the sergeant stops him and lectures him before sending him to rejoin his platoon, we see Hickman in profile, close up, a chinless, embarrassed young man, a humiliated, downturned grin acknowledging his awkwardness and completely failing to charm the sergeant.

Wiseman cuts to the marching platoon, with Hickman now marching along at the rear, excruciatingly, comically, out of step. "You're out of step, Hickman. You're out of step, Hickman. You're out of step, Hickman. Change step, Hickman. Change step, Hickman. To your right. To your right." Hickman droops along out of step, arms hanging uselessly at his sides, hopelessly tagging along with his competently, stolidly marching comrades. Then the marching gets more complicated, as the drill sergeant calls for a rapid series of about-faces, and soon many of the men are confused as they turn about and turn about again, losing track of their direction, as Hickman swings this way and that, now with a wide smile on his face.

The scenes of Hickman's marching are a small gem of comic relief, a welcome oasis of stereotyped laughter in the midst of the developing series of scenes of rifle and bayonet training. When we cut away from the scene on the jumble of about-faces, Hickman's smile even seems to identify with our own laughter. Hickman's smile concedes the joke in his own incompetence and perhaps forgives us the pleasure we have taken in seeing him simply as a comic stereotype.

The relatively extended scenes of Hickman's marching have another small, but significant, effect on the structure of the film. Wiseman uses brief scenes of marching men, both before and after this sequence, as transitions. They are simple and convenient as transitions and inconspicuously reinforce a sense of the narrative continuity of the film by knitting sequences to each other in time and space. After Hickman's marching scenes, however, we cannot see the marching scenes as merely punctuation: they, too, are an accomplishment, a problematic and significant part of army training, an icon of regimentation, but also a symbol of initiation into the mysteries of soldiery. The scene allows us to discover for ourselves that nothing can be taken for granted as simply part of the background. The difference this makes alters the way we see every scene in the film.[22]

It is a mark of Wiseman's gift that his films are full of seemingly anomalous details, bits of human oddity, and yet that nothing seems wasted. Wiseman creates a way of seeing that has room for the details, the accidents, and the repetitions of daily life. Somehow, the films maintain a felt coherence, in which these details seldom seem simply extraneous or self-indulgent on Wiseman's part, and yet the coherence is not ever merely tidy or neatly symbolic. There are scenes in Wiseman films that resist reduction to thematic paraphrase and yet seem fitting, both in the way they are joined to the scenes that precede and follow them and in the way they jar our expectations and at the same time demand our assent—yes, that's odd, but that happens, that is the way people behave.

Hickman, having performed his comic turn, and having altered our perception of all those scenes of marching, may seem to have served his purpose as a vignette, one of those isolated characters who is featured in a scene in a Wiseman film and then disappears, never to be seen again. But we do see Hickman again. His reappearance is arranged with a formal complexity that is characteristic of Wiseman. Let us go back to the point where we left the trainee from the rifle rack, who was reprimanded for being too enthusiastic in pugil training. The pugil scene is numbered 37 in the Zipporah transcript. At this point, we have followed the trainee from the rifle rack (scene 23) through the rifle range (scene 25) and bayonet training (scenes 34–36) to the pugil demonstration (scene 37) and in the meantime have seen the introduction of Hickman in the marching scenes (scenes 29–31). The pugil demonstration ends with the rifle-rack trainee being reprimanded by his instructor. Another scene of marching immediately follows, in which a soldier, perhaps not Hickman, seems to be out of step, and we cut within the scene to a close-up of marching boots. Then we cut to a shot over the shoulder of a man seated at a desk, as a soldier presents himself and says, "Private Booker reporting to service, sir." We cut to a close-up of the officer at the desk and discover that it is Lieutenant Hoffman, who, in scene 15, had told the men of his company that to get along they needed to go along. Hoffman tells the private that he is being punished for fighting and that his punishment will consist of forfeiture of pay and seven days of correctional custody. "You're not back on the block. You do not go around just beating up people. And hitting them. You do as you're told, you do what you're told, when you're told. . . . You just do what you're told, as you're told, and don't cause trouble, and you'll have no problems."

Hoffman's reappearance here creates another thread of narrative continuity, just as the punishment of Private Booker seems to establish a continuity of content with the brief reprimand of the rifle-rack soldier in the pugil scene that has come a moment before. Hoffman's repetition of his rule—"do what you're told, as you're told, when you're told"—seems as much a magical formula for himself (he repeats it here, as if clinging to its familiarity) as it is advice to his subordinate. Hoffman tells Booker that he is not "back on the block. You do not go around just beating up people." This reference to "the block" as a place where "beating up people" is normal behavior seems both a square's appropriation of street language and a casual bit of racism— Hoffman is white; Booker is black—in its assumptions about Booker's background.

When Booker is dismissed by Lieutenant Hoffman, he is sent to the first sergeant, who again explains his punishment and warns him about the seriousness of his offense. The first sergeant is used as the bridge to the next scene (scene 41), where we see him crouching at the feet of Hickman, the out-of-step soldier, showing him how to tuck his trousers into his boots. The first sergeant is mild, fatherly, concerned.

FIRST SERGEANT: Where's your hat?
PRIVATE HICKMAN: I forgot it, First Sergeant.
FIRST SERGEANT: Okay, then, go and get it. Did you eat breakfast this morning?
PRIVATE HICKMAN: No, First Sergeant, I didn't.
FIRST SERGEANT: Why?
PRIVATE HICKMAN: Upset stomach. Couldn't go anything.

The scene ends, without explanation, and, in what is evidently a new scene, without any obvious connection to the previous one, we cut to a close-up of the first sergeant talking on the telephone. Continuity is maintained by the fact that this is the third scene in a row featuring the first sergeant. We do not learn who the first sergeant is speaking to, but it seems clear that he is speaking about a trainee.

He's got, I suspect, a family problem, and he's trying to relate it to training, that he wouldn't be, that he wasn't able to keep up with training. He's got suicidal tendencies and [he pauses, as the person on the other end evidently asks him to clarify]—suicidal tendencies. In other words, it seems like he wants to knock hisself off. He's got a separate family. His mother and father are separated, and I suspect it's a deep-seated problem there, and I'd appreciate it if you could see him, talk to him. And, we had a little problem with him before, this motivation problem. But outside of that there really hasn't been any serious problem. He performs quite well. Of course, he has a normal trainee tendency to miss some of it. Some of it he has to go back and get again. This bothers him quite a bit, and, ah, he needs to see you, and I'd like to have your recommendation from there, cause I'm gonna send him back to mental hygiene again after he gets through with you.

Somebody is in trouble—we don't know who—and is being sent for help, though the mode of cutting focuses our attention on the first sergeant, who is the basis of the scene's continuity with the film at this point. The first sergeant's use of psychological jargon ("suicidal tendencies," "deep-seated problem," "motivation problem") is undermined by the way he translates his diagnosis into "he wants to knock hisself off." The sergeant's assessment of the unknown trainee's performance also cuts both ways: he seems familiar with the trainee's record, and patient about his mistakes, but as he himself says the trainee sees it differently, and so the sergeant reminds us of the gulf in point of view between army and trainees.

We cut from the close-up of the sergeant on the phone to a midshot of Hickman seated in a chair, listening to an off-screen voice, which asks, "What do you feel that you're messin' up on, Hickman?" Hickman responds, " 'Bout everything, I guess."

Suddenly it is clear to us that the trainee the first sergeant has been describing in the previous scene is Hickman, and so, in retrospect, a direct continuity of this and the previous two scenes is established, a narrative connection we can make only after it occurs. Given the rules of continuity that Wiseman has already employed in the film, it would have been perfectly consistent for Wiseman to have strung together these three scenes without any such narrative connection. That is, the trouser-tucking scene between Hickman and the first sergeant and the following scene of the first sergeant on the telephone could—and, so far as we know when we first see them, do—refer to different trainees. The two scenes do not require the next scene to be connected temporally or causally; they would still have satisfyingly context-dependent meanings, relevant to the development of the film as a whole, if the third scene in the series were, say, of marching men, followed by whatever comes after that. It is not an adequate test of the coherence of a Wiseman film, however, to notice that a given scene could be missing without utterly destroying the continuity of the film. That is, just because a scene could be missing without creating incoherence does not mean that the film as it stands must therefore lack coherence. Rather, this structural quality is a clue to the way in which almost any scene is tied to other scenes by multiple strands of association, each of which deepens the meaning both of a single scene and of the film as a whole. That this should be so is part of what gives Wiseman's documentaries their seeming authenticity to the rhythms and textures of everyday life, and at the same time their sense of aesthetic elegance and pleasure.[23] But the new Hickman scene goes beyond simple narrative coherence. We continue to watch Hickman, weighed down with depression, as he answers:

HICKMAN: 'Bout everything, I guess.   *Midshot of Hickman, seated in chair.*

[Voice off-screen]: You're not messing up on everything there, because, like I said the first sergeant told me

you're doing pretty well in some things.

As he answers, Hickman nervously passes his hand across his chin, then pulls at his ear lobe. His hat is in the other hand.

Cut to a midshot, from slightly above, of a large black man reclining in an office chair, his hands clasped behind his head. It is his voice we hear talking to Hickman throughout this scene.

What kind of problem did you have last night, or yesterday, when was it?

Cut to close-up of Hickman.

HICKMAN: Last night, I guess, the guys, they bugged me quite a bit, 'cause I can't do things exactly right, you know. So all they ever do is bug me about it. And

[Voice]: Bug you about what? I don't understand.

HICKMAN: Well, every time something goes wrong, and they're all asking, you can't do this, you can't do that. They come up, I don't know, they just act like they, just think I'm helpless or something, I don't know.

Hickman passes his hand across his forehead, then strokes the back of his neck.

[Voice]: You can't do anything. Give me an example. What did they do? What did they tell you?

HICKMAN: Well, last night, 'bout making the bed. They sure got mad. Folding things, you know, seems like I was having a little trouble with that. They threatened to give me a blanket party if I didn't do right, anything right, you know. Threaten me and everything. I don't know.

Hickman strokes his upper lip, then the back of his neck.

[Voice]: In other words, they feel like you're messin up the company or somethin?

The camera begins to zoom out to a midshot of Hickman.

HICKMAN: Yeah, I guess so. It's what they say

[Voice]: You felt that to solve your problem you just, you'd just put yourself to sleep, huh?

HICKMAN: Yes, well, I—

[Voice]: Is that the way you usually solve your problems?

HICKMAN: No, found that out.

[Voice]: Huh?

HICKMAN: No.

[Voice]: Well, I would much rather you come in here and tell me, "Mr. Chaplain, I'm a little depressed today, Chaplain, I'm running into some difficulties," than to, just to, swallow a bunch of pills and just say I'm gonna forget the whole thing. That doesn't sound like somebody who's really trying, really trying to get to the top. [Long pause] Does it?

Cut to tight close-up of the man who has been talking to Hickman. [It is here, for the first time, that we realize Hickman has been talking with the chaplain.]

HICKMAN: Guess it doesn't.

The chaplain smiles a heartily encouraging smile and stares at Hickman, his face in close-up.

CHAPLAIN: All of life is really a lot of ups and downs, isn't it?

Cut to Hickman.

HICKMAN: Unh [he nods assent].

CHAPLAIN: And I don't care how good a person is. He has those days when he's not as good as he wants to be. Not as good as he has been. Right? And the difference, the difference between us, is not so much whether we lose today or whether we win today, but what we do as a result of having won or lost. And if we gonna go around feeling sorry for ourselves, then, you know, there's no hope for us.

Now, the doctor can help you, mental hygiene can help you, and I can help you, but you have to be

Cut to a shot from over Hickman's shoulder. Hickman is at screen right; the chaplain is at screen left, his body

willing to help yourself, too, hmm? If you fall down in the mud, you have to be willing to get up. See? If you flunk one test, you've gotta be willing to stay in the arena. Keep struggling, keep fighting and go at it again. Okay?

oriented to the center of the screen, his head turned to address Hickman.

HICKMAN: Okay.

CHAPLAIN: All right. Now I'll be out there, in the training area, and if you need to see me, or want to stop and talk

Cut to a close-up of Hickman. He squeezes his nostrils, then twists his lower lip between two fingers.

Cut to a tight close-up of the chaplain, his head resting on his hand.

I'll be willing to do that. And I'm gonna be checking up on you to find out how you're coming in your training. All right?

Cut to a close-up of Hickman; as the chaplain rises, the camera zooms out to include him in the shot; Hickman rises and shakes the hand offered by the chaplain; then he shrinks backwards, recognizing his cue to leave.

Well, I'm gonna probably be seeing more of you during the week. Okay? And now, you take care of yourself, and, go back over and see the first sergeant, and he'll tell you what to do.

HICKMAN: Okay.

CHAPLAIN: Okay, and I'll talk with you again, at your convenience, all right?

HICKMAN: All right.

Hickman turns to open the door, but has trouble with the knob. The chaplain leans past him and opens the door for him, then stands watching in the doorway after Hickman leaves.

He looks at his watch. Cut.

Hickman's scene with the chaplain is complex and disturbing. Points of view that viewers had perhaps felt safe in assuming as, if not their own, at least the film's—and therefore their own on a tentative, provisional basis— are challenged and subverted. Most central, perhaps, is the transformation of Hickman, whom we had at first been encouraged to view as a stereotype present in the film for our amusement. Suddenly it becomes clear to us, from Hickman's own agonized description, that his fellow trainees have stereotyped him, too, and that this has led to a suicide attempt. Hickman's comrades, he says, "just think I'm helpless or something." Our own callous amusement at Hickman's ineptitude in the marching scenes, an amusement authorized, perhaps, by the way we were able to read it as narrative, as vaguely fictional, is suddenly given the jolt of reality and is identified as an attitude that almost cost Hickman his life.

Hickman's narrative requires other adjustments in our point of view. If we have been tempted to read the film as a story of oppressors and victims, with the recruits cast as the victims, we must now acknowledge that at least some of the trainees are also victimizers. If we read the discipline of Private Booker as possibly unjust, as punishing him for fighting in a setting in which fighting is the agenda and bound to leak into unauthorized contexts, the Hickman scenes force us to take fighting among the trainees as a serious matter, and one that, even if it can be blamed on the context, must not be permitted. If we were encouraged to explain away the disciplining of Booker as a case of racial victimization, stemming from Hoffman's (and therefore the army's) racial stereotypes of blacks as prone to violence, the presence of the black chaplain as an agent of the army undermines that simple assumption. The Hickman-chaplain scene strips away from us what seems a highly likely strategy in reading the opening scenes of the film, the strategy of sentimentalizing either blacks or trainees.

What is the effect of allowing the Hickman-chaplain scene to proceed so far before the chaplain is identified? Surely the chaplain could have been identified earlier, so that we would start the scene knowing his identity. The chaplain was briefly seen very early in the film, as one of the party of officers sharing the stage with the general during scene 13; perhaps he was introduced to the men during that session and perhaps even said a prayer on the occasion. Or Wiseman could have unobtrusively preceded the interview with a shot of a sign on the chaplain's door or desk that identified him. A minor effect of the late identification of the chaplain—and it is characteristic of the position into which a spectator is put in this and other Wiseman films—is that we are constantly encountering reality as if by surprise (when in fact this mode of encountering "reality" is created by a particular narrative mode, in this case withholding information from us that is shared by the characters, just as, at other points, we are given information that is withheld from one or more characters).

As the Hickman-chaplain scene opens, we can recognize it as vaguely therapeutic and may wonder whether it signals that Hickman is either going to be helped or even given a release from the army. But the questioning, if therapeutic, is also vaguely argumentative ("Is that the way you usually solve your problems?"). The argumentativeness of the question hints that this man is working primarily for the army, and not for Hickman, and that he is taking it as his task to convince Hickman to adapt to the army's way. It is just after the chaplain has identified himself (to us) that he launches into his advice to Hickman, and he at once makes it clear that Hickman will find no escape from his problem with this man, who is assuming that "reality" is the army. The chaplain's advice, indeed his whole performance in this scene, unfolds as rigidly foreordained, as a scripted bit of theatre often performed for the army: ask the trainee what his problem is, cast doubt on his behavior, deliver a pep talk, and get him out of the office. That the chaplain is black and a man of religion, which might, given the film up to this point, give us a momentary expectation that he either would or should in some measure stand apart from the army's values, does not seem to influence his bland acceptance of the army—though it may reinforce our sense that he is a sellout or a hypocrite. The cliches that he offers Hickman seem agonizing and irrelevant, and they are contextualized in a way that seems to require Hickman to give his assent to them, allowing the script of the scene to proceed, at the surface, to its smooth conclusion, describing his problem with embarrassment and pain, then finding himself required to nod, to rise when bidden, shake hands, and return to his problem. The chaplain's glance at his watch ends the scene on a note of bitterness, underscoring the feeling that the Hickman interview is a piece of theatre that the chaplain routinely conducts.

We have stated our disapproval of the chaplain strongly, perhaps too strongly, as a way of reaching into what may be happening in the experience of a willing spectator.[24] But it must also be said that Hickman plays his own part in the scene with apparent willingness, and it may be that any sort of encouragement is better than none for him at this point. Scene after scene reminds us that, for better or worse, these men are in the army and that the army will employ every sort of discourse it can to mold them to its uses and will in fact do nothing that is not part of this relentless art of control. For us as spectators, this evokes, progressively, a growing astonishment at the variety of the army's modes of control, but perhaps it also wears away at our hope that it can be avoided. We have been told explicitly, and shown repeatedly, that once in this army these men are destined for combat. No matter what our fantasies of escape from the army (on behalf of Hickman), or our darker, narrative sense (which also functions as a desire for something terrible to happen, as a formal fulfillment) that Hickman may come to a bad end, we may also gradually, grudgingly come to agree, even if against our will, that if they are stuck in the army, these men should learn its ways, learn to avoid trouble, learn to survive the hell that it is preparing them for. It is a measure of the film's complexity, and in many ways its gift to us, that it encourages us to entertain these opposing feelings and points of view all at once and does not ask us merely to choose one from among them, although it seems likely that a considerable amount of our energy, as spectators, is going into constructing these dilemmas of logic and feeling and seeking in ourselves and in the film a way through them. The film engages our energies and desires in contradictory ways; and it engages our reflections in seeking the wisdom to grasp complexity without forfeiting judgment, to see institutional life as difficult but not simply to give up or to cut through the difficulties by acts of despair or willful impatience.

As Hickman leaves the chaplain's office, we find ourselves with an attitude toward what we have seen but with no clear narrative agenda. This might, of course, be said at almost any moment in a Wiseman film, and it in large part accounts for the feeling of openness in the film's structure and for the sense that we work harder at a Wiseman film than at a typical narrative, where most of the continuity can simply be taken for granted. But the hard work we put into Wiseman's films is not simply a matter of modernist "difficulty." It is not that the film makes no sense without deep study. Rather, it is that the film's narrative structure and its deepening thematic reflections read as much backwards as forwards, each scene helping us to make sense of what we have seen before, but not seeming to obligate the filmmaker to any particular scene in what follows. When the scene that does follow is seen to fit what has come before, even though it has not been required by what came before, the formal satisfactions are considerable, lending aesthetic pleasure, rhetorical force, and a sense of documentary authenticity.

We cut from the chaplain looking at his watch to a nearly blank screen, which we may recognize as an exterior shot looking down at an empty field. We hear a shout, and then a large group of men runs beneath the camera, entering from the top of the screen, and the men line up. Again a cut, this time to men who are joined in couples. One man in each couple has his arms about the other, and an off-screen voice instructs the man who is held in how to join his hands, bend his knees, and strike the other man in the groin. In the foreground, seeming to enjoy the practice, is Hickman, who hits his opponent in the groin and, on command, steps over the fallen man and mimics stomping him in the throat. The groin-hitting scene is brief, as was the preceding lineup scene, and, although the presence of Hickman lends narrative continuity, we can gather that we are again in a series of transitional scenes, waiting again for another extended episode. Another cut reveals a field full of men, again coupled, wearing light gloves and boxing. They slap at one another's faces. They seem enthusiastic, and there is laughter in the background, but they are still awkward, throwing swings but holding their heads instinctively back out of range. The faces of the men who dodge and bob through the foreground of the scene are serious with concentration and anticipated pain. This is followed by a shot, from above, of men crawling, much as they did in scene 21, but now they seem more practiced, and there is no sergeant shouting at them from off-screen. Is this an intimation that they are making progress?

The crawling scene is followed by shots of the men, outdoors, eating and then resting under trees. Then a close-up of a sergeant, as he disciplines a trainee. The sergeant wears sunglasses and a campaign hat, and he speaks with a belligerence we have not yet heard from the instructors, although it is in many ways what fictional films have featured as the typical tone for drill instructors. Wiseman's handling of the scene demonstrates again how narrative structures underlie and give coherence to a scene that has survived the cutting process presumably because of its thematic weight. The scene is another variation on the issue of how the army exerts discipline and control over the trainees; narratively, it illustrates how continuity of time and character shape our perception of how things fit together.

DRILL SERGEANT: Any time during questioning, you can have time—

Close-up of two sergeants, looking towards screen left. One of them is talking.

TRAINEE: [says something barely audible]

DRILL SERGEANT: I didn't ask you to speak, I'm explaining something to you. Shut up.

Wipe that smile off your face.

As the sergeant begins these words, the camera pans left to a close-up of the trainee.

Stand at attention.

The trainee, helmeted, looks down as if to see whether his feet are in the proper position. As his head comes up again, the camera pans back to the right, to the two sergeants.

Now you think you're real hot today. Come out here with a soda in your pocket, trying to sneak one through. Then you're caught reading Unit Fund property out here on the range when it belongs in the day room. Has no business being out here near the range. Your little stint in CC doesn't seem to have done you any good, does it? You'd like to go to stockade, wouldn't you? Cause you're trying your best to get there. And I got news for you. I'm gonna try my best to put you there

and if you don't wipe the smile off your face I'm gonna knock your goddamn teeth out. Have you got that?

As these words begin, the camera starts to zoom in to a close-up of the sergeant.

TRAINEE: Yes, Drill Sergeant.

DRILL SERGEANT: Have you fired on this range yet?

TRAINEE: No I haven't. I'm still waiting.

DRILL SERGEANT: You go up there to the top of the hill, and you stand at parade rest until such time as I call your firing order. And if I see that smirk come to your face one more time, me and you are gonna take a walk.

The camera pans left to a close-up of the trainee.

Execute an about face. Get out of here.

The trainee turns to face screen left, and then on the order leaves the screen. The camera pans quickly to the right, to a close-up of the drill sergeant, then zooms out to include the drill sergeant who has been standing next to him all during this scene. The two are seen in a midshot.

SECOND SERGEANT: He just snuck in the day room this morning and got that?

DRILL SERGEANT: Yeah, he just went in the day room right after he came back from sick call, cause he's got bad teeth, to git him a soda. Then he tried to sneak it inside his shirt, inside his trouser pockets, and bring it out here on the range.

The drill sergeant is holding a magazine in his hands.

The drill sergeant turns and puts the magazine on a table.

SECOND SERGEANT: I imagine the First Sergeant be

Cut to a close-up of the drill sergeant.

very happy to see him. Don't you think?

DRILL SERGEANT: I'll see him.

SECOND SERGEANT: Huh?

DRILL SERGEANT: I'll see him.

Cut to a long shot of the trainee, who is standing at parade rest, on a knoll.

Cut to a midshot of Hickman, sitting against a tree and turned to look at something off-screen right.

The form of this scene with the drill sergeant calls upon our narrative attention in a number of ways. The point of view of the camera is, most of the time, upon the face of the drill sergeant, who is deliberately menacing. The camera first pans to the trainee in time to watch his reaction to the order to "wipe that smile off your face," and we can feel the difficulty of the position this puts him in, whatever the merits of his alleged offense. The camera is on him once again when the drill sergeant warns him about the smile—a smile that we never see with any certainty, though we can certainly see the trainee's efforts to keep his face straight and can hear the theatrical outrage of the drill sergeant. These choices about what we will see are made by the cameraman (and preserved by the editor) and are followed by another crucial choice of point of view. When the drill sergeant dismisses the trainee, we do not see him go, but instead stay with the sergeants and hear the drill sergeant provide us with a narrative of the trainee's offense. Whatever the instinct of the camera that led to this choice, the effect is to make the drill sergeant not only the key actor in the scene but, in a sense, its narrator, as, instead of going forward with the action of the trainee taking his punishment, we pause on the sergeant as he tells briefly of time past. A crucial and virtually invisible cut then occurs as the drill sergeant's narrative ends. The second sergeant begins to speak, and in the middle of his line, we cut to a close-up of the drill sergeant. In actuality, something must be missing here, as the film is being shot with a single camera. But although real time is compressed, narrative time appears to be continuous and has the effect of keeping the force of the scene upon the drill sergeant, and upon his threat—"I'll see him"—which has the effect of pointing now to future time. Then another cut, this time to the trainee standing where he has been positioned. Perhaps some time has passed, because he seems at a little distance and yet has had time to go where he was ordered and take up his parade rest. But it does not appear that much time has passed, and perhaps the time is even taken as, in effect, continuous, for when we cut to Hickman, sitting under a tree, a dramatic shift in point of view occurs, and it is implied that Hickman is looking at the trainee, soberly witnessing the punishment, and, since he is so sober, it also appears that he has probably witnessed the entire scene we have just watched. Hickman, whom we know to be fearful, must seem in context to be quietly watchful and worried by what he has witnessed. The scene's narrative frame has shifted not simply to include Hickman, but to become itself, retrospectively, included in Hickman's point of view about the army. In staying with the drill sergeant and later cutting to Hickman, the film embeds the sergeant's narrative within its own narrative and then in turn embeds it into Hickman's. The appearance of Hickman serves to provide a retrospective narrative coherence, a continuity with the scenes in which he has appeared earlier and which adds to the menace of the drill sergeant by reminding us how he must look to Hickman. Further, in staying with the sergeants when the trainee marches off, we are—to a degree unprecedented so far in the film—invited to look behind the curtain. A hint of the curtain and what was behind it occurred with some force in the early scene of the general's orientation, but here our glimpse is direct and seemingly privileged. In the general's orientation, Wiseman drew attention to the backstage by irony; here he intrudes directly into the backstage itself. It is, perhaps, a small moment, but it is only the second moment in the film in which we see either trainees or trainers without their counterparts. (The first moment is the scene in which the first sergeant describes Hickman's problem on the telephone.) The glimpse is sufficiently rare to give it some force, and of course when we realize that Hickman himself may have overheard it as well, its force is magnified, as our voyeurism is compounded by being identified with Hickman's timid eavesdropping.

Hickman's isolation as a lonely witness to the drill sergeant's menace is underscored by what immediately follows. As Hickman watches the punished trainee, we cut to shots of other trainees asleep under the trees or gathered in small groups talking to each other. Within the same implied after-lunch rest period follow two scenes that could stand alone as classics of folk rhetoric. But instead of standing alone, they add to the rich texture of the film's social observation, extending the sense of oddness that is always so near at hand in the film and deepening its patterns of identification and division. In the first of the two scenes, a trainee describes a recreational trip to Louisville; in the second, a sergeant describes to other sergeants the theory of karma.

In the first of these scenes, a trainee seated on the ground with a few other trainees seated or standing nearby tells about a sexual encounter. The story seems both vividly human and depressingly dehumanizing, as an instance of the sexual talk of men in groups. Once again, narrative is used to justify behavior—the trainee starts the story by suspecting his wife and then describes his experience with a prostitute. It is important to the tone of the scene that the story is told as if comic, but the comedy clearly seems to be redeemed out of anger, and that in itself appears to be an achievement both of the narrative and the situation.

The scene opens with a two-shot. Two trainees, shown in close-up, are seated on the ground. The trainee on the right (whom some viewers may remember as the toe-tapping tooth-brusher from the dental scene) is telling the story. At his right (screen left, and slightly in the background), the second trainee, a smile on his face, listens. We appear to start the scene after the story has begun.

TRAINEE: I sat up there all night, waiting on my wife, waiting on my

The second trainee, the listener, smiles and, with the off-screen listeners, to

wife. It was about eleven o'clock when I got back to the company. I knew that something had happened, so I went and called home. My wife answered the damn phone. I said, "What the hell you doing at home?" "We had car trouble."

whom he looks up at intervals, laughs slightly.

The listening soldier laughs uncertainly.

I said, "Uh hum."

The smile fades from the listening trainee's face, as he seems unsure how to react to the story, which is still seeking its own tone, between comedy and anger. He turns his head to look away from the speaker, and this takes his face out of the frame. The listening soldier's uncertainty about how to react to the story is shared by the viewer, but is compounded by his actual presence at the scene: a wrong reaction could be offensive. (How do you respond when a man tells you, in a semipublic situation, framed as a funny story, a tale of his wife's probable infidelity? Does it make a difference that the speaker is black, the listener white?)

I called home early. My grandmother said they left around six o'clock. That was eleven o'clock, and they just got home. You know that's a bunch of shit. But I got some loving anyhow. Car trouble.

The camera pans right for a close-up of the storyteller.

[A voice off-screen]: Did you ask her who the "we" was?

TRAINEE: You damn right. "We had car trouble." I said, "Yes, I know what kind of car trouble. Was it bed trouble, too?" Damn right, man. I spent my money going to Louisville and then had to spend fifteen dollars for a piece of ass,

Cut to a more distant shot of the two trainees sitting by the tree. In the section of the story that follows, the second soldier is laughing again, with the off-screen listeners.

and I was fucked up when I got home. Ask Varelli. Varelli said, Varelli said, [a name, inaudible] "Did you see your wife?" I said, "Unh, unh, but I seen something that looked like her." I was fucked up, boy.

Cut to a close-up of the trainee who is telling the story.

If I'da had, if I'da had my knife I would have cut it out and brought it on back with me. Fifteen dollars a whop and you're only in there three minutes because she already got it ready for you. She pat you on the ass and say, "Let's go, that's it brother." She pat you on the ass, that's right, and she know when you get through. She pat you on the ass.

"That's it, you can get up."

"Wait a minute, I ain't through."

"You through. I know you're through; I felt it." [Off-screen laughter.]

That's what she told me. I said, "I ain't through yet."

She said, "You're a liar, I felt it. Get up."

At this line, the trainee hands his rifle to another trainee and begins to rise to his feet.

I said, "Lord, I got a wet ass, she got a wet ass, and I had to pay fifteen dollars." It's a shame, boy. You pay fifteen dollars for a shot, for one shot of ass. You get, she get just as much results out of it as you do. She get more. That's right.

He picks up his pack and puts it on.

I tried to steal my fifteen dollars back, but I couldn't get it. I was leaning on her. She say, "Unh, unh, get your hand out."	*He laughs and illustrates trying to steal his money back by leaning on the trainee who is holding his rifle and reaching towards his chest.*
I had my fun in Louisville, anyhow. I ain't lying. I'm going back there this weekend.	*He turns away and laughs, then takes his rifle and slings it on his shoulder.*

As the trainee's story ends, there is an immediate cut to a sergeant, standing and talking informally to a small group of sergeants. He appears to be in midstory. During the whole scene, we hear rifle shots in the background.

SERGEANT: He has a cousin, well, he has several of them, in Happensville; one of his cousins came to my Sunday school class and talked about him. He has this theory called karma. That's his term for it. That's where this reincarnation come from. Supposedly, there is, when God created earth, he created a certain number, an infinite number of souls. Just souls. Okay. These souls come to earth. They live their life. They sin. They live another life to make up for these sins that they had in a former life. He said you'll always be a human. You may be a different sex. You may be a different race. For example, if you get somebody that's prejudiced, extremely prejudiced, hates colored people—

SERGEANT #2: You might come back as—

SERGEANT: You'll come back as a—

SERGEANT #2: Negro.

SERGEANT: Negro. You oughta seen the people in our class when he said that. He also predicted—

[Voice off-screen]: What about something, somebody else?

SERGEANT: What?

[Voice off-screen]: Do you think you can be somebody else?

SERGEANT: Well, did you see the movie *Patton?*

[Voice off-screen]: No, I didn't see it.

SERGEANT: Have you heard about it? You know, Patton's theory really was a whole lot of reincarnation. He said, "I was here."

SERGEANT #2: I have been here, right.

SERGEANT: I have been here. I firmly believe it.

The sergeant's appeal to the oddness of things that are believable is consistent with the tone of this odd film, even the oddness of these down-to-earth men speculating about karma. The two scenes presented together seem to suggest the likeness of the trainees and the sergeants, both groups of whom are shown trading stories, the division of trainees versus sergeants transcended by the shared culture of men in groups. And the story about karma seems also to hint at a fundamental identification of souls. The sense of identification is balanced and perhaps strengthened by a strong undercurrent of division—whatever the contrasts between the trainees and the army, these men are all in the army now, and the outside world exists across a gulf. The trainee's story about his trip to Louisville exerts a ritual force of male bonding as both wives and prostitutes are declared to be adversaries, and the objects of stories. The story about karma seems not so much to transcend barriers as to point out where they are—these white sergeants quickly name blacks and women as the most extreme examples of people different from themselves. And what is the spectator's relation to these men? There seems an uneasy balance between the forces of our identification with them and division from them, just as there may be an uneasy sense of an underlying challenge to stereotypes about racial or hierarchical victimizations: it is the black trainee who portrays himself as a knowing negotiator of the battle of the sexes; it is a white sergeant who credulously tells the tale of karma he heard at Sunday school. In both cases, stereotypes are challenged by presentations of self that themselves are undermined by irony.

In a scene that follows soon after, a trainee meets with his family, and one feels strongly that for all their admiration of the army, his family is now separated from this young man. Even as his mother and father cheer and scold the young man to better performance, and tell him the army will make a man of him, we hear the parents' ignorance of what is happening to him and feel—again at the level of identification—what is implicit in the Louisville prostitute and the karma scenes: we, and these trainees, are now looking at the world from inside the army.

In the next two scenes, the narrative point of view that implicitly identifies with the army is put to a severe test—even, perhaps, reversed. If we are correct in our analysis of the structure of *Basic Training* as it has developed to this point, the film has created a dialectical tension between a narrative that gradually and imperceptibly locates at least part of our point of view within the army and a clinically neutral or even somewhat hostile analysis of the army's methods of indoctrination. The two perspectives both inform and undermine one another and, as we have tried to show, display a variety of tensions both within and between themselves.

In scene 57, Lieutenant Hoffman is conversing with a private. "I understand that this morning you failed to make reveille formation with the rest of the company. It is my intention as your commanding officer to give you an article 15 for failing to make reveille. Now, I inform you that you do not have to accept this article. You may, if you wish, request a trial by court martial. This is up to you."

To the lieutenant's evident surprise, the private says he would rather take the harsher course and just "go to jail, period." The private seems discouraged, depressed, and bent on self-destruction, and the lieutenant finds himself in the curious position of counseling the private to take the lesser punishment. We cannot tell whether the lieutenant is urging the article 15 as opposed to a court martial out of a genuine concern for the private's welfare, or because it would simply be less trouble for himself, or because it would signify that the private was accepting the army's control. Despite the lieutenant's repetition of his cliches about going along and doing "what you were told," the narrative force of this scene seems to side with the lieutenant, whatever his motives: we surely hate to see this young man get himself into more trouble, and so we find ourselves hoping that he will accommodate the lieutenant and accept his relatively minor administrative punishment. If we are right about this reading of the scene, then we have found ourselves identifying with, and becoming part of, the process of accommodation ourselves—it seems so easy to give way on this small matter rather than buying into bigger trouble.

Scene 58 seems at first to present an exactly parallel case. A private, along with a sergeant and another trainee taking a break from waxing a floor, is discussing the choice between accepting an article 15 and asking for a court martial.[25] If we have already decided, in the previous scene, that accepting the article 15 is the easier course, we might find ourselves wanting this private, too, to be persuaded by the amateur lawyering of the sergeant and the other private to accept his punishment. The sergeant explains that a court martial would stay on the private's record and follow him into civilian life, possibly affecting his chances of getting a job. But this argument does not persuade the private, who, as we begin our analysis, below, assumes center stage in the discussion of his case, which, for a moment, had gone on over his head, between the sergeant and the other private. In contrast to the private in the previous scene, who was dogged and stubborn but relatively uncommunicative, this private is a natural debater and concedes nothing. Like the private in the previous scene, this private is black. As the private speaks, we see him over the shoulder of the sergeant. He is half-seated on a desk in what appears to be an office.

PRIVATE: I'm takin' the court martial. Anyway, court martial, the thing that I did, it wouldn't,

The camera begins to zoom in to a close-up of the private.

actually, what I did, it's minor. It's less than minor.

He looks with a pained expression in the direction of the sergeant.

SERGEANT: No, you don't say it's less than minor now.

The private looks away.

PRIVATE: Technicality, if you use technicality no, it's not—

The private looks back at the sergeant.

SERGEANT: You slept on fire guard. Right?

PRIVATE: No, I just, I refused fire guard.

SERGEANT: You refused fire guard. That means somebody else had to

The private drinks from a canteen.

pull your load. Right? Somebody
else had to do your job.

PRIVATE: It's cause I thought I was
done a misjustice. As a matter of
fact, I think that everybody should
have participation in taking fire
guard.

SERGEANT: Right. Everybody should
have participation in fire guard.

PRIVATE: They didn't.

SERGEANT: The thing is, if you've been
done an injustice, like I told you
before, if you think that somebody
is doing you an injust,

*Zoom out to a two-shot of the private
and the sergeant.*

the army way is that you do what
you're told, and then you act after.
You tell them, "I think I was done
an injust." And see higher
personnel, like going to the first
sergeant, say, "First Sergeant, I believe I was done an injust. I've
pulled so much duty, and this man
didn't pull so much duty." And the
first sergeant would check into this.
And you wouldn't be in this spot
today.

PRIVATE: All this is good and well if I
thought that way. But I just don't
think that way. That's all. To each
his own.

Zoom in to a close-up of the private.

SERGEANT: Right. To each his own.

PRIVATE: [laughs]

Private drinks from the canteen.

PRIVATE #2: Don't look at me, man.

SERGEANT: But the army way is you do
what you're told, and then you find
out after.

PRIVATE: Some things you do what
you're told, you, you might not live
to come back and tell it

*As this speech begins, camera zooms
out to a midshot of the private.*

SERGEANT: That's affirmed.

PRIVATE: Right.

SERGEANT: That's right. That's right. What you did—

PRIVATE: Well, now, I'm still here to, say that I, that I was done a misinjustice.

SERGEANT: Right, but in a combat situation, if you don't do what you're told sometimes, you can be shot, too.

The sergeant is visible at the right edge of the screen.

PRIVATE: But we're not in war. You're talking about being at war.

PRIVATE #2: In other words, if you do it here, you do it while you're in war. That's what he's trying to get over to you.

The camera pans left and zooms in to find the second private.

PRIVATE: No, not necessarily.

SERGEANT: Not necessarily, but, but, he might be a very good soldier in combat, and be on the line—

PRIVATE #2: He might be a good soldier.

PRIVATE: I don't want no medals. I don't want to be here, period. I don't want no medals. I want my life. That's my medal, and my heart. I want to function, out in society, not in here. Outside.

Pan right to resume the two-shot of the private and the sergeant.

The camera pans slightly left to isolate the private in midscreen.

SERGEANT: This is your country, too.

PRIVATE: No, it's not. No, it's not. Now you, now let's just be frank with each other. Now you know it's not my country.

[Voice off-screen]: Right! Right! Right!

PRIVATE: Why are you gonna say that? How you gonna tell me that this is my country?

SERGEANT: Which one do you claim, then?

PRIVATE: I don't claim nothin'. I don't claim nothin'.

SERGEANT: A man without a country, huh?

PRIVATE: Right.

[Pause]

SERGEANT: Well, see the First Platoon, and get that floor waxed in there.

Break time is over.

Zoom out; the sergeant enters the screen from the right and turns to look off-screen, as if at a clock. He passes off-screen left.

PRIVATE: Got the wax?

SERGEANT: Right, I got the wax, right here.

Hey, you got some of that wax in there? You don't, huh? [From the sound of his voice, it appears that the sergeant has passed into another room.]

PRIVATE: He trying to break me. He gonna try to break me. That's just like tryin' to bend steel. He's gonna wear his own self out.

The private drinks from his canteen. Cut.

There are several ways to read this scene. From a certain perspective, it is startling and climactic. The private's calm refusal to accept the proposition that "this is your country, too" suddenly throws the film's consideration of racial relations into a wholly new context, and at the same time it provides us with a wily and dignified adversary of the army's system of control. The challenge to the army's disciplinary system, coupled as it is with its assertion of resistance to racial oppression in the country at large, would be startling in any context. But if we are right in our description of the shape of the film up to this point, we have, as its audience, gradually been drawn into conceding that the racial question is fuzzy and that the army's educational and disciplinary mission is more or less successful and inevitable. Hence the effect of the private's refusal to concede is intensified not only by its contrast to the scenes in which other trainees have in various ways made their peace with war, but also by its reminder of what we, as viewers, have so relatively easily let ourselves believe. The private's unhesitating reply to the sergeant that his blackness means that this is not his country is stated not simply as a matter of his own black experience but in an appeal to the sergeant's common sense: "Now let's be frank with each other. Now you know it's not my country." That appeal to common sense is, in context, an appeal to our common sense as well, and we may feel it as an implicit rebuke to our own accommodation to the appeals of the narrative. The private's eloquence and independence are thus not merely an exception but, as placed in the film, a direct subversion of the narrative work we have been performing in apparent collaboration with the filmmaker, and a challenge to repudiate that collaboration.

The scene epitomizes the film as a whole, in the way it evolves as a miniature debate between the sergeant's appeal to short-term pragmatism, to equity, patriotism, brotherhood, and the need to conform to "the army way." The private replies in kind, with his own appeals to equity, justice, truth, personal dignity, to an implicit racial brotherhood, and to common sense. Both men seem to agree that all these principles apply and that their right application is a difficult matter which, paradoxically, requires both careful debate and independent judgment: they argue with each other as if arguments matter, and yet agree with the private's maxim: to each his own. Surely the same forces are at work for us as viewers of Wiseman's film: the film calls upon us to work our way through the constitutional tensions among various conflicting ways of judging what we see; it calls upon us to see ourselves as a community of viewers who may rightly debate the meaning of the film and the institution it depicts; and yet it paradoxically reminds us by formal and thematic means that we are all responsible for our own perceptions and judgments. This simultaneous avidity for debate and distrust of discourse is typical of Wiseman's characters and of his films. It is seemingly underscored by the way the debate ends: it reaches no resolution; the sergeant steps back from the context, resumes his role in the hierarchy, and orders the men back to work; the routine goes on.

Of course there are other ways to read the scene. The private could be dismissed as a mere barracks-room lawyer, playing a scene for the camera and his comrades. The very dramatic presence that makes him such a compelling character could also be used to read the scene as evidence that he is being merely dramatic, playing for effect. And, because of the subtlety with which Wiseman has constructed our relations with all the characters in the film—and with ourselves as its self-conscious viewers—we might notice that even as the scene invites us to celebrate the private's rebelliousness, the context of the scene reminds us that we are taking narrative pleasure in a situation that could mean lifelong trouble for a real human being.[26] But of course not all of this film's viewers, first on television and, later, in the college classrooms where Wiseman's films are shown so often, are white middle-class liberals. Black viewers, for example, might have quite other readings of the scenes in this film that involve racial issues—ranging from stronger identification with the rebellious private, to embarrassment at the self-satisfied black chaplain, to anger at Wiseman for, it might be claimed, taking that black chaplain out of the context in which his speech and actions would take on a more sympathetic aspect. For us to offer a single reading of the film as authoritative, or to offer a demographically segmented list of variant readings based on differences of race, gender, class, or political perspective would be, it seems to us, both condescending and self-defeating. It would, on the other hand, be irresponsible for us to write about the film without offering a critically reasoned interpretation. Simply indulging in description and, in effect, saying that each viewer interprets the film in his or her own peculiar way strikes us as hiding behind a half-truth and avoiding an obligation of the critic: to offer and account for readings that the film seems to invite us to share and to welcome discussion of variant readings.[27]

The scene of the private without a country cuts immediately to a small ceremony in which Lieutenant Hoffman, in the presence of his wife, mother, and child, is promoted to captain. As in scene 56, in which a trainee visits with his family, the presence of these outsiders at an army ceremony emphasizes that, proud as they are of the success of their soldier, they are entirely outside the club. This feeling is emphasized in the wife's ineptness at pinning on the captain's new bars and in the mother's chat with another officer, during which she smooths the hair of the small child in her arms. Hoffman himself perhaps demonstrates this best, as, in close-up, he beams with pleasure and embarrassment and seems a different person from the company commander he has played before his men. The worlds of his wife, mother, and child simply do not fit with the world of the army, and the mixed context leaves him speechless.

Hoffman's promotion is followed by an informal speech delivered by a sergeant who is returning for another tour of duty in Vietnam. We have seen this sergeant before: it was he who instructed the trainee in how to clean the sinks and urinals in scene 17; it was his voice that urged the men through their first crawl in scene 21; and it was he who told the black private that this was his country, too. He tells the trainees:

No matter where they put me over there, I'll do my best. And if some of you men come over there, I'll risk my life to save yours if you're in a spot. And I expect the same from any one of you, 'cause that's the way I was trained, and that's the way I'm trying to train you. We take care of our people over there, believe you me. I know. I've seen a lot of young men like you that didn't make it. They were fine, real fine, upstanding soldiers. They went out there to do a job. I've seen some of them try to save another life, and they got it. This is part of combat. The part we don't like.

Despite the hanging question left by the slightly ridiculous moment at which this speech ends (what part of combat *do* we like?), the sergeant's sincerity seems unquestionable, and the men seem to take him with utter seriousness. And the scene states again, explicitly, as an overt rhetorical appeal, a line of argument that has been progressively implicit in the narrative subtext of the film: the theme that the army is a special brotherhood in which, whatever its demerits as a hierarchical and violent institution, these men's lives depend upon each other and are expected to be offered up willingly.

The men march once more and then find themselves being exposed to tear gas, as a sergeant orders them to stand—stinging, drooling, and weeping—until dismissed. Weeping, they once again look like children, and though they try to obey, and do obey, the order not to leave until dismissed, each successive pair of men turns to leave too soon and is admonished to stand at attention, eyes open, until told to leave. They suffer, and they anticipate their cues and begin to leave before being ordered to, but they appear to have grown in discipline, and they pass their test—after which we see them coughing and spitting in the clear air. Then they march again and appear in an auditorium, where we hear a sergeant tell them about two films they are about to see (and which we do not see). The sergeant, who is standing on the stage of the auditorium, is shot from a low angle, his belt line at the bottom of the frame, his belly sagging over it. The sergeant makes a joke out of army training films before he falls back into his canned exhortation. "Good afternoon, men, and welcome once again to movie matinee. This afternoon we got two big pictures for you, I know you've been wanting to see all week. . . . The objectives of these two movies are first of all for the first one, to find out the winning traditions we have in the United States Army. . . . The United States Army has never lost a war. It is undefeated. Think about that. That's quite a record, and you're part of this army at this time. And it's up to you to carry on this tradition."[28] Again the men march. Their marching is by now robust and competent, and Wiseman emphasizes this by the way he follows their marching songs and their coordinated steps.[29] In this marching shot, we hear a drill sergeant calling off the left-right-left as we see men, shot from the waist down, marching right to left past a fixed camera; in the background is a church. Then we cut to a mysterious shot that unrolls in silence. The shot reveals a glass doorway, shot at an angle. The doorway is narrow, but two men pause and then squeeze through it. Then another man, then another. The glass surface of the doorway has the effect of making each man's image converge from both sides of the screen toward the center, as the man enters screen right and his reflection enters from screen left: then both images disappear as the man passes through the doorway into an unseen and unidentified interior space. The silence of the men's entry into the mirror echoes the sacramental overtones of the rifle-rack scene, here with a new twist. A cut makes it plain that the men have been entering a church or chapel: in close-up, we see the chaplain, in midsermon.

The chaplain says, "Some theologians claim, and I think rightfully so, that the church has been of far more value to men when it had far less in the realm of material goods. . . . . 'Silver and gold have I none,' sayeth the church this morning, but such as I have I offer it unto you. God loves you this morning. God has the power to heal you this morning." With pompous self-satisfaction, the chaplain tells his listeners that it is not the church, but God, who can not only get them through "these two or these three years that now face you, but God has the power to call you to stand and live a renewed life. A life in His son, Jesus Christ."

As the chaplain finishes his sermon, the logic of which seems to be that money is not important, but that God can provide redemption, he has moved from the pulpit and stands beneath a cross. As he speaks the last sentence, Wiseman cuts to a close-up of a collection plate, full of money. It is in the hands of a trainee, standing at the back of the chapel's main aisle, next to another trainee also bearing a collection plate. As the doxology is sung, the two trainees march down the aisle to present the collection plates to the chaplain; the camera follows them in a traveling shot. Remaining at the head of the aisle, before the chaplain, the camera pans right after the two trainees, who turn and walk back down the aisle; the camera stays on the congregation until the end of the doxology, then pans left to the chaplain, who is seen from behind in a head-and-shoulder shot; the collection plates are raised above his head, toward a cross. He offers this prayer: "Oh Lord, we offer you, unto you at this time, our sweat, our work, our joys, our hostilities, and our very souls, congealed and solidified in the form of money. Accept these, our tokens, and accept us in your service. Through Jesus Christ, our Lord, and for Your sake we pray. Amen."

We have argued that in his first appearance, the chaplain was contextualized as a hypocrite in the service of the army's system of institutional control. If that is so, it seems probable that the way Wiseman has cut the chapel scene would reinforce and extend that perception of the chaplain, who, after condemning materialism, seems to offer salvation in exchange for a full collection plate.

The chaplain's prayer is immediately followed by an extended shot in which a trainee seated at a piano in the darkened chapel, framed on the screen by a spotlight that throws dramatic light and shadow across his face, croons a hymn in praise of Jesus. The hymn cuts to an outdoor shot, flooded with sunlight, in which the men, calling out the cadence in unison, march along a road away from the camera.

A detailed description of a Claymore mine ("responsible for approximately 8 percent of all the casualties we inflict on the enemy in Vietnam") is followed by instruction in hand-to-hand combat, as the men kick and punch at dummies.

In scene 72, a sergeant is explaining how to kill an enemy with a blackjack or his own helmet. The scene opens with a shot of a large company of trainees seated under trees and listening to the demonstration; when it cuts to a close-up of the sergeant and his trainee-demonstrator, who serves as the victim for these attacks, we see that it is Hickman. The shot is framed from in front of Hickman; the sergeant stands behind him. Hickman smiles as the sergeant jokingly describes the killing blows and then dismisses Hickman. "Thank you, demonstrator. Give the demonstrator a big hand." As Hickman walks toward the trainees and sits in an empty space in the front row, the men cheer him good-naturedly. Hickman seems to be in good spirits and looks fit. Are we to feel pleasure and surprise that he is still here and that he is apparently accepted as one of the men?

The men march again, singing, "Mr. Nixon, drop the bomb, 'cause I don't want to go to Nam. If I get my orders now, I'm goin' AWOL back to Mom." The marching song is sung responsively—a phrase is sung by a single soldier, then repeated by the men, and so on. As the line of marching soldiers passes by the camera, the solo singer comes into the frame, and the camera tracks along to keep him in close-up as he sings: it is the soldier who told his comrades about the Louisville prostitute in scene 53. No longer are the sergeants counting cadence for the marching: the men, apparently increasingly competent and integrated into the army, are providing their own singers. As the men march by, the camera pans down to watch their shadows striding along.

From the marching shadows, the film cuts to a close-up of Hickman, his glasses off, squinting in the sunshine as someone applies camouflage makeup to his face. A short series of close-ups shows other trainees being made up, the whites becoming darker, the blacks lighter. One of the camouflaged soldiers is the rifle-rack soldier from scene 23. He, too, is still here.

The makeup scene begins a series of scenes that present themselves as dress rehearsals for war. These dress-rehearsal scenes last some seven and a half minutes on the screen, but contain virtually no speech: the scenes (numbered 74 to 79 in the Zipporah transcript) take up less than half a page in the thirty-six-page transcript of the film. The skills that have been taught to the men as isolated moves are now integrated into something that resembles actual combat. Speech, which has been so crucial to the film and to these men, tied to each other through the language of greeting, ordering, instructing, persuading, complaining, debating, exhorting, and pontificating, now gives way to the speechless stealth of the combat zone, as the makeup scene gives way to a scene in which the men practice moving in coordinated slow motion, communicating by hand signals, and creeping slowly forward. We cut to a close-up of a hand, swiftly and yet with careful delicacy creeping back and forth, the fingers crablike on bare earth, presumably to detect enemy devices. The only sound over these close-ups is that of insects in the Kentucky woods. The sounds of the insects carry on uninterruptedly as the scene changes to night, with the men performing the same silent exercises. In close-up, a hand dances over the bare earth; then a hand feels its way along a low wall. Another hand, in close-up, this time with the palm up, slides forward along the ground, encounters a line of barbed wire and slides underneath; then the soldier's arm and face come into the frame. The camera tracks his silent progress under the wire. We cut to the muzzle of an automatic rifle shining against the black background, and the night explodes with bursts of fire. A line of trainees, rifles cradled in their arms, rolls over a low wall. They creep forward, then roll onto their backs when they come to the barbed wire. The machine gun continues to fire, apparently just over their heads. Wiseman stays with the scene, cutting back and forth between shots of the machine gun firing, the men squirming along on their backs under the wire, and more soldiers rolling over the wall and crawling forward. Then a cut to a line of marching men, moving away from the camera; there is a very low undertone of conversation. Cut to a ground-level shot, looking up through a screen of long grass as a line of silent men strides by the camera. Then a burst of voices and fast motion. A soldier is running fast, rifle in his hands, from left to right, as the camera pans with him; a voice is shouting, "I'll move; you cover." Men run over open ground, then crouch for cover; a man throws a hand grenade; another man rushes forward with the repeated cry, "I'll move; you cover." Then a man marches forward at a walking pace through the small grassy valley, firing his rifle as he goes. Another shout, and another soldier races forward, the camera panning with him.

We find ourselves on a forest path, the hand-held camera walking along behind a line of men dressed in protective clothing, hats, and glasses. The men move quietly along, scanning the woods on either side. Then a cut, a rustle of leaves, and a figure rises from the ground to a crouching position and fires a rifle past the camera. We cut back to the line of walking men as the first man in line dives to the ground. Twice more the sniper in the woods fires at the line of men; grenades explode with a plume of smoke. The trainees take cover, then rise and continue moving forward. They come upon a clearing in the woods; one of the men descends some steps to investigate an underground bunker. A few yards further on, they advance towards what we take to be a Vietnamese hut. There is an explosion somewhere in the woods. As a soldier advances slowly toward the hut a figure with a rifle steps from the hut, fires at him, then jumps back into the hut. In a long shot, several men fan out around the hut, preparing to attack it. They are laughing. One soldier crouches outside the door, and the man inside jumps out again, fires, and retreats; he jumps out again to grab for the attacker's rifle, then pops back into the hut. The men continue to laugh. Suddenly these wary soldiers have become boys at play. In the woods, a man with a rifle in his hands and another slung on his back strides past the camera, looking from side to side; the camera pans with him, then stops panning and allows him to exit the frame as a commanding voice says, "Sound entrance call," and we hear a bugle. Wiseman cuts to the bugler, and, as he finishes and a marching band begins to play, to a drum, and then to a bandleader.

The film cuts to a long shot, and we see that we are at a parade ground in bright daylight. Men in ranks parade formally behind color guards. Then a cut to Captain Hoffman, the company commander, who is speaking into a microphone.[30] As Hoffman speaks—he is reading from a text—the film cuts to shots of civilians in the audience. Hoffman describes the American Spirit of Honor Award and introduces the private to whom it is to be awarded. Then we cut to a close-up of a young soldier. In the background stands an older officer, gazing impassively into the middle distance. The soldier begins to speak, acknowledging the general, two colonels, "officers and men of the Sixteenth Battalion, Ladies and Gentlemen." As the private continues, his speech becomes a classic American high-school valedictory speech. In the ironic context of this film, the speech seems an uproarious celebration of the patriotic cliche. But in the context of the graduation ceremony of which it is a part, featuring the earnest wholesomeness of this blandly handsome ideal soldier, and cutting for reaction shots to the ranks of sergeants and privates standing at attention, the speech seems to stand as an appropriate rhetoric for the demands of the occasion. As a classic American speech, and in the context of this film's emphasis on the everyday rhetoric of social control, the speech deserves to be reread as a whole.

Whether one prefers to call today's exercises "graduation" or "commencement," it matters not. But may I suggest you keep both words in their individual connotative and denotative meanings in mind today. "Graduation" signifies an end, while "commencement" is of course a beginning.

Basic combat training has now ended for us of the Sixteenth Battalion. We came here from different places with different backgrounds, from Michigan, Kentucky, Pennsylvania, Indiana, Alabama. Entering the army as farm and factory workers, mechanics, college students, and professional men, we arrived in blue jeans, sandals, tennis shoes, and t-shirts. We are now emerging as trained fighting men in the uniform of the United States Army.

We are now at the end of basic training. We leave the classes we've had, the weapons we've fired, the friends we've made, and the officers and drill sergeants who have gained our respect.

On the other hand, we are but embarking on our army careers. For some, it may be a sojourn of a year or two, for others a way of life. However, it is now up to each of us to carry on in the tradition of those who have gone before. The award which I have the honor and pleasure to receive today is entitled "The American Spirit of Honor Award." This is what we are now entrusted with and must carry forth. The American spirit of honor. It was born in the snow of Valley Forge, nurtured midst the smoke of Gettysburg and San Juan Hill. The doughboys of World War I found it lying in the trenches of France and Belgium. When fascism reared its ugly head, the American spirit came forth and slew the dragon. The 38th Parallel saw the American spirit march forth under the flag of the United States peace-keeping force. And now Southeast Asia. Laying aside the political controversy surrounding this conflict, we see once again displayed that American spirit of honor. Fighting men dying for their nation and democracy. It is up to us to continue the fight, to take up the banner. It is our task to go forth with courage and pride, and respond in the manner of our forefathers. Lord, give us the strength to meet the challenge. I thank you.

As the private finishes his speech, we cut from a close-up of his face to a long shot of the platform, as the commanding general shakes his hand and murmurs, "Well said, son." The camera pans quickly to the left to show the small audience of applauding civilians. There is a howl of feedback from the microphone, and the band strikes up another march. Cut to a phalanx of men marching away from the camera; the camera pans as it discovers more ranks of marching men and the band, trailed by a rotund tuba player. To the strains of the march, the men pass in review before the general, who stands on the stage, the flag of his rank flapping behind him in the breeze. A drum major leads the band toward the camera, pumping a large baton, and as the music continues, the film abruptly comes to an end, and the credits are shown to the accompaniment of the continuing music.

The film's conclusion seems deliberately abrupt, though its abruptness is in some ways diminished by the continuation of the diegetic music of the graduation scene into the credits. The energy of that music bridges the transition from the world of the film to the simple graphics of the credits. The music creates a sense of bustling forward movement, and it carries us through the credits, fading out on the next-to-the-last credit card.

> THIS FILM WAS MADE AT FORT KNOX,
> KENTUCKY, IN THE SUMMER OF 1970.
> SINCE THAT TIME, CHANGES HAVE
> TAKEN PLACE IN BASIC TRAINING,
> WHICH IS CONSTANTLY EVOLVING
> AND CHANGING.
>
> GRATEFUL ACKNOWLEDGEMENT IS
> MADE TO THE DEPARTMENT OF THE
> ARMY FOR ITS ASSISTANCE.[31]

But there is perhaps another sense in which the ending of the film catches us unawares. We have argued that *Basic Training* is constructed partly as a narrative, though a peculiarly attenuated narrative. Narrative continuity is maintained within some scenes by continuity of character or by intercutting that creates a sense of simultaneous movement from one camera shot to another. In addition, narrative continuity is to some degree maintained by the reappearance of some characters from one scene to the next: Hickman is the character to whom this happens most often, though it also occurs with the rifle-rack soldier, with Hoffman, with the sergeant who first appears in the shaving scene, and with some other privates, sergeants, and officers. And underlying the whole film, which so clearly begins at the beginning of a cycle of basic training, is the sense that the film moves gradually forward through the duration of this cycle, even if it does not follow the progress of particular characters.

How does the film's final scene fit into the film's architecture? As viewers, we can recognize the graduation ceremony as a formal conclusion and as an indication that the film is coming to an end, although, especially in a Wiseman film, we never have the feeling that we know exactly at what point any scene will conclude. Even so, our generic expectations as viewers, despite Wiseman's refusal so far in the film to accept the full burdens of conventional narrative and documentary forms, must lead us to expect, at the graduation ceremony, that we will see close-ups of the trainees we have come to recognize and that, conversely, those whose faces we do not see can be assumed to have failed to graduate. But though we see sergeants who have appeared before, none of the trainees we know is clearly visible at the commencement. We are refused the comfort of simple narrative, or of conventional fulfillment of our generic expectations. This film is not about Hickman, or the rifle-rack soldier, or the man who hired a prostitute in Louisville. It is about a system of basic training that, whatever happens to those particular men, will continue. And whatever the fate of Hickman and the others, some of the men we see marching on the parade ground are going to Vietnam, and some of them are going to get killed.[32]

The force of Wiseman's graduation ceremony is not in any implicit claim that documentary should ignore individuals in favor of a curiosity about institutions. Rather, it seems to us, Wiseman's films depend for their effect upon the way in which they play against conventional narrative and documentary. It is not that we should not be curious about Hickman, Wiseman seems to say, but that whatever the fate of Hickman, whose fate we have been made to care about, the institution will continue to do its work. It is in this sense that the meaning of *Basic Training* is not simply in the film as the portrait of an institution, but also in ourselves, as viewers whose longing to know more about the individuals we have seen here, to know whether they graduate, whether they survive Vietnam, is deliberately ignored by the film, as it is ignored by the institution of basic training. Wiseman could not have brought us to this understanding of basic training without the resources of narrative; and he could not have done so without turning narrative against itself and against the grain of our desire for completion that he has aroused and abandoned.

In practice, Wiseman's "reality fiction" is something more complex and subtle than a phrase with which to rebuke the pontifical claims of cinema verite and direct cinema; and it is something more complicated than the implicit acknowledgment of a method that shoots reality and then edits it by the rules of fiction. The "reality-fiction" slogan is inherently unstable, and perhaps ironic, and yet it points to the methods of the films, which are rooted not in a theory or formula, but in the use of aesthetic means to discover the structures and the feeling states of our institutions. The films themselves depend upon dialectical opposition, paradox, irony, and associative and comparative thinking, and they are full of surprises, recognitions, indignation, and comedy. In the experience of a Wiseman film, author and viewers gain at least a temporary freedom from the voice of habit and accommodation that shouts, "Get in step. Get in step. You're out of step."

Chapter 5

Psychology, Religion, and Law as Social Order
Essene and *Juvenile Court*

In 1961, *The American Journal of Psychiatry* published an article by Frederick Wiseman entitled "Psychiatry and Law: Use and Abuse of Psychiatry in a Murder Case." Wiseman, who was identified in the article as a "Lecturer-in-Law, Boston University Law School, Boston, Mass.; Russell Sage Foundation residency, Dept. of Social Relations, Harvard University," had earlier read the paper at the annual meeting of the American Psychiatric Association in Chicago, in May 1961. The article offers a fascinating insight into the thinking of the young lawyer, who was still six years away from making his first documentary, *Titicut Follies*. Framed as a case study of the murder trial of Jim Cooper, who shot his former fiancee, Connie Gilman, the article sets forth three claims. "1. Psychiatric expert testimony is too complex, both emotionally and intellectually for a jury and judge to understand, accept and use to make a just disposition of a particular case; 2. The technical phrasing of the legal test of criminal responsibility is less important than the attitude toward crime represented by the test; 3. The courtroom confrontation of psychiatrists with different theoretical orientations leads only to chaos, disrespect and interference with the needs of the community and the disposition of the unique problem of each offender."[1]

Wiseman's narrative of the Cooper case seems in many ways to treat both the legal system and the psychiatric community with ridicule and contempt, by showing how the law in effect requires expert psychiatric witnesses to oppose one another in court, and to resort to a technical jargon that neither the judge nor the jury can understand. But it is not so much that the law or psychiatry are contemptible, Wiseman seems to argue, as that they have no business being forced into the relationship that they occupy in trials where the defendant's sanity is in question. The jury, as lay persons, have no business trying to ascertain the sanity of a defendant, because they have no way of understanding the technical issues involved in modern psychiatry.

Psychiatry, conceived as a procedure to provide treatment for people in need, instead participates in a charade that dangerously delays the defendant's access to treatment. Wiseman summarizes the contradictions:

> In the Cooper case the State used one set of psychiatrists to prove that Cooper was "perfectly sane" and therefore "responsible" and the defense, other psychiatrists, to show that Cooper was sick and therefore "not responsible." The lay jury chose the testimony it could understand and which corresponded with their own sentiments and Cooper was convicted of a murder he admitted. The only flaw in this successful manipulation of psychiatric expertise was the State's ambivalence. Since there was much moral sentiment against capital punishment Cooper could not be executed and State proceeded to use its first team of psychiatrists to rationalize the decision not to execute.[2]

Wiseman laconically describes Cooper's fate, after the state psychiatrists recommended against execution. "When Cooper was told the Governor was about to approve their recommendations he hanged himself."[3]

Wiseman's article shows characteristic patterns of thought that he later transformed and put to use in his films. Throughout the films, he reveals institutions becoming confused or tyrannical when they mix their social agendas, or when they attempt to combine incompatible domains of thought. In *Titicut Follies*, Wiseman directly explores the "use and abuse of psychiatry," where psychiatry and law are mixed, although, whether because of a change in his own thinking or simply because of the difference between an academic essay and a personal documentary, his thinking in *Titicut Follies* seems to develop his sense of narrative and of the conflict of law and psychiatry, but seems to be less programmatic in suggesting solutions. In the 1961 essay, Wiseman suggests what, in view of the ambiguity and pessimism of his films, seems an unrealistically straightforward way of curing the problem by ridding it of its ambiguities.

> I would not question the value of the psychiatrist to weed out the grossly disturbed offender in the pre-trial competency examination but why not let the law have its own archaic way with the rest. . . . The function of a jury in a murder trial should be limited to a finding that an accused did or did not commit the offense charged. Once guilt is established, a Sentencing Authority composed in part of psychiatrists and other professionally trained people, should, in the absence of capital punishment, decide what combination of treatment and/or punishment is appropriate to the individual offender.[4]

Wiseman's later films are so full of ambiguity and dialectical comedy that one is sometimes tempted to imagine him as a pure storyteller, swept away by the textures and the surrealities of everyday life. It is well to be reminded, as we are by his 1961 essay, that his fascination with ambiguity, hypocrisy, and narrative—what we might see as his mature, "artistic" side—finds its beginnings and is grounded in a simpler, angrier sensibility and intelligence. We see in the early Wiseman a counterbalancing impatience with blandly routinized procedures that work their ways upon society's victims and misfits, with the pretensions of socially concerned middle-class intellectuals, with "modish verbal formulas," with all that is expert, ambiguous, modern, and artificially complex. And, in that early Wiseman, we see a longing, despite his self-conscious hedging that "it is perhaps out of place for me as a lawyer to talk of rational Utopias,"[5] for a simple, unambiguous solution. When he became a filmmaker, Wiseman developed a mode of discourse in which he was able to be more ambiguous than an advocate and in which it was arguably his responsibility to be more interpretive, if less reliable, than a witness.

We do not mean to shift the focus of attention here from the films as social discourses to Wiseman as an auteur, a biographical subject, or a psychological case. But even to consider the films as contributions to social discourse requires some attention to their sources of thought. Our concern in this examination of Wiseman's films is to see them as at once art and social discourse, and that requires us, we think, to explore the films as rhetorical action—as invitations to their audiences to think and feel. It also requires us to suggest the social and historical contexts out of which the films arise, because those contexts inevitably constrain the form and the thought of the films. We cannot expect to encompass all the constraining personal and social forces that shape the films, though the most obvious of those forces—legal, economic, technical—surely have to be taken into account in using the films as social documents. What, then, are we to make, in considering Wiseman's early and enduring concern with the conflict of law and psychiatry, of the fact that his father was a lawyer, his mother an administrator at the department of psychiatry at Boston Children's Hospital? Ignoring this fact might suppress a vital piece of evidence that helps to explain Wiseman's art. But having mentioned it, we find ourselves reluctant to take it any further. We are not competent psychohistorians, nor does it seem to us that it would be particularly useful to reduce Wiseman's important contributions to the struggles of an infant psyche to regulate the relations of father and mother.

In the speculative, ironic context of Wiseman's films, it is perhaps worth reflecting that even to mention Wiseman's 1961 essay, or his parents' occupations, invites exactly the sort of "psychologizing" about which his films are so suspicious, or the sort of "fictionalizing" with which the films are so rich. In speeches and interviews, Wiseman energetically resists any suggestion that his films are in any way conditioned or constrained either by his own personal background or by the agencies that fund and distribute his films. And yet he joked to Alan Westin, apparently in reference to his parents, that "I had more than the usual doctor/lawyer conflicts for a middle-class Jewish boy. Fortunately I worked my way out of both professions."[6]

Whatever the origins of Wiseman's sense of the conflict between law and psychiatry, he has returned to the theme, with various permutations, again and again, in his investigation of the construction of social order in American institutions. In *Essene* (1972), a monastic community bases personal commitment and a rule of life on religious devotion and authority. In *Juvenile Court* (1973), children who are delinquent, abused, or abandoned are dealt with in the context of civil and criminal law.[7]

But in both of these documentaries, the rules of religion and law that provide the official rationale for social order are variously reinforced and contradicted by the claims of "psychology." The psychology at work in these institutions is pictured as both "expert" and colloquial, and as both a system of explaining and a system of controlling human behavior. In *Essene*, the authority of religious dogma and the consolations of Christian community are reinforced by various appeals to mental hygiene and psychotherapy, in which the sacrament of confession competes with interrogations and group exercises in self-disclosure conducted in the name of adjustment.

In *Juvenile Court*, psychology and law are related in complex and contradictory ways. Psychological commonplaces are used in judicial reasoning about issues of guilt and motivation. Meetings between counselors and juvenile offenders develop a confounding rhetoric of appeals to legal authority and blandishments about happiness and adjustment. In some cases, a system of double jeopardy confronts young defendants, who are, in effect, told that they must either confess to their crimes and accept psychological help or deny their crimes and accept harsh legal penalties—either choice leads to the equivalent of guilty verdicts and incarceration. Denial is psychologically unhealthy and compounds the crime. Confession is psychologically healthy but still counts as an admission of both criminal guilt and psychological "problems." Wiseman seems to suggest that the juvenile court system uses psychological double talk as a way of serving its own convenience and preconceptions. In both films, Wiseman invites his viewers to understand psychology both as a subversion of the traditional ends and methods of religion and law, and as a rhetoric by which the institutions maintain social order.

In this chapter, rather than tracing the development of the two films as complete formal units in themselves, we shall attempt to examine how Wiseman displays, in the context of the films, the permutations of "psychology" as a force in contemporary institutions.

Essene

Essene begins in a curious way, with its title in archaic type, followed by a shot of a man in a bathing suit raking leaves on a large lawn. Then a cut shows us two men in monkish robes kneeling and silently praying. The film's third shot introduces a scene in which one robed man is reading to others. We have not been told where we are, though it seems clear that we are in some sort of monastery. We are not told anything directly about the status of the various men we see, though it is clear that they are "religious." Are they priests? As the film proceeds, it appears that some are. They do not all share the same status; some seem more senior, or more permanent than others. Some are addressed or referred to as "father," others as "brother." We do not mean to say that information about status is unavailable, or even that it might be altogether unfamiliar to some viewers. But the film makes no explicit attempt to explain either the religious rituals or the formal pattern of governance of this institution.[8] Nevertheless, it is exquisitely attentive to nuances of status and to the conduct of ritual.

Wiseman's films are typically dialectical in structure. Instead of straightforwardly imparting a unified body of "information" or advocating a linear and coherent "argument," they invite us to make meaning by finding the patterns of association and contrast among the people, words, and actions that we see and hear. In some of the films, these dialectical patterns consist of open and dramatic clashes. In all of them, however, even the most dramatic conflicts are further split into yet more subtle dialectics, whose tone becomes not so much that of self-confident debunking as of fascinated irony. In *Essene*, although there are some notable disagreements among the characters, the primary levels of manifest action seem relatively uneventful, sober, low-key; the underlying dialectics seem correspondingly contemplative and reflective, in contrast to the public urgency of some of Wiseman's subjects. Still, there are surface dramas and underlying fault lines of contradiction that provide much of the unity and interest of the film.

Let us return now to the first words in the film, spoken by a priest who reads to the others. As he reads, the camera watches him and seeks out the faces of his listeners. A pattern of camera work is established early: many large close-ups of priests and brothers, alone in the frame, every facial feature and texture pressingly visible, the background usually a blank whiteness. The visual style of these shots appears to echo Carl Dreyer's *Passion of Joan of Arc* (1928), though with very different effects. In the first speech, two key themes are forthrightly asserted: life here is about religion and about rules.

> *The Rule of Our Holy Father Benedict,* chapter 49, "On the Observance of Lent." The life of a monk ought at all times to be Lenten in its character, but since few have the strength for that, we therefore urge that in these days of Lent the brethren should lead lives of great purity and should also in this sacred season expiate the negligences of other times. This will be worthily done if we refrain from all sin and apply ourselves to prayer with cheer, to reading, to compunction of heart, and to abstinence. Let each one, over and above the measure prescribed for him, offer God something of his own free will in the joy of the Holy Spirit. Let each one, however, tell his abbot what he is offering and let it be done with his consent and blessing. Because what is done without the permission óf the spiritual father shall be prescribed to presumption and vain glory and not reckoned meritorious. Everything therefore is to be done with the approval of the abbot.

Attentive viewers will have gathered from this speech that this is a Benedictine monastery.[9] They might also notice that the first words are not only about authority, but speak through a person who is reading the words of authority, rather than speaking in his own voice. We may expect that this film will explore how it is that religious authority is exercised, mild though this first hint in that direction is.

The logic of the reading, with its emphasis on the abbot as the immediate authority for this community, may lead us to suppose that the next speaker will be the abbot. We are presented with a close-up of a large, round face; it is full of comfortable authority, though the eyes are directed humbly, prayerfully downward. As only the abbot could do, he develops a revisionist interpretation of the abbot's power, describing it as shared, while at the same time reminding us of the authority that declares it to be so. "If it is true today that authority is more of a shared responsibility, then this abbot's approval becomes more and more a community awareness of what we are doing. Not secret and private matters of each person, but as we try in these chapter sessions to become more conscious and more aware of what we are doing and why, this brings us into a higher level of corporate consciousness and, finally, a corporate approval of our life."

The abbot, speaking the language of enlightened capitalist management, here authoritatively disavows authority. His very choice of words, calling for a "corporate consciousness," gives him the aspect of a humane chief executive officer who wishes to run his business according to the most advanced principles of psychology, putting aside "authority" and the "secret" and "private" in favor of "community," "awareness," "responsibility," "sharing," and "consciousness."

We do not mean to argue, nor do we think Wiseman argues, that the abbot is in bad faith. But the question of bad faith is inescapably raised by the apparent contradictions and associations among psychology, law, and religion as they are spun out in *Essene*. Wiseman draws our attention to the mix of psychological and religious talk in every one of the major speeches early in the film.

From the abbot's short speech, Wiseman cuts to a meeting of young men that appears to be a mix of prayer and group psychotherapy. The first young man speaks of trying to combine Christian love of all people with love and acceptance of individuals.

> And it's through living together, through growing together, through accepting that person, not just for what he is at the moment, but for what he is becoming, and this is why so often the little egocentric habits that we have, which bug us all, in time really endear you to that person, because it is part of him. And you begin to see the changes taking place in each other over a period of time, and this also endears you, because that person is becoming, and at the same time you are becoming, and you're watching this growth. It's like a flower blooming through a process of slow motion. You're watching a person begin to blossom and come to real life.

What sort of real life is the becoming person blossoming into? The language is the language of psychological development, and the context is that of a religious order. Is the person finding psychological adjustment? Or God? Are the two somehow related? Or does one undermine the other? Wiseman's inclusion of these speeches has made some religious viewers of the film uncomfortable, and angry. When we have shown the film to students, some who have strong commitments to traditional religion comment that Wiseman seems to be prying into something they do not want to know about and that he seems to be saying that people are seeking God for the wrong reasons— for their own psychological adjustment rather than from purely religious motives. These viewers experience the film both as an invasion of privacy— theirs, as well as the priests'—and a demystification of religious experience.

Another young man in the same meeting, filmed in a low-angle shot, his eyes closed in prayer, the camera so close that his large nostrils and cleft chin are uncomfortably emphasized, explicitly refers to psychotherapy:

> I'd like to ask my brothers this morning to remember the name of Elizabeth Faire. Elizabeth Faire is a lay analyst in New York City with whom I've had contact, and I was under her care for several months, and it was quite a wonderful experience at the time. I was able to share the experience of analysis and group therapy with people with whom I was working in an experimental program. And I was also able to share the experience with about forty other patients in New York City and develop a sense of community together with forty other people. . . . And I really felt that I was led by God to this person and to this experience in community; because it has certainly prepared me for community life here. And very often I feel at our chapter sessions, and occasionally even our prayer meetings become, as Elizabeth would say, "Let's have a little group," and it is extremely therapeutic and it all relates to the emphasis on healing that we have here at the monastery and the emphasis on healing in our prayer life.

As his speech ends, the camera, in a characteristic gesture, pans downward to his clasped hands, fingers interlaced in prayer. Is this brother equating the experience of religious community in the monastery with the experience of "community" in his earlier group therapy program? Does his explicit reference to an earlier therapeutic experience type him as a seeker after treatment—of which this monastery is simply one in a series? Many scenes in the film contribute to the stirring of such speculations, especially given the placement early in the film of so many instances of the language of psychology, which contextualize our reading of later scenes.

Seated among a group of middle-aged men in monks' robes, the abbot discusses the sources of minor dissensions, which he ascribes to a failure to "listen to the spirit," leading to a pattern in which "we continue to shift the ego battles from one question to another."

The next major scene is one of the pivotal encounters in the film—an extended discussion between the abbot and a man, perhaps in his sixties, whose name is revealed during the conversation to be Brother Wilfred. It is the issue of his name that seems to initiate the conversation, though it is clear from the context that the conversation is already in progress when the scene begins. The scene opens with a two-shot of Brother Wilfred and the abbot. The camera looks past the abbot, who is on the right foreground, to Brother Wilfred, who faces the camera from the left background of the frame, his back to the wall. The two men are seated by a desk. Brother Wilfred is at the "owner's" side of the desk, the abbot in the "client's" chair at the side of the desk. Hence, in the struggle that follows, Brother Wilfred has the advantage of his office (room) and the abbot that of his office (role).

BROTHER WILFRED: To me, the use of a first name doesn't necessarily mean respect at all; in fact, rather the lack of it.

There's an old English saying, how old I don't know, but anyway an English saying, "Familiarity breeds contempt."

Zoom in to a loose close-up of Brother Wilfred, leaning back in his chair, arms folded across his chest. There is a wall telephone next to his head. During most of this speech, Brother Wilfred gazes into empty space in front of himself.

ABBOT: Right.

WILFRED: You've probably heard it. I can assure you that it does. I do not feel the same respect for the person I can first-name just like that, that I would for him that has a title to his front name,

a title or a handle, call it, we won't use the word title there,

Cut to a close-up of the abbot, gazing sympathetically to screen left, toward Brother Wilfred.

and of course, as I've said, for my part I don't readily accord the privilege of first-naming me, and I do consider it a privilege, and I do consider that it can only be accorded by myself. Now that's the, what do we call it—

Cut back to the former shot of Brother Wilfred.

the ethical?—

Brother Wilfred glances at the abbot.

you put the name to it, I don't know what it is. Part of it, there's also the matter of convenience.

If the community had only one person of a name and guests and

Zoom in to a tight close-up of Brother Wilfred.

things were not involved, or else
they were referred to as Mr. or
Mrs., or whatever it happens to be,
the difficulty would not arise, you
see. But now on deck here we have
already two Davids, we've got Dom
David and David Ramm,

and at times we have other Davids.   *Brother Wilfred looks at the abbot.*

And who's to know which David it   *Brother Wilfred shifts his glance to*
is?   *screen left, as if appealing to an unseen*
                                       or imaginary listener.

The thing, of course, originally I
suppose was a matter of being a baptismal name

                                       Cut to a wide shot of Brother Wilfred
                                       and the abbot at the desk.[10]

and many years ago baptismal   *Cut to former close-up of Brother*
names were the thing, but even   *Wilfred.*
then they found it a little
inconvenient and added descriptions
to distinguish one person from another one—Eric the Red, or
William apt Jones, which is son of,
and even in biblical times there was
Judas, not Iscariot, so obviously the
necessity—   *Brother Wilfred glances up.*

there are flies coming in here—

the necessity to distinguish one from
another was felt.

Brother Wilfred begins his speech with a reference to himself, and it appears that his is some sort of obscure complaint to the abbot about people using his first name, because he speaks at first in the tone of an injured party. But then he begins to lecture the abbot on names in general, and his tone becomes stiffly pedantic and condescending, since what he is saying about the history of names could hardly be news to the abbot. If, as it seems, Brother Wilfred is saying all this as a way of supporting his objection to being first-named by others, his speech sounds slightly obsessive, and it is weakened by its invocation of so many different justifications for his position: he claims to be supported by the rules of the order, etiquette, personal preference, history, etymology, ethics, and convenience. The abbot now responds with an apparent attempt to shift and focus the definition of the situation. "What does it, aside from this point in the rule, of which I think we could spread out on a broader basis, what does it feel like to you when someone just uses your first name?" Brother Wilfred at first appears to accept the abbot's attempt to shift the issue from propriety to feelings, from rules of interaction and naming to psychological issues, and replies, "It's disrespect sort of, and I accept it that way." But though Brother Wilfred answers the abbot's question, he shifts the meaning from himself to the utterance: "It's disrespect." The disrespect, Brother Wilfred implicitly argues, is in the first-naming itself, and not merely in his own interpretation of it—he merely accepts the meaning. The abbot pursues his therapeutic agenda, which becomes clearer as he pushes his inquiry from the issue of what it feels like to where the feeling came from.

ABBOT: Has it always been that way?
BROTHER WILFRED: Yes. It has always been that way.

Brother Wilfred's answer is direct, but then the abbot seems to realize that the "it" in his question and Brother Wilfred's answer may not be the same. The abbot seems by "it" to refer to Brother Wilfred's feelings, and then to realize that Brother Wilfred may mean, by "it," that first-naming is disrespectful. He nudges the conversation toward the personal issue again.

ABBOT: I mean before you got Wilfred.
BROTHER WILFRED: Yes, it has always been that way. And another thing I never cared for very much when I was in the world known as Edmund, I did not care to be known as Ed or Eddie or whatever else you want to call the thing, except among my very close chums, of which there were five. Anyone beyond that, they'd be put down in short order.

Brother Wilfred has again evaded the abbot's suggestion to make the issue personal. Brother Wilfred accepts the abbot's push in the direction of talking about his earlier experiences of first-naming, which we and apparently he, too, recognize as attempts at making the issue one of personal therapy. The abbot clearly seems to be suggesting to Brother Wilfred that he talk about the matter in such a way as to make it not a matter of rules, nor of what other people may have done to violate those rules, but of Wilfred's "problem" with the situation: a classic therapeutic tactic of helping the client to understand how he feels about the problem, where it came from, and that he can solve it only by making it his own problem. But Brother Wilfred is a wily adversary in this struggle for definition of the situation, and even as he accepts the abbot's invitation to discuss his childhood memories of first-naming, he manages to describe those memories as constituting a precedent, a confirmation of what is acceptable and normal behavior, rather than as his own, individualized difficulty. In the classic sense, and from the abbot's point of view, he is resisting therapy, and he is very good at it. His subtle shifting of the grounds of the discussion from himself to the rules succeeds in distracting the abbot from the therapeutic agenda.

ABBOT: What's the difference between your close friends and—

BROTHER WILFRED: Chaps I grew up with, went to school with. Friends are friends; the rest are acquaintances.

Again Wilfred shifts from answering the biographical question to stating a rule; he also shifts the tense from the biographical past to the universal present: "Friends are friends; the rest are acquaintances." The abbot continues to be drawn into a fruitless discussion of the logic of Brother Wilfred's system.

ABBOT: Why would they have that privilege?
BROTHER WILFRED: Well, because, as I say, I've known them always.
ABBOT: So that using a first name implies access to you or having spent a lot of time with you.

Now Brother Wilfred seems to recognize the abbot's new tactic. Having failed to achieve a definition of the matter as Brother Wilfred's psychological problem, the abbot is trying to get inside Brother Wilfred's logical system, in an apparent attempt to argue with him on his own grounds. Brother Wilfred sees the flanking tactic and resists. His response is at first wary, then outright disruptive and distracting.

As well it might be. Just as Brother Wilfred's first speech supported his position with too many arguments, the abbot has now shifted from a therapeutic to a logical or argumentative mode. Implicitly he seems to be trying to find a way to convince Brother Wilfred to abandon his complaint about being first-named. So long as his discourse is purely therapeutic, he might be able to convince Brother Wilfred, and us, that his concern is solely for Brother Wilfred. But as soon as he shifts his ground, he casts doubt on his motives. His therapeutic maneuver, we may now suspect, is being used not simply for Brother Wilfred's benefit but as a way to manage a source of contention within the community. If this is so, then the abbot is using therapy for his own convenience, in his role as the leader of the institution, rather than simply as a healing art.

Of course, the abbot's shift from Brother Wilfred's feelings and experience to their underlying logic may be regarded as part of a single and sincere line of therapeutic discourse. From this point of view, the abbot's intentions are to adjust Wilfred to the community, and Wilfred is resisting logic, healing, and charitable accommodation.

Wiseman's evenhandedness throughout this encounter allows us to see the dialogue from the points of view of both participants. Brother Wilfred, we might argue, is resisting the bad faith of a therapy that has ulterior motives, in the name of a freedom from psychological manipulation and false intimacy that he finds in a more conservative interpretation of the rule of the order. From this point of view, the abbot might be seen as using his position of authority paradoxically, to invoke a modern doctrine of psychological adjustment in a way that both disavows and reinforces his control of the order. Brother Wilfred, on the other hand, could be seen as conservative, fussy, evasive, and disruptive, refusing either to accept the authority of the abbot or to take responsibility for his own problem. Running throughout the scene is the irony characteristic of Wiseman's films. In this scene, the abbot exercises control by disavowing it; Brother Wilfred takes responsibility for his own interpretation of the situation by refusing to concede to the abbot that that is what he is doing. The elderly conservative is cast as the rebel in a drama where change becomes the new rule, as he answers, "You could call it that if you wish." But, Brother Wilfred implies, I am not going to concede your renaming of my argument to grounds upon which you can defeat it. Naming, which has been the subject of the discussion between Brother Wilfred and the abbot, now becomes an issue within the discussion, as Brother Wilfred contends with the abbot over how to name the problem.

ABBOT: In a parallel way—

Brother Wilfred gazes upward, apparently watching something. Brother Wilfred then leans forward, out of the frame, and the camera zooms out to reveal that he has opened a desk drawer, from which he takes a fly swatter.

BROTHER WILFRED: You don't mind if I exercise a fly swatter here?

ABBOT: Why, help yourself.

Swatter in hand, Brother Wilfred leans back in his chair.

BROTHER WILFRED: In a who?

ABBOT: In a parallel way, that is time spent with people,

Brother Wilfred brings the fly swatter down on his desk with a loud smack, then sweeps the fly from the desk with the swatter. He leans forward and replaces the fly swatter in his desk drawer.

you might spend actually more time with some religious brother.

BROTHER WILFRED: But why should he not be known as "Brother"

Brother Wilfred settles himself back into his leaning posture, squirming a little against the back of his chair to find a comfortable position, and folds his arms once more across his chest. As the camera resumes its loose close-up

*of Brother Wilfred, he looks boldly at
the abbot.*

ABBOT: Well, I'm not arguing against
that, I was just putting those two
ideas together.

This statement of the abbot's may come as something of a surprise, since
he has apparently been suggesting an argument about just this point. The
commotion of the fly swatting, created as an apparent diversion by Brother
Wilfred, also diverts attention from the abbot's arguing, while claiming not
to argue. For the moment, Brother Wilfred accepts the responsibility of
carrying the burden of proof.

BROTHER WILFRED: I think he has earned the title, as far as that goes. He's gone
through a long way to get it.
ABBOT: Yeah, but the common denominator is a mutual experience, that is a mutual
experience helps people feel that there is respect.
BROTHER WILFRED: I would think so.
ABBOT: Whatever names are used.
BROTHER WILFRED: Another thing too on that score: there is so much a tendency
today for something to be taken up at once. I'm addressed by a first name by
somebody in the community who may or may not have the right to do so, and
immediately some guest or other with whom he is starts doing the same thing,
with no grounds, no basis, no nothing whatever, absolutely nothing whatever.
ABBOT: Right. Basically I—

Brother Wilfred interrupts the abbot in midsentence. This is the third
time he has used interruption as an essentially disruptive tactic in the conversation; he does this a total of four times. The disruptiveness of Brother
Wilfred's interruptions appears to be of two sorts: sometimes it cuts off a
speech of the abbot's that might be dangerous to his position; sometimes, as
in the next interruption, it also seems to assert that he was not ready to hand
over his own turn, as he continues with his former line of thought as if the
abbot had not spoken. This places the abbot in the position of having seemed
to interrupt Brother Wilfred. Control of timing and turn taking is crucial
throughout the conversation. The abbot not only never interrupts Brother
Wilfred, but waits out some long pauses in Brother Wilfred's speeches. The
abbot does, on several occasions, insert an apparently reinforcing "right" or
"unh huh" into Brother Wilfred's turns.

BROTHER WILFRED: That's a bad example.
ABBOT: You're saying you don't have a common experience with this person who
takes up your first name.
BROTHER WILFRED: Well, if you put it that way. I don't understand half of what you
say sometimes, but if that's your understanding of it, let's put it that way.

Brother Wilfred continues to resist the abbot's argument, which seems to boil down to something like this: you object to people here using your first name; you say that as a boy you allowed people who had known you for a time and shared experience with you to call you by your first name; your fellow members of this community share with you the most fundamental experience of all, experience of Christ; hence, your position is illogical and you should abandon your objection to their first-naming you.

But Brother Wilfred's resistance continues. The abbot has not yet called attention to it as resistance, but it must be clear to him and to us that Brother Wilfred is avoiding the issue. He at first concedes to the abbot the right to name the situation as he wishes, but without agreeing to see it that way himself. He then claims not to understand the abbot, but does not ask for an explanation, which seems to reveal his response not simply as a statement of his confusion but as an unwillingness to accept a premise that will win the abbot's point.

ABBOT: It seems to fit with your earlier experience, that you had no difficulty with first name or even abbreviated nickname because you had a common experience with those friends.
BROTHER WILFRED: If you wish to put it that way, put it that way. If that's how you understand it.
ABBOT: I was thinking that's what you said. Now you're feeling trapped, as if I were cornering you with an argument.

Finally the abbot calls attention to Brother Wilfred's resistance, which he does by interpreting Brother Wilfred's feelings. It is a bold move in the conversation, and it gives Brother Wilfred the option of saying, yes, he does feel that the abbot is trying to trap him—a feeling that we might, at this point, partly endorse. But to admit that he feels trapped would have tactical disadvantages. Either it would concede the weakness of his position, or it would force him to accuse the abbot of trying to trap him. He tries to refuse the gambit.

BROTHER WILFRED: I'm at the end of anything on that.
ABBOT: I was just trying to illuminate what you were actually saying. I'm not trying to trap you.

The abbot's direct reference to his own good faith of course calls attention to the issue of his good faith, and to the tactical advantage that he has in the conversation—where his position as abbot would make this virtually a forbidden charge. So that even if the abbot is in good faith, and even if we believe that he is, he has made it an issue and has put it to use in the struggle with Brother Wilfred. Brother Wilfred now simply tries to end the conversation.

BROTHER WILFRED: I have told you all I can tell you on that.
ABBOT: Well, do you want to go on to another subject?

BROTHER WILFRED: Anything you wish.
ABBOT: Well, if you don't mind, I think I can illuminate your understanding.
BROTHER WILFRED: Illuminate.
ABBOT: That in the growing-up process, the common experience—
BROTHER WILFRED: Yes, you've said that; you've said it ad nauseam.

Brother Wilfred now seems desperate indeed. He tries to end the conversation. Then he in effect tells the abbot to continue the conversation without him. He echoes the abbot's request that he be allowed to illuminate with a graceless, clipped invitation: "Illuminate." As soon as the abbot begins to do so, Brother Wilfred interrupts the abbot with a strongly worded accusation that he is just repeating himself.

ABBOT: Right. Well, isn't that true? That's what you're saying.
BROTHER WILFRED: Okay. Yes, if you think so, that's fine.
ABBOT: So what would seem to be the parallel in our case here is the common experience of Christ would be the equivalent.
BROTHER WILFRED: No. I don't think so.
ABBOT: What's the difference?
BROTHER WILFRED: I don't know.
ABBOT: It just is different?
BROTHER WILFRED: It's different.
ABBOT: Unh huh.

The abbot begins again, and Brother Wilfred adopts yet another tactic. After repeating his ploy of telling the abbot he can call the situation anything he wishes, Brother Wilfred refuses to agree with the abbot, and then refuses to explain his disagreement. Stalemate.

The encounter between Brother Wilfred and the abbot ends inconclusively, but that partly enhances the scene's contribution to the film as a whole, in which the dialectical tensions aroused by the introduction of psychological principles to the monastery's mission of personal healing and corporate management result in a standoff between a sixth-century religious order and a twentieth-century psychological perspective.

Variations on these associations are played out through the rest of the film. One of the great pleasures and contributions of *Essene* is that as a speculation on rule, religion, and psychology it does not take sides or distract us with a situation in which bureaucrats contend with social victims or delinquents. The film's lack of clamor and conflict, its contemplative richness and ambiguity, give it an important place in the body of Wiseman's work as a whole.

Juvenile Court

In his very next film, *Juvenile Court*, Wiseman returns to the world of public institutions. But different as the Memphis, Tennessee, Juvenile Court is from a Benedictine monastery, Wiseman continues in this film his inquiry into the way we mix law, religion, and psychology in the maintenance of public order. We do not wish to reduce *Juvenile Court* to this single theme, nor to suggest that *Juvenile Court* and *Essene* are or mean the same thing. Wiseman is more ambitious than that. We shall try to show how in the context of *Juvenile Court* Wiseman uses the possible conflict of law, psychology, and, to a smaller extent, religion to frame his exploration of the institution. In *Juvenile Court,* the mixed agenda of the court to administer justice and to seek the welfare of its juvenile clients at times results in confusion or contradiction, and at times threatens due process itself.

The early scenes of *Juvenile Court* locate the film and establish the initial questions that a viewer might take to later, more extended sequences.[11] We see the Memphis skyline, the Memphis Municipal Juvenile Court building, a police car. A policeman removes a pair of handcuffs from a boy's wrists: this is a place where the institution has an extraordinary degree of immediate physical power over its clients. In a brief scene, a boy says into a telephone, presumably to his parents, "If you love me, why don't you come up here and get me out, cause I ain't done nothing." And so at once, to the issue of the institution's control over children are added the issues of guilt and innocence, truth and lies, and the mysteries of family love, with the obligations and disappointments they imply. But we are not given time to absorb or reflect on these matters, as the film continues to sort through short introductory scenes. A boy cries, repeatedly, "Mama, I don't want to go," but both mother and police officer deny his appeal. A police officer phones in a shoplifting report, the narrative of the arrest made bleaker by the jargon of the trade. A boy on probation is questioned about his illegal possession of a knife and told repeatedly that his story is just not going to be believed. A man informs a girl accused of shoplifting of her Miranda rights, a recital made newly strange to television viewers who have heard it on TV cop shows by its application here to an accused juvenile petty thief. A boy is photographed and searched. Three boys are given short haircuts.

These are scenes of intake and process, establishing for us the formal role of the institution in apprehending children, separating them from their parents and other outside connections, processing them legally, searching and shearing them. We see a room full of boys gazing at a television set; then a prison yard filled with boys being led in calisthenics. These opening scenes, with their chilling routine of separation and confinement, buzzing hair clippers and clanging doors, are only part of the story, however; we soon see that the institution is also in the complicated double business of seeking the truth and trying to control and change human beings.

The processing continues and moves to a still more intrusive level, introducing for the first time in the film the issue of psychology as a tool in the institution. In a small bare office, a man and boy are seated on opposite sides of a desk. The man speaks in a bored singsong that implies how many young people have been through his office, and how the regular recital of a formal speech is asserted to stand for the impartiality, objectivity, and expertness of the diagnostic procedure.

PSYCHOLOGIST: And now, Charles, I'm going to show you some cards that are anything, everything, or nothing. They're whatever you think they are, they're whatever they look like to you. As long as the cards remind you of something— and it can be anything, everything, or nothing, it can be the whole card or part of the card—as long as the card reminds you of something, I want you to tell me what. When they no longer remind you of anything, you tell me that. Can you do that? Do you understand now? Here is your first card. What does it remind you of?

CHARLES: A butterfly.

PSYCHOLOGIST: Anything else?

CHARLES: A bat.

PSYCHOLOGIST: A bat? Does it remind you of anything else?

CHARLES: A bird.

PSYCHOLOGIST: A bird. Does it remind you of anything else?

CHARLES: No.

To make sense out of this brief diagnostic scene, we must attend to it at several levels at once. We do not possess the expert knowledge that may permit the psychologist to make sense of the test, but part of our curiosity may be directed to intepreting the boy's answers from the psychologist's point of view. What do his answers reveal? And what of the boy's point of view? He is presumably trying to see what he can in the cards, but he must also understand that anything he says is subject to interpretations that are outside his control. This is dangerous territory, in which any answer might get him into various difficulties. Would we have said that the cards looked like a butterfly, a bat, a bird? What would that do to our chances of getting out of here? Following so closely upon the heels of the Miranda warning in an earlier scene, this diagnostic scene alerts us to the possibly expanding dimensions of the warning that "anything you say can and will be held against you."

If the inkblot scene has alerted us to the hazards of psychological testing, the next scene builds upon it. The psychologist we heard in the previous scene is sitting at a desk with a probation officer. He says to her, "Okay, on the basis that you have given about your reason for referral and on the basis of the background information that we have in regard to this eleven-year-old female black. The testing, I'll go over with you in loose terms and then we'll put it into written form if it fits, for your purposes in court, and then we'll make some additional recommendations." If we presuppose no special knowledge on the part of viewers of the procedures of the legal system, it must seem strange that the psychologist seems to offer to negotiate his report with the probation officer and turn in a written form suited to the probation officer's judgment of what she might want to accomplish in court. Is the psychology a genuine form of inquiry or merely an accessory mode of persuasion, called in to bolster judgments that the system has arrived at by other means? Why is it relevant that the girl is black, and why does the psychologist comment that the self-portrait that forms the basis of his diagnosis is not shaded to indicate her color?

The next two extended sequences are full of sadness and perplexity. An eleven-year-old girl charged with violating parole is separated from her mother and assigned to a foster home. This is evidently the girl whose self-portrait was being diagnosed by the psychologist and the probation officer in the earlier scene. As the sequence opens, the weeping girl is being led down a corridor and into court by the probation officer, who admonishes her, "Don't cry yet. You haven't even been to court." In the courtroom before the hearing begins, the probation officer tells the girl, "We want to help you, but for some reason your mama can't make you mind. And you know Dr. Lee, the man you talked to yesterday? He thinks you need a home, where you'd have a mama that would really make you toe the line and stay out of trouble. Cause you're not a bad little girl. Would you rather be in a home than in an institution?" The girl replies, weeping, in a way that gives an entirely different meaning to the word "home," revealing as she does so the euphemistic rhetoric of the system, "I want to go home."

Wiseman places us in a position to recognize the circular pattern of decision making here. In this scene, the probation officer justifies the recommendation for a foster home by saying that it was Dr. Lee's advice. But in the earlier scene with Dr. Lee, it seemed clear that Dr. Lee was willing to recommend whatever the probation officer thought was best. The decision can hardly be argued, because it is not clear where it has come from. Even less is it arguable by an eleven-year-old girl.

The girl has been truant from the sixth grade and has lower than average grades. This, and unconfirmed speculation about prostitution, is taken as evidence of "lack of supervision." As she weeps, she is told not to run away from the foster home or she will be sent to an institution—a training school. Then she is offered a kleenex. We see the girl and her mother in a corridor, allowed a last visit, weeping.

In the judge's chambers, a lawyer and social worker discuss a case of child abuse with the judge. A three-year-old boy has been badly beaten, while naked, with a belt, by the mother's fiance. The judge concludes, "Well, it looks like this prospective stepfather just got carried away, a little over-zealous in correcting the child." The lawyer supports the judge's opinion by quoting a psychiatrist, who apparently stated, "I think his response to the child's behavior was an overreaction. . . . Essentially what we have here is a man who suddenly has the responsibility of disciplining a child of three-and-a-half years old, after no previous experience. I think his response to the child's behavior was an overreaction, but I do not see him as a future threat to this child or any other." The judge now moves toward the decision that we have seen coming almost from the beginning of the conference:

JUDGE: Well, it doesn't appear to be a willful thing then and he just, uh, overdid the job of punishment and spanked the child with a child's belt, which if corporal punishment is in order wouldn't appear to be an unusual instrument, would it?
SOCIAL WORKER: No.
JUDGE: We've seen so many cases in here where a child, children have been beaten with ironing cords and bed slats, and tortured in various other ways, and no prosecution then is recommended at this time and we'll, and your recommendation is that the child will be placed back with the mother under the protective supervision of the welfare department, and hopefully everyody's learned a lesson from this experience.
SOCIAL WORKER: Yes.
JUDGE: Okay, we'll do that, then.

In these sequences of the truant girl and the beaten boy, we see the retrospective and prospective logics of the system, trying to determine what happened, and why, and trying to devise a system for controlling the behavior of the participants in the future. In both cases, the judgments are necessarily based not simply upon facts but upon assessments about human motivation—the domain of psychology. Unlike many of Wiseman's films, *Juvenile Court* has several episodes in which the characters arrive at and announce decisions. Even so, the episodes are inconclusive, since judgments about the past, even when supported by expert psychological testimony, are made on the basis of probabilities and commonplaces and since we cannot know the consequences of these decisions in the future that lies beyond the end of the film. Although it would of course be possible for Wiseman, or perhaps this book, to reveal something of the later lives of these children, it is important to notice that that is not the point of the film. Although the effect of the film depends upon our caring about these children, it also depends upon our understanding how difficult it is to make just and wise decisions about their lives. The film's biographical interest is incidental—Wiseman prefers to direct our attention to the institutional decision-making process, and, without apparently denying the at least normal goodwill and competence of the participants, to make plain its limits. Wiseman does not go outside the frame of the film to confirm or deny the accuracy of the court's decisions, though he does, by editing, encourage a style of comparative thinking that allows us to attend to the constraints and limits of the institutional process. In the juxtaposition of the truancy and child-abuse cases, for example, we are able to see that the court's decisions are made in a framework of values that believes in discipline and intervention in the lives of children and on these grounds sends a truant to a foster home but sends a child beater home for another chance. The product of this institution is decisions, and we often sense the urgency that moves the workers here to collaborate in the disposition of a case so that they can clear the way for the next case—a classic institutional ulterior motive. Psychological understandings, both expert and locally commonsensical, form an essential resource for these processes.

Juvenile Court looks briefly at a number of cases. Three cases, all involving white male teenagers, come in for extended treatment. Two of them begin early in the film and appear again later; the third case runs uninterrupted as the final long sequence of the film.

Because the juvenile court acts as both a judicial and a helping institution, it is forced to negotiate its way through occasionally clashing agendas. The case of Robert Y. is an example. We first meet Robert when he is in confinement, charged with selling drugs and being counseled by two ministers from the Teen Challenge program. One of the ministers, who says he is a former drug user, tells Robert that the only way to change is to accept religion. "You need Jesus. You need a power greater than the power that you are serving now—the devil, sin, and drugs. The only greater power in the world is, and the ultimate power in the world is, Jesus himself." Robert agrees and is led through a prayer. Several scenes later, we see Robert again, talking to his mother. He speaks of trying to get into the navy, says he has learned his lesson, and tells his mother about Teen Challenge: "They gave me a Bible and everything." His mother is skeptical. "But Bob, they did that before and you didn't do anything about it."

After several intervening sequences we see Robert Y. again, this time in court. The bailiff introduces the judge, Kenneth A. Turner, and then Robert Y. is presented, charged with "unlawful possession and sale of LSD." A public defender, who throughout the scene appears to be a little at a loss, says that Robert denies the charge. After hearing a narrative of the charge, the judge says he sees no reason not to refer Robert as an adult to the criminal court system. The public defender attempts to argue that the charge ought to be dismissed, since the police have not even attempted to prove their charge. Then the Teen Challenge ministers ask to be heard. They narrate their own criminal records and ask to be allowed to work with Robert. The judge asks to hear from Robert, telling him that "if I have to send you and a thousand like you to the penitentiary [to prevent drug selling] this court's prepared to do it."

Robert denies that he sold the drugs. And here the judge, who has admonished the public defender that this is not a trial over Robert's guilt or innocence, replies to Robert, "Well, the police say they have pretty good proof that you did." The judge asks the police officer who presented the charges whether they can be substantiated and is told that the alleged crime was witnessed by undercover agents, who cannot be brought into court. It suddenly becomes clear that Robert and the public defender have made a dangerous choice. The judge rules that since Robert will not confess to the charges, he is not properly remorseful and therefore not a candidate for the Teen Challenge program. Before making the ruling final, the judge asks whether the probation officer has any comment. The probation officer, revealing apparently confidential information Robert told him during the course of counseling, says that Robert has admitted to selling other drugs, but not those he is accused of. "But, Bobby, you know, told me the other day that he has sold things on the street but he does deny this LSD. But to me, it's kind of a fine point. . . . I think he definitely needs a structured adult-level program to work in, where somebody can work with him on an individual therapy level." Hence, from the judge's point of view, Robert is not entitled to the therapies of the juvenile court system unless he confesses to a crime he denies. The probation officer supports the judge's decision by offering a therapeutic rationale that apparently breaks the confidence of the counseling relationship in order to send Robert to a criminal court so that he can be sentenced to an adult penal institution and its therapy program. As viewers, we have no way of knowing whether the judge and the juvenile court system are making a wise decision about Robert Y., but Wiseman makes it quite clear that he is in a no-win condition of double jeopardy. What the boy told a probation officer in a counseling setting is used against him in a decision leading to criminal proceedings. When the boy denies the charges against him, this is taken as evidence of his resistance to therapy, and so he is ordered to stand trial in an adult criminal court so that he can get therapy.

Robert's lawyer seems marginally competent, and, in the outcome, seems to have ignored the judge's hint that, if he would plea bargain, Robert could get off with a lesser charge. Even the Teen Challenge advocates, who are there ostensibly to support Robert, seem primarily interested in vividly testifying before the judge about their own former depravity—which makes a good story but does not seem to win much sympathy from the judge. Robert, lost in the shuffle and marked by a past history of involvement with the juvenile court, is sent off to be tried as an adult.

In the next extended case, a fifteen-year-old boy named Tommy is accused of sexually molesting a very young girl for whom he was baby-sitting. We first see Tommy in an early scene in which he is asked by an adult, apparently a psychologist, in an interview room, what he is charged with. Tommy replies in legal jargon, which seems precocious and perhaps suspicious in such a young person, but when the interviewer asks that Tommy state the matter in his own words, that, too, sounds problematic, because he is asking Tommy to describe in his own words a crime that Tommy denies.

PSYCHOLOGIST: You want to tell me just a little bit about the reason you're here?
TOMMY: Ah, yes, they got me here for, let's see, assault and battery to a minor under twelve with intent to sexually fondle.
PSYCHOLOGIST: I'm not too interested in our jargon, but I'm interested in how you perceive it, so tell me in your own words what you think you're here for.
TOMMY: Ah, they say—
PSYCHOLOGIST: I'm not concerned with what they say, I'm concerned with what you say. What do you say about it?

TOMMY: Ah, it's all a bunch of bunk because I'm here for no reason at all, really.
PSYCHOLOGIST: Do you, do you know what the charge sheet reads?
TOMMY: Yes.
PSYCHOLOGIST: Are these charges true?
TOMMY: No.

This conversation with the psychologist appears very peculiar, because of the way the psychologist changes directions. He tells the boy not to use the jargon of the court, but when Tommy's vernacular response is a simple denial, the psychologist returns to the court's language, which a moment earlier he said he was not interested in. This peculiar behavior may, particularly in the context of the film as it develops, make us suspicious about the use of psychologists to extract confessions of guilt in a diagnostic or therapeutic session, which are then applied in a situation of criminal liability. Reflection might tell us that it is the responsibility of the psychologist to determine whether the boy understands the charges against him, but this technical matter is not explained in the film, and so a developing suspicion about the role of psychology appears to be confirmed.

In the more extended later sequence, Tommy appears in court, and then the scene shifts almost immediately to the judge's chambers for an informal conference, first with the mother of the allegedly molested child, then with Tommy. The two opposing lawyers and a probation officer are present at both of these conferences, but it is the judge who leads the interrogation. From the moment that the courtroom scene opens, the issue of expert and commonsense psychology runs through the inquiry. Tommy's lawyer requests a lie detector test, suggesting it might lead to appropriate psychiatric care if Tommy should prove guilty; the judge responds with a reference to the psychiatric report on the case and then agrees to the lawyer's request for a conference in the judge's chambers.

With her allegedly molested daughter seated in her lap, the mother tells her story to the judge—who sits at his desk with his arm about the girl's only slightly older brother. The mother's story is somewhat inconclusive, since it is based primarily on her recollections of the half-articulate story told to her by a very young child, and since it is clear that she was, as Tommy's lawyer later points out, preoccupied with the possibility of sexual molestation. The judge asks her what should be done if the boy is found guilty.

MOTHER: Well, he's got to be sick or disturbed to do anything like that, and, uhm, he needs attention. He needs psychiatric help. It would keep him from hurting some other little girl. And, uhm, it's like this, she's my daughter. Ah, I'm not, I hate to see any of these children up here, they're kids to me, you know. I don't care if I am a few years older I hate to see them up here and getting in this trouble, but when somebody hurts one of my children, I want them punished. Ah, you know what I'm talking about?
JUDGE: Sure.
MOTHER: Now, the boy is sick and I feel sorry for him. To that extent, you know, for

any sick person, but I can't bend over double for somebody, you know, like that. I've got to think about my children.

JUDGE: The psychologist says that the young man has hostility towards his father. And, uhm, seems to be striving for appropriate adjustment in sexual areas, but is hampered and fearful of the male role as a result of conflicts he has with his father.

MOTHER: Well, he told me.

JUDGE: He's a mixed-up kid.

Wiseman presents us here with a welter of seeming improprieties. Why would the judge, who has not yet interviewed Tommy, seem to presume his guilt and, worse, share a psychological report with the mother? Once again, psychology is used as a way to prop up what seems to be a predisposition on the part of the court to assume the guilt of a juvenile offender. This theme continues to play itself out when the mother leaves and the judge interviews Tommy. "Now, you're accused of fondling this little girl, Tommy. Now, I'll tell you right now, regardless of whether you did it or not, we've concluded that you do need some help, you do need to talk to a counselor, have a psychiatric counseling to help you straighten out your thinking, you see."

Wiseman presents us with no particular information that would force us to conclude that Tommy is innocent, nor, though the case was resolved after the shooting but long before the release of the film, does he inform us of the outcome. His purpose, clearly, is not to persuade us that one side or the other is right, but to contemplate the process by which a decision is reached. And about that process he induces doubts. In case after case, psychological testimony is used in such a way as to place due process in jeopardy. In scene after scene, the court seems to presume that children are more likely to be guilty than adults are. Earlier in the film, after we have first met Tommy being interrogated by the psychologist but before his case is heard by the judge, Wiseman presents us with a contrasting scene, in which an allegation of child molestation against a stepfather is dismissed as hardly worth examining. In that scene, the probation officer describes her conversation with the stepdaughter, who had also attempted suicide, and says, "I told her, you could have cut a little bit deeper." And in the scene immediately following the judge's interview with Tommy, a terrified and heavily bandaged young boy is shown in an office with a probation officer, who addresses him from across a desk in a loud, public voice. "Okay, well, I guess we'll have to wait until your grandmother comes in to get any more information, but you say that your uncle poured hot grease on you. You didn't knock it off the stove, did you? Or did you? You say he poured it on you. Now, what did you do, son, to make him pour this on you, did you do anything to him? Or did you do anything to him? All right, we'll certainly be in touch with him and see what caused this. See what happened."

Juvenile Court ends with a long sequence, occupying approximately half an hour, in which we hear the case of another young man named Robert, this one accused of armed robbery. Wiseman asks us to use all that we have learned earlier in the film as we watch this complex drama unfold. The hearing on the case begins in the courtroom and then moves to the judge's chambers. During the opening courtroom deliberations, the prosecutor requests a probable cause hearing and asks that Robert be remanded for trial as an adult. Robert's lawyer asks that Robert be treated as a juvenile and suggests that the court hear favorably Robert's claim that he was along for the robbery as a driver and that he went along only because the other defendant threatened his life. After the presentation of the facts of the case by a police officer, the judge reminds those in attendance that he, too, was once a policeman and suggests a conference. It will soon become clear that the judge is going to push the two attorneys into plea bargaining. The scene in the courtroom seems to take place among judge, attorneys, and police officer. We twice see Robert, but he does not speak during these proceedings, and is not given a chance to speak until his case has been, in effect, decided.[12]

In the judge's chambers, the phrase "plea bargaining" is never uttered, but that is clearly what is taking place. The process begins by a softening up of the defendant's position: the judge indicates his potential willingness to consider some course other than sending Robert to trial as an adult, and the prosecutor indicates that if Robert were tried as an adult for armed robbery he thinks a conviction could be obtained—which might subject Robert to a twenty-year sentence. Robert's past counts against him. He has apparently admitted to experimenting with drugs, and he has previously had a brush with the juvenile court, when he briefly ran away from home. The earlier association with the court is clearly a history that counts against him, and his lawyer volunteers that "the boy has a psychological problem. Now I understand from the parents that the boy was seeing a clinical psychologist even before he came to this jurisdiction." In reply, the judge makes it clear what he is willing to offer the defendant. "Course, I think you know now the only question we're trying to determine here is whether or not this boy will be sent to a state correctional school as a juvenile or whether or not he will be held for action by the grand jury and tried as an adult." After some additional consideration of Robert's background, the prosecution asks whether the defendant's lawyer would be willing to forego a request for probation if the state did not object to Robert's being treated as a juvenile. The defense attorney replies:

LAWYER: Of course I'd leave that entirely up to the discretion of the judge. I feel like sometimes we don't necessarily do or strictly follow what is prescribed by law books, but the end result of what we're trying to achieve here, of what I'm trying to achieve here, is the manifest best interest of this boy. Now I have to tell you candidly, whether that means putting his parents down, or whatever is involved, obviously they're partially responsible for whatever the boy is today. And I'm interested in doing whatever is in the best interest of the boy. Now I just can't believe that the best interest of this society and this boy lies in his being sent down here and thrown into that county jail and being tried as a criminal, ah, for armed robbery. I don't believe, as Mr. Herbert said, this boy just has no concept of that. And, and, I think his best interests would be served in whatever the court feels would be necessary. Now strictly thinking, he doesn't think that he's guilty of any armed robbery because he didn't have any intent in his mind of doing this, but as the court has pointed out so often the defendant doesn't realize that he can be guilty of a lesser offense, and so forth. To be specific and answer Mr. Graves, yes, I'd be willing to enter a plea of guilty if the court saw fit to retain jurisdiction of this young man in whichever way that it would be in the court's mind as to what would be in his best interest and the best interest of the society.

JUDGE: You want to plead him guilty to simple robbery, two counts, and I'll send him to the training school.

Robert's lawyer asks for a moment to confer with Robert and his parents, and we see him in a hurried conference, at which we hear Robert speak for the first time. He asks, "Can't we fight it out in court and prove that I'm innocent?" Back in the judge's chambers, from which Robert and his parents are again excluded, the deal is struck, despite Robert's objections. The legal professionals agree that they are acting in Robert's best interests. Back in the courtroom, the judge for the first time interrogates Robert directly, but the decision, we know, in a dramatic irony rare in Wiseman's narrative technique, has already been reached.

Robert, I think you've been doing some rationalizing and you've convinced yourself that what you're saying is true, but you haven't been able to convince anybody else. Under the circumstances, Robert, you stand before this court charged with robbery with a deadly weapon, two counts. You know what the penalty is for robbery with a deadly weapon? The maximum penalty under law is death in the electric chair. That's how serious this matter is, and if this court were to waive jurisdiction and allow you to be tried in the criminal court, I think the least you could get off of this would be about twenty years in the penitentiary. Your lawyer knows that, and I know it, and I don't want to see you face that. Because that's what's gonna happen to you, that's what would happen to you. Now I don't think that you're a mean or vicious person. And your parents, your lawyer, and this court want to do what's in your best interest and at the same time protect the community. We have to follow the law, so, at this time, I'm going to find you guilty of the lesser offense of robbery, two counts, and order that you be committed to the Tennessee Department of Correction for an indefinite period of time. Now, you're going to go to the State Vocational Training School for Boys. You can make it easy on yourself there or hard on yourself there. And how long you stay there will just depend on you. And in time, Robert, I'm sure you'll realize that what is being done here today is in your best interest.

The court recesses, and we see a hurried conversation afterward. A probation officer tells Robert how lucky he has been.

PROBATION OFFICER: Robert, we did a miracle today. Now, they want to hit you with twenty years. Now, they did this to a boy about two months ago, and all, and he was a driver, and they gave him the electric chair. Bob, he's sitting on death row, and he was a driver. Now, this was a white boy, he was a driver and they gave him the electric chair. We did a miracle. I know this is a hell of a blow. But, Bob, this can be erased. This can be erased, this record can be erased. Ten years from now this will be a bad dream. But the other way, Bob, it will follow you, it would have followed you to the grave. So help me. So we did a miracle. I want you to look at it that way. I know it's hard to look at it that way, but we did a miracle. Because that man is after your skin.

ROBERT: But why must they lie? Why?

PROBATION OFFICER: Because you were a driver. It didn't matter if you were a lookout, or just a participator, or what. Now, let's handle this like a man, because you're approaching adulthood. I know this is a bitter pill to swallow. But it can be erased. This is America, believe me.

The probation officer's consolatory speech presents not the justice but the luck of the decision, in which the system could otherwise have done much worse. It is accepted, and pressed, as a natural fact, that although the system is harsher to black defendants (Robert is white), that system was out to get Robert, and he was saved only by a miracle. The key to his salvation is that he is to be treated as a juvenile and deprived of the power to participate in the deal. But then he is asked to take it like a man. Still, we may believe that all of these things, which must count in the narrative as ironic, may be true: that Robert is better off being treated as a juvenile, that he would have been worse off if he were black, and that he should be encouraged to act like a man. It may be harder for us to believe that "this can be erased," since the film is full of cases, including this one, in which the disposition rests both upon a narrative of the case at hand and upon the system's apparently ineradicable memory for disciplinary or psychological "records." Wiseman has made it clear to us that to visit the juvenile court to discuss a disciplinary problem, or to visit a psychologist, is going to constitute grounds for assuming the worst if the juvenile involved is ever brought before the court on a criminal matter.

Robert, his parents, and the probation officer exit. The sequence, and the film, end soon after the prosecutor and Robert's lawyer meet on their way out.

PROSECUTOR: You did a good job.

LAWYER: Thank you.

The lawyers and several other men exit in comradely fashion, and the camera returns to a long shot of the exterior of the courthouse. End of film.

What are we to make of Wiseman's use of psychology in these films? In one sense, he has again shown us something about the rules of art and logic that govern the construction and invited interpretation of his films, each of which recreates at the stylistic level the mode in which we are asked to apprehend it. He also seems to be speaking substantively, if indirectly, about both institutional experience and institutional processes. In his essay cited at the beginning of this chapter, Wiseman said that juries were not capable of the complicated technical judgments that psychological testimony required of them. And yet, in *Essene* and *Juvenile Court* Wiseman is asking his own audience to make extraordinarily complicated judgments about the material he places before them. Is he being inconsistent? How can he so distrust juries and so trust his audience? The answer to this question speaks directly to the ethics and aesthetics of Wiseman's films. The films seem to suggest, singly and together, in substance and in style, the difficulty of finding the truth and to suggest that, whatever the truth, everyday routine and everyday suffering must somehow be met.

We do not wish to suggest that *Essene* and *Juvenile Court* are reducible to attacks on psychology. Both films are about larger matters, but in both Wiseman employs psychology, and our attitudes about it, as a way into those larger matters. In his suspicion of psychology and psychiatry, Wiseman draws upon tradition in film and in everyday, commonsense folklore. The same suspicion of psychology surfaces clearly in cinema as early as *The Cabinet of Dr. Caligari* (1919) and is represented again and again in mainstream Hollywood cinema: as for example in Hitchcock's *Spellbound* (1945) and *Psycho* (1960). But the films are not merely a put-down of psychology. Rather, as the suspicion of psychology as a healing art subordinated to the aims of a brotherhood of the spirit or an overburdened bureaucracy of juvenile justice deepens and grows, it leads us to themes that digress and take on separate substance.

The matter of psychology intersects with but does not altogether account for the separate issue of narrative itself. In both films, psychology is used as a way of interrogating the past, on the one hand by attempting through narrative to account for the psychological present, and on the other by using a present-tense assessment of a person's psychological condition to make a judgment about the accuracy of an account about the past. In the case of Brother Wilfred, the abbott probes Wilfred's present feelings by trying to find their origin in a narrative of Wilfred's childhood. But in the case of the alleged offenders in *Juvenile Court*, the judge again and again seems to base a determination of the facts of the case upon what seems probable given a report from the psychologists. Partly for this reason, *Juvenile Court* seems to offer a more deeply reflective understanding of judicial process than Wiseman's earlier law review article, which advised that psychological assessment and the determination of the facts of the case be kept separate: as he shows in *Juvenile Court*, they cannot be kept separate, since, in the absence of perfectly compelling evidence of the facts of the case, a determination of the facts must partly be based upon what seems probable given what we can know of the defendant. Such judgments, whether commonsense or expert, are inevitably partly "psychological," as Aristotle argued in *The Rhetoric* in the fourth century B.C..

In *Juvenile Court*, the question of narrative takes on a life of its own, since narrative is at the heart of almost every dispute we witness in the film and since Wiseman, in this film, presents more fully developed narrative sequences than in almost any other film. For example, one striking feature of the film's structure is that the narratives into which it inquires are in virtually every case those of its juvenile clients and defendants. It is they who have a past into which the court and we inquire; it is they who have a future that the court is responsible for molding.[13] But the institution and its officers seem to exist in a continuing present tense. Their past is not open to our inspection, nor is their future in question. The filmmaker exists in the same present tense—what we learn of the past we learn only because its recital is enacted during the term of Wiseman's visit to the institution; we are told nothing of the eventual disposition of these cases in the future beyond the visit. What is the effect of this exemption of the institution and the filmmaker from history?

What do we know of the judge? He mentions in passing, late in the film, that he was once an investigator: neither he nor Wiseman tell us that Judge Kenneth Turner was formerly a captain of detectives.[14] Wiseman does not mention in the film what he later told an interviewer who inquired how Tommy did on his lie detector test: that the lie detector test became unnecessary when the boy confessed "a couple of weeks" after Wiseman left Memphis.[15]

What of the filmmaker? Like most Americans, but unlike most of the children in *Juvenile Court*, Fred Wiseman is granted by artistic license and social convention a large measure of control over his presentation of himself. Wiseman was trained as a lawyer, taught occasional courses to law students, and was trained as a court reporter during his army service. He was the losing defendant in a bitter and highly publicized trial involving his first documentary film. He has sometimes described his G.I.-bill years in Paris as devoted to study and service in an attorney's office, but details of that period have never been revealed.

We do not mention these bits of biography about Kenneth Turner and Frederick Wiseman to suggest that they should somehow have been included in the film, but that the choice of leaving them out is part of the rhetorical design of the film. Especially in *Juvenile Court*, and to a lesser extent in *Essene* and *Welfare*, those who tell the stories of their past are at the bottom of the social hierarchy. In his films, Wiseman thus uses narrative in a reflexive and ironic way, in which our suspicion of institutional hierarchy extends to a suspicion of narrative itself, so that both appear likely to be unreliable and to be a distraction from the reality that is present before us. In *Juvenile Court*, the facts of the case are not what may have happened in a Kentucky Fried Chicken holdup on a Memphis midnight; the facts are in the courtroom we see before us at the present moment in the film. It is in the present tense, Wiseman seems to tell us, that we have our only chance to act, however absurd our choices.

Chapter 6

Justifying Curiosity
Primate

The mission of rhetorical critics is to pay close attention to the communicative potentials of symbolic forms, to understand not only the forms themselves but also what listeners, readers, and watchers are likely to make of those forms. Rhetorical critics inquire into meaning, not simply in an artifact but also in the pragmatics of that artifact: that is, in how a human being can, or did, or should use that artifact. Rhetorical critics are interested not only in *what* meaning emerges from a text or artifact, but also in *how* it emerges. This is a complicated matter, but it seems apparent, at least, that a critical account must do more than propose a reduction of its text to a theme or an effect: the game of critical truth or consequences. In rhetorical situations, the connections among referent, author, text, and reader are always mutual.

Even if focused pragmatically on the "effect" of a text, a rhetorical critic is usually going to do best if he or she is attentive to the details of the text; to the contexts, both internal and external, that give that text meaning; and to the forms and processes that connect to create meanings. For modern rhetorical criticism, a meaning-centered approach brings to the text a curiosity not simply about the structure of the text, or about the clues to the author revealed by the text, or about the extent to which the text mirrors "reality," but also about the ways in which the text invites an audience to make meanings. The text implies its audience and the interpretive actions of its audience.

In this chapter, we propose to examine the rhetoric of *Primate*, arguing that the film is a rhetorical documentary about the implications of human curiosity in an institutional setting—a primate research center. Wiseman uses comparison, sequence, and sound-image relations to employ and transcend filmic and rhetorical genres, enabling him to engage the viewer in a reflective exploration of human being. *Primate* (1974) demonstrates how facts can be recontextualized into complex meanings and how audiences can be actively engaged in the process of constructing meanings. Wiseman helps us to understand how meanings are made by audiences and how audiences turn "facts" into symbols with which to comprehend their world.

To understand how Wiseman's *Primate* works, and its significance to studies in rhetoric and film, we need to see it as part of a developing tradition, a continually evolving dialogue in the arts and social sciences of the past century. To place Wiseman fully into the context of Western cultural developments is beyond the scope of this chapter and so we propose instead to begin with a brief discussion of two authors who are precursors of Wiseman. Anthony Trollope, a nineteenth-century master of political realism and personal romance, and James Agee, a twentieth-century documentarist who turned facts into imaginative activities, help us trace the development of the issues of audience action and the transformation of facts.

Anthony Trollope understood that fictions are made by authors in collaboration with their audiences. In the first of his Palliser novels, *Can You Forgive Her?*, Trollope addresses his reader directly, starting with the title itself. He has been describing how his heroine, Alice Vavasour, jilted the virtuous John Grey because she felt she might have fallen in love with her own cousin, the scoundrel George Vavasour. She even promises to marry her cousin, thinking she can help him. But she soon discovers her mistake and understands that she can never love George—and, of course, that she cannot permit herself to return to John Grey. In the midst of Alice's muddle occurs this passage: "She had done very wrong. She knew that she had done wrong. . . . She understood it now, and knew that she could not forgive herself. But can you forgive her, delicate reader? Or am I asking the question too early in my story? [We are on page 384 of an 800-page novel.] For myself, I have forgiven her. . . . And you also must forgive her before we close the book, or else my story will have been told amiss."[1] Trollope here asserts what every author of fiction knows: that the novel is not simply the invention of the actions of its characters, but also the invention of the actions of its readers.[2] The *meaning* of Trollope's novel is not simply in the story of Alice's redemption, but in the pleasure we take in wishing for and welcoming that redemption.

Another short passage from Trollope bears on our second methodological point: that critics need to attend both to details and to contexts in constructing a balanced account of meaning. Alice is in the Alps with her cousins. The idle George Vavasour is described as lounging on a "bench, looking at the mountains, with a cigar in his mouth." George expresses his contempt for hikers who climb the mountains for exercise, or for study. "They rob the mountains of their poetry," says George, "which is or should be their greatest charm."

> "The poetry and mystery of the mountains are lost to those who make themselves familiar with their details, not the less because such familiarity may have useful results. In this world things are beautiful only because they are not quite seen, or not perfectly understood. Poetry is precious chiefly because it suggests more than it declares. Look in there, through that valley, where you just see the distant little

peak at the end. Are you not dreaming of the unknown beautiful world that exists up there;—beautiful, as heaven is beautiful, because you know nothing of the reality? If you make your way up there and back to-morrow, and find out all about it, do you mean to say that it will be as beautiful to you when you come back?"

"Yes—I think it would," said Alice.[3]

By this point in the novel, we have come to recognize Alice's virtue and George's sinfulness, and so Alice's simple "yes" carries considerable force. It is clear from the discussion that Alice, and Trollope, invite the reader to take pleasure and wisdom from the details of everday reality, and from the relations of those details, and even from the effort that it takes us to trudge up the mountain for a clearer view of them. Trollope's invitation to detail has nothing in common with that other sort of nineteenth century amateur scientism that reduced the world to a statistic.[4] For Trollope, the alternative to George Vavasour's vague and lazy romanticism is not science, but a commonsense and feeling willingness to face the details of the world and to see their relations and their consequences.

Americans have had an especially interesting time trying to cope with "the facts." Our literature, journalism, and popular arts have been dominated in this century by various forms of flight to and from facts. From Upton Sinclair to Norman Mailer, from Robert Flaherty to *60 Minutes,* from the newsreels to *Real People,* we have searched after the facts and have found that facts are not enough, even if we could agree on what "the" facts are. Artists have told us over and over again that art may be too disconnected, and science too reductive, to bring us into a proper relation with our world.

The issue is posed with special poignancy by James Agee, in a passage from his documentary book on Depression sharecroppers in Alabama, *Let Us Now Praise Famous Men.* "If I could do it, I'd do no writing at all here. It would be photographs; the rest would be fragments of cloth, bits of cotton, lumps of earth, records of speech, pieces of wood and iron, phials of odors, plates of food and of excrement. Booksellers would consider it quite a novelty; critics would murmur, yes, but is it art; and I could trust a majority of you to use it as you would a parlor game."[5]

And yet Agee is writing a book, and not simply trading in objects, as his writing shows very well. In a later passage, Agee describes the dresses of one of the tenant farm women.

> Mrs. Gudger: I have spoken already of her dresses. I think she has at most five. . . . Three are one-piece dresses; two are in two pieces. By cut they are almost identical; by pattern of print they differ, but are similar in having been carefully chosen, all small and sober, quiet patterns, to be in good taste and to relieve one another's monotony. I think it may be well to repeat their general appearance, since it is of her individual designing, and is so thoroughly a part of the logic of her body, bearing, face and temper. They have about them some shadow of nineteenth-century influence, tall skirt, short waist, and a little, too, of imitation of Butterick patterns for housewives' housework-dresses; this chiefly in the efforts

at bright or "cheery," post-honeymoon-atmosphere trimming: narrow red or blue tape sewn at the cuffs or throat. But by other reasons again they have her own character and function: the lines are tall and narrow, as she is, and little relieved, and seem to run straight from the shoulders to the hem low on the shins, and there is no collar, but a long and low V at the throat, shut narrowly together, so that the whole dress like her body has the long vertical of a Chartres statue.[6]

The passage is remarkable not simply for its factuality, its close attention to detail, but also for the way it relates those details, gives them a meaning in the life of the person whose dresses are being described, and calls on us to bring to the description a cultural sophistication that is almost certainly unfamiliar to Mrs. Gudger—that final reference to the statues of Chartres Cathedral is only the most explicit indication that the entire passage is addressed to educated and prosperous readers, and not to the tenant farmers with whom Agee in so many ways identifies himself imaginatively.

The issues raised by Anthony Trollope in the 1860s and by James Agee in the 1930s are still with us, though transformed. Certainly in the past two decades, Frederick Wiseman has been one of the most profound inquirers into American facts. Wiseman's films have much to teach us about the uses to which we can put "the facts" about everyday reality, and about the rhetorical actions that filmmakers and their audiences perform.

Primate, shown on public television for the first time in 1974, was shot at the Yerkes Regional Primate Research Center in Atlanta. Immediate and later reaction to *Primate* was sharply divided between those who charged that Wiseman had unfairly attacked the Yerkes scientists and those who applauded the film as a profound attack against vivisection. That is to say, the majority of commentators for and against the film seemed to recognize it as a rhetorical act in the narrowest sense: as persuasive discourse in the forensic and deliberative modes, accusing a group of particular scientists of cruelty to animals and attacking the policy of public support for animal research.

Rhetorical critics could sensibly and conveniently proceed through the film on these narrow grounds. We would extract from the film its implicit accusations and propositions, examine the proofs Wiseman offers to support them, and attempt to assess both the extent to which the film might be persuasive and the extent to which we, as critics, could support the proofs as "good reasons" to accept the propositions and accusations. Nothing could be more straightforward.

But such a critique, though it would have its uses, would be seriously incomplete, because it would fail to account for the way the audience is likely to understand the film. Rhetorical critics in the last two decades have discovered that nonoratorical persuasive actions can be analyzed with the rigorous tools of traditional rhetorical criticism. But they have also followed Kenneth Burke in understanding that all symbolic actions, and not just those most narrowly didactic, can be encompassed by a rhetorical criticism that is interested in the whole enterprise of sharing meanings in human communication.[7] It is this latter, larger sense of rhetorical criticism to which we must turn, we think, to understand how Fred Wiseman's *Primate* invites us to share its meanings.

What does Wiseman's *Primate* mean? *Primate* invites us to experience a horrified, comic rage at the arrogance, hypocrisy, banality, and destructiveness of our fellow humans and ourselves. Like most of Wiseman's films, *Primate* is not simply accusatory, it is paradoxical, and this of course contributes to the frustration of Wiseman's opponents, both in the film community and in the various institutions that he has explored in his documentaries. *Primate* is addressed not to particular crimes, nor even to social policy, but to our attitudes about human action. The film is not merely forensic or deliberative, it is existential.

Primate is 105 minutes long—feature length—and contains, according to an analysis by Liz Ellsworth, 569 shots.[8] That works out to an average of eleven seconds per shot for *Primate,* approximately half of the average shot length of twenty-three seconds in Wiseman's *High School,* and a third of the average shot length of thirty-two seconds in *Titicut Follies.*[9]

The unusually large number of shots in *Primate* is not simply a fact, but a clue, both to the rhythm of the film and to its method of building meanings. We would expect that with briefer shots the meanings would emerge to a great extent from the structural relations among shots—from editing or montage—and that the shots themselves would be very likely to be highly condensed in their imagery and iconography. This pattern of condensation and montage does much to account for Wiseman's method.

We propose to get closer to the film's method by examining how certain major structural features of the film invite us to construct meanings. We will discuss three major structures: comparison, sequence and continuity, and sound-image relations. Rather than treat these structural features separately and sequentially, we will layer them in the discussion that follows, because they work together to achieve Wiseman's effects.

The effect of *Primate* depends very heavily upon the family of rhetorical structures that may be collected under the heading of comparison: analogy, contrast, metaphor, identification, irony, and comparison itself. Our response to the film depends upon our willingness to compare men to apes and to judge their relations in terms of the increasingly complex comparisons we are invited to draw. The film opens with a long series of shots in which we may first notice the ambiguity of the film's title, which applies equally well to men and apes. We see a large composite photograph, with portraits of eminent scientists, hanging, presumably, on a wall at the Yerkes Center. Wiseman cuts from the composite portrait to a series of eight individual portraits, in series, then to a sign identifying Yerkes Regional Primate Research Center, a bust of a man on a pedestal, an exterior shot of the center, and then a series of four shots of apes in their cages. The comparison is obvious, though not particularly forceful, and it depends for its meaning both upon the structure Wiseman has chosen to use—at least he does not intercut the apes and the portraits—and upon our own predictable surprise at noticing how human the apes look.

Slightly later in the film, still very near the beginning, a pair of sequences occur that are crucial to how we will experience the rest of the film. Researchers are watching and recording the birth of an orangutan. The descriptive language is objective, but not altogether free of anthropomorphism: for example, it is hard not to refer to the female giving birth as the "mother."

Immediately following the birth sequence, we watch women in nursing gowns mothering infant apes: the apparatus of American babyhood is evident—plastic toys, baby bottles, diapers, baby scales, and a rocking chair. To reinforce the comparison, we hear the women speaking to the infant apes. "Here. Here. Take it. Take it. Come on," says the first woman, offering a toy to an infant ape. Then another woman enters the nursery, also dressed in gown and mask. "Good morning, darlings. Good morning. Mama's babies? You gonna be good boys and girls for Mommy?" A moment later she continues, "Mama take your temperature. Come on, we'll take your temperature. It's all right. It's all right. It's all right. It's all right." Then a man enters and hands cups to the infants. He says, "Come on. Come on. Here's yours."

The rhetorical effect of this scene is to reinforce our sentimental identification with the apes. And this scene, by comparison, makes even more frightening a scene that follows close upon it, in which a small monkey is taken from its cage, screaming, as a man with protective gloves pins its arms behind its back and clamps his other hand around its neck.

After these scenes, every image in the film invites us to continue enacting comparisons, as part of the process by which we actively make meanings out of the images. Those who object to Wiseman's methods argue that his comparison of apes and people is a cheap shot, an obviously sentimental ploy to make monkeys out of primatologists. Although there is something to be said for this view, since it is quite clear that Wiseman is showing us comparisons whose meanings are predictable, the problem is complicated. Wiseman's comparisons do not stay at the simple level of the infant sequence, but grow increasingly complex throughout the film. The infant sequence not only predisposes us sentimentally, it also rehearses us in the exercise of comparative thinking. The researchers themselves invite the comparison. Their use of the dramatic apparatus of American baby care is not something Wiseman forced upon them, though admittedly he takes advantage of it. And at a deeper level, those scientists who object to a sentimental willingness to object to vivisection are placed in the paradoxical situation that the primary justification for their research is that, biologically, apes are such close relatives of people. The defenders of such research must seek funding for their research on the grounds that apes are biologically analogous to humans; but they must also seek to justify their practices upon those apes by arguing that, ethically, apes are not analogous to humans. *Primate* makes it very difficult for viewers to buy that argument, by inviting them to identify with the apes at an aesthetic, subjective level. This is why comparison is so central to Wiseman's film: comparison both justifies and condemns the research, and Wiseman exploits that comparison not simply to attack vivisection, or scientific research in general, but also to engage us in actively considering the paradoxes of our institutions and ourselves.

And this is why those scientists and reviewers who attacked *Primate* had such a frustrating time of it. Wiseman invites his audience not simply to condemn particular scientists for foolishness or cruelty to animals, and not just to reason about the policy of animal research. Instead, Wiseman reframes the whole question, inviting us to look with our common sense at the whole context of human action at Yerkes, to employ our own abilities to identify with the apes, and to feel horror and shame as we identify with the actions of our fellow humans.

There is a paradox for Wiseman here, too. His rhetorical method in *Primate* not only casts doubt upon the primatologists' justifications for their work; it casts doubt upon the rhetoric of justification itself, by showing us how often justification is offered as a way of masking what is actually happening. But if we are to dismiss justification as essentially a distraction, how are we to evaluate *Primate?* Must we not concede that a sympathetic appreciation of *Primate* is framed partly as a *justification?* That is, we recognize that Wiseman's rhetoric refuses to take entirely into account the point of view of the primatologists, but we justify his actions on the grounds that he is pursuing an equally important issue of his own. Hence, Wiseman denies justification as a tactic to his subjects, but claims it for himself, or puts us in the paradoxical position of doing it for him. What is a critic or a viewer to make of this? We could perhaps accept Wiseman's justification as of a higher moral order than that of the primatologists. We could accuse him of unfairness and inconsistency. Or we could recognize that, as an ironist, he himself has created this paradox more or less deliberately and that our consideration of the issue is itself part of his rhetoric—making the film not so much a condemnation of primate research as a complex speculation about the paradoxes of inquiry. This reflexive reading, in which our curiosity justifies unfairness, by condemning scientists who justify their unfairness on the grounds of curiosity, places Wiseman and his viewers in much the same position as the scientists, an irony from which he offers us no escape.

Wiseman's peculiar rhetorical talent is to help his audiences identify with oppressors and oppressed: we feel pity, fear, and rage on behalf of the victims, with whom we identify. And we feel the shock of horrified recognition in realizing that the oppressors are acting in our name, as members of this society: teaching our children, butchering our meat, administering our institutions, and toying with the generation and termination of life in a primate research center.

Comparison works in another way in the film. Wiseman establishes a dialectic between acts that we are likely to perceive as kindness to the apes and acts that we are likely to perceive as cruelty. Do the acts of kindness balance the acts of cruelty? Is there a journalistic attempt at fairness here? Not really. We understand that in this institution, the apes are subject to human domination, mutilation, and termination. In such a situation, the acts of kindness do not balance the acts of heartless research. Rather, kindness is reduced to hypocrisy, a lie told to ease the consciences of the scientists and to keep the apes under control. Far from balancing the harshness of the research scenes, the scenes of kindness turn the research into a cruelty and a betrayal.

We can perhaps forgive Wiseman his unsympathetic methods, because we realize that the shame and rage we direct at the primate researchers is directed at them as representatives of ourselves. It is not that we cannot forgive them—we cannot forgive ourselves. And what makes Wiseman's films so devastating is that there is no easy liberal solution. Wiseman's films are not about corruption. They are about something that is much more nearly indivisible from our daily lives, and about institutions that—even when they have some modifiable policies—are never going to be able to resolve the paradoxes they were set up to deal with. Problem films are almost always optimistic, in that every problem implies a solution. Wiseman's films do not imply any solution to the enterprise of being human.

And here we have another reason why *Primate* is so frustrating to the scientists who have attacked it. They realize that they must defend themselves on the deliberative issue of the justification for their research. But *Primate* goes beyond deliberation—one cannot expunge the effect of *Primate* on a susceptible viewer with an argument addressed to policy. And yet—and here's the rub—Wiseman's film is relevant to that deliberative issue, even as it goes beyond it. The rhetoric of nonoratorical forms frequently presents us with this paradox: that it implies a stance toward deliberative matters that its opponents cannot refute adequately with a deliberative reply.

Let us examine briefly another sequence in *Primate*. It is the climactic sequence of the film, a little over twenty minutes and over one hundred shots long. In it, researchers remove a gibbon from its cage, anesthetize it, drill a hole in its skull, insert a needle, then open its chest cavity, decapitate it, crack open its skull, and slice the brain for microscope slides. It is a harrowing sequence. From a structural standpoint, Wiseman uses the techniques we have noticed earlier. The images are often highly condensed, with close-ups of needles, drills, scalpels, the tiny beating heart, the gibbon's terrified face, scissors, jars, vises, dials, and so on.

We are invited to engage in our continued work of making comparisons and metaphors: the gibbon is easy to identify with, in its terror of these silent and terminal medical procedures. We are the gibbon, and we are the surgeons. At another level, we see the gibbons' cages as a sort of death row and call upon our memories of prison movies when we see the helpless fellow gibbons crying out from their cages as the victim is placed back into its cage for a twenty-five-minute pause in the vivisection.

Wiseman has carefully controlled progression and continuity in this section of the film, first by placing the sequence near the end of the film, so that it becomes the climax of the preceding comedy, and then by controlling its internal structure for maximum effect. The sequence is governed by the rules of both fiction and documentary. We do not know until almost the very last second that the gibbon is certainly going to die. Earlier in the film we have seen monkeys with electrodes planted in their brains, so we are able to hope that the gibbon will survive. We keep hoping that it will live, but as the operation becomes more and more destructive of the animal, we must doubt our hopes. And then, with terrible suddenness, and with only a few seconds' warning, the surgeon cuts off the gibbon's head. We feel a terrible despair that it has come to this. But the sequence continues through the meticulous, mechanical process of preparing slides of the brain. Finally we see the researchers sitting at the microscope to examine the slides for which the gibbon's life has been sacrificed. And for us, as viewers, the discovery ought to be important if it is to redeem this death. The two researchers talk:

FIRST SCIENTIST: Oh, here's a whole cluster of them. Here, look at this.
SECOND SCIENTIST: Yeah. My gosh, that is beautiful.
FIRST SCIENTIST: By golly, and see how localized. No fuzzing out.
SECOND SCIENTIST: For sure it does not look like dirt, or—
FIRST SCIENTIST: No, no, it's much too regular.
SECOND SCIENTIST: I think we are on our way.
FIRST SCIENTIST: Yeah. That's sort of interesting.

The whole operation, which viewers are invited to experience as pitiable and frightening, seems to have been indulged in for the merest idle curiosity, and, if the scientists cannot distinguish brains from dirt, at the lowest possible level of competence. Our suspicions are confirmed a few minutes later when a group of researchers seated at a meeting reassure each other that pure research is always justified, even if it seems to be the pursuit of useless knowledge.

We have already mentioned the sound-image relationships in this sequence in discussing the structural uses of comparison and continuity. But let us point to some special issues that relate to Wiseman's use of sound. At many places in the film, people talk to apes, creating a dramatic fiction that the apes can understand and respond to human speech. But in the vivisection sequence, no word is spoken to the victim. This silence is almost as disturbing as the operation itself, because a bond of identification offered earlier is now denied. Its denial, in this context, becomes part of an action that we see as sadistic. It is interesting that Wiseman's critics in the scientific community object that he has made a misleading use of sound. Their argument is that one cannot understand scientific research just by watching it take place and that the audience needs to be told what it is seeing and why it is justified in scientific terms. The absence of a narrator forces us to see the film as an existential drama and to believe in the reality of the gibbon's death as important in and of itself. But that is the point. This is not a debate between Wiseman and the primatologists on the costs versus the benefits of vivisection. Presumably there are good reasons to be offered by both sides of that debate. Wiseman works at a different level, inviting us to question whether any verbal justification is relevant to what we have seen. Wiseman uses his "reality fictions" to address our subjective consciousness, and his films do not depend for their effect upon objective accuracy (whatever that is) or immediate political utility.

Although Wiseman has frequently referred to himself as a documentary filmmaker, he has never professed to provide an objective description of reality. In fact, he seems to have coined the term "reality fiction" as a partly tongue-in-cheek way of declining to be described as part of the cinema verite tradition, with its implied claims of transparency and unmanipulated reality. Wiseman has frequently described his editing method as a process of fiction making in which bits and pieces of photographed actuality are reassembled to see what can be found in the material.

And yet a very large percentage of the praise and detraction of Wiseman's films centers on the issue of accuracy. Those who praise the films often seem to accept them as literally true and discuss not the films but the people in them. And those who object to the films often do so on the basis of their alleged inaccuracy or lack of objectivity. Wiseman usually brushes aside both the praise and the blame. He allows his admirers the meanings they find in the films, and he typically responds, as he did to an objection made by Geoffrey H. Bourne, director of the Yerkes Center, that Bourne did not object to the film when he saw it for himself, but only after he began to see how he looked to others.[10]

Yerkes continues to object to the film. In a symposium on "Animals and Research: A Film Forum" at Drexel University in 1986, a showing of *Primate* was followed by a discussion featuring Wiseman and the current director of Yerkes Regional Primate Research Center, Frederick A. King. In his talk, King supported his objections to the film by showing slides that presented the center's version of its research, and he distributed a "fact sheet" summarizing the Yerkes case against *Primate*. The materials presented by King demonstrate once again both how the meanings of Wiseman's films are different for different audiences and how subjects are likely to feel misrepresented when Wiseman is at his most critical. Many of the themes that were voiced by the subjects and their institutional sponsors in *Titicut Follies* and *High School* surface again in the objections of the Yerkes Center. King's speech and handout provide useful information about the larger context and the purposes of the research at Yerkes, and they remind the audience of Wiseman's statements that the film is "fictional," that he did not see cruelty to animals at Yerkes, and that "these animals are vital to research."[11] And yet, King says, Wiseman's film makes it appear that animals are treated cruelly, and for the most trivial reasons.

One of the more interesting objections to Wiseman's accuracy is made by Karl Heider. An anthropologist and ethnographic filmmaker, Heider argues that one of the primary attributes of a successful ethnographic film is that it will "show the structure of a whole act."[12] One of Heider's key examples of a film that fails to depict whole acts is Wiseman's *Primate*.

> A major weakness of Frederick Wiseman's 1974 television film, "Primate," was that, although he spent one month shooting and two hours of screen time on bits of scientific experimentation at the Yerkes Primate Research Center in Atlanta, the film never followed a single experiment as a whole act. The approach had interestingly different effects on different viewers. Laymen (including television critics) were simply horrified by the picture of senseless butchery in the guise of science; one friend of mine who is familiar with that sort of research could fill in the gaps for himself and was fascinated by the film; more thoughtful viewers reacted strongly against the film itself on the grounds that it made no attempt to communicate an understanding of primate research by presenting whole acts, but only used scenes of gore to play on the audience's emotions and turn them away from such research.[13]

Heider's objections deserve careful scrutiny, and there are five important considerations that deserve to be mentioned. First, it is curious that in a passage in which he is describing the importance of "wholeness," Heider does not provide a full description of *Primate*, thus denying to Wiseman the structural completeness he proposes as his standard of accuracy. Second, and obviously, Wiseman does not present his films as ethnographic documents, and so it is not clear why the standards Heider proposes for ethnography should be applied to *Primate*.[14]

Third, Wiseman does provide, in at least one case, a dramatic account, with beginning, middle, and end, of one experiment. The vivisection of the gibbon takes approximately twenty minutes of screen time: it begins when the gibbon is taken from its cage; it provides some background on the stated desire of the scientists to check some previous research; it proceeds through the surgery to the examination of slides and the agreement that the procedure has been a success. Of course, Wiseman's account is anything but neutral, but it does have the three-act structure that Heider accuses the film of lacking.

Fourth, it is interesting to note that in developing his case against *Primate*, Heider devotes very little space to the film itself and concentrates instead on audience reactions to the film. Implicitly, Heider seems to be struggling with the difficulty that philosophy, science, and rhetoric have recently begun to reexamine in a new light. Is Heider implying that the standard of a film's accuracy is to be found not in its correspondence to an "objective" reality, but in what an audience makes of it? Apparently not, because Heider pre-judges the matter in favor of the primatologists—the lay audience's reactions to the film are dismissed as "emotional." Heider seems to imply that if the audience had the whole story, they would understand and support primate research.

A major difficulty of ethnographic—or any other—film is that accuracy cannot be measured simply in terms of the correspondence of the film to the actuality it describes. Every theorist of ethnographic film, including Heider, recognizes that completeness is impossible. Every film that explains one culture to another must confront the dilemma of point of view: if the film is made purely from the point of view of the subject culture, it will be unclear to the audience; if the film is translated into the point of view of the audience, it will necessarily introduce elements that are unfamiliar to, and therefore untrue for, the subject culture. Hence the question of accuracy often reduces itself to the struggle over point of view. Clearly it would have been possible for a filmmaker to make a film sympathetic to the point of view of the primatologists: but that was not the point.

But, fifth, by far the most interesting and challenging of Heider's argu-ments is his standard of "whole acts." The chief danger of Heider's "whole act" standard is that it can easily reduce a sensible principle to a naive and inappropriate technical reductionism. In principle, Heider is convincing when he argues that it is a mistake to focus on what he calls the "peak" of a cultural event, "that part of the act which involves the most energy and activity and draws the most attention."[15] Even if the peak activity is the focus of one's interest, that peak cannot be properly understood without some context, and in ethnographic reporting, the cultural context would include some placement of the activity in its natural setting in time and space, including the relevant events that led up to and succeeded the event. A full understanding of the whole act might require not simply extended observa-tion but verbal commentary about the invisible and implicit cultural substruc-tures that give meaning to the act. Clearly, from the point of view of the scientists, Wiseman withholds from his audience the contextual information that might either distract us from the horrors or justify the horrors in the name of scientific knowledge or human use.

But why should Heider assume that the "act" being described by *Primate* is scientific research as understood by scientists? Heider's argument rests on the unsupportable assumptions that the ethnographer is explaining "them" to "us"; and that any social action is, firmly, finally, and naturally what it is. Wiseman correctly violates both assumptions, in our view. *Primate* is not about a "them"—it is about us. The scientists are not a foreign culture but our agents, acting like us, and on our behalf. And what a social action "is" is a matter of definition, duration, and point of view. A behavior may possibly be what it is, but an action is a socially constructed human product, subject to understandings (and misunderstandings) from a variety of perspectives, more than one of which can be accurate.

A human action, as rhetoricians from Aristotle to Kenneth Burke have told us, is a behavior waiting for a name. If a man kills another, it is for others to judge whether the act is an accident, manslaughter, or murder. From the point of view of the victim, the act is the end of life. From the point of view of the perpetrator, the act may be the culmination of a quest (revenge) or the beginning of an ordeal. From the point of view of the community, the act is a legal fact, to be dealt with as a matter of justice and given its proper name. Any one of these points of view is capable of being understood as a "whole act," and yet they are obviously different renderings of a single set of events, variously understood (and not by any means necessarily misunderstood).

Similarly, in the narrative arts, the form of the whole work guides the reader in defining the action that is represented. In her novel *July's People*, Nadine Gordimer describes the experiences of a white South African family hiding in the bush with their former servant, July, during a revolution. It is not at all clear that the family will survive the ordeal. The novel ends when the wife runs off, alone, to seek rescue from a helicopter. From one point of view, the novel is disastrously incomplete, since we do not learn whether she is actually rescued or what happens to her husband and children. The novel seems to end too soon, before its action has been completed. But that is just the point. It is only when the novel has ended that we realize that the action of the novel is not, as we had thought it might be, about the escape, successful or not, of this family. Rather, we see, when it ends in the woman's headlong flight through the bush, that the action of the novel is the woman's transformation from a housewife to "a solitary animal at the season when animals neither seek a mate nor take care of young, existing only for their lone survival, the enemy of all that would make claims of responsibility."[16] The strong feeling that Gordimer's novel is incomplete forces us, as readers, to reevaluate what we take the novel to be about, while at the same time recognizing our own predispositions toward melodrama.

Let us cite one other example, to show how the process may work in a different way. American student viewers almost always feel that Sergei Eisenstein's *Potemkin* (1925) is too long. The fourth "act" of the film climaxes with the famous massacre on the Odessa steps, which is capped, briefly, by the answering guns of the Potemkin coming to the aid of the victims. Then comes a fifth "act," in which the Potemkin cruises off from Odessa and goes to meet the fleet. It is not clear to the mutineers on the Potemkin whether the fleet will open fire on them. At the last moment, the sailors of the fleet refuse to fire. Why does the film seem too long to American students, and why would Eisenstein have mishandled his dramatic forms? It is a question of what *Potemkin* is *about*. American students are inclined to see *Potemkin* as melodrama, in which a mutiny leads to the massacre on the Odessa steps and the vengeance of the Potemkin's reply. At that point, the story, if it is to be taken as a conventional melodrama of victimage and revenge, is over. The meeting with the fleet is an anticlimax, an emotional letdown, and a narrative flaw. Did Eisenstein include the last act because historical facts constrained him to do so? Probably not, since he took many liberties with history in fashioning the film. Again, it is a question of what the film is about. For Eisenstein, the film is about the achievement of revolutionary solidarity. Seen from this point of view, the meeting with the fleet becomes a dramatic and ideological extension that follows logically and meaningfully from the scene on the Odessa steps. A film that appears, if regarded as a bourgeois melodrama, to be too long, appears to fit the structure of a "whole act" if it is redefined as a drama of revolutionary solidarity.

Primate is a film with a point of view, and it is certainly not sympathetic to scientific research. But Heider's "whole act" standard is both misleading and misapplied. Wiseman records, constructs, and communicates a whole act that transcends vivisection as a political issue to examine the experience of being human. The whole act that Wiseman records, and in which he invites his audience to participate, is an act of identification with both the scientists and their victims.

The act of identification that we perform as viewers of Wiseman is not undifferentiated, not simply a sympathetic embrace of all that is. We identify with the apes and the scientists, but in different ways. In identifying with the apes, we are able to feel the horror and helplessness of their position; in identifying with the scientists, we are able to feel responsible. There is, of course, another identification possible, and one which may complicate the matter further. Do we not also identify with "Fred Wiseman," the implied author of *Primate*?[17] The implied author of *Primate* is not simply saddened or outraged at the apes' victimage, nor does he seek redemption in political reform.

Wiseman's elusive narrative point of view, depending upon strategies of action and identification, places a strain upon critical language. Throughout this chapter, we have employed the first-person plural pronoun in discussing audience response. We the authors have said that "we" the audience read the film in this way or that. We have done so partly as a way of identifying with the reader whose actions we are proposing to describe, and as a way of pointing to the way in which Wiseman's method hinges upon identification and division among his audience, himself, and his subjects. The use of the first-person pronoun has the disadvantage, in academic and critical argument, of seeming both overly familiar and presumptuous and may even seem to beg the question of effect, presuming that "we" the viewers will see the film as "we" the critics describe it. But a third-person usage does not avoid the problem of critical question begging and may distort not only the critical perspective but the critical interpretation by suggesting an objective assessment by the critic about how "they" will read the film. The meaning of a film, that is, the meaning "in" or "intended by" a film, even when understood by its audience, is not irresistible.

Primate achieves its peculiar effects with a curious combination of generic styles that include both comedy and horror. The comedy of the early birth and baby scenes is magnified and pushed in a less sentimental direction by the many scenes in which the scientists observe, discuss, and manipulate the sex lives of the apes. The distortion of sexual behavior, in the name of understanding sexual behavior, sometimes reduces sexuality to mechanics, as in the many scenes where apes are stimulated to erection and ejaculation by means of electrodes implanted in their brains, or the scene in which a technician masturbates an ape with a plastic tube in one hand while distracting the ape with a bottle of grape juice in the other. At other times, the scientists seem gossipy, as they sit and whisper about sex outside a row of cages. The effect of the sex scenes is comic and undermines the dignity of the presumably scientific enterprise we are watching.

But along with the comedy, there is an undercurrent of horror, at times straightforward, at times almost surrealistic. Sometimes the horror occurs in small moments: a technician tries to remove a small monkey from its wire cage. He reaches inside the door of the cage and grasps the monkey, which tries to evade capture by clinging to the front of the cage next to the door, an angle that makes it difficult for the technician to maneuver it out of the door. The technician reaches up with his other hand and releases another catch, revealing that the whole front of the cage is hinged. The front of the cage swings open, and the technician grasps the clinging monkey from behind, as our momentary pleasure at the comedy of the impasse gives way to a small despair: there is no escape.

At other times, the scientists are framed to seem sinister, as when the surgeon who vivisects the gibbon is shot in close-up, from a low angle, a large surgical light shining over his shoulder. And because of the structure of the film, in which a seemingly observational point of view is maintained, we are never quite sure what will happen next. The camera and editing do not take a purely observational point of view, however; instead they place us, as spectators, in a state of tension, making us feel as if we were watching an unfolding reality controlled by someone else—the subjects in the enactment and Wiseman in the telling. We are often surprised by events, as when the gibbon's head is snipped off, but we also experience a sense of foreboding throughout the film, very similar to what might be experienced in a horror film, where suspense is created by foreshadowing devices. Wiseman accomplishes this both by repetition and by camera and cutting styles that often place him ahead of the action. This produces a conundrum: a strictly literal, observational film would presumably *follow* the action, not anticipate it. But a skilled cameraman like William Brayne can often place himself ahead of the action by anticipating it, enhancing our sense of understanding the filmed experience but paradoxically risking the accusation that a particular shot was a setup, a collaboration between camera and subject.[18] It quickly becomes clear to us that the scientists, for all their expressed good will, are capable of anything, and so we approach even the mildest procedures with dread, not knowing what horror they are likely to reveal. We can identify with the scientists as our representatives—even, perhaps, as analogies for Wiseman, who is, after all, observing the observers—but we do not trust them.

And for all of his unobtrusiveness as a narrator, Wiseman puts a considerable distance between himself and his subjects. From very early in the film, Wiseman adopts a convention of sound-image relationships that makes for an ironic distance. In an early scene, we observe a resident scientist talking with another man about gorilla sexuality. As we continue to listen to their conversation, the camera begins to gaze about on its own. We *hear* the official line, but we begin to *see* other things. That wandering camera begins to stand for Wiseman's—and our—free curiosity, refusing to be locked into the conventions of place and point of view.[19] A profound relation is thus established, in which filmic consciousness, and our consciousness, is willing to be interested in its own questions, rather than just those suggested by the speakers. Wiseman's use of sound-image relations here is something far more sophisticated than the heavy-handed cinema verite rhetoric that zooms in on the nervous hands of a speaker we are thus invited to doubt. Wiseman does not obviously use cutaways as a method of bridging gaps in continuity or as a way of underlining possibly deliberate misrepresentations. He rarely cuts, within a scene, to images that cannot be accounted for as literally part of the immediate context. But when he does do so, the effect is one of irony rather than of mere continuity or confirmation. The typical Wiseman effect of narrative, temporal continuity within episodes is, of course, an illusion, since, in a film shot with one camera, no cut from one shot to another can ever be temporally continuous; that illusion of continuity not only makes the films readable at the narrative level, but also contributes to the rhetorical illusion of Wiseman as a detached observer of ongoing reality. He makes us active participants in the process of building meanings by wandering beyond the speaker's concern to the context in which it occurs, or, conversely, by gazing uninterruptedly at the actuality of everyday institutional reality rather than brushing actuality aside in favor of its rationale or product.

Wiseman looks at the "facts" of social reality and reveals the structures that underlie them. There is a danger for Wiseman here. He is skating very close to the thin ice of despair, and of that currently fashionable despair which adopts an antipolitical cynicism as a substitute for responsibility to social particulars.[20]

We said at the outset that Wiseman could not accurately be pigeon-holed as the filmic equivalent of a forensic or deliberative orator, suggesting that he has gone beyond indicting his subjects or offering a policy. Part of Wiseman's usefulness to us as viewers is the way he resists the sterility of fixed genres. But it may be that we can understand Wiseman as offering us something akin to Lawrence Rosenfield's notion of epideictic.[21] Rosenfield writes of epideictic rhetoric as a celebration of the radiance of being, and he wisely notes that even condemnatory rhetoric can function as an affirmation of Being's excellence and availability. When Wiseman's films work for us, we are perhaps experiencing, through the comedy and the cruelty, a larger sense that comedy and cruelty are recognizable to us as alternatives to the human excellence that they imply by denying. If, as Karl Wallace wrote, the substance of rhetoric is good reasons,[22] Wiseman's *Primate* offers us good reasons to look more honestly at ourselves.

Chapter 7

Good Films from Bad Rules
The Ethics of Naming in *Welfare*

Both of us spend at least part of our time teaching courses in film and television criticism, often to students who are planning to become filmmakers and television producers. When we teach the films of Frederick Wiseman to these students, we find ourselves in a dilemma: the films are compelling and original investigations of American institutional life, rightly inspiring to our students. And yet, when examined at the level of techniques and procedures, Wiseman's films seem to violate many of the most elementary rules one finds in responsible texts on film making. Wiseman sometimes invites us to regard his subjects with ridicule; he has made films that outrage his subjects; he fragments and rearranges the actualities of time and space; he provides no commentary that would reveal and take responsibility for his own point of view or supply historical and other contexts for his treatment. Wiseman's films seem to present genuine difficulties at ethical and epistemological levels.

Wiseman breaks the textbook rules of documentary. His own apparent rules would seem to be bad rules for most of our students to try to follow. And yet we admire the films, as do our students. How do you talk to a sophomore filmmaker about using Frederick Wiseman's films as a model? One soon exhausts the usual answers. We hate to hear ourselves resorting to the empty advice so often offered by adults to teenagers: "First learn the rules, and then you will be able to break them." Or, "Geniuses can break the rules, but the rest of us need some sort of procedures to be responsible to, so follow the textbook." Our students, it seems to us, are rightly suspicious of such appeals to genius and authority. And yet as critics and teachers we do not want to say that there are no workable rules of ethics or of knowing: the result of calling off all attempts to arrive at some sort of principled approach to documentary would be to place the whole power of self-knowledge through film beyond discussion, saying, in effect, that good documentary is whatever you can get away with. As appealing as that might sound to a sophomore, such an argument would, in practice, do less to liberate genius than to disable all argument against the abuses of mass media controlled by money or political authority.

In this chapter, we shall try to play out the perhaps simple-minded notion that if Wiseman is making good films, he must be doing something right, despite the fact that he evidently breaks many of the rules of documentary. We admire Wiseman's work. But we do not want to act simply as his advocates or apologists: he does not need that, nor do we wish to commit ourselves to an abandonment of all critical judgment in an attempt to justify at all costs everything in Wiseman's films. We shall, instead, try to discover where, if at all, Wiseman's films do break the rules of documentary ethics, aesthetics, and epistemology, and where, if at all, he is working by other rules. Wiseman's films do not offer a recipe for documentary production, nor shall we try to derive recipes from them. In the spirit of Dwight Macdonald (who himself invoked Groucho Marx), we shall try to keep in mind that we are merely critics and that we "wouldn't want to see a movie by a director who had to learn to make movies from [our] reviews."[1] In the spirit of documentary itself, we shall try to work out the argument by a close examination of Wiseman's work, rather than by a direct appeal to abstractions.

Frederick Wiseman's elusive point of view presents audiences with an accumulation of behaviors waiting to be named. In *Welfare*, Wiseman turns facts into imaginative activities and social judgments. Wiseman's documentary rhetoric of "reality fiction" implies that subject, filmmaker, and spectator share cultural and ethical responsibility for the construction of meaning.

Wiseman's methods—creating context through fragmentation, abstraction through attention to social detail, identification through irony, and an open form through construction—provoke ethical questions regarding his procedures and his results, yet finally give substance to the paradoxical position taken in this chapter: Wiseman makes good films from bad rules.

Welfare (1975) is an inquiry into social truth at two distinct levels of discourse. At the level of film content, *Welfare* attends to the process by which the search for the truth at the Waverly Center in New York City is, in the name of accuracy and equity, reduced to a formula, a set of rules, a "welfare system." The evident result is that the system seems to pay more attention to the cases people make for themselves, and the way they document and enact those cases in terms of the requirements of the welfare system, than it pays to providing help itself. While Wiseman's film invites us to speculate about the truth of the claims made on the welfare system, the documentary also invites us to observe the evident distress of its clients. As spectators, we cannot distinguish who is deserving, but we can see who is in need—everybody.

At the level of documentary product, *Welfare* participates in a genre devoted to the search for social truth. Yet, through his series of films examining American institutions, Wiseman has emerged as a central figure in the development of a documentary form that refuses to follow the constraints of traditional journalism or conventional television documentary. Wiseman violates many of the rules of accuracy and equity with a paradoxical result: he helps audiences search for other truths.

Welfare illustrates how Wiseman casts familiar rules into new perspectives. Wiseman challenges the conventional rules of knowing and naming not by avoiding them, but by confronting them, thus making the rules, and their results, visible and, therefore, open to debate and judgment.

Any discussion of documentary "rules" must attend to the interaction of human agents with differing interests and points of view and to several levels of rules: artistic conventions, laws, ethical guidelines, ways of construing art, forms of social behavior, and so on.[2] The "rules" of documentary film may be clustered according to subject, filmmaker, and audience. They comprise:

1. The (extrafilmic) social rules that the film's subjects may seem to be enacting (or violating).
2. The procedural, formal, and technical conventions of film form, and of documentary in particular, that have come to possess a certain force in defining documentary as a genre and in organizing meaning in documentary film. These rules of documentary construction are influenced by the "laws of the marketplace," ideological and legal constraints, and federal regulations that are followed by the mass media systems that finance and distribute documentary films.
3. The "rules" by which audience members understand films. These are practices of construal based on experiences with both (1) and (2), which often result in conflicting expectations that may prevent as well as promote understanding of a documentary film and its subjects.

Subject Rules

In discussions of his documentaries, Wiseman has often mentioned his recurrent concern with "the gap between ideology and actual practice, between the rules and the way they are applied."[3] *Welfare* explores that gap more explicitly than any other Wiseman documentary. At the level of surface action, the film presents the application of welfare rules at the Waverly Center in New York City. Wiseman uses those specific social details as material to build abstract propositions about the institution of welfare in contemporary America. One assumes that the creation of a welfare system by a society grows from humane intentions, yet the practicing system pictured in *Welfare* is often far from humane. Rules set up to administer compassion often seem impossible to administer and far from compassionate. Still, Wiseman presents something more complicated than institutional hypocrisy in *Welfare*.

Social psychologists, rhetorical critics, sociolinguists, and poets all remind us of the importance of labels to self image and the social construction of reality. Charles Horton Cooley described in 1902 a process that he called "the looking-glass self." "We always imagine, and in imagining share, the judgments of the other mind."⁴ Wiseman's *Welfare* is about social judgments of a particular sort. One group of individuals is pictured seeking a label, another is seen making determinations regarding that label. "Who's next? Is there a next?" we hear from a (usually off-screen) voice. The spectator wonders who will next be named eligible—or ineligible—for welfare. *Welfare* turns on the terrible irony that moves the welfare system: to be successful as a welfare recipient—to be eligible—one must be lacking in some fundamental way and be able to document that failure. The documentation often takes the form of notarized letters in which parents or children or spouses or roommates have stated that the applicant is unwanted. For the welfare applicants, the looking-glass self is reflected from the distorted mirror of eligibility. Let us turn to examples from the film to see how Wiseman pulls us into the web of judgment regarding identification and eligibility, how he presents the practice of welfare.

Welfare opens with images of individual faces, the sounds of a camera, voiced instructions regarding a photography session, and images of the still camera itself. As usual in a Wiseman picture, there is no explanation of the action, yet most Americans recognize the ritual of identification card making. It is part of familiar rules of eligibility. Within minutes, we are confronted with a situation that illustrates how problematic familiar rules can become. A man who has an assistance check complains that he cannot get it cashed, because he has no ID. He wants to obtain one at Waverly, but he is told he cannot get one because he is not on the Waverly rolls. According to him, the agency that issues his checks does not issue identification cards. The man claims that he is being discriminated against as an Indian when he is "a human being like anybody. Like a white or black or something like that." The welfare worker tries to be helpful, yet concludes, "Waverly is not responsible." The applicant mentions having escaped from a reservation in Washington. He is clearly dislocated and confused. He seems caught in an absurd Catch–22 regarding identification rules, yet he also gives indications that he might have difficulty following more reasonable rules, too.

The world of welfare is a maze of rules. Almost every scene in the film is built around a confrontation with those rules and the rules of the larger society that surrounds and flows into the life at Waverly. There are frequent references to other agencies, and their complicated rules, resulting in a network of procedures that seem contradictory and often inexplicable even to the welfare staff. A worker seems to take delight in announcing to his client that "Miss Horowitz has made a mistake." Deep into the film a worker advises a client, "Since welfare is really based upon what clients say, they really have to believe what you tell them—until it's proved otherwise." Consequently, all the applicants label themselves "eligible." They offer stories as proof. *Welfare* is full of stories—people trying to find the right story to tell the social worker. Some of the staff try to find out the truth; some do not care: they either will not believe or regard belief as irrelevant to their attempt to meet the formal rules. And we try to find out the truth; and we wonder if it is the truth that matters, or the evident suffering. Wiseman engages us in the act of trying to discern the truth based on the evidence before us, but he does not let us see the conclusion of the action (which, in the case of *Welfare*, is usually a judgment about eligibility).

Sometimes we think we know an outcome and then are reminded that "outcome" may be too decisive a term for human actions that are connected one to another. For instance, there is a couple seen in five different sections of *Welfare*. They are among those waiting outside the building in the second scene of the film (after the photo session and before the ID complaint). The fourth scene is an "emergency interview" in which we hear their individual and collective stories at length. In the course of the interview, the woman mentions that she and the man are both married—to other people. He denies he is married.

WORKER: So what gave her the impression that you were?
MALE CLIENT: Maybe it's a wish that she had that—
FEMALE CLIENT: Maybe it could be a wish, I don't know. I haven't eaten in a couple of days and I'm hungry and I'm, you know, I get a little excited. So I'm sorry, Larry, okay?

Although the welfare worker points out that marital status affects eligibility rules, and the man does not seem to be telling the truth about his wife (and perhaps other things), the worker "accepts" them. Why? Does she believe the man's denial? Is she overlooking the rules for a man who claims he was formerly a welfare worker? Has she decided that a greater truth—need— transcends procedural rules? If she has violated the welfare rules, is this independent action admirable, detrimental, irresponsible, inconsequential? Wiseman puts us in a position of watching a judgment being made. We have not heard everything, but, in another sense, neither has the worker. The information we have for making judgments about other people is never complete. Nor are the outcomes of the judgments we make certain. We hear the couple being told by the social worker to go to housing on the fifth floor and employment on the fourth. We see them three other times in the film, presumably in these locations, presumably waiting for other interviews, and other judgments.

Again and again, we observe bureaucratic procedures that make truth seeking difficult, if not impossible, and truth telling risky, if not equally impossible, in the world of *Welfare*. A woman petitions a social worker regarding the announced closing of her case. She denies that her husband is living with her, which the worker may or may not believe; his supervisor does not believe the woman. The social worker weaves through several levels of procedure to halt the closing. He manages this, not by discovering "the truth," but by calling the supervisor on a technicality.

WORKER: Excuse me, is this Miss Horowitz's office? And you agree that the case should be closed. Is that what this means?

MISS HOROWITZ: "Client working for five years." Yes, that's what it means, whatever action is necessary. Because I have no proof that this man is, has left the home. In fact, I don't believe he has.

WORKER: Well, no, but she was asked to bring in the pay stubs. Right. That is what the closing is for. She says she brought them and there is a copy of them in here. Did she show you that?

MISS HOROWITZ: She asked me to change the budget and put it back in her name. But he's not living with her.

WORKER: I mean, is this what she brought me? Is that sufficient? Does that answer the closing notice?

MISS HOROWITZ: It's more involved than what the man is making.

WORKER: Yes, I know, there is more involved. I agree with you. But we have to go by what is on this paper here. And it says we are closing it because for the last five years you have never brought your pay stubs. See, she's bringing them now.

MISS HOROWITZ: Yeah.

WORKER: So you have to leave it open.

Once again, it would seem that the matter is settled when the worker returns to tell the client that her case will not be closed. But the interview continues. The client discovers that her worker, who has handled the formidable Miss Horowitz, cannot give her an emergency check for food. He says, "It's not my responsibility, money matters."

The general notion of welfare as a "system" draws on ideals of shared responsibility, yet in *Welfare* we see the frustrating dilemmas caused by responsibility that is divided, overlapping, and generally confused. Frequent references to other aid programs and other social services indicate the bureaucratic nightmare of programmed responsibility. The ubiquitous promise of "39 Broadway" (a nearby welfare center) runs through the film as a leitmotif of responsibility shunted.

One of the central absurdities of the situation is that the welfare system has been designed to help people who have problems handling their lives independently, that is, responsibly. Yet the system has become a labyrinth that challenges personal responsibility and aggressiveness. Some meet that challenge and even get the better of it (as when two supervisors discuss "our friend Curtis Rosser," a man who gets aid under three names), but most of the people we see are overwhelmed by it. Some of the attempts of clients to assume responsibility are ludicrous (a young man petitions for a greater housing allowance because he "has responsibilities" toward his dog).

The abstract theme of responsibility can be located in the specific language of *Welfare*. Here are examples from three different scenes:

WORKER: I didn't give you a check.

CLIENT: I'm talking out—Now, now, you that tech-, you're that technical, that you know—you understand what I'm saying, when I say "you," I'm not speaking about you.

CLIENT: How do you contest it?
WORKER: You file for a fair hearing—
CLIENT: Okay. That's insane.
WORKER: Your beef is not with me. Your beef is with the law.

FRIEND: Valerie, Valerie, Valerie, Valerie, Valerie, Valerie, you not going to get nowhere up here arguing with him. He's doin' his job. A man can't do no more than—
VALERIE: I was here Friday. I was here last Wednesday, I was here on the second.
FRIEND: Baby, he only got a certain amount of authority. You can't fight with him. Come off with me.

It is easy to see, to hear, to feel the responsibilities unmet in *Welfare*. It is quite another thing for the subjects—or the spectators—to know who should be held accountable.

At the center of the film, in six different scenes, clients turn to each other or to people outside the Waverly system for attention, if not aid. A young woman, talking on the telephone, recalls her unsatisfactory interview at Waverly. "I said, lady, what do I do for the weekend? I am sick. I was discharged Monday from a psychiatric institute for manic depression. This is friendly New York for you and the New York Welfare Department. Maybe she thinks I could sleep in Port Authority for the weekend. Yeah, that's what they—oh, first said even down at the state department, or whatever it is, she said, women's shelter. She said, but you really couldn't go there. There's a lot of sickies there." Her solution to the dilemma widens the circle of responsibility: "What the hell do they expect me to do? What? Yeah. That's not a bad idea. Well, I'm writing a letter to *The Village Voice*. Yeah, maybe I'll call Hillary, too. Geraldo Rivera? Okay. Yeah. I think he might be very interested in it."

Like all Wiseman films, *Welfare* suggests the changeable nature of roles, and the importance we attach to them. The woman on the telephone, who threatens to call Geraldo Rivera, labels herself "sick" when asking for aid, but clearly dissociates herself from "the sickies" who depend on welfare. In the emergency interview described earlier, we learn that the possibly married male applicant had been a supervisor in social services. In the last developed scene in the film, Hirsch, an after-hours supplicant, confronts the center with his suffering, and with his urgent sense of roles and rules; he is a man "with twenty-two years of education . . . with seventeen years of service to this state," who now labels himself "poor. In fact, destitute, not poor." Hirsch arrives at the center as it is closing for the day; it is too late for an interview. But of course the problems that bring people to the center do not end with office hours. Hirsch launches into several long speeches, first to the assistant director of the center and then to God. A woman seated next to him on the waiting bench seems decidedly uncomfortable as Hirsch self-consciously describes his wait "for something—Godot" and indicates his willingness "to suffer for everybody who's gone before." Hirsch is articulate, theatrical, and quite possibly mad.[5] Wiseman uses his anger and his sorrow as a climax to *Welfare*. The last images of the film, a reprise of clients waiting, many of them now familiar, return us to the opening scene and close the circle of *Welfare*.

When asked if he thought it right to steal, Hirsch replies, "I said it was necessary. There's a difference between right and necessary." Certainly many of the rules, and certainly the ways they are applied, don't seem "right" in *Welfare*.

The welfare system that is presented in Wiseman's film is a profoundly fatiguing and demoralizing apparatus. Social workers and their clients cling to a system that usually seems unsatisfactory from both points of view. In an extended sequence near the end of the film, a daughter tries to act as an advocate for her mother. We will conclude this section with a long passage from that scene, which captures the endless and dizzying search for help and for the locus of responsibility.

SOCIAL WORKER: You'll have to apply for a fair hearing.
DAUGHTER: Oh, in the meantime, what they going to do with the fair hearing? What they going to do? Starve to death? He's in the hospital. She's sick. She's got diabetes. She's got arthritis. She's got heart trouble. What she supposed to do while she waiting for a fair hearing?
SOCIAL WORKER: Wait a minute.
DAUGHTER: Since November I been walk—running around with this woman.
SOCIAL WORKER: You know, you're making it sound like my fault. I'm tellin—
DAUGHTER: It's not my fault either.
SOCIAL WORKER: I'm tellin—
DAUGHTER: It's not his fault. He's in the hospital. It's not her fault. She's sick. Whose fault is it?
SOCIAL WORKER: I'm telling you what they're telling me. They have, they have—
DAUGHTER: Who's responsible for her?
SOCIAL WORKER: Who's responsible—
DAUGHTER: If her husband is sick, he's in the hospital. And she's sick.
SOCIAL WORKER: He's getting disability payments from the union.
DAUGHTER: Can she take the—can she take the check from him?
SOCIAL WORKER: He's legally responsible for her support.
DAUGHTER: That's why she's taking him to court, 'cause he doesn't take care of his legal responsibility.
SOCIAL WORKER: The responsibility is in the hands of the court.
DAUGHTER: The court says they here, I have a letter from the court telling her to come here.
SOCIAL WORKER: This was given—Now this was before the case was rejected, the case was rejected, on the twenty-fourth, and this was given to her—
MOTHER: The same day I came here.
DAUGHTER: When you rejected her, she had this letter.
MOTHER: They told me to go here, Social Security, and that's where I went.

DAUGHTER: She went to Social Security and Social Security sent her back here. They ain't going to take care of her.

SOCIAL WORKER: Well, Social Security is evaluating your application. That's a different thing altogether.

DAUGHTER: Okay. But the new—well, who's responsible for her?

SOCIAL WORKER: Mr. Gaskin.

DAUGHTER: But he's in the hospital as you very well know.

SOCIAL WORKER: I, ah—I understand he's in the hospital.

DAUGHTER: Now what is she supposed to do?

SOCIAL WORKER: Check upcoming—

DAUGHTER: Go down there and take checks that don't belong to her? They belong to him.

SOCIAL WORKER: He has a responsibility—

DAUGHTER: He don't want to give them to her.

SOCIAL WORKER: I — I—

SUPERVISOR: I'll bring it up.

DAUGHTER: We're going into a vicious cycle again. And I'm getting tired of it.

SOCIAL WORKER: Well, as I said before, you have to apply for a fair hearing.

DAUGHTER: How long's a fair hearing going to take and what's she going to do in the meanwhile, while she's waiting for the fair hearing? She's been here—she's been coming here since the fifth, since November.

SOCIAL WORKER: It's her responsibility to try to get the—

DAUGHTER: What do you think she's trying to do?

SOCIAL WORKER: Well—

DAUGHTER: Why do you think she's going to court?

SOCIAL WORKER: You keep shouting at me and you don't—

DAUGHTER: You sending me around in a vicious cycle. I'm trying to tell you, honey, I'm tired—

SOCIAL WORKER: I'm not sending you—

DAUGHTER: She is sick. He is sick. Who is going to take care of them?

SOCIAL WORKER: I am not sending you anywhere.

Film Rules

The documentary or nonfiction film tradition is as old as film itself.[6] Often traced to the nineteenth-century work of film pioneers such as the Lumière brothers and W. K. L. Dickson, documentary film embraced the styles, techniques, and aspirations of earlier media forms interested in dealing with reality artistically.[7] Not only did documentary film inherit the goals of other art forms devoted to mimesis, but it also adopted many of the procedures and ideals of journalism and social science. By the late 1920s, the seminal work of two English-speaking filmmakers shaped the boundaries of documentary purpose and style. Although forced dichotomies underestimate the complex work of both filmmakers, there are distinctions between the lyrical humanism of Robert Flaherty and the socially committed manifestoes of John Grierson.[8]

By the 1970s, the American nonfiction film had developed a style sufficiently formulaic for Barsam to offer this description:

> Generally, the nonfiction film stems from, and is based on, an immediate social
> situation: sometimes a problem, sometimes a crisis, sometimes an undramatic and
> seemingly unimportant person or event. It is usually filmed on the actual scene,
> with the actual people, without sets, costumes, written dialogue, or created sound
> effects. It tries to recreate the feelings of "being there," with as much fidelity to
> fact as the situation allows. The typical nonfiction film is structured in two or three
> parts, with an introduction and conclusion, and tends to follow a pattern from
> problem to solution. Even more typically, it is in black-and-white, with direct
> sound recording (or simulated sound), a musical score written expressly for the
> film and conceived as part of a cinematic whole, and, often as not, a spoken
> narration. Its typical running time is thirty minutes, but some films run less and
> some are ninety-minute feature-length films.[9]

Explicit and implicit rules on how to make such films as Barsam describes
appear consistently in standard documentary textbooks and interviews with
filmmakers.[10]

Sections on "breaking the rules" are predictable parts of the most conservative guides to film making. In *The Technique of Documentary Film Production*, published about the time Wiseman was working on *Welfare*, W. Hugh
Baddeley writes, "Having now laid down a number of rules and conventions
that should be observed in the directing, shooting and editing of factual films,
I am going to repeat that they can, on occasions, all be broken." Yet Baddeley
goes on to caution that "rules can be broken, and broken successfully. But it
is nevertheless vitally important to know what the rules are. It is one thing
to break rules for a carefully calculated reason; it is quite another thing not
to know that there are any rules at all!"[11]

Rules of documentary film were inherited by television producers and
directors, who revived and expanded a form that was in serious decline by
the late 1950s.[12] Once television networks became the primary distributor/
exhibitor of documentary film, another layer of rules constrained the genre.
Bound by commercial considerations and closely regulated by formalized
codes of "fairness," the television documentary has been closely linked with
network news programming and its tradition of objectivity as the journalistic
ideal. Most televised documentaries are in-house productions of network
news divisions and are closely regulated by network guidelines.[13] Av Westin,
a network producer, offers this analysis of the current status of television
documentary as constrained by the sometimes competing demands of money
and reputation:

> Understand this about documentaries on television: They are troublesome to
> advertisers and special interest groups. Despite poll after poll that shows the
> public wants more of them on the air, the fact is that the public turns them off
> when they appear. A documentary can average about 30 percent less in the ratings

than the program it replaces, and because documentaries cost more to produce than other forms of informational programming—in the eighties, a one-hour documentary was budgeted at $235,000 in production money, plus another $200,000 in administrative overhead costs—they seldom earn back their expenses in sponsor revenues. Why do the networks take the heat? For the prestige, which is substantial; for the awards, which are meaningful; and occasionally to get out of trouble with vociferous public interest groups or the Federal Communications Commission.[14]

Commercial television, in the ABC "Close-Up" series, sponsored the early work of Drew Associates. Made possible by technical advances (such as the development of lightweight, portable cameras, synchronous sound equipment, and fast film stock), the move toward cinema verite/direct cinema was highly political in its rejection of what was considered the rigid authoritarianism of the traditional documentary. Public television, the primary sponsor and outlet for cinema verite and direct cinema, has its own rules, dictated by private philanthropy and inconsistent governmental support. Stephen Mamber stresses the deliberate attempt of cinema verite to change the rules:

> Cinema verite as we are speaking of it, then, is an attempt to strip away the accumulated conventions of traditional cinema in the hope of rediscovering a reality that eludes other forms of filmmaking and reporting. Cinema verite is a strict discipline only because it is in many ways so simple, so "direct." The filmmaker attempts to eliminate as much as possible the barriers between subject and audience. These barriers are technical (large crews, studio sets, tripod-mounted equipment, special lights, costumes and makeup), procedural (scripting, acting, directing), and structural (standard editing devices, traditional forms of melodrama, suspense, etc.). Cinema verite is a practical working method based upon a faith in unmanipulated reality, a refusal to tamper with life as it presents itself. Any kind of cinema is a process of selection, but there is (or should be) all the difference in the world between the cinema-verite aesthetic and the methods of fictional and traditional documentary.[15]

Despite what Mamber says about the total stripping away of old conventions, rules die hard. In the section that follows, we shall try to illustrate, with examples from *Welfare*, how Fred Wiseman follows, breaks, and transcends the rules of fiction and nonfiction film to create his own rules for a form he calls "reality fiction."

Wiseman's Rules

Wiseman's procedural and formal rules for documentary are revealed in his films and in the accounts he has given of those films in a series of lectures and interviews and in sworn testimony in *Commonwealth v. Wiseman*.[16]

Wiseman as a filmmaker and direct cinema as a film style were familiar to avid documentary watchers by the time that *Welfare*, Wiseman's ninth film and the seventh funded by WNET/13, was broadcast on PBS in the fall of 1975. But many members of a more general television audience in 1975, and later, expect a documentary to have off-screen, voice-over narration. Wiseman has frequently compared his abandonment of narration to the breaking down of the proscenium arch, an analogy that acknowledges the essentially dramatic nature of his films and at the same time stakes their claim as "art." Wiseman remarked to Atkins that narration is "like having a butterfly collection with everything labelled."[17] This lack of labeling has led some to fault Wiseman for violating rules of clarity and political commitment.[18] Donald Brieland challenges the clarity—and ultimately, the fairness—of Wiseman's method. "Viewing [*Welfare*] almost two years after the change [elderly, blind, and disabled clients were transferred from state-administered categorical programs to a federal program under the social security office], one cannot comprehend the reason for either the change or for the confusion. The result is to make a bad system look worse because of the concentration on one historical event. Wiseman's method is to let people tell their own stories; however, a little narration would have been useful to explain the transition."[19]

Another standard expository device that Wiseman rejects is the staged interview. In a memo to his staff on the function of interviews, network news president Reuven Frank wrote:

> It is natural and human and in many ways commendable that most of us recoil at being personally unpleasant to our fellow men. In conversation we take answers on faith, and even when that is not possible we do not express incredulity rudely or press our partners into confessions of dissimulation. This is part of good manners. But an interviewer is not an individual human in conversation. He is the representative of the curiosity of an audience, presumably its legitimate curiosity. His supposed good manners are often the means of denying information to his fellow citizens. An interview which is not more than a conversation is less than an interview. You are wasting our time, and we are invading the dullness and superficiality of your privacy. . . . To be sententious about it, the essence of professionalism is discipline. Interviews too often are broadcast before they are edited, before they are disciplined. The best interviews are of people reacting—not people expounding. Joy, sorrow, shock, fear—these are the stuff of news. No important story is without them.[20]

In many respects, *Welfare* is an interview film; but Wiseman does not stage any interviews. He simply uses the interviews conducted at the Waverly Center as the major material of his film, working inside and outside the news interview boundaries. The result is something not at all simple.

The curiosity—and identification—of the audience that Frank describes as lodged in the persona of the interviewer as audience surrogate is more likely to be free-floating in *Welfare*. Frank calls for joy, sorrow, shock, and fear and appears to think that they need to be motivated by an aggressive interviewer. In a Wiseman film, the joy, sorrow, shock, and fear reveal themselves as products of a world that the film is merely observing. It is an important part of Wiseman's aesthetic that he does not seem to describe, explain, or motivate the actions and feelings of his subjects. Because Wiseman avoids direct address and does not show production staff on camera, the interviews in *Welfare* resemble action in the illusionary or fictional cinema more than traditional documentary. Certainly the interviews are edited. Wiseman follows many of the conventions for single-camera news editing in his heavy reliance on cutaways for smooth editing of portions that have been deleted; however, because he does not direct the profilmic event and does not stage reaction shots (although he "takes" them), Wiseman must be especially ingenious in editing to achieve the illusion of temporal and spatial continuity and to maintain thematic coherence. Wiseman freely admits to editing together images and sounds out of chronological order.

Welfare is full of the emotional reactions that Frank encouraged his staff to provoke and that are the staples of news and fiction. Yet Wiseman's "bad manners" differ from those of the network interviewers. The provocations in *Welfare* are subject-induced; the incredulity is first theirs, and then ours. Here two welfare workers confront the issue directly:

WORKER 1: I don't think my, I don't put clients through a, through a hoop.
WORKER 2: Well, are you assuming that we are?
WORKER 1: What?
WORKER 2: Are you assuming that we are?
WORKER 1: I assume that you are. If you're, if you're, if you're interviewing her and torturing her by asking her about her, about her husband and so forth when the client—
WORKER 2: I don't think that is a torture.
WORKER 1: I think it is.
WORKER 2: Ah, ho. Well, I don't think it's torture to ask somebody—
WORKER 1: Well, close to it, anyway.
WORKER 2: Okay, okay. But, look.

Although (and perhaps because) Wiseman does not stage or himself label the "tortures" of his films, his use of shocking material is often seen as a violation of rules of taste and ethical standards.[21] Nichols maintains that "Wiseman disavows conventional notions of tact, breaking through what otherwise would be ideological constraints of politeness, respect for privacy, queasiness in the face of the grotesque or taboo, the impulse to accentuate the positive, etc. . . . Wiseman's 'tactlessness' allows him not to be taken in by institutional rhetoric. . . . But this lack of tact also pulls Wiseman's cinema toward the realm of voyeurism and visual pleasure."[22]

Wiseman's films all tread the line between voyeurism and the "presumably legitimate curiosity" of Frank's imagined audience. Wiseman's sometimes unsympathetic attitude toward his subjects has led some of his critics—and some of his subjects—to accuse him of breaking normal rules of documentary ethics. Closely linked to the implied attitude—a matter internal to the films but sufficiently consistent in twenty years of work to constitute a sort of "rule"—is the issue of how he negotiates permission to get his subjects on film. With *Titicut Follies* and from time to time with other films, there have been complaints that Wiseman has violated the expectations of informed consent and that he has exploited the good will of his subjects. Wiseman's standard reply, which now amounts to his summary of his rules of procedure, is that he obtains consent by approaching the head of an institution, relying on the head to tell its members that the institution has consented to Wiseman's presence. Then, he says, he obtains consent at the moment of shooting or just after, recording it on film and/or tape; if a person objects to being filmed then and there, he does not use the material; but if a person fails to object at the time of shooting, Wiseman says, he considers that consent cannot be withdrawn. Questions regarding consent and exploitation raised about other Wiseman films are echoed by Coleman regarding *Welfare*. "Wiseman's most extreme play upon our emotions centres round a WASP supervisor who finds herself—natural liberal that she is—abruptly lost, out of control, unsympathetic to us, the viewers. How he gained her approval of herself on screen is not merely a mystery . . . but a bother. Mr. Wiseman has both the gall and the empathy . . . to produce these astonishing affairs, and one begins to wonder how he lives with himself after such liberations of rawness: at least two of his people in this were evidently of unsound mind and played for the camera."[23]

Coleman's response to *Welfare* exhibits many familiar patterns. He labels the actions of someone in the film as unsympathetic, assumes other audience members agree, and goes on to presume that the individual will have a predictable response to that label. It is difficult to know which people Coleman meant by unsound (Hirsch? The woman on the telephone? The man who plans to marry a Rockefeller?), but he assumes that an ethical rule or law dictates that incompetents should not be photographed. Still, he obviously admires *Welfare*. His solution: he attributes to Wiseman both empathy and gall. By implication, Coleman praises and condemns Wiseman for rule violations.

Contradiction is at the heart of all of Wiseman's "reality fictions." Part of their dialectical energy flows from the configuration of different film-making rule systems. This quality of what Clifford Geertz has called "blurred genres" creates energy—and confusion.[24] Like all of Wiseman's films, *Welfare* is constructed with two quite different organizational patterns. At the level of the scene or sequence, action conforms to the rules of time and space followed by traditional narrative films. Time is compressed, but continuity-style editing dictates that the "action" be easily followed by the audience. Scenes are progressive, both in the sense of causal motivation and through time/space. On the level of the scene, the viewer's response to *Welfare* is more akin to the affective bond created in "illusionary cinema" than in the traditional narrated documentary, although scenes typically do not come to a "conclusion" or lead narratively to the scene that follows.

But at the level of the film as a whole, Wiseman avoids both the guided-exposition or the problem-solution structure of traditional documentary and the narrative rise and fall of fictional films. *Welfare* is metaphorical, thematic, and episodic in structure. Sequences are connected to one another by form and theme, usually by several forms and themes at the same time. This modernist structure is also modernist in the coolness of its tone. Its collage structure is nonlinear and abstract. "Continuity" becomes a thematic construct, emerging from the repetition, restatement, and variation of themes and forms. This ultimately self-conscious form requires an active, intellectual, reflective reading by audiences, but also operates powerfully at the level of feelings, in its refusal to cushion viewers within a structure of explicitness, narrative, and authority.

Despite the associational collage structure of his films, Wiseman follows many basic rules of dramatic construction, such as foreshadowing, introducing characters and connecting them to place, building to a climax, and so forth. "If you abut major sequences, you lose meaning," he told Ellsworth.[25] Wiseman claims he makes his films with no intended audience in mind, to please his own personal standards, yet his desire to "make a film that works in film terms" connects in practice to shared rules of art/craft/entertainment/journalism.[26] Before he made *Welfare*, he spoke of working with a rough cut of a film that, at two and a half hours, was "not a movie yet."[27] *Welfare* exceeded that length, thereby breaking many of the rules of broadcast programming and audience patience. Nevertheless, Wiseman's willingness to construct longer films has not automatically resulted in adherence to Karl Heider's proposed ethnographic rule that the filmmaker convey the sense and structure of "whole acts." Wiseman's style of compression continues to violate both the rules of ethnographic purists regarding fidelity to natural time and space and the rules of Hollywood and network television pacing.

Wiseman frequently advertises his contempt for the conventions of journalistic documentary and has been blunt about his disdain for film-making schools. He says, "it is a total waste of time to major in film production. The kids are not getting an education. They don't know how to read. The film technology is really very easy. The question is what to do with it. The way to know that is to have some experience in other things beside filmmaking. A good filmmaker has to have some ideas in response to the world."[28]

Still another documentary convention is the exclusion of the comic, unless the entire tone of the piece is light-hearted. Irony is rare in documentary and subtle irony is even more rare. Documentarian Ed Pincus says that the delicate problem of tone in documentary is linked to class. He suggests that the upper-middle-class sensibilities of many documentary filmmakers can easily cross the line from detachment to ridicule. Pincus describes Wiseman as sharing this problem, but lacking a sense of humor.[29] The laughs in Wiseman's films often make audiences uncomfortable. When asked about whether he felt the need for comic relief in his films, Wiseman replied, "I'm interested in the comic aspects of some of these things, but not so much at the expense of the people in the films. A lot of the scenes in the films are situational comedy of a very high order."[30] Once again, Coleman captures the sense of contradiction one feels in responding to *Welfare* as he describes the "emergency interview": "Their encounter with the interviewer is terribly funny—and the word terribly is used advisedly: it is a peculiarly sad and loopy event."[31]

Wiseman has mentioned Eugene Ionesco and nineteenth-century novels as particularly influential in shaping his sense of dramatic construction. Wiseman claims, "I've learned more about filmmaking from reading than I have from other films. The best book I ever read about filmmaking was a collection of Eugene Ionesco's essays in which he talked about playwriting and construction."[32] The contradictions in tone and style between Ionesco and George Eliot are incorporated into *Welfare*, which results in a blend of theater of the absurd, social commentary, and melodrama, and a hovering sense of grand philosophical and ethical ambition.

No documentary rule looms larger than that of "fairness." Wiseman claims that he tries to be fair to "the subject" in all his films but he scorns the forced equity of broadcasting codes that has resulted in superficial point/counterpoint statements followed by a stated conclusion that the truth lies somewhere in between.[33] Common sense reminds us that Wiseman's films are not the last word or the only word on the topics he addresses. Common sense also reminds us that rules of art should be like constitutions, rather than checklists. The rules of art are constitutional in two major senses. First, constitutional rules are established not as absolute, but on the understanding that the constitution will usually be appealed to in difficult cases where two or more constitutional rules are in conflict. Hence, the Supreme Court does not simply apply or construe the Constitution, it contributes to the evolution of constitutional law.[34] Second, constitutions govern competing human interests, where freedom or benefit for one person may result in contraint or harm to another, and where a decision affecting the parties in a particular case may have consequences for the community as a whole. Constitutional rules are fundamentally and thoroughly social and essentially dynamic. All questions about the aesthetic or ethical merit of documentary film in general and *Welfare* in particular should be rule-governed in these "constitutional" senses.

Just as ethical and aesthetic boundaries should not be absolute, so, too, should the epistemological rules of documentary resist absolutism. Wiseman maintains a vexing elusiveness, in the films and in interviews, about the meanings of his films. Audiences and critics sometimes complain that Wiseman is insufficiently committed, or insufficiently clear, about his views—meaning, usually, his political views—of the institutions he examines. Wiseman has stated, "My only commitment to documentary is that I like to do it."[35] Wiseman's refusal to commit himself may be vexing, but it is an essential part of his contribution. He is not merely being coy; nor is he defending the "purity" of art by contending—explictly in interviews and implictly in the films—that it is not his point of view that is at issue, but what audiences are able to make of the films. Paradoxical though it may be, Wiseman's films become public through his dogged privatism. An apprehension of the political insights Wiseman offers us depends upon our achieving them through our own active experience of the films, rather than by comparing them to some hidden "thesis" that Wiseman has buried in the film for us to discover.[36] One of the paradoxes Wiseman presents us with is that the political value of the films depends upon our experiencing them apart from a paraphase, and yet, because the insights of the films are profoundly social and political, it becomes the responsibility of Wiseman's viewers to carry on the work of rendering the issues he raises into debatable, propositional terms.

We do not think that Wiseman evades the political responsibility of his films, but that he rightly understands that his responsibility is to explore the means by which documentary film may help to illuminate the connections of subject, filmmaker, and audience. The audience must share the burden— and opportunity—of representation and meaning. The ethics of documentary do not end with the filmmaker, but neither does saying this attempt to shift the whole burden of meaning, and of ethical responsibility, to the audience. Wiseman's methods do not shift the burden of documentary ethics to his subject or his audience; rather, they enlarge the burden and the opportunities of the documentary enterprise.

Audience Rules

Welfare provokes two levels of audience debate and judgment: (1) judgments of the film's individual "subjects" and of the "subject" of welfare and (2) judgments of the film *Welfare*. The social behaviors at the surface of the film are waiting to be named; the film itself also awaits naming. Thus, the silence of direct cinema implicates the spectator in the act of naming.

What, then, are the rules of documentary spectatorship? If spectators have independence and are active participants in constructing and construing meaning, do they have an ethical responsibility for careful attention, maturity, fairness, even imagination? One presumes that spectators will employ complicated sets of social standards to make judgments regarding welfare and will bring equally complicated standards and expectations about art, journalism, social science, entertainment, and so forth to use as criteria for judging *Welfare*. Because of Wiseman's methods, and the habits of audiences, the two levels of judgment necessarily combine.

The labels audience members and critics put on the individuals and the institutional subjects of Wiseman's films often create another version of the looking-glass self. Edgar Z. Friedenberg claims that "the delayed development of hostile reactions by the subjects of Wiseman's films is one of the more revealing social responses his work evokes."[37] Critics sometimes judge the subjects of *Welfare* harshly, but more often they engage in discussions of the "system" as something beyond the participants and find that system woefully lacking. Often reviewers reach to previous Wiseman films for technical, structural, and intentional rules and standards, but they also apply rules from other sources. Pulling a single word from a review is a perverse truncation, but the following labels of the film give capsule judgments of what critics assume as its intentions and accomplishments: catalogue (O'Connor), study (Arnold, Coleman), examination (Arnold), dissection (Waters), glimpse (Meyer), look (Stein, Coleman), stare (Coleman), eavesdropping (Arnold), vision (Wolcott), portrait (Lewis, Kilday), epic (Brieland), art (Rosenblatt), event (Feldman), ordeal (Shain), and indictment (Kilday).[38]

And what of the film's general audiences? We cannot know, of course, what Wiseman's audiences make of the film. Certainly the film seems to leave room for a range of political judgments concerning the welfare system, from a resigned turning away from the whole muddle, to a condemnation of eloquent malingerers, to an equally fervent condemnation of a bureaucratic system that seems to turn its back on fellow citizens in need.

But an attempt to make a rhetorical reading of *Welfare* commits itself not merely to a formal reading of the film as a text, but also to an attempt to read the film for the actions of interpretation it invites in its readers. Our response to art is dependent upon our general propensity to seek form in symbolic action and to seek that form in terms of our expectations. Audiences bring to *Welfare* not only ideas about public policy (which may be challenged by the film), but also ideas about documentary film (ideas which may also be challenged by the film).

A central, perhaps *the* central, rule for documentary, from the audience's point of view, seems to be "it should be objective." In a discussion with school administrators attending a showing of *High School*, Wiseman was charged with claiming the mantle of documentary but of not living up to its rules of objectivity.

SCHOOLMAN: Why did you concentrate on such unattractive teachers and show so many uncomplimentary close-ups? Were you trying deliberately to set the tone for a grotesque picture?

WISEMAN: That comment indicates the degree to which we are all sold on the Hollywood myth. We all expect to see beautiful people in films. But "High School" is a documentary and most people in real life simply aren't as good looking as Hollywood stars.

SCHOOLMAN: You use the word "documentary" but I don't see this as an accurate, objective reporting job on what high schools are like today. Your techniques are biased and your message is very far off the mark.

WISEMAN: Every documentary film is subjective. I don't know how to make an objective one.[39]

Wiseman's comments in reply to the "schoolman" may seem disingenuous, self-protective, and even contradictory, a problem that seems to be central to his description of his films as "reality fiction."

Documentary filmmakers and communication theorists almost unanimously agree that objectivity is a false and impossible standard, but they inevitably work in an arena where audiences are supposing that a documentary is or should be "objective." In such an arena, it is not especially useful for filmmakers to dismiss the standard of objectivity with a flat assertion of the subjectivity of their work. Audiences and their protectors of course mean a great many things by objectivity, and although, in the section which follows, we shall attempt to demonstrate some of the difficulties of "objectivity" as a standard, we do not, in principle, mean to deny the possibility or the desirability of fairness or impartiality, nor of a range of responsible modes of representation, from conscientiously neutral reporting, to avowed and explicit advocacy, to suggestive and intuitive personal expression.[40]

The naive standard of objectivity is often applied inappropriately to understandings of film subjects, the film process, the filmmaker, and the film audience. The subject of documentary film, and of fiction film as well, is human action, a world that is constructed as and by symbolic action. Human action is thus, itself, an interpretation, since it is constructed in terms that imply an understanding of what is happening, an understanding that is of human subjects rather than of merely material objects in motion.[41] Human action, the subject of documentary, is motivated by understandings, rather than by unmediated facts. Hence any treatment of these subjects that is objective in the sense of treating them as objects would be unable to account for or even describe the *actions* of the subjects except at the minimal level of objective motion.

The whole apparatus of film and television, from the mechanisms of recording and transmission to genres and formulas shaping what gets produced and in what formats, inevitably imposes constraints on our knowing. Documentary is necessarily interpretive even at the mechanical level because it is both selective and constructive. The film apparatus records sound and image from a point of view. The filmmaker is in one place rather than another, directs the camera one way rather than another, and turns the camera off part of the time. The editing process imposes further reductions upon the flow of the original events. But of course film making is not simply a process of reducing reality—it is the *construction* of a reality. Even when audiences understand that film is selective, they seldom understand fully how it constructs an interpretation, a difficulty that cannot be resolved by appeals to "objectivity," as if that would relieve the filmmaker of the responsibility of constructing meaning. So far we have claimed that *what* is known by documentary and *how* it is known through film is necessarily interpretive. The filmmaker and audience are part of the same process.

Human knowing is, by definition, subjective. In a comprehensive recent discussion of this issue, Richard Gregg argues that "the rhetorical function of [symbolic] inducing is a part of all knowing."[42] The viewer of a film *must* view it through the human means of responding to symbols, through an active process of subjective knowing, in which both feelings and logical categories are necessarily human inventions.[43] What Paul Ricoeur says of the writing of history, in his essay on "Objectivity and Subjectivity," applies to documentary film as well. Ricoeur argues that for the historian, "the justification of his enterprise is man—man and the values he discovers and develops in his civilizations. And this reminder sometimes rings as an awakening when the historian is tempted to repudiate his fundamental intention and yield to the *fascination for a false objectivity*—that of a history in which there would no longer be men and human values but only structures, forces, and institutions." Ricoeur continues, "For reflection constantly assures us that the *object* of history is the human *subject* itself."[44]

If we tell our film-making students that objectivity is impossible, does that mean that anything goes? Is absolutism as regards truth or representational correspondence replaceable only by anarchism or totalitarianism? What is the nature of the subjectivism that has replaced objectivism in the films of Frederick Wiseman?

In our view, the necessary element of subjectivity in human knowing does not relieve subject, filmmaker, or audience of the responsibility for knowing. It is possible to reduce both objectivity and subjectivity to ethical evasions. To say that human knowledge is not absolute, automatic, objective, and universal is not to say that it must be, on the other hand, arbitrary, accidental, idiosyncratic, and particular. Human knowing is based in material reality and expressed through particulars and individuals, but it is mediated by social beings capable of communicating with one another and therefore responsible for what they do and what they share. The necessity for interpretation, for regarding documentary and the response to it as human action, is what makes ethical discussion of documentary possible at all. It is only because all the elements of the process—subjects, filmmakers, and audiences—are capable of actively sharing the responsibility of making meanings that choices are possible. To assign ethical responsibility only to the filmmaker is to undermine documentary as report, as advocacy, or as interpretation, and to reduce subjects and audiences to objects, manipulated by filmmakers themselves robbed of ethical dimensions by the isolation thus imposed, and by the assumption of a mechanics of knowing that is objective in the sense that it is outside of human interpretation. Hence, ethics and objectivity become mutually exclusive conceptions.

To assert the subjectivity of documentary is not to give way to anarchy of knowledge, the sort of radical relativism that our hypothetical sophomore refers to in saying that "if documentary isn't objective, that means everybody's opinion is just as good as everybody else's." Rather, in our view, subjectivity imposes the burden of human action within the constraints of subjectivity, and of a mutual search for the truths of our shared social lives.

One of the things that makes Frederick Wiseman's films so compelling is that they take on directly the subjective-objective issue and that they create a rich sense of the mutually interpretive actions of subjects, filmmaker, and viewers. Wiseman's films are capable, in fact, of a richness on this issue that goes far beyond what he has articulated in words, perhaps underlining the special genius he brings to documentary.

From very early on, Wiseman chafed at the pretensions of documentary to objective knowledge. Certainly the label "cinema verite" was an unfortunate one, for it implied a standard, a rule, that was clearly impossible. In an early interview, Wiseman made the following comment on audience expectations of objectivity: "I think this objective-subjective stuff is a lot of bullshit. How can any intelligent person think [films are] anything but [subjective]? . . . I mean you can't put a subtitle on: 'For the wary viewer, for the novitiate, all films are subjective.' You can't do it. It might be fun to do it as a joke, but for no other reason." Wiseman goes on, in the same interview, to dismiss his obligation toward the novice who assumes objectivity. "That's education in another area that somebody else has to deal with. I don't know how to deal with that."[45] What Wiseman says in this quotation sounds very much like an attempt to evade responsibility, but, in practice, his films are partly remarkable for the way they invite a sense of shared responsibility. Objectivity may be denied, but the burden of interpretation is shared, and usually, in a Wiseman film, it is *felt* and *understood* to be shared.

Wiseman's films display something of the existential horror at self-satisfied liberal humanism that Jean-Paul Sartre made famous in *Nausea*. In Sartre's novel, his hero, Antoine Roquentin, meets a liberal humanist in a restaurant and savagely attacks the humanist's optimistic, abstract refusal to attend to the reality that is all about him. The humanist claims to love everyone, including all the people in the restaurant. Roquentin asks, "Whom must you love? The people here?"

> "They too. All" [says the Self-Taught Man, as Roquentin, the narrator, refers to the humanist].
> He turns towards the radiant young couple: that's what you must love. For a moment he contemplates the man with white hair. Then his look returns to me: I read a mute question on his face. I shake my head: "No." He seems to pity me. "You don't either," I tell him, annoyed, "you don't love them."

The Self-Taught Man objects. "So, those two young people behind you," says Roquentin, "—you love them?" The Self-Taught Man fences for a moment, then replies, "I see they are young and I love the youth in them. Among other things, Monsieur." Roquentin pursues the matter:

"You turn your back on them, what they say escapes you. . . . What colour is the woman's hair?"

He is worried:

"Well, I . . ." He glances quickly at the young couple and regains his assurance. "Black!"

"So you see!"

"See what?"

"You see that you don't love them. You wouldn't recognize them in the street. They're only symbols in your eyes. You are not at all touched by them: you're touched by the Youth of the Man, the Love of Man and Woman, the Human Voice."

"Well, doesn't that exist?"

"Certainly not, it doesn't exist! Neither Youth nor Maturity nor Old Age nor Death. . . ."

The face of the Self-Taught Man, hard and yellow as a quince, has stiffened into a reproachful lockjaw.[46]

Wiseman's existential paradoxes in *Welfare* turn the objectivity of the liberal welfare system on its head. For in *Welfare*, it is Wiseman and his audience, if they are prepared to take the leap with him, who face the anguished burden of existence as it is borne by the applicants before the welfare system, a system which represents the love of society for its members in quite a different sort of objectivity, the objectivity of eligibility that has translated its avowed humanism into a depressed and inept bureaucracy.

In a Wiseman film, it is subjectivity that faces existential reality, and objectivity that evades reality behind a mask of neutrality, received authority, and nominal justice. Wiseman's subjectivity is not fantasy or radical individuality, but a direct confrontation with the felt reality of concrete human experience. In the typical Wiseman institution, objectivity is not about objects, or about reality; it is, rather, about managing humans by a strategy of naming them as if they were objects. For Wiseman, an objectivity that consists in fixing humans into labels is at the heart of all his films, displayed as a strategy by which humans evade the pain and the responsibility of actually looking at one another.

There is no way, of course, to simply cut through the paradox. Wiseman himself employs abstract, symbolic strategies to reveal the strategies of institutions, and he employs his human subjects to serve his own symbolic, artistic ends. Wiseman does not offer to make our lives more simple; he does offer us a way of noticing the ethical dimensions of naming in the lived experience of American institutions, and in the startling experience of watching his films.

In *Welfare*, Wiseman helps us see the absurdity that can result from the mechanical application of rules that have lost their connection to meaning or purpose. Early in his career, Wiseman said he was drawn to the filming of institutions because this subject seemed "to be very fresh material for film."[47] He wanted a topic that "hadn't been overworked," yet he wanted to avoid seeming to claim that his films were the definitive statement on a given institution or theme. Although certainly not the only, or even the first, filmmaker to shape the rules of direct cinema, Frederick Wiseman has arguably influenced the form more than any other single individual. Wiseman is now in danger of being the victim of his success. His rules, originally innovative, have come to seem mechanical to some other filmmakers. In the decade since *Welfare*, there has been a growing complaint that Wiseman's documentaries have turned in on themselves and lost their thematic energy and creative power. But there is a more positive side to this. Impatience with Wiseman is partly his gift to us, in the sense that he has brought us to the place where it is possible to articulate differences. Yet his willingness to keep—and to keep faith in—his own rules while exploring variations on a personal vision that has a core, but changes, is an immeasurable contribution to how audiences and filmmakers understand American institutions and American film making. Wiseman has used his luck, used his rules. He has made it possible for others to see those rules and thus to build on them, or break them. His achievement has made possible a debate that could not have existed otherwise. We can learn much about good films and bad rules from Frederick Wiseman.

Chapter 8

Standing on Ceremony
Believing as Seeing in *Canal Zone*

The conquest of the earth, which mostly means the taking it away from those who have a different complexion or slightly flatter noses than ourselves, is not a pretty thing when you look into it too much. What redeems it is the idea only. An idea at the back of it; not a sentimental pretence but an idea; and an unselfish belief in the idea—something you can set up, and bow down before, and offer a sacrifice to.

—Joseph Conrad, *Heart of Darkness*

About halfway through *Canal Zone* occurs a scene of a little over seven minutes in which a young married woman takes a thematic apperception test administered by a man seated at a desk. The woman is shown a series of rather ambiguous still pictures and asked what is happening in them. She makes up stories, speculates about who the characters are, what motivates them, how they are feeling, how they are related to one another, and how their stories will turn out. Her talk is full of romance, of partings and reconciliations, and of optimistic predictions. The psychologist shows the woman one in the series of pictures, and asks her, "How about this one?"

WOMAN: I think maybe she is this woman's husband's lover and she caught 'em. And she's running away.

PSYCHOLOGIST: What brought this event about in terms of her catching them? Or was she looking? Or what?

WOMAN: Yeah, I think, I think maybe she just stumbled up upon them. Maybe they were out in the woods or something, I don't know. She might have just stumbled up upon them and she watched 'em.

PSYCHOLOGIST: And how does she feel about that?

WOMAN: Maybe she feels like she's less of a woman because she can't please her husband and hold on to him. Maybe he has to turn to somebody else. Because this one, she looks younger than the wife.

PSYCHOLOGIST: And how does she feel? The other woman?

WOMAN: I guess she feels like she's been caught. Ha. She's been caught in the act.

PSYCHOLOGIST: And what's going to come out of all this?

WOMAN: I think maybe it will draw maybe the husband and wife closer together. I think it will make her want to try even harder to be a good wife and to hold on to her man.

Later, the psychologist asks the woman about another picture which she has described as a couple about to be married.

PSYCHOLOGIST: And how will things go?
WOMAN: I think they'll go good. I think they'll have a happy life. I think they'll have their ups and downs but basically a happy life. Probably have kids right away. That's about it.

The thematic apperception test scene works in *Canal Zone* at a number of levels, as do all scenes in Wiseman's films. Wiseman is unusual in the length of time he gives his subjects, often allowing conversational interactions, arguments, and speeches to endure on the screen long after other filmmakers would have cut to new material, responsive to that conventional, but internalized, urgency to keep things moving.[1] But for all their felt quality of duration and "everydayness," Wiseman's films are formally very dense and tend to draw more attention to themes than to the ongoing stories of particular people. The scenes of Wiseman's films do not simply accumulate, or "add up" to a meaning. Rather, he structures every scene, and even transitional shots, so that they reverberate within a complex structure of meaning, reaching out to other shots and scenes at multiple levels of significance. It appears that no scene survives Wiseman's editorial process that does not serve more than one purpose in the organization and meaning of the film as a whole. So it is with the TAT scene.

At the ostensibly descriptive level, the TAT scene amplifies and seemingly confirms an issue that is introduced in the scenes that precede and follow it. In the preceding scene, a woman tells an audience that the high stress of life in the Canal Zone results in an unusually high rate of child abuse. And so we are prepared to see the TAT scene, immediately following, as another example of a mental health problem presumably caused by stress. There is no particular evidence within the TAT scene to indicate that the client is disturbed, but because we have just been told about stress and abuse, we are likely to perceive the woman as getting, and requiring, therapy. This relatively literal, narrative reading of the TAT scene is supported by the scenes that follow, in which we see a gateway with a large sign reading "Mental Health Center" and then a group of apathetic souls in an institution, gazing at a television set playing an old Abbott and Costello movie dubbed into Spanish, which is interrupted by an ad, also dubbed into Spanish, for Kentucky Fried Chicken.

As description, although it lacks sufficient detail and context to count as scientific evidence of any ethnographic point about the particular woman or the psychologist, the TAT scene stands in the film as evidence that residents of the Canal Zone suffer from emotional problems and that some attempt is made to alleviate those problems. But in a Wiseman film, irony and reflexivity carry the significance of each scene beyond the descriptive level. In the relatively modest and unobtrusive TAT scene, many of the formal and thematic issues of *Canal Zone* are potentially revealed.

The TAT scene comments upon the level of manifest action (the client and the psychologist), the level of the culture (the world of the Canal Zone as revealed in *Canal Zone*), the level of the film as a formal structure, and the level of the spectator of the film. These levels (or we might think of them as concentric zones) are defined by the assumption of the thematic apperception test: the images that are shown to the client are merely stimuli; the true significance of the test is that it allows the client to project what is inside her head. She is not describing the pictures, she is describing her own preconceptions. And this, of course, is exactly what *Canal Zone* seems to be about—a culture busily, fixedly, cooperatively projecting its preconceptions. And, as an ironist, Wiseman reminds us not only that we and he are doing the same thing in constructing and decoding the meanings of the film, but also that we are necessarily doing it as we create the culture and symbol system that permit us to realize that we are creating our culture and symbol system.

Canal Zone is about the construction of belief. In the conventional sense, scene after scene shows how human beings propagandize their fellow human beings to join them in a system of belief, so that seeing and hearing become believing. But in another sense, it is clear that the whole structure of beliefs is an invention projected upon the world: believing is seeing. Culture, in this view, consists of the stories we tell when we consult the pictures in our heads.

Taken in the context of the film as a whole, the TAT scene poses the dialectical pairs that run throughout the film in an ever-changing series of clusters and oppositions. The Panama Canal is an enormous engineering accomplishment, a feat of reason, technology, money, and will power. The scene upon which the canal is imposed is a land of jungle and swamp, a fevered tropical zone. The oppositions in the film between North America and Central America, between technological and backward, might be read in the TAT scene as clustering about the psychologist and his client, in which the client represents all that is female, passive, irrational, tropical, romantic, imaginative; and the psychologist all that is male, active, rational, Northern, scientific. The romantic visions of the client are offered up to the bland stare of science, and the implicit promise of the scene is that reason will redeem the wilderness of her fantasies. All this is latent in the TAT scene. Of course, in reading these meanings into the scene, we are, perhaps, engaging in exactly that rapture of significance—in which everything means something and everything fits—that constitutes the difficulty that brings the client to the psychologist's office. Just so. That is part of the joke Wiseman plays on his readers, who are allowed to speculate upon the meanings of his films, while being reminded that that is what they are doing. But if the irony includes the viewer, it also intentionally and persuasively subverts the dialectic of forces between client and psychologist, between fantasy and technology. For the whole pattern of *Canal Zone* demonstrates that the technology that is the canal is itself a fantasy projected upon the tropics and sustained by a culture that is, in its turn, a metaphor, that is, a trope. The effect of Wiseman's film is of a potentially terrifying, or perhaps liberating, dislocation, in which what we are used to taking for granted as routine and natural is thrown into relief as merely symbolic.

In his *Tropics of Discourse*, Hayden White argues that human living and modes of understanding it inevitably proceed in terms of metaphorical thinking, rather than by absolute knowledge. Borrowing from the rhetorical tradition the idea of a trope as a figure of thought or speech, White claims that argument, or discourse, in the human sciences is therefore necessarily tropical.[2] The discourse that sustains the *Canal Zone* is, in Hayden White's sense, tropical, essentially an invention and a projection, difficult to maintain, and in fact maintained largely by material culture and discursive appeal.[3]

Canal Zone was filmed in the Canal Zone in the spring of 1976—the year in which the United States was celebrating its bicentennial. 1976 was also a presidential election year, and one of the issues by which Ronald Reagan attempted to wrest the Republican nomination from President Gerald Ford had to do with a treaty to cede to Panama the Canal Zone and the operation of the Panama Canal. *Canal Zone* was first shown on public television on October 7, 1977. Several reviewers commented on the timeliness of a film about the Canal Zone, though it is not clear that timeliness works in favor of the film, since the political context might encourage viewers to see the film as something it is not. Because the Panama Canal treaty was still an issue for some Americans, it might seem natural that Wiseman's film ought to be held accountable for contributing to the debate. James Wolcott, writing in the *Village Voice*, begins his largely negative review of the film by invoking the political context:

> Perfect timing. Frederick Wiseman's documentary *Canal Zone*—which premieres locally this Friday (October 7) on Channel 13—arrives just as interest in the Panama Canal is at its perihelion. David McCullough's magisterial history, *The Path between the Seas,* is notched on the bestseller lists; conservative coneheads, led by Senators Strom Thurmond and Jesse Helms, are mobilizing antitreaty offensives; and nearly every day brings dispatches from the embattled American community there (a recent *Washington Post* report was headlined "Gun Sales Rise in Zone"). Even at his most clairvoyant, Wiseman couldn't have anticipated such a consciousness-raising convergence of events.[4]

Wolcott finds *Canal Zone*, however, to "have no special bearing on the current situation." The film, says Wolcott, "is famished when it comes to information" and "moves in a historyless void."[5] Wolcott compares *Canal Zone* with Wiseman's more recognizably political films, *Titicut Follies* and

High School, and complains that *Canal Zone* fails to offer the sort of political analysis offered by the earlier films.

Wolcott's analysis of *Canal Zone* forces the issue of whether the film contributes to the debate about the politics of the Panama Canal treaty. The film does not, in our view, provide, or attempt to provide, a balanced, discursive analysis of all the strategic, economic, and historical issues that would need to inform a decision. In other ways, however, the film makes a contribution to the debate. For example, the film seems to undermine the argument that the canal should be retained by the United States because it has become a naturalized extension of North America: the U.S. residents of the zone we see in the film are clearly out of context. But the immediate political issues do not entirely account for *Canal Zone.* Concentration on the topicality of the Canal Zone as a political issue can prevent an adequate reading of the film. Other reviews of *Canal Zone* were more sympathetic and noticed its status as a cultural analysis of American colonialism.[6]

Wolcott's review, with its admiring mention of Wiseman's earlier films, raises also the notion that what was admirable in those films was Wiseman's exposure of oppression—and he is disappointed not to find a clear depiction of oppression in *Canal Zone.* Other critics have shared Wolcott's disappointment in commenting on other Wiseman films that have dealt with "cultural" themes outside the context of more clearly oppressive institutions, a trend that increases in the films following *Canal Zone.* The issue Wolcott raises is an important one, reaching to the purpose of documentary as a generic enterprise and to issues of what justifies the money and the air time it takes to prepare and broadcast a Wiseman film, or any documentary, on public television. Further, the ethical issues of consent and attitude become more sharply visible when Wiseman is not dealing with victimization. In films like *Titicut Follies* or *High School,* Wiseman's evident disapproval of the institution, as well as the cinematic irony he employs to draw us to share his disapproval, seems to justify itself by its politics. But what position does Wiseman put his audience in when he takes away that justification? If Wiseman is making cultural comedy, what justifies his intrusion on the privacy of his subjects and his making them the target of his ridicule? The answers that seem implicit in Wiseman's work (answers that his recent films reveal as uneasy for Wiseman as well as his audiences) suggest that the issue of victimization may be a distraction as well as a justification; that, after all, the subjects in the films consented to be filmed; that it is naive to keep returning in film after film to a liberal, reformist exposure of oppression; that an oppressive culture cannot be resisted unless we understand it, which requires that we understand a wide variety of institutions; that part of the mechanism by which institutions exert oppression is through the "tropicality" of symbolic representation, a political process that Wiseman helps us to understand; or that the films are cultural investigations and comedies at base and that audiences can take them or leave them. So Wiseman seems to say in his films and in various interviews. Wolcott's questions are not altogether answered by these replies, which leave a variety of issues unresolved. But Wiseman's films, from this point of view, are broadly consistent and a deliberate challenge to the naive idealism and self-satisfaction he seems to see in traditional documentary.

Canal Zone lends itself to an anticolonialist (and to that degree, political) interpretation, but it does not take on the burden of admiring the indigenous Panamanian culture. For the most part, the Panamanians we see in the film are background figures, peddling tourist trinkets on street corners or performing menial chores. It is made to appear that the U.S. residents of the zone isolate themselves from the Panamanians. At one point, we see an absurdly short television lesson in Spanish, and at another we hear advice offered on a radio spot about how to avoid Panamanian purse snatchers. Early in the film, after an extended series of scenes on the impressive technology of the canal, there is a distinctly unsentimental scene of a group of Spanish-speaking men unloading bananas, chickens, and cows from a small boat. Their marginal effectiveness and casual brutality are in contrast to the bland, large-scale technological mastery of the canal operators. Without seeming to approve of the colonial situation, Wiseman seems to ally himself here with the tone taken toward "native" brutality in such writers as George Orwell, Graham Greene, Joseph Conrad, and Joan Didion.[7]

Here is Orwell, for example, describing how, as a subdivisional colonial police officer in Burma, he came to shoot an elephant that had killed a coolie.

> As soon as I saw the elephant I knew with perfect certainty that I ought not to shoot him. . . .
> But at that moment I glanced round at the crowd that had followed me. . . . And suddenly I realized that I should have to shoot the elephant after all. . . . A sahib has got to act like a sahib; he has got to appear resolute, to know his own mind and do definite things. To come all that way, rifle in hand, with two thousand people marching at my heels, and then to trail feebly away, having done nothing— no, that was impossible. The crowd would laugh at me. And my whole life, every white man's life in the East, was one long struggle not to be laughed at.[8]

Orwell's reflection on colonialism here is both a refusal to sentimentalize "the natives," who are willing to have the elephant suffer for their entertainment, and a further, deeper, refusal to blame them for the larger pretensions of colonialism. Orwell comments that the imperialist "wears a mask, and his face grows to fit it."[9]

Wiseman's scene of the unloading of the boat might have been written by Orwell, contextualized as it is by an extended speculation on the mask of the displaced colonial and focusing on an observation of "natives" inflicting a recreational brutality upon their animals. The scene is packed with significance by the political context a viewer brings to the film and ends in puzzling questions rather than pat answers: Can the Panamanians run the canal if we leave? Do the U.S. residents of the Canal Zone (and we) feel more sympathy for the animals than for the humans? Does the gulf between the U.S. and Panamanian residents justify or condemn U.S. ownership of the canal? Wiseman does not answer these questions, or even address them explicitly, but he does trigger the emotional responses that are at the heart of the colonial experience and makes them, through art rather than through discourse, available for examination in the context of felt experience.

Canal Zone is in this sense political, though it does not address directly the deliberative issues of the canal treaty or engage in polemics about colonialism. It is crucial to an understanding of Wiseman's developing methods as an observer of American institutions to see that he is noticing, and inviting us to notice, the cultural and social dimensions of our institutions. But he is not, for all his coolness as an observer, impersonal. In his special way, he addresses the sense in which the personal is political, but, even more pointedly, he enables us to speculate about the ways in which the political is personal—that is, the ways in which institutional life works itself out in concrete, subjective, human experience.

In *Canal Zone*, Wiseman gives us a remarkably full anthology of American public speeches. We have counted twenty-four speeches, taking up just under 74 minutes, or about 42 percent of a film that runs 174 minutes (see figure 8-1).[10] These speeches, which constitute the core of the bicentennial celebration that Wiseman observed and recorded in the Canal Zone in 1976, are used in the film to convey the impression, in a comic frame, that American culture, all culture, is tropical, invented. In *Canal Zone*, the substance of reality is rhetorical.

The speeches in *Canal Zone* begin with an innocuous pair in which first a canal guide and then the governor of the Canal Zone explain the history and operation of the canal. These two speeches, totaling about thirteen and one-half minutes, serve to provide us with essential establishing information, but in a way that differs markedly from the usual way of doing such things in television documentary, where, as a matter of course, the preliminary overview of the canal and its operations would be spoken by an authoritative off-screen narrator. These speeches are contextualized in the film as naturally occurring social behavior, addressed to other persons who are listening to them for reasons of their own having nothing to do with the making of the film. The speeches are authenticated as part of the work of the guide and the governor, and they in their turn serve to authenticate the many speeches that follow and to establish our relationship as spectators to the world of the film: whatever explanations we get are going to occur within that world, rather than as Wiseman's commentary. This has the curious effect of keeping us at a distance from what we are seeing and hearing, since we do not have Wiseman's voice to bridge the gap between viewer and subject, but, at the same time, it lessens the gap and plunges us directly into the world of the Canal Zone, to make of it what we can.

Figure 8–1

Major Speeches in *Canal Zone*.

---

1. Canal guide. (3:30).
2. Governor. (9:53).
3. Reverend John Kennedy at Law Day. Invocation. (1:23).
4. Judge at Law Day. (1:50).
5. Crime prevention tip on radio cassette. (0:30)
6. Fashion show announcer. (2:51).
7. Ham radio operator on short wave. (4:30).
8. Police youth officer on child abuse. (5:56).
9. President of VFW Ladies Auxiliary. (0:48).
10. Colonel Oronstein addresses VFW Ladies Auxiliary. (2:16).
11. Civic council meeting; speaker reads letter that has been sent to Mr. Vesey. (4:58).
12. Marriage counselor. (7:48).
13. Boy Scout award dinner: master of ceremonies. (0:36).
14. Boy Scout award dinner: Jim Hatrig presents Silver Beaver Award. (2:25).
15. Boy Scout award dinner: award recipient Frank Castle. (0:10).
16. Boy Scout award dinner: master of ceremonies; closing ceremonies. (0:45).
17. Preacher in church. (8:05).
18. Man in church. Benediction. (0:33).
19. High-school graduation. Boy speaker. (3:33).
20. High-school graduation. Girl speaker. (3:05).
21. On boat. Chaplain prays. (0:25).
22. On boat. Man reads Gettysburg Address. (1:44).
23. Cemetery. Memorial Day speech by Sidney Kaufman. (4:40).
24. Cemetery. Memorial Day ceremonies. Benediction by priest. (0:18).

The entire first section of *Canal Zone* is devoted to an observation of the workings of the canal itself, the speech of the guide, the scene of the unloading of the banana boat, and the speech of the governor. We spend long, quiet moments watching a pilot guide a ship through the canal, and other technical operations. This leisurely introduction prepares us, if we are willing to stay with the film at all, for a long film. Wiseman is in no hurry. Nor are the workers we observe: the pilot and the governor are equally deliberate and rational in their guidance of the enormous ships and the enormous technical, financial, and administrative apparatus needed to sustain the canal.

Americans have come to regard speechmaking as an art that is well lost. Even during the heat of a presidential campaign or an important congressional debate, television and newspapers give only very abbreviated reports of the speechmaking, and these are typically reported not so much as legitimate attempts to deliberate as disingenuous exercises in mystification.[11] Part of the difficulty is that the speeches we do see on television are usually constructed, at least in part, not for their immediate audiences but for the television coverage of them. Wiseman places his viewers in a different relation to the speeches in *Canal Zone,* for they are speeches genuinely addressed to the immediate audience, and not with an eye on us, watching at home.

Many of the speeches in *Canal Zone* are ceremonial, and yet even these ceremonial speeches often seem to be closely tied both to their immediate contexts and to the ceremonial occasions of which they are a part. These ceremonial speeches are doing the work of restating the values of the community, though as viewers not connected to the immediate interests of that community we can often hear signs of trouble. At a courtroom observation of Law Day, the judge makes some quite predictable remarks welcoming official guests, and then thanks the local Elks Lodge for loaning the court a bicentennial flag for the occasion. He continues:

> We Americans are a tough breed, I think, and we know how to meet adversity. We're adaptable. Our nation has succeeded in the heat and disease of the tropics and in the bitter cold winds of the Alaskan frontier. The American people, they're tough. They will meet adversity and they will survive. I think another thing that I would be remiss in not alluding to and that is the fact that we, on this Law Day, have splendid law enforcement in the Canal Zone. People can walk the streets of the Canal Zone at night and are sure of being well protected all the time. It's, uh, excellent to live in a community like that.

The judge's remarks about safe streets have an ominous ring. At first, they may sound like the sort of small-town boosting that compares its safety to the dangerous life of the big city—or, in this case, the mainland. But the judge does not say that the zone is safe because people can be trusted; he says it is safe because it is competently protected. From whom? In the next scenes, we see a police van, and then a breakfast line at a prison. A few moments later, a radio voice offers a "crime tip," reminding women listeners to keep their car windows rolled up and doors locked to prevent purse snatchings. From what the judge and the radio have said about street safety, it may appear that North-American residents are concerned primarily with protecting themselves from Panamanians. But in a later speech, a police youth officer tells an audience that the Canal Zone has an unusually high rate of child abuse, "three times above the national average," and that the primary offenders appear to be young U.S. military families who are suffering the stresses of isolation, large families, worry about their jobs, and a possible Panamanian revolution. The enemy may be the tropics, but, again, the tropics is in us, as well as surrounding us.

Wiseman allows the themes of patriotism, family, colonialism, and crime to emerge in a widening pattern of complexity through the speeches. It soon becomes clear that not all the speeches are merely ceremonial and that even the ceremonial speeches are drawing attention directly to deeply felt community issues. The speeches describe and sustain the community's civic vision, and they help to define, in old-fashioned ways, civil religion, gender roles, public safety, and the obligations of citizenship.

The issue of religion occupies a curious place in Wiseman's films. In *Hospital*, the appearance of a priest in an emergency room seems less an assurance of eternal life than a whiff of impending death, a sign that the energetic medical procedures are about to fail. In *Basic Training*, an army chaplain seems less a spiritual counselor than a special pleader for going along with the system that had brought a draftee to a suicide attempt. Later in the same film, the chaplain makes an especially inept transition, during a worship service, from the subject of his love of Jesus to the matter of the materialization of that love in contributions to the collection plate. In *Essene*, a religious community's adherence to order is sustained not so much by mysticism or spiritual commitment as by a curious blend of authoritative tradition and the judicious application of group therapy. And in *Canal Zone*, too, the church speaks not simply for spirituality but for social order. The first formal public speech in *Canal Zone*, that of the judge at Law Day, is preceded by an invocation, and the last speech, at Memorial Day ceremonies in a cemetery, is followed by a benediction, incidentally framing the film's speeches as a single, extended ceremony. Neither the invocation nor the benediction are explicitly political in content, but by their mere presence at civil ceremonies, and by their appeal to God to bless the law and preserve the peace, they constitute what Robert Bellah has called "civil religion."[12]

Another scene ties together the themes of woman's place, religion, and belief in a way that reaches to the roots of the film with a vivid and compelling human performance and a startling formal compactness. Wiseman has shown, in the TAT scene, how the issue of woman's place stands as a metaphor for the conquering of the tropics. At the same time, he demonstrates how the TAT as a process of projection stands for the subordination of perception to belief. Religion, too, which reaches out to frame the film in an invocation and benediction, speaks to the issues of belief and woman's place.

We see a church exterior, then a congregation inside the church. The preacher describes the links among religion, sex, and belief.

> Be you not underneath the yoke together with unbelievers, God told the Jews. Don't marry Gentiles. Why? Because they worship heathen gods, strange gods. . . . Remember that, when Adam was created, he had no partner, then God, before he was given a partner, created all the animal life. And he created the horses and the cows, all the birds and the animals, and he watched God make male and female, male and female. . . . So that after he names the cow, after he names all the animals, after he names every bit of life, God says, "It's not good for man to dwell alone." And Adam looked over every animal. There wasn't an animal that suited him, and so then God says, "I'll make for you a helpmate," and man, when he brought Eve out, I'm sure Adam said something like this, "Hey, Man, I've been looking for her all my life." And you know the thing about Adam was he didn't have a choice, heh, heh, he didn't have to choose. That must have been so easy. What I mean is, ha, ha, there was no choice, there was one, that was enough for him. See? But the Bible says, He made for Adam a completor, a man without

a bride is incomplete. After he made male and female for all the animals, he finally got around to Adam and said, "All right, Adam, I see you're lonely. I see there's no one understands you. No one can counsel with you, no one can comfort you; besides, there's no one to sew your socks, an alligator can't do that. And so, Adam, you need a helpmate." And so he made Eve. And this is where it all began. . . . God's plan: one man, one woman, together they worship the same Lord. Man under the headship of Christ, woman under the headship of a man led by Christ. . . . Now this is the plan of God. There is nothing vexes me, and, oh, I'll just have to use it, it's not a good expression, that gripes me more, than what the women's lib and everything is saying about marriage and children and husbands and all the rest. There's nothing vexes me more than this. Because it's, all of it, out of the pit of Hell. It's Satan's way of breaking up homes, destroying what God has set up and his plan. Beloved, when there's things wrong in the home, mark it down, it's because of one or the other of you are wrong with Jesus Christ. You're not in good relationship with him. Because may I say this compatibility with Jesus Christ makes every other incompatibility of really no importance. When you're compatible in Christ, she can burn the toast or not, it doesn't make any difference to you.

The particulars of marital adjustment are different for various speakers in *Canal Zone*, although, for each of them, it appears that adjustment will be possible if only right belief and right relationship can be maintained. A marriage counseling team (working, apparently, under the sponsorship of army chaplains) offers adjustment through a "marriage enrichment" workshop, in which a ritualized public expression of positive feelings sets the stage for twenty-four hours of "intimacy," "feelings," and "communication on a very deep basis."

At a high-school graduation ceremony near the end of the film, the boy speaker says to his listeners, "In the distant future when we've become mellow in our old age and decide to settle down and get married, remember this definition of happiness. Happiness is being married to your best friend." The boy orator is followed immediately by a girl speaker who says that "nothing in life that is worthy is ever too hard to achieve if we have the courage to try and the faith to believe. . . . You can do what you believe you can do. . . . Believe in America. . . . Believe in life with a big yes and a small no. Thank you."

In *Canal Zone*, a series of orators exert their eloquence to persuade their listeners to believe in belief. The Canal Zone thus becomes a land of Oz, in which these displaced midwesterners discover that belief is the key to having a heart, a brain, courage—even to recovering Kansas itself, here in a remote tropics beyond the rainbow.

Wiseman shows us how one of the great technological marvels of modern engineering, the Panama Canal, this enormous *fact* set down in the brutal fact of a fevered tropical isthmus is a construction not just of mud and steel but of belief. In this world, believing is seeing, and the substance of reality is rhetorical.

Wiseman's films all make meanings out of contrasts, and one of the most puzzling and fruitful contrasts, as a source of cultural speculation, occurs in *Canal Zone*, which may be read at one level as a comedy in which a lost tribe of 1950s Reader's Digest Americans attempts by the magic of civic and patriotic ritual, of Boy Scout awards and home-sewn fashion shows, of sports, insecticide, and lawn mowers, to imagine together the fiction of an America that is disappearing. As a comedy, *Canal Zone* is funny in a way that reflects an affection for the innocent dreams of small-town and suburb, and a pathos that arises from the futility of the rituals and ceremonies, which cannot prevent the certain displacement of these colonial Americans. The film is saved from viciousness by the further certainty that these colonials are us, that they are living in a way that is at bottom a highly disciplined imitation, a performance and a projection of our culture and its process.

Chapter 9

Materialism and Symbolic Action
The Store

Frederick Wiseman set his seventeenth documentary, *The Store* (1983), in the Neiman-Marcus flagship store in Dallas, Texas. In *The Store*, Wiseman investigates sales and shopping as institutional materialism and considers how the promises of private consumption bind us together as a society. Wiseman encourages us to attend to the meanings of our objects and actions, and to the processes by which they are brought into being. *The Store* seems to require an examination of the issue of materialism as it relates to Wiseman's films—an issue that is made inescapable both because of the nature of the film and because of the sorts of critical attention Wiseman's films have received from scholars and reviewers.

The December 14, 1983, PBS broadcast of *The Store* provoked a degree of journalistic attention uncommon for a televised documentary, but increasingly common for a Wiseman production.[1] Television critics for the popular press, many of whom had attended a prebroadcast screening of *The Store* and a subsequent press conference with the producer-director, had been encouraged by WNET press releases to treat *The Store* as part of a celebrated series. The reviews were mixed. Most of the journalists, predictably and reasonably, reached to the director's previous work for clues to meaning and standards of judgment. Some others turned, also predictably, but less reasonably, to an idealized generic form—cinema verite—as Wiseman's implied standard.

Three related complaints emerge from reviews of *The Store*. The documentary is faulted for: (1) concentrating on a trivial topic; (2) presenting nonrepresentative subjects; and (3) missing an opportunity to criticize a vulgar, if not corrupt, institution. A variant of the third criticism claims that the director has abdicated his responsibility to express a clear judgment.

Marvin Kitman's review of *The Store* is typical of a view shared with Bill Carter, John Corry, and Fred Rothenberg: that the film lacks clarity and accountability. "As usual, Wiseman says nothing about the mass of material he is presenting. Is this institution gross or wonderful? Wiseman shrugs at all the material, as usual. He is only the camera, the open vessel for images. It all pours in one end and out the other."[2]

The red herring of cinema verite—a term that Wiseman has consistently disavowed, but which has, nevertheless, consistently reappeared—is dragged out by several critics as a standard not met. Karen Rosenberg asks, "Should we believe that cinema verite has lived up to its name and delivered truth on a platter?"[3]

Several reviewers claim that Wiseman has left something out that must have been there to see. Critics often play the game of "missing data" with documentary, and especially with Wiseman, who frequently presents unexpected or idiosyncratic views of an institution. Jack Thomas's review charges that "Wiseman has not captured the bizarre nature of Neiman-Marcus, as shown in its famous catalog." Karen Rosenberg doubts a "camera [that] finds only employees who identify totally with their company." Carter finds the documentary sexist because "the entire show deals only in items aimed at women."[4]

Some critics of Wiseman's earliest films accused him of exploiting helpless subjects and unfairly criticizing the beleaguered staffs of institutions in crisis. Some critics of The Store now charge him with creating an elaborate commercial for the extravagantly successful Neiman-Marcus store. Usually the complaint of complicity is cast as a comparison. Thomas writes that, in contrast to Wiseman's "powerful, probing, often controversial and frequently unflattering examinations of American institutions . . . this time, the institution wins."[5]

Other reviewers of The Store seem to agree with Thomas that Wiseman is at his best when condemning institutions, but they see The Store as fitting the pattern. The Store, says Hilary DeVries, "starts out a deceptively discursive exploration . . . [and] ends up a significant, if subtle, indictment of yet another group ethic." Harry Waters says that The Store "offers viewers the season's most precious gift, a pungent antidote to Yuletide hyperglycemia." John Donohue writes that the "film might seem simply to show, not to tell. . . . Mr. Wiseman is, however, a moralist as well as an artist, and he edits his materials with both insight and conscience. . . . What Frederick Wiseman has brought back [from Neiman-Marcus] is a homily for Advent. It's fabulous."[6]

Whether in response to the tradition of the documentary of social indignation, to Wiseman's (somewhat undeserved) reputation as a muckraker, or to some personal or shared sense of anti-institutionalism, many critics expected, and desired, a sermon from The Store. Some find the film not tough enough on others; some find it not tough enough on themselves. Karen Rosenberg argues that "by focusing on the rich who shop at a swanky store, Wiseman lets the rest of us off the hook." Rothenberg casts his complaint somewhat differently, describing the film pejoratively as an "elitist examination" in which Wiseman "merely showcases the wealthy without analyzing their excessive tastes . . . so it shouldn't surprise him that his highfalutin' film may offend shoppers who aren't excited by $45,000 sable jackets and $65,000 pitchers."[7]

In a number of ways, reviewers assail *The Store* as an essentially trivial film that not only has narrowed its social view but also "is not telling us anything new."[8] Rather, argues this group of critics, the film is tedious (Rothenberg), dull (Carter), and boring (Thomas). Let us use these criticisms, which we have admittedly abbreviated and clustered, to notice some of the expectations regarding documentary that critics bring to their viewing of *The Store*, and to notice how various critics differ in their assessments of Wiseman's success in fulfilling these expectations.

1. *Expectations of significance and profundity.* Is *The Store* trivial? Perhaps it is too easy to dismiss charges of triviality against *The Store* by comparing it with the prime-time broadcasts of the three commercial networks on December 14, 1983. Commercial programs included a two-hour episode of *The Fall Guy*, an adventure drama, on ABC; two animated cartoons, *Frosty the Snowman* and *'Twas the Night Before Christmas*, and a made-for-TV movie, *Drop-Out Father*, on CBS; *The Real People Christmas Show* and weekly episodes of two situation comedies, *Facts of Life* and *Family Ties*, on NBC.

In addition to being nonfiction at one important level, *The Store*, as a cultural product, presents an account of what Stuart Ewen calls the "social roots of consumer culture."[9] *The Store* shows us that much of what we are concerned with in our everyday lives is trivial, but that we invest that everydayness with a moral and social significance that is important to us. As individuals, and as a culture, we convert the trivial into something "deep," in cultural anthropologist Clifford Geertz's phrase. Geertz has shown how cultural practices that may seem trivial, like cockfighting, are forms of "deep play" because of the seriousness with which the social actors invest them. Geertz reports that "in the cockfight . . . the Balinese forms and discovers his temperament and his society's temper at the same time."[10] Wiseman suggests that American shoppers, and American salespeople, may go through a similarly deep process of cultural discovering and forming. On these grounds, we agree with Unger that Wiseman "has delved deeply and wisely into seemingly superficial subject matter and come up with a subtly informative—and incidentally entertaining—tract that will likely be of sociological importance for generations to come."[11] Wiseman himself was clearly thinking about the question of triviality when he said that *The Store* "is just as, if not more, revealing of our society" as his earlier films.[12]

2. *Issues of identification and representation.* The issues of identification and representation are always important in film, but especially in documentary, where questions of "us" and "them" have particular force. Does Wiseman, in choosing to make a film about shopping and selling at Neiman-Marcus, simply tell "us" about "them," or is he telling us something about

ourselves? Karen Rosenberg, for example, argues that *The Store* loses its moral force because it lets its audience off the hook when it chooses to focus on the rich.

Who would "us" be for a Wiseman film? Demographically, it is the audience of public television, presumably an educated, liberal elite. The secondary audience, those who see the films in college classrooms now, and in the future, will bring a variety of contexts to the films and may, in a decade or two, gradually convert the films into recollections about the past rather than speculations about a present. Does Wiseman invite his audience to identify with those on the screen, to believe that the social actors in his films somehow represent the viewers?

Early Wiseman films in which there was a strong sense of victimage or social problems did not directly implicate the audience. We are not the inmates of Bridgewater or their guards (*Titicut Follies*). We are not the Kansas City police or their suspects (*Law and Order*). We are not those dislocated residents of the Canal Zone (*Canal Zone*). But in two important senses we are these people. First, we are represented metaphorically by the roles in these films. Aspects of our consciousness or actions are displayed for us to examine apart from ourselves—a traditional function of cathartic drama. The very abstractness of the Canal Zone inhabitants' dogged efforts to maintain *Saturday Evening Post* America so far from home throws our own cultural assumptions into an unfamiliar perspective. And in the films of oppression, we can recognize the structures of victimage in our own lives, just as we can recognize our own ways of victimizing others. Second, even when we are not literally the cop, the conscript, the guard, the butcher, or the vivisectionist, we can recognize that what is done by the authorities in these films is done in our name. The law is enforced on our behalf; soldiers are trained for our defense; meat is slaughtered for our tables; monkeys are sacrificed to protect our health. The victimizers act as our representatives and, so long as we are silent, on our sufferance.

Still, for Wiseman's audiences, apart from those occasions when the films are used, as they often are, for example, in the training of social workers (*Welfare*) or other specialists, the cops and the down-and-out are not us, and although watching them may arouse in us an appropriate sense of self-awareness or a realistic sense of social responsibility, the effect may also degenerate into a morally complacent exoticism, an upper-middle-class version of moral signs and wonders. Wiseman treats the institution as a social matrix, frequently cutting across demarcations of social class and role. We see physicians in *Titicut Follies*, administrators in *High School*, attorneys in *Juvenile Court*, social workers in *Welfare*, and so on. There are middle-class professionals in most of the films, though their consciousness, as enacted in the films, is very different from the one Wiseman seems to assume and invite for his audiences. Wiseman's bemused curiosity, his obsessive detachment, and his growing unwillingness, after *Titicut Follies* and *High School*, to follow the path of muckraking social reformer raises the question of whether any of his films precisely target either us or himself.

It is easy for a critic to put Wiseman, or any documentary filmmaker, in a no-win position regarding choice of subjects. If Wiseman made all of his films about his audience, critics might accuse him, with some justice, of being excessively narrow in his interests. If he were to make films only about "others," critics could accuse him of exoticism. The ideal, never entirely achieved in practice and never stable in its subject matter, is for artists to show us how to identify ourselves in and with others. It seems to us that Wiseman, even when he does not literally show us ourselves, encourages his audiences to take responsibility for the meanings they make of his films, even as he shows them how to make those meanings; and he invites us to identify with people and actions shown in his films, even when we are encouraged to disapprove of those actions. This invitation to identify is not at all the same thing as asking us to sympathize with people and actions. That is partly why the experience of watching Wiseman's films is so uncomfortable, and often so funny. Action and identification, both within the world of the film and between the film and its audience, help to account for the enormous appeal of the films, and for the way viewers and critics appropriate Wiseman's images for their own speculations.

3. *Expectations of clarity and commitment.* Is *The Store* unclear? Weisman argues persuasively that *The Store* "acts as a kind of litmus test of the viewer's own attitudes about that most indigenous of American behaviors—shopping." Corry complains that *The Store* "does not exist as art in itself; it exists as art only if we bring something to it." *The Store* does "demand a critical, savvy audience."[13] Are Wiseman's demands on his audience inappropriate or unreasonable? We think not. Too frequently, Wiseman's critics trust his audiences less than he does, thereby casting themselves adrift from their own readers. A spectator obviously cannot change the material film itself but by extending and developing one's attention to it one can extend cultural inquiry into the significance of seemingly trivial, everyday events. Wiseman encourages such active readings of his films, but he does so partly at the risk of seeming coy and irresponsible, or of seeming to ridicule his subjects simply for his own amusement. Wiseman's films are clearly ironic, but when viewers look into the ironic structure of a Wiseman film for a stable point of view from which the irony originates, Wiseman has disappeared, leaving viewers to form their own conclusions. Looking through Wiseman's window on the world, we discover a mirror.

Although Wiseman's films make unusual demands on television audiences, they "get considerable ratings," by public broadcast standards, according to WNET vice-president Robert Kotlowitz. "The audience turns it on and it's still there two and a half hours later. There is nothing else like it on television."[14] Wiseman pushes the capacities of his audiences by creating a series of rhetorical paradoxes: he invites individual readings of a seemingly open text; he creates a rhetorical structure in which the ironic locus of his own attitudes remains elusive; and he simultaneously poses a critique of American institutions.

Wiseman's journalistic reviewers have praised or criticized *The Store* on a fairly consistent and limited array of issues. In what follows, we shall try to show that, in order to come to terms with Wiseman's work, with the gaps left by his journalistic critics, and with the uses that might be made of *The Store* by its viewers, two strategies of critical analysis are needed to bring together a rhetorical understanding: a thematic and formal reading of the film and a placement of the film in its cultural context as a speculation about materialism.

Part of the logic by which a viewer is invited to understand *The Store* hinges on implied reasonings about materialism. Of course, the identification of materialism as a theme is a reduction of the film, naming only one thematic thread out of several woven throughout the film. Not all viewers would see the film in the way we describe it, though we consider that a rhetorical analysis of the sort we are undertaking here commits itself to the burden of arguing that viewers are invited to experience the film as we describe it.

Four senses of materialism are relevant to a discussion of *The Store:* (1) *philosophical materialism:* the doctrine that reality is material; (2) *dialectical and historical materialism:* Marxism; (3) *material:* as a way of referring to the content/form and object/subject debate in film in general and documentary in particular; (4) *"materialistic":* materialism in its ordinary language sense used to describe consumers as seekers after money and objects. These four senses of materialism are related, both linguistically and logically, but they are by no means synonymous. By accident or design, however, they are all involved in coming to terms with *The Store.*

All the senses of materialism we have cited are, at least in part, accounts of causation or motivation; that is, they explain not only how things are, but why things happen. For a comprehensive inventory of motivation in social and artistic structures we turn to Kenneth Burke's *A Grammar of Motives.* As Burke puts it, "We shall use five terms as generating principle of our investigation. They are: Act, Scene, Agent, Agency, Purpose. In a rounded statement about motives, you must have some word that names the *act* (names what took place, in thought or deed), and another that names the *scene* (the background of the act, the situation in which it occurred); also, you must indicate what person or kind of person (*agent*) performed the act, what means or instruments he used (*agency*), and the *purpose.*[15] In a later passage, Burke identifies how various philosophical approaches to motive derive from their allegiance to one or another of the terms of the pentad:

> For the featuring of *scene,* the corresponding philosophic terminology is *materialism.*
>
> For the featuring of *agent,* the corresponding terminology is *idealism.*
>
> For the featuring of *agency,* the corresponding terminology is *pragmatism.*

For the featuring of *purpose*, the corresponding terminology is *mysticism*.
For the featuring of *act*, the corresponding terminology is *realism*.[16]

Insofar as human actions in *The Store* are presented as being motivated by the scene, evoking what Burke has called the scene-act ratio, they imply some version of materialism. Where other ratios are noted, the dominance of materialism is called into question. In our analysis, we are not trying to determine what actually motivated the social actors in real time and space; rather, we are examining the rhetoric of the film as a constructed depiction of human motivation, a "reality fiction."

Philosophical materialism, as it is usually termed, "is the name given to a family of doctrines concerning the nature of the world which give to matter a primary position and accord to mind (or spirit) a secondary, dependent reality or even none at all. Extreme materialism asserts that the real world consists of material things, varying in their states and relations, and nothing else."[17] Materialism need not deny the existence of mental activity, but does argue that mental activity can be explained on the basis of physical and chemical motions. Does *The Store* imply such an extreme materialism?

There is much evidence in Wiseman's documentary films that circumstances (the scene) can govern actions. Individually, and especially as a series, the films focus on the institution—prison, school, hospital, factory, and so on—as the locus of action and, hence, partly, of motive. Wiseman's institutions are the settings for the routine exercise of power. Nevertheless, the films are, in a variety of ways, fundamentally opposed to materialism and behaviorism.

Wiseman's films are not philosophical arguments, they are aesthetic texts. Although they do not display a linear and assertive logic, the films do suggest attitudes toward the tension between materialism and its alternatives. For example, Wiseman's films display a continuing strategy of exposing institutional hypocrisy by juxtaposing the statements of institutional leaders with their actions. The implication of hypocrisy and the implication that it matters are claims upon a common-sense logic of idealism. The human habit of misrepresenting motive both honors the virtues it betrays and concedes that responsibility is unavoidable.[18]

And yet in *The Store* hypocrisy seems much less present than it has been in earlier Wiseman films. True, the salespeople court their customers with appeals to vanity, and courtliness is always fundamentally hypocritical. But in the many sales meetings, morally sleazy as they may seem, the objective of the institution is clearly stated: sales. Taking his cue from that bluntness, Wiseman chooses as his first extended scene a staff meeting of department heads. Here are the first audible words we hear inside *The Store:*

VICE-PRESIDENT: There's one word. The reason for it all.
WOMAN: What?
VICE-PRESIDENT: Sales. A simple little word and that's why we have the building.

The aesthetic structure of *The Store* does much to reinforce the influence of the store as a scene. The film opens with an extreme long shot of the city of Dallas. Then, in a series of shots, the camera explores the street in front of the Neiman-Marcus building. It might appear that we are viewing the context that controls the store itself, but once we cut inside the store we seem to be in another world. The people in the street outside walk past Neiman-Marcus without paying much attention to it. The world inside the store is isolated from the street sounds by its own canned music, and from the sights of the streets by its own designed atmosphere. Early and later images reinforce the power of the store as scene by conferring upon the building itself metaphors of motivation: elevator doors close upon shots, sealing off our vision, then open to reveal the next location; escalators carry passive shoppers from floor to floor. The building literally (hence metaphorically) moves human beings and literally (hence metaphorically) reveals and obscures what we see. On two "literal" levels, the frequent images of elevators and escalators are useful for Wiseman: they re-present movement between floors and departments, simulating the experience of being in a department store, and they also function as cutaways or connective material for assembling disparate scenes into a coherent collage. Sometimes these distinctions and uses blend, as, for example, when a person dressed as Ronald McDonald drifts through the frame on an escalator. But instead of suggesting a literal materialism, these animations of the scene transcend materialism to produce a pronounced quality of magic and surrealism—what might be called, in Wiseman's films, the surrealism of the normal. In a radio interview on *The Store*, Wiseman said that "the great subject of documentary filmmaking is normalcy and sometimes normalcy turns out to be more bizarre than anything else. It may even be the true surrealism."[19] And, building upon the elevator doors and the escalators, Wiseman includes scenes in which the building, with the aid of mirrors, magically whisks people on and off camera and even doubles them. For example, in one scene, a man appears, center-screen, from behind a wall, walking obliquely towards and to the left of the screen, as his image—in what we only then realize is a mirror—leaves him and marches off to our right. There are certainly many ways to interpret what these scenes may "symbolize," but their general experiential influence at the very least seems to temper literalism with imagination, positivism with fantasy. It appears, then, that materialism is a strong force in the world of *The Store*, but that plain materialism does not entirely account for the actions of its inhabitants.

Dialectical and *historical materialism*, the Marxist versions of materialism, are an evolving and by no means settled philosophy, particularly when used as covering terms to describe "materialist" perspectives toward the criticism of contemporary culture. Although *The Store* is clearly, in part, about economic matters and although Wiseman often employs dialectical structures, the film cannot be reduced to a portrait of class struggle without entirely distorting its form and content.

Marxism has been changing as a basis for social criticism in Western society. Classical or orthodox Marxism regarded culture as a "superstructure" built upon and wholly determined by the economic "base." Frank Lentricchia tells the story of how Kenneth Burke, speaking at the American Writers' Congress in Madison Square Garden in 1935, was angrily rejected by the audience of Marxist writers for proposing the importance of "revolutionary symbolism" as opposed to a "strictly materialist point of view."[20] Lentricchia is careful not to argue that Burke was and is a better reader of Marx than the "strictly materialist" left of the 1930s, but does argue that Burke anticipated a view that showed up a generation later when American Marxists became familiar with the work of Lukacs and Gramsci. Lentricchia continues:

> The political work of the hegemonic, as well as that of a would-be counter-hegemonic culture, Burke saw (as Marx did not) as most effectively carried through at the level of a culture's various verbal and nonverbal languages. In 1935 Burke was saying to America's radical left not only that a potentially revolutionary culture should keep in mind that revolution must be culturally as well as economically rooted, but, as well, and this was perhaps the most difficult of Burke's implications for his radical critics to swallow, that a revolutionary culture must situate itself firmly on the terrain of its capitalist antagonist, must not attempt a dramatic leap beyond capitalism in one explosive, rupturing moment of release, must work its way through capitalism's language of domination by working cunningly within it, using, appropriating, even speaking through its key mechanisms of repression. What Burke's proposal in 1935 to America's intellectual left amounts to is this: the substance, the very ontology of ideology—an issue that Marx and Engels engaged with little clarity, to put it charitably—in a broad but fundamental sense is revealed to us *textually* and therefore must be grasped (read) and attacked (reread, rewritten) in that dimension.[21]

In the generation since Burke's 1935 speech, and especially since World War II, American and European critics have discovered what Steven Smith calls an "array of Marxisms" concerned "with cultural and philosophical matters, or, to use the Marxist term, 'superstructural' problems, which until recently would have been unthinkable within the orthodox Marxist framework."[22] In American and British academic circles, a variety of neo-Marxisms have been invoked as a base for conducting mass media research.[23]

In a persuasive account of *Model*, Dan Armstrong argues that Wiseman's work can be interpreted from a variety of Marxist perspectives, from the neo-Marxism of Georg Lukacs to the emphasis on cultural production in the perspective developed by Louis Althusser. Armstrong sketches a Marxist analysis that retains its radical social aspirations while at the same time tempering its reliance upon material determinism by making room for culture as a social force. For some recent Marxist critics, both the means of production and the aesthetics of consumption maintain the status quo of capitalism, the "ideological and cultural hegemony of the Professional-Managerial Class (PMC) over the subordinate working class."[24] For these Marxists, it is no longer impossible for the individual to alter the forces of the dialectic: since the means of production are a human invention and are maintained by cultural methods, they can be altered by artists and critics who demystify and thereby break the grip of capitalist social propaganda.

Armstrong sees *Model* as a description and critique of the means by which capitalism, through the fashion industry, celebrates a mystifying ideology of personality and glamor that masks a reality of collective passivity and domination. Armstrong avoids the literal materialism of orthodox Marxism, while retaining in his language a Marxist rhetoric that strikes an equivocal note of robustness; thus, Marxism now speaks of "cultural production," to preserve the nineteenth-century flavor of work as the source of class struggle, and Armstrong evokes "the work of co-producing meaning"—another oxymoron from the point of view of strict materialism. The Marxist struggle to bridge the worlds of material and symbolic is signaled, too, in Armstrong's admiration for Bill Nichols's description of Wiseman's films as "mosaics," a form in which recognizably distinct bits of material reality combine to take on iconic and symbolic significance.[25]

The Marxist analyses of Wiseman proposed by Nichols and Armstrong are sufficiently convincing to amount to a prima facie case that a Marxist analysis should be extended to the rest of Wiseman's work, perhaps with special emphasis on *The Store*.[26] *Model* shows us the work of preparing images for consumers, and *The Store* goes the next step along the process to explore the world of sales and shopping. *The Store* is balanced between scenes of shoppers seeking gratification in relation to material objects and salespeople working with ingratiating volubility on the sales floor and anxiously cultivated pretensions to elegance in the executive suite. Occasional scenes of silently toiling tailors, jewelers, packagers, and custodians remind us of the base upon which the superstructure is raised.

Still, *The Store* is not earnestly propagandistic. It is a complex, witty film that avoids a doctrinaire hostility towards consumer culture while nevertheless critically interpreting a successful institution. According to Wiseman, the staff at Neiman-Marcus liked *The Store*.[27] Wiseman's disdain for sloganeering and his affection for the eccentric are apparent in his films, and in this comment: "You want something on my politics? Well, they're kind of anarchic. As the saying goes, the Marx is more Groucho than Karl."[28] And yet a reflective viewer is encouraged to experience what Armstrong describes as alienation from the vanities of fashion and pleasure in the seeking of fresh perspectives, as we shall try to demonstrate when we turn to a detailed analysis of the film. Wiseman's work can in many ways support a Marxist interpretation, but Wiseman seems by no means a Marxist in his views, expressed or implied, nor do his films seem to induce particularly Marxist views in his audience. Wiseman encourages us to attend to the meanings of our objects and actions, and to the processes by which they are brought into being in our institutions. In those institutions—educational, legal, religious, recreational, commercial—Wiseman observes the politics of organizational, personal, economic, and cultural life. It is no wonder that his work is of interest to Marxist critics, as it is to others with broadly humanistic and social scientific interests. In *The Store*, Wiseman creates a vehicle for analysis that provides a uniquely valuable ground upon which to unite Burkean rhetorical criticism with Marxist media criticism.[29]

The notion of materiality has another sense that speaks to the interpretation of *The Store*. Paralleling Kenneth Burke's five sources of motivation are Aristotle's four kinds of causes: the efficient (which corresponds to Burke's agency); the formal (which corresponds to the act, in the sense of the form into which something is changed or transformed); the final (which corresponds to purpose); and the material, by which Aristotle refers to the material out of which something is made, as with the stone out of which a statue is carved. In the case of a film, we may locate the material cause in two places: the observed reality that supplies the filmmaker with sounds and images, and the material (tape and film) upon which those sounds and images are re-corded, and which are shaped by sound recording, camera work, and editing into a formal product, the final film. In film theory, there have been many ways of arguing the issue of the ways in which film does or should remain faithful to the materiality of the subject world and the materiality of film itself.

Self-consciousness about the material causes of film form has a variety of precedents. In a discussion of the development of theatrical scenery into an ideology of environment, Mordecai Gorelik draws attention to the importance Marxist theatre places on scene and its relation both to stage action and to propaganda. "It is characteristic of Soviet theatre that it looks upon stage form not as a kind of aesthetic envelope for stage productions but as something having a highly important social propaganda of its own."[30] Gorelik's emphasis upon scene as a materialist locus of motivation, and upon audience as the point of the exercise, captures the dually "scientific" and "revolutionary" spirit of early materialist theatre. Scene motivates and hence explains the actions taking place on stage; what happens on stage exists to change the audience.

It is conventional in film history to point to a bifurcated myth of origins in which the materially realistic films of Louis and Auguste Lumière compete with the fancifully imaginative visions of Georges Melies. The history of Western thought is so thoroughly imbued with the vocabularies of realism vs. idealism and mind vs. body and nature vs. culture that film aesthetics could not have expected to escape them.

Peter Bondanella discusses how, in Italian cinema, the realistic treatment of social themes is related to the use of scene. "Visconti achieved in *Obsession*

[1942] a magnificent linkage between his tragic protagonists and their environment. . . . Extremely lengthy medium shots, a typical feature of Visconti's mature style, allow the director to follow Gino and Giovanna . . . as their destinies unfold and become shaped by their surroundings."[31] Most recent critics of the Italian film have pointed out that the "realistic" tendencies of neorealism, "realistic treatment, popular setting, social content, historical actuality, and political commitment," are themselves conventions.[32] For these Italian directors, the scene does not merely *express* theme, it also embodies theme by motivating action. Even so, it is very difficult for a critic to argue against naive realism without employing a vocabulary that preserves the distinction between realism and formalism. In film theory, the realist aesthetic was most systematically stated by Siegfried Kracauer and Andre Bazin. Kracauer argued that film was essentially a photographic art and as such lent itself to "the redemption of physical actuality." The more a film imposed form on straight observation, the less it was truly cinematic.[33]

The realist-formalist distinction is often carried over into discussions of documentary cinema verite, which Stephen Mamber describes as "an attempt to strip away the accumulated conventions of traditional cinema in the hope of rediscovering a reality that eludes other forms of filmmaking and reporting."[34] Wiseman has disavowed the labels direct cinema and cinema verite in favor of the intentionally paradoxical *reality fiction*, a term meant to acknowledge the inevitable perspective imposed by a filmmaker in recording and restructuring social action, the form imposed on the material.

Realist film directors, and especially documentarists, face the paradox that their realistic descriptions of political and social actualities may make the conditions they depict seem natural and inevitable—they may seem so individuated as to resist criticism or so universal as to be impervious to merely social and political amelioration. Even when Wiseman's films have dealt with "social problems" (*Titicut Follies, High School, Law and Order, Juvenile Court*), and especially when they have dealt with more broadly cultural topics, as in (*Essene, Canal Zone, Model, The Store*), they have a striking feeling for the gestures and structures of everyday life, which they then put in the service not of journalism but of a more abstract artistic vision. Wiseman's films certainly raise as many problems as they solve, from aesthetic and political points of view, but his whole body of work is an astonishing accomplishment of deepening documentary's explorations of both realism and formalism, and the relations between the two.

Everywhere evident in *The Store* is observation of American *materialism* in its ordinary language meaning as the pursuit of money and material goods. Shoppers and sellers consider the qualities of clothing, furs, jewelry, cosmetics, food, and household furnishings in scene after scene. When we consider the film from the perspective of its examination of consumer materialism, we can see how Wiseman ties together his ethical, cultural, and economic critique. The many scenes of executive conferences help to define the institution as a force in the lives of its inhabitants. The many scenes of shopping and selling help to define the material goods as a force in contemporary American culture. In neither case does Wiseman reduce his analysis to literal materialism; instead, he suggests a wide variety of motivations that cluster around the issues of institution as scene and material goods as cultural products.

Early in the film, a male customer is being shown a selection of sable coats.

CUSTOMER: It is pretty. Jim, on something like this, where can it be worn? How formal is it is what I am asking.

SALESMAN: I'll tell you, it's like whenever anybody asks me, well, I want a sable jacket, where can I wear it, I don't mean to sound flippant about it but it's that's the kind of thing you could wear anywhere. The old story of the bear, where can he go—anywhere you want.

CUSTOMER: Anyplace.

SALESMAN: Anywhere you want to go. You're talking. I think sable is a great Texas coat because of the weight number 1, because of the luxury factor number 2 and it just—I could see this with jeans, I can see this with the most elegant evening gown, lunch, cocktails, dinner. There is just no limitation on something like this. It's just a true work of art.

This scene, like so many others in Wiseman films, illustrates the adage that good documentarists are lucky. It would be difficult to compose an exchange of speeches that would so economically express the concern of the buyer, not for the materiality of the coat but for its social appropriateness and, by extension, for the gratification that it would provide for him and the woman he plans to give it to. The reply of the salesman is equally eloquent: he begins by reaffirming his subordination ("I don't mean to sound flippant") —but in a way that manages to sound subordinate to the customer and still invoke a respectful decorum in the presence of a coat that is going to cost from $37,500 to $45,000. Then the salesman—for the customer, the coat, or the camera, we cannot tell—refers to, but euphemizes, the story of the bear in the woods, another gesture of power and decorum, asserting, at the same time, the desire of the customer to rise above the constraints of the scene, of materialism, by exercising the power of his money. In an ambiguous gesture, the salesman displays the coat by draping it partly on the carpet, emphasizing its visual and tactile beauty and at the same time the immaculateness of the store and the casualness with which this lovely and expensive object may be treated. The salesman's reference to the "luxury factor" and his enumeration of the occasions on which the coat is appropriate return to a theme of pragmatism, and the speech ends with a peroration to art for its own sake—"It's just a work of art."

This first extended scene of shopping and selling is characteristic of the themes and relations that we see repeatedly in *The Store*. What stands out most strongly is the sheer sociality of the act of shopping, and the mostly social motives that the eventual purchase would be designed to serve. Shopping in

The Store is seen as a social activity, mainly performed by women or for women.[35] Even the sales staff at Neiman-Marcus become buyers. An elegant department head appears early in the film advising, and yet finally deferring to, a strong-willed customer. Later, the same saleswoman reappears as a customer in the photography studio, where she instructs the photographer, "I want to look like a soft, feminine, noncareer lady. I want to look soft. I stay at home all day. I play cards."

As in most Wiseman films, we are put into a very peculiar position as spectators. The absence of a clearly narrative structure encourages us to watch each scene with a special focus on its presence, its existential reality. In addition, we look beyond the particular scene for ways to knit our experience of the film into a coherent whole and discover that we can do so, in the absence of narrative, only by moving to a speculative plane, where we notice the formal and thematic relations among the scenes.

In Wiseman's films, people collaborate or conflict in pursuit of ends that are clearly important to them, but as spectators we almost never see the outcomes. So it is with *The Store*. We see repeated scenes of shopping and selling, but very little buying; we see repeated discussions of executive policy, but very few decisions; we see an extended job interview, but do not learn the outcome. The absence of outcomes encourages us, in a variety of ways, to attend to the motives, both expressed and implicit, of the actors in the scenes. Because, as spectators, we do not have an easy narrative line to carry us from scene to scene, we are never sure where a shot or scene is likely to end, and we must work hard to cope with the informational enrichment that Wiseman's method forces upon us. In narrative, especially most television narrative, the story is so dominant that the visible experience of the text becomes subordinate—we hardly have to watch at all. But Wiseman's text forces us to attend more actively. As the camera browses about the store, we cannot know from one shot to the next which bit of behavior will be extended into a major scene and which will give way to Wiseman's impulse to wander to another location. And once in a major scene, we are constantly on the watch for the sort of significance that will provide a punch line, leading Wiseman to conclude the scene and wander on. One effect of this technique is to encourage us to listen and watch very closely for the shape of the scene itself, so that we can lend ourselves to the material form of the film and make sense out of what we are watching. Another effect is to encourage us to see each succeeding scene not so much as a development from the preceding scene but as a variation: meaning is built up, layer by layer, dialectically, through repetition and variation, comparison and contrast.

Let us turn to three major scenes—a job interview, a birthday party, and a banquet—all placed late in the film, to note their shape and sense as discrete units and, even more importantly, as parts that connect with other scenes in suggesting how the promises of private consumption bind us together as a society.[36]

More clearly than any other scene in the film, the job interview presents an articulation of personal motives, whose connections to the goals and processes of corporate business are unmistakable. The applicant is a young black female, the interviewer a slightly older white male. Tensions of class, role, race, and gender, although never mentioned, are part of the subtext of the woman's direct appeal to enter the managerial class. Unabashedly selling herself as a product, she is the embodiment of the ideology of the store. Her sales pitch displays aggressiveness, self-confidence, ingratiation, and coquetry. Here she responds to a question about what she is "particularly proud of":

Ah, the thing that's coming to mind, right now, that I'm particularly proud of, is that the company, you don't know how much I respect and appreciative this company is. And the reason I am here with this company—Neiman-Marcus has a principle that I always believed in and that is that a sale is not a good sale for this company unless it is a good buy for the customer. And I appreciate that. I appreciate how this company differentiates itself from other companies, you know, in the same field. I mean, we do everything for the customer. We pamper the customer with our greenhouse; we give them personal assistance; we will even do the shopping for them, personal shoppers. You know the clientele system, the nylon club, fortnight, The Christmas Book. I mean we do so much for the customer. I appreciate that. And I think that a person who really appreciates what this company is all about, a person who can really understand what's going on in the economy, a person who can work with numbers, understand that we're here to make a profit and keep our expenses down low, a person who can respect Stanley Marcus. I mean highly respect him. A person who is willing to learn more about the company—I think I'm that person—belongs here. And I feel like I'm that person. I feel like I deserve executive training—more so than anyone. I mean, I have paid my dues. I have the educational and background. And the reason why I got an education is because it prepared me to understand what I was going to do for a career. It made me more intelligent as a person, it refined me, then I worked with the finest merchandiser, your finest customer under Kay Gladder, then I worked in the highest volume area. And I am doing a great job.

One expects the scene to end after the interviewer delivers a speech on the rigors of retailing and tells Sabrina how and when the decision will be made and that it was nice to meet her. But it does not. As so often happens in Wiseman's films, important information comes after the supposed punch line. What seems to be a climax is no assurance of closure, thus recasting our definitions of meaning and motive. In what functions as a coda, Sabrina condenses her motives to pure desire: "And listen, I want you to recommend me. I want you to highly recommend me because I want it."

Alone, the scene would be powerful, but it accumulates meaning and functions as both narrative and abstraction, act and purpose, particularly because it is positioned directly after a montage of silently working, mostly dark-skinned seamstresses, tailors, pressers, and loaders, and only a few minutes before a vice-president tells new buyers that their position "is perceived, by 90 percent of the retail community, and damn near everybody outside the retail community, as a tremendously elitist position. . . . [To be with Neiman-Marcus is] the one great attribute that you never have to apologize for. It's so damn neat."

It is the business of business to transform desire into consumption. "America teaches its children," writes John Updike, whose novels have chronicled American middle-class desire, "that every passion can be transmuted into an occasion to buy."[37] Personal longing and the inevitable failure to satisfy that longing promote the cultural narcissism described by Christopher Lasch.[38] *The Store* plumbs the archaeology of that narcissism. The principles of conspicuous consumption and conspicuous waste move private passions into the realm of the public.[39] Nationalized and ritualized, holidays are created or exploited as occasions for buying.

The Store was filmed in 1982 during the annual American shopping orgy— the month before Christmas. We observe women dropping hints, hear sales-clerks taking telephone gift orders, and see packagers wrapping Christmas presents. Wiseman and cinematographer John Davey found a moment when a gift was actually received on that other major American excuse for gifts, the birthday party.[40] The recipient is a woman of a certain age, a clerical worker who is apparently surprised, but not shocked, by her birthday gift—a singing telegram delivered by a young man in a chicken costume. He asks her a series of questions, prompting straight lines for his sexually provocative remarks that are climaxed by a striptease while he sings "Let Me Entertain You." Lasting six minutes and nine seconds, the scene is the longest in the film. It feels much longer.

In the birthday party scene, the camera sometimes zooms out to include other office employees, but usually our attention is directed to Margaret Murphy and her gift. She is a good sport. She laughs and jokes along, but gift getting is obviously a little fatiguing. She sits down at her desk halfway through the chicken's routine, perhaps from the strain of maintaining her delight for her office colleagues, who are presumably the gift givers.

In the birthday party, we see how the practice of giving impractical, fanciful gifts—a practice everywhere evident in the scenes of Christmas shopping throughout the film—has trickled down from the wealthy customers to the pink collar workers. The gift is absurd and, although sexually sugges-tive, entirely impersonal. Its public presentation in the work place by ersatz family is an exercise in distraction and amusement. Gift giving becomes an entertainment and a waste, the logical conclusion of the custom of the birth-day party. The empty wastefulness of the gift is underlined by our growing awareness of the burden of appreciation that is thrust upon the recipient. As the scene lengthens, our attention shifts from the performing chicken to Margaret Murphy. Wiseman leaves the scene on the screen long enough for us to grow uneasy with her extended performance, where a condensed version of the scene could easily have appeared as a mere grotesquerie. In a culture where our most profound expressions of desire and its satisfactions are often confined to the thirty seconds of a television commercial, the hollowness of Margaret Murphy's extended, obligatory performance of gratification does what generations of Marxists have been unable to do in earnest class propaganda: it makes consumption visibly, and as a felt experience, demoralizing.

Among other challenges in direct cinema is the demand for a satisfactory ending. With no story line to resolve and no voice-over narrator or authoritative interviewee to offer summary comments, Wiseman still manages to restate the major themes of *The Store* in the cluster of scenes that form its conclusion. The scenes of the Neiman-Marcus seventy-fifth anniversary celebration function as summation, yet open themselves to various resolutions.

In the banquet hall, we recognize a face we have seen earlier in the film, and finally Stanley Marcus is named, not by subtitles or an off-screen narrator, but in a speech. The tension and clarity of drama combine with the immediacy and authenticity of spontaneous event as Marcus is introduced near the end of the film.

Marcus first appears in the "medley" that opens *The Store*.[41] In two extremely brief shots, Marcus is photographed signing an elegantly bound book, and then his signature is shown. Combined, the two shots last only five seconds. This introduction of Marcus moves so quickly that a first-time viewer would probably not be able to discern the signature (let alone notice that the action could not have been naturally seen as it is presented, since the first shot is a head-on view of Marcus signing the book, and the second has been taken over his shoulder, making the signature, but for its brevity, potentially legible). Several minutes later in the film, the same elderly, bearded man, dressed in a red tie, white shirt, and blue suit, seated in front of an abstract poster, gives advice to buyers: unscrupulousness is bad for business. A viewer could easily fail to recognize this man, yet still recognize his importance. The trainees remain hushed while he talks, then laugh immediately and heartily at a mildly funny joke he tells. Wiseman frames the executive's advice with two extremely short reaction shots (two and three seconds) of the attentive buyers. During the rest of the scene, Marcus— photographed at a respectful low angle, with the only variation that of focal distance—remains on center screen. The camera isolates him from the scene as it isolates no other individual in *The Store*.

Why this man has been given such respect becomes obvious in the concluding scenes of the film. It also becomes obvious, if there has ever been any doubt, that the influence of the store extends beyond its physical space. Leaving the Neiman-Marcus building and the street in front of it for the only time in the documentary, we travel to a Dallas hotel for the anniversary banquet.

Wiseman shows us the labor that makes the elegant dinner possible. We go into the hotel kitchens where hurried directions are issued, usually in Spanish. Our attention is directed to the head table and three dinner companions seated near its center. They can be seen as merchant prince, dowager, and jester; as representatives of the power of business, government, and the press; or simply as Stanley Marcus, Lady Bird Johnson, and Art Buchwald. They respond to each other as friends and equals. The camera presents them individually, in couples, and as a trio, yet the central focus is on Stanley Marcus.

Before Marcus goes to the podium, he is praised by Buchwald. "Your interest in art, culture, and international affairs have made you a worldwide figure. You made Dallas a better place to live for everybody. During the McCarthy era, you took many unpopular political stands which cost your stores customers and business, but your devotion to this country's freedom far exceeded your desire for bigger profits."

Stanley Marcus's turn on the podium is also abundant with contradictions. His self-deprecating, self-congratulatory performance is ludicrous, yet the normal behavior of the honored retiree:

> I have chosen to emulate one of the great singers, Frank Sinatra, and the only song that suits the occasion is "My Way," which I hope to sing to you in the manner of a man called Rex Harrison. Professor, an arpeggio, please. Whatever the hell that may be.
>
>> It's my delight to say how right I think all this is. To state, I think it's great to celebrate with love and kisses. The praise, the cheers for all the years I do accept, and in no shy way. I can't disclaim the family name. I did it my way.

Predictably, we see Marcus accepting his applause, waving to his employees and friends. But the film does not end on Stanley Marcus. The last image is of cars driving in the Dallas night. The scene scatters.

Watching for motive and form in *The Store* is likely to show us that a variety of motives shape the actions before us. Certainly, the store itself, as an institutional setting for its workers, and the goods and money that form the media of exchange uniting buyers and sellers provide the primary account of why and how these people act together. And so, in the Marxist and in the Burkean senses, the world of *The Store* is doubly *scenic* and *material* in its motivation. And yet, in their different ways, Burke and the Marxist media critics provide us with ways of noticing that *The Store* is not simply a world of class conflict and exploitation, of deprivation and suffering, or of sheerly material determinism. Rather, it is a world in which our most profoundly social desires are achieved in terms of scenes and goods, where we are moved by material not in its own right but for the sake of symbolic ends. If Wiseman seems less generous than Burke in his view of the human barnyard, and less systematic, earnest, and dogmatic than self-professed Marxist media critics, it is partly owing to his greater particularity. Wiseman is sometimes angry, sometimes contemptuous, sometimes, it must be admitted, vulnerable to the temptations of a vision that can be unfair, or that can slide off into a by turns weary or vigorous surrealism. Still, through it all, Wiseman catches our dreams of power and our stifled desires, our suspicious and stubborn search for truth, our constantly reiterated rhetoric of justification and social control, and he gazes at them with a paradoxical refusal of the undeniable, a repeated astonishment at the mundane.

As Burke said, symbolic action is "the dancing of an attitude."[42] What would it mean to read and respond to an action or a text as the dancing of an attitude? In part, one would experience the form of the dance, and in part one would read it as the expression of another's view of things: as a description, an argument, a fantasy, a feeling. But a dance is not simply the expression of an attitude, any more than a text is simply the "expression" of an "ideology." A dance is an "interpretation" of, a giving form to, an attitude, and an invitation to a watcher to reinterpret the dance, either by simply taking pleasure in it or by responding with a dance of one's own. One's own dance is not simply an imitation of the other's; to dance with another is to dance a corresponding, not an identical form. And to dance after, or elsewhere, quite differently or not at all, is also to dance an attitude. Similarly, a rhetorical reading of Wiseman's film text requires us not simply to search for Wiseman's ideology, his attitude, but to read beyond that to the attitude it implies for us or makes possible for us as its readers and users. For Wiseman, as for Burke, to dance an attitude is not to insist on that attitude, but to give form to an idea, or a feeling, or a perception—an attitude—that others may put to use. What Frank Lentricchia refers to as the "vulgar Marxism" of 1930s intellectuals, who tried and failed to appeal to a nonexistent proletariat, has perhaps been superceded by a pragmatic formalism that is energetically and critically post-Marxist, speaking in a rhetoric that echoes Emma Goldman's famous line, "If I can't dance, I don't want to be part of your revolution."

Chapter 10

Let's Talk When I'm Eighty
Reality Fiction in Midcareer

We have offered a preliminary account of the documentary films of Frederick Wiseman, centering on close readings of representative films and contextualizing the readings with an inquiry into how some of the films were made and how they were received by viewers, subjects, and, in the case of *Titicut Follies*, the courts. Wiseman has made his career in film by working along the fault lines between art and social discourse, documentary and fiction. His work is ironic, paradoxical, and dialectical, generating its formal and thematic power by a strategy that invites his audiences to experience the tensions of everyday life in American institutions.

Wiseman's films seem to have challenged the assumptions of an earlier documentary tradition. And yet, fundamentally, they contribute directly to the agenda set for documentary film by Robert Flaherty and John Grierson, who both knew, as does Wiseman, that documentary is not so much about transmitting information as it is about transforming actualities into attitudes, teaching us to see the world differently. Wiseman is no social reformer, and he clearly scorns ingenuous didacticism, and yet his films would lack their characteristic energy and interest if it were not for his curiosity about the exercise of power and desire, and his radical insistence on seeing behind the facade of institutional routine.

Behind a body of work that is built upon the exploitation of contradictions, Wiseman himself lurks as a figure of contradiction, whose own facade has seldom been penetrated. Fred Wiseman once responded to a question about his work with the remark that if he were eighty and had stopped making movies he could comment more freely.[1] Wiseman, of course, is entitled to his privacy, and he has maintained a carefully conventional silence, for the most part, about himself and his working methods. But there are a variety of ways in which critical curiosity about Wiseman seems a natural part of understanding his work. His documentaries are built upon a method of film making that deliberately courts questions of invasion of privacy—to watch the films is often to feel that we are seeing deeply into other people's private experience. In the *Titicut Follies* case, the issue of invasion of privacy became a legal issue; in all the films, it is an ethical and aesthetic issue. But the privacy issue has other dimensions, as well. Wiseman's access to others' lives partly depends upon their not knowing too much about his reputation. His presentation of himself to institutions as a lawyer-filmmaker who is making a documentary for public television uses a legitimate aspect of his reputation to gain consent to enter the institution, but the occasional complaints that have marked such films as *Titicut Follies, High School,* and *Primate* and the general critical view that Wiseman often treats his subjects unsympathetically are matters that must be kept in the background.

It is now possible to piece together a fairly complete description of the production, mediation, and distribution of Wiseman's films and to see how these processes contribute to the reception and interpretation of the films. The issue of how the films are produced, mediated, and distributed goes beyond matters of credit or biography. The audience's experience does not usually include a strong sense of the films' authorship except as a hypothetical construct. And yet the films are as they are because of a complicated process that includes craft, collaboration, and institutional constraints and supports. If Wiseman's films are to be taken seriously as speculations about artistic, political, social, and cultural matters, then it is important to understand not only what they offer us, and the rhetorical means by which their meanings are constructed, but also to understand the process by which naturally occurring social life is discovered, reconstructed, and presented to us.

Over the years, Wiseman has given a number of interviews and lectures; some to which we have access have never been published. Those interviews and lectures, although they are in some ways incomplete, do provide a basic description of Wiseman's working methods, as well as a sense of how he manages his persona as a public figure. We have been able to fill out our understanding of Wiseman's working methods in interviews with all four of Wiseman's cameramen, with some of his other associates, and with some members of institutions in which he has worked.

Fred Wiseman has been unusually aggressive and successful in managing the related problems of funding and distribution. The first five films, according to Wiseman, were filmed by juggling various loans, grants from foundations and public television, lab credits, and the assistance of various unpaid friends. In 1971 Wiseman signed the first of two five-year, five-film contracts with WNET. In the same year, he formed his own distribution company, Zipporah Films, named after his wife. Under the terms of the WNET contract, half the money for a particular film would be advanced to Wiseman when the subject was approved, and the other half when the film was delivered. In 1982, Wiseman was awarded a five-year MacArthur foundation grant of $248,000, which financed the preliminary costs of several films that were later sold one at a time to WNET. Public broadcasting typically purchases, in funding the films, the right to broadcast the films—usually four plays in three years (a play is defined as an unlimited number of broadcasts in a one-week period). Rights to all subsequent distribution are retained by Wiseman, who rents and leases prints and videotapes. No prints or tapes are sold outright; a lease runs for five years.

College and university rentals are a major source of income for Zipporah Films; the film rentals are sometimes supplemented in a lecture by Wiseman at which he delivers extemporaneously what appears to be a fairly standard speech, with variations, on how he makes his films, and answers the by now predictable questions of his audiences with what have become more or less formulaic answers. Wiseman chooses institutions as his subjects, he says, because that is what interests him and because, after twenty years of working, he sees his films as constituting one large film. The institutions, sometimes tax-supported, are "generally speaking . . . thought to be doing a good job."[2] Next Wiseman negotiates permission to film. "Generally, what happens is I get permission because I try to locate somebody who is familiar with the institution, either is currently active in it or is a consultant to it or . . . at least knows something about it, and that person tells me who I should get in touch with, who the people are who have the actual authority to give me permission and what the politics are of getting permission and that person becomes a kind of advocate or an advisor or consultant to me on the politics of getting permission."[3] Wiseman makes it clear that once permission to film in the institution is granted, and acknowledged by signing a copy of Wiseman's letter describing his procedure, then "nobody will be photographed who doesn't want to be photographed, but they must indicate that they don't want their picture taken or their voice recorded either just before the sequence is shot or just after." From that point on, editorial control is entirely in Wiseman's hands. "You can never give anybody any control over your film if you're in fact going to call it your film." Shooting begins at once, "primarily because, one, I'm anxious to do the film and, two, I'm concerned that the people who gave me permission may change their minds." "And I don't do any research in advance. . . . All I try to do is get a sense of the geography of the place before I start. So usually I'll spend a day or a day and a half just walking around the halls. . . . I will request the director to put in the daily bulletin or the newspaper or bulletin board, if all of those exist at a place, an announcement that the film is going to be made. I try to demystify the filmmaking process in advance."[4] During filming, Wiseman looks for situations where one member of the institution is likely to be explaining or justifying its procedures. In *High School*, "the dean of discipline felt obliged to rationalize, to explain to the students why they were getting the punishment. So his statements became statements of value, ideological statements. . . . And there's the kind of situation you always look for, because you need that kind of abstraction to help the final audience of the film understand why the people who are the subject of the film are doing what they're doing. So there's one of the ways you try and get over the absence of traditional narration." As Wiseman well knows, the juxtaposition of institutional rationalizations with institutional routines results in an ironic structure. Hence, a narrative convenience is, for Wiseman, also an ideological practice.

Wiseman's crew consists of three people: a cameraman, an assistant who carries fresh film magazines, and Wiseman himself, who records sound. In a typical day, Wiseman and his crew spend from twelve to fifteen hours in the institution, recording at most about two hours of film. Wiseman says that, "for reasons I don't understand, I don't think that the presence of the camera and tape recorder changes people's behavior very much."[5] But the issues of privacy and verisimilitude, of informed consent and artistic freedom, are sometimes placed in a paradoxical conflict: Wiseman must claim that the presence of a film crew and equipment does not alter the ongoing social actuality they are recording; but he must also claim, and often has, that the film crew is clearly obtrusive enough that no one is ever filmed unknowingly. Social scientists refer to the phenomenon of a research subject's behavior being shaped by the observer, rather than as part of the natural setting, as the "reactivity" problem. In Wiseman's films, the reactivity problem is often played very close to the line. Wiseman has often, in public appearances, adopted from his cameraman William Brayne the claim that his camera has a "bullshit meter" and that he throws away any footage that he detects as performed for the camera. And yet Wiseman's films often depend for their effect upon allowing the viewer to detect subtle tones of inauthenticity in his subjects—inauthenticity that the viewer presumably attributes to the world within the film but that cannot with absolute assurance be ruled out as an artifact of the subject's awareness of the camera. Once filming has begun, "in the course of usually four to six weeks about a hundred to a hundred and twenty thousand feet of film is shot, which is fifty to sixty hours." Each day, Wiseman makes notes on what he is recording. After the day's filming, Wiseman and his crew view the silent rushes from three days before.[6] The film is then sent back to Cambridge, where an assistant synchronizes the picture and sound tracks.

Back in Cambridge after the four to six weeks of shooting, Wiseman reviews the assembled footage and prepares a log, cross-indexed "for situation and character." Out of the preparation of the log comes Wiseman's "goodies list . . . those sequences which I think are going to be important for the final film. . . . And then I try to figure out a tentative beginning and a tentative end." The process of editing, as Wiseman describes it, consists of "internal" and "external" editing. Internal editing occurs within sequences; external editing is the process of ordering the completed sequences together into a larger whole. At the early stages, most of the editing is internal, as Wiseman condenses and shapes sequences from his "goodies list." Later, he experiments with ways of assembling the sequences into a film of one and a half to three hours. In the last weeks of an editorial project that can take up to a year, as the film takes shape, the effort grows more intensive.

And it's funny because at the same time as you're involved very intensely in the effort to finish the film you have to learn to be very cold and detached from the material. Because otherwise you can't even begin to make the choices that you have to make in order to edit it down from sixty hours. . . . I have developed a capacity to totally detach myself from the film, to think of the experience as material, which is not to say that I've given up whatever sympathy I have for some of the people and some of the situations they're in, but I have to think of it solely in terms of how it works on film. Because the only thing that matters is whether, at that point, I can make a film that I'm pleased with, that has a dramatic structure, that conveys the themes that I'm interested in conveying in a film form.

And then, says Wiseman, when the film has been edited, "you go into a sound studio and you do the mix, which means you adjust the levels of the sound track and you make an optical track which can be printed with the negative that's matched to the work print that you've edited over the last eight months and then you go into the lab and spend forty to fifty thousand dollars getting answer prints and internegatives, whatever you may need for the film, and you finally have a print of the film. And then PBS, in its infinite wisdom, schedules the film anywhere from one to five years after you've finished it."

Wiseman is entitled to credit as the essential creative and organizational force behind his films. But he is not the sole intelligence or influence on the films, as he typically portrays himself to be. Chief among his collaborators have been his four cameramen, who are always clearly mentioned in the film credits but virtually never mentioned in Wiseman's lectures and interviews except with the claim that it is always Wiseman who acts as director on the scene, selecting with an elaborate set of subtle signals what should be filmed.[7] In interviews with each of the cameramen, we asked them to describe their recruitment, their working relationships, and their creative collaboration with Fred Wiseman.[8]

Wiseman's cinematogaphers recall being recruited with a minimum of fuss—he appears to have offered each of them work without any sort of extensive interview. Marshall says that "Fred just called me up one night. He said he was doing this film and he said, 'Do you want to shoot it?' And I said, 'Sure.' " Wiseman's other three cinematographers have all worked with Allan King Associates and were recruited through that organization. Richard Leiterman recalls, "I'm not sure how it came about. It came through Allan King's office, a job offer." William Brayne remembers that Wiseman had seen Brayne's work on *Warrendale* and simply called one day with an offer to shoot the film that became *Law and Order*. When Brayne left, he recommended John Davey, who was recruited, apparently, with a similar lack of preliminaries.

Each of the cinematographers recalls that Wiseman said little about how or what to shoot, either before or during the shooting. They understood that Wiseman was working in the Drew-Leacock-Pennebaker direct cinema style,

with which each of them had experience, sometimes distinguished experience, but remember being told little about style or subject matter, except
that they were to "float" in the institution and to "hang in there," which
translated to shooting long takes. Usually, they recalled, takes consumed
entire ten-minute rolls. Although the cinematographers directly contradicted
Wiseman's claim to be choosing and directing the image-making process,
they all recalled that Wiseman was enthusiastic and encouraging about their
work and that they felt a strong sense of rapport. Marshall: "We clicked. . . .
We hit it off." Leiterman: Our minds "were in sync, . . . working in absolute
parallel." Brayne: "We kept an eye on each other," using "very simple signals.
. . . We had a rapport." Davey: Working with Wiseman is "fascinating,
interesting, rewarding." We are "in sympathy." "We were both brought up
in entirely different cultures, Fred and myself, but we share the same jokes
and sense of humor."

We asked whether the camera changed the behavior it was observing, and
how the cinematographer interacted with subjects.

MARSHALL: [referring to the scene in *Titicut Follies* in which a man sings "Chinatown"
in front of a TV set]: We sort of half set the shot up and half didn't. . . . I got him
to stand in front of the TV, because that seemed like an idea. . . . A lot of that
stuff is half and half. People would turn on. We'd come out there and they'd turn
on, because you live in a place like that and this is what you can do. It's half
mockery; it's half cynical.

LEITERMAN: The camera does something really wild to people. People that you've
never known before, except for a half hour and you've sat in a sitting room and,
all of a sudden, they're doing all kinds of things. Why? It's the thing that goes
through our heads continually. Why do people do this?

BRAYNE: There was no manipulation whatsoever at any time between the subject and
the camera. . . . I have a thing on the camera called a bullshit meter. [There is]
always a danger [of performance for the camera]. . . . If in doubt, it would be
sorted out in the editing process. We do not impinge in any way, shape, or form
on the natural occurrences within any situation.

DAVEY: Nothing is ever, ever set up. . . . You can always, always tell when you're
filming someone whether they're saying it for the benefit of the camera and they're
playing a role. . . . If I become aware of people playing up to the camera or
reacting in an unnatural way, we just quietly turn off, until it gets right. You might
shoot that footage, but, you know, we'll have a discussion afterwards.

Although all four cinematographers seem to share a deep sense of the
direct cinema ideals of descriptive fidelity and unobtrusive technique, they
all acknowledge the fundamentally narrative and dramatic structure of much
of their work. Marshall speaks of the tension in documentary between "shooting pictures of events . . . like playing ping pong" and seeking out "images
that you want." Marshall clearly thinks that the "pictures of events" is a more
authentic approach, but one that is constantly threatened by the filmmaker's
temptation to control things, to make "a story movie."

Richard Leiterman speaks of how, especially in *High School*, the newly introduced possibilities of fast zoom lenses and the strong ideas of the film-makers about the process of schooling led them to search for "symbolism."

> It was a long time ago, but I know I was enraptured by the close-up. Hands are expressive. . . . Eyes are always real expressive. Mouths, the set of a mouth, are expressive. And it was so new and refreshing and perhaps even a little stylistic to go into something like that and to say, "Hey, I see a marvelous pair of hands, look what's happening over there. Why not just pick it up?" If it's in context, such as that example where you're traveling up something, or go to a hand because that hand is expressing something that may be more expressive than what he's saying. He's pointing the finger at somebody. And what's coming out of his mouth is secondary. The movement of the hand, or the set of the mouth I think is pretty exciting stuff. I certainly did then; considering that that was twenty years ago this was very, very new stuff, new material. And I think when you're on to something like that, there's no limit as to what you can get away with. You're looking for, I suppose, symbolism, all those things you learn that are important in cinema. That's a long time ago.

The cinematographers understood that they were not just there to take pictures, however authentic, but to provide Wiseman, as editor, with the materials out of which to construct coherent scenes. Brayne commented, "There's a very basic grammar in film, and even in this type of film making, cinema verite, hand-held camera, available lights, you have to adhere to a certain degree to that elementary grammar, or you attempt to follow an elementary grammar, and it's not that much different from just drama shoot-ing. You know you have to establish a scene. You know you have to find out what the scene is about and come to some sort of resolution. It's quite, quite simple. I mean, if you leave out those parts, the chances are you don't have a successful scene."

But despite the inevitable artificiality of symbolism and narrative, the four cinematographers—even Marshall, who is most dubious on this point— seem to believe that Wiseman is getting at something authentic in everyday experience. John Davey made the point strongly: "I've shot dozens and dozens of documentaries and I think working on Wiseman's films is the nearest to the truth that one can ever get. . . . I go to the British Film Theatre and see the films for the first time . . . and it really does sort of take me back and it reminds me of exactly how it was, and I've never had that feeling with any of the other films I've worked on."

Clearly, Wiseman's most important artistic collaborators have been his cinematographers, whose skills and vision have shaped his films in every image. But Wiseman has had other, even less visible collaborators. A key feature of Wiseman's large body of work is that most of it has been prepared under the sponsorship of American public television, which gave him an extraordinary measure of creative freedom. How was that freedom gained? When Wiseman has spoken of public television, it has often been in disparagement: he entertains audiences with images of bureaucrats who worriedly count dirty words and who schedule his films long after they have been completed. Presumably Wiseman has often had to fight to maintain his independence, and certainly his work has merited the support of American public television. But he has not gained his position in public television single-handedly. Several key figures have apparently made it their business to act as Wiseman's advocates within the system of American public television. One of Wiseman's most important institutional advocates has been Robert Kotlowitz, vice-president and director of programming at WNET in New York.[9] When Kotlowitz joined WNET in 1971, Wiseman had recently embarked upon his first five-film contract with the station. From the first, Wiseman seems to have been given a unique creative freedom, according to Kotlowitz:

> I was managing editor of *Harper's* magazine before I came here, and that was a very comfortable way for me to operate, [but] it's not the way I operated with most producers. Fred seemed to me so unique in his approach, and so unique in what he had already achieved, that anything that I might have to say conceptually would be absolutely gratuitous. . . . So the agreement was that we would provide him with a certain amount of production money every year which came out of our discretionary funds. . . . So the funding was assured, and Fred would call from Cambridge and say, "I want to do a juvenile court," or "I want to do a study of welfare." And I would say, "Terrific." And there was no clearance. I mean, I didn't have to go to anybody, and I did not have Fred report in to any of our executive producers here because it just seemed to me that he was just too special and, besides, it interested me professionally and personally, so I sort of retained it for myself. . . .
>
> Well, you know, Fred was a pretty strong advocate of himself. He loves to speak up and he did speak up. But I was his advocate with PBS, yes.

In his descriptions of his work, vivid and convincing as they often are, Wiseman has been reticent about his artistic and institutional collaborators. Similarly, Wiseman is usually reticent about the interpretation of his films, and increasingly so after the early years. He makes the films to satisfy himself, he says, and adds that it is up to audiences to make of the films what they can. Wiseman thus takes the conventional stance of the romantic and modern artist as the sole progenitor of his works and the sole source of their meaning, who, having created his works, can comment on them only at the risk of interfering with their influence upon an audience. This stance of Wiseman's is inevitably paradoxical, since he places the burden of interpretation upon the audience but refuses to relinquish to the audience—and especially to critics—the "meaning" of the films. Our own critical analysis of Wiseman's films, of course, faces much the same difficulty: we have employed a rhetorical perspective to seek in the films the response that Wiseman seems to invite. And yet the "meaning" of the films is not simply in Wiseman, nor even in the films themselves, but also in the various interpretations Wiseman's viewers make of the films. A rhetorical reading of the films cannot in itself replace Wiseman's meanings with its own, but at best contribute to the interrogation of the subject. For critic and viewer, engagement with Wiseman films necessarily goes beyond guessing what the films mean in and of themselves, or as evidence of Wiseman's thoughts and feelings. As Terry Eagleton remarks in discussing the critical theories of Hans-Georg Gadamer, "What the work 'says' to us will in turn depend on the kind of questions which we are able to address to it, from our own vantage point. . . . All understanding is *productive*: it is always 'understanding otherwise,' realizing new potential in the text, making a difference to it."[10]

Insofar as his films are social documentaries—and, with Wiseman's films, that phrase is not an exact fit—Wiseman illustrates a peculiar difficulty, because, in part to preserve the rhetorical effect of the films, he chooses not to engage in a full dialogue with his audiences or subjects about the issues he deals with in his films. Hence, a form of film making that is essentially demystifying in its rhetorical appeal, unmasking social institutions and practices, depends for its effect on a mystification of the filmmaker.

Part of the special appeal of Wiseman's films is that they convey a vivid and recognizable sense of institutional life by employing fictional techniques but avoiding progressive, narrative development at the level of the whole film. Instead, Wiseman replaces progressive narrative by a series of more or less self-contained narrative episodes contextualized spatially in the institution and thematically by issues of power and institutional routine. The avoidance of progressive narrative structure, for the most part, allows Wiseman to direct our attention to the institution and to various issues, instead of being distracted by plot or character; but at the same time we are presented with a gallery of memorable characters engaged repetitively in familiar human actions that he makes strange by his prolonged gaze.

Wiseman has often said that he avoids the conventional support of a voice-over narrative because he wants to place the audience in the position of working out its own relation to the material, as if it were placed in the institution and had to figure out for itself what was going on. Part of the pleasure and excitement of watching a Wiseman film is the feeling that we are figuring it out for ourselves. Of course, that, too, is partly an illusion, a rhetorical construction of the filmmaker. Wiseman locates us not in the institution, but in his film; our experience is the experience of coming to terms with his fiction. Moreover, the information that we are given to work on is radically different from that of any actual participant in the situation. As audience members, we know much less about the structural and circumstantial situation than the institution's staff or clients, and less than Wiseman. The feeling that we experience—of being dropped into the institution—is a feeling we could not get by visiting the institution. We can get it only through the film, which allows us the luxury of staring and speculating, and the unobtrusive guidance of Wiseman's highly formal filmic structures.

But although the films employ fictional techniques, their usefulness and their effect depend on our knowing that they are not simply fictions, in the sense that they are made about ongoing institutions that exist outside of Wiseman's films about them and that are inhabited by real people. Wiseman's vision of social reality is achieved through fictional techniques; at the same time, his aesthetic sophistication achieves its most satisfactory expression in its union with documentary realism, as his largely unsuccessful venture into pure fiction with *Seraphita's Diary* demonstrates.

The experience of a Wiseman film is in a fictional present tense. This present-tense quality of the films is one of the rhetorical accomplishments that permits him to direct our attention at what is actually happening before us, refusing to be distracted by the subjects' justifications, or by what might have come before, or what might be about to happen. As a formal achievement, Wiseman's present-tense, existential cinema offers rich aesthetic pleasures. As social documentary, the films have made a considerable contribution, and at the same time reveal their own limits.

Wiseman's films strongly convey the sense that they are about the politics of everyday institutional life. Their present-tense structure allows us to look directly at the day-by-day experience of life in the institution, to see how power relations are maintained by various devices of rationalization, justification, confusion, salesmanship, misdirected therapy, and outright command. The mechanisms of social control and their effect as human experience have never been as fully explored in documentary film. And yet, in focusing our attention on the present, Wiseman's films necessarily neglect the historical contexts that brought the institutional situations into being, and sometimes they seem to drift away from the fundamental promise of social documentary that human institutions can be changed by human action. An implicit difficulty of the sardonic, present-tense existential Wiseman comedies is that they court a contemptuous despair—they seem to show us a world that is not likely to change, that is ultimately a subject for fictional speculation but not for pragmatic debate. Hence the paradox of Wiseman's politics: he shows us, as we have never before seen it in documentary, the politics of institutions, enacted in the present tense, made visible by a sophisticated rhetoric of defamiliarization, but he does so at the possible expense of placing the films beyond politics altogether. This is perhaps a limit of Wiseman's films, but it is not necessarily a weakness. His task is to help us see, and that he has done. Our task, as his audience, is to see what is in the films, but it is as surely our task to move beyond the films, to put them to our own uses. To make full use of Wiseman's films as social documentaries would mean, it seems to us, an answering series of documentaries that finds a way to use Wiseman's penetrating vision while restoring history and politics to that vision; it would also mean that audiences in their own spheres of political engagement carry the sensibilities Wiseman has taught us but at the same time recall that politics demands more of us than irony. Prudential public action demands an understanding of history and a willingness to cooperate to change the future. These are, in a sense, beyond what Wiseman addresses in his films, and although it is the critics' job to press this argument, it is not meant as a disparagement of Wiseman's contributions. An honest respect for Frederick Wiseman's films makes them part of a debate that will ultimately go beyond Wiseman's films and beyond Wiseman himself. Fred Wiseman has changed the history of documentary film. At midcareer, the history of his own films remains unfinished.

Appendix: Filmography
Notes
Bibliography
Index

Appendix
Filmography

Titicut Follies

Producer/ Director/ Editor: Frederick Wiseman
Co-director and photographer: John Marshall
Associate Editor: Alyne Model
Associate Producer: David Eames

Filmed at Massachusetts Correctional Institution-Bridgewater, between 22 April and 29 June 1966
First public showing: New York Film Festival, 28 September 1967
Running time: 89 minutes; black and white

High School

Producer/ Director/ Editor: Frederick Wiseman
Photographer: Richard Leiterman
Associate Editor: Carter Howard
Camera Assistant: David Eames

Filmed at Northeast High School, Philadelphia, Pennsylvania, in the spring of 1968
First WNET/13 broadcast: October 1968
Running time: 75 minutes; black and white

Law and Order

Producer/Director/Editor: Frederick Wiseman
Photographer: William Brayne
Associate Editor: Carter Howard
Camera Assistant: David Martin
Editing Assistant: Andrea Green
Production Assistants: Robbin Mason and Susan Primm

Filmed at Admiral Street Precinct, Kansas City, Missouri, in the autumn of 1968
First NET broadcast: 2 March 1969
Running time: 81 minutes; black and white

317

Hospital

Producer/ Director/ Editor: Frederick Wiseman
Photographer: William Brayne
Associate Editor: Carter Stanton-Abbot
Sound Mixer: Richard Vorisek
Camera Assistant: David Martin
Assistant Editor: Susan Primm
Production Assistants: Robbin Mason and Margaret Anderson

Filmed at Metropolitan Hospital Center, New York City, in May 1969
First NET broadcast: 2 February 1970
Running time: 84 minutes; black and white

Basic Training

Producer/ Director/ Editor: Frederick Wiseman
Photographer: William Brayne
Associate editor: Pat Thomson

Filmed at the U.S. Army Training Center at Fort Knox, Kentucky, in the summer
    of 1970
First PBS broadcast: 4 October 1971
Running time: 89 minutes; black and white

Essene

Producer/ Director/ Editor: Frederick Wiseman
Photographer: William Brayne
Associate Editor: Spencer Bruskin
Camera Assistant: Oliver Kool

Filmed in an Anglican Benedictine monastery in Three Rivers, Michigan, in the
    summer of 1971
First PBS broadcast: 13 November 1972
Running time: 86 minutes; black and white

Juvenile Court

Producer/ Director/ Editor: Frederick Wiseman
Photographer: William Brayne
Camera Assistant: Oliver Kool
Production Assistants: James Medalla and Rene Koopman

Filmed in the Juvenile Court of Memphis and Shelby County, Memphis,
    Tennessee, in February and March 1972
First PBS broadcast: 1 October 1973
Running time: 144 minutes; black and white

Primate

Producer/ Director/ Editor: Frederick Wiseman
Photographer: William Brayne
Camera Assistant: James Medalla
Assistant Editor: Oliver Kool
Synchronization: Ken Sommer
Mix: Richard Vorisek

Filmed at Yerkes Regional Primate Research Center, Emory University, Atlanta, Georgia, in January and February 1973
First PBS broadcast: 5 December 1974
Running time: 105 minutes; black and white

Welfare

Producer/ Director/ Editor: Frederick Wiseman
Photographer: William Brayne
Camera Assistant: Oliver Kool
Synchronization: Ken Sommer
Mix: Richard Vorisek

Filmed at Waverly Welfare Center, New York City, in early 1974
First PBS broadcast: 24 September 1975
Running time: 167 minutes; black and white

Meat

Producer/ Director/ Editor: Frederick Wiseman
Photographer: William Brayne
Assistant Editor: Oliver Kool
Camera Assistant: Oliver Kool
Synchronization: Ken Sommer

Filmed at the Monfort Packing Company, Greeley, Colorado, in November 1974
First PBS broadcast: 13 November 1976
Running time: 113 minutes; black and white

Canal Zone

Producer/ Director/ Editor: Frederick Wiseman
Photographer: William Brayne
Camera Assistant: James Hallowell
Assistant Editor: Oliver Kool
Synchronization: Stephanie Tepper

Filmed in the Panama Canal Zone, in the spring of 1976
First PBS broadcast: 8 October 1977
Running time: 174 minutes; black and white

Sinai Field Mission

Producer/ Director/ Editor: Frederick Wiseman
Photographer: William Brayne
Camera Assistant: Ali Kul
Assistant Editor: Stephanie Munroe
Synchronization: Herve Schneib and Andy Lane

Filmed in the Sinai Buffer Zone, in the summer of 1977
First PBS broadcast: 17 October 1978
Running time: 127 minutes; black and white

Manoeuvre

Producer/ Director/ Editor: Frederick Wiseman
Photographer: John Davey
Camera Assistant: Oliver Kool
Synchronization: Patricia Cahalan and Charles Scott
Assistant Editor: Stephanie Munroe

The NATO field maneuver, Operation Autumn Forge, filmed at Fort Polk,
Louisiana, and in West Germany, in the autumn of 1978
First PBS broadcast: 20 March 1980
Running time: 115 minutes; black and white

Model

Producer/ Director/ Editor: Frederick Wiseman
Photographer: John Davey
Camera Assistant: Oliver Kool
Assistant Editor: Diane Hodgman

Filmed at Zoli Management, Inc., New York City, in the autumn of 1979
Shown at the London Film Festival, November 1980
First PBS broadcast: 16 September 1981
Running time: 129 minutes; black and white

Seraphita's Diary

Producer/ Director/ Editor/ Screenwriter: Frederick Wiseman
Photographer: John Davey
Sound: David John
Hair, Makeup, and Animals: Anthony Clavet
Camera Assistants: James Hallowell and Anne M. O'Toole
Best Boy: Eric Wiseman
Synchronization: Stephanie Munroe and Shelia Bernard
Costumes: Glorgio Di Sant'Angelo and Alberta Wright of Jerzebel,
Private Collections

Additional Costumes: John Eric Broaddus, Mimi Trujillo, and
Bob Colbath
Accessories: Barbara Turk
Additional Styling: Freddie Lieba
Jewelry: David Webb and Judith Van Amring
Set Designer: Michael Booth
Still Photographers: Ara Gallant and Hans Feurer
Production Photographers: Willie Chu and Ollie Kool
Credits: Jean Evans
Timing: David Pultz
Columbian Music Consultant: Jane Safer

Seraphita: Appolonia Van Ravenstein
Seraphita's Friends: Rory Bernal, Eric Boer, John Eric Broaddus,
Willie Chu, Ara Gallant, Suzy Guilder, Todd Irvin,
Carlin Jeffrey, Barbara Lantz, Tommy McCarthy, Russell Todd,
and Kery Warn

Filmed in the summer and in October 1981 at the Sylvan Bookshop, Studio 54,
and the Robert Whittington and the Gary Gross studios
First public showing: Boston, October 1982
Running time: 90 minutes; color

The Store

Director/ Producer/ Editor: Frederick Wiseman
Photographer: John Davey
Additional Photography: Kevin Burke
Camera Assistant: Ollie Hallowell
Assistant Editor/ Synchronization: Stephanie Munroe
Editorial Assistant: Bonnie E. Waltch

Filmed at Neiman-Marcus, Dallas, Texas, during the Christmas shopping season,
1982
First PBS broadcast: 14 December 1983
Running time: 118 minutes; color

Racetrack

Director/ Producer/ Editor: Frederick Wiseman
Photographer: John Davey
Camera Assistants: David B. Wiseman and Ollie Hallowell
Assistant Editor: Stephanie Munroe
Synchronization: Mary Jo Wheatley, Susanne Simpson, and
Jeanne Jordon

Filmed in and around Belmont Park, Elmont, New York, in May and June 1981
Shown at the Boston Film Festival, 13 August 1985

First PBS broadcast: 4 June 1986
Running time: 114 minutes; black and white

Deaf; Blind; Multi-handicapped; Adjustment and Work

Director/ Producer/ Editor: Frederick Wiseman
Photographer: John Davey
Camera Assistants: Ollie Hallowell and Evan Eames
Assistant Editor: Stephanie Munroe
Assistant Editors (Synchronization): Alexandra Anthony and
Diane Hodgman

Filmed at the Alabama Institute for the Deaf and Blind, Talladega, Alabama, in
the fall of 1984
Shown at the London Film Festival, November 1986
First PBS broadcast: June 1988 as a miniseries, *Deaf and Blind*
Running times: 164 minutes, 132 minutes, 126 minutes, and 120 minutes; color

Missile

Director/ Producer/ Editor: Frederick Wiseman
Photographer: John Davey
Camera Assistant: Evan Eames
Assistant Editors (Synchronization): Stephanie Munroe, Trish
Cahalan, and Alexandra Anthony
Editorial Assistants: Lynn Gaza and Lindsay Mofferd

Filmed with the 4315th Training Squadron of the Strategic Air Command at
Vandenberg Air Force Base, California, in January and February 1986
Shown at the US Film Festival, Park City, Utah, January 1988
First PBS broadcast: 31 August 1988
Running time: 118 minutes; color

Other Film and Theatre Work

At various points in his film career, Wiseman has been at the edges of what is commonly known as fiction filmmaking. He was an investor in *The Connection* (1962), directed by Shirley Clarke. He produced *The Cool World* (1963), also directed by Clarke. He was an (uncredited) screenwriter on *The Thomas Crown Affair* (1968). He wrote the first script for *The Stunt Man* (1980), but it was put aside unread by the final screenwriter and director. He has written a screenplay based on Anne Tyler's novel *Celestial Navigation,* which he has said he hopes to produce and direct.

In 1982 Wiseman produced, directed, edited, and "adapted" *Seraphita's Diary* with model Appolonia Van Ravenstein (who appears in *Model)* as Seraphita. Ravenstein plays multiple parts—an old man who discovers Seraphita's diary, various people in Seraphita's life, and various versions of Seraphita. Some evidence indicates that portions of Wiseman's script for the film were improvised by Van Ravenstein.

In the fall of 1986 Wiseman went on stage himself as the documentarian Frederick Wiseman in the American Repertory Theatre adaptation of Luigi Pirandello's *Tonight*

We Improvise. Adapted and directed by Robert Brustein, the Loeb Drama Center production in Cambridge, Massachusetts, included the onstage creation of a video documentary shot by Wiseman and simultaneously displayed on monitors while the actors were "improvising," and the presentation of an interlude film, a parody travel documentary supposedly shot in Sicily—the setting of the Pirandello play—and portentously narrated by Wiseman from behind a lectern.

In May 1988 *Life and Fate*, a play adapted from a chapter in Vasily Grossman's novel of the same name, was presented by the American Repertory Theatre at the Agassiz Theatre in Radcliffe Yard, Cambridge. Wiseman directed and adapted the material, which he had reportedly seen in a French version in Paris in February 1987. The French production featured two characters. Wiseman's one-act, one-character adaptation, running about an hour, depicts a Russian Jewish doctor, caught up by the German invasion, writing a last letter to her son before her death in the Holocaust. The part of the mother was played by Ruth Maleczech.

All of Frederick Wiseman's films are available for rent or lease from Zipporah Films, One Richdale Avenue, Unit #4, Cambridge, MA 02140 (telephone 617 576–3603).

Chapter 1. *Reality Fictions*

1. See John Grierson, *Grierson on Documentary*, ed. Forsyth Hardy, rev. ed. (Berkeley: University of California Press, 1966). For other accounts of Grierson's work, see especially Paul Rotha, *Documentary Film*, 3d ed. (New York: Hastings House, 1963); Erik Barnouw, *Documentary: A History of the Non-Fiction Film*, rev. ed. (New York: Oxford University Press, 1983). For Grierson, the "creative treatment of actuality" was not a matter of turning life into art, but of using the art of cinema to address the needs of society. Grierson was the first to use the term *documentary* as a description of film, in a review of Robert Flaherty's *Moana*. In the same review, Grierson described *Moana* as a "poetic record," a phrase that addresses some of the same paradoxes as "reality fictions." John Grierson, "Flaherty's Poetic *Moana*," *New York Sun*, 8 February 1926; reprinted in Lewis Jacobs, ed., *The Documentary Tradition*, 2d ed. (New York: Norton, 1979), 25. Wiseman's films bear a strong generic similarity to the form of documentary generally called "direct cinema," a "type of location, non-fiction, close observation cinema in which lightweight cameras and sound recorders are used to record action as it actually happens with indigenous sound only" (*Glossary of Film Terms* [Philadelphia: University Film Association, 1978], 27). Direct cinema was pioneered in American film by Robert Drew, Richard Leacock, Donn A. Pennebaker, Albert and David Maysles, and, slightly later, Frederick Wiseman, and in Canada by Allan King and several of his associates, including Richard Leiterman and William Brayne (Leiterman and Brayne later working as Wiseman's cinematographers). A parallel development, developed by Jean Rouch and Edgar Morin, is the *cinéma vérité* documentary, which, as developed by Rouch and Morin, typically involved active interviews and interventions by the filmmakers and the use of nonsynchronous sound. In practice, the terms are often used interchangeably to refer to modern (since about 1960) documentary, beginning with the Drew-Leacock *Primary* (1960) and the Rouch-Morin *Chronique d'un été* (1961). For histories of these developments see, for example, Erik Barnouw, *Documentary: A History of the Non-Fiction Film* (New York: Oxford University Press, 1974); Stephen Mamber, *Cinema Verite in America: Studies in Uncontrolled Documentary* (Cambridge: MIT Press, 1974). In a letter of application to the Fifth International Film Festival, Wiseman described *Titicut Follies* as "done in the 'cinema verite' style" (26 April 1967, exhibit 44 in *Commonwealth v. Wiseman*). In this book we shall follow the common practice of using *cinema verite* (without italics or accent marks) as the covering term for the two forms and their many variants, *direct cinema* as the somewhat narrower term usually used to refer only to the Anglo-Canadian-American movement. In this usage, common in the documentary movement as well as in writings about it, cinema verite includes direct cinema but direct cinema does not include *cinéma vérité*.

2. Capote's use of the phrase "nonfiction novel" was made in reference to his *In*

Cold Blood (New York: Random House, 1965). Norman Mailer's history-as-novel is invoked in his *Armies of the Night* (New York: New American Library, 1968); Wiseman used the phrase "reality dream" in a 1970 interview with John Graham, "There Are No Simple Solutions," reprinted in *Frederick Wiseman*, ed. Thomas R. Atkins (New York: Monarch Press, 1976), 35–36; Wiseman used the term *reality fictions* in a 1974 interview with Thomas Atkins, in Atkins, ed., *Frederick Wiseman*, 82. In a 1970 article, Beatrice Berg wrote that there is no correct term for what Wiseman does, but "perhaps film intellectuals will manufacture a new label" ("I Was Fed Up with Hollywood Fantasies," *New York Times*, 1 February 1970, sec. 2, 26). In 1971, M. Ali Issari reported that Wiseman was calling his films "new documentaries," in an apparent parallel to the "new journalism." M. Ali Issari, *Cinema Verite* (East Lansing: Michigan State University Press, 1971), 125. Wiseman is a highly original film artist, but his flirtation with the term *reality fiction* also underscores another theme that is repeated in almost all of his interviews and lectures: an anxiety not to be thought naïve or commonplace.

3. Wiseman, in an unpublished interview with Randall Conrad, circa 1978.

4. For recent, fairly comprehensive overviews of contemporary rhetoric and its place in communication studies generally, see Carroll C. Arnold and John Waite Bowers, eds., *Handbook of Rhetorical and Communication Theory* (Boston: Allyn and Bacon, 1984); Thomas W. Benson, ed., *Speech Communication in the 20th Century* (Carbondale: Southern Illinois University Press, 1985); Gerard A. Hauser, *Introduction to Rhetorical Theory* (New York: Harper & Row, 1986); for a survey of the extension of the rhetorical tradition to the study of film and other media, see Martin J. Medhurst and Thomas W. Benson, eds., *Rhetorical Dimensions in Media: A Critical Casebook*, rev. printing (Dubuque: Kendall/Hunt, 1986).

5. We do not wish to imply that cinematography is or should be a male domain, but because Wiseman's cinematographers have been men, we shall use the terms *cameraman* and *cameramen* throughout.

6. Leiterman started as the cinematographer on *Law and Order*, in Los Angeles, but the project was aborted when the police department withdrew its blanket permission to observe and record police activities. By the time Wiseman made arrangements to film in Kansas City, Leiterman was committed to shoot *A Married Couple* (1969) (according to Leiterman in an interview with the authors, Mont Tremblant, Quebec, 17 August 1986).

7. Limitations of space have required us to exclude from the present book analyses of Wiseman's other films. For an analysis of *Model*, see Thomas W. Benson and Carolyn Anderson, "The Rhetorical Structure of Frederick Wiseman's *Model*," *Journal of Film and Video* 36, no. 4 (1984): 30–40.

Chapter 2. *Titicut Follies*

1. In an interview with Alan Rosenthal in *The New Documentary in Action: A Casebook in Filmmaking* (Berkeley: University of California Press, 1971), Wiseman claimed, based on his attorney's research, that *Titicut Follies* was the only American film with court-imposed restrictions for reasons other than obscenity (68). More recently, Karen Konicek, director of distribution at Wiseman's company, Zipporah Films, said that *Titicut Follies* is the only film in the United States censored for reasons other than obscenity or national security (Helen M. Wise, "Coursework vs.

Career Choices: Two Roads Taken," *The Alumnus* [University of Massachusetts], August–September 1987, 6). Harvey Silvergate, president of the Civil Liberties Union of Massachusetts (CLUM), described the *Titicut Follies* case by saying that "twenty years ago the state judiciary for the first (and still the only) time in modern American history issued an unprecedented order, a prior restraint injunction that suppressed a motion picture neither legally obscene nor a 'clear and present danger' to the national security" ("President's Column: *Titicut Follies* Revisited," *The Docket* [CLUM] 17, no. 4 (1987): 3). Legal scholars on a *"Titicut Follies:* 20 Years Later" panel held at the University of Massachusetts-Boston, 14 May 1987 repeated the claim about the film's unique legal status ("Film on State Hospital Provocative after 20 Years," *New York Times,* 17 May 1987, 27). Other American films have had unusual restrictions placed on their exhibition. For example, although the Rolling Stones, a rock music group, had commissioned Robert Frank to film their 1972 U.S. tour, they sued to block the release of Frank's documentary, *Cocksucker Blues.* "Litigation on the part of the Rolling Stones has guaranteed the film can be shown only a few times a year and only when Frank is in attendance" (Sean Elder, "Darkness Visible: Robert Frank and the Real Rolling Stones," [Berkeley] *Express,* 30 October 1987, 6). Marlaine Glickman claims that Frank's film "remains banned (by legal order) to this day" ("Highway 61 Revisited," *Film Comment* 23, no. 4 [1987]: 33). For a comprehensive review of restrictions on film exhibition see Edward De Grazia and Roger K. Newman, *Banned Films: Movies, Censors, and the First Amendment* (New York: R. R. Bowker, 1982).

2. Bridgewater has been referred to for many years as the "state hospital for the criminally insane" by professionals and lay people. Robert H. Weber, executive director of the Mental Health Legal Advisors Committee, and his legal intern David Twohig have argued that the "phrase 'criminally insane' is an inaccurate and oxymoronic description of Bridgewater's clientele" since "those who are judged insane are, by definition, excused from criminal responsibility." The managing editor of the *Boston Globe* was sufficiently impressed by their argument to issue a directive that the state's most influential newspaper would revise its style book to eliminate the objectionable phrase (Robert L. Kierstead, "Dropping a Stigmatizing Phrase," *Boston Globe,* 2 November 1987, 18).

3. "Frederick Wiseman on the Films of Frederick Wiseman," an appearance sponsored by the Student Cultural Events Organization, University of Massachusetts-Boston, 6 April 1977.

4. Wiseman, U-Mass-Boston, 6 April 1977.

5. Mass. Gen. Laws Ann., ch. 127, sec. 36 (1958).

6. Wiseman, as quoted in Alan Westin, " 'You Start Off with a Bromide': Wiseman on Film and Civil Liberties," *Civil Liberties Review* 1, nos. 1 and 2 (1974): 65.

7. Christina Robb, "Focus on Life," *Boston Globe Magazine,* 23 January 1983, 17 and 26; Robb's is the most detailed published account of Fred Wiseman's background and early years.

8. In December 1957, in Paris, a mutual friend of Wiseman's and Phil Green's explained Wiseman's absence from the social activities of the group by telling Green that "Freddy had gone to Algeria to do documentaries for French TV." Green was never able to ascertain any more about the alleged project, nor have we. Interview with Professor Philip Green by Carolyn Anderson, Northampton, MA, 26 September 1986.

9. Wiseman, as quoted in Robb, 27. In *Commonwealth v. Wiseman*, when asked about his occupation, Wiseman replied, "I am a filmmaker, an attorney, and a consultant on social problems" (trial transcript, vol. 13, p. 4; in *Commonwealth v. Wiseman*, Suffolk Superior Court, no. 87538 Equity). All subsequent references to this trial transcript will be by speaker, volume, and page number only (for example, Wiseman, Tr. 13:4). References will be placed within the text when the speaker is easily identified therein. Wiseman describes his hope for *The Cool World* in "The Talk of the Town: New Producer," *The New Yorker*, 14 September 1963, 33–35. Wiseman and an associate formed a social-science consulting company in the spring of 1966.

10. Gaughan, Tr. 4:12.

11. Charles Gaughan, "History of MCI-Bridgewater," p. 3, enclosure in correspondence with Carolyn Anderson, 9 May 1977.

12. Michael Perleman, psychiatrist, made this comment as a participant in a panel discussion after the exhibition of *Titicut Follies* at Hampshire College, Amherst, Massachusetts, 5 April 1977.

13. Robert Perrucci, *Circle of Madness: On Being Insane and Institutionalized in America* (Englewood Cliffs: Prentice-Hall, 1974), 27.

14. Gaughan, tr. 4:86, 5:82.

15. Wiseman, U-Mass-Boston, 6 April 1977.

16. Exhibit 1, *Commonwealth v. Wiseman*. Subsequent references to exhibits will be noted in the text.

17. The issue of competency later became crucial. Wiseman's defense took the position that he and the state agreed that competency would be determined at the time of shooting, as a procedural matter. The state took the position that it had a continuing obligation to determine the competency of subjects in the film. Wiseman's letter could support either interpretation.

18. The plaintiffs did not enter the proposal with Wiseman's letter in their original petition against Wiseman. The defense introduced the proposal in Wiseman's reply to the Bill in Equity.

19. Commonwealth of Massachusetts Suffolk Court for Civil Business, Equity no. 87538. "Findings, Rulings, and Order from Decree," docket entry no. 75, entered 4 January 1968, 3–4. Subsequent references to this file will be by docket number only.

20. Christopher Lydon, "Richardson Victory Fruit of Shrewd Analysis and Action," *Boston Globe*, 5 November 1964, 11.

21. Jerome M. Mileur and George T. Sulzner, *Campaigning for the Massachusetts Senate: Electioneering outside the Political Limelight* (Amherst: University of Massachusetts Press, 1974), 4.

22. Brooke, citing 41 Am. Jur. 888.

23. Gavin, "Hearings on the Bridgewater Film before the Special Commission on Mental Health," Boston, 17 October–9 November 1967, 28 (quoted by counsel for the defense, tr. 3:104–5). Subsequent references to the legislative hearings will cite "Hearings" and page number only.

24. Eames, tr. 6:167–68. Interview by Carolyn Anderson with John Marshall, Cambridge, 13 April 1984.

25. For a brief account of the circumstances that led to a remarkable family research project that has continued for over three decades, see Lorna Marshall, *The !Kung of Nyae Nyae* (Cambridge: Harvard University Press, 1976), 1–4.

26. Wiseman, tr. 13:143.

27. According to Pacheco's testimony, he never worked at the hospital before his escort assignment; he was a sanitation officer in the alcoholic section (Tr. 10:27).

28. Marshall interview (1984).

29. Kozol, memorandum, 2 May 1966. Exhibit 14.

30. Wiseman, tr. 13:121; Eames, tr. 6:114.

31. During the *Commonwealth v. Wiseman* trial, the Commonwealth tried to demonstrate that subjects were sometimes unaware of the recording of picture or sound. George Caner, questioning David Eames about the capabilities of a directional mike, asked, "And thus, to the extent that when it is directed at an object it screens out sounds coming from elsewhere, to that extent, it is able to pick up meaningful sounds that your ear might not be able to pick out?" Eames replied, "That is correct" (Tr. 7:55). In a memorandum to the authors, Wiseman said it was inaccurate to assume that "the mike could pick up sounds the ear could not. I think it is difficult not to notice a camera, tape recorder, mike, a bag with film and magazines and 3 strangers" (4 August 1987). In another context, Alan M. Dershowitz has noted that in Massachusetts in the mid–1980s "it is a felony to 'secretly record' conversations. Massachusetts also makes it a crime to disclose surreptitiously recorded conversations" (*Reversal of Fortune: Inside the von Bulow Case* [New York: Random House, 1986], 266n.).

32. Wiseman, tr. 13:108; Joseph F. Moran, tr. 6:79.

33. George J. Lepine, Jr., tr. 5:125; Wiseman, tr. 13:126; Marshall interview (1984).

34. Wiseman and Marshall have differing current memories about Marshall's independence while shooting. In various published interviews, Wiseman has claimed he directs the shooting on all his films. He noted to us that "Marshall stated in [his] deposition that he did all camera work under my direction" (4 August 1987 memorandum). The Marshall deposition is not included in the public file of *Commonwealth v. Wiseman*. In his trial testimony, Wiseman said, "We might be seven or eight feet apart. Mr. Marshall might be in one place with a camera and I would be in another place with a tape recorder" (Tr. 14:153).

35. Marshall interview (1984). See Lisa Henderson, "Photographing in Public Places" (Thesis, University of Pennslvania, 1983). Following Goffman, Henderson provides an analysis of strategies and justifications used by still photographers.

36. According to Wiseman, "during the trial a letter was received from Vladimir giving his consent" (memorandum to the authors, 4 August 1987).

37. See Anthony J. Lucas, *Common Ground: A Turbulent Decade in the Lives of Three American Families* (New York: Knopf, 1985).

38. Bud Collins, "Marty and Benny Show Tries Out," *Boston Globe*, 24 April 1967, 10. See also "King Begins Anti-War Bloc Here," *Boston Globe*, 24 April 1967, 1, 22.

39. Ronald A. Wysocki, "Bridgewater Lacks Medics," *Boston Globe*, 2 January 1967, 1.

40. Bailey, as quoted in Ray Richard, "Bridgewater: An Emergency Situation," *Boston Globe*, 21 January 1967, 1, 4.

41. Gaughan, as quoted in Wysocki, "Strangler Escapes—Manhunt On," *Boston Globe*, 24 February 1967, 1.

42. Edward G. McGrath, "Public Reaction: Disgust," *Boston Globe*, 24 February 1967, 1.

43. Gaughan, tr. 4:200–201.

44. Moran, tr. 6:86–88, 90–91; Pacheco, tr. 10:31–35.

45. Wiseman, tr. 13:6.

46. Wiseman, as quoted in Westin, "You Start Off with a Bromide," 62.

47. Wiseman, tr. 13:76

48. Marshall interview (1984). Marshall repeated this account of his role in the editing process in an interview with the authors, 27 December 1986, in Peterborough, New Hampshire. During the trial, Wiseman said that sometimes Eames and Marshall gave their views on what had been edited (Tr. 13:140). In a memorandum to the authors, Wiseman said that "Marshall and Eames did not see the film (apart from rushes) until I screened a rough cut for them. Marshall played no part in the editing and does not have co-editor's credit. I gave Marshall co-director's credit in appreciation for his working without pay and providing equipment free" (memorandum to authors, 4 August 1987).

49. Liz Ellsworth, *Frederick Wiseman: A Guide to References and Resources* (Boston: G. K. Hall, 1979), 33.

50. Ira Halberstadt, "An Interview with Frederick Wiseman," *Filmmaker's Newsletter* 7, no. 4 (1974): 22.

51. Wiseman, in Randall Conrad, "An Interview with Frederick Wiseman," unpublished transcript, circa 1978, 15.

52. Eames, tr. 7:41, 44; Wiseman, tr. 15:15; John Marshall, Hearings, 821–29; Heather Marshall, Hearings, 868–74.

53. Eames, tr. 7:42. According to Marshall, the company existed primarily to protect Wiseman from potentially overlapping liabilities with *The Cool World* (interview with authors, Peterborough, New Hampshire, 27 December 1986).

54. Shirley Clarke, who directed *The Cool World*, produced by Wiseman, was one of three directors of the Film Maker's Distribution Cooperative. As early as 1966, she complained about Wiseman's distribution arrangements for *The Cool World*, charging that he turned out to be much like other purely commercial producers and that she had never seen any of the profits from the film. See "What Is the New Cinema? Two Views—Paris and New York," *Film Culture*, no. 42 (1966): 59.

55. Wiseman, letter to the Fifth Moscow International Film Festival, 26 April 1967. Exhibit 44..

56. Wiseman, description of film sent to Mme. Flavia Paulon, Venice, 26 May 1967. Exhibit 51.

57. Wiseman, tr. 13:172.

58. Gaughan, tr. 4:54; Wiseman, tr. 13:178.

59. Wiseman, as quoted in Thomas R. Atkins, ed., *Frederick Wiseman* (New York: Monarch Press, 1976), 62.

60. Richardson, as quoted in Atkins, *Frederick Wiseman*, 68.

61. Wiseman, as quoted in Atkins, *Frederick Wiseman*, 73.

62. Wexler, in Ernest Callenbach and Albert Johnson, "The Danger Is Seduction: An Interview with Haskell Wexler," *Film Quarterly* 21, no. 3 (1968): 7.

63. In his testimony, Wiseman described himself as "one of the authors of a feature film shot in Boston last summer . . . [then titled] *The Crown Caper*" (Tr. 13:9). Wiseman does not list this film in his curriculum vitae. Wiseman recalls, "I met Haskell Wexler for the first time when he was in Boston as Director of Photography

for *The Thomas Crown Affair*. I worked solely on the script of the film and had nothing to do with the production" (memorandum to the authors, 4 August 1987).

64. See Leonard Maltin, *Behind the Camera: The Cinematographer's Art* (New York: New American Library, 1971), 57–60; and Dennis Schaefer and Larry Salvato, *Masters of Light: Conversations with Contemporary Cinematographers* (Berkeley: University of California Press, 1984), 247–66. Later, Wexler was the cinematographer for Milos Forman's film of Ken Kesey's novel, *One Flew over the Cuckoo's Nest*, about a mental hospital. Wiseman told us that the producers of *Cuckoo's Nest* rented a print of *Titicut Follies* and screened it repeatedly for the cast and crew before shooting began (Wiseman, in conversation with Thomas W. Benson, Bucknell University, 12 November 1985).

65. Wexler, in Callenbach and Johnson, "The Danger Is Seduction," 7.

66. Rossett deposition in *Commonwealth v. Wiseman*, 10 November 1967, 15–16.

67. *Attorney General v. The Book Named "Tropic of Cancer,"* 1984 N.E. 2d 328 (1962); 345 Mass. 11 (1962). Other relevant cases involving Grove Press include *Grove Press, Inc., v. Christenberg,* 276 F. 2d 433 (1960); *Grove Press, Inc., v. Gerstein,* 378 U.S. 577 (1964); *A Book Named "John Cleland's Memoirs of a Woman of Pleasure" v. Attorney General,* 86 S. Ct. 975 (1966).

68. De Grazia and Newman, 123. According to the 1975 Rockefeller Commission Report, Grove was the only American publisher whose activities were monitored.

69. Rossett deposition, 19.

70. Rossett deposition, 20.

71. In *Film as a Subversive Art* (New York: Random House, 1974), Vogel labels *Titicut Follies* "a major work of subversive cinema" (187).

72. Richardson, in Atkins, *Frederick Wiseman*, 68.

73. Richardson, in Atkins, *Frederick Wiseman*, 68.

74. By order of the Supreme Judicial Court of Massachussets, a statement regarding improvements at Bridgewater was added to the film in 1971.

75. Exhibit 1, p. 2.

76. Breitrose, review of *Documentary*, by Erik Barnouw, *Film Quarterly* 28, no. 4 (1975): 38.

77. Bill Nichols, *Ideology and the Image: Social Representation in the Cinema and Other Media* (Bloomington: Indiana University Press, 1981), 209.

78. Rouch, as quoted in G. Roy Levin, *Documentary Explorations: 15 Interviews with Film-Makers* (Garden City: Doubleday, 1971), 141–42.

79. Nichols, *Ideology*, 198.

80. Kalus, "Findings, Rulings, and Order for Decree," 4.

81. Wiseman, U-Mass-Boston, 6 April 1977.

82. Robb, "Focus on Life," 26.

83. Wiseman, in Conrad, "An Interview."

84. Eames, "Watching Wiseman Watch," *New York Times Magazine*, 2 October 1977, 102.

85. Jean-Claude Bringuier, as quoted in Louis Marcorelles, *Living Cinema* (New York: Praeger, 1973), 98. See Mark Roskill and David Carrier, *Truth and Falsehood in Visual Images* (Amherst: University of Massachusetts Press, 1983) for a cogent analysis of visual "truth" by an art historian and a philosopher.

86. Wiseman, as quoted in Atkins, *Frederick Wiseman*, 35–36.

87. Wiseman, as quoted in Halberstadt, "An Interview," 22.

88. Wiseman, as quoted in Deckle McLean, "The Man Who Made *Titicut Follies*," *Boston Sunday Globe Magazine*, 27 July 1969, 13.

89. Memorandum to authors, 4 August 1987.

90. Marshall interview (1984).

91. Dowd, "Popular Conventions," *Film Quarterly* 22, no. 3 (1969): 29. Dowd's speculation flows from confusion about the suicide discussion early in the film. It is not the body pictured on the television monitor, but the man being led to his cell who is (mistakenly) described as suicidal.

92. Ellsworth, 12–14. Heyer, "The Documentary Films of Frederick Wiseman: The Evolution of a Style" (Thesis, University of Texas, 1975), 28–42. We have created an outline from Heyer's lucid prose, using her vocabulary.

93. Marshall interview (1986).

94. Marshall interview (1984).

95. Cf. Robert Phillip Kolker, *A Cinema of Loneliness* (New York: Oxford University Press, 1980), 103. Kolker equates uncertainty with meaninglessness. He makes a distinction between openness and ambiguity and argues that open films engage viewers in constructing plural meanings, while ambiguous films promote passivity.

96. Wiseman, tr. 13:149. The amount of footage that was usable attests to Marshall's skill as a (direct) cinematographer.

97. Wiseman, panel discussion as part of a Wiseman retrospective at the Institute of Contemporary Art, Boston, 30 October 1977.

98. Wiseman, as quoted in Halberstadt, "An Interview," 22.

99. Elizabeth Jennings [Liz Ellsworth], "Frederick Wiseman's Films: A Modern Theory of Documentary" (Thesis, University of Wisconsin-Milwaukee, 1975), 199.

100. See Barry Salt, *Film Style and Technology: History and Analysis* (London: Starword, 1983), 345. The *Titicut Follies* averages are based on the figures provided by Ellsworth, 14–32.

101. Marshall interview (1984); Wiseman, tr. 14:117–19.

102. Wiseman, as quoted in Janet Handelman, "An Interview with Frederick Wiseman," *Film Library Quarterly* 3, no. 3 (1970): 7.

103. Wiseman, tr. 14:28, 30; Greenman, tr. 12:13–14, 53, 61; Richardson, tr. 12:118–20.

104. Arthur Knight, "Cinema Verite and Film Truth," *Saturday Review*, 9 September 1967, 44. In his testimony before the legislative hearings, Gavin called the publication *The Saturday Evening Review* (Hearings, 17).

105. Wiseman, tr. 14:29.

106. Wiseman, tr. 14:30, 33.

107. Wiseman, tr. 14:31.

108. Wiseman, memorandum to the authors, 4 August 1987.

109. Greenman, tr. 12:94.

110. Greenman, tr. 12:20, 88, 92–93.

111. Richardson, tr. 12:119.

112. Greenman, tr. 4:76.

113. Richardson, as quoted in a letter by Gavin to Volpe, itself quoted in the *Sunday Herald Traveler*, 15 October 1967, 6C.

114. Gavin, tr. 3:57.

115. Bill in Equity, docket entry no. 1, 22 September 1967, 5.

116. Equity no. 87538, docket entry no. 2, 25 September 1967. On 16 October 1967, the plaintiffs further amended their bill by adding as a party plaintiff James C. Bulcock, appearing by Gaughan.

117. Memorandum from Wiseman to the authors, 4 August 1987.

118. Wiseman, as quoted in William McGrath, " 'Titicut' Winner at Film Festival," *Boston Herald Traveler*, 15 October 1967, 7.

119. Wiseman testimony before the legislative commission, as reported by David B. Wilson, "Producer of 'Titicut' Denies Doublecross," *Boston Globe*, 25 October 1967, 25.

120. As reported by Sara Davidson, "N.Y. Justice Denies Bridgewater Film Ban," *Boston Globe*, 29 September 1967, 9.

121. "N.Y. to Show Film on Bridgewater," *Boston Herald Traveler*, 29 September 1967, 3.

122. Street, as quoted in Peter Lucas, "What Are the Rights of the Insane?" *Boston Herald Traveler*, 16 October 1967, 15.

123. Eames, tr. 7:72–73; Marshall interview (1984). In his testimony, Eames recalled a discussion, probably on September 21, at which Wiseman told him of a newspaper story reporting a claim by Gaughan that the film was subject to state approval (Tr. 7:73).

124. Eames, tr. 7:147; Marshall interview (1984). According to Wiseman, he had "shown the almost completed film to Mr. and Mrs. Marshall, Mr. and Mrs. Eames, and my wife," sometime before 27 June 1967 (memorandum to authors, 4 August 1987). Eames testified that he saw the finished film in May 1967 (Tr. 7:14).

125. Wiseman, tr. 15:36; Marshall interview (1984).

126. The figures are from Gallen's deposition, 10 November 1967, 5; the quotation is from a memo of 25 September 1967, exhibit 22. Wiseman's advance on *The Cool World* had been six thousand dollars (Wiseman, Hearings, 375).

127. Zornow deposition, 10 November 1967, 12.

128. Exhibit 22.

129. This delicate term is from the "Brief for the Respondents," 23.

130. Eames, tr. 7:76; Wiseman, tr. 15:61.

131. Rossett deposition, 20.

132. Rossett deposition, 20–21.

133. *Burstyn v. Wilson*, 343 U.S. 495 (1952). See De Grazia and Newman, *Banned Films*, 231–33.

134. "Statement by Arthur L. Mayer," in Mary Batten, "An Interview with Ephraim London," *Film Comment* 1, no. 4 (1963): 2, 19.

135. Wiseman, tr. 15:49.

136. Exhibits 24 and 23.

137. Wiseman, tr. 15:40; Eames, tr. 7:110. The Marshalls had a family fortune to protect. John's father, Laurence Kennedy Marshall, founded the Raytheon Company in 1922 and was its president until his retirement in 1950. In a memorandum to the authors, Wiseman wrote, "Marshall was frightened that his own assets would be involved. They never were. He failed to support the film because of his fear. His failure to stand by the film was extremely damaging to the defense" (4 August 1987). Marshall explained his resignation to us differently: "I didn't know what Fred had said to various people. I didn't know the obligations he'd undertaken, with respect to the film or with respect to the state, or the institution at Bridgewater, or Charlie

Gaughan. I didn't know what he'd said. And Heather and I were holding the bag on the corporation. We were the majority of this corporation and, in theory, if it was a real corporation, we would have to say 'yea' or 'nay' as to whether the film was to be released or how or what was to become of it and I didn't want to be in that position not knowing all the facts. And I had, besides that, a personal reason—that I didn't know what would happen about some of the people who had been in the film. In these hearings with that guy Robey, they are basically being evaluated to see if they're crazy, or sane enough to stand trial. And I thought, you know, what if it gets around and somebody who's going to be on the jury someday sees them in the film and thinks they're crazy or they make a bad impression on the juror and they go in the slammer when they shouldn't or the lawyers say, well, you know, we'll never get a fair trial in Massachusetts for these people and they just keep putting it off and putting it off— putting their trial off. In Bridgewater, you go there and stay there until you are adjudged competent to stand trial and it's a way of putting people away forever. It's one of the glaring loopholes, in our country anyway, in which you can get incarcerated and you go to jail, basically to jail, without ever meeting your accusers, without ever going before a court, before God and the people. And I thought, well, hell, if somebody has to spend another three years in Bridgewater because their trial keeps being postponed because of a film, that seems a little extreme. So the real reason was I just didn't know, and that was in my deposition. I think they didn't ask me to come to court because, on the one side, Fred's lawyers would be afraid I'd just tell the truth and, on the other side, because they knew I didn't have any—I thought the film was a good film. I thought it should not be changed or varied or censored" (interview with the authors, Peterborough, New Hampshire, 27 December 1986).

138. Marshall interview (1984).

139. According to Willard Van Dyke, tr. 17:10–17, *Titicut Follies* was screened either 2 or 3 September 1967. The annual seminar, in honor of Robert Flaherty, is devoted exclusively to documentary film.

140. Sara Davidson, " 'Titicut Follies' Switches Moods," *Boston Globe*, 29 September 1967, 8.

141. Advertisement, *New York Times*, 3 October 1967, 55.

142. Gallen affidavit in opposition, *Commonwealth v. Lincoln Center*, index no. 15866/67, 3.

143. Gallen affidavit, 4.

144. Information obtained from Zornow deposition, 27, *Commonwealth v. Wiseman;* and Vincent McNally, theater manager of Carnegie Hall Cinema, as quoted in Peter Lucas, "Follies Doing Only 'Fair' Business in New York," *Boston Herald Traveler,* 19 October 1967, 3.

145. Thomas C. Gallager, "Furor Sure Over 'Follies,' " *Boston Herald Traveler,* 4 October 1967, 34.

146. Advertisement, *New York Times*, 14 October 1967, 13.

147. "Brief for the Petitioners as Cross-Appellants," 7. These figures are drawn from records of Grove and Titicut produced in the course of discovery. See also tr. 18:8–16.

148. "Never Termed 'Titicut Follies' Film Superb, Says Richardson," *Boston Herald Traveler,* 30 October 1967, 6.

149. Zornow deposition, 22, 26.

150. Wiseman (Tr. 15:62) testified that he neither arranged nor knew of this

screening. Eames often traveled to Rhode Island, but the circumstances of the exhibition were not pursued in his examination.

151. Van Dyke, tr. 17:10.

152. Joseph Goldstein, tr. 16:147.

153. Zornow deposition, 24–25.

154. Wiseman interview in Rosenthal, *The New Documentary in Action*, 68.

155. Robert Healy, "Mrs. Hicks Collects the 'Anti' Votes," *Boston Globe*, 27 September 1967, 1.

156. Bud Collins, "Louise, Luis Fan Eight Batters Apiece," *Boston Globe*, 27 September 1967, 23.

157. Kane, letter to the editor, *Boston Herald Traveler*, 3 October 1967, 28.

158. Cornelius J. Noonan, "Gavin, Gaughan Face Questioning on Bridgewater Hospital Film 'Indiscretions,' " *Boston Globe*, 9 October 1967, 13.

159. "Blunder at Bridgewater," *Boston Herald Traveler*, 2 October 1967, 16.

160. Gallager, "Furor Sure Over 'Follies,' " *Boston Herald Traveler*, 4 October 1967, 34.

161. Gallager, "Where Are the Liberals?" *Boston Herald Traveler*, 6 October 1967, 18.

162. Gallager, "More Answers Required," *Boston Herald Traveler*, 12 October 1967, 26.

163. Frank Reilly and John Sullivan, "Hospital Film Maker Hit," *Boston Record American*, 12 October 1967, 2.

164. Peter Lucas, "Follies 'Double Cross' Charged," *Boston Herald Traveler*, 12 October 1967, 1.

165. Wiseman, as quoted in " 'Titicut Follies' Producer Blasts Atty. Gen. Richardson," *Boston Herald Traveler*, 13 October 1967, 10.

166. Ray Richard, "Richardson Backed Filming, Gavin Says," *Boston Globe*, 15 October 1967, 1.

167. Gallager, " 'Follies' Film Could Cost State Millions," *Boston Herald Traveler*, 17 October 1967, 20.

168. Richard, "Tuesday's 'Titicut Follies' Showing May Cause Legislative Fury," *Boston Globe*, 15 October 1967, 39.

169. Reilly, "Bridgewater Hearing Set," *Boston Record American*, 13 October 1967, 10.

170. John H. Fenton, "Film Stirs Furor in Massachusetts," *New York Times*, 18 October 1967, 40.

171. Richard, "Film Probers Seek Information in N.Y.," *Boston Globe*, 21 October 1967, 4; H. Marshall, Hearings, 872.

172. Ronald A. Wysocki, "Gaughan Says State Tricked by Titicut Showing," *Boston Globe*, 18 October 1967, 3.

173. Reilly and Gordon Hillman, "Sex Criminals Filmed after Doctor's Bar," *Boston Record American*, 27 October 1967, 5.

174. Reilly and Hillman, "Top 'Follies' Figures in Heavy Grilling," *Boston Record American*, 27 October 1967, 5.

175. Bob Creamer, "Wiseman Assails Prober," *Boston Herald Traveler*, 23 October 1967, 3.

176. Lucas, "Wiseman Says Volpe Barred from Preview," *Boston Record American*, 31 October 1967, 3.

177. "Claim Follies Filmed Just to Make \$\$," *Boston Record American*, 31 October 1967, 3.

178. "Claim Follies Filmed Just to Make \$\$," *Boston Record American*, 31 October 1967.

179. On four occasions (at a funeral mass for a prisoner and at three rehearsals or performances of the variety show "The Titicut Follies"), Asch and Marshall both operated cameras. According to documentary filmmaker Ed Pincus, his partner David Neuman took sound one day with the BFC crew. Pincus interview in Levin, 367.

180. Richard, "Cameraman Told to Get a Lawyer," *Boston Globe*, 3 November 1967, 10.

181. Richard, "Cameraman," 10.

182. Wiseman, press conference held 14 October 1967.

183. Gallager, *Boston Herald Traveler*, 18 October 1967, 66.

184. Robert F. Muse, counsel for the plaintiffs in *Cullen v. Grove* was one of several who used the expression.

185. Senator Beryl Cohen, as quoted in Richard, "Cameraman Told to Get a Lawyer."

186. Lucas, " 'Follies' Aide Filmed Fernald," *Boston Herald Traveler*, 4 November 1967, 1.

187. Richardson, as quoted in "State to Probe Fernald Filming," *Boston Globe*, 5 November 1967, 2.

188. Asch, as quoted in " 'Titicut' Cameraman Denies Taking Fernald School Pix," *Boston Herald Traveler*, 8 November 1967, 72.

189. Gavin, tr. 3:28.

190. Wiseman, tr. 14:29–30.

191. Eames, tr. 7:111; Marshall interview (1984).

192. *Boston Herald Traveler*, 15 October 1967, 6

193. *Boston Herald Traveler*, 27 October 1967, 1.

194. Wiseman, as quoted in Richard, "Richardson 'Excluded' Volpe from Seeing Film—Wiseman," *Boston Globe*, 27 October 1967, 16.

195. St. Clair, tr. 3:124.

196. *Boston Record American*, 18 October 1967, 29. Harold Banks quoted Wiseman: "Since I grew up in a household where 'things legal' were discussed with some frequency, neither my family nor myself were particularly surprised when I decided to become a lawyer. It would not be honest if I did not admit that this familial condition probably determined my choice. Coupled with this seemingly negative reason is a strong desire to spend my time at a profession that will require the active use of my mind in solving technical and difficult legal problems, as well as affording some chance to become skillful in understanding—coping with human problems. I, of course, did not overlook the possibility of remunerative reward."

Wiseman's sponsors at the bar were attorney David M. Watchmaker and Superior Court Judge Lewis Goldberg. Both men were long-time friends of attorney Jacob L. Wiseman, the applicant's father, and had known Fred Wiseman, then twenty-four years old, since his birth. Wiseman took the Massachusetts Bar Examination in July 1954 and December 1954. He passed the December 1954 exam. His applications (nos. 54175 and 54439) are filed in the office of the clerk of the Supreme Judicial Court in Boston.

197. Reporters returned to their filed accounts of the 24 April 1967 visit.

198. Harold Banks, *Boston Herald Traveler*, 1 November 1967, 20.

199. Richard, "Confident Film Maker," *Boston Globe*, 26 October 1967, 2.

200. Gallager, "Rep. Kane Was Financial Backer for Earlier Wiseman Documentary," *Boston Herald Traveler*, 22 October 1967, 2.

201. "Confident Film Maker," 26 October 1967, 2.

202. "Tempest in a Snakepit," *Newsweek*, 4 December 1967, 109.

203. "Comr. Gavin Guarded after Acid Threat," *Boston Record American*, 21 October 1967, 1.

204. See Anderson, "Documentary Dilemmas: An Analytic History of Frederick Wiseman's *Titicut Follies*" (Ph.D. diss., University of Massachusetts, 1984), 284–91, for a more complete description of newspaper coverage.

205. *Boston Globe*, 30 September 1967, 6.

206. *Boston Globe*, 18 October 1967, 23; 19 October 1967, 17; 20 November 1967, 14.

207. *Boston Globe*, 29 October 1967, 26.

208. Although supportive enough to appear as a witness for the defense in *Commonwealth v. Wiseman*, Boston print and television newsman Louis Lyons made no mention of the *Titicut Follies* story in his history of the *Globe* told through an examination of its most important stories. *Newspaper Story: One Hundred Years of the Boston Globe* (Cambridge: Belknap Press, 1971).

209. The academic was G. D. Wiebe, " 'Follies' Film Neither Lurid Nor Shocking," *Boston Herald Traveler*, 2 November 1967, 21; the analysis was by James Southwood, "The Story behind 'Titicut Follies' Row," *Sunday Herald Traveler*, 8 October 1967, 57.

210. National press attention to *Titicut Follies* from the fall of 1967 through 1969 included: Arthur Knight, "Cinema Verite," 44; "Bay State in Move to Bar Prison Film," *New York Times*, 27 September 1967, 42; "Cinema: Festival Action, Side Show Action, *Titicut Follies*," *Time*, 29 September 1967, 101; "Court Here Refuses to Bar Film at New York Film Festival," *New York Times*, 29 September 1967, 55; "Controversial Film to Have Six Day Run at Cinema Rendezvous," *New York Times*, 30 September 1967, 27; Vincent Canby, "The Screen: *Titicut Follies* Observes Life in a Modern Bedlam," *New York Times*, 4 October 1967, 38; Linda Searbrough, " 'Follies' Is Jolting Film about Insane," *New York Daily News*, 4 October 1967, 89; reviews of *Titicut Follies* by "Byro" in *Variety* and Judith Crist on "Today," NBC-TV, reprinted in *FilmFacts* 60 (1967): 314–16; John H. Fenton, "Film Stirs Furor in Massachusetts," *New York Times*, 18 October 1967, 40; review of *Titicut Follies* in *Film Society Review*, October 1967, 17–19; William Wolf, "A Sane Look at an Insane Situation," *Cue*, 21 October 1967; Joseph Morgenstern, "Movies: Bedlam Today," *Newsweek*, 23 October 1967, 100–101; Brendan Gill, "The Current Cinema," *The New Yorker*, 28 October 1967, 166–67; Robert Hatch, "Films," *The Nation*, 30 October 1967, 446; review of *Titicut Follies* in *Films in Review*, November 1967, 580; Andrew Sarris, review of *Titicut Follies* in *The Village Voice*, 9 November 1967, 33; "*Titicut Follies*," *America*, 11 November 1967, 539; Richard Schickel, "The Frightful Follies of Bedlam: *Titicut Follies*," *Life*, 1 December 1967, 12; "U.S. Court Refuses to Ban *Titicut Follies* to Public," *New York Times*, 1 December 1967, 52; "Tempest in a Snakepit," *Newsweek*, 4 December 1967, 109; Robert Coles, "Stripped Bare at the Follies," *The New Republic*, 20 January 1968, 18, 28–30; separate "Correspondence" from Ronald Kessler, Elliot Richardson, and Robert Coles, *The New Republic*,

10 February 1968, 35–36; Wilfred Sheed, "Films," *Esquire,* March 1968, 52, 55; Deac Rossell, *"Titicut Follies," Christianity and Crisis,* 18 March 1968, 43–45; Harvey G. Cox, "Massachusetts Movie Ban," in "The Playboy Forum," *Playboy,* March 1968, 45; *"Titicut* Ban Affirmed," in "Forum Newsfront," *Playboy,* April 1968, 62; "Film-Festival Firsts for *Follies,*" in "Forum Newsfront," *Playboy,* June 1968, 54; Paul Bradlow, "Two . . . But Not of a Kind, A Comparison of Two Controversial Documentaries about Mental Illness, *Warrendale* and *Titicut Follies," Film Comment* 5, no. 3 (1969): 60–61; Dowd, "Popular Conventions," 28–31; *"Titicut Follies* Is Banned to Bay State Public," *New York Times,* 25 June 1969, 41.

211. Docket entry no. 15, 7.

212. Wiseman, "Letters: Focusing again on *Titicut Follies," Civil Liberties Review* 1, no. 3 (1974): 151.

213. Letter to Carolyn Anderson, 11 October 1979.

214. Gallager, "Where Are the Liberals?" *Boston Herald Traveler,* 6 October 1967, 18.

215. Gallager, "Beatniks Aided, Insane Aren't," *Boston Herald Traveler,* 18 October 1967, 66. For the same criticism, more calmly stated, see "Titicut Follies: A Grotesque Invasion," *Boston Herald Traveler,* 20 October 1967, 18.

216. Berlin, as quoted in Harold Banks, "Today's Periscope: Baron Watch Went Deep," *Boston Record American,* 28 October 1967, 19.

217. Wiseman, as quoted in Westin, "You Start Off with a Bromide," 64, 66.

218. See Aryeh Neier (executive director of ACLU), "Letters," *Civil Liberties Review* 2, no. 2 (1975): 151.

219. Berlin's deposition was taken on 9 November 1967. See docket entry no. 36. The deposition transcript is not included in the case file.

220. " 'Titicut Follies' Movie Case Presents Complicated Issues," *Civil Liberties in the Bay State,* Winter 1968, 5. All subsequent quotations are from this source. See also "Civil Liberties Union Postpones Stand on 'Follies,' " *Boston Globe,* 29 October 1967, 26, and Bill McGrath, "CLU Explains Its Silence on 'Follies' Film," *Boston Herald Traveler,* 29 October 1967, 20.

221. 356 Mass. 251, 249 N.E. 2d 610 (1969).

222. Wiseman, as quoted in Westin, "You Start Off with a Bromide," 66. The *Titicut Follies* controversy goes unmentioned in the *American Civil Liberties Union Annual Reports,* vol. 7 (New York: Arno Press and The New York Times, 1970).

223. "Elliot Richardson on Titicut Follies," a letter originally appearing in the *Civil Liberties Review* 1, no. 3 (1974): 150, and reprinted in Atkins, *Frederick Wiseman,* 67.

224. Wiseman, in Atkins, *Frederick Wiseman,* 69.

225. Feingold, *"Titicut Follies* and Competing Rights," *Civil Liberties Review,* 2, no. 2 (1974): 145–51.

226. Telephone interview between Carolyn Anderson and Roberts, 3 June 1977. Attached to Wiseman's personal affidavit on behalf of his 1987 motion to remove the ban from exhibiting *Titicut Follies* to the general public was a letter of support sent to Wiseman from Harvey A. Silvergate, president of the CLUM Board of Directors. See docket entry no. 2512, 20 July 1987. While Wiseman's July 1987 motion was under consideration, CLUM was a plaintiff in court action against the Commonwealth. On 14 September 1987, Suffolk Superior Court Judge James P. Lynch, Jr. ordered changes in procedures used for isolating violent and suicidal patients at Bridgewater State Hospital in response to the CLUM suit, one of a series of Bridgewater maltreat-

ment suits filed by CLUM since the late sixties. See "CLUM Wins Major Victory in Bridgewater State Hospital Suit," *The Docket* 17, no. 4 (1987): 1, 6; and Diane E. Lewis, " 'Pain in the Neck' Lawyer Reaps Gains for Bridgewater Patients," *Boston Globe*, 6 December 1987, 37, 42, 43.

227. Richardson, in response to a series of questions asked by Carolyn Anderson during Richardson's U.S. Senate campaign appearance at the University of Massachusetts-Amherst, 27 April 1984.

228. Reitman, "Past, Present, and Future," in *The Pulse of Freedom: American Liberties, 1920–1970s*, ed. Alan Reitman (New York: Norton, 1975), 334.

229. "How CLUM's Legal Program Works," *The Docket* 13, no. 3 (1983): 2.

230. N.Y. Civil Rights Law 50, 51 (Mc Kinney 1948).

231. 276 F. Supp. 727 (S.D.N.Y. 1967).

232. Muse, as quoted in "4 Guards File Suit vs. Movie," *Boston Globe*, 2 November 1967, 9.

233. Crist, *Filmfacts*, 316.

234. Plaintiffs, as quoted in the Mansfield decision, attached as Appendix B to the Wiseman-BFC brief on appeal before the Massachusetts Supreme Judicial Court, in *Massachusetts Reports, Papers, and Briefs*, 356, part 5 (20–24 June 1969), 362–66.

235. 385 U.S. 374 (1967).

236. As paraphrased by Mansfield, 364.

237. Gallager, " 'Follies' Film Could Cost State Millions," *Boston Herald Traveler*, 17 October 1967, 29.

238. "Comment: The 'Titicut Follies' Case: Limiting the Public Interest Privilege," *Columbia Law Review* 70, no. 2 (1970): 360, n. 4.

239. Richard W. Daly, "Guards Plan Suit in N.Y. to Block 'Titicut Follies,' " *Boston Herald Traveler*, 31 October 1967, 1.

240. "5 Million Sought in 'Titicut Follies' Case," *Boston Globe*, 4 November 1969, 33.

241. Sullivan, as quoted in Joseph Harvey, "Titicut Follies Survives $5M Suit," *Boston Globe*, 2 March 1972, 10. Subsequent quotations from the Sullivan decision are from this article.

242. Donald M. Gillmor and Jerome A. Barron, *Mass Communication Law: Cases and Comment*, 4th ed. (St. Paul: West Publishing Company, 1984), 311.

243. Telephone interview between Carolyn Anderson and Ellen Feingold, 23 May 1977. Attorney Feingold was the instructor of the class mentioned.

244. Ford's order is docket entry no. 21, filed 23 October 1967. A pretrial conference was held on 17 November 1967; the trial began 20 November 1967.

245. Nathan Cobb, "James St. Clair," *Boston Globe*, 13 February 1983, A17–18. Much less well known is the fact that St. Clair was also approached to serve as chief litigator for the prosecution of the Nixon case.

246. St. Clair, tr. 1:23. See docket entry no. 55, "Petition for Removal," Civil Action no. 67–846-F.

247. Holmes, from *The Common Law* (1881), cited in Arthur R. Miller, *The Assault on Privacy: Computers, Data Banks and Dossiers* (Ann Arbor: Michigan University Press, 1971), 210.

248. Kalus's obituary headline ("Judge Harry Kalus, 76—He Barred Showing of 'Titicut Follies' in Mass," *Boston Globe*, 8 October 1980, 49) speaks to the importance

of this case in his judicial career. The *Boston Herald American* obituary (8 October 1980, C10) does not mention the case.

249. Interview between Carolyn Anderson and Francis X. Orfanello, executive secretary to administrative judges, Suffolk Superior Court, 17 February 1984.

250. Perry made the objection (noted) to a question asked of G. A. Wiebe, tr. 16:133; Kalus, tr. 16:192.

251. Hanify, tr. 2:22.

252. See docket entry no. 14. The Marshall deposition was scheduled for 2 November 1967. See Marshall's testimony before the legislative hearing, also 2 November 1967, 800–840, 852–67.

253. The length is described in William F. Doherty, "Wiseman Tells His Side in 'Titicut Follies' Dispute," *Boston Herald Traveler*, 6 December 1967, 2.

254. Tartakoff, tr. 8:92.

255. The count is by a correction officer, George J. Lepine, Jr., who saw the film in New York City and dictated a description into a tape recorder as he viewed *Titicut Follies*, tr. 5:96–117.

256. See Ellsworth, shots 53–57, pp. 20–21.

257. Docket entry no. 35; the deposition was scheduled for 16 November 1967. The absence of a deposition in the case file does not prove that none was taken, only that its contents were not used as part of the trial record. It seems fair to assume that Bulcock would not have been permitted to leave Bridgewater for his deposition.

258. See David M. O'Brien, *The Public's Right to Know* (New York: Praeger, 1981), for an elaboration of this thesis.

259. The affidavit was filed in U.S. District Court, New York (Civil Action no. 4246). See Wiseman, tr. 15:113–15.

260. Kalus, tr. 15:158–9. See Barbara Sweeney, "The Use of Social Science Research in Supreme Court Opinions Related to Obscenity" (Ph.D. diss., University of Massachusetts, 1981).

261. Kalus [paraphrased], tr. 17:52–54.

262. Don R. Pember, *Mass Media Law*, 3d ed. (Dubuque: Brown, 1984), 10.

263. "Findings, Rulings, and Order for Decree," 4–5.

264. Findings, 13.

265. Findings, 5–6.

266. Findings, 14.

267. Docket entry no. 106.

268. "Brief for the Petitioners as Cross-Appellants," 17, *Commonwealth v. Wiseman*, 356 Mass. 251, 249 N.E.2d 610 (1969). All subsequent references to the appeal are to this source.

269. "Brief for the Respondents," 101–3.

270. "Brief for the Petitioners as Appellees," i–ii.

271. "Brief *Amicus Curiae* of the American Sociological Association, Inc.," 1–11.

272. "Brief for *Amicus Curiae* of the American Orthopsychiatric Association," 21–22.

273. "Brief *Amicus Curiae* of the Civil Liberties Union of Massachusetts," 1–23.

274. 249 N.E.2d at 615, 356 Mass. at 258.

275. 249 N.E.2d at 619, 356 Mass. at 264.

276. 249 N.E.2d at 619, 356 Mass. at 263. Wiseman added the required statement

about "changes and improvements," but he preceded the statement with the order itself.

277. David L. Bennett and Philip Small, "Case Comments," *Suffolk Law Review* 4, no. 1 (1969): 204.

278. "Recent Cases," *Harvard Law Review* 83, no. 7 (1970): 1730–31, n. 42.

279. "Comment: The 'Titicut Follies' Case: Limiting the Public Interest Privilege," 359, 371.

280. "Producers Sue to Show Film," *Boston Globe*, 1 July 1971, 25. The headline is an error, in that it was not Wiseman who sued. Wiseman did not initiate the court action and he said he was unaware of its existence (telephone conversation with Carolyn Anderson, 9 May 1977).

281. According to Judge Murray's clerk, the case (Civil Action no. 71–1341-M) was dismissed 31 March 1972.

282. See docket entries no. 1183, 1184.

283. Wiseman, in telephone conversation with Carolyn Anderson, 14 November 1983.

284. 385 U.S. 374 (1967).

285. 398 U.S. 960 (1970); 400 U.S. 954 (1970).

286. 398 U.S. at 961–63.

287. In a memorandum to the authors, Wiseman recalled the circumstances of Douglas's absence from the vote: "Douglas recused himself because Gerald Ford had instigated hearings in Congress in an attempt to impeach Douglas. Douglas was being very careful and was cautious even about such a remote connection as publishing a chapter of a book in the Evergreen Review" (4 August 1987).

288. "Public ban stays on 'Titicut' film," *Boston Globe*, 7 December 1970, 3.

289. "Brief for the Respondent Wiseman in Support of Motion to Amend Final Decree After Rescript," docket entry no. 2511, 23 July 1987.

290. "Response of Commonwealth of Massachusetts to Motion to Amend Final Decree After Rescript," docket entry no. 2522A, 12 August 1987.

291. "Order," Judge Andrew G. Meyer, docket entry no. 2604, 17 December 1987, 2.

292. *Boston Herald*, 4 January 1988, 38; *Boston Globe*, 4 January 1988, 4; *Daily Hampshire Gazette*, 4 January 1988, 28.

293. Telephone interview between Carolyn Anderson and Stephen A Jonas, deputy chief, Public Protection Bureau, Department of the Attorney General, 4 April 1988.

294. "Order," docket entry no. 2604, 5.

295. Kent Carroll, telephone interview with Carolyn Anderson, 12 April 1977.

296. Carroll interview.

297. Wiseman, in Levin, *Documentary Explorations*, 327.

298. Wiseman, in Westin, "You Start Off with a Bromide," 67.

299. 275 N.E.2d at 148.

300. These instructions are printed in the fall 1987 promotional brochure from Zipporah Films, 15. Since 1977, directions have varied only slightly, the greatest substantive change being the receipt of the statement of intent from ten to twelve days. Before 1983, rental instructions for *Titicut Follies* were mailed separately and were not included in the Zipporah brochure itself. All subsequent references to

Zipporah prices and policies use these annual brochures as their source of information, unless otherwise indicated.

301. Bradlow, "Two, But Not of a Kind," 60.

302. Telephone interview between Carolyn Anderson and Kevin Crain, director of the Center for Media Development, University of Massachusetts-Boston, 13 April 1977.

303. *Five College Calendar* 15, no. 8 (March 29–April 16, 1977).

304. Interview between Carolyn Anderson and Jerry Sousa, 6 May 1982. See also Alice Dembner, "Prison Reform Ex-Con's Goal," *Daily Hampshire Gazette* (Northampton, MA) 24 January 1983, 1, 7.

305. Information provided by Zipporah director of distribution, Karen Konicek, 5 April 1984.

306. Telephone interview between Carolyn Anderson and Iris Berry, secretary at Zipporah Films, 26 April 1977.

307. Wiseman, in Rosenthal, *The New Documentary in Action*, 68. *High School* was broadcast on WNET-TV. On 25 August 1987, ABC-TV broadcast a special *Nightline* report on *Titicut Follies* and the conditions at Bridgewater State Hospital. Included in the program were clips from what host Ted Koppel called a "bootleg print" of *Titicut Follies*. Wiseman, one of several people interviewed on the show, objected to this use of *Titicut Follies*. See Diane E. Lewis, " 'Nightline' Airs Segments from 'Titicut Follies,' " *Boston Globe*, 27 August 1987, 66. Scenes from *Titicut Follies* were rebroadcast (28 September–2 October 1987) during a five-part series, "Inside Bridgewater," produced by WCVB-TV, the Boston ABC affiliate. According to reporter Ron Allen, the local station obtained "unlimited access" to Bridgewater while filming its report. Footage from the WCVB series was combined with clips from *Titicut Follies* on a *World News Tonight* (ABC-TV) report on Bridgewater on 12 October 1987.

308. Brochure for Zipporah Films, Fall 1987, 14. Wiseman's minimum lecture fee is $1,700, plus expenses.

309. Information regarding these showings was obtained in interviews by Carolyn Anderson with John Morrison, co-owner of the Pleasant Street Theater, on 1 March and 9 May 1977.

310. In a memorandum to the authors, Wiseman wrote, "Neither I nor Zipporah Films had any connection with the flyer or the advertisements other than to insist that restrictions on the audience be made absolutely clear" (4 August 1987).

311. Telephone interview between Carolyn Anderson and Michael Leja, 4 October 1977.

312. Interviews between Carolyn Anderson and Deac Rossell, May 1980 and July 1982. Rossell, Film Coordinator, Boston Museum of Fine Arts, and co-organizer of the Boston 350 screenings, provided an account of the actions of the attorney general's office.

313. Fran Weil, "Jack Lemmon Kicks Off Jubilee 350 Film Festival," *Boston Herald American*, 7 May 1980, 85.

314. Michael Blowen, "What Do Jack Lemmon, the Brink's Job, and Thirty Five Cents Have in Common?" *Boston Globe* "Calendar," 8 May 1980, 12.

315. Fran Weil, " 'Titicut Follies' Showing Set in Hub, Despite Ban," *Boston Herald American*, 8 May 1980, A 3.

316. "Movie Banned in 1967 Will Be Shown," *Daily Hampshire Gazette,* 9 May 1980, 4.

317. *Boston Herald American,* 11 May 1980, D 11.

318. Docket entry no. 1184, 2.

319. Docket entry no. 1183.

320. Michael Blowen, "Some Told Lies to See 'Titicut,' " *Boston Globe,* 13 May 1980, 17.

321. Unidentified spokesperson from Zipporah Films, as quoted in Blowen, "Some Told Lies," 17.

322. "Commonwealth's Request for Production of Documents," docket entry no. 1193, 2.

323. Docket entry no. 1193, 2–3.

324. Ned Rifkin, "Drama of the Real: The Films of Frederick Wiseman," program notes at Wiseman retrospective sponsored by the Institute of Contemporary Art, Boston, 13–28 October 1982.

325. The file, last checked 27 May 1988, listed docket entry no. 2726, dated 27 May 1988, as its most recently entered item. The number 2726 refers to the total number of entries in the case file. Beginning with entry no. 139, dated 17 July 1974, the entries are all exhibition statements, until entry no. 2511, filed 23 July 1987. (Entry no. 2511 was a motion by Wiseman to amend the "Final Decree after Rescript.") Other motions, an affidavit, and two orders pertaining to Wiseman's motion of July 1987 were also entered in 1987 and 1988. Usually, but not always, there are two entries for each showing of *Titicut Follies.* The first is a statement from Zipporah Films indicating date, place, and audience for a scheduled screening. The second statement indicates that a showing took place or, less often, that it was canceled.

326. See Levin, *Documentary Explorations,* and Alan Rosenthal, *The Documentary Conscience: A Casebook in Film Making* (Berkeley: University of California Press, 1980).

327. Galliher, "The Life and Death of Liberal Criminology," *Contemporary Crises* 2 (1978): 251.

328. Galliher, "Social Scientists' Ethical Responsibilities: Looking Up Meekly," *Social Problems* 27 (1980): 298–308.

329. Wiseman, as cited in Westin, "You Start Off with a Bromide," 64; Levin, *Documentary Explorations,* 319–20; Atkins, *Frederick Wiseman,* 43–44; and telephone conversation with Carolyn Anderson, 14 November 1983. According to cinematographer John Davey, consent was obtained from the parents of handicapped children in the *Deaf* and *Blind* series (interview with the authors, London, 14 October 1986).

330. Murray Wax, "Paradoxes of 'Consent' to the Practices of Fieldwork" *Social Problems* 27 (1980): 282.

331. Karl Heider, *Ethnographic Film* (Austin: University of Texas Press, 1976), 120–21.

332. See Charles Cooley, "Looking-Glass Self," in *Symbolic Interaction: A Reader in Social Psychology,* ed. Jerome Manis and Bernard Meltzer, 3d ed. (Boston: Allyn and Bacon, 1978), 169–70.

333. Pryluck, "Ultimately We Are All Outsiders: The Ethics of Documentary Filming," *Journal of the University Film Association* 28, no. 1 (1976): 28.

334. Gaughan, personal correspondence with Carolyn Anderson, 9 May 1977.

335. Chasen, as quoted in Peter Lucas, "Film Harms Inmates, Says Doctor," *Boston Herald Traveler*, 24 October 1967, 1.

336. Telephone interviews between Carolyn Anderson and Dave Haley, assistant director, Department of Correction, 4 May and 9 May 1977.

337. Telephone interview between Carolyn Anderson and Ken Colpan, counsel to the psychiatric staff, Institute of Law and Psychiatry, McLean Hospital, 17 May 1977.

338. Telephone interview between Carolyn Anderson and Michael Perleman, Director of Mental Health for Western Massachusetts, 1971–74, 7 May 1977.

339. Information on changes obtained from Charles Gaughan, "Bridgewater State Hospital," 29 April 1977, enclosure in correspondence with Carolyn Anderson.

340. Wiseman, as quoted in Atkins, *Frederick Wiseman*, 56.

341. Wiseman, panel discussion at the Institute of Contemporary Art Retrospective, Boston, 3 October 1977.

342. "Affidavit of Frederick Wiseman," docket entry no. 2512, 20 July 1987, 6. In other contexts, Wiseman continues to describe his early notions about the film's role in social change as naive. In December 1987, he told a North Adams State College audience that "there is no direct correlation between any work and social change" (David Tyler, "Bridgewater Filmmaker Defends His Freedom of Expression," *The Transcript*, 2 December 1987, 3).

343. Gilligan, as quoted in Robb, "Focus on Life," 30–31.

344. Wiseman, as quoted in Robb, "Focus on Life," 30.

345. Robb, "Focus on Life," 31.

346. Richardson, *The Creative Balance: Government, Politics, and the Individual in America's Third Century* (New York: Holt, Rinehart & Winston, 1976).

347. Kane, telephone conversation with Carolyn Anderson, 16 June 1982.

348. Marshall interview (1984).

349. John Marshall and Emilie De Brigard, "Idea and Event in Urban Film," in *Principles of Visual Anthropology*, ed. Paul Hockings (The Hague: Mouton, 1975), 138.

350. Eames, "Watching Wiseman Watch," 102.

351. Exhibit 3, 3.

Chapter 3. *High School*

1. Ira Halberstadt, "An Interview with Fred Wiseman," in *Nonfiction Film: Theory and Criticism*, ed. Richard Meran Barsam (New York: Dutton, 1976), 303.

2. Wayne C. Booth, *The Rhetoric of Fiction*, 2d ed. (Chicago: University of Chicago Press, 1983).

3. Among the critics of *High School*, see Richard Meran Barsam, *Nonfiction Film: A Critical History* (New York: Dutton, 1973), 275–77. But Barsam garbles some of the details of the film and misses the point of others. Stephen Mamber, *Cinema Verite in America: Studies in Uncontrolled Documentary* (Cambridge: MIT Press, 1974), 224–29, has a fuller commentary on *High School* but fails to integrate the elements of the film, partly because of an a priori claim that "the events in cinema verite are uncontrolled and editing generally attempts to avoid the imposition of value judgments" (228). Our view of the film differs from the quantitative generic analysis offered by Bruce Gronbeck in "Celluloid Rhetoric: On Genres of Documentary," in

Form and Genre: Shaping Rhetorical Action, ed. Karlyn Kohrs Campbell and Kathleen Hall Jamieson (Falls Church, VA: Speech Communication Association, 1978), 139–61. See also Thomas R. Atkins, "The Films of Frederick Wiseman: American Institutions," *Sight and Sound* 43 (1974): 232–35; Donald E. McWilliams, "Frederick Wiseman," *Film Quarterly* 24, no. 1 (1970): 17–26; Stephen Mamber, "The New Documentaries of Frederick Wiseman," *Cinema* 6, no. 1 (1970): 33–39; Bill Nichols, "Fred Wiseman's Documentaries: Theory and Structure," *Film Quarterly* 31, no. 3 (1978): 15–28; Susan Swartz, "The Real Northeast," *Film Library Quarterly* 6, no. 1 (1972–73): 12–15.

4. In an interview with Alan Rosenthal, Wiseman spoke at length about the theme of power. "A high school, like any institution, is a self-contained society and you have to hunt out the places where power is exercised. That's where you're going to find the real values of the institution expressed. In one way the film is organized around the contrast between the formal values of openness, trust, sensitivity, democracy, and understanding, and the actual practice of the school which is quite authoritarian." Rosenthal, *The New Documentary in Action: A Casebook in Film Making* (Berkeley: University of California Press, 1971), 71.

5. Rosenthal, *The New Documentary in Action,* 70.

6. The illustrations in figure 3–2 are line drawings representing frames from *High School.* Subsequent references to numbered frames will be to the drawings in figure 3–2.

7. Rosenthal, *The New Documentary in Action,* 73.

8. This administrator is referred to in the transcript and in various Wiseman interviews as the "dean of discipline," but this phrase never appears in the film itself, and so we will not use it in the text, since the audience, whose responses we are trying to track, does not learn of it.

9. For descriptions of the double bind see Gregory Bateson, Don D. Jackson, Jay Haley, and John Weakland, "Toward a Theory of Schizophrenia," *Behavioral Science* 1 (1956): 251–64; John H. Weakland, "The 'Double-Bind' Hypothesis of Schizophrenia and Three-Party Interaction," in *The Etiology of Schizophrenia,* ed. Don D. Jackson (New York: Basic Books, 1960), 373–88; Albert E. Scheflen, with Alice Scheflen, *Body Language and Social Order: Communication as Behavioral Control* (Englewood Cliffs, NJ: Prentice Hall, 1972), 184–98; Carlos E. Sluzki and Donald C. Ransom, eds., *Double Bind: The Foundation of the Communicational Approach to the Family* (New York: Grune and Stratton, 1976); Milton M. Berger, ed., *Beyond the Double Bind: Communication and Family Systems, Theories, and Techniques with Schizophrenics* (New York: Brunner/Mazel, 1978). An especially clear explanation of the double bind and its relation to paradoxical communication is found in Paul Watzlawick, Janet Helmick Beavin, and Don D. Jackson, *Pragmatics of Human Communication* (New York: Norton, 1967), 187–229. We are not arguing that Wiseman imposes the double-bind theory on his material. In fact, in describing his working methods, Wiseman has often said, disparagingly, that he makes little use of social science. But Wiseman has discovered (or created) a structure in his material that is remarkably similar to the double bind. Wiseman's structure and the double-bind hypothesis do seem to offer some confirmation of one another and are likely to exercise a forceful appeal to audiences whose own experience of social institutions has been double binding.

10. Albert E. Scheflen, "Quasi-Courtship Behavior in Psychotherapy," *Psychiatry*

28 (1965); reprinted in Shirley Weitz, ed., *Nonverbal Communication: Readings with Commentary* (New York: Oxford University Press, 1974), 192–93.

11. Desmond Morris, Peter Collett, Peter Marsh, and Marie O'Shaughnessy, *Gestures: Their Origin and Distribution* (New York: Stein and Day, 1979), 100–105.

12. Scheflen, "Quasi-Courtship Behavior in Psychotherapy," 186.

13. Barsam, *Nonfiction Film: A Critical History*, 276; Gronbeck, "Celluloid Rhetoric," 147; Mamber, *Cinema Verite in America*, 227–28; Ed Pincus in G. Roy Levin, *Documentary Explorations: 15 Interviews with Film-makers* (Garden City: Doubleday, 1971), 366; Harvey G. Cox, "High School," *Tempo* 1 (15 June 1969): 12; Charles E. Fager, "Sweet Revenge," *Christian Century*, 3 September 1969, 1142; Joseph Featherstone, "High School," *The New Republic*, 21 June 1969, 30; Pauline Kael, "High School," *The New Yorker*, 18 October 1969, 202–3.

14. Janet Handelman, "An Interview with Frederick Wiseman," *Film Library Quarterly* 3, no. 3 (1970): 6. For a criticism of the film by a former student, see Swartz, "The Real Northeast."

15. Wiseman, in Westin, " 'You Start Off with a Bromide': Wiseman on Film and Civil Liberties," *Civil Liberties Review* 1, nos. 1 and 2 (1974): 61.

16. Wiseman, in Westin, "You Start Off with a Bromide," 58.

17. Rosenthal, *The New Documentary in Action*, 66–75.

18. The periods after "however" are in the original letter, which we reprint without omissions.

Chapter 4. *Basic Training.*

1. Liz Ellsworth, *Frederick Wiseman: A Guide to References and Resources* (Boston: G. K. Hall, 1979), 2. In her discussion of *Law and Order,* Ellsworth mentions that it was financed by the Ford Foundation and the Public Broadcasting Laboratory (Ellworth, 58). She later says that *Hospital* was funded by the Corporation for Public Broadcasting through a grant to NET (Ellsworth, 62). At this time, PBL was receiving its funding through the Ford Foundation (Wiseman, in telephone conversation with Thomas W. Benson, September, 1986).

2. Wiseman, quoted in Alan Westin, " 'You Start Off with a Bromide': Wiseman on Film and Civil Liberties," *Civil Liberties Review,* 1, nos. 1 and 2 (1974): 57; the interview is reprinted in *Frederick Wiseman,* ed. Thomas R. Atkins (New York: Simon and Schuster, 1976), 47–66. See also "Reminiscences of a Film Maker: Fred Wiseman on *Law and Order,*" *The Police Chief* (September 1969), 32—35.

3. Westin, 1974, "You Start Off with a Bromide," 62.

4. Bill Nichols, "Frederick Wiseman's Documentaries: Theory and Structure," in *Ideology and the Image: Social Representation in the Cinema and Other Media* (Bloomington: Indiana University Press, 1981), 220. This chapter is a slightly revised and expanded version of an essay that first appeared in *Film Quarterly* 31, no. 3 (1978): 15–28.

5. Nichols, *Ideology,* 234.

6. Nichols, *Ideology,* 235.

7. Nichols, *Ideology,* 235.

8. Wayne C. Booth, *The Rhetoric of Fiction,* 2d ed. (Chicago: University of Chicago Press, 1983).

9. Wolfgang Iser, *The Implied Reader: Patterns of Communication in Prose Fiction from Bunyan to Beckett* (Baltimore: Johns Hopkins University Press, 1974); Edwin Black, "The Second Persona," *Quarterly Journal of Speech* 56 (1970): 109–19; Umberto Eco, *The Role of the Reader: Explorations in the Semiotics of Texts* (Bloomington: Indiana University Press, 1979).

10. Wiseman, as quoted in Westin, "You Start Off with a Bromide," 56–57.

11. Aristotle, *Rhetoric*, 2.21.1395b; quoted from Lane Cooper, trans., *The Rhetoric of Aristotle* (New York: Appleton-Century-Crofts, 1932), 153–54. The antibureaucratic stance qualifies as an American bromide partly because it is used not only by antiestablishment rhetors but also, traditionally, by politicians of both the left and right, including presidential candidates of both parties, who run against "the bureaucracy."

12. Kenneth Burke, *Attitudes Toward History* (1937; reprint, Boston: Beacon Press, 1961), 225–29.

13. Paul Goodman, "Introduction to the 1970 Edition," in Alexander Berkman, *Prison Memoirs of an Anarchist* (New York: Schocken Books, 1970), n. p. Originally published in 1912, by the Mother Earth Publishing Association.

14. Nichols, *Ideology*, 208–236; Nichols, "The Voice of Documentary," *Film Quarterly* 36, no. 3 (1983): 17–30. We attribute the structural description *mosaics* to Nichols, not because he was the first critic to use this term, but because he has developed the metaphor more than any other analyst of Wiseman's films. See Stephen Mamber, "The New Documentaries of Frederick Wiseman," *Cinema* 6, no. 1 (1970): 33; and Thomas R. Atkins, "The Films of Frederick Wiseman: American Institutions," *Sight and Sound* 43, no. 4 (1974): 233, for earlier uses of the term *mosaics* applied to Wiseman's films. But Wiseman himself seems to have been the first to apply the term *mosaic* to his films. "I'm writing a script with a grant from the American Film Institute. I would like to adapt documentary techniques to a feature, using a mosaic technique so the film will not have the conventional story line with beginning, middle, and end, but will reveal the relationships of the characters to each other" (Janet Handelman, "An Interview with Frederick Wiseman," *Film Library Quarterly* 3, no. 3 [1970]: 9).

15. Ellsworth, 90. See also Elizabeth Jennings [Liz Ellsworth], "Frederick Wiseman's Films: A Modern Theory of Documentary," Master's thesis, University of Wisconsin-Milwaukee, 1975.

16. We do not wish to imply any carelessness on Ellsworth's part here. Her book is an exemplary reference work, indispensable to Wiseman scholarship, and she describes her reasons for choosing the four films for which she includes shot lists (Ellsworth, *Frederick Wiseman*, ix). She includes synopses, as well, for the four films for which she presents the more detailed shot lists. Furthermore, her critical discussions of Wiseman's work are compact, judicious, and perceptive. Figure 4–1 is from Ellsworth, *Frederick Wiseman*, 90–92. In this Figure, we have quoted directly from Ellsworth's numbering and titling of parts, from her shot numbers, and from her timings of parts. We have added, in square brackets, the corresponding scene numbers from the Zipporah transcript.

17. In figure 4–2, from the Zipporah transcript of the film, "scenes" appear to be identified from the filmmaker's perspective, as separate pieces of camera work for the editor's assembly. It seems likely that spectators would see some of these separate scenes as united. For example, scenes 18 and 19 feature instruction in dental care and appear, it seems to us, as one scene in the finished film. But because they are in

separate "locations," interior and exterior, the transcript lists them as separate. Similarly scenes 62–64 show the men's ordeal of chemical warfare training and appear, narratively, as one united scene, but the transcript lists them as three scenes: outside, inside, outside. This is not to argue with the Zipporah transcript, but simply to indicate that the most probable audience reading of the film would be likely to contain fewer than the eighty-one scenes of the Zipporah transcript.

18. This chapter makes extensive, though usually implicit, use of recent theoretical and critical work in literary and filmic narration. Rather than burden an already-long chapter with an extended review of this work, we list here several works that the reader might find helpful in pursuing further the theoretical and methodological issues raised by analysis of narrative form, but which are not cited elsewhere in the chapter. These works are only a partial list, and they do not represent a single theoretical position. They differ markedly from each other, and sometimes from the critical position elaborated in our treatment of Wiseman. Peter Brooks, *Reading for the Plot: Design and Intention in Narrative* (New York: Knopf, 1984); Seymour Chatman, *Story and Discourse: Narrative Structure in Fiction and Film* (Ithaca: Cornell University Press, 1978); Gerard Genette, *Narrative Discourse: An Essay in Method,* trans. Jane E. Lewin (Ithaca: Cornell University Press, 1980); Fredric Jameson, *The Political Unconscious: Narrative as a Socially Symbolic Act* (Ithaca: Cornell University Press, 1981); Wallace Martin, *Recent Theories of Narrative* (Ithaca: Cornell University Press, 1986); Robert Scholes, *Semiotics and Interpretation* (New Haven: Yale University Press, 1982); Robert Scholes and Robert Kellogg, *The Nature of Narrative* (London: Oxford University Press, 1966); Jane P. Tompkins, ed., *Reader-Response Criticism: From Formalism to Post-Structuralism* (Baltimore: Johns Hopkins University Press, 1980). Major sources on narration in film include: David Bordwell, *Narration in the Fiction Film* (Madison: University of Wisconsin Press, 1985); Edward R. Branigan, *Point of View in the Cinema: A Theory of Narration and Subjectivity in Classical Film* (Amsterdam: Mouton, 1984); John L. Fell, *Film and the Narrative Tradition* (1974; reprint, Berkeley: University of California Press, 1986); Bruce F. Kawin, *Mindscreen: Bergman, Godard, and First-Person Film* (Princeton: Princeton University Press, 1978); George M. Wilson, *Narration in Light: Studies in Cinematic Point of View* (Baltimore: Johns Hopkins University Press, 1986). A renewed interest in narration in rhetorical studies has been summarized by Walter R. Fisher, "Narration as a Human Communication Paradigm: The Case of Public Moral Argument," *Communication Monographs* 51 (1984): 1–22; Walter R. Fisher, "The Narrative Paradigm: An Elaboration," *Communication Monographs* 52 (1985): 347–67; Walter R. Fisher, "The Narrative Paradigm: In the Beginning," *Journal of Communication* 35, no. 4 (1985): 74–89. The *JOC* essay is part of a special symposium on *Homo narrans.* Fisher's argument has been extended in his *Human Communication as Narration: Toward a Philosophy of Reason, Value, and Action* (Columbia: University of South Carolina Press, 1987). Replies to Fisher have appeared in Robert C. Rowland, "Narrative: Mode of Discourse or Paradigm," *Communication Monographs* 54 (1987): 264–75, and Barbara Warnick, "The Narrative Paradigm: Another Story," *Quarterly Journal of Speech* 73 (1987): 172–82. It appears that Fisher is interested in narrative insofar as it serves conventionally "rhetorical" or persuasive purposes; as should be clear from our analysis of Wiseman, we are using both *rhetoric* and *narrative* in somewhat different senses.

19. *Basic Training* was photographed by William Brayne, whose work adds in

immeasurable ways to the richness and complexity of the film; in this and most other critical passages about the films, we refer to the work as "Wiseman's" as a convenient way of naming the composite implied author.

20. The political controversy surrounding the Vietnam War places special difficulties in the way of trying to construct an audience-sensitive reading of the film itself, but it does not, in principle, we think, force the critic to choose between writing about the viewer of 1971 and the viewer of, say, 1988. The film is different for these viewers, as we shall try to suggest: for example, in 1971, the whole issue of the Vietnam War was *contingent*, subject to uncertainty and to human choice. Now the war is behind us, and *Basic Training* may seem to viewers to be about a time remembered. These differences are real, and it would be self-defeating critical reductionism to write as if the text of the film timelessly determined reader response. On the other hand, there is no end to the consideration of audience differences, on the basis of gender, class, age, race, political opinion, and so on. We have tried to avoid the simplistic extremes of regarding response to Wiseman's films as either universal (determined entirely by the text) or particular (determined entirely and idiosyncratically by each individual viewer). For the point of view of the viewer in 1971, and especially for the way in which the media formed a context to which Wiseman's film might have been compared, see especially: Gilbert Adair, *Vietnam on Film: From "The Green Berets" to "Apocalypse Now"* (New York: Proteus, 1981); Steven F. Fenwick, *"Hearts and Minds:* A Case Study of a 'Propaganda' Film," 2 vols. (Ph.D. diss., University of Michigan, 1982); Todd Gitlin, *The Whole World Is Watching: The Mass Media in the Making and Unmaking of the New Left* (Berkeley: University of California Press, 1980); Daniel C. Hallin, *The "Uncensored War": The Media and Vietnam* (New York: Oxford University Press, 1986); John Hellmann, *American Myth and the Legacy of Vietnam* (New York: Columbia University Press, 1986); Timothy J. Lomperis, *"Reading the Wind": The Literature of the Vietnam War* (Durham, NC: Duke University Press, 1987); Kathleen J. Turner, *Lyndon Johnson's Dual War: Vietnam and the Press* (Chicago: University of Chicago Press, 1985). For the place of the Vietnam War in the American imagination and experience, see also Mark Baker, *Nam: The Vietnam War in the Words of the Men and Women Who Fought There* (New York: Morrow, 1981); John Balaban, *Coming Down Again* (San Diego: Harcourt Brace Jovanovich, 1985); C. D. B. Bryan, *Friendly Fire* (New York: Putnam, 1976); Philip Caputo, *A Rumor of War* (New York: Holt, Rinehart & Winston, 1977); John M. Del Vecchio, *The 13th Valley* (New York: Bantam, 1982); Gloria Emerson, *Winners and Losers: Battles, Retreats, Gains and Losses from the Vietnam War* (New York: Random House, 1976); Peter Goldman and Tony Fuller, with Richard Manning, *Charlie Company: What Vietnam Did to Us* (New York: Morrow, 1983); Michael Herr, *Dispatches* (New York: Knopf, 1977); Tim O'Brien, *Going After Cacciato* (New York: Delacorte, 1978); Tim Page, *Nam* (New York: Knopf, 1983); Al Santoli, *Everything We Had: An Oral History of the Vietnam War by Thirty-Three American Soldiers Who Fought It* (New York: Random House, 1981). But although the Vietnam War must certainly have colored responses to the film in 1971, *Basic Training* is not about the war itself, nor is the film typically mentioned in histories of popular culture about the war. But the failure to include *Basic Training* in discussions of Vietnam films may in part be owing to the larger and more general neglect of documentary film; for example, histories of Vietnam-War films also typically omit mention of such documentaries as *The Anderson Platoon* (1969) and *Time of the Locust* (1966).

21. On defamiliarization, see Robert H. Stacy, *Defamiliarization in Language and Literature* (Syracuse: Syracuse University Press, 1977); for an application of defamiliarization to film criticism, see Kristin Thompson, *Eisenstein's "Ivan the Terrible": A Neoformalist Analysis* (Princeton: Princeton University Press, 1981). On perspective by incongruity, see Kenneth Burke, *Permanence and Change: An Anatomy of Purpose*, 3d ed. (Berkeley: University of California Press, 1984), 89–96.

22. Even if it altered only our way of viewing the marching scenes, it would be a big difference: in the numbering of the Zipporah transcript, out of eighty-one scenes in the film, seventeen are devoted to marching or running.

23. In this sense, Wiseman's films transcend the "formative" and "realistic" tendencies asserted by Siegfried Kracauer, using highly complex and pleasing formal strategies that inquire into the politics of institutional life without losing the "realistic" feeling for everyday life as "unstaged," "fortuitous," "endless," and "indeterminate." Siegfried Kracauer, *Theory of Film: The Redemption of Physical Reality* (New York: Oxford University Press, 1960), 30–40, 60–74.

24. Our reading of the chaplain, as of all other characters in the films we discuss, is conjectural. Further, we are reading the chaplain in the narrative context constructed by the filmmaker and claim no special knowledge of these characters as actual people. We realize, of course, that this disclaimer does not entirely resolve the issue we raise here: the chaplain is a real person, and we are making judgments based on the actions of that real person, and useful only if true for real situations.

25. Ellsworth's synopsis mistakenly identifies the privates in scenes 57 and 58 as the same man, Private Johnson. Ellsworth, *Frederick Wiseman*, 91.

26. It has by now become impossible for the viewer to ignore, at some level of awareness, the issue of race in *Basic Training*; it has, perhaps, by now also become inappropriate for the authors of this book not to acknowledge that one's readings of this set of themes may well depend upon one's own racial identification. The authors are, partly by accident of birth and circumstance, white middle-class liberals, writing about the film of a white middle-class filmmaker. In an interview with Beatrice Berg in 1970, Wiseman referred to himself, and presumably his audience, as "we liberals." (" 'I Was Fed Up with Hollywood Fantasies,' " *New York Times*, 1 February 1970, sec. 2, 25).

27. For an account of the experience of black Americans in Vietnam, see Wallace Terry, *Bloods: An Oral History of the Vietnam War by Black Veterans* (New York: Random House, 1984); Stanley Goff and Robert Sanders, with Clark Smith, *Brothers: Black Soldiers in the Nam* (Novato, CA: Presidio Press, 1982); Morris J. MacGregor, Jr., and Bernard C. Nalty, eds., *Blacks in the United States Armed Forces*, especially vols. 12 and 13 (Wilmington: Scholarly Resources, 1977); Robert W. Mullen, *Blacks and Vietnam* (Washington: University Press of America, 1981); Bernard C. Nalty, *Strength for the Fight: A History of Black Americans in the Military* (New York: Free Press, 1986).

28. For many viewers, and perhaps for the men who were hearing these words, the sergeant's claim that the army was undefeated may have carried a special meaning in 1970–71, when American confidence in the Vietnam War was at a low ebb, when war protests continued at home, and when, according to Wallace Terry, even the troops in the field had decided they were fighting "a war they knew they would never win in the conventional sense" (Terry, *Bloods*, xvi). At the end of 1968, there had been 540,000 American troops in Vietnam; by the end of 1971 (*Basic Training* was

first broadcast in October 1971), President Nixon's policy of Vietnamization had reduced American troop strength to 140,000; the last American troops left Vietnam on March 29, 1973. Saigon fell on April 30, 1975. (These dates are from Stanley Karnow, *Vietnam: A History* [New York: Viking, 1983], 684–87.) These events, of course, are variously interpreted. For some Americans who fought in Vietnam, and for many others, there was often a sense that the loss in Vietnam was not a defeat for the army, which, they claimed, had never been allowed to employ the full resources of American power. But the army left without winning, and that, added to the notorious neglect of returning veterans, created a legacy of bitterness.

29. Though the men's marching is progressively more competent, as Wiseman displays it, there are some shots in which the rhythm of the marching feet is not in step with the left-right-left of the drill sergeants. Usually this occurs in shots so brief that the anomaly is probably not noticed by the audience, and in these scenes the rhythm is on the beat, though on the wrong foot.

30. In an apparent oversight, the Zipporah transcript identifies the speaker here as "General."

31. Wiseman declined to answer our question about whether his acknowledgment to the army was part of the process of negotiating consent to film. John O'Connor says that both the army and WNET retained the power to cut the final film. "Given Wiseman's past involvements in controversy, it may seem a bit odd that the U. S. Army gave him permission to infiltrate its basic training procedures. But, especially on the basis of *Law and Order* and *Hospital*, the army was convinced that he would be fair. It retained the right of review for questions of security and 'balance,' but the film was recently approved intact. . . . It was approved despite the fact that it did include bellowing sergeants and confused recruits and obvious racial tensions. The Army, it seems, has recognized that it must deal with problems and it feels that there is no harm in the public knowing about those problems. As for the Army as an institution, the viewer can decide for himself. . . . One footnote for the television record: the version that will be seen on TV is not intact. One brief scene—a recruit vividly describing his sex life—has been cut to protect the innocent and pacify the nervous television powers that be" (John J. O'Connor, " 'The Film Is about Killing,' " *New York Times*, 3 October 1971, sec. 2, 17). A *Life* review of the film also mentions the cutting of the scene from the television version: Cyclops, "Snapshots of the Old Army Game," *Life*, 1 October 1971, 10. Wiseman is frequently asked by audiences whether he has been forced to make cuts by public television; he replies that generally he has not. In a question-and-answer session following a lecture at Bucknell University in 1985, Wiseman said there were only two instances in which he had conflicts with television executives over possible alterations in the films: In *Law and Order*, a young man being thrashed by police officers

> calls them "motherfuckers." And . . . he calls them "motherfucker" nineteen times. . . . PBL, in its infinite wisdom, without consulting me, cut, and I discovered this about 24 hours before the broadcast, cut it so it went "mother thhhp, mother thhhp." And I got quite agitated and I made them, they wouldn't restore it to its pure form, but I made them introduce the film and end the film with the statement that the cuts were made without my knowledge, and when I found out about it, against my will, and that it was unfair to the participants in the film and to the Kansas City police department. There was a slight effort with *Hospital*, too. But they didn't succeed. In *Hospital*, . . . there's one sequence where a young man

has taken some mescaline and is then given an overdose of ipecac to throw up the mescaline. He throws up all over the place and he says "shit" a few times. I, again, never counted. And over a lobster newburg lunch at one of Boston's finest restaurants the executives of Channel Thirteen, not the people currently running it but an older group, said that they counted five "shits" and the first three were okay, but the last two were gratuitous. So I said that if they insisted that I cut those I would have a press conference and put out a press release saying that shit was okay 60 per cent of the time on public television, and that was the end of it. Those are the only two minor incidents. (Frederick Wiseman, "Twenty Years of Documentary Filmmaking," Bucknell University, 12 November 1985)

Although Wiseman allowed, or was forced to make, cuts in *Basic Training*, he has not been willing to make drastic cuts in order to have his films shown on commercial television. In a 4 June 1986 interview with Carol Rissman on WBUR-FM's *Evening Edition,* Wiseman recalled that he "has been approached a couple of times by the commercial networks." After *Basic Training* and *Welfare* were broadcast on public television, "CBS wanted to run them on *60 Minutes,*" if he would cut them to fifty-two minutes each. Wiseman said no, "because it would be a different film in fifty-two minutes." On another occasion, Wiseman withdrew from negotiations on a film deal because he was unwilling to submit to network control. Producer Dean Hargrove recalled that in 1970 or 1971 he became interested in making a movie of the novel *The Stunt Man*.

I got in contact with a producer named William Castle, who controlled the rights at that time, and they had, I believe, a screenplay done by Frederick Wiseman, who was going to direct this picture. Castle seemed to be interested in disposing of the rights, but for one reason or another I was never able to acquire them. However, the notion of Frederick Wiseman being the director of a theatrical film sounded like an interesting idea to me, so I got his phone number and I called him and I told him that I was a television producer and that I had a notion for doing a two-hour movie, which would be about a film documentarian, and the notion would be that he would actually make a documentary inside this theatrical film. . . . And I think the background I suggested was welfare, but I'm not sure. So I got hold of his phone number from someone and I called him and I told him what the idea was and he told me that he was interested in doing it. So I contacted, I think it was NBC at the time, and they were interested. It all fell apart because Wiseman, most properly, did not want to allow anyone to exercise any form of editorial control over the documentary that would be within the theatrical film— the documentary that this documentarian who would be the leading character in the narrative would be making. And, of course, that raises problems with television networks when you have to consider their broadcast standards, specifically the language, and no television studio or network is going to turn over that right to a filmmaker. They're going to reserve the right to edit the film, if necessary. And Wiseman would not accept that, which was understandable, and that was the end of that. (Dean Hargrove, interviewed by Carolyn Anderson, Chicago, 16 November 1986).

According to the eventual director of *The Stunt Man*, Richard Rush, he and screenwriter Lawrence B. Marcus knew that Wiseman had written an earlier screenplay based on the same source, but Rush and Marcus deliberately refrained from reading Wiseman's version before, during, or after production of the film (interview with Richard Rush by the authors, Boston, MA, 26 March 1988).

32. It is quite possible, even likely, that the actual reason we do not see recruits we recognize in the graduation scene is that Wiseman and his crew were not at the base long enough to record a complete cycle of basic training and were forced, therefore, to record the graduation of a different group of trainees. We have been unsuccessful in our attempts to confirm or deny this explanation. But whatever the actual case, the film itself does not prompt an explanation of its form based on a merely practical constraint. Rather, it presents itself throughout as having been designed deliberately, and therefore as inviting interpretation on that basis. It is typical of Wiseman's methods that his films invite themselves to be experienced and interpreted, not to be explained.

Chapter 5. *Essene* and *Juvenile Court*

1. Frederick Wiseman, "Psychiatry and Law: Use and Abuse of Psychiatry in a Murder Case," *The American Journal of Psychiatry* 118, no. 4 (1961): 289. Wiseman had earlier published another article about law and psychiatry: "Lawyer-Client Interviews: Some Lessons from Psychiatry," *Boston University Law Review* 39, no. 2 (1959): 181–87. When he was in his second year at Yale Law School, Wiseman wrote, with his roommate, a paper entitled "The Psychiatrist's Role in Criminal Movies." It was the first time Wiseman wrote about film (Christina Robb, "Focus on Life," *The Boston Globe Magazine*, 23 January 1983, 26). In 1975, the *American Bar Association Journal* published an interview with Wiseman on the relation between his films and his training as a lawyer: Philip and Elizabeth Nicholson, "Meet Lawyer-Filmmaker Frederick Wiseman," *American Bar Association Journal* 61, no. 3 (1975): 328–32. See also "Wiseman on *Juvenile Court*," *Journal of the University Film Association* 25, no. 3 (1973): 48–49, 58.

2. Wiseman, "Psychiatry and Law," 298.

3. Wiseman, "Psychiatry and Law," 298.

4. Wiseman, "Psychiatry and Law," 298, 299.

5. Wiseman, "Psychiatry and Law," 298.

6. Wiseman, in Alan Westin, " 'You Start Off with a Bromide': Wiseman on Film and Civil Liberties," *The Civil Liberties Review* 1, nos. 1 and 2 (1974): 52. Westin describes Wiseman's mother Gertrude as "administrative head" of the department of psychiatry at Boston Children's Hospital. One of the fullest biographical accounts of Wiseman is found in Robb's *Boston Globe Magazine* article; see also Silvia Feldman, "The Wiseman Documentary," *Human Behavior*, February 1976, 64–69.

7. The juvenile justice system is typically separated from the "criminal justice" system applied to adults. But Wiseman's film clearly seems to regard the distinction as a mere euphemism.

8. In this chapter, we shall try to conduct our analysis from the point of view of the audience, though we shall necessarily be pointing to patterns explicitly that the audience may only be attending to implicitly or partially—or not at all. There are cases where a transcript, or a later scene in the film, or a study guide or review, provides inside knowledge of a person or procedure that is not revealed to the audience in the film itself. In such cases, we shall, for the most part, leave aside such information, or refer to it only in a note, or remind the reader of its status as

outside the viewer's experience. In *Essene*, this matter is complicated further by the fundamental division in the audience between those who are familiar with the religious doctrines and rituals and those who are not. We will try to remain aware of this, and for the most part will assume not very much specialized religious training on the part of viewers and readers. In some ways, Wiseman's typical refusal to supply contextual information is made a special point in *Essene*, since most viewers are unlikely to be familiar with the word Wiseman chooses as the film's title, which refers to a monastic Jewish sect of the second century B.C. to the second century A.D. But although the obscurity of the word *essene* makes a special point of the issue of inside knowledge, it is also clear that every Wiseman film potentially divides its spectators between insiders and outsiders, and according to general social and political attitudes—an issue that cannot be swept aside by attention to "ideal" or "invited" or "intended" interpretations.

9. *Essene* was filmed at an Anglican monastery in Three Rivers, Michigan. The twenty Benedictines of this religious community "make up the sole order of this devotional and prayer group associated with the Episcopalian Church" (Robert Steele, "*Essene*," *Film News* 30 [September 1973]: 24). According to Wiseman, he attempted to film at three or four Roman Catholic monasteries, but was denied access (Eugene Rice, "*Essene*: A Documentary Film on Benedictine Community Life," *The American Benedictine Review* 24, no. 3 [1973]: 382). At the monastery in Three Rivers, the abbot said that the film making was all right with him, but that the brethren had to vote. He left Wiseman alone for the afternoon, during which time Wiseman met with each of the senior people individually. A couple of weeks later, Wiseman got a letter from the abbot saying the brethren had voted their permission (Randall Conrad, "An Interview with Frederick Wiseman," circa 1978, 10). During the filming, Wiseman and his crew were housed and fed at the monastery, according to Thomas Meehan, "The Documentary Filmmaker," *Saturday Review*, 2 December 1972, 14, 18.

10. Why this cutaway? During this two-shot of the abbot and Brother Wilfred, there is no sound. It appears that the shot is used to redirect our attention and to reestablish the convention that there are only two people present in the room, after Brother Wilfred's glance in the previous shot, perhaps at Wiseman, who was recording sound.

11. In most of this book, we have used the word *scene* to describe a dramatic unit longer than a single shot. A scene is taken to be a unit of narrative development occurring with more or less the same group of characters, in the same place, in more or less continuous time. A sequence would usually be understood to be a group of scenes, in which, for example, a group of characters were seen in a sequential dramatic unit that might involve changes in location and fairly short breaks in time. Larger breaks in time or space or dramatic action would move us to a new sequence. In most of Wiseman's films, groups of scenes do not add together into narrative sequences —from a narrative point of view, the scenes are the sequences. *Juvenile Court* presents several exceptions to this usual Wiseman construction, because here scenes do extend into narrative sequences in several key dramatic units. The language of shot-scene-sequence is borrowed from fictional feature films and is in many ways a bad fit for documentary films, whose structure is often episodic (if narrative at all) or thematic. But it would further obscure the realities of the viewer's experience, it seems to us, to second-guess the film by describing it in terms of "thematic sequences" as a way of getting to an organizational level beyond the scene.

12. The boy's parents are also not clearly identified until late in the sequence, when the lawyers and the judge have agreed to a plea-bargain arrangement. But during Robert's attorney's opening remarks, Wiseman shows cutaways of various faces in the courtroom audience; just as the lawyer refers to Robert's nineteen-year-old adult codefendant with the words, "the adult defendant," Wiseman cuts to a close-up of Robert's father. Wiseman has often talked of the importance to his editing of filming a great many cutaway shots. In *Juvenile Court,* according to the recollection of Judge Turner, Wiseman at times used two cameras simultaneously during courtroom scenes: one camera, on a tripod, focused on the judge at the bench, the other, carried by Bill Brayne, followed the action (Kenneth A. Turner, interviewed by the authors, Memphis, TN, 9 April 1988).

13. Later, the film itself became an issue in the future of these juvenile clients, prompting objections to the showing of the film. WNET/13 vice-president and director of programming Robert Kotlowitz recalled that "a set of parents" whose child appeared in *Juvenile Court* raised "a question of clearance" before the broadcast of the film. Kotlowitz said, "We dealt with it right up to broadcast time" (interview with the authors, New York City, 13 June 1985). After the 1 October 1973 PBS broadcast of *Juvenile Court,* television critic Les Brown wrote that the initial broadcast of the documentary had raised questions of invasion of privacy and that the film "had been withheld from television until the legal issue was resolved." According to Brown, "the resolution has been to omit the city of Memphis, where all the film had been shot, from all future national telecasts of the two-hour and 20-minute program. At issue in Memphis was whether it was fair for the film to come back to haunt the youngsters who were on trial in Judge Kenneth Turner's juvenile court there two years ago, when the film was shot. . . . Several of the young people involved had moved to new neighborhoods to escape the taint of the personal scandals recorded in the film" ("Documentary to Change The Second Time Around," *New York Times,* 15 December 1973, 63). Writing several years later, Bob Kalin claimed that "*Juvenile Court* is an extremely difficult film to see because the litigation involving one of the film's subjects forced it to be withdrawn from circulation for quite awhile" ("Frederick Wiseman: From *Titicut Follies* to *Model,*" *Film News* [Fall 1981], 8). In a 1988 interview with the authors, Judge Turner recalled that the teenage babysitter shown in the film "on his own" had contacted "free legal services" after the 1 October 1973 broadcast of *Juvenile Court* (Judge Kenneth A. Turner, interviewed by Thomas W. Benson and Carolyn Anderson, Memphis, TN, 9 April 1988). Rebroadcasts of the documentary scheduled for 6 October 1973 on WKNO-TV Memphis and on the PBS network were cancelled (*Memphis Press-Scimitar,* 8 October 1973). Judge Turner's files on the film include correspondence from Wiseman's attorney, Blair L. Perry, indicating that on 30 October 1973 Perry met the Memphis legal services lawyers in their offices in Memphis to discuss the boy's complaint.

14. Nicholson and Nicholson, "Meet Lawyer-Filmmaker," 331. Turner was an elected judge and had served on the bench for ten years when *Juvenile Court* was made. At that time, Turner's was the only juvenile court for Memphis and Shelby counties. Turner's annual case load was seventy-one thousand. The year before Wiseman filmed *Juvenile Court,* Turner campaigned for mayor of Memphis and was defeated by only several hundred votes. Looking back on that election, state senator and juvenile court referee Curtis Person said he thinks strong community approval of Turner as a judge contributed to his defeat "because a lot of people wanted him to

stay in the juvenile court" (interview with the authors, Memphis, TN, 9 April 1988).
Recalling the film years later, Judge Turner said that the film had shown him things
about his own court that he had not known. Referring to the scenes in which two
ministers from Teen Challenge counsel Robert Y., Judge Turner said that "I learned
some things myself about what was going on that I would not have ordinarily in the
course of a day had a chance to observe. And that was one of them that I stopped
immediately. I don't like all the emotionalism. . . . I don't believe in jailhouse
conversions. . . . We got rid of those people. Teen Challenge itself is a respectable
outfit, but at that particular point they had apparently got into drug counseling and
picked up some ex-druggies to work with them and they were giving the organization
a pretty bad name. . . . I think the people who support Teen Challenge would hate
to think they were being represented by the likes of what we saw on that tape"
(Kenneth A. Turner, interviewed by the authors, Memphis, TN, 9 April 1988).
Turner's file on the film includes a letter from the executive director of Teen Challenge
of Memphis, Tim Waters, dated 18 October 1973, in which Waters wrote that he
"enjoyed seeing the program on Television" and "was impressed with the whole
operation of the Court." Waters also told Turner that he felt "very honored that you
are a member of our Teen Challenge Advisory Board."

15. "Wiseman on *Juvenile Court*," 48.

Chapter 6. *Primate*

1. Anthony Trollope, *Can You Forgive Her?* vol. 1 (1864; reprint, Oxford: Oxford
University Press, 1973), 383–84.

2. This is the sort of relationship that Kenneth Burke refers to as "a communicative
relationship between writer and audience, with both parties actively participating."
Kenneth Burke, "Antony in Behalf of the Play," *The Philosophy of Literary Form*, 3d
ed. (Berkeley: University of California Press, 1973), 329.

3. Trollope, *Can You Forgive Her?*, 44–45.

4. The theme is a common one in nineteenth- and twentieth-century British and
American fiction. For example, Charles Dickens, especially in *Hard Times*, shows us
the terrible consequences of the misplaced love of facts, and John Fowles uses another
facet of this mentality in two of his best novels, *The Collector* and *The French
Lieutenant's Woman*, both of which are in large part variations on his theme of the
horror of the impulse to factualize, possess, name, count, and fragment the world
of nature, to reduce it to our order and our use. Fowles states the same theme
autobiographically and polemically in his text for *The Tree*. John Fowles and Frank
Horvat, *The Tree* (Boston: Little, Brown, 1979), n. p.

5. James Agee and Walker Evans, *Let Us Now Praise Famous Men* (1941; reprint,
New York: Ballantine Books, 1966), 12.

6. Agee and Evans, *Let Us Now Praise*, 250. See also Charles Wolfe, "Direct
Address and the Social Documentary Photograph: 'Annie May Gudger' as Negative
Subject," *Wide Angle* 9, no. 1 (1987): 59–70.

7. See, for example, Martin J. Medhurst and Thomas W. Benson, ed., *Rhetorical
Dimensions in Media: A Critical Casebook*, rev. printing (Dubuque, Iowa: Kendall/
Hunt, 1986).

8. Liz Ellsworth, *Frederick Wiseman: A Guide to References and Resources* (Boston: G. K. Hall, 1979), 102–58.

9. Ellsworth, *Frederick Wiseman*, 11–57.

10. Frederick Wiseman, *New York Times*, 22 December 1974, D 33. Les Brown in "Scientist Angrily Cancels TV Discussion of 'Primate,' " *New York Times*, 7 December 1974, 59, and Christine Russell in "Science on Film: The 'Primate' Controversy," *BioScience* 25 (March 1975): 151–54, 218–19, provide details about responses to the broadcast of *Primate*. The 5 December 1974 broadcast scored exceptionally high ratings for WNET/13. During the program, WNET received 149 complaints, one bomb scare, and a threat on Wiseman's life. Nationwide, only 81 of the 222 Public Broadcasting Service stations aired *Primate* on December 5. Many stations scheduled it for a later date; others never broadcast it.

Then-director of Yerkes Geoffrey Bourne prepared a three-minute statement explaining some of the procedures shown in *Primate* and defending their use. WNET refused to append Bourne's statement to the *Primate* broadcast and suggested the director appear on a special program with Wiseman, an offer which he first accepted and then declined after he saw the film a second time. Atlanta station WETV, which had taped the Bourne statement, is the only PBS station that ran it in conjunction with the *Primate* broadcast.

The *NOVA* staff at WGBH, Boston's public television station, organized a panel discussion following its delayed broadcast of *Primate*. Filmed in December, but withheld until the 3 January 1975 broadcast of *Primate*, the discussion was moderated by *NOVA* science editor Graham Shedd. Participants were Wiseman, Yerkes researcher Adrian Perachio, biologists Richard Lewontin of Harvard and David Baltimore of MIT, and Harvard philosopher Robert Nozick. WNET aired the WGBH-produced discussion when it rebroadcast *Primate* on 6 January 1975. An abbreviated transcript of that discussion has been published as "Can Some Knowledge Simply Cost Too Much?" *The Hastings Center Report* 5 (February 1975): 6–8.

11. Frederick A. King, "Yerkes Center Fact Sheet on the Film 'Primate,' " and "The Facts about the Film 'Primate,' " 9–11 April 1986. It is difficult to track down the reactions of Wiseman's subjects to his films. When asked, he usually says that his subjects have been pleased with the films. But from time to time, complaints about the other films manage to surface. Two members of the audience of the 7 November 1985 showing of *Racetrack* at a Documentary Film Week sponsored by Valley Filmworks at the Carnegie Hall Cinema in New York told us that the celebratory atmosphere preceding the screening turned to mumbling and then even boos by the end of the film. Several members of the audience who were either subjects in the film or claimed they spoke for subjects voiced strong objections that Wiseman had presented the institution unfairly (interview with Hal Himmelstein, 9 October 1986, Philadelphia; Jemethy MacKaye, 30 January 1987, by telephone).

12. Karl Heider, *Ethnographic Film* (Austin: University of Texas Press, 1976), 82.

13. Heider, *Ethnographic Film*, 84. We have quoted Heider at some length to try to do justice to the shape of his argument. Heider refers to *Primate* at two other points in his book: once in a table on p. 108 that restates the charge of fragmentation; and once on p. 121, where, in a discussion of consent, he notes the exchange of charges between Wiseman and Geoffrey Bourne in the *New York Times*.

14. Still, Wiseman does encourage the use of his films by anthropologists. The 1987 Zipporah brochure suggests that all the films in the collection are appropriate for classes in sociology and anthropology.

15. Heider, *Ethnographic Film*, 85.

16. Nadine Gordimer, *July's People* (New York: Viking Press, 1981), 160.

17. The concept of implied author refers not to the actual author of a text but to the consciousness that is implied as controlling the point of view of the work. See Wayne C. Booth, *The Rhetoric of Fiction*, 2d ed. (Chicago: University of Chicago Press, 1983), 71–76.

18. This structural issue often turns up in criticism of Robert Flaherty's documentary work. Flaherty studied his subjects' repeated behaviors so often that he could anticipate their actions, and his camera work is for this reason tuned to the rhythm of the subjects, able to move with or ahead of them. On the other hand, Flaherty often *did* set up scenes artificially, and, whatever the merits of that practice, it cast doubt on the literal, observational accuracy of some scenes that were probably not artificially staged. We do not offer these speculations to imply that Wiseman typically set up his scenes: Wiseman, his cameramen, and his subjects testify that this is not the case, with some exceptions. As a matter of documentary rhetoric, this is a fine line, but the issue of constructing a compromise between following and anticipating the action cannot be legislated away by insisting upon an unattainable objectivity or a point of view that is always surprised by the events unfolding before the camera.

Primate does contain one scene that is unusual for a Wiseman film, in which a scientist talks directly to the camera, explaining his research in an "interview" format. The scene violates Wiseman's usual practice of seeming to be invisible to his subjects. Frederick King, director of the Yerkes Center, specifically charges that Wiseman promised other interviews, and promised to include them in the film. From King's point of view, such interviews would have been a clear opportunity to put the Yerkes research into context as science, and Wiseman's failure to do this is made, in his account, to stand as evidence both of Wiseman's deliberate unwillingness to contextualize the research and of Wiseman's violation of his agreements with Yerkes. Further, King charges that one scene presented in the film as naturally occurring was a setup—the roundtable discussion among the scientists, immediately following the vivisection scene, in which then-director Bourne and others justify "pure" research. King writes, "Although the film producer's technique supposedly is to record events as they occur, several scenes in the film were staged at his request. In one scene, a group of scientists discuss the importance of basic research. Their conversation is stilted because it was artificial. Scientists do get together to 'brainstorm,' to discuss their findings, new ideas and approaches. But this is not shown" (King, "Fact Sheet," 5).

19. The independent gaze of the camera, in this scene, appears to be established by cutting rather than by camera movement, making it a choice of the implied author and film editor, rather than simply the decision of the cameraman. Wiseman also employs cutaways during the scene in which one of the scientists speaks directly to the camera; as the sound track rolls along with the apparently continuous voice of the speaker who is addressing the camera, Wiseman intercuts shots of the same scientist working in his laboratory with one of the apes.

20. See William Stott's discussion of social documentaries versus human documents. "Human documents show man undergoing the perennial and unpreventable in experience, what happens to all men everywhere: death, work, chance, rapture, hurricane, and maddened dogs; as John Grierson said, the theme of such documents is 'la condition humaine.' Social documentary, on the other hand, shows man at grips with conditions neither permanent nor necessary, conditions of a certain time and

place: racial discrimination, police brutality, unemployment, the Depression, the planned environment of the TVA, pollution, terrorism" (William Stott, *Documentary Expression and Thirties America* [New York: Oxford University Press, 1973], 20).

21. Lawrence W. Rosenfield, "The Practical Celebration of Epideictic," in *Rhetoric in Transition: Studies in the Nature and Uses of Rhetoric*, ed. Eugene E. White (University Park: The Pennsylvania State University Press, 1980), 131–55.

22. Karl Wallace, "The Substance of Rhetoric: Good Reasons," *The Quarterly Journal of Speech*, 49 (1963): 239–49.

Chapter 7. *Welfare*

1. Dwight Macdonald, *On Movies* (1969; reprint, New York: Berkley, 1971), 13.

2. For an overview of rules theories of communication, see Stephen W. Littlejohn, *Theories of Human Comunication*, 2d ed. (Belmont, CA: Wadsworth, 1983), 45–73; see also Donald P. Cushman, "The Rules Perspective as a Theoretical Basis for the Study of Human Communication," *Communication Quarterly* 25, no. 1 (1977): 30–45; Stuart J. Sigman, "On Communication Rules from a Social Perspective," *Human Communication Research* 7 (1980): 37–51; Susan B. Shamanoff, *Communication Rules: Theory and Research* (Beverly Hills, CA:Sage, 1980); W. Barnett Pearce and Richard L. Wiseman, "Rules Theories: Variations, Limitations, and Potentials," in *Intercultural Communication Theory*, ed. William B. Gudykunst (Beverly Hills, CA: Sage, 1983). Shimanoff defines a rule as "a followable prescription that indicates what behavior is obligated, preferred, or prohibited in certain contexts" (57).

3. In Alan Westin, " 'You Start Off with a Bromide': Wiseman on Film and Civil Liberties," *Civil Liberties Review* 1, nos. 1 and 2 (1974): 60.

4. Cooley, "The Looking-Glass Self," in *Symbolic Interaction: A Reader in Social Psychology*, ed. Jerome G. Manis and Bernard M. Meltzer, 3d ed. (Boston: Allyn & Bacon, 1978), 169. Extending the concept of the looking-glass self developed by Cooley, contemporary symbolic interactionists have argued for the explanatory power of a "labeling theory," especially as a way of understanding deviance. See James Wilfrid Vander Zanden, *Social Psychology*, 2d ed. (New York: Random House, 1981), 180–181; and John P. Hewitt, *Self and Society: A Symbolic Interactionist Social Psychology*, 3d ed. (Boston: Allyn & Bacon, 1984), ch. 7, for overviews; and Howard Becker, *Outsiders*, rev. ed. (New York: Free Press, 1973), 177–212, for a discussion of the issues surrounding labeling theory written by one of its major proponents. For a discussion of naming as rhetorical strategy and interpretive action, see Richard M. Weaver, *Language Is Sermonic: Richard M. Weaver on the Nature of Rhetoric*, ed. Richard L. Johannesen, Rennard Strickland, and Ralph T. Eubanks (Baton Rouge: Louisiana State University Press, 1970); Jane Blankenship, "The Search for the 1972 Democratic Nomination: A Metaphorical Perspective," in *Rhetoric and Communication*, ed. Jane Blankenship and Hermann G. Stelzner (Urbana: University of Illinois Press, 1976), 236–60; Shirley Keddie, "Naming and Renaming: *Time* Magazine's Coverage of Germany and Russia in the 1940s" (Ph.D. diss., University of Massachusetts, Amherst, 1985). All these critics build on the collective work of Kenneth Burke. Much of current sociolinguistic research assumes (as did the earlier work of general semanticists) the social importance of naming. See Dell H. Hymes, *Foundations in Sociolinguistics* (Philadelphia: University of Pennsylvania Press, 1974), for a general introduction. Adrienne Rich brings a poet's sensibility to the discussion in *Critical*

Essays (New York: Norton, 1977). Ursula Le Guin offers a similar argument as satire in "She Unnames Them," *The New Yorker*, 21 January 1985, 27.

5. At a theatre conference, as part of the presentation "Drama and Documentary Art," Wiseman showed clips from five of his documentaries, ending with the scene of Hirsch from *Welfare*. Wiseman said he considers himself privileged to have recorded such "spectacular performances." Nonetheless, he insisted, as he does consistently, that the camera had not changed the subject's behavior. Wiseman claimed that Hirsch was equally "theatrical" in other situations in which he was not filmed (Theatre Communications Group National Conference, Northampton, MA, 14 June 1986). For a developed analysis of the theatre of daily life, see the work of Erving Goffman, especially *The Presentation of Self in Everyday Life* (New York: Doubleday, 1959) and *Relations in Public: Microstudies of the Public Order* (New York: Harper & Row, 1971).

6. We have followed conventional usage in employing the terms *documentary* and *nonfiction film* as synonymous, generic terms. Barsam uses *nonfiction film* as his general classification and then breaks the genre into three main approaches: documentary film, factual film, and direct cinema. For Barsam, documentary differs from factual film in that it has "a message." Richard Meran Barsam, *Nonfiction Film: A Critical History* (New York: Dutton, 1973), 4.

7. See Paul Rotha, *Documentary Film*, 3d ed. (New York: Hastings House, 1963), and *Robert Flaherty: A Biography*, ed. Jay Ruby (Philadelphia: University of Pennsylvania Press, 1983); Barsam, *Nonfiction Film;* Erik Barnouw, *Documentary: A History of the Non-Fiction Film* rev. ed. (New York: Oxford University Press, 1983); Lewis Jacobs, ed., *The Documentary Tradition*, 2d ed. (New York: Norton, 1979).

8. Arthur Calder-Marshall, *The Innocent Eye: The Life of Robert J. Flaherty* (New York: Harcourt, Brace & World, 1966); Elizabeth Sussex, ed., *The Rise and Fall of British Documentary: The Story of the Film Movement Founded by John Grierson* (Berkeley: University of California Press, 1975).

9. Barsam, *Nonfiction Film*, 4.

10. G. Roy Levin, *Documentary Explorations: 15 Interviews with Film-Makers* (Garden City: Doubleday, 1971); Alan Rosenthal, *The New Documentary in Action: A Casebook in Filmmaking* (Berkeley: University of California Press, 1971); Rosenthal, *The Documentary Conscience: A Casebook in Film Making* (Berkeley: University of California Press, 1980). See also Lisa Henderson's account of still photographers at work, in "Photography in Public Places" (Master's thesis, University of Pennsylvania, 1983).

11. W. Hugh Baddeley, *The Technique of Documentary Film Production*, 3d ed. (New York: Focal Press, 1973), 113, 115.

12. See William A. Bluem, *Documentary in American Television: Form, Function, Method* (New York: Hastings House, 1965); Charles Montgomery Hammond, Jr., *The Image Decade: Television Documentary: 1965–1975* (New York: Hastings House, 1981); Raymond L. Carroll, "Television Documentary," in *TV Genres*, ed. Brian G. Rose (Westport, CT: Greenwood Press, 1985), 237–56.

13. Fred W. Friendly, *Due to Circumstances beyond Our Control* (New York: Random House, 1967); Edward Jay Epstein, *Between Fact and Fiction: The Problem of Journalism* (New York: Vintage Books, 1975); Av Westin, *Newswatch: How TV Decides the News* (New York: Simon and Schuster, 1982). Before the opening of the trial of *Westmoreland v. CBS*, the "Benjamin Report," an in-house investigation of

the documentary *The Uncounted Enemy: A Vietnam Deception* (broadcast 23 January 1982) was released at the direction of the court. In the report, Burton Benjamin, a senior executive producer at CBS, made public both CBS documentary guidelines and what CBS would consider violations of those guidelines. On 17 February 1985, Westmoreland withdrew his libel suit against CBS before the trial jury had reached its decision.

14. Westin, *Newswatch*, 180. In contrast to the nearly half-million dollars per hour for the production and administrative costs of network documentary in the late 1970s and early 1980s, Frederick Wiseman was producing documentaries, sometimes up to three hours long, on his second five-year contract for WNET/13 for $150,000 per film. (Robert Kotlowitz, interviewed by the authors, New York City, 13 June 1985; and telephone interview with Robert Kotlowitz by Carolyn Anderson, 17 February 1987). Kotlowitz said that these costs were "not expensive, not high cost" compared to other public affairs programming on public television. The fees Wiseman charged WNET were arrived at, apparently, by comparing them in a general way with the costs of similar programming. Did Kotlowitz or others at WNET ever examine Wiseman's budgets? "There was no point to. His job was to make the program within the limits of the money so that he could cover his costs and acquire some profit. And that's how it was." Wiseman has said that his films cost $30,000 to $50,000 in 1967, and about $200,000 in 1985. (Wiseman, in answer to a question during a public appearance at Bucknell University, 12 November 1985). In 1988, Wiseman received a grant of $171,172 from the MacArthur Foundation to partially underwrite *Missile* (*Boston Globe*, 29 January 1988, 2).

15. Stephen Mamber, *Cinema Verite in America: Studies in Uncontrolled Documentary* (Cambridge: MIT Press, 1974), 4; see also James Blue, "Direct Cinema," *Film Comment* 4, nos. 2 and 3 (1967): 80–81; Louis Marcorelles, *Living Cinema: New Directions in Contemporary Filmmaking*, trans. Isabel Quigly (New York: Praeger, 1973); M. Ali Issari and Doris A. Paul, *What Is Cinema Verite?* (Metuchen, NJ: Scarecrow Press, 1979); Brian Winston, "Hell of a Good Sail . . . Sorry No Whales: Direct Cinema, the Third Decade," *Sight and Sound* 52, no. 4 (1983): 238–43.

16. Interviews with Wiseman appear in Thomas Atkins, ed., *Frederick Wiseman* (New York: Monarch Press, 1976); Beatrice Berg, "I Was Fed Up with Hollywood Fantasies," *The New York Times*, 1 February 1970, sec. 2, p. 25; Silvia Feldman, "The Wiseman Documentary," *Human Behavior* 5, no. 2 (1976): 64–69; John Graham, "Frederick Wiseman on Viewing Film," *The Film Journal* 1, no. 1 (1971): 43–47; Ira Halberstadt, "An Interview with Fred Wiseman," *Filmmaker's Newsletter* 7, no. 4 (1974): 19–25; Janet Handelman, "An Interview with Frederick Wiseman," *Film Library Quarterly* 3, no. 3 (1970): 5–9; G. Roy Levin, *Documentary Explorations: 15 Interviews with Film-Makers* (Garden City: Doubleday, 1971), 313–28; Stephen Mamber, "The New Documentaries of Frederick Wiseman," *Cinema* 6, no. 1 (1970): 33–40; Donald E. McWilliams, "Frederick Wiseman," *Film Quarterly* 24, no. 1 (1970): 17–26; Philip Nicolson and Elizabeth Nicolson, "Meet Lawyer-Filmmaker Frederick Wiseman," *American Bar Association Journal* 61 (March 1975): 328–32; Christine Robb, "Focus on Life: The Films of Frederick Wiseman," *Boston Globe Magazine*, 23 January 1983, 15–17, 26–34; Alan Westin, "You Start Off with a Bromide," 52–67.

17. In Atkins, *Frederick Wiseman*, 45.

18. See Allan T. Sutherland, "Wiseman on Polemic," *Sight and Sound* 47, no.

2 (1978): 82. Youdelman and Nichols provide general discussions of the political consequences of abandoning voice-over narration in contemporary documentaries. Jeffrey Youdelman, "Narration, Invention, and History," *Cineaste* 12, no. 2 (1982): 8–15; Bill Nichols, "The Voice of Documentary," *Film Quarterly* 36, no. 3 (1983): 17–30.

19. Donald Brieland, "Welfare," *Social Work* 20, no. 6 (1975): 498.

20. Reuven Frank, "The Function of Interviews." Memorandum on the Half-Hour NBC Network News Program. Unpublished mimeo.

21. ABC, NBC, and CBS have put program practices and standards into writing and made them public. See Diane Mermigas, "CBS Draws Up a Set of Standards," *Electronic Media*, 2 May 1985, 3, 12, 37.

22. Bill Nichols, *Ideology and the Image: Social Representation in the Cinema and Other Media* (Bloomington: Indiana University Press, 1981), 209.

23. John Coleman, "Films: Long Look," *New Statesman*, 7 November 1975, 590.

24. Clifford Geertz, *Local Knowledge* (New York: Basic Books, 1983).

25. Liz Ellsworth, *Frederick Wiseman: A Guide to References and Resources* (Boston: G. K. Hall, 1979), 3.

26. Halberstadt, "An Interview," 22; Atkins, *Frederick Wiseman*, 33.

27. Atkins, *Frederick Wiseman*, 36.

28. Feldman, "The Wiseman Documentary," 68.

29. In Levin, *Documentary Explorations*, 368.

30. In Mamber, "The New Documentaries of Frederick Wiseman," 39.

31. Coleman, "Films," 590.

32. Robb, "Focus on Life," 28.

33. In Atkins, *Frederick Wiseman*, 38.

34. See Kenneth Burke's discussion of the rhetoric of constitutions in *A Rhetoric of Motives* (1950; reprint, Berkeley: University of California Press, 1969).

35. Ellsworth, *Frederick Wiseman*, 4.

36. David Thomson finds "something pusillanimous in this restrained conflict of motives" and offers a strong rejection of the argument we present here; see his *Biographical Dictionary of Film*, 2d ed. (New York: Morrow, 1981), 668–69.

37. Edgar Z. Friedenberg, "Ship of Fools: The Films of Frederick Wiseman," *New York Review of Books*, 21 October 1971, 20.

38. John O'Connor, "Wiseman's 'Welfare' Is on Channel 13 Tonight," *The New York Times*, 24 September 1975, 91; Coleman, "Films," 589–90; Gary Arnold, "Wiseman's 'Welfare': Compelling Case Study," *Washington Post*, 24 September 1975, sec. C, 1–2; Harry F. Waters, "Wiseman on Welfare," *Newsweek*, 29 September 1975, 62–63; Karl Meyer, "Television: Report from Purgatory," *Saturday Review*, 20 September 1975, 52; Benjamin Stein, "Close-Up on Welfare," *Wall Street Journal*, 24 September 1975, 24; James Wolcott, " 'Welfare' Must Be Seen," *The Village Voice*, 29 September 1975, 126; Caroline Lewis, "Welfare," *Monthly Film Bulletin*, March 1976, 65; Gregg Kilday, "The Woes of Welfare," *Los Angeles Times*, 22 September 1975, sec. 4, 1, 17; Donald Brieland, "Welfare," *Social Work*, November 1975, 498; Roger Rosenblatt, "Frederick Wiseman's 'Welfare,' " *The New Republic*, 27 September 1975, 65–67; Feldman, "The Wiseman Documentary," 64–69; Percy Shain, "Latest Wiseman Film a Stark View of Welfare," *Boston Globe*, 24 September 1975, 55.

39. "The High School: How Much Change—And How Fast?" *School Management*, December 1969, 57–58.

40. For discussions of objectivity, see Theodor W. Adorno, "Subject and Object," in *The Essential Frankfurt School Reader*, ed. Andrew Arato and Eike Gebhart (New York: Continuum, 1985); David Altheide, *Creating Reality: How TV News Distorts Events* (Beverly Hills, CA: Sage, 1976); Edward Jay Epstein, *Between Fact and Fiction;* and *News from Nowhere: Television and the News* (New York: Vintage Books, 1974); Glasgow University Media Group, *Bad News* (London: Routledge & Kegan Paul, 1976); Bernard Roshco, *Newsmaking* (Chicago: University of Chicago Press, 1975); Philip Schlesinger, *Putting "Reality" Together: BBC News* (London: Constable, 1978); Michael Schudson, *Discovering the News: A Social History of American Newspapers* (New York: Basic Books, 1978); Michael Tracey, *The Production of Political Television* (London: Routledge & Kegan Paul, 1977); Gaye Tuchman, *Making News: A Study in the Construction of Reality* (New York: Free Press, 1978); and "Objectivity as Strategic Ritual: An Examination of Newsmen's Notions of Objectivity," *American Journal of Sociology* 77 (1972): 660–79; Charles Winick, ed., *Deviance and Mass Media* (Beverly Hills, CA: Sage, 1978). For a full discussion of the history and application of the Fairness Doctrine and its effects on public affairs programming, see Don R. Pember, *Mass Media Law*, 3d ed. (Dubuque: William C. Brown, 1984), 538–53. For an overview of broadcast regulation, including an analysis of the equal-time requirement, see Donald M. Gillmor and Jerome A. Barron, *Mass Communication Law: Cases and Comment*, 4th ed. (St. Paul: West, 1984), 771–1033.

41. See Kenneth Burke, *A Grammar of Motives* (1945; reprint, Berkeley: University of California Press, 1969) and *A Rhetoric of Motives*.

42. Richard B. Gregg, *Symbolic Inducement and Knowing: A Study in the Foundations of Rhetoric* (Columbia: University of South Carolina Press, 1984), 136.

43. Gregg, *Symbolic Inducement;* also Robert Joyce, *The Esthetic Animal: Man, the Art-Created Art-Creator* (Hicksville: Exposition Press, 1975).

44. Paul Ricoeur, *History and Truth*, trans. Charles A. Kelbley (Evanston, IL: Northwestern University Press, 1965), 40.

45. In Levin, *Documentary Explorations*, 321.

46. Jean-Paul Sartre, *Nausea*, trans. Lloyd Alexander (New York: New Directions, 1964), 118–20.

47. Rosenthal, *The New Documentary in Action*, 69.

Chapter 8. *Canal Zone*

1. On conventional editing, see Dai Vaughan, *Television Documentary Usage* (London: British Film Institute, 1976).

2. Hayden White, *Tropics of Discourse: Essays in Cultural Criticism* (Baltimore: Johns Hopkins University Press, 1978).

3. See Roy Wagner, *The Invention of Culture*, rev. ed. (Chicago: University of Chicago Press, 1981).

4. James Wolcott, "Wiseman's Panamania," *The Village Voice*, 10 October 1977, 45. See David McCullough, *The Path between the Seas: The Creation of the Panama Canal, 1870–1914* (New York: Simon and Schuster, 1977); and J. Michael Hogan, *The Panama Canal in American Politics: Domestic Advocacy and the Evolution of Policy* (Carbondale: Southern Illinois University Press, 1986).

5. Wolcott, "Wiseman's Panamania," 45.

6. Richard A. Blake, "From Poland to Panama," *America*, 8 October 1977, 217–

18; Shepherd Bliss, " 'Canal Zone': An American Way of Death," *Christianity and Crisis*, 28 November 1977, 286–87; Frank Rich, "A Sunny, Nightmare Vision," *Time*, 10 October 1977, 103; Peter Sourian, "Television," *The Nation*, 15 October 1977, 381–82.

7. See George Orwell, "Shooting an Elephant," in *Collected Essays* (London: Secker & Warburg, 1961), 15–23; Graham Greene, *Another Mexico* (New York: Viking, 1964), originally published in 1939 as *The Lawless Roads; Journey without Maps* (1936; reprint, New York: Penguin, 1978); and the more sympathetic *Getting to Know the General* (New York: Simon and Schuster, 1984); Joan Didion, *Salvador* (New York: Simon and Schuster, 1983); Joseph Conrad, *Heart of Darkness*, originally published in *Youth and Two Other Stories*, 1903 (New York: Signet, 1950).

8. Orwell, "Shooting an Elephant," 18–20.

9. Orwell, "Shooting an Elephant," 19–20. Orwell takes up the same theme in his celebrated essay "Marrakech" and again uses the strategy of "Shooting an Elephant" to compare the colonialist's sympathy for animals and inability to identify with native humans. Orwell says in "Marrakech," "When you walk through a town like this—two hundred thousand inhabitants, of whom at least twenty thousand own literally nothing except the rags they stand up in—when you see how the people live, and still more easily how they die, it is always difficult to believe that you are walking among human beings. All colonial empires are in reality founded upon that fact. The people all have brown faces—besides, there are so many of them! Are they really the same flesh as yourself? Do they even have names?" (*Collected Essays*, 24). For a discussion of the legacy of this colonial consciousness, see Philip Rogers, *"No Longer at Ease:* Chinua Achebe's 'Heart of Whiteness,' " *Research in African Literatures* 14, no. 2 (1983): 165–83.

10. These measurements would vary if counted differently, and other choices might have been made about what to count as a "speech." In timing the speeches, we have started with the beginning of the speaker's words and stopped counting when the speaker stopped. Timings would be longer, for instance, if we were to count as the timing of a speech the entire ceremony of which some of the speeches form a part. Similarly, some of what we count as speeches might have been left out, or others included. For example, we count as a speech a radio message about how to avoid purse snatching, but do not count an announcement about the week's local movies and other entertainment, or a television interview with Keeno, the drug-sniffing dog, and his handler. The main point of measurement here is to notice an order of magnitude, rather than to construct a categorical base for quantitative content analysis. Timings in fig. 8–1 are approximate—made by hand with a stopwatch. In some scenes, sound starts before picture; in others, a speech is interrupted by questions or interpolations from other speakers.

11. Thomas W. Benson, "Implicit Communication Theory in Campaign Coverage," in *Television Coverage of the 1980 Presidential Campaign*, ed. William C. Adams (Norwood, NJ: Ablex, 1983), 103–116.

12. Robert N. Bellah, "Civil Religion in America," *Daedalus* 96, no. 1 (1967): 1–21; *Beyond Belief: Essays on Religion in a Post-Traditional World* (New York: Harper & Row, 1970); "American Civil Religion in the 1970s," *Anglican Theological Review* 1, no. 3 (1973): 8–20, reprinted in Russell E. Richey and Donald G. Jones, eds., *American Civil Religion* (New York: Harper & Row, 1974); *The Broken Covenant: American Civil Religion in A Time of Trial* (New York: Seabury Press, 1975); *Varieties*

of Civil Religion (San Francisco: Harper & Row, 1980). See also Roderick P. Hart, *The Political Pulpit* (West Lafayette: Purdue University Press, 1977); Michael W. Hughey, *Civil Religion and Moral Order: Theoretical and Historical Dimensions* (Westport, CT: Greenwood Press, 1983); Martin J. Medhurst, " 'God Bless the President': The Rhetoric of Inaugural Prayer" (Ph.D. dissertation, The Pennsylvania State University, 1980).

Chapter 9. *The Store*

1. Jim Baker, "Tonight's Wiseman Film Is a Riveting Look at 'The Store,' " *Boston Herald*, 14 December 1983, 51; Bill Carter, "Neither a Portrait nor a Polemic," *Baltimore Sun*, 14 December 1983, B 6; John Corry, "TV: 'The Store,' A Wiseman Film," *The New York Times*, 14 December 1983, C 34; Hilary DeVries, "Fred Wiseman's Unblinking Camera Watches How Society Works," *Christian Science Monitor*, 1 May 1984, 25–27; John W. Donohue, "An Advent Homily from Neiman-Marcus," *America*, 10 December 1983, 374; Marvin Kitman, "The Marvin Kitman Show Starring Neiman-Marcus," *Newsday*, 14 December 1983, 80; Otile McManus, "Inside the Store," *Connoisseur*, December 1983, 45–46; Steven Reddicliffe, "The Heart and Soul of The Store," *Dallas Times Herald*, 11 December 1983; Glenn Rifkin, "Wiseman Looks at Affluent Texans," *The New York Times*, 11 December 1983, sec. 2, 37, 44; Howard Rosenberg, "Show of the Week," *Los Angeles Television Times*, 11 December 1983, 3; Karen Rosenberg, "The Store," *The Nation*, 17 December 1983, 642–43; Fred Rothenberg, "A Tedious Documentary," *Daily Hampshire Gazzette*, 14 December 1983, 35; Jean Saylor, "Shopping at 'The Store,' " *Des Moines Register*, 14 December 1983, 4 T; Tom Shales, "Best Li'l Store in Texas," *Washington Post*, 17 December 1983, B 1, 4; Jack Thomas, "Wiseman without Bite," *Boston Globe*, 14 December 1983, 87, 90; Arthur Unger, "Wiseman Aims His Camera at the Neiman-Marcus Way of Life," *Christian Science Monitor*, 13 December 1983, 32; Harry F. Waters, "Inside a Shopping Shrine," *Newsweek*, 19 December 1983, 81–82; Mary-Lou Weisman, "Neiman-Marcus, the Movie," *The New Republic*, 31 December 1983, 25–26. We will refer to these reviews in the text by citing in parenthesis the last name of the reviewer. PBS rebroadcast *The Store* on 26 December 1984.

2. Kitman, "The Marvin Kitman Show," 80.

3. Karen Rosenberg, "The Store," 642.

4. Thomas, "Wiseman without Bite," 90; Karen Rosenberg, "The Store," 642; Carter, "Neither a Portrait," B 6.

5. Thomas, "Wiseman without Bite," 87.

6. DeVries, "Unblinking Camera," 25; Waters, "Inside a Shopping Shrine," 81; Donohue, "An Advent Homily," 374.

7. Karen Rosenberg, "The Store," 643; Rothenberg, "Tedious Documentary," 35.

8. Corry, "TV: 'The Store,' " C 34.

9. Stuart Ewen, *Captains of Consciousness: Advertising and the Social Roots of the Consumer Culture* (New York: McGraw-Hill, 1976); see also Erik Barnouw, *The Sponsor: Notes on a Modern Potentate* (New York: Oxford University Press, 1978).

10. Clifford Geertz, *The Interpretation of Cultures* (New York: Basic Books, 1973), 451.

11. Unger, "Wiseman Aims," 32.

12. Rifkin, "Wiseman Looks," 44. Dan Armstrong discusses the charge of triviality

in the case of Wiseman's *Model* and argues that, both as work and as a force maintaining cultural hegemony, fashion modeling is nontrivial as it is depicted by Wiseman. See Armstrong, "Wiseman's *Model* and the Documentary Project: Toward a Radical Film Practice," *Film Quarterly* 37, no. 2 (1983/84): 2–10.

13. Weisman, "Neiman-Marcus," 25; Corry, "TV: 'The Store,' " C 34; Karen Rosenberg, "The Store," 643.

14. Robert Kotlowitz, interviewed by the authors, New York City, 13 June 1985.

15. Burke, *A Grammar of Motives* (Berkeley: University of California Press, 1969), xv. Our choice of Burke as a check upon a bias toward materialism carries its own bias. Burke's account of human motive is distinctly opposed to philosophical materialism as an adequate account of human behavior. For Burke, the distinction between humans who act and objects that move is fundamental.

16. Burke, *Grammar*, 128. To complicate matters, Burke further expands his list of philosophical schools to *rationalism* and *nominalism*, arguing that they do not belong to one or the other of the terms of the pentad but, variously, to all. Later Burke suggested turning the pentad into a hexad by adding *attitude*.

17. Keith Campbell, "Materialism," in *Encyclopedia of Philosophy*, ed. Paul Edwards, vol. 5 (New York: Macmillan, 1967) 179.

18. See Thomas W. Benson and Gerard A. Hauser, "Ideals, Superlatives, and the Decline of Hypocrisy," *The Quarterly Journal of Speech* 59 (1973): 99–105.

19. Wiseman, interviewed on "All Things Considered," National Public Radio (14 December 1983). Surrealism itself is partly another version of materialism, insofar as it suggests the dominance of the unconscious as a force motivating human action. But surrealism's materialism is also tempered by its fascination with "magic, accident, irrationality, symbols, and dreams." Alan Bullock and Oliver Stallybrass, eds., *The Fontana Dictionary of Modern Thought* (London: Fontana, 1977), 615.

20. Frank Lentricchia, *Criticism and Social Change* (Chicago: University of Chicago Press, 1983), 21–23.

21. Lentricchia, *Criticism*, 23–24.

22. Steven Smith, *Reading Althusser: An Essay on Structural Marxism* (Ithaca: Cornell University Press, 1984), 17. See also Raymond Williams, *Problems in Materialism and Culture* (London: NLB, 1980).

23. A useful account of recent developments in Marxist analysis of mass media is Samuel L. Becker's, "Marxist Approaches to Media Studies: The British Experience," *Critical Studies in Mass Communication* 1 (1984): 66–80; see also J. M. Bernstein, *The Philosophy of the Novel: Lukacs, Marxism, and the Dialectics of Form* (Minneapolis: University of Minnesota Press, 1984); R. W. Bologh, *Dialectical Phenomenology: Marx's Method* (Boston: Routledge & Kegan Paul, 1979); Christopher Butler, *Interpretation, Deconstruction, and Ideology: An Introduction to Some Current Issues in Literary Theory* (Oxford: Clarendon Press, 1984); Peter Davison, Rolf Meyersohn, and Edward Shils, *Literary Taste, Culture, and Mass Communication*, vols. 13 and 14 of *The Cultural Debate* (Cambridge: Chadwyck-Healey, 1980); Andrew Feenberg, *Lukacs, Marx and the Sources of Critical Theory* (Totowa, NJ: Rowman and Littlefield, 1981); George Gerbner and Martha Siefert, eds., "Ferment in the Field," *Journal of Communication* 33, no. 3 (1983); Lawrence Grossberg, "Strategies of Marxist Cultural Interpretation," *Critical Studies in Mass Communication* 1 (1984): 392–421; Stuart Hall, "Signification, Representation, Ideology: Althusser and the Post-Structuralist Debates," *Critical Studies in Mass Communication* 2 (1985): 91–

114; Robert L. Heath, "Kenneth Burke's Break with Formalism," *Quarterly Journal of Speech* 70 (1984): 132–43; David Held, *Introduction to Critical Theory: Horkheimer to Habermas* (Berkeley: University of California Press, 1980); Michael C. McGee, "A Materialist's Conception of Rhetoric," in Ray E. McKerrow, ed., *Explorations in Rhetoric: Studies in Honor of Douglas Ehninger* (Chicago: Scott Foresman, 1982), 23–48; McGee, "Secular Humanism: A Radical Reading of 'Culture Industry' Productions," *Critical Studies in Mass Communication* 1 (1984): 1–33; Michael Real, "The Debate on Critical Theory and the Study of Communication," *Journal of Communication* 34, no. 4 (1984): 72–80; William H. Rueckert, *Kenneth Burke and the Drama of Human Relations*, 2d ed. (Berkeley: University of California Press, 1982); Phillip K. Tompkins, "On Hegemony—'He Gave It No Name'—and Critical Structuralism in the Work of Kenneth Burke," *Quarterly Journal of Speech* 71 (1985): 119–31. For a discussion of ideological analysis in the context of twentieth-century rhetorical theory, with special emphasis on the contributions of Michael McGee, see Michael Leff and Margaret Organ Procario, "Rhetorical Theory in Speech Communication," in *Speech Communication in the 20th Century*, ed. Thomas W. Benson (Carbondale: Southern Illinois University Press, 1985), 23–26. Leff and Procario make clear McGee's commitment to the idea that rhetorical action is itself "material," not in the sense that it is a physical object, but rather that it is "as omnipresent as air and water," a "gestalt of relationships" that constitutes the experience of social life. This notion of materiality as the everyday experience of life, and as the basis of ideology, casts rhetoric as "the creative management of distortion and illusion . . . to effect social control" (24–25). Wiseman's curiosity about the experience of everyday social reality and its function as social control have much in common with the rhetorical materialism of McGee.

24. Armstrong, "Wiseman's *Model*," 3. See also Thomas W. Benson and Carolyn Anderson, "The Rhetorical Structure of Frederick Wiseman's *Model*," *Journal of Film and Video* 36, no. 4 (1984): 30–40.

25. Armstrong, "Wiseman's *Model*," 2; Bill Nichols, *Ideology and the Image: Social Representation in the Cinema and Other Media* (Bloomington: Indiana University Press, 1981), 211. Neo-Marxism tried to soften the strict economic determinism and materialism of later Marx by reference to a supposedly utopian and idealistic element in the early Marx. Louis Althusser, whose work has had a profound influence on Marxist studies of media, rejected the work of the neo-Marxists and argued that Marx himself rejected his alleged early humanism. Louis Althusser, *For Marx*, trans. B. Brewster (New York: Pantheon, 1969). Gary Teeple claims that Marx was a materialist from the beginning. Teeple, *Marx's Critique of Politics: 1842–1847* (Toronto: University of Toronto Press, 1984).

26. See Ronald Tuch, "Frederick Wiseman's Cinema of Alienation," *Film Library Quarterly* 11, no. 3 (1978): 9–15, 49, for a Marxist reading of *Meat*.

27. Telephone interview with Carolyn Anderson, 14 November 1983. Kitman described *The Store* as a "two-hour commercial for Neiman-Marcus aimed at the public television audience" (Kitman, "The Marvin Kitman Show," 80). Wiseman showed *The Store* at a special advance screening (8 December 1983) cosponsored by the Annenberg School of Communications and the Graduate School of Business Administration at the University of Southern California. Wiseman has said, "Stanley Marcus is a terrific guy. He is very funny, smart, and irreverent. . . . He is very good at what he does. He sells. People buy" (quoted in McManus, "Inside the Store," 46).

28. Wiseman, as quoted in Alan Westin, " 'You Start Off with a Bromide': Wiseman

on Film and Civil Liberties, *Civil Liberties Review* 1, no. 1 and 2 (1974): 55. Wiseman told Thomas R. Atkins that many viewers are "looking for the literal—something ideologically trendy and socially conscious in a simplified form. And that doesn't interest me" (Wiseman, in Thomas R. Atkins, ed., *Frederick Wiseman* [New York: Monarch, 1976], 78). Wiseman has taken special pains to indicate his antipathy to Soviet communism. In the program notes for his stage production of a chapter from Vasily Grossman's *Life and Fate*, we are told that "the novel hammers home the fundamental similarity between Nazism and Stalinism—two totalitarian systems based on contempt for human life." On the other hand, Wiseman was so taken with Dan Armstrong's neo-Marxist analysis of *Model* that he strongly encouraged Armstrong to write about his other films, sent him study prints without charge, and wrote a letter in support of his past and prospective work on Wiseman's films.

29. Burke himself comments on the usefulness of Marx in grounding rhetorical criticism in *A Rhetoric of Motives* (Berkeley: University of California Press, 1969), 101–110. Hugh Dalziel Duncan and Don Abbott discuss Burke's relation to Marx: Duncan, *Communication and Social Order* (New York: Bedminster, 1962); Don Abbott, "Terminology and Ideology: Marxist Influences on the Rhetorical Theory of Kenneth Burke (Ph.D. dissertation, University of Massachusetts, 1973), and "Marxist Influences on the Rhetorical Theory of Kenneth Burke," *Philosophy and Rhetoric* 7 (1974): 217–33. See also Heath, Lentricchia, Rueckert, Tompkins, and Ray E. McKerrow, "Marxism and a Rhetorical Conception of Ideology," *Quarterly Journal of Speech* 69 (1983): 192–205. The newly "rhetorical" path of the Marxist media critics brings them still closer to Burke's position.

30. Gorelik, *New Theatres for Old* (New York: Samuel French, 1940), 366.

31. Bondanella, *Italian Cinema: From Neorealism to the Present* (New York: Frederick Ungar, 1983), 28.

32. Bondanella, *Italian Cinema*, 31, citing Geoffrey Nowell-Smith. See also Roy Armes, *Film and Reality: An Historical Survey* (Baltimore: Penguin Books, 1974); Pierre Leprohon, *The Italian Cinema*, trans. Roger Greaves and Oliver Stallybrass (New York: Praeger, 1972); Mira Liehm, *Passion and Defiance: Film in Italy from 1942 to the Present* (Berkeley: University of California Press, 1984); R. T. Witcombe, *The New Italian Cinema: Studies in Dance and Despair* (New York: Oxford University Press, 1982).

33. Siegfried Kracauer, *Theory of Film: The Redemption of Physical Reality* (New York: Oxford University Press, 1960); Andre Bazin, *What Is Cinema*, 2 vols., trans. Hugh Gray (Berkeley: University of California Press, 1967, 1971). For an introduction to the debate over the theories of Bazin and Kracauer, see J. Dudley Andrew, *The Major Film Theories: An Introduction* (New York: Oxford University Press, 1976); Brian Henderson, *A Critique of Film Theory* (New York: Dutton, 1980); Andrew Tudor, *Theories of Film* (New York: Viking, 1974).

34. Stephen Mamber, *Cinema Verite in America: Studies in Uncontrolled Documentary* (Cambridge: MIT Press, 1974), 4.

35. Carter labels *The Store* sexist. McManus thinks the "documentary reflects the ironies inherent in a consumer culture and raises questions about the lives of shoppers, predominately women, who have so much time and money at their disposal" ("Inside the Store," 46).

36. In the Zipporah transcript's terminology and numbering, the three scenes are: reel 3, scene 8, personnel office; reel 4, scene 4, birthday party; and reel 4, scene 14,

banquet hall. Wiseman's transcript for *The Store* labels most scenes, usually by the "scene" in which they take place (personnel office, banquet hall), less often by "act" (birthday party), rarely by "agent," "agency," or "purpose."

37. John Updike, *The Witches of Eastwick* (New York: Knopf, 1984), 102.

38. Christopher Lasch, *The Culture of Narcissism: American Life in an Age of Diminishing Expectations* (New York: Norton, 1978).

39. See Thorstein Veblen, *The Theory of the Leisure Class* (1899; reprint, Boston: Houghton Mifflin, 1973); John Kenneth Galbraith, *The Affluent Society*, 2nd ed. (Boston: Houghton Mifflin, 1969); J. M. Gutman, *Buying* (New York: Bantam, 1975); Chandra Mukerji, *From Graven Images: Patterns of Modern Materialism* (New York: Columbia University Press, 1983). On politics as the ritual of conspicuous waste in the public realm, see Richard B. Gregg and Gerard A. Hauser, "Richard Nixon's April 30, 1970 Address on Cambodia: The 'Ceremony' of Confrontation," *Speech Monographs* 40 (1973): 167–81.

40. "Wiseman considers [the birthday party] 'a key scene' in the film but, characteristically, won't say why" (Shales, "Best Li'l Store," B 4).

41. Far less common than the term *montage*, the word *medley*, used in the Zipporah transcript, captures the sense of assorted content and also the editing rhythm of the film. The transcript lists sixty-three scenes and twenty-six medleys.

42. Kenneth Burke, *The Philosophy of Literary Form*, 3d ed. (Berkeley: University of California Press, 1973), 9.

Chapter 10. Let's Talk When I'm Eighty

1. Telephone interview with Carolyn Anderson, 14 November 1983.

2. Wiseman's description of his film making in the paragraphs that follow is drawn from published and unpublished interviews given over the course of his career. Unless otherwise noted, direct quotations in this section are from "Twenty Years of Documentary Filmmaking," a lecture delivered by Wiseman at Bucknell University, Lewisburg, PA, 12 November 1985. The lecture and the following question-and-answer session were recorded by Thomas W. Benson and Len Siebert, with the permission of Wiseman, with the provision that he be given an opportunity to correct the transcript for grammar and accuracy before the authors quoted it. He later declined to offer any corrections to the transcript. The Bucknell talk follows closely the explanations Wiseman has given of his working methods since his earliest interviews and represents the basic speech he takes on the road to various colleges and universities. In addition to the Bucknell appearance and the published interviews referred to in this chapter and throughout the book, we rely on appearances by Wiseman at Auburn University (February 1986) and Lycoming College (April 1987). Another version of this basic speech appears in Frederick Wiseman, "A Filmmaker's Choices," *The Christian Science Monitor*, 25 April 1984, 30.

3. Wiseman at Auburn University, Alabama, February 1986.

4. Years earlier, Wiseman told Alan Westin, "I don't believe in doing very much research before going in to shoot. The shooting of the film is the research. The editing is like writing the book. The research instead of being on 3-by-5 cards is on film. The final film is the product of studying and thinking about how you are going to structure, order, and find a form for the chaotic raw material of the research. In this process, 100,000 feet of film are reduced to 3,000 feet, and the film emerges." Wiseman, in

Alan Westin, " 'You Start Off with a Bromide': Wiseman on Film and Civil Liberties," *Civil Liberties Review* 1, nos. 1 and 2 (1974): 56. Amplifying his remarks about demystification, Wiseman told his audience at Auburn, "What you try to do as much as you can is demystify the process, so that you have the opportunity to just blend into the woodwork, so to speak. And you try to present yourself in a nonthreatening way. My bland, leprechaun look, I suppose, has helped me from time to time" (Wiseman at Auburn, February 1986).

5. Wiseman, in a lecture at Lycoming College, Williamsport, PA, 15 April 1987.

6. It appears to be Wiseman's current practice to view and discuss rushes with his crew, a practice that he did not follow with Richard Leiterman on *High School*.

7. For example, see Wiseman's comments in Ira Halberstadt, "An Interview with Frederick Wiseman," *Filmmaker's Newsletter* 7, no. 4 (1974): 19.

8. The quotations from Wiseman's four cinematographers in this chapter, unless otherwise cited, are from the following interviews conducted by the authors: John Marshall, Peterborough, New Hampshire, 27 December 1986; Richard Leiterman, Mont Tremblant, Quebec, Canada, 17 and 18 August 1986; William Brayne, London, England, 11 October 1986; John Davey, London, England, 14 October 1986. All four of these cinematographers, who have contributed so much, through Frederick Wiseman's films, to the understanding of American culture, were in some sense apart from the culture of the United States: Marshall had spent crucial early years in Africa with his family; Leiterman and Brayne are Canadians (Brayne has for many years been living in England); Davey is an Englishman. Hence, each of them brings to the films the eyes of an outsider, and of a trained observer.

9. Quotations from Robert Kotlowitz are from an interview conducted by the authors at WNET, New York, 13 June 1985.

10. Terry Eagleton, *Literary Theory: An Introduction* (Minneapolis: University of Minnesota Press, 1983), 71.

Bibliography

Abbott, Don. "Marxist Influences on the Rhetorical Theory of Kenneth Burke." *Philosophy and Rhetoric* 7, no. 4 (1974): 217–33.

Adair, Gilbert. *Hollywood's Vietnam*. New York: Proteus, 1983.

Adorno, Theodor W. "Subject and Object." In *The Essential Frankfurt School Reader*, edited by Andrew Arato and Eike Gebhart, 497–511. New York: Continuum, 1985.

Affron, Charles. *Cinema and Sentiment*. Chicago: University of Chicago Press, 1982.

Agee, James, and Walker Evans. *Let Us Now Praise Famous Men*. 1941. Reprint. New York: Ballantine Books, 1966.

Alexander, William. *Film on the Left: American Documentary Film from 1931 to 1942*. Princeton: Princeton University Press, 1981.

Altheide, David. *Creating Reality: How TV News Distorts Events*. Beverly Hills, CA: Sage, 1976.

Althusser, Louis. *For Marx*. Translated by B. Brewster. New York: Pantheon, 1969.

American Civil Liberties Union Annual Reports. Vol. 7. New York: Arno Press, 1970.

Anderson, Carolyn. "The Conundrum of Competing Rights in *Titicut Follies*." *Journal of the University Film Association* 33, no. 1 (1981): 15–22.

———. "Documentary Dilemmas: An Analytic History of Frederick Wiseman's *Titicut Follies*." Ph.D. diss., University of Massachusetts, 1984.

———. "The *Titicut Follies* Audience and the Double Bind of Court-Restricted Exhibition." In *Current Research in Film: Audiences, Economics, and Law*, edited by Bruce A. Austin, vol. 3: 189–214. Norwood, NJ: Ablex, 1987.

Anderson, Carolyn, and Thomas W. Benson. "Direct Cinema and the Myth of Informed Consent: The Case of *Titicut Follies*." In *Image Ethics: The Moral Rights of Subjects in Photography, Film, and Television*, edited by Larry Gross, John Katz, and Jay Ruby. New York: Oxford University Press, 1988.

Andrew, Dudley. *The Major Film Theories: An Introduction*. New York: Oxford University Press, 1976.

Aristotle. *Rhetoric*. Translated by Lane Cooper. *The Rhetoric of Aristotle*. New York: Appleton-Century-Crofts, 1932.

Armes, Roy. *Film and Reality: An Historical Survey*. Baltimore: Pelican Books, 1974.

Armstrong, Dan. "Wiseman's *Model* and the Documentary Project: Toward a Radical Film Practice." *Film Quarterly* 37, no. 2 (1983/84): 2–10.

Arnold, Carroll C., and John Waite Bowers, eds. *Handbook of Rhetorical and Communication Theory*. Boston: Allyn and Bacon, 1984.

Arnold, Gary. "Wiseman's 'Welfare': Compelling Case Study." *Washington Post*, 24 September 1975, C 1–2.

Atkins, Thomas R. "The Films of Frederick Wiseman: American Instititutions." *Sight and Sound* 43, no. 4 (1974): 232–35.

———. *Frederick Wiseman*. New York: Monarch Press, 1976.

Baddeley, W. Hugh. *The Technique of Documentary Film Production*. 3d ed. New York: Focal Press, 1973.

Baker, Jim. "Tonight's Wiseman Film Is a Riveting Look at 'The Store.'" *Boston Herald*, 14 December 1983, 51.

Baker, Mark. *Nam: The Vietnam War in the Words of the Men and Women Who Fought There*. New York: Morrow, 1981.

Balaban, John. *Coming Down Again*. San Diego: Harcourt Brace Jovanovich, 1985.

Barnouw, Erik. *Documentary: A History of the Non-Fiction Film*. Rev. ed. New York: Oxford University Press, 1983.

———. *The Sponsor: Notes on a Modern Potentate*. New York: Oxford University Press, 1978.

Barsam, Richard Meran. *Nonfiction Film: A Critical History*. New York: Dutton, 1973.

———, ed. *Nonfiction Film: Theory and Criticism*. New York: Dutton, 1976.

Barthes, Roland. *Mythologies*. 1957. Reprint. Translated by Annette Lavers. New York: Hill & Wang, 1972.

Bateson, Gregory, Don D. Jackson, Jay Haley, and John Weakland. "Toward a Theory of Schizophrenia." *Behavorial Science* 1 (1956): 251–64.

Batten, Mary. "An Interview with Ephraim London." *Film Comment* 1, no. 4 (1963): 2–19.

Bazin, Andre. *What Is Cinema?* 2 vols. 1958–1965. Reprint. Translated by Hugh Grey. Berkeley: University of California Press, 1967, 1971.

Becker, Howard. *Outsiders*. Rev. ed. New York: Free Press, 1973.

———, ed. *Exploring Society Photographically*. Evanston, IL: Northwestern University Press, 1981.

Becker, Samuel L. "Marxist Approaches to Media Studies: The British Experience." *Critical Studies in Mass Communication* 1 (1984): 66–80.

Bellah, Robert N. "American Civil Religion in the 1970s." *Anglican Theological Review* 1, no. 3 (1973): 8–20.

———. *Beyond Belief: Essays on Religion in a Post-Traditional World*. New York: Harper & Row, 1970.

———. *The Broken Covenant: American Civil Religion in Time of Trial*. New York: Seabury Press, 1975.

———. "Civil Religion in America." *Daedalus* 96, no. 1 (1967): 1–21.

———. *Varieties of Civil Religion*. San Francisco: Harper & Row, 1980.

Bennett, David L., and Philip Small. "Case Comments." *Suffolk Law Review* 4, no. 1 (1969): 197–206.

Benson, Thomas W. "Implicit Communication Theory in Campaign Coverage." In *Television Coverage of the 1980 Presidential Campaign*, edited by William C. Adams. Norwood, NJ: Ablex, 1983.

———. "*Joe*: An Essay in the Rhetorical Criticism of Film." *Journal of Popular Culture* 8 (1974): 608–18.

———. "The Rhetorical Structure of Frederick Wiseman's *High School*." *Communication Monographs* 47 (1980): 233–61.

———. "The Rhetorical Structure of Frederick Wiseman's *Primate*." *Quarterly Journal of Speech* 71 (1985): 204–17.

————, ed. *Speech Communication in the 20th Century*. Carbondale: Southern Illinois University Press, 1985.

Benson, Thomas W., and Carolyn Anderson. "Good Films from Bad Rules: The Ethics of Naming in Frederick Wiseman's *Welfare*." In *Visual Explorations of the World: Selected Papers from the International Conference on Visual Communication*, edited by Jay Ruby and Martin Taureg. Aachen, West Germany: Radar Verlag (Edition Herodot), 1987.

————. "The Rhetorical Structure of Frederick Wiseman's *Model*." *Journal of Film and Video* 36, no. 4 (1984): 30–40.

Benson, Thomas W., and Richard Barton. "Television as Politics: The British View." *Quarterly Journal of Speech* 65 (1979): 439–57.

Benson, Thomas W., and Gerard A. Hauser. "Ideals, Superlatives, and the Decline of Hypocrisy." *Quarterly Journal of Speech* 59 (1973): 99–105.

Berg, Beatrice. " 'I Was Fed Up with Hollywood Fantasies.' " *New York Times*, 1 February 1970, sec. 2, 25.

Berger, Milton M., ed. *Beyond the Double Bind: Communication and Family Systems, Theories, and Techniques with Schizophrenics*. New York: Brunner/Mazel, 1978.

Berger, Peter L., and Thomas Luckman. *The Social Construction of Reality: A Treatise in the Sociology of Knowledge*. 1966. Reprint. Garden City, NY: Doubleday, 1967.

Bernstein, J. M. *The Philosophy of the Novel: Lukacs, Marxism, and the Dialectics of Form*. Minneapolis: University of Minnesota Press, 1984.

Black, Edwin. "The Second Persona." *Quarterly Journal of Speech* 56 (1970): 109–19.

Blake, Richard A. "From Poland to Panama." *America*, 8 October 1977, 217–18.

Blankenship, Jane. "The Search for the 1972 Democratic Nomination: A Metaphorical Perspective." In *Rhetoric and Communication*, edited by Jane Blankenship and Hermann G. Stelzner, 236–60. Urbana: University of Illinois Press, 1976.

Bliss, Shepherd. " 'Canal Zone': An American Way of Death." *Christianity and Crisis* 28 November 1977, 286–87.

Blue, James. "Direct Cinema." *Film Comment* 4, nos. 2 and 3 (1967): 80–81.

Bluem, A. William. *Documentary in American Television: Form, Function, Method*. New York: Hastings House, 1965.

Blumenberg, Richard. "Documentary Films and the Problem of 'Truth.' " *Journal of the University Film Association* 29 (Fall 1977): 19–22.

Bologh, R. W. *Dialectical Phenomenology: Marx's Method*. Boston: Routledge & Kegan Paul, 1979.

Bondanella, Peter. *Italian Cinema: From Neorealism to the Present*. New York: Frederick Ungar, 1983.

Booth, Wayne C. *The Rhetoric of Fiction* 2d ed. Chicago: University of Chicago Press, 1983.

Bordwell, David. *Narration in the Fiction Film*. Madison: University of Wisconsin Press, 1985.

Bradlow, Paul. "Two, But Not of a Kind." *Film Comment* 5, no. 3 (1968): 60–61.

Branigan, Edward R. *Point of View in the Cinema: A Theory of Narration and Subjectivity in Classical Film*. Amsterdam: Mouton, 1984.

Breitrose, Henry. "Review of *Documentary*." *Film Quarterly* 28 (Summer 1975): 38.

Brieland, Donald. "*Welfare.*" *Social Work* 20, no. 6 (1975): 498.

Brooks, Peter. *Reading for the Plot: Design and Intention in Narrative.* New York: Knopf, 1984.

Brown, Les. "Scientist Angrily Cancels TV Discussion of 'Primate.' " *New York Times,* 7 December 1974, 59.

Bryan, C. D. B. *Friendly Fire.* New York: Putnam, 1976.

Bullock, Alan, and Oliver Stallybrass, eds. *The Fontana Dictionary of Modern Thought.* London: Fontana, 1977.

Burke, Kenneth. *Attitudes toward History.* 1937. Reprint. Boston: Beacon Press, 1961.

———. *Counter-Statement.* 1931. Reprint. Berkeley: University of Calfiornia Press, 1968.

———. *A Grammar of Motives.* 1945. Reprint. Berkeley: University of California Press, 1969.

———. *Permanence and Change: An Anatomy of Purpose.* 3d ed. Berkeley: University of California Press, 1984.

———. *The Philosophy of Literary Form,* 3d ed. Berkeley: University of California Press, 1973.

———. *A Rhetoric of Motives.* 1950. Reprint. University of California Press, 1969.

Burstyn v. Wilson. 343 U.S. 495 (1952).

Butler, Christopher. *Interpretation, Deconstruction, and Ideology: An Introduction to Some Current Issues in Literary Theory.* Oxford: Clarendon Press, 1984.

Calder-Marshall, Arthur. *The Innocent Eye: The Life of Robert J. Flaherty.* New York: Harcourt, Brace, & World, 1966.

Callenbach, Ernest, and Albert Johnson. "The Danger Is Seduction: An Interview with Haskell Wexler." *Film Quarterly* 21, no. 3 (1968): 3–14.

Campbell, Keith. "Materialism." In *Encyclopedia of Philosophy,* edited by Paul Edwards. New York: Macmillan, 1967.

Campbell, Russell. *Cinema Strikes Back: Radical Filmmaking in the United States, 1930–1942.* Ann Arbor: UMI Research Press, 1982.

"Can Some Knowledge Simply Cost Too Much?" *The Hastings Center Report* 5 (February 1975): 6–8.

Canby, Vincent. "The Screen: *Titicut Follies* Observes Life in a Modern Bedlam." *New York Times,* 4 October 1967, 38.

Capote, Truman. *In Cold Blood.* New York: Random House, 1967.

Caputo, Philip. *A Rumor of War.* New York: Holt, Rinehart & Winston, 1977.

Carroll, Raymond L. "Television Documentary." In *TV Genres,* ed. Brian G. Rose, 237–56. Westport, CT: Greenwood Press, 1985.

Carter, Bill. "Neither a Portrait nor a Polemic." *Baltimore Sun,* 14 December 1983, B 6.

Casebier, Allan. "Idealist and Realist Theories of the Documentary." *Post Script* 6, no. 1 (1986): 66–75.

Cater, Douglass, ed. *The Future of Public Broadcasting.* New York: Praeger, 1976.

Cavell, Stanley. *Pursuits of Happiness: The Hollywood Comedy of Remarriage.* Cambridge: Harvard University Press, 1981.

Chatman, Seymour. *Story and Discourse: Narrative Structure in Fiction and Film.* Ithaca: Cornell University Press, 1978.

"Cinema: Festival Action, Side Show Action, *Titicut Follies.*" *Time,* 29 September 1967, 101.

Coleman, John. "Films: Long Look." *New Statesman,* 7 November 1975, 589–90.

Coles, Robert. "Stripped Bare at the Follies." *The New Republic,* 20 January 1968, 18, 28–30.

"Comment: The 'Titicut Follies' Case: Limiting the Public Interest Privilege," *Columbia Law Review* 70, no. 2 (1970): 359–71.

Commonwealth v. Wiseman. 356 Mass. 251, 249 N.E.2d 610 (1969); cert. denied, 398 U.S. 960 (1970); rehearing denied, 400 U.S. 954 (1970).

Conrad, Joseph. *Heart of Darkness.* New York: Signet, 1950. Originally published in 1903 in *Youth and Two Other Stories.*

Conrad, Randall. "An Interview with Frederick Wiseman." Unpublished transcript, Boston, circa 1978.

Cooley, Charles Horton. "The Looking-Glass Self." In *Symbolic Interaction: A Reader in Social Psychology.* 3d ed. Edited by Jerome G. Manis and Bernard M. Meltzer. Boston: Allyn & Bacon, 1978.

Corner, John, ed. *Documentary and the Mass Media.* London: Edward Arnold, 1986.

Corry, John. "TV: 'The Store,' A Wiseman Film." *New York Times,* 14 December 1983, C 34.

Cox, Harvey G. "Massachusetts Movie Ban." *Playboy,* March 1968, 45.

———. "High School." *Tempo* 1 (15 June 1969): 12.

Crain, Jane Larkin. "TV Verite." *Commentary,* December 1973, 70–75.

Cullen v. Grove Press, Inc. 276 F.Supp. 727 (S.D.N.Y. 1967).

Curry, Timothy Jon. "Frederick Wiseman: Sociological Filmmaker?" *Contemporary Sociology* 14, no. 1 (1985): 35–39.

Cushman, Donald P. "The Rules Perspective as a Theoretical Basis for the Study of Human Communication." *Communication Quarterly* 25, no. 1 (1977): 30–45.

Davidson, David. "Direct Cinema and Modernism: The Long Journey to *Grey Gardens.*" *Journal of the University Film Association* 36, no. 1 (1981): 3–13.

Davison, Peter, Rolf Meyersohn, and Edward Shils. *Literary Taste, Culture, and Mass Communication.* Vols. 13–14 of *The Cultural Debate.* Cambridge: Chadwyck-Healey, 1980.

De Grazia, Edward. *Censorship Landmarks.* New York: Bowker, 1969.

De Grazia, Edward, and Roger K. Newman. *Banned Films: Movies, Censors, and the First Amendment.* New York: Bowker, 1982.

Del Vecchio, John M. *The 13th Valley.* New York: Bantam, 1982.

Dershowitz, Alan M. *Reversal of Fortune: Inside the Von Bulow Case.* New York: Random House, 1986.

Desilet, E. Michael. "Fred Wiseman: *Titicut* Revisited." *Film Library Quarterly* 4, no. 2 (1971): 29–33.

DeVries, Hilary. "Fred Wiseman's Unblinking Camera Watches How Society Works." *Christian Science Monitor,* 1 May 1984, 25–27.

Didion, Joan. *Salvador.* New York: Simon and Schuster, 1983.

Donohue, John W. "An Advent Homily from Neiman-Marcus." *America,* 10 December 1983, 374.

Dowd, Mary Ellen. "Popular Conventions." *Film Quarterly* 22, no. 3 (1969): 28–31.

Duncan, Hugh Dalziel. *Communication and Social Order.* New York: Bedminster, 1962..

Eagleton, Terry. *Literary Theory: An Introduction.* Minneapolis: University of Minnesota Press, 1983.

Eames, David. "Watching Wiseman Watch." *New York Times Magazine,* 2 October 1977, 96–102, 108.

Eaton, Mick. *Anthropology-Reality-Cinema: The Films of Jean Rouch.* London: British Film Institute, 1979.

Eco, Umberto. *The Role of the Reader: Explorations in the Semiotics of Texts.* Bloomington: University of Indiana Press, 1979.

Elder, Sean. "Darkness Visible: Robert Frank and the Real Rolling Stones." [Berkeley] *Express,* 30 October 1987, 6.

Ellsworth, Liz. [Elizabeth Jennings.] *Frederick Wiseman: A Guide to References and Resources.* Boston: Hall, 1979.

Emerson, Gloria. *Winners and Losers: Battles, Retreats, Gains, Losses and Ruins from the Vietnam War.* New York: Random House, 1976.

Epstein, Edward Jay. *News from Nowhere: Television and the News.* New York: Vintage Books, 1974.

———. *Between Fact and Fiction: The Problem of Journalism.* New York: Vintage Books, 1975.

Ewen, Stuart. *Captains of Consciousness: Advertising and the Social Roots of the Consumer Culture.* New York: McGraw-Hill, 1976.

Fager, Charles E. "Sweet Revenge." *Christian Century,* 3 September 1969, 1142.

Featherstone, Joseph. "High School." *New Republic,* 21 June 1969, 30.

Feenberg, Andrew. *Lukacs, Marx, and the Sources of Critical Theory.* Totowa, NJ: Rowman and Littlefield, 1981.

Feingold, Ellen. "*Titicut Follies* and Competing Rights." *Civil Liberties Review* 2, no. 2 (1974): 145–51.

Feldman, Silvia. "The Wiseman Documentary." *Human Behavior* 5, no. 2 (1976): 64–69.

Fell, John L. *Film and the Narrative Tradition.* 1974. Reprint. Berkeley: University of California Press, 1986.

Fenwick, Steven F. "*Hearts and Minds:* A Case Study of the Propaganda Film." 2 vols. Ph.D. diss., University of Michigan, 1982.

"Film-Festival Firsts for *Follies.*" *Playboy,* June 1968, 54.

"Film on State Hospital Provocative After 20 Years." *New York Times,* 17 May 1987, 27.

Fisher, Walter R. *Human Communication as Narration: Toward a Philosophy of Reason, Value, and Action.* Columbia: University of South Carolina Press, 1987.

———. "Narration as a Human Communication Paradigm: The Case of Public Moral Argument." *Communication Monographs* 51 (1984): 1–22.

———. "The Narrative Paradigm: An Elaboration." *Communication Monographs* 52 (1985): 347–67.

———. "The Narrative Paradigm: In the Beginning." *Journal of Communication* 35, no. 4 (1985): 74–89.

Fowles, John, and Frank Horvat. *The Tree.* Boston: Little, Brown, 1979.

Friedenberg, Edgar Z. "Ship of Fools: The Films of Frederick Wiseman." *New York Review of Books,* 21 October 1971, 19–22.

Friendly, Fred W. *Due to Circumstances beyond Our Control . . .* New York: Random House, 1967.

Galbraith, John Kenneth. *The Affluent Society.* 2d ed. Boston: Houghton Mifflin, 1969.

Galliher, John. "The Life and Death of Liberal Criminology." *Contemporary Crises* 2, no. 3 (1978): 245–63.

———. "Social Scientists' Ethical Responsibilities to Superordinates: Looking Up Meekly." *Social Problems* 27, no. 3 (1980): 298–308.

Geertz, Clifford. *The Interpretation of Cultures.* New York: Basic Books, 1973.

———. *Local Knowledge.* New York: Basic Books, 1983.

Genette, Gerard. *Narrative Discourse: An Essay in Method.* Translated by Jane E. Lewin. Ithaca: Cornell University Press, 1980.

Gerbner, George, and Martha Siefert, eds. "Ferment in the Field." *Journal of Communication* 33, no. 3 (1983).

Gilbert, Craig. "Reflections on 'An American Family.' " *Studies in Visual Communication* 8, no. 1 (1982): 24–54.

Gill, Brendan. "The Current Cinema." *The New Yorker,* 28 October 1967, 166–67.

Gillmor, Donald M., and Jerome A. Barron. *Mass Communication Law: Cases and Comment.* 4th ed. St. Paul: West, 1984.

Gitlin, Todd. *The Whole World Is Watching: The Mass Media in the Making and Unmaking of the New Left.* Berkeley: University of California Press, 1980.

Glasgow University Media Group. *Bad News.* London: Routledge & Kegan Paul, 1976.

———. *More Bad News.* London: Routledge & Kegan Paul, 1980.

Glicksman, Marlaine. "Highway 61 Revisited." *Film Comment* 23, no. 4 (1987), 32–39.

Glossary of Film Terms. Philadelphia: University Film Association, 1978.

Goffman, Erving. *Asylums.* Garden City, NY: Doubleday, 1961.

———. *Gender Advertisments.* Cambridge: Harvard University Press, 1979.

———. *The Presentation of Self in Everyday Life.* New York: Doubleday, 1959.

———. *Relations in Public: Microstudies of the Public Order.* New York: Harper & Row, 1971.

Goldman, Peter, and Tony Fuller, with Richard Manning. *Charlie Company: What Vietnam Did to Us.* New York: Morrow, 1983.

Goodman, Paul. "Introduction to the 1970 Edition." In *Prison Memoirs of an Anarchist,* by Alexander Berkman. 1912. Reprint. New York: Schocken Books, 1970.

Gordimer, Nadine. *July's People.* New York: Viking Press, 1981.

Gorelik, Mordecai. *New Theatres for Old.* New York: Samuel French, 1940.

Graham, John. "Frederick Wiseman on Viewing Film." *The Film Journal* 1, no. 1 (1971): 43–47.

Greene, Graham. *Another Mexico.* New York: Viking Press, 1964. Originally published in 1939 as *The Lawless Roads.*

———. *Getting to Know the General.* New York: Simon and Schuster, 1984.

———. *Journey without Maps.* 1936. Reprint. New York: Penguin, 1978.

Gregg, Richard B. "The Criticism of Symbolic Inducement: A Critical-Theoretical Connection." In *Speech Communication in the 20th Century,* edited by Thomas W. Benson, 41–62. Carbondale: Southern Illinois University Press, 1985.

———. *Symbolic Inducement and Knowing: A Study in the Foundations of Rhetoric.* Columbia: University of South Carolina Press, 1984.

Gregg, Richard B., and Gerard A. Hauser. "Richard Nixon's April 30, 1970, Address on Cambodia: The 'Ceremony' of Confrontation." *Speech Monographs* 40 (1973): 167–81.

Gronbeck, Bruce. "Celluloid Rhetoric: On Genres of Documentary." In *Form and Genre: Shaping Rhetorical Action*, edited by Karlyn Kohrs Campbell and Kathleen Hall Jamison, 139–61. Falls Church, VA: Speech Communication Association, 1978.

Gross, Larry, John Katz, and Jay Ruby, eds. *Image Ethics: The Moral Rights of Subjects in Photography, Film and Television*. New York: Oxford University Press, 1988

Grossberg, Lawrence. "Strategies of Marxist Cultural Interpretation." *Critical Studies in Mass Communication* 1 (1984): 392–421.

Gutman, J. M. *Buying*. New York: Bantam, 1975.

Halberstadt, Ira. "An Interview with Frederick Wiseman." *Filmmaker's Newsletter* 7, no. 4 (1974): 19–25.

Hall, Stuart. "Signification, Representation, Ideology: Althusser and the Post-Structuralist Debates." *Critical Studies in Mass Communication* 2 (1985): 91–114.

Hallin, Daniel C. *The "Uncensored War": The Media and Vietnam*. New York: Oxford University Press, 1986.

Hammond, Charles Montgomery, Jr. *The Image Decade: Television Documentary: 1965–1975*. New York: Hastings House, 1981.

Handelman, Janet. "An Interview with Frederick Wiseman." *Film Library Quarterly* 3, no. 3 (1970): 5–9.

Hardy, Forsyth, ed. *Grierson on Documentary*. Rev. ed. Berkeley: University of California Press, 1966.

Hart, Roderick P. *The Political Pulpit*. West Lafayette: Purdue University Press, 1977.

Hatch, Robert. "Films." *The Nation*, 30 October 1967, 446.

Hauser, Gerard A. *Introduction to Rhetorical Theory*. New York: Harper & Row, 1986.

"Hearings on the Bridgewater Film before the Special Commission on Mental Health." Massachusetts General Court, Boston, 17 October - 7 November 1967.

Heath, Robert L. "Kenneth Burke's Break with Formalism." *Quarterly Journal of Speech* 70 (1984): 132–43.

Hecht, Chandra. "Total Institutions on Celluloid." *Society* 9, no. 6 (1972): 44–48.

Heider, Karl. *Ethnographic Film*. Austin: University of Texas Press, 1976.

Held, David. *Introduction to Critical Theory: Horkheimer to Habermas*. Berkeley: University of California Press, 1980.

Hellmann, John. *American Myth and the Legacy of Vietnam*. New York: Columbia University Press, 1986.

Henderson, Brian. *A Critique of Film Theory*. New York: Dutton, 1980.

Henderson, Lisa. "Photographing in Public Places." Master's thesis, University of Pennsylvania, 1983.

Herr, Michael. *Dispatches*. New York: Knopf, 1977.

Hewitt, John P. *Self and Society: A Symbolic Interactionist Social Psychology*. 3d ed. Boston: Allyn and Bacon, 1984.

Heyer, Susan J. "The Documentary Films of Frederick Wiseman: The Evolution of a Style." Master's thesis, University of Texas, 1975.

"The High School: How Much Change—And How Fast?" *School Management*, December 1969, 56–62.

Hockings, Paul, ed. *Principles of Visual Anthropolgy*. The Hague: Mouton, 1975.

Hogan, J. Michael. *The Panama Canal in American Politics: Domestic Advocacy and the Evolution of Policy*. Carbondale: Southern Illinois University Press, 1986.

Hughey, Michael W. *Civil Religion and Moral Order: Theoretical and Historical Dimensions*. Westport, CT: Greenwood Press, 1983.

Hymes, Dell H. *Foundations in Sociolinguistics*. Philadelphia: University of Pennsylvania Press, 1974.

Iser, Wolfgang. *The Implied Reader: Patterns of Communication in Prose Fiction from Bunyan to Beckett*. Baltimore: Johns Hopkins University Press, 1974.

Issari, M. Ali. *Cinema Verite*. East Lansing: Michigan State University Press, 1971.

Issari, M. Ali, and Doris A. Paul. *What Is Cinema Verite?* Metuchen, NJ: Scarecrow Press, 1979.

Jacobs, Lewis, ed. *The Documentary Tradition*. 2d ed. New York: Norton, 1979.

Jameson, Fredric. *The Political Unconscious: Narrative as a Socially Symbolic Act*. Ithaca: Cornell University Press, 1981.

Jennings, Elizabeth. [Liz Ellsworth.] "Frederick Wiseman's Films: A Modern Theory of Documentary." Master's thesis, University of Wisconsin-Milwaukee, 1975.

Joyce, Robert. *The Esthetic Animal: Man, the Art-Created Art-Creator*. Hicksville: Exposition Press, 1975.

Kael, Pauline. "High School." *The New Yorker*, 18 October 1969, 202–3.

Kalin, Bob. "Frederick Wiseman: From *Titicut Follies* to *Model*." *Film News*, Fall 1981, 6–12.

Karnow, Stanley. *Vietnam: A History*. New York: Viking, 1983.

Kawin, Bruce. *Mindscreen: Bergman, Godard, and First-Person Film*. Princeton: Princeton University Press, 1978.

Keddie, Shirley. "Naming and Renaming: *Time* Magazine's Coverage of Germany and Russia in the 1940s." Ph.D. diss., University of Massachusetts, 1985.

Kierstead, Robert L. "Dropping a Stigmatizing Phrase." *Boston Globe*, 2 November 1987, 18.

Kilday, Gregg. "The Woes of Welfare." *Los Angeles Times*, 22 September 1975, sec. 1, pp. 1, 17.

Kitman, Marvin. "The Marvin Kitman Show Starring Neiman-Marcus." *Newsday*, 14 December 1983, 80.

Knight, Arthur. "Cinema Verite and Film Truth." *Saturday Review*, 9 September 1967, 44.

Kolker, Robert Phillip. *A Cinema of Loneliness*. New York: Oxford University Press, 1980.

Kracauer, Siegfried. *Theory of Film: The Redemption of Physical Reality*. New York: Oxford University Press, 1960.

Lasch, Christopher. *The Culture of Narcissism: American Life in an Age of Diminishing Expectations*. New York: Norton, 1978.

Leff, Michael C., and Margaret Organ Procario. "Rhetorical Theory in Speech Communication." In *Speech Communication in the 20th Century*, edited by Thomas W. Benson, 3–27. Carbondale: Southern Illinois University Press, 1985.

Le Guin, Ursula K. "She Unnames Them." *The New Yorker*, 21 January 1985, 27.

Lentricchia, Frank. *Criticism and Social Change*. Chicago: University of Chicago Press.

Leprohon, Pierre. *The Italian Cinema*. Translated by Roger Greaves and Oliver Stallybrass. New York: Praeger, 1972.

Levin, G. Roy. *Documentary Explorations: 15 Interviews with Film-Makers*. Garden City, NY: Doubleday, 1971.

Levin, Murray B., and George Blackwood. *The Compleat Politician: Political Strategy in Massachusetts*. Indianapolis: Bobbs-Merrill, 1962.

Lewis, Caroline. "Welfare." *Monthly Film Bulletin*, March 1976, 65.

Lewis, Diane E. " 'Nightline' Airs Segments from 'Titicut Follies.' " *Boston Globe*, 27 August 1987, 66.

Liehm, Mira. *Passion and Defiance: Film in Italy from 1942 to the Present*. Berkeley: University of California Press, 1984.

Litt, Edgar. *The Political Culture of Massachusetts*. Cambridge: MIT Press, 1965.

Littlejohn, Stephen W. *Theories of Human Communication*. 2d ed. Belmont, CA: Wadsworth, 1983.

Lomperis, Timothy J. *"Reading the Wind": The Literature of the Vietnam War*. Durham, NC: Duke University Press, 1987.

Lovell, Alan, and Jim Hillier. *Studies in Documentary*. New York: Viking Press, 1972.

Lucas, Anthony J. *Common Ground: A Turbulent Decade in the Lives of Three American Families*. New York: Knopf, 1985.

Lyons, Louis M. *Newspaper Story: One Hundred Years of "The Boston Globe."* Cambridge: Belknap Press, 1971.

McCullough, David. *The Path Between the Seas: The Creation of the Panama Canal, 1870–1914*. New York: Simon and Schuster, 1977.

Macdonald, Dwight. *On Movies*. New York: Berkley, 1971.

McGee, Michael C. "A Materialist's Conception of Rhetoric." In *Explorations in Rhetoric: Studies in Honor of Douglas Ehninger*, edited by Ray E. McKerrow, 23–48. Chicago: Scott, Foresman, 1982.

———. "Secular Humanism: A Radical Reading of 'Culture Industry' Productions." *Critical Studies in Mass Communication* 1 (1984): 1–33.

McKerrow, Ray E. "Marxism and a Rhetorical Conception of Ideology." *Quarterly Journal of Speech* 69 (1983): 192–205.

McLean, Deckle. "The Man Who Made *Titicut Follies*." *Boston Sunday Globe Magazine*, 27 July 1969, 11–15.

McLuhan, Marshall. *The Mechanical Bride*. Boston: Beacon Press, 1976.

McManus, Otile. "Inside the Store." *Connoisseur*, December 1983, 45–46.

McWilliams, Donald E. "Frederick Wiseman." *Film Quarterly* 24, no. 1 (1970): 17–26.

Mailer, Norman. *The Armies of the Night*. New York: New American Library, 1968.

Maltin, Leonard. *Behind the Camera: The Cinematographer's Art*. New York: New American Library, 1971.

Mamber, Stephen. "The New Documentaries of Frederick Wiseman." *Cinema* 6, no. 1 (1970): 33–40.

———. *Cinema Verite in America: Studies in Uncontrolled Documentary*. Cambridge: MIT Press, 1974.

Marcorelles, Louis. *Living Cinema: New Directions in Contemporary Filmmaking.* Translated by Isabel Quigly. New York: Praeger, 1973.

Marshall, Lorna. *The !Kung of Nyae Nyae.* Cambridge: Harvard University Press, 1976.

Martin, Wallace. *Recent Theories in Narrative.* Ithaca: Cornell University Press, 1986.

Massachusetts Reports, Papers, and Briefs. 356 part 5 (20–24 June 1969): 362–66.

Medhurst, Martin J. " 'God Bless the President': The Rhetoric of Inaugural Prayer." Ph.D. diss., Pennsylvania State University, 1980.

Medhurst, Martin J., and Thomas W. Benson, eds. *Rhetorical Dimensions in Media: A Critical Casebook.* Rev. printing. Dubuque: Kendall/Hunt, 1986.

Meehan, Thomas. "The Documentary Maker," *Saturday Review,* 2 December 1972, 12, 14, 18.

Mermigas, Diane. "CBS Draws Up a Set of Standards." *Electronic Media,* 2 May 1985, 3, 12, 37.

Meyer, Karl. "Television: Report from Purgatory." *Saturday Review,* 20 September 1975, 52.

Mileur, Jerome M., and George T. Sulzner. *Campaigning for the Massachusetts Senate: Electioneering Outside the Political Limelight.* Amherst: University of Massachusetts Press, 1974.

Miller, Arthur R. *The Assault on Privacy: Computers, Data Banks, and Dossiers.* Ann Arbor: University of Michigan Press, 1971.

Morgenstern, Joseph. "Movies: Bedlam Today." *Newsweek,* 23 October 1967, 100–101.

Morris, Desmond, Peter Collett, Peter Marsh, and Maire O'Shaughnessy. *Gestures: Their Origin and Distribution.* New York: Stein and Day, 1979.

Mukerji, Chandra. *From Graven Images: Patterns of Modern Materialism.* New York: Columbia University Press, 1983.

Neier, Aryeh. "Letters." *Civil Liberties Review* 2, no. 2 (1975): 151.

Nichols, Bill. "Fred Wiseman's Documentaries: Theory and Structure." *Film Quarterly* 31, no. 3 (1978): 15–28.

———. *Ideology and the Image: Social Representation in the Cinema and Other Media.* Bloomington: Indiana University Press, 1981.

———. "The Voice of Documentary." *Film Quarterly* 36, no. 3 (1983): 17–30.

Nicholson, Philip, and Elizabeth Nicholson. "Meet Lawyer-Filmmaker Frederick Wiseman." *American Bar Association Journal* 61, no. 3 (1975): 328–32.

O'Brien, David M. *The Public's Right to Know.* New York: Praeger, 1981.

O'Brien, Tim. *Going after Cacciato.* New York: Delacorte, 1978.

O'Connor, John J. " 'The Film Is about Killing.' " *New York Times,* 3 October 1971, sec. 2, p. 17.

———. "Wiseman's 'Welfare' Is on Channel 13 Tonight." *New York Times,* 24 September 1975, 91.

Orwell, George. "Shooting an Elephant." In *Collected Essays,* 15–23. London: Secker & Warburg, 1961.

Page, Tim. *Nam.* New York: Knopf, 1983.

Pearce, W. Barnett, and Richard L. Wiseman. "Rules Theories: Variations, Limitations, and Potentials." In *Intercultural Communication Theory,* edited by William B. Gudykunst. Beverly Hills. CA: Sage, 1983.

Pember, Don R. *Mass Media Law*. 3d ed. Dubuque: William C. Brown, 1984.

Perrucci, Robert. *Circle of Madness: On Being Insane and Institutionalized in America*. Englewood Cliffs, NJ: Prentice-Hall, 1974.

Press, Aric, with Daniel Shapiro and Tom Schmitz. " 'Titicut Follies': An Asylum with a Past." *Newsweek*, 20 July 1987, 57.

Pryluck, Calvin. " 'Seeking to Take the Longest Journey': A Conversation with Albert Maysles." *Journal of the University Film Association* 28, no. 2 (1976): 9–16.

———. "Ultimately We Are All Outsiders: The Ethics of Documentary Filming." *Journal of the University Film Association* 28, no. 1 (1976): 21–29.

Ray, Robert B. *A Certain Tendency of the Hollywood Cinema: 1930–1980*. Princeton: Princeton University Press, 1985.

Real, Michael. "The Debate on Critical Theory and the Study of Communication." *Journal of Communication* 34, no. 4 (1984): 72–80.

"Recent Cases." *Harvard Law Review* 83, no. 7 (1970): 1722–31.

Redicliffe, Steven. "The Heart and Soul of 'The Store.' " *Dallas Times Herald*, 11 December 1983.

Reitman, Alan, ed. *The Pulse of Freedom: American Liberties, 1920–1970s*. New York: Norton, 1975.

Renov, Michael. "Re-thinking Documentary: Toward a Taxonomy of Mediation." *Wide Angle* 8, nos. 3 and 4 (1986): 71–77.

"Review of *Titicut Follies*." *Films in Review*, November 1967, 580.

Review of *Titicut Follies*. *Film Society Review*, October 1967, 17–19.

Rice, Eugene *"Essene*: A Documentary Film on Benedictine Community Life." *The American Benedictine Review* 24, no. 3 (1973): 382.

Rich, Adrienne. *Critical Essays*. New York: Norton, 1977.

Rich, Frank. "A Sunny, Nightmare Vision." *Time*, 10 October 1977, 103.

Richardson, Elliot L. "Letters: Focusing Again on *Titicut Follies*." *Civil Liberties Review* 1, no. 3 (1974): 150.

———. *The Creative Balance: Government, Politics and the Individual in America's Third Century*. New York: Holt, Rinehart, & Winston, 1976.

Ricoeur, Paul. *History and Truth*. Translated by Charles A. Kelbley. Evanston, IL: Northwestern University Press, 1965.

Rifkin, Glenn. "Wiseman Looks at Affluent Texans." *New York Times*, 11 December 1983, 37, 44.

Robb, Christina. "Focus on Life." *Boston Globe Magazine*, 23 January 1983, 15–34.

Rogers, Philip. *"No Longer at Ease:* Chinua Achebe's 'Heart of Whiteness.' " *Research in African Literature* 14, no. 2 (1983): 165–83.

Roscho, Bernard. *Newsmaking*. Chicago: University of Chicago Press, 1975.

Rosenberg, Howard. "Show of the Week." *Los Angeles [Television] Times*, 11 December 1983, 3.

Rosenberg, Karen. "The Store." *The Nation*, 17 December 1983, 642–43.

Rosenblatt, Roger. "Frederick Wiseman's 'Welfare.' " *The New Republic*, 27 September 1975, 65–67.

Rosenfield, Lawrence W. "The Practical Celebration of Epideictic." In *Rhetoric in Transition: Studies in the Nature and Uses of Rhetoric*, edited by Eugene E. White, 131–55. University Park: Pennsylvania State University Press, 1980.

Rosenthal, Alan. *The Documentary Conscience: A Casebook in Film Making*. Berkeley: University of California Press, 1980.

———. *The New Documentary in Action: A Casebook in Film Making*. Berkeley: University of California Press, 1971.

———, ed. *New Challenges to Documentary*. Berkeley: University of California Press, 1988.

Roskill, Mark, and David Carrier. *Truth and Falsehood in Visual Images*. Amherst: University of Massachusetts Press, 1983.

Rossell, Deac. "*Titicut Follies*." *Christianity and Crisis*, 18 March 1968, 43–45.

Rotha, Paul. *Documentary Diary: An Informal History of the British Documentary Film, 1928–1939*. London: Secker & Warburg, 1973.

———. *Documentary Film*. 3d ed. New York: Hastings House, 1963.

Rothenberg, Fred. "A Tedious Documentary." *Daily Hampshire Gazette*, 14 December 1983, 35.

Rothman, William. *Hitchcock: The Murderous Gaze*. Cambridge: Harvard University Press, 1982.

Rowland, Robert C. "Narrative: Mode of Discourse or Paradigm?" *Communication Monographs* 54 (1987): 264–75.

Ruby, Jay. "The Image Mirrored: Reflexivity and the Documentary Film." *Journal of the University Film Association* 29, no. 4 (1977): 3–11.

———, ed. *A Crack in the Mirror: Reflexive Perspectives in Anthropology*. Philadelphia: University of Pennsylvania Press, 1982.

———, ed. *Robert Flaherty: A Biography*. Philadelphia: University of Pennsylvania Press, 1983.

Rueckert, William H. *Kenneth Burke and the Drama of Human Relations*. 2d ed. Berkeley: University of California Press, 1982.

Russell, Christine. "Science on Film: The 'Primate' Controversy." *Bioscience* 25, no. 3 (1975): 151–54, 218–19.

Salt, Barry. *Film Style and Technology: History and Analysis*. London: Starword, 1983.

Santoli, Al. *Everything We Had: An Oral History of the Vietnam War by Thirty-Three American Soldiers Who Fought It*. New York: Random House, 1981.

Sarris, Andrew. "Review of *Titicut Follies*." *The Village Voice*, 9 November 1967, 33.

Sartre, Jean-Paul. *Nausea*. 1938. Reprint. Translated by Lloyd Alexander. New York: New Directions, 1964.

Saylor, Jean. "Shopping at 'The Store.'" *Des Moines Register*, 14 December 1983, 4T.

Schaefer, Dennis, and Larry Salvato. *Masters of Light: Conversations with Contemporary Cinematographers*. Berkeley: University of California Press, 1984.

Scheflen, Albert E. "Quasi-Courtship Behavior in Psychotherapy." In *Nonverbal Communication: Readings with Commentary*, edited by Shirley Weitz, 192–93. New York: Oxford University Press, 1974.

Scheflen, Albert E., with Alice Scheflen. *Body Language and Social Order: Communication as Behavioral Control*. Englewood Cliffs, NJ: Prentice-Hall, 1972.

Schickel, Richard. "The Frightful Follies of Bedlam: *Titicut Follies*." *Life*, 1 December 1967, 12.

Schlesinger, Philip. *Putting "Reality" Together: BBC News*. London: Constable, 1978.

Scholes, Robert. *Semiotics and Interpretation*. New Haven: Yale University Press, 1982.

Scholes, Robert, and Robert Kellogg. *The Nature of Narrative.* London: Oxford University Press, 1966.

Schudson, Michael. *Discovering the News: A Social History of American Newspapers.* New York: Basic Books, 1978.

Schutz, Alfred. *Collected Papers.* 3 vols. Edited by Maurice Natanson. The Hague: Nijhoff, 1962–1966.

Searborough, Linda. " 'Follies' Is Jolting Film about Insane." *New York Daily News,* 4 October 1967, 89.

Shain, Percy. "Latest Wiseman Film a Stark View of Welfare." *Boston Globe,* 24 September 1975, 55.

Shales, Tom. "Best Li'l Store in Texas." *Washington Post,* 17 December 1983, B 1, 4.

Sheed, Wilfred. "Films." *Esquire,* March 1968, 52, 55.

Shimanoff, Susan B. *Communication Rules: Theory and Research.* Beverly Hills, CA: Sage, 1980.

Sigman, Stuart J. "On Communication Rules from a Social Perspective." *Human Communication Research* 7 (1980): 37–51.

Silvergate, Harvey. "President's Column: *Titicut Follies* Revisited." *The Docket* [Civil Liberties Union of Massachusetts] 17, no. 4 (1987): 3.

Sluzki, Carlos E., and Donald C. Ransom, eds. *Double Bind: The Foundations of the Communicational Approach to the Family.* New York: Grune and Stratton, 1976.

Smith, Steven. *Reading Althusser: An Essay on Structural Marxism.* Ithaca: Cornell University Press, 1984.

Snyder, Robert L. *Pare Lorentz and the Documentary Film.* Norman: University of Oklahoma Press, 1973.

Sobchack, Vivian. *"No Lies:* Direct Cinema as Rape." *Journal of the University Film Association* 29, no. 4 (1977): 13–18.

Sontag, Susan. *On Photography.* New York: Farrar, Straus & Giroux, 1978.

Sourian, Peter. "Television." *The Nation,* 15 October 1977, 381–82.

Stacy, Robert H. *Defamiliarization in Language and Literature.* Syracuse: Syracuse University Press, 1977.

Steele, Robert. "Essene." *Film News,* September 1973, 24.

Stein, Benjamin. "Close-Up on Welfare." *Wall Street Journal,* 24 September 1975, 24.

Stott, William. *Documentary Expression and Thirties America.* New York: Oxford University Press, 1973.

Sullivan, Patrick J. " 'What's All the Cryin' About?' The Films of Frederick Wiseman." *Massachusetts Review* 13, no. 3 (1972): 452–69.

Sussex, Elizabeth, ed. *The Rise and Fall of British Documentary: The Story of the Film Movement Founded by John Grierson.* Berkeley: University of California Press, 1975.

Sutherland, Allan T. "Wiseman on Polemic." *Sight and Sound* 47, no. 2 (1978): 82.

Swartz, Susan. "The Real Northeast." *Film Library Quarterly* 6, no. 1 (1972–73): 12–15.

Sweeney, Barbara. "The Use of Social Science Research in Supreme Court Opinions Related to Obscenity." Ph.D. diss., University of Massachusetts, 1981.

Szasz, Thomas S. *The Myth of Mental Illness: Foundations of a Theory of Personal Conduct.* Rev. ed. New York: Harper & Row, 1974.

"The Talk of the Town: New Producer." *The New Yorker*, 14 September 1963, 33–35.

Teeple, Gary. *Marx's Critique of Politics: 1842–1847*. Toronto: University of Toronto Press, 1984.

"Tempest in a Snakepit." *Newsweek*, 4 December 1967, 109.

Terry, Wallace. *Bloods: An Oral History of the Vietnam War by Black Veterans*. New York: Random House, 1984.

Thomas, Jack. "Wiseman without Bite." *Boston Globe*, 14 December 1983, 87, 90.

Thompson, Kristin. *Eisenstein's "Ivan the Terrible": A Neoformalist Analysis*. Princeton: Princeton University Press, 1981.

Thomson, David. *A Biographical Dictionary of Film*. 2d ed. New York: William Morrow, 1981.

"Titicut Ban Affirmed." *Playboy*, April 1968, 62.

"*Titicut Follies*." *America*, 11 November 1967, 539.

Tompkins, Jane P., ed. *Reader-Response Criticism: From Formalism to Post-Structuralism*. Baltimore: Johns Hopkins University Press, 1980.

Tompkins, Phillip K. "On Hegemony—'He Gave It No Name'—and Critical Structuralism in the Work of Kenneth Burke." *Quarterly Journal of Speech* 71 (1985): 119–30.

Tracey, Michael. *The Production of Political Television*. London: Routledge & Kegan Paul, 1977.

Trollope, Anthony. *Can You Forgive Her?* 1864. Reprint. Oxford: Oxford University Press, 1973.

Tuch, Ronald. "Frederick Wiseman's Cinema of Alienation." *Film Library Quarterly* 11, no. 3 (1978): 9–15, 49.

Tuchman, Gaye. "Objectivity as Strategic Ritual: An Examination of Newsmen's Notions of Objectivity." *American Journal of Sociology* 77 (1972): 660–79.

———. *Making News: A Study in the Construction of Reality*. New York: Free Press, 1978.

Tudor, Andrew. *Theories of Film*. New York: Viking Press, 1974.

Turner, Kathleen J. *Lyndon Johnson's Dual War: Vietnam and the Press*. Chicago: University of Chicago Press, 1985.

Unger, Arthur. "Wiseman Aims His Camera at the Neiman-Marcus Way of Life." *Christian Science Monitor*, 13 December 1983, 32.

Updike, John. *The Witches of Eastwick*. New York: Knopf, 1984.

Vander Zanden, James Wilfrid. *Social Psychology*. 2d ed. New York: Random House, 1981.

Vaughan, Dai. *Television Documentary Usage*. London: British Film Institute, 1976.

Veblen, Thorstein. *The Theory of the Leisure Class*. 1899. Reprint. Boston: Houghton Mifflin, 1973.

Vogel, Amos. *Film as a Subversive Art*. New York: Random House, 1974.

Wagner, Roy. *The Invention of Culture*. Rev. ed. Chicago: University of Chicago Press, 1981.

Wallace, Karl. "The Substance of Rhetoric: Good Reasons." *Quarterly Journal of Speech* 49 (1963): 239–49.

Warnick, Barbara. "The Narrative Paradigm: Another Story." *Quarterly Journal of Speech* 73 (1987): 172–82.

Waters, Harry F. "Inside a Shopping Shrine." *Newsweek*, 19 December 1983, 81–82.

———. "Wiseman on Welfare." *Newsweek*, 29 September 1975, 62–63.

Watzlawick, Paul, Janet Helmick Beavin, and Don D. Jackson. *Pragmatics of Human Communication*. New York: Norton, 1967.

Waugh, Thomas, ed. *"Show Us Life": Toward a History and Aesthetics of the Committed Documentary*. Metuchen, NJ: Scarecrow Press, 1984.

Wax, Murray L. "Paradoxes of 'Consent' to the Practice of Fieldwork." *Social Problems* 27, no. 3 (1980): 272–83.

Weakland, John H. "The 'Double-Bind' Hypothesis of Schizophrenia and Three-Party Interaction." In *The Etiology of Schizophrenia*, edited by Don D. Jackson, 373–88. New York: Basic Books, 1960.

Weaver, Richard M. *Language Is Sermonic: Richard M. Weaver on the Nature of Rhetoric*. Edited by Richard L. Johannesen, Rennard Strickland, and Ralph T. Eubanks. Baton Rouge: Louisiana State University Press, 1970.

Weisman, Mary-Lou. "Neiman-Marcus, the Movie." *The New Republic*, 31 December 1983, 25–26.

Westin, Alan. " 'You Start Off with a Bromide': Wiseman on Film and Civil Liberties." *Civil Liberties Review* 1, nos. 1 and 2 (1974): 52–67.

Westin, Av. *Newswatch: How TV Decides the News*. New York: Simon and Schuster, 1982.

"What Is the New Cinema? Two Views—Paris and New York." *Film Culture*, no. 42 (1966): 56–61.

White, Hayden. *Tropics of Discourse: Essays in Cultural Criticism*. Baltimore: Johns Hopkins University Press, 1978.

Williams, Raymond. *Problems in Materialism and Culture*. London: NLB, 1980.

Wilson, George M. *Narration in Light: Studies in Cinematic Point of View*. Baltimore: Johns Hopkins University Press, 1986.

Winick, Charles, ed. *Deviance and Mass Media*. Beverly Hills, CA: Sage, 1978.

Winston, Brian. "Documentary: I Think We Are in Trouble." *Sight and Sound* 48, no. 1 (1978/79): 2–7.

———. "Hell of a Good Sail. . . . Sorry, No Whales: Direct Cinema, the Third Decade." *Sight and Sound* 52 (1983): 238–43.

Wise, Helen M. "Coursework vs. Career Choices: Two Roads Taken." *The Alumnus* [University of Massachusetts], August–September 1987, 6.

Wiseman, Frederick. "A Filmmaker's Choice." *The Christian Science Monitor*, 25 April 1984, 30.

———. "Lawyer-Client Interviews: Some Lessons from Psychiatry." *Boston University Law Review* 39, no. 2 (1959): 181–87.

———. "Letters: Focusing Again on *Titicut Follies*." *Civil Liberties Review* 1, no. 3 (1974): 151.

———. "Psychiatry and Law: Use and Abuse of Psychiatry in a Murder Case." *American Journal of Psychiatry* 118, no. 4 (1961): 289–99.

———. "Reminiscences of a Film Maker: Fred Wiseman on *Law and Order*." *The Police Chief*, September 1969, 32–35.

———. "Time to Unlock the 'Titicut Follies." *Boston Sunday Globe*, 7 June 1987, A 2.

"Wiseman on *Juvenile Court*." *Journal of the University Film Association* 25, no. 3 (1973): 48–49, 58.

Witcombe, R. T. *The New Italian Cinema: Studies in Dance and Despair*. New York: Oxford University Press, 1982.

Wolcott, James. " 'Welfare' Must Be Seen." *The Village Voice*, 29 September 1975, 126.

———. "Wiseman's Panamania." *The Village Voice*, 10 October 1977, 45.

Wolf, William. "A Sane Look at an Insane Institution." *Cue*, 21 October 1967.

Wolfe, Charles. "Direct Address and the Social Documentary Photograph: 'Annie Mae Gudger' as Negative Subject." *Wide Angle* 9, no. 1 (1987): 59–70.

Youdelman, Jeffrey. "Narration, Invention and History." *Cineaste* 12, no. 2 (1982): 8–15.

Zimmermann, Patricia R. "Public Television, Independent Documentary Producers and Public Policy." *Journal of the University Film and Video Association* 34, no. 3 (1982): 9–23.

Index

Thomas W. Benson is professor of speech communication at The Pennsylvania State University.

Carolyn Anderson is assistant professor of communication at the University of Massachusetts, Amherst.